Creating Environments for Learning

Birth to Age Eight

Third Edition

Julie Bullard
University of Montana

PEARSON

Boston Columbus Indianapolis New York San Francisco Upper Saddle River
Amsterdam Cape Town Dubai London Madrid Milan Munich Paris Montréal Toronto
Delhi Mexico City São Paulo Sydney Hong Kong Seoul Singapore Taipei Tokyo

Vice President and Editorial Director: Jeffery W. Johnston
Executive Editor: Julie Peters
Editorial Assistant: Pamela DiBerardino
Development Editor: Krista Slavicek
Executive Field Marketing Manager: Krista Clark
Executive Product Marketing Manager: Christopher Barry
Program Manager: Megan Moffo
Project Manager: Janet Domingo
Manufacturing Buyer: Carol Melville
Art Director: Diane Lorenzo
Media Project Manager: Michael Goncalves
Full-Service Project Management: Raja Natesan/ Lumina Datamatics Inc.
Editorial Production and Composition Services: Lumina Datamatics, Inc.

Credits and acknowledgments for materials borrowed from other sources and reproduced, with permission, in this textbook appear on the appropriate page within the text.

Library of Congress Cataloging-in-Publication Data

Bullard, Julie.
Creating environments for learning : birth to age eight / Julie Bullard, University of Montana.—Third Edition.
pages cm
ISBN 978-0-13-401455-5
ISBN 0-13-401455-3
1. Classroom learning centers. 2. Early childhood education—Activity programs. I. Title.
LB3044.8.B85 2017
372.13—dc23

2015030222

13 2019

ISBN 13: 978-0-13-401455-5
ISBN 10: 0-13-401455-3

For my sister, Nancy Boothe, who displayed courage, fortitude, an indomitable spirit, and a positive attitude in spite of severe disabilities and life-threatening illnesses. She was an inspiration to everyone who knew her.

About the Author

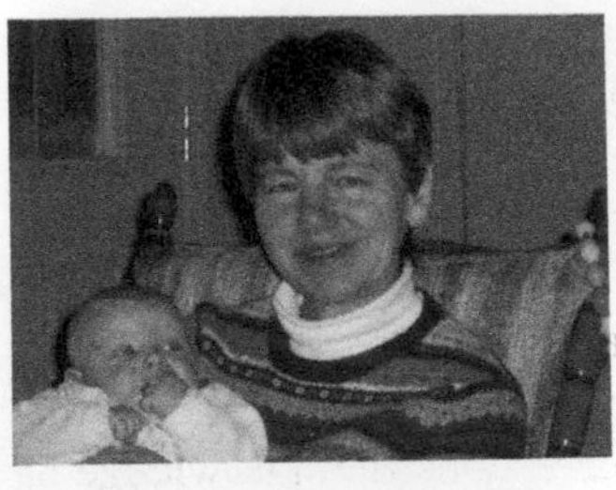

Julie Bullard is an early childhood professor at the University of Montana. During her 35 years in the early childhood field, she has been a preschool and elementary teacher, childcare director, and Head Start administrator, and has taught adults receiving CDAs, associate degrees, and bachelor's degrees in early childhood as well as students receiving master's degrees in curriculum and instruction. Julie has taught higher education coursework both face-to-face and online for over 20 years and was named the Carnegie Professor of the Year for Montana in 2011. She also received the 2015 National Association of Early Childhood Teacher Educators (NAECTE) Outstanding Early Childhood Teacher Educator Award.

Julie has had a passion for the importance of the early learning environment since completing coursework in architecture more than 30 years ago. She also has a special interest in curricular standards and has served on several state and national committees that are working on developing and implementing standards using play-based curriculum. She has served on the National Association for the Education of Young Children (NAEYC) Professional Development Panel, as a national reviewer of early childhood higher education programs, and on an oversight committee for NAEYC/NCATE accreditation. Julie served on an NAEYC committee to revise the national early childhood higher education standards. She was on the National Council for Accreditation of Teacher Education Board of Examiners (NCATE BOE), is a Council for the Accreditation of Educator Preparation (CAEP) reviewer, and is on the editorial board for the *Journal of Early Childhood Teacher Education*. She has been involved in the development of the Montana early childhood knowledge base, infant–toddler guidelines, preschool guidelines, kindergarten standards, and early childhood and elementary higher education standards. Julie received her doctorate from Montana State University.

Preface

Creating Environments for Learning: Birth to Age Eight is designed for college courses taught at 2- and 4-year institutions that focus on quality early childhood learning environments and curriculum. The book's content spans the birth to age 8 range and is appropriate for teachers-in-training as well as practicing teachers in family childcare homes, childcare centers, preschools, or elementary schools.

How did this book come to be written? Philosophically, I value play as the primary way of learning for young children and have become increasingly alarmed that children's time for play is disappearing. Through play, children construct knowledge by engaging in self-chosen, integrated experiences at their ideal levels of development. Play is a time-honored, tested, and valued method of learning in early childhood.

Why has play diminished in early childhood settings? I believe this has occurred for several reasons. As we've entered the era of accountability, teachers worry about whether children will be able to achieve all the standards or outcomes if they are involved in self-chosen activities. Additionally, children now spend many more years in group settings. Children may find the same materials present for several years as they stay in the same classroom or even when they move from classroom to classroom. Boredom due to lack of challenging and interesting environments results in children displaying behavioral issues. Teachers often mistakenly reduce the amount of play in favor of more teacher-controlled groups, hoping to manage children's behavior. Finally, in an overemphasis on safety and cleanliness, we've often stripped children's environments and lives of many types of experiences and challenges.

In the past, many teachers believed that play was the only catalyst for learning. However, most teachers now realize that children's learning through play is profoundly affected by the social and physical environments. If we want to prevent boredom and help children meet outcomes primarily through play, we need to intentionally design environments that provide children with the materials, tools, and challenges that allow development to flourish. For children to gain the most from play, we also need to be available to scaffold children's learning.

I believe that if we want to preserve play, we must ensure that teachers are able to integrate developmental and curricular outcomes into play-based learning. To do this, teachers must have a deep understanding of the outcomes they want to achieve, know how to design a "rich" environment to realize the desired outcomes, and understand their role as facilitators. Quality environments are the foundation upon which a quality, play-based curriculum is built.

Important Elements in a Resource for Designing Environments for Learning

How do we learn about quality environments? Our Montana early childhood higher education program demonstrates the belief in the importance of the environment by requiring a course on early childhood learning environments. The following are the criteria we want a textbook resource to possess. In developing and writing this textbook, I have strived to meet each of these criteria:

We want a textbook that not only provides basic information on environments, but also helps students to see environmental possibilities. To enhance children's learning, teachers must be able to develop "rich" environments, but to do so teachers must have a firm foundation of knowledge. The book provides students the foundation of knowledge they need to design "rich" environments.

We want students to consider early childhood theories, child development, current research, and curriculum standards and outcomes in designing environments. For students to understand the importance of these areas, they are transparent in the textbook, with specific research information and citations. Research and theory are then translated into practice and are written in user-friendly language. Since many early childhood programs struggle with financial barriers, the book contains many practical, inexpensive ideas.

It is also important that the interests, developmental levels, and cultural and geographic backgrounds of the children in the classroom be considered in establishing environments. The book provides information and an abundance of examples that assist students in seeing that every effective early childhood environment will be unique based upon these criteria and that a cookie-cutter approach will not be effective.

Finally, the book needs to cover the entire early childhood age range, from birth to age 8. Even if students will work exclusively in pre–K programs, they need to understand the full early childhood age range since many pre–K children will be developmentally advanced and ready for more challenging activities. The book covers the entire early childhood range.

New to This Edition

This book continues to meet the philosophy previously stated and the goals set forth for earlier editions of the book. However, this third edition expands upon this foundation by providing **additional information about how this philosophy translates into K–3rd grade classrooms.** Current and future teachers must also be prepared to use the latest research as they design their early childhood environments, plan curriculum, and defend the use of play as a teaching method. Therefore, this revised edition provides the most up-to-date **information on research, curriculum standards, and play-based learning**. Furthermore, this edition continues to focus on creating a resource that is **practical, interesting, and understandable through examples and photos**. An addition to this third edition is a section in most chapters on **designing your own teaching and learning materials**. An exciting aspect of this new book is the **opportunity for students to continually assess their understanding of key concepts** through pop up short-answer and multiple-choice quizzes in the Pearson eText, which has been enhanced since the last edition. Here is a list of the key changes to this edition:

- **Additional sections on meeting the needs of children K–3** were added to many chapters. These sections assist students in understanding how this philosophy applies to children in elementary schools.
- Twenty percent of the **research** cited in the book is new. This includes 180 new research references. It is crucial that students receive up-to-date information that is supported by research, allowing them to make research-informed decisions and to defend their practices based upon research.
- **Thirty-six new or updated figures and tables** call attention to important and timely information. For example, a new figure on strategies for working with dual-language learners will assist students to meet the needs of this group of children.
- There is more **emphasis on the Common Core State Standards (CCSS)** and the addition of **new curriculum standards** in this textbook. For example, new national standards on the arts were incorporated into the music and art chapters. As a result of these new standards, dance was added to the music chapter. To preserve play, students must understand the standards and how these standards can be integrated into a play-based environment.

- In addition to an updated chapter on technology, **technology resources** have been integrated throughout the chapters. For example, there is a section on choosing e-books in the literacy chapter and apps to accompany different units in the science chapter. Technology, when well chosen, can assist in the learning process. It is important that students are able to effectively critique technology and use it wisely.
- **Short answer "Check Your Understanding" assessments (in the Pearson eText) at the end of each major heading** allow students to continually assess their understanding of chapter content and concepts. These authentic tasks and scenarios allow students to apply what they have just learned. For example, when learning about appropriate schedules, the student is then asked to critique a schedule. Answers and feedback are immediately available so that students can determine whether they understand the section or whether they should review it again.
- **A short, digital multiple-choice quiz at the end of each chapter in the Pearson eText** allows students to assess their overall understanding of chapter concepts. In addition to providing the correct answer, the student receives feedback about why this is the correct answer and why the other answers are incorrect. This helps to reinforce understanding.
- A new special section in most chapters called **"Create Your Own"** provides photos and directions for creating teaching tools that are inexpensive, durable, appropriate for a range of ages, hands-on, and rich in play value. For example, the "Create Your Own Ball Roll" is made from empty water bottles and magnetic tape. The ball rolls are placed on an auto magnetic drip pan, allowing children to experiment with different patterns as they arrange the ball rolls.
- **Additional videos** are embedded throughout the chapters, allowing students enhanced learning opportunities and the ability to learn using more than one modality.
- **More theorists** have been added to the textbook, including information on Steiner, Maslow, and Erickson, providing a context for students' learning.
- A pop-up **glossary** has been added to the Pearson eText, permitting students to easily check or clarify the meaning of a term.

Features of This Text

This textbook combines "the basics" or foundational information about how to arrange an environment with an exploration of the characteristics and abundant examples of centers rich with materials and possibilities. Several themes and features are embedded throughout the book.

- **Content and examples from each age group**—infants and toddlers, preschoolers, and primary grades—in the entire early childhood age span provide information on how to work with a variety of age groups.
- **Scenarios about children and teachers in classrooms** introduce each chapter, illustrating how research appears in practice.
- **Photos** from a variety of programs across the country are interwoven throughout the chapters, helping to illustrate points and bring theory and principles to life.
- The specific **role of the teacher** in relationship to each center provides information on how to facilitate learning (specifically, in promoting concept development and using and developing children's vocabulary unique to each center).

- **Research citations** help students to understand the knowledge base upon which learning environments and curriculum are built.
- Specific topics and strategies assist students in understanding and meeting the needs of **diverse learners**, such as special sections on English language learners and children with attention deficit hyperactivity disorder.
- **Curricular standards** and **children's developmental progression** related to each learning center assist students in understanding the goals and content to be facilitated in each learning center.
- Numerous examples provide information about how teachers consider children's **individual needs and interests** when designing the environment and curriculum.
- Inexpensive **tips** for environmental design and materials and the "Create Your Own" feature provide practical ideas.
- **"Pop-up," Interactive "Check Your Understanding" quizzes, end-of-chapter exercises**, and **Apply Your Knowledge** boxes found throughout the text help students apply and demonstrate their learning.
- **Embedded video links** help to deepen students' understanding of concepts they've read about by seeing what they are reading about.
- Comprehensive **Environmental Checklists** at the end of each chapter provide a tool to assess early childhood environments and review chapter content.
- Content and examples from **a variety of settings**, such as special sections on family childcare and afterschool programs, allow students to see the application of information to different environments.

Throughout the book you will notice the term ***teacher***. This is used as an inclusive term to designate providers, educarers, educators, and practitioners, whether working with infants, toddlers, preschoolers, or elementary-age children in home, center, or school settings. I hope that this text will inspire teaches to design environments for miracles where children learn through play, explore friendships, experience wonder and joy, and continually make new discoveries as they meet standards and learn needed content.

Instructor Resources

The following instructor resources are available for instructors to download at www.pearsonhighered.com. Click on *Educators*, then click on the *Download Instructor Resources* link.

- **Online Instructor's Manual (013401460X).** The *Instructor's Manual* gives professors a variety of helpful resources supporting the text. These include chapter overviews, teaching strategies, classroom activities, and discussion questions.
- **Online Test Bank (0134037235).** The *Test Bank* contains multiple-choice and essay (short-answer) questions. The items are designed to assess the student's understanding of concepts and application to classrooms.
- **Online PowerPoint® Slides (0134015401).** A collection of PowerPoint® slides is provided for each chapter.
- **Computerized Test Bank Software (0134014618).** Known as TestGen, this computerized test bank software gives instructors electronic access to the Test Bank items, allowing them to create and customize exams. TestGen functions in a variety of learning management system (LMS) formats.
  - **Course Management.** The assessment items in the Test Bank have been converted to operate in a variety of LMS formats.

Acknowledgments

There is a saying that it takes a village to raise a child. The same may be said about writing a textbook. A book is not written by an individual in isolation. Books build upon the research and knowledge of others. Others also provide support, encouragement, critiques, and examples. It would be impossible to list all of those who provided inspiration, support, and encouragement in writing this book. However, I would like to mention a few people who provided outstanding assistance. First, I want to thank my daughter, Lisa Bullard. Lisa reviewed, critiqued, and edited chapters; made trips across the country with me for photo shoots; provided sketches and personal photos; and provided examples of practice from her experience in a range of early childhood settings. Danny, Scott, and Christopher Bullard (my sons); Cassie Bergum and Cassie Schmit (their significant others); Justin O'Dea (my son-in-law); and Dave Browning (a special friend) also deserve thanks for the many ways they assisted with the book—creating props, and providing ideas, computer assistance, and photos—and for their patience with my preoccupation and the countless hours that I spent writing. I also want to thank my grandchildren (Seamus Bullard, Ember Bullard-O'Dea, Michael Stufflebean, and Suzi Stufflebean), who continue to be a source of delight, inspiration, photo subjects, and willing participants in trying out new ideas. Special thanks needs to go to Suzi, who is a wonderful illustrator and drew the fairies for the fairy garden. Finally, I want to thank my sister, Marysue Davis, for her dedication and strong commitment to family.

In addition to my family, many others deserve special recognition. I want to thank Eve Malo, my long-term mentor and friend who edited several chapters and provided wise advice about writing and this book. Cathy Jackson also deserves special thanks for being a masterful, creative teacher who contributed photos and inspiration for the book. I wish to thank the following reviewers for their helpful comments: LaDonna Atkins, University of Central Oklahoma; Kim Doyle, Whatcom Community College; Jill E. Gelormino, St. Joseph's College; Jeff Leffler, University of Southern Mississippi; and Sarah Ann G. Pugh, Gadsden State Community College. I also wish to thank Janis Bullock and the University of Montana Western early childhood faculty members, especially Jeff Jensen, Libby Hancock, Lucy Marose, Jen Gilliard, and Pat Adams, who provided thoughtful comments and reviews of chapters. Others who provided important support include Dawn Zimdars, Susan Parker, and Sheila Roberts. Invaluable input and encouragement were also provided by editor Julie Peters.

There were also many early childhood programs, teachers, and students who provided inspiration for the book. I want to especially thank the programs that allowed me to photograph their settings for this book, including Blessings Abound Family Child Care Center; Bozeman HRDC Head Start; Jen Gilliard's Child and Family Development Institute; Davey Hagland's Starting Small Preschool; Brenna Randall's Little Buckaroos; Cardinal Bernardin Early Childhood Center; Spokane Community Building School; Karl Wolf's Central School kindergarten classroom; Elly Drigger's Central School kindergarten classroom; Curious Minds: Early Care and Education Center; Helen Gordon Child Development Center; Mentor Graphics Child Development Center at Wilsonville, Oregon; North Idaho College Children's Center; Opal School; Renaissance School of Arts and Science; Salish-Kootenai College Child Care Center; Silver Bow Montessori; A.W.A.R.E. Inc. Early Head Start Program; Spirit at Play Center; Cozy Kid's Corner; and Middle Creek Montessori. Without their cooperation, generosity, and dedication to contributing to the field, this book would not be the same product that it is.

JULIE BULLARD
University of Montana

Brief Contents

Contents

Chapter 1

Understanding the Importance of the Environment

Learning Outcomes

After reading this chapter, you will be prepared to:

- Explain why the environment is important in children's learning
- Explain the importance of play-based learning
- Describe how an effective environment supports developmentally appropriate principles
- Explain how behavioral issues can be reduced through environmental design
- Discuss how major theorists and early childhood approaches confirm the importance of the environment
- Describe the role of the teacher in creating effective learning environments

Cathy Jackson

Close your eyes and visualize an environment from your childhood that evoked positive emotions. Remember how you felt when you spent time there. Think of the sounds, smells, and experiences in this place. Now sketch this special space, compose a brief poem depicting this place, or write a list of descriptive words that capture the essence of this environment.

Over the past years, I have asked hundreds of students to engage in this exercise. There are common threads in the students' descriptions of their favorite places. These special places typically include exploration, rich sensory experiences often involving nature, and freedom to choose activities. This place was a refuge that the student had in some way personalized or made his or her own. Is this true of your special environment?

Do the children you know or work with today have environments that meet these needs? This book will explore ways that allow us to create rich environments that become the kinds of places that children will remember as their favorites; places of rich sensory experiences, exploration, choice, and freedom—a personalized, pleasant refuge.

Why Is the Environment Important for Children's Learning?

The environment we are in affects our moods, ability to form relationships, effectiveness in work or play—even our health. In addition, the early childhood group environment has a very crucial role in children's learning and development for two important reasons.

First, young children are in the process of rapid brain development. In the early years, the brain develops more synapses or connections than it can possibly use. Those that are used by the child form strong connections, while the synapses that are not used are pruned away. Children's experiences help to make this determination. The National Scientific Council of the Developing Child compares the development of the brain to constructing a house, stating, "Just as a lack of the right materials can result in blueprints that change, the lack of appropriate experiences can lead to alterations in genetic plans." They further state, "Building more advanced cognitive, social, and emotional skills on a weak initial foundation of brain architecture is far more difficult and less effective than getting things right from the beginning" (National Scientific Council of the Developing Child 2007, p. 1). Because children's experiences are limited by their surroundings, the environment we provide for them has a crucial impact on the way the child's brain develops (Strong-Wilson & Ellis, 2007, p. 43). Not only does experience affect the development of the brain, but new research also reveals that the environment affects whether or how genes are expressed (National Scientific Council on the Developing Child, 2010).

Watch the video to learn more about early brain development. How does experience shape brain development?

https://www.youtube.com/watch?v=VNNsN9IJkws

The second reason that the early childhood group environment has such a strong role in children's development is because of the amount of time children spend in these environments. Many children spend a large portion of their wakeful hours in early childhood group settings. For example, a baby beginning child care will spend up to 12,000 hours in the program. This is more time than he or she will spend in both elementary and secondary school (Greenman, 2005a, p. 1). Children will typically spend another 4,000 hours in kindergarten through third-grade classrooms. It is important that these environments are high quality since this affects children's short- and long-term development. For example, many studies show that children in lower quality early learning environments have higher cortisol levels than children in higher quality environments. High cortisol levels are an indication of stress. Chronic levels of stress can have detrimental impacts on children's physical health, learning, and development (Sajaniemi et al., 2014).

The early childhood environment that this baby enters will reflect the teacher's philosophy, values, and beliefs about children and learning through either deliberate design or lackadaisical overlook. It provides messages to all those who enter—children, parents, and staff. Is this a place where I am welcomed and where my physical, social, and intellectual needs will be met? Is this an environment where I am seen as worthwhile and competent? Do I passively receive information in this environment, or am I actively engaging in the construction of knowledge? Is this a play-based environment? Does

Julie Bullard

Clear glass containers highlight these natural and recycled materials. What is the message that this light table and materials provide to children?

someone think I am special enough to provide a beautiful environment for my benefit? Anita Rui Olds, a well-known environmental designer, believes that we should design our early childhood environments for miracles, not minimums. She states:

> Children are miracles. Believing that every child is a miracle can transform the way we design for children's care. When we invite a miracle into our lives, we prepare ourselves and the environment around us. We may set out flowers or special offerings. We may cleanse ourselves, the space, or our thoughts of everything but the love inside us. We make it our job to create, with reverence and gratitude, a space that is worthy of a miracle! Action follows through. We can choose to change. We can choose to design spaces for miracles, not minimums. (Olds 2001, p. 13)

In this chapter we will examine the environment with regard to play-based learning and developmentally appropriate practice, discuss how environments reduce behavioral issues, review environments through the eyes of theorists, examine early childhood approaches that emphasize the environment, and finally examine the teacher's role in the environment. This chapter builds the foundation for the remaining chapters in the book, helping us on our quest to design environments for miracles.

Check Your Understanding 1.1
Click here to gauge your understanding of section concepts.

Why Is Play-Based Learning Important?

Importance of Play

A well-designed environment allows children to participate in in-depth play opportunities. The environment "is the backdrop to play, supplying content, context, and meaning" (Cosco & Moore, 1999, p. 2). What is play? Although there are many definitions, most contain the following: play is voluntary, requires active involvement of the participants, involves **symbolic activity** (pretend is involved), is free from external rules with rules being determined by the players, focuses on the **process** (the act of creating) rather than the **product** (the final result), and is pleasurable (Sluss, 2005).

Why is play important? Play promotes social-emotional, literacy, cognitive, and self-regulation skills. In fact, many argue that for young children it may be one of the best vehicles for doing so. The value of play has a long history within early childhood. In the early 1800s, Froebel, often called the father of kindergarten, stated, "Play is the highest expression of human development in childhood for it alone is the free expression of what is in the child's soul" (Froebel, 1912, p. 50). Play continues to be valued in early childhood today as exemplified by its inclusion in the Developmentally Appropriate Practices principles, which were developed by the National Association for the Education of Young Children (NAEYC).

Play has been recognized globally as not only an important learning tool but also an important right for children. For example, play is included in the United Nations Convention on the Rights of the Child (1989), an international, legally binding instrument. Worldwide, all children engage in play. However, the cultural context determines how play is expressed, the role of adults in the play, the type of play that is encouraged (whether individual or group), and gender roles in play (Johnson, Christie, & Wardle, 2005). Play allows children to practice cultural roles and to try out new roles. "During play, children not only explore and reproduce cultural roles and expectations of gender, race, and class, but also test and resist these cultural conventions as they set up and break down boundaries in their play groups" (Wohlwend, 2005, p. 78).

Through play, children learn the rules for social interaction, build social competence, practice cooperation, and gain confidence in working with others. While playing, they can adopt the persona of another, trying out their role and seeing a new perspective. Play allows children to "construct meaning from emotionally challenging experiences" (Haight, Black, Ostler, & Sheridan, 2006, p. 210). Additionally, play can help to alleviate stress (Hirsh-Pasek, Golinkoff, Berk, & Singer, 2009).

Play in a rich environment also provides the vehicle for optimal cognitive development (Hirsh-Pasek et al., 2009). During play, children actively participate in an integrated activity that is motivating and rewarding. This often involves solving complex dilemmas. Because the players control the action and the play script, the play is at the child's ideal developmental level (Johnson et al., 2005). Play also encourages flexibility in thinking and risk taking (Sluss, 2005). Lev Vygotsky, a famous Russian theorist, believed that play served several additional purposes. First, play encourages abstract thought by separating meaning from an object. For example, a building block might become a boat, house, or phone. Second, play allows learning to be supported or scaffolded by more competent peers. Third, play encourages self-talk, which leads to greater self-regulation (Johnson et al., 2005). Self-regulation is critical for academic success allowing children to focus, pay attention to what is important, and exercise self-control (Johnson, Sevimli-Celik, & A-Mansour, 2013). Play also provides children with authentic reasons to use cognitive skills, such as writing an order while playing restaurant.

Children also gain language and literacy skills as they play using speech to define plots and to designate props. A research study that followed 74 children found that three dimensions accounted for later literacy success. These were extended discourse, exposure to varied vocabulary, and home and school environments that are cognitively and linguistically challenging (Dickinson & Tabors, 2002). A well-designed early childhood environment promotes all three of these dimensions. As children play in a rich environment, they engage in extended discourse in play. Varied vocabulary is enhanced as adults facilitate learning through items they place in the environment. The well-designed environment provides a variety of activities that offers challenges for children with different interests and developmental levels.

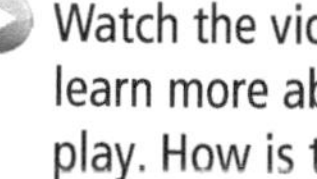

Watch the video to learn more about play. How is the value of play supported by research?

https://www.youtube.com/watch?v=vnH4ljen7Ol&index=6&list=PLyizHCAockpoWzLf4kDaq3BirJXl5mEpR

Play, particularly outdoors, is linked to many health benefits. Playing outdoors increases physical fitness and exercise, reduces obesity, and improves motor development and health outcomes. But, did you know that playing outdoors also enhances academic performance, social skills, and mental health (Gill, 2014)? See Chapter 17 for more information.

What Are the Outcomes for Children in Play-Based Programs Versus Programs That Focus on Teacher-Directed Learning?

A long-term study examined the outcomes of preschool children that used a play-based approach versus direct instruction. The curriculums were:

- DISTAR—a direct instruction model with scripted lessons
- High/Scope—children learned through play in a well-developed environment; engaged in active learning of key experiences individually, in small groups, and in whole-class groups; used a plan, do, and review process
- traditional Nursery School—loosely structured setting where teachers' responded to children's self-initiated play, and used themes or topics of study

Although initially each of the models produced similar results in academic performance, longitudinal evidence showed differences between these models. These differences began to surface when children were examined at age 15 and were more pronounced when the same group was examined at age 23. For example, at age 23, the DISTAR group had three times as many felony arrests. Additionally, only 6% of children in the Nursery School model and the High/Scope model needed treatment for emotional disturbance compared to 47% in the DISTAR group (Schweinhart & Weikart, 1997). Researchers believe that the play-based learning promoted social competence and organizational skills in children that produced these long-term results (Heckman, Pinto, & Savelyev, 2013; Schweinhart & Weikart, 1997).

Another example is found when comparing preschools in Germany. In Germany in the 1970s many kindergartens began to use a more academic, teacher-directed approach. This change allowed researchers to examine the difference in achievement between children in 50 centers who were play-based versus children in 50 centers who were more teacher-directed. The study found that by the age of 10, children in the play-based programs had higher skills in math, reading, oral expression, and creativity. They also had better social and emotional adjustment (Darling-Hammond & Snyder, 1992). The results of this study caused most programs in Germany to return to play-based learning.

Another interesting large-scale study examined 632 programs and 1897 children in 10 different countries including the United States and countries in Europe and Asia. The study found that children in preschool settings where the predominant activity was free choice had better language performance at age 7 than programs where pre-academic activities or group social activities predominated. Children's cognitive performance at age 7 was higher when children spent less time in whole group activities and when the number and variety of materials available increased (Montie, Xiang, & Schweinhart, 2006).

But, what about primary-age children, can they still learn what is needed through a play-based environment? Let's look at one study that examined this. In this study the achievement of elementary children who were in a HighScope program were compared with children who were in other comparable classrooms. Most of the comparison classrooms used a more teacher-directed approach while in HighScope the children used play-based learning centers, where they engaged in self-initiated activities. The HighScope program also involved families. The children in the HighScope programs scored higher on achievement tests in the areas of reading, writing, language, math, science, and social studies (Schweinhart & Wallgren, 1993). Throughout the book, we will be looking at many more studies that examine play-based learning.

Concerns about Lack of Play Opportunity. Worldwide there is concern about the opportunity for children to participate in play. Poverty, violence, an overreliance on media entertainment, inadequate space, and an overemphasis on academics affect children's ability and time for play (Milteer et al., 2012). For example, studies in child care centers between 1982 and 2002 found that the prevalence of pretend play had dropped from 41% to 9% (Hirsch-Pasek et al., 2009).

In addition, time for play is reduced by changing cultural values, including valuing arranged, structured activities over free play. The International Play Association (1989), in response to these alarming trends, developed a Declaration of the Child's Right to Play. They stress that play is critical for children's physical health, mental health, and education, and that we must ensure that children have the opportunity to play in educational, family, and community settings. The American Academy of Pediatricians, also alarmed by the decreasing opportunities for play, developed a position statement stressing that play is needed for healthy development. They further state that while play promotes emotional development, the lack of play and free time can lead to stress, anxiety, and possibly depression in children (Ginsburg, 2007, p. 285).

Do children have the opportunity to play in early childhood environments? In pre-K programs, it is common for teachers to provide learning centers where children can play (Early et al., 2010). However, there is concern that this is not as evident as children get older. In *Crises in the Kindergarten: Why Children Need to Play in School*, the authors examined a variety of studies, including large studies conducted in New York City and Los Angeles. They found that while most classrooms have blocks, dramatic play materials, and art supplies, children have little time to use them. For example, in most classrooms children in full-day kindergarten had 30 minutes or less for choice time and some had none (Miller & Almon, 2009).

However, this is not true for all kindergarten children. In Boston public schools, kindergarten children participate in a play-based program where rich, interdisciplinary centers are at the heart of the curriculum. Children spend 80 minutes in the centers, with a small-group pull-out during that time. They also participate in a circle time before the center time where the teacher introduces and helps children plan for center work and a circle after center time where the children reflect upon what they have learned. In addition to centers, children meet in small and large groups, participate in writing and storytelling workshops, and engage with math investigations. To learn more about this program see the Boston K2 website.

Play, engaged in by children throughout the world, is a critical vehicle for children's development. A rich environment can support children's play, providing social, emotional, physical, and cognitive benefits.

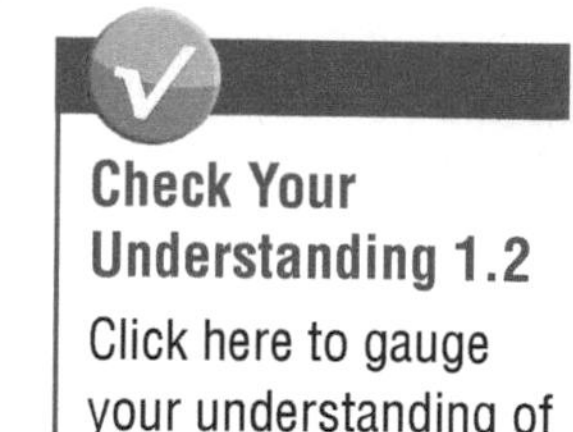

Check Your Understanding 1.2
Click here to gauge your understanding of section concepts.

How Does an Effective Environment Support Developmentally Appropriate Principles?

Drawing upon the views of a variety of theorists, NAEYC, the largest early childhood association in the world, wrote a position statement titled *Developmentally Appropriate Practice in Early Childhood Programs* (Copple & Bredekamp, 2009). In addition to play, several developmental principles set forth in the DAP position statement relate to the environment. See Table 1.1 to explore these principles and relationships.

Table 1.1 How a Well-designed Environment Support DAP Principles

Developmental Principles	A well-designed environment:
Active Learning Is Important	provides children with multiple opportunities to construct their knowledge through first-hand experiences and through interactions with peers and teachers. Teachers facilitate children's learning as they use the environment, individualizing their interactions to meet each child's needs.
Domains Are Related and Influence Each Other	allows integrated learning. For example, as children play with blocks they use gross and fine motor skills, practice cooperative and language skills, and use cognitive skills (problem solve building issues, learn about shapes, weight, and balance). The well-designed environment encourages children to be independent, to exercise control, and to build competence and mastery, assisting children in developing a healthy self-concept. When children have a healthy self-concept, they are more likely to be successful socially and academically.
Learning Follows Well-Documented Sequences, Becoming More Complex over Time	provides materials at a variety of levels meeting the needs for different levels of complexity. A preschool math center would contain materials for children working on one-to-one correspondence, counting, recognizing numerals, and adding and subtracting.

(Continued)

Table 1.1 How a Well-designed Environment Support DAP Principles *(Continued)*

Developmental Principles	A well-designed environment:
Development Is Variable	provides a variety of materials and activities that meet the needs and interests of individual children with varying abilities. Allows the individual child to work at different levels in different areas. For example, the child may be able to read simple books but be very low in math skills.
Social and Cultural Contexts Influence Learning	assists in cultural understanding by accurately reflecting the lives of children and families in the program through classroom materials, photos, and written and spoken language. Multicultural books, pictures, music, art, manipulatives, and dramatic play props representing children in the classroom as well as other cultures expand the children's understanding.
Biological Maturation and the Environment Interact	provides a range of challenges, so that as a child successfully completes a challenge, another one awaits. The child controls the amount of time engaged in a particular activity and whether to work alone or with others. This freedom allows children to be self-directed learners, learning from both the physical and the social world. It also recognizes and honors the individual child's maturity level.
Practice Advances Development	provides opportunities for children to practice skills in an authentic way (using skills in a real-life context rather than through drill). Authentic tasks are more engaging and a more effective way to learn than those same tasks performed through drill or direct instruction (Cooper, Capo, Mathes, & Gray, 2007).
Development Occurs in the Context of Secure, Consistent Relationships	provides a place where children and adults can find sanctuary, nurturance, comfort, compassion, and community (Greenman, 2005a). Relationships flourish as children have the opportunity to play with peers in self-chosen activities. The one-on-one time with an adult that occurs as children interact in learning centers facilitates positive relationships.
Experiences Shape Future Dispositions and Behaviors	provides multiple ways of learning the same skill through different learning centers. This allows children to choose the learning modality that is most effective for them, while exposing them to a wide range of different learning options. Persistence and initiative are increased when children have the opportunity to learn in ways that are interesting and motivating to them.
Early Experiences Are Critical	allows children to participate in activities that that are ideally matched to the child's interests and development, thus providing a solid foundation for current and future learning.

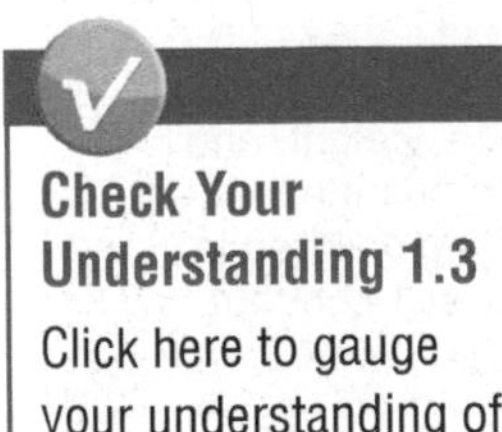

Check Your Understanding 1.3
Click here to gauge your understanding of section concepts.

How Does an Effective Environment Support Positive Behaviors?

In addition to helping support play and developmental principles, a well-designed environment reduces behavioral issues, allowing children to spend more time engaged in learning and teachers to spend more time scaffolding children's learning. The environment can help prevent behavioral issues in five ways. The well-designed environment:

1. provides children with many choices at different developmental levels allowing children's unique skill levels, preferred learning styles, and interests to be addressed. Children who are actively engaged in developmentally appropriate, interesting activities that they choose usually display fewer behavioral issues.

2. reduces stress by allowing children to learn in developmentally appropriate ways and by providing private spaces where children can escape. When children have private areas to retreat, they learn more and have lower levels of stress.
3. includes a variety of activities that assist children to manage emotions such as soothing water play, pounding on clay, or dancing to music.
4. promotes positive relationships. Research shows that there is a link between appropriate classroom environments and secure, positive relationships between the teacher and children (Howes, Fuligni, Hong, Huang, & Lara-Cinisomo, 2013).
5. is intentionally designed to prevent common behavioral issues.

Julie Bullard

After a family who is Chinese introduced the children to a tea ceremony, the teacher extended their learning with these dramatic play materials.

To prevent common behavioral issues:

- Teachers design learning centers (dedicated areas, indoors or outdoors, that have intentional purposes) that allow small groups to work together, without interruption from others.
- Dividers are placed between areas to provide a protected space for play, and to assist children to stay focused.
- Clear boundaries keep materials in one area from interfering with other areas. For example, shelves are placed between the art and block areas, which prevents trucks from running under the easels.
- Fighting over limited resources is prevented by having a sufficient number of materials (for very young children, exact duplicates are often necessary).
- Interesting, enticing materials keep children from being bored.
- Making sure each center is well-stocked with enticing materials keeps children from all congregating in one place.
- Organized and labeled shelves allow children to keep materials orderly and to locate the materials that they need.
- Materials and books are in good condition and beautifully displayed, creating the desire in children to want to care for them.
- The floor plan is developed to prevent children from seeing it as a racecourse. For example, when an obvious circular path is available it invites children to run (see Chapter 5 for sample floor plans).

Julie Bullard

This retreat space was developed by children and their teacher at Spirit at Play when they were completing a project on birds.

- Density (the number of children in a given space) is reduced, since crowding increases the likelihood of aggressive behavior (see Chapter 6 for research and information on density).
- Children's health and safety needs, including restful places to sleep or relax, are planned for.

If you have behavioral issues in your class, first examine the environment to see if a change could solve the problem. For example, I was a consultant to a program where the following occurred:

The teachers were very frustrated because three children were running their large Tonka trucks (housed in the block area) under the art easels. The day before I arrived, one of the easels had fallen, splattering paint everywhere. The teachers had placed the children involved in time-out, but the next day they again drove the trucks under the easel. At this point, the teachers banned these children from the block area for one week. When I arrived, I observed that there was no clear division between the art and block area. In my opinion, the children crawling on the floor may have been focusing on their play and oblivious to the easels. After our discussion, the teachers redesigned the room, placing clear dividers between the art and block area. This solved the problem, where the punitive approach did not.

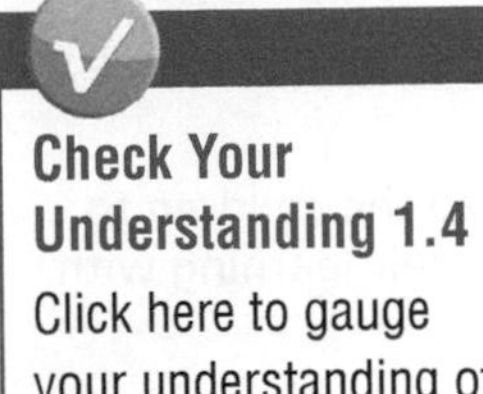

Check Your Understanding 1.4
Click here to gauge your understanding of section concepts.

We have seen how the well-designed environment supports play-based learning and developmentally appropriate practice and how it can reduce behavioral issues, allowing the caregiver to concentrate on positive interactions with children. Now we will examine the historical roots of the environment as a key early childhood learning element.

Early Childhood Theories and Approaches: What Is the Role of the Environment?

Early childhood theories and approaches support the need for a rich environment. Just what does a "rich" environment mean? What are its characteristics? We will begin our discussion with Maria Montessori, who is credited with designing and promoting beautiful, child-size environments filled with engaging materials. Maria Montessori's philosophy influenced both Piaget's and Vygotsky's theories (Mooney, 2000), which we will examine next. We will then discuss the perspective of Loris Malaguzzi, who built upon the work of Piaget and Vygotsky as well as other theorists to develop the Reggio Emilia approach (Rankin, 2004). Finally, we will examine Steiner and the Waldorf approach. Examining the theorists and approaches assists us in understanding the historical and philosophical foundations for designing learning environments.

Montessori

As we prepare orderly, clean, aesthetic environments using child-size furnishings and beautiful materials, we can thank Dr. Maria Montessori, an Italian physician, who was the first advocate of such settings. The carefully prepared environment is a key component of Montessori's philosophy. She states:

> The immense influence that education can exert through children, have the environment for its instrument, for the child absorbs his environment, takes everything from it, and incarnates it in himself. (Montessori, 1995, p. 66)

According to Montessori, the child must find the environment motivating, so he or she is interested in pursuing the available activities. The child will then want to "conduct his own experiences" (Montessori, 1995, p. 92).

Montessori stressed that the environment needs to liberate the spirit, promote independence, allow activity, and be beautiful, safe, and orderly. It is necessary that the environment be orderly to prevent children from wasting their energy seeking materials (Standing, 1957). Additionally, Montessori believed that when children play in an orderly environment, this desire for order becomes part of the child.

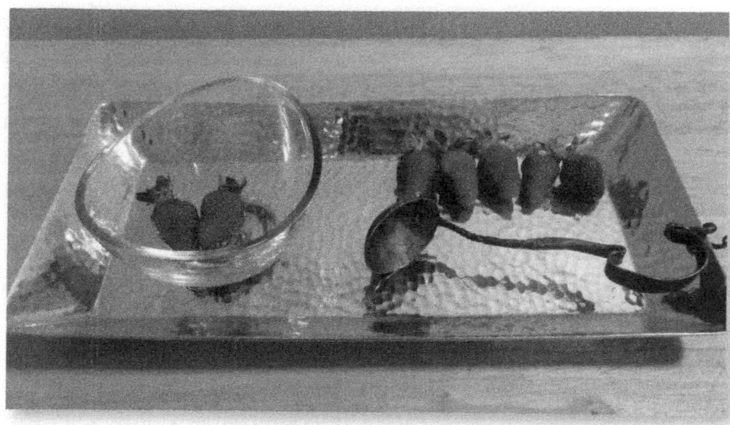

Julie Bullard

This aesthetic practical life activity for toddlers allows them to use tools found within a kitchen.

Child-size environments, according to Montessori, applied to not only furnishings but also the proportions within the entire building (windows that are near the ground, low door handles, shallow steps) (Standing, 1957). She promoted using low, open shelves to display self-correcting materials (e.g., knobbed cylinders to seriate by size are placed in a frame that will only allow the correct-sized cylinder to fit). Maria Montessori also advocated providing real working tools (knives and scissors that cut, shovels and trowels that actually dig holes, quality paints and clay) to children.

She also believed in beauty. According to Montessori, the environment and materials should be clean and have harmonious colors. However, she also stressed that materials should be practical. For example, she replaced several expensive, beautiful marble tables that had been donated to the Montessori center with more practical, simpler, wooden tables that could be easily moved by the children.

The goal of the environment according to Montessori is, "As far as it is possible, to render the growing child independent of the adult. That is, it is a place where he can do things for himself—live his own life—without the immediate help of adults." In this environment the child becomes "increasingly active, the teacher increasingly passive. It is a place where the child more and more directs his own life: and in doing so, becomes conscious of his own powers. As long as he is in a state of dependency on the adult he cannot grow as he should" (Standing, 1957, p. 267). However, Montessori also felt that the teacher plays a very critical role, since children only have access to the materials that the teacher provides (Montessori, 1995). In addition, teachers observe children, provide very specific guidance to children on how to use the materials, and support them when needed. However, they show respect for the worker and do not interrupt unless it is necessary. The competent teacher "must make her presence felt by those who are seeking; and hide from those who have already found" (Standing, 1957, p. 280).

Piaget and the HighScope Approach

Piaget. Like Montessori, Piaget believed that children learn through play, with curiosity driving their learning. He stressed that children construct their knowledge through active involvement. As stated by Piaget, "Experience is always necessary for intellectual development . . . but I fear that we may fall into the illusion that being submitted to an experience (a demonstration) is sufficient for a subject to disengage the structure involved" (Duckworth, 1964, p. 174).

However, more than just experience is required. "The subject must be active, must transform things, and find the structure of his own actions on the objects" (Piaget, 1964, p. 4). In addition to experimentation, the child must be interested in the learning experience (DeVries, 2004). Without interest, the child will not exert the effort to make sense of the experience. Piaget believed that cooperation is also helpful for active learning. Cooperation helps people experience moral dilemmas and conflicts, and to become aware of differences in opinions and viewpoints, thereby creating cognitive disequilibrium (Bullard & Hitz, 1997). **Disequilibrium** is an uncomfortable state where new information challenges one's existing knowledge, beliefs, or assumptions. When this occurs one might **assimilate** the information, working it into his current thinking and belief system, or the person might **accommodate** or modify her thinking or belief. For example, a child might see a horse for the first time and think "cow," assimilating this new animal into their current thinking. However, if someone tells the child it is a horse she might create a new category of animal, accommodating or changing her thinking. Piaget stressed, "Active physical and mental interactions of the child with the environment (physical and social interactions) that permit construction are seen as the most important school-related factor in cognitive development" (Wadsworth, 1989, p. 165). Piaget also believed that the child needs to be able to transform space. This includes looking at things from a different angle, such as looking down upon a scene on the classroom floor from a loft.

According to Piaget, the teacher is a guiding mentor, who encourages initiative, experimentation, reasoning, and social collaboration. She arranges safe, supportive environments for spontaneous exploration where learners are free to choose from many alternatives (Bullard & Hitz, 1997). Like Montessori, Piaget believed that to be effective the teacher needs to be a careful observer, so that he can set up environments and experiences that challenge children.

HighScope. Developed in the 1970s by David Weikert and his colleagues, HighScope is based on the child development ideas of Jean Piaget. HighScope is undoubtedly the most researched early childhood curriculum, showing positive results in both social and emotional as well as cognitive skills. Today the curriculum is used throughout the world and serves infants and toddler, preschoolers, and elementary-aged children. At the heart of the curriculum is a belief in active learning where children construct their knowledge through their experiences and through reflection. As children engage in active learning they participate in key developmental indicators, facilitated by teacher interactions. A strong emphasis is placed on the learning environment, which is divided into interest areas and supplied with plentiful materials. In addition to commercial materials, teachers seek out natural, found, and recycled materials. Authentic items that represent children's lives outside the classroom are viewed as being especially critical (HighScope, 2015). Daily routines such as the planning, working, and recalling (plan, do, review) assist children to reflect on the learning in the centers. The HighScope model encourages beginning planning with toddlers, believing that planning and recalling helps children to "call up mental pictures of themselves in action, to connect their ideas with actions, to communicate their intentions to others, and to begin to organize their past actions into a simple narrative" (Post & Hohman, 2000 p. 260).

Watch the video to learn more about HighScope. How does HighScope help children to learn through play-based environments?

Vygotsky and Tools of the Mind

When you think of Vygotsky, you probably think of his best-known theory, the **zone of proximal development**. This zone is the difference between what we can independently accomplish and what we can accomplish with assistance from a more competent peer or teacher. This assistance is called **scaffolding**. Like that of a construction crew, this support helps us to reach a higher level.

Like Piaget, Vygotsky also believed that children actively construct their own knowledge, and that play is a vehicle for doing so. Both theorists believed that play promotes both cognitive and social learning. According to Vygotsky, play, especially pretend play, should be the leading activity for preschool and kindergarten-aged children.

Vygotsky defined play as an activity that involves an imaginary situation created by the children in which they take on roles and follow a set of rules related to those roles (Bodrova & Leong, 2007). As children play, they use language to negotiate roles, enact scenes, and determine processes, furthering their development (Mooney, 2000).

In addition to play, preschool children should also engage in what Vygotsky called productive activities, such as storytelling, block building, and art and drawing. Pre-academic skills are considered beneficial, but only if they emerge from children's interests, are considered meaningful to children, and occur in a developmentally appropriate social context (Bodrova & Leong, 2007). According to Vygotskians, motor activities (statues and stop-and-start games) can also assist with development, especially self-regulation and attention.

When children enter first grade, learning activities become the leading activity. "Learning activities are adult-guided activity around specific, structured, formalized content that is culturally determined" (Bodrova & Leong, 2007, p. 210). However, children at this age still use models (manipulatives and graphic representations). Vygotskians also stress that children themselves need to understand the learning goal and learn to judge their work according to a standard or acceptable level of performance.

To follow the Vygotskian approach you must be a careful observer who uses the information learned to plan hands-on, interactive environments and to scaffold children's learning. Since Vygotsky believed that learning occurs in a social setting, you would provide opportunities and encouragement for children to work together (Mooney, 2000). In addition, Vygotskians often support the quality of children's play through helping them develop play plans (see Chapter 7 for more information).

Tools of the Mind Curriculum. Designed for preschool and kindergarten the Tools of the Mind curriculum is based upon Vygotsky's philosophy, as discussed previously. If you were to visit a classroom using this curriculum, you would find children engaged in playful learning, using make-believe play as a primary means of developing self-regulation. Pre-K children develop play plans that guide the first few minutes of dramatic play while kindergarten children develop learning plans that guide children's work as they use the activity centers. The teacher assists children to develop mature play, where an elaborate theme is maintained over a long period of time, with complex roles and role speech (Leong & Bodrova, 2012).

Children are taught specific skills to support peer scaffolding and to create classroom community. For example, children are taught how to provide encouragement and to give constructive feedback to their partners.

Props and toys are chosen that provide for **open-ended** use. For example, large pieces of cloth rather than specific dress-up clothes might be found in the dramatic play area. However, specific props related to the child's current type of play might also be available, helping children to remember their roles. For example, if playing restaurant, the cook might have a chef hat while the waiter has an apron (Bodrova & Leong, 2007).

Malaguzzi and the Reggio Emilia Approach

Malaguzzi, the "philosophical leader" of the Reggio Emilia inspired approach, scaffolded his approach upon the work of other theorists including Montessori, Piaget, and Vygotsky (Fraser & Gestwicki, 2002, p. 9; Rankin, 2004). Like the previous theorists, he believed that children construct knowledge through active engagement with the environment. Similar to Vygotsky, he stressed the importance of social interaction in developing children's mental constructions.

In the Reggio approach, teachers base the educational environment and activities upon the **image of the child**. The child is seen as unique, curious, capable, competent, having potential, relationship seeking, an active constructor of knowledge, and a

possessor of rights rather than needs (Fraser & Gestwicki, 2002; Gandini, 2004). This image affects the way that teachers work with children. They view themselves as co-constructors of knowledge, or as partners in children's learning.

Apply Your Knowledge What adjectives would you use to describe your image of the child? How does this image affect the way you interact with the child?

The Reggio Emilia environments are referred to as the "third teacher" (the parents and teachers are considered the other two teachers). Several principles support this concept (Fraser & Gestwicki, 2002; Gandini, 2012). In the Reggio Emilia approach, the environment:

- Is aesthetic, containing beautiful materials and spaces. There is intense attention to detail in every environmental feature, with no overlooked corner, wall, ceiling, or floor.
- Is highly personalized, reflecting the culture and interests of the inhabitants through photos, materials, artwork, and transcriptions (Gandini, 2004).
- Promotes active learning through abundant **affordances**, or opportunities to learn that include many choices, provocative displays, and a variety of open-ended, intellectually stimulating materials. The school is a "workshop for research and experimentation, a laboratory for individual and group learning, a place of construction" (Ceppi & Zeni, 1998, p. 14).
- Encourages interaction with materials through the use of **provocations** (activities, materials, or questions that provoke thought, problem solving, and creativity), many different types of objects (realistic objects, colorful beautiful objects, natural objects, authentic furniture, tools, and utensils), beautiful displays that highlight materials, and mirrors that are placed to see objects in new ways (Strong-Wilson & Ellis, 2007).
- Encourages children to represent their ideas in many different types of media. Each center has an **atelierista** (a trained visual arts teacher) and an **atelier** (shared arts studio). In addition, many classrooms have mini-ateliers. Malaguzzi gave art a new meaning by using art as a tool to express one's ideas, thoughts, and knowledge, and also to further one's thinking. As one creates art, knowledge, ideas, and thoughts become visible and new questions, ideas, and thoughts emerge.
- Welcomes children, families, and teachers and views them as the three subjects of education. As stated by Rinaldi, "everything that happens to one affects the other" (Rinaldi 2001, p. 53). The Reggio community is characterized by empathy, close bonds, a sharing of knowledge, fears, and hopes, and a construction of common values and shared meanings (Ceppi & Zeni, 1998, p. 11).

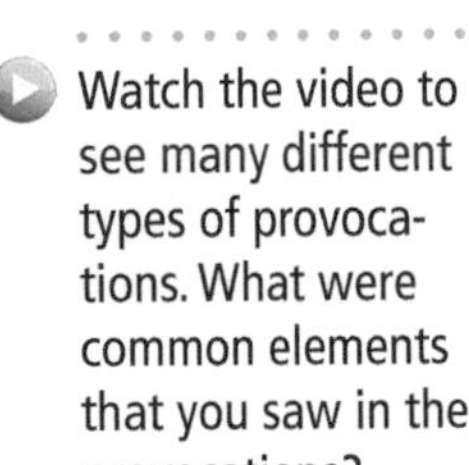

Watch the video to see many different types of provocations. What were common elements that you saw in the provocations?

https://www.youtube.com/watch?v=CCb2KD6X8BU&list=PLaNtPP95UBnzGnYlGjkQp3n6i3cJc3OBY&index=38

Julie Bullard

This light activity for infants and toddlers at North Idaho College Children's Center is an example of a provocation.

- "Fosters encounters, communication, and relationships" (Gandini, 2004, p. 17) through the design of activities and space. Spaces are available for children to work in small groups, and to work individually if they choose. Common areas, such as a central piazza, encourage children, parents, and teachers from different groups to interact. The environment is also rich in documentation of group efforts. It is a "living testimony to interactions that happen in the environment" (Strong-Wilson & Ellis, 2007, p. 42).
- Provides rich sensory experiences that encourage "investigation and discovery using the whole body." The environment itself (walls, floors, ceilings) is also multisensory, with different sensory media so each individual person's needs can be met (Ceppi & Zeni, 1998, p. 8).
- Provides transparency. Light is everywhere, shining through low windows; reflected in shiny mobiles and mirrors hung from ceilings, walls, and lofts; shining from interesting light features; flowing through transparent fabric, beautiful glass objects, colored transparency film in windows, and child-created murals on plastic sheets; and explored with light tables. Children can look from one space to another, outside, or into another classroom. It is also a metaphor for openness and transparency in sharing learning through documentation (Fraser & Gestwicki, 2002).
- Brings the outside world in. This includes the natural world and the social world (the community and culture). The program experiences "osmosis with the world outside. A school should not be a sort of counter world, but the essence and distillation of society surrounding it, it is a part of the larger world" (Ceppi & Zeni, 1998, p. 6).
- Supports flexibility and creativity through encouraging children and adults to use objects and space in imaginative ways.
- Provides reciprocity. The environment is not passive; instead, it is like a living being, conditioning and being conditioned by children's and adult's actions (Fraser & Gestwicki, 2002; Gandini, 2012).

The Reggio Emilia teacher is a keen observer who is an active listener and interpreter. She uses this knowledge to design flexibly planned curriculum and to establish provocations that help children think more deeply and to question their assumptions. The curriculum occurs at a leisurely pace and flows naturally from the children's and teachers' ideas (Gandini, 2004). The teacher also collaborates with children, coworkers, families, and the community to form a "community of learners" (Fraser & Gestwicki, 2002).

Steiner and the Waldorf Approach

Ruldolph Steiner was an Austrian scientist and philosopher who developed the Waldorf Approach. Like the Montessori and Reggio Approach, the Waldorf Approach was designed following the devastation of war, in this case World War I. With each of these approaches the goal was to create a better society. Initially this coeducational school was founded for the Waldorf-Astoria cigarette factory. Today there are Waldorf schools throughout the world serving children from preschool through high school. As stated in a lecture by Steiner, "Every education is self-education, and as teachers we can only provide the environment for children's self-education. We have to provide the most favorable conditions where, through our agency, children can educate themselves according to their own destinies" (Steiner & Trostli, 1998).

For the young child, imaginary play is viewed as critical. Teachers nurture the imagination through storytelling and preparing rich environments for imaginative

Watch the video to learn more about the Waldorf and the Montessori approach. How does the environment support the children's learning in these two approaches?

play. Environments are beautiful, warm, home-like, and filled with natural materials. For example, in a Waldorf preschool environment you might find tree branch blocks, bark, stones, wool, beeswax, and plant-dyed sheep's wool. As stated by Dora Dolder from the International Waldorf Kindergarten Association, "It is important that one uses beautiful, pure material to awaken the artistic senses and sensibilities" (Dolder, 2007, p. 22).

Teachers who follow the Waldorf approach believe that much of what children learn is through imitating adults. "The child will imitate not only the words and gestures of the teacher, but will also imitate the teacher's inner mood" (Oppenheimer, 2007, p. 31). The teacher therefore plays a critical role. As stated by Susan Howard, "Thus the essential element in early childhood education is actually the educator, who shapes and influences the children's environment, not only through the furnishings, activities, and rhythms of the day, but most important, through the qualities of her own being and her relationships to the children and other adults in the kindergarten, to the parents, to daily life in the kindergarten, and to living on earth" (Howard, n.d., p. 1).

Current Elementary School Initiatives

The Partnership for 21st Century Skills and the Association for Supervision and Curriculum Development (ASCD) Whole Child Initiatives also support learning through the environment. Nineteen states have joined in the Partnership for 21st Century Skills, which is designed for preschool through college age students. The goals stress the need for children to not only learn academic subjects but also learn other skills that they will need to be successful in the 21st century. These skills include learning to think and work creatively with others, implement innovations, effectively communicate and collaborate, engage in critical thinking and problem solving, and gain information, media, and technology skills. Learner-centered curriculum based on student needs and interests, integrated curriculum, project-based learning, collaborative groups, developing curriculum around big ideas and essential understandings, and space divided into learning zones are emphasized in schools subscribing to this philosophy.

The ASCD's Whole Child Initiative also examines skills that children will need in the 21st century, believing that a narrow focus on academics alone will not promote long-term success or development. In addition to challenging, comprehensive curriculum in core subjects, the initiative stresses the need for skills in reasoning, problem solving, critical thinking, and technology. The Initiative, designed for early childhood through high school, is endorsed by over 70 national organizations and several international groups. In schools subscribing to this philosophy you would see an emphasis on physical and emotional safety; physical and emotional health and well-being; engaged children involved in inquiry, project-based, and experiential learning; cooperative learning as well as individualized learning guided by assessment; child decision making and goal setting; learning within the community; and families as partners. Learning centers are a way that this vision can effectively be implemented.

Montessori, Piaget, Vygotsky, Malaguzzi, and Steiner all valued the environment as an important teacher of young children. They each also valued the teacher as an environmental designer and as a scaffolder of children's learning. Throughout the book, we will learn more about these theorists. We will also be learning about other theories such as Smilansky's theory of play, Maslow's hierarchy of needs, and Erickson's stages of psychosocial development. Current initiatives in elementary schools such as the 21st Century Skills and the Whole Child Initiatives are also favoring a child-centered approach, consistent with learning through centers. In the next section, we will further examine the teacher's role in supporting children's learning.

Check Your Understanding 1.5

Click here to gauge your understanding of section concepts.

What Is the Role of the Teacher in Facilitating Learning Through the Environment?

Teaching effectively through the environment requires the teacher to be concurrently aware of the children in her classroom (their developmental levels, cultural backgrounds, interests, learning styles, dispositions, and behavioral nuances) and the early learning guidelines, curriculum standards, and program outcomes appropriate for her age group. She must use this information to design relevant, engaging environments and to make needed environmental changes as the year progresses. Finally, she must be available as children use the environment to scaffold their learning. In this section, we will discuss the prerequisites for establishing the environment, some key points for environmental design, and the teacher's role once she has designed the environment. See Figure 1.1.

We will examine these roles through four cases. Each of these points will be further explained in chapters throughout the book.

Prerequisites to Effective Environmental Design: Sanya's Story

Sanya, a Head Start teacher is newly hired as a substitute to teach three-year-olds in a Head Start classroom, while their teacher, Veronica, goes on maternity leave. Veronica encourages Sanya to change the environment to meet children's changing needs. Although Sanya is very familiar with both child development and developmentally

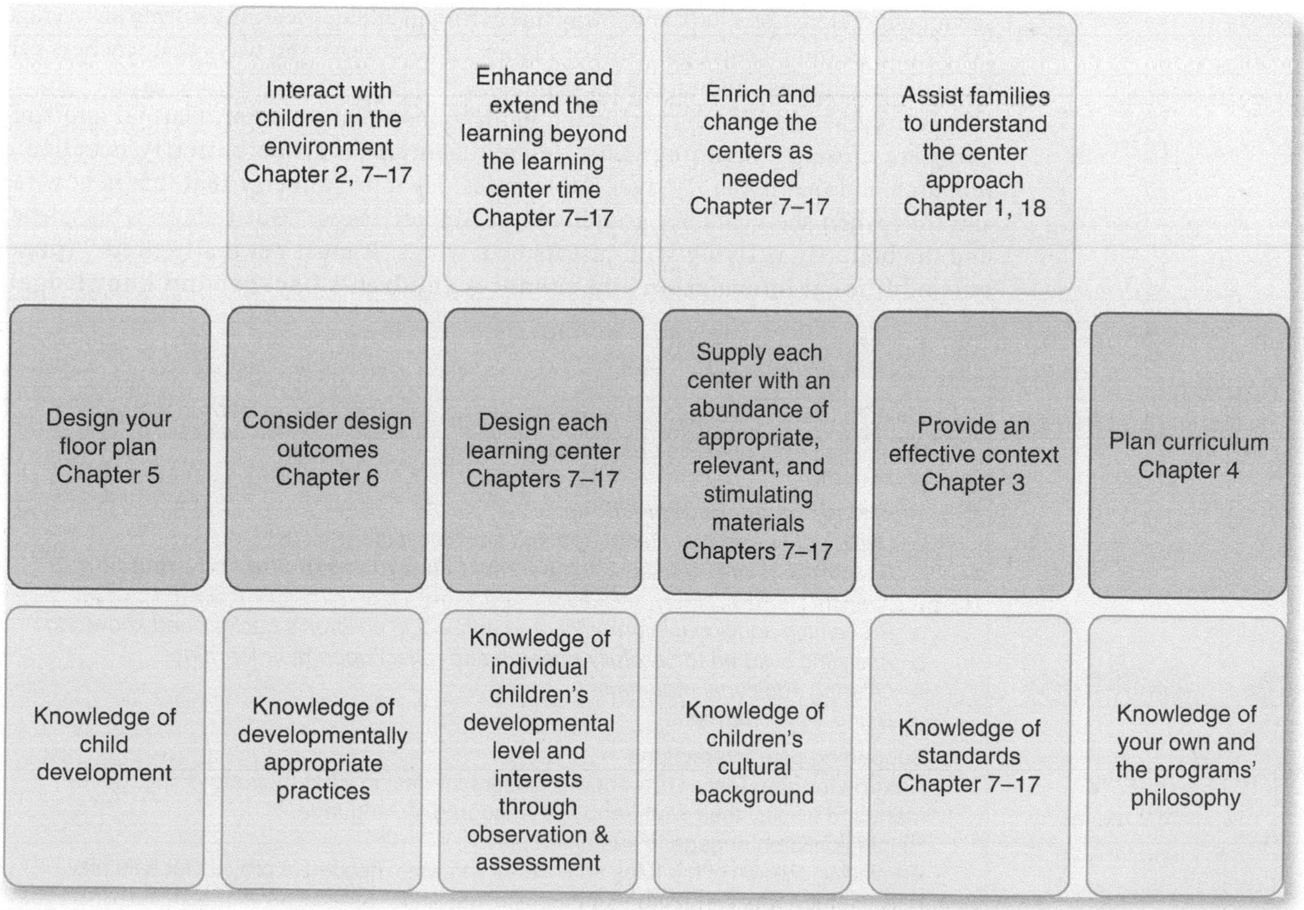

	Interact with children in the environment Chapter 2, 7–17	Enhance and extend the learning beyond the learning center time Chapter 7–17	Enrich and change the centers as needed Chapter 7–17	Assist families to understand the center approach Chapter 1, 18	
Design your floor plan Chapter 5	Consider design outcomes Chapter 6	Design each learning center Chapters 7–17	Supply each center with an abundance of appropriate, relevant, and stimulating materials Chapters 7–17	Provide an effective context Chapter 3	Plan curriculum Chapter 4
Knowledge of child development	Knowledge of developmentally appropriate practices	Knowledge of individual children's developmental level and interests through observation & assessment	Knowledge of children's cultural background	Knowledge of standards Chapter 7–17	Knowledge of your own and the programs' philosophy

FIGURE 1.1 The Role of the Teacher: Environmental Designer and Facilitator of Learning

appropriate practice, she must get to know these individual children and their families. She reviews the children's assessments, spends time getting to know individual children, and makes home visits to families. Like an ethnographer, she tries to understand the community, the families, and the children. Since she has not worked for Head Start before, she must also become familiar with the Head Start Outcomes Framework, the standards used by Head Start. While Sanya knows that an important part of her own philosophy is play-based learning, she must also learn about the Head Start's philosophy. She learns that they use the HighScope method, so she begins to study this including how to implement planning, working, and recalling. Sanya must understand these prerequisites before she can begin to design an effective environment or curriculum.

Supporting Learning as the Children Use the Centers: Jeffrey's Story

Jeffrey, a first-grade teacher who has been teaching for several years, has become increasingly dissatisfied with teaching. He'd entered the teaching field because he enjoyed facilitating children's learning. But, lately, teaching has seemed like drudgery for himself and for the children. After taking a workshop on active learning, he has decided to redesign his room into learning centers. As children use the centers, he wants to take the opportunity to interact with them individually and in small groups, recapturing the role he treasured as a facilitator of learning. After three weeks, both Jeffrey and the children seem invigorated. Let's look at the way that Jeffrey facilitates learning during an average 60-minute learning center period (see Figure 1.2 to observe the ways that teachers can facilitate learning as children use the centers).

Jeffrey has added a butterfly and moth to the science center. Garmai and Amberly are closely examining them. Jeffrey mentions that the butterfly is called a monarch and that it can fly over 2,000 miles. He tells Amberly that this is how far she flies when she visits her grandmother. Amberly says, "But I am in a big plane, and the butterfly is flying with just its own wings. It must get really tired." **(presents additional information and enhances children's background knowledge)**.

FIGURE 1.2 Facilitating Children's Learning

As children use learning centers teachers interact with them in the following ways:

- ❑ Scaffolding or supporting children's learning
  - ❍ ***Modeling***
  - ❍ *Asking* ***open-ended questions***
  - ❍ *Using rich, descriptive language and new vocabulary*
  - ❍ *Encouraging language by using* ***parallel talk,*** *and* ***expanding*** *and* ***extending*** *speech*
  - ❍ *Presenting additional information and enhancing children's background knowledge*
  - ❍ *Assisting children to carefully observe and reflect upon their learning*
  - ❍ *Offering additional materials*
  - ❍ *Being a play partner*
- ❑ Supporting peer interactions

  Acknowledging learners—show a sincere interest in what they are doing, document and display their work, and use encouraging language.

  Helping children engage in sustained play

  Reminding children of the rules and intervening when needed to provide for safe play

  Purposefully observing and documenting learning

  Meeting children's individual needs

Jeffrey says to Garmai and Amberly, "Look at the butterfly's and moth's antennas." The children look through magnifying glasses, noting that the butterfly has a round club at the end of its antenna while the moth does not. Jeffrey next asks the children if they would like to look at the butterfly and moth through the digital microscope **(provides additional material)**. Finally, Jeffrey asks the children if they would like to draw the butterfly and moth **(helps children observe and reflect upon their learning)**. Jeffrey takes a photo of the children observing the butterfly to post with their sketches **(documents learning)**.

Jeffrey next goes to the art area where three children are working with clay. One of the children is trying unsuccessfully to attach an arm to her clay figure. Jeffrey demonstrates how to score and then use a slip to attach the clay **(models and provides new vocabulary)**. Another child says, "Look, look." Jeffrey says, "Wow, you figured out how to make your figure stand" **(acknowledges learner)**.

Jeffrey hears a commotion in the block area. Two children are tugging on opposite ends of a block, both wanting the same block for their respective block constructions. Jeffrey goes to the area and helps the children resolve the issue **(supports peer interactions, intervenes when needed to provide for safe play)**. He notices that Sarah, a new child, is watching the children build but seems uncertain of what to do. Jeffrey sits near her and begins to build. He asks Sarah if she would like to join him **(play partner)**. When she nods yes, he asks her what type of building they should create **(asks an open ended question)**. (See examples of open-ended questions in Table 1.2.) She says, "Hospital." Jeffrey replies, "Do you want to build a hospital like your mother works in, one with a lot of stories?" **(encourages language by expanding and extending speech)**. As you can see, Jeffrey used many different techniques to support children during the learning center time. He has become excited about teaching again as he sees children actively engaged in learning.

Open-ended questions encourage multi-word responses that have more than one correct answer. They invite conversation, require thinking and problem solving, and ask children to share ideas, theories, thoughts, emotions, and reasoning (Kostelnik, Whiren, Soderman, & Gregory, 2012). **Closed-ended questions** ask the child to recall factual information, provide a correct answer, answer yes or no, or state a preference.

Table 1.2 Sample Closed and Open Questions

Closed Questions	Open Questions
What shape is this?	In what ways are circles and ovals the same or different?
What color is the bird?	Why do you think the bird is brown?
Should we skip or hop across the room?	What are other ways that we can move across the room?
Is this a moth or butterfly?	How are the butterfly and the moth the same? How are they different?
Will the salt affect the ice?	What are ways that we can make the ice melt faster?
Can you make applesauce from apples?	What are other things that we could make with the apples?

Apply Your Knowledge Two children have spent the entire center time building a multi-floor castle. They are proudly showing the castle to you. What are some encouraging remarks you could say to the children?

Enhancing and Extending the Learning Beyond the Learning Center Time: Veronica's Story

To take full advantage of the environment as a learning tool we need to extend the learning beyond the center time (see Figure 1.3). One technique is to use small- or large-group discussions to introduce center activities and materials, build excitement, provide relevant background experiences, introduce challenges, plan and recall experiences, encourage children to share their work, and synthesize and discuss children's learning. Let's visit Veronica's preschool classroom to see how she does this. Veronica was introducing a bubble center that was going to be in the sensory table. She set out a variety of objects (funnels, sieves, regular spoons, slotted spoons, forks, a tea strainer, and a potato masher) and asked the children what they thought you might do with these materials. After a lively discussion and many guesses, Veronica brought out a bubble wand and asked again. Several children then guessed that they were going to make bubbles **(introduced center activities and built excitement)**. Veronica had the children vote on whether each item would make bubbles or not and graphed their answers. Since children were going to be sorting items and creating a graph at the bubble center this allowed Veronica to teach the children how to make a picture graph **(provided relevant background experiences)**. Children were eager to see if their hypotheses were correct and to try the different materials. Over the course of the next several days, all of the children voluntarily visited the center. After a few days, Veronica challenged the children to create as small a bubble as they could and as large a bubble as they could **(introduced challenges)**. At another circle time children shared what tools they had used to create their smallest and their largest bubble and Veronica listed this information on a chart that was posted in the center **(encouraged children to share their work)**. After the children had used the bubble center for a couple of weeks, Veronica again discussed the bubbles. She and the children re-examined their initial predictions and reviewed what they had found out. Veronica placed all the items that made bubbles in one area and all those that did not in another. She asked the children what was similar about the items that made bubbles. By having this circle, Veronica was able to help children analyze and express what they had learned **(synthesized and discussed children's learning)**. As you can see it is important that teachers know the children, the standards, and their own and the program's philosophy to design an effective programs.

FIGURE 1.3 Enhancing and Extending the Learning Beyond the Learning Center Time

To take full advantage of the environment as a learning tool the teacher needs to:

- ❑ Introduce Center Activities and Materials
- ❑ Build Excitement
- ❑ Provide Relevant Background Experiences
- ❑ Introduce Challenges
- ❑ Plan and Recall Experiences
- ❑ Encourage Children to Share Their Work
- ❑ Synthesize and Discuss Children's Learning

They also need to facilitate learning as the children use the centers, and expand and extend the learning beyond the learning center time. It is also important to help others understand the learning center approach.

Helping Families Understand the Learning Center Approach

It is also the responsibility of the teacher to assist families in understanding developmentally appropriate practices, and to keep families informed about what their children are learning. Families are often concerned about whether their children will be successful in the next level of schooling. Some parents associate worksheets with learning. When they do not see these sent home each night they become worried. Here are several techniques teachers have used to provide information to families.

Jeremy has a family night at the beginning of each year. He introduces the center approach by having the families complete activities in each learning center. Jeremy tries to choose activities that would be appropriate for children and also interesting for adults. For example, in the manipulative area, Jeremy places a collection of office items with a sign asking families to sort them in as many ways as they can think of. One year, four parents became very engaged in this activity and found 50 different ways of classifying the materials. At the end of the evening, the families and teachers gather together to reflect upon what they have learned.

Teresa makes signs to place in each center that list skills and knowledge that children acquire through using the center. She also regularly sends "Today I learned" notes to the families. While children interact in centers, she will observe and write a short note to families to tell what their child has learned that day. For example, "Chin used both math and science skills to make a block structure with a turret today. He experimented with many ideas (hypotheses) before solving the problem of how to create a turret that would balance on top of his tower." Teresa has created a check-off sheet so that she can easily track who she has sent notes to. By keeping a tracking sheet, Teresa can make sure that she regularly sends notes to each child's family.

Teachers may also display children's artifacts (samples of children's "work") on the wall or in digital picture frames. Many teachers also send artifacts and other forms of documentation from center work home. These include photos of children participating in an activity, artwork and recording sheets the child has created, or audio recordings of children reading or telling a story. At least occasionally, it is helpful to include information that describes and interprets what children learned. Many teachers save some of this work to place in portfolios. The portfolio will include artifacts with a description and interpretation for each artifact. Portfolios are typically shared with parents during parent-teacher conferences or home visits.

Rhonda, a teacher of kindergarten children, develops a booklet that describes the learning centers in her classroom. There is a photo of each classroom center, a description of what children learn in the center, and the state standards that are addressed in the center. Each year she gives the booklet to each family and the school administrators. She states, "Before I did this, families and the administrators were concerned about whether the children would be ready for first grade if they spent so much time playing. However, now that they understand that children can enjoy school and still be meeting the standards, they have become advocates for this approach."

Programs that use the project approach often have **culminating events** to conclude a project. Culminating events allow the children to share what they have learned with parents and other community members. For example, one program had completed a project on "Our Body," and decided to have their culminating event at a community health fair. They set up displays that included webs of what the children knew before and after the project, questions the children had, art they had created, stories they had written, and materials they had used. Pictures and narratives described the center materials, children's activities, and learning throughout the project. They also invited the public to try out a sensory walk that the children had created. For the sensory walk, the children decorated 14 flat boxes and placed a different item in each box (e.g., sand, bubble wrap, sandpaper). Participants could walk barefoot through each of the boxes. The teachers in each of these scenarios helped families and others to understand what children learn as they use a learning center approach.

Teachers play a crucial role in children's learning by designing a rich, stimulating environment, interacting with children as they use the environment, expanding and extending the children's learning beyond the center time period, and changing centers and adding materials to provide for more in-depth learning. In addition, teachers assist families and administrators to understand the learning center approach. In each chapter of this book, you will find many other examples of specific ways that teachers are involved in children's learning.

Check Your Understanding 1.6

Click here to gauge your understanding of section concepts.

In this chapter, we have discussed the importance of the learning environment, how the environment supports play-based learning and developmentally appropriate practices, the crucial role of the teacher, and the recognition by theorists and early childhood founders of the importance of the environment. It seems only fitting to end this chapter with a quote from Maria Montessori, who first created the child-sized environment and filled it with beautiful, thoughtfully planned learning materials. In discussing children's cognitive development she states, "The first lesson we must learn is that the tiny child's absorbent mind finds all its nutriment in its surroundings. Here it has to locate itself, and build itself up from what it takes in. Especially at the beginning of life must we, therefore, make the environment as interesting and attractive as we can" (Montessori, 1995, p. 97).

Chapter Quiz 1

Click here to gauge your understanding of chapter concepts.

Sample Application Activities

1. You began this chapter by imagining your favorite childhood environment. Now think of your favorite environment today. Are there commonalities between your favorite environment as a child and your favorite environment today? What aspects of your favorite environment could you share with children through your classroom environmental design?
2. Review the Developmentally Appropriate Practices position statement on the NAEYC website.
3. Visit a classroom and observe how the environment is affecting children's behavior.
4. You have just been hired to teach a kindergarten class in a public school with K–5 classes. Write a one-page letter to parents describing why developmentally appropriate practices and learning through play are important in kindergarten.
5. Visit the Alliance for Childhood website to learn more about the importance of play and studies that support it.

6. Using the information in the text, compare and contrast the Montessori, Reggio Emilia, Tools for the Mind, HighScope, and Waldorf approaches. For additional information, review the organizations associated with each of these approaches.
7. Visit an early childhood facility. What do you see in the environment that was influenced by Montessori, Vygotsky, Piaget, Malaguzzi, or Steiner? Observe the teacher and record examples of the ways she is scaffolding the children's learning.

Chapter 2

Establishing an Emotionally Supportive and Equitable Environment

Learning Outcomes

After reading this chapter, you will be prepared to:

- Discuss the importance of supportive relationships
- Define an emotionally supportive, equitable environment using the Circle of Courage framework
- Describe the foundations of an emotionally supportive and equitable environment
- Discuss the teacher's role in supporting the Circle of Courage

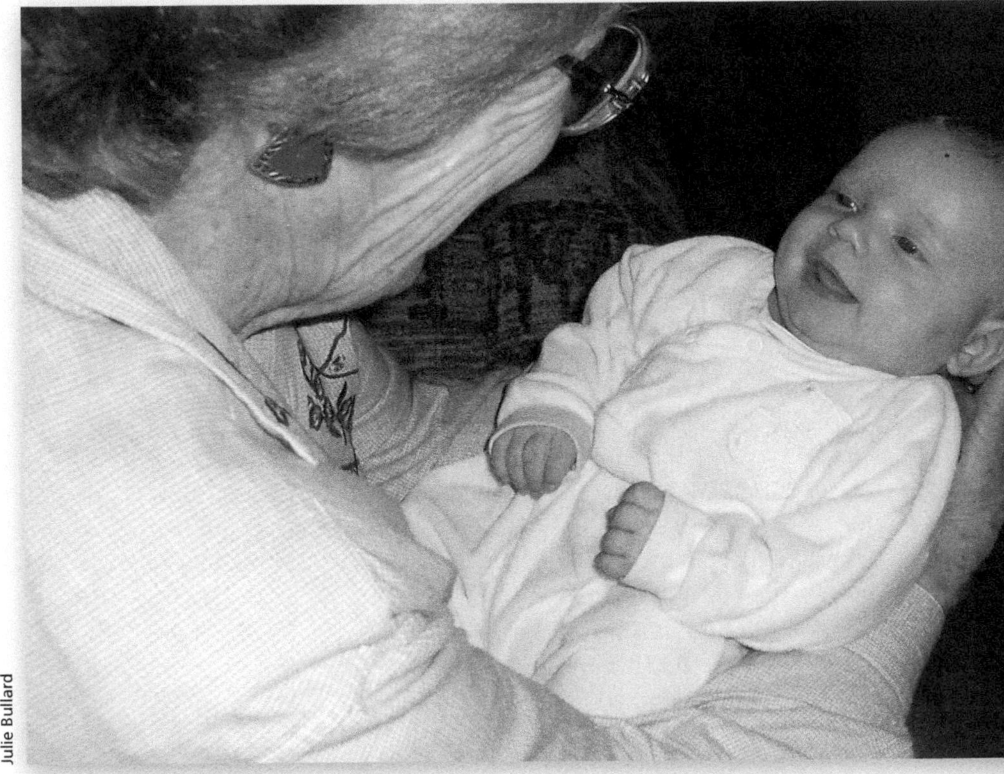

Julie Bullard

It was November when Kamiko's parents enrolled her in preschool. They had just arrived from Japan to work on a ranch in an extremely isolated, rural, Caucasian community. Alisha, Kamiko's teacher, knew that she should have materials in the environment that reflected Kamiko. However, she could not easily find any books or nonstereotypical images of Japanese children. She finally ordered some books, and when they arrived several weeks later she placed them in the reading area. Kamiko was elated when she discovered the books. She carried one of the books with her all day, saying "me, me" to everyone she met. She even slept with the book at nap time. The next day she again carried the book with her, showing the pictures to each parent and child as they arrived.

It was a vivid reminder to Alisha of the importance of having materials and images representing all the children in the classroom. When Alisha saw Kamiko's reaction, she began to examine all the classroom materials. There were multicultural dolls in the dramatic play area, but none were Asian. The same was true for the multicultural figures in the block area. A multicultural poster adorned the wall, but again none of the children were Japanese. Alisha replaced the multicultural poster with photos of children in the classroom, she ordered Asian dolls, and she visited with Kamiko's parents to see if they had any materials that she could add to the classroom. The parents brought in some empty food containers, a children's dish set, and a Japanese newspaper for the dramatic play area. This recognition by Alisha of the family's culture helped to build relationships. As the year progressed, Alisha continued to learn more about Kamiko's culture and to build relationships with Kamiko and her family.

Importance of Supportive Relationships

Relationships are the heart of an early childhood program. Just as a plant needs to experience both sunlight and rich soil to produce a healthy plant, a child needs to experience both quality *relationships* and quality *instruction* to be successful (Ray, Bowman, & Brownell, 2006). Relationships affect children's social skills, academic success, and brain development (National Scientific Council on the Developing Child, 2004b, 2007; Ray et al., 2006). They also affect children's and families' feelings about the program.

Relationships between staff and children, staff and families, among children, and among staff define the climate of a program. High-quality climates assist children to feel safe, increase positive behavior, and reduce absenteeism from the program. When children are in emotionally supportive environments in the early years their achievement increases, resulting in higher social, math, and reading scores. Additionally, supportive relationships positively influence work habits and improve educational resiliency. This is especially true for children who are at risk of school failure (Ray et al., 2006).

Emotional responsiveness (acknowledging and responding to children's emotions and needs), particularly in the early years, even affects brain development and the biochemistry of the brain. Similarly, unresponsive care can alter the brain's biochemistry. Here's how this works: when we feel stress, our bodies produce the hormones adrenaline and cortisol. Both hormones help the body to respond to threat. However, when these hormones are activated either frequently or for long periods, they can produce negative effects on the brain. For example, long-term elevations of cortisol can change the architecture of the brain, leading to memory and learning problems. Because young children's brains are "particularly malleable," stress is especially harmful for this age group (National Scientific Council on the Developing Child, 2004b, p. 2).

The child's early experiences also determine how the stress system reacts to subsequent stress. High levels of stress can result in a stress system that responds at a lower threshold of stress and remains stressed for a longer period of time. As stated by the National Scientific Council on the Developing Child, "Like the immune system, which defends the body

Table 2.1 Maslow's Hierarchy of Needs

Hierarchy Levels	Needs	Examples
8	Transcendence	Helping others achieve self-actualization
7	Self-actualization	Self-fulfillment, personal growth
6	Aesthetic	Beauty, order, symmetry
5	Cognitive	Knowledge, understanding
4	Esteem	Achievement, confidence, responsibility
3	Love and belonging	Friendship, affection
2	Safety and security	Protection, stability
1	Physiological	Food, sleep

against threatening infections but can cause autoimmune disease when it turns against the body's own cells, a poorly controlled response to stress can be damaging to health and well-being if activated too often or for too long" (National Scientific Council on the Developing Child, 2004b, p. 2). Elevated stress can lead to an increased vulnerability for stress-related disorders (depression, anxiety, cardiovascular problems, stroke, and diabetes).

However, high-quality care in the early years leads to a lessened stress response. In addition, as you will learn in this chapter, when a child does experience stress, the responsive teacher can dramatically buffer the child's stress response through her relationship with the child (National Scientific Council on the Developing Child, 2004b).

While teachers have limited influence over the other environments that children are in, they do have control over their classroom. When the classroom environment is emotionally supportive, children experience less stress, there is reduced absenteeism, and they learn more. But, why is this? One way of understanding this is to view these results through the lens of the hierarchy of needs identified by Maslow, a humanistic psychologist. According to Maslow, the lower needs must be met before we can begin to work on higher needs (Maslow, 1970; McLeod, 2007). You would not be able to concentrate on learning, if you were in an unstable environment with unpredictable adults. For young children, the adults in their lives exert almost complete control over their physiological needs and safety needs, and finally as stated earlier strongly influence their feelings of belonging. See Table 2.1 for Maslow's hierarchy.

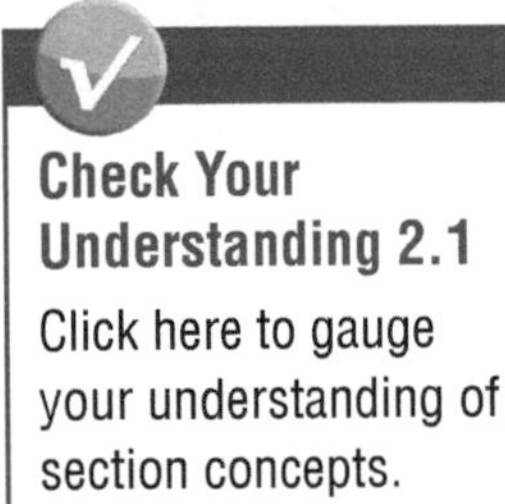

How do we create an emotionally supportive environment? We will examine this question next.

Circle of Courage: Defining an Emotionally Supportive, Equitable Environment

Realizing the importance of the emotionally supportive, equitable environment, many curriculum developers have designed excellent models to assist teachers. In this chapter, we view the supportive environment through the lens of one of these models, the Circle of Courage. This model, simple to remember and yet profound, provides a unifying theme for services to children in multiple settings. The model, which incorporates resiliency (Brendtro & Larson, 2006) and self-worth research (Coopersmith, 1981), is used worldwide in educational, mental health, youth and family services, treatment facilities, and juvenile justice settings.

The Circle of Courage, based on Native American philosophy, is compatible with beliefs from many cultural groups. The philosophy is based on four needs (the need to belong, to achieve mastery, to be independent, and to be generous). Brendtro, Brokenleg, and Van Bockern (2002), the authors of the Circle of Courage, describe these in the following ways:

- The child who experiences the spirit of belonging knows "I am loved." This is essential for meeting all other needs. To experience the spirit of belonging, children must have mutual connections or positive relationships characterized by deep respect. Since belonging is cyclical, the child who expresses this ideal also knows how to identify and relate to others.
- The child who experiences the spirit of mastery knows that "I can succeed." This includes both academic and social competence. Mastery assists a child to have a positive self-concept.
- The child who experiences the spirit of independence knows "I have the power to make decisions." This provides individual control and inner discipline, and allows the child to establish and attain goals. As stated by the authors of the Circle of Courage, "Even when it might be easier for the adults to 'take over,' adults will respect children enough to allow them to work things out in their own manner" (Brendtro, Brokenleg, & Van Bockern, 2002, p. 53).
- The child who experiences the spirit of generosity knows "I have a purpose for my life." Generosity allows the child to take "responsibility for the welfare of others in the community" and to contribute positively to the group through being caring and empathetic (Brendtro et al., 2002, p. 59).

According to the authors of the model, when these needs are not met or are out of balance the child becomes discouraged and loses a sense of purpose, leading to a downward spiral. Adults often have a difficult time forming relationships with discouraged, disengaged children, and may respond to them punitively. This leads the child to react in an even more discouraged way. However, using the Circle of Courage as a guiding framework for interacting with children, designing our environments, and planning our curriculum can help children to avoid this downward spiral.

Check Your Understanding 2.2

Click here to gauge your understanding of section concepts.

Circle of Courage Foundations

In order to meet the needs of belonging, mastery, independence, and generosity, children need foundational skills. These foundational skills include attachment, self-regulation, and social skills (empathy and friendship skills). We will examine each of these foundational skills next.

Attachment

Secure **attachment** is at the heart of the spirit of belonging. "Attachment describes a strong emotional bond between a baby or young child and a caring adult who is part of the child's everyday life—the child's attachment figure" (Honig, 2002, p. 2). The attachment figure greatly influences a child's beliefs about relationships. These beliefs become internalized templates for behavior and have a "profound effect throughout life" (Honig, 2002, p. 3). Attachment grows over time, beginning at birth and progressing through the early years. It involves a two-way interaction, with the child affecting the caregiver and the caregiver affecting the child.

Securely attached children use the adult attachment figure as a home base, feeling comfortable to explore or try new things, but returning to the caregiver for reassurance and guidance. Children who are securely attached to at least one adult have better current and future academic and social outcomes. They are also more resilient (Center on the Developing Child, 2015). About 70% of young children display secure attachments to one or both parents (Riley, San Juan, Klinkner, & Ramminger, 2008). However, these children also benefit from having a secure attachment to their childcare provider or teacher. There is no indication that the relationship between the child and caregiver negatively affects parental attachment. Instead, outcomes are more positive if the child is attached to both the parents and the early childhood teacher. Attachment to the teacher is even more crucial for children who do not have a secure attachment with their parents (Riley et al., 2008). While attachment is critical for young children, it is very difficult if they must detach and reattach to important people in their lives. This can cause stress and "enduring problems" (National Scientific Council on the Developing Child, 2004a, p. 4). Therefore, we must try to reduce the number of times that children are moved to new classrooms or programs or experience new teachers within the same classroom. For example, many infant/toddler programs practice *continuity of care* and permit teachers to move with more mobile infants into the toddler room when they become ready for this transition.

Attachment is a universal developmental aspect in all cultures. However, the way that responsiveness is demonstrated may differ from culture to culture (Riley et al., 2008). Cultural discontinuity between the child's home and childcare or school setting can cause the child to be vulnerable to stress (Espinosa, 2006). Therefore, it is important that we observe how parents promote secure attachment, so that we can support the child and family by using similar routines and techniques (Riley et al., 2008).

Secure attachment is a critical component of the Circle of Courage, forming the basis for the spirit of belonging. The spirit of belonging is essential for meeting the other needs—mastery, independence, and generosity.

Self-Regulation

Self-regulation is the ability to control one's emotions, actions (impulsivity), and thinking (focusing attention and planning). The ability to self-regulate predicts both immediate and long-term success. Children who have good self-regulation skills display higher self-esteem, increased academic performance, better social skills, and the ability to handle emotions constructively (Riley et al., 2008, p. 67).

Watch the video to examine how toddlers learn to regulate emotions. How do adults assist or hinder this crucial skill?

Regulating Emotions. Gaining the ability to regulate emotions is one of the tasks of the early childhood years. By the end of the preschool years, most children are able to anticipate and discuss their feelings. This is very important because "when children can label a feeling, they can make the leap from unconscious experience to conscious control" (Riley et al., 2008, p. 86). Poorly managed feelings can impair learning, attention, decision making, planning, and problem solving (National Scientific Council on the Developing Child, 2004b).

Culture affects the way that children display their emotions (Day, 2006). For example, some cultures view it as inappropriate to display anger in public while other cultures do not. In some cultures, physical affection is openly displayed, whereas in others this is viewed as inappropriate. Children learn the culturally acceptable ways to display emotions through imitation, feedback, and direct instruction (Kostelnik, Gregory, Soderman, & Whiren, 2012).

Regulating Actions and Thinking. Self-regulation of actions and thinking is also developing during the early childhood years. Self-regulation often involves delaying gratification or exercising self-control. A study that followed 1,000 children until the age of 32, found that the degree of self-control as a preschool child predicted criminal behavior, health, finances, and substance abuse as an adult. The degree of self-control was nearly as strong a predictor of adult outcomes as the child's intelligence or social class (Moffitt et al., 2011).

Cathy Jackson

To regulate emotions, we must be able to identify and express emotions in an acceptable way. At times, it is easier to express emotions when you can become someone or something else.

It is easier for children to learn self-regulation if they are in a predictable environment. I once worked as a houseparent for children who were abused and neglected. At mealtime, many of the children overate. Even though snacks were readily available, several of them hid food in heater vents, under pillows, and in dresser drawers. They were unable to delay gratification for eating because they had lived in unpredictable environments where food was not consistently available.

In addition to providing a predictable environment and routines, we can assist children to develop self-regulation skills by helping them develop successful techniques. One successful technique that children often use in delaying gratification is to distract themselves. Self-talk (verbalizing what you are doing or the next steps to take) is another technique that children use to assist in regulating both actions and thinking. A third technique that assists with self-regulation is planning. For example, we might incorporate "plan, do, review" (see information in Chapters 1 and 3 on the HighScope method) as a way of helping children learn planning skills.

Teachers also need to be aware of typical development and make referrals to specialists where appropriate when development is atypical. Even very young children have deep and intense feelings and can experience severe mental health problems (National Scientific Council on the Developing Child, 2004b). If there are mental health concerns, teachers need to discuss these concerns with the family and refer the child to a specialist. Early intervention can be critical for current and future well-being.

Learning to regulate one's emotions, thoughts, and actions are important goals for the early childhood years. Self-regulation is a foundation for achieving mastery and independence, and for interacting successfully with others or displaying generosity.

Social Skills

Children's social skills build upon their self-regulatory skills. Researchers contend that social skills and knowledge are as important for school success as academic skills (Ray et al., 2006). To form and maintain successful relationships, children must identify, regulate, and manage their feelings in a constructive manner. In addition, they must develop empathy and friendship skills (National Scientific Council on the Developing Child, 2004b).

Developing Empathy. To develop **empathy**, children must first be able to engage in social perspective-taking (understanding another's wants and thinking) and emotional perspective-taking (understanding another's feelings). With empathy, the child experiences an emotional response as he views things from the other's perspective (Riley et al., 2008). When 3-year-old Julian sat down and cried next to his friend Kirsten, who was sad that her mother had left, he was displaying perspective-taking and empathy. He understood Kirsten's feeling of loneliness and demonstrated an emotional response to her sadness.

Developing Friendship Skills. To make friends children must learn communication, negotiation, and play entry skills. In addition, they must demonstrate the attributes of a friend. Children often learn these attributes, such as cooperation, faithfulness, and loyalty, from more competent peers or adults.

Even during the first year of life, children begin to recognize another child as a social partner. As toddlers, they begin to have reciprocal social interactions (Honig & Thompson, 1994). For example, Tabi and Tenile were washing dolls in the water table. Tabi said, "Baby wet." Tenile handed her a towel and said, "Dry baby." Tabi said, "Thank you." The friendships formed in the toddler and preschool years can be quite stable over time (Dunn, 2004). One study found that 50% to 70% of children's friendships lasted through the next year (Howes, 1989). The concept of friends changes from preschool to elementary school to adolescence. However, children typically choose friends that are similar to themselves in race, gender, behavioral characteristics, play behaviors, and attitudes (Kostelnik et al., 2012).

"The quality of peer relationships in early childhood predicts later success in intellectual growth, self-esteem, mental health, and school performance" (Riley et al., 2008, p. 42). Why do friendships affect children's outcomes? While interacting with friends, children develop interaction skills, practice reciprocity and fairness, and learn to value other's feelings. Research also indicates that children's interactions with groups of friends are more positive than when they interact with other peers. In addition, a group of friends is often pursuing a mutual goal, leading to discussion, negotiation, and cooperation. This leads to more problem solving and complex thinking (Riley et al., 2008, p. 43). Friends can also be helpful in coping with new situations. For example, when children move to a new classroom at the same time as a friend, the transition is easier. Having a friend in an established group also helps pave the way for other friends to join the group.

However, the peer group rejects some children. Rejected children often exhibit inappropriate social skills (Honig & Thompson, 1994), particularly communication skills (Hazen & Black, 1989). Children who are not popular are more likely to perform poorly in school and ultimately drop out (Riley et al., 2008). Children who do not have friends are also at serious risk for detrimental developmental effects (National Scientific Council on the Developing Child, 2004a, p. 3).

Check Your Understanding 2.3
Click here to gauge your understanding of section concepts.

Teachers have a responsibility to assist children in developing the foundations for the Circle of Courage: attachment, self-regulation, and social skills. How can teachers accomplish this? We will examine the teacher's role in assisting children to develop these skills in the next section.

The Teacher's Role in Supporting the Circle of Courage

The teacher plays a crucial role in helping the child to feel a sense of belonging, mastery, independence, and generosity. The teacher models these characteristics, establishes an environment that assists children in achieving these values, and supports children through informal and formal techniques.

Creating a Spirit of Belonging

The teacher sets the stage for the child to feel a sense of belonging by displaying a warm, accepting attitude. This helps the child to form an attachment to the teacher. She also creates a welcoming and caring classroom community. Finally, she is responsive to all children, including those who are from cultures different from her own, children who come from low-income families, and children with disabilities.

Forming an Attachment with Each Child. "Throughout the early childhood years, most learning depends on the formation of a nurturing relationship" (Riley et al., 2008, p. 8). When this is absent, developmental delays can occur. For example, studies of children reared in orphanages have demonstrated that the lack of attachment and responsive care results in developmental delays in social, emotional, cognitive, and language development (Rosas & McCall, 2009). In addition, attachment to a primary caregiver in early childhood settings appears to reduce the levels of the child's cortisol. Cortisol is typically highest in the morning and decreases throughout the day. However, research has shown that when children are in childcare, cortisol often rises throughout the day. This can be reduced when the child has a consistent, responsive caregiver that they are attached to (Badanes, Dmitrieva, & Watamura, 2012).

Children are more likely to form attachments to adults who are sensitive, warm, and nurturing (Riley et al., 2008), and who show unconditional positive regard for the child (Gartrell, 2011). To help form attachments, the adult needs to show genuine interest in the child and spend quality time with him. For example, the adult converses with the child, listening attentively as he speaks, and asks questions to get to know the child's preferences. As the child and adult spend time together, they learn to "read each other," and it becomes easier for the adult to know how to assist the child (Riley et al., 2008). In addition, children gain their feelings about their own self-worth from the adults in their environment. When the adult is warm and responsive, the child feels valuable and worthwhile. Children who experience warmth from their caregiver display greater social competence, have fewer behavioral issues, achieve more academically, and show increased reasoning skills. They are more excited about school and are more self-confident (National Scientific Council on the Developing Child, 2004a). For example, a recent study found that children's math development was related to the relationship between the teacher and child. This may be because children who have a closer relationship with the teacher get more individualized attention and encouragement (Choi & Dobbs-Oates, 2014).

In addition to displaying warmth, the adult must also be responsive to the child. The responsive adult treats children with respect and responds quickly to their needs. For example, the infant teacher responds to a baby's cries. She also uses appropriate pacing during interactions, taking cues from the baby (Riley et al., 2008). Like a conversational dance she follows the baby's lead, talking to the baby and then pausing, waiting for a reply. She might also describe the baby's nonverbal actions, "Oh, you're yawning, are you tired?" From the baby's cues, such as turning his head away, the teacher recognizes that he is trying to escape the stimulation and respects this. The teacher creates a responsive environment and schedule that allows time and space for emotionally supportive interactions. It is very important that the teacher is consistent in his or her interactions. Research shows that the more consistent the teacher is the better the academic, social, and emotional outcomes are for children. The authors of the study speculate that when children have to exert less effort to monitor the teacher's moods, they have more attention to devote to learning (Bailey, Zinsser, Curby, Denham, & Bassett, 2013).It takes time for attachments to develop. Secure attachment is more likely when there is an ongoing sustained relationship between the caregiver and child (Honig, 2002, p. 22). Unfortunately, high teacher turnover rates in early childhood programs can negatively affect attachment by not allowing time for the attachment to develop, and by creating negative impacts when the attachment ends. In addition, frequent moves from classroom to classroom can also have negative impacts on the child. There is a relationship between the number of lost caregivers and socially withdrawn or aggressive behavior on the part of the child

Table 2.2 Erikson's Stages of Psychosocial Development During the Early Childhood Years

Stage of Development	Age	How Adults Assist in Development
Trust vs. Mistrust	Birth–1	Provide a predictable, warm, loving environment with predictable caregivers
Autonomy vs. Shame and Doubt	Toddlers	Allow children choices and control, avoid shaming the child over accidents
Initiative vs. Guilt	Preschool	Allow children to plan and initiate activities and to explore interpersonal skills through play
Industry vs. Inferiority	Elementary	Provide encouragement, allow children many opportunities to be successful

(Howes & Hamilton, 1993). The child who loses a person she is attached to may act depressed and have difficulty forming new relationship. Erik Erikson, a theorist known for developing stages of psychosocial development, states that the most important goal of the child under one is the establishment of trust (Erikson, 1964). When children continually lose providers, their ability to learn to trust is diminished. See Table 2.2 to learn more about Erickson's stages.

What can early childhood programs do to assist with attachment? In addition to reducing turnover, programs can provide time for relationship development by assigning primary caregivers and keeping children with the same caregiver for multiple years (Riley et al., 2008). Smaller child/adult ratios also assist with attachment. We will next examine another way to create a sense of belonging.

Developing a Classroom Community. We often hear about the need to develop a sense of community, but what exactly does this mean? When there is a sense of community, there is an emotional connection among members. They encourage, support, and influence each other. Members depend on each other and feel like insiders within the group. To create a sense of community, you can:

- Make sure that all staff, children, and families are represented in the classroom displays and materials.
- Help children get to know each other and to bond together as a cohesive group. Many programs begin the year with "All About Us," where children learn about themselves and others in the classroom. This time is also devoted to many group-building activities.
- Allow time for children to systematically share with each other (see Figure 2.1), and to spend time interacting in both formal and informal small groups.
- Set up the classroom environment to encourage children to work together. For example, provide two phones in the dramatic play area, multiple earphones to listen to a CD, two doll buggies for strolling together, wagons for pulling each other,

The morning meeting, a component of the Responsive Classroom, is designed to assist children to feel welcome; form respectful, trusting relationships; create a sense of community; and enhance social and academic skills (Kriete & Davis, 2014; Roser, 2012). These meetings are often child led. They typically consist of:

- ❑ A greeting where each child's name is used
- ❑ Sharing of personal news
- ❑ A brief, lively activity to build group cohesion
- ❑ A morning message about what will happen today

FIGURE 2.1 Developing a Sense of Belonging Through the Morning Meeting

rocking boats and swings, easels side by side with paint that is shared, two chairs at the computer center, large floor puzzles, and board games.

- Be realistic about sharing. Even adults have difficulty sharing favored possessions or items they are using. Make sure that you have duplicate materials and enough materials so that all children can be actively engaged using materials that interest them.
- Develop activities where children work together to complete a goal. For example, children might create a garden, paint a mural, build a house from straw bales, move together like a centipede, or make a ball bounce on a parachute.
- Develop a unique sense of place in the program, one that represents the children, adults, and community in which you live. To create a sense of place, you can display photos of staff, children, and families. Also, you can provide materials that reflect the uniqueness of the environment in which you live. For example, if you live near a beach, your playground might include driftwood that children can use for building. Many programs develop a special sense of place by encouraging children to name the classroom and develop a class mascot.
- To create a sense of belonging we must form attachments to each child and develop a classroom community. We must also be responsive to all children. We will examine this next.

Julie Bullard

When these early elementary-aged children begin school at the Renaissance School of Arts and Sciences in Portland, Oregon, they create their own bucket. They use these buckets to carry art materials and their lunch when they go on field trips.

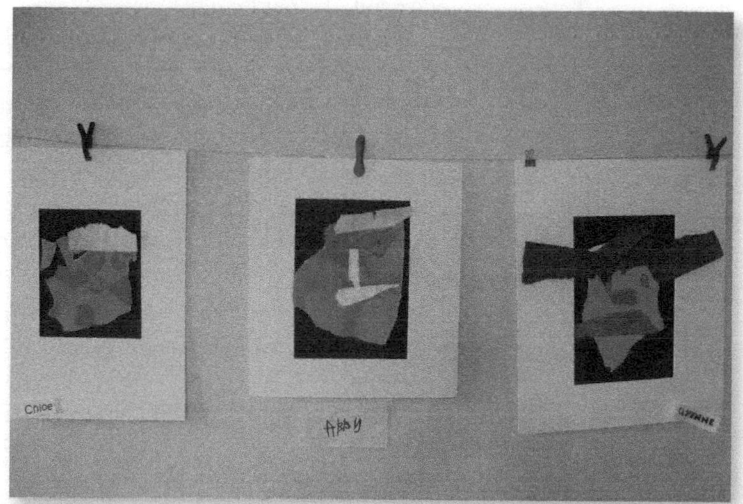

Julie Bullard

These preschool children created their faces out of torn paper as part of the beginning of the year "getting to know you" project.

Being Responsive to Children from All Cultures. "Culture is defined by the values, traditions, social and political relationships, and worldview shared by a group of people bound together by a combination of commonalities that include one or more of the following: history, geographic location or origin, language, social class, or religion" (Wolpert, 2005, p. 53). Culture is learned, often being passed on from generation to generation. However, members are embedded in the cultural group to different degrees. Culture is dynamic, changing over time due to influences from cultural members as well as outside forces. However, there is also cultural stability. The desire of a system to maintain the status quo tends to prevail over change. Culture is a template that influences all aspects of our lives: our goals, expectations, relationships, values, roles, and perspectives. Through our culture, we learn rules that govern the way we think, act, and feel, allowing us to behave in ways that are acceptable to the group (Day, 2006, p. 29). It is critical that we understand the children's and families' cultures in our classrooms.

When there is a mismatch between the teacher's culture and the child's, there is the possibility that misunderstandings will occur (Ray et al., 2006). The difference in cultural lens, or the way we view the world because of our culture, may cause teachers to misinterpret children's abilities or behaviors, and this may negatively affect the teacher's ability to establish rapport with the child. This may also make it more difficult to understand the child's needs and interests, which will affect the teacher's ability to deliver effective curriculum. In addition, *cultural discontinuity* (a difference in the learning preferences, practices, and behaviors valued at home and school) can cause children to have a more negative perception of themselves as learners, readers, writers, and speakers (Garcia, 1993).

Watch the video to learn more about making cultural assumptions. Which assumption did this teacher make?

In the United States, the population of children is becoming more diverse. For example, over 26% of Head Start children (Hulsey et al., 2011) and 21% of school-age children speak a language other than English at home (Federal Interagency Forum on Child and Family Statistics, 2011). Additionally, statisticians estimate that by the year 2023, 50% of children in the United States will be children of color (Nieto and Bode, 2012). However, the population of teachers does not reflect this same diversity, with 82% of elementary teachers being White, 7% Black, and 8% Hispanic. The typical elementary teacher is also female, middle income, and monolingual (speaking English only) (Aud et al., 2011).

In addition to concern about lack of continuity between the children's home and school culture, there is also danger from bias. According to Day (2006), "Institutional bias that are manifested in monocultural, monoracial assumptions and representations in books, materials, testing, and tracking for example can cause repeated and cumulative harm to children's growth, development and academic achievement" (Day, 2006, p. 30).

The mismatch between teacher's and children's culture as well as individual and institutional bias can contribute to some children being less successful in the classroom. Achievement gaps occur between children who are Black, Latino, and Native American and their White peers (Day, 2006, p. 23). For example, fewer children who are African American, Latino, or poor graduate from high school or attend college (Chapman et al., 2011). As reported by Linda M. Espinosa (2006), an early childhood researcher and professor, the Latino population, the largest and fastest growing ethnic minority in the United States, is the group with the lowest academic performance. She states that children who are Latino start kindergarten behind their White peers in reading and math, and these differences continue to widen as children progress through school, leading to high dropout rates. So how can we reverse this trend?

To change these statistics, we must provide an equitable education and help children experience a sense of belonging in our classrooms. Each of us has cultural scripts

Julie Bullard

These puppets are an example of multicultural materials. Also note the child-created sign advertising a puppet show.

that guide us in our interactions, behaviors, and thinking. These scripts become our "undeniable reality" and are often unchallenged, particularly if we are a member of the dominant culture (Maschinot, 2008). We must begin cultural awareness by examining our own cultural scripts. This helps us to uncover our own worldview. For example, if you are a member of the mainstream United States you will most likely value individualism. However, recent immigrants are more likely to value interdependence (Maschinot, 2008). Think about how early childhood programs might be different if interdependence rather than independence were stressed.

After we examine our own cultural scripts, we are ready to learn about the children's cultures. Teachers can learn about the cultures of children in their classrooms in a variety of ways. They can discuss goals, beliefs (for example, about routines, celebrations, family roles, gender roles, food, discipline), and traditions with children and families; ask parents and children to share songs, stories, food, customs, and family activities with the class; and observe the interactions of children and their families. They can also interview community members and review research and other written materials pertaining to the culture (Ray et al., 2006).

As we learn about culture, we must remember that there is great variety within a particular culture. Children and their families are individuals, and we must be cautious about attributing specific characteristics to them simply because they belong to a particular cultural group. In other words, we must not stereotype. As stated by Day (2006), "Because we are human we share predictable, universal patterns of change with all other humans; because we are social beings, we share predictable patterns of behavior with members of our group or groups; and because we are individuals, each of us is unique and idiosyncratic" (Day, 2006, p. 24).

We can use the information we have learned about individual children and their culture to arrange inclusive environments, plan appropriate activities, and adapt our interaction styles. This is critical if we are going to help all children to succeed.

Apply Your Knowledge Throughout this chapter, we have been reading about how essential it is to affirm each child and the child's culture. As a frequent volunteer in my daughter's first-grade classroom, the teacher asked me to help with a Halloween party. I noticed that Sarah did not participate in the costume parade, play the games, or eat the treats. Instead, she sat quietly at her desk with tears streaming down her face. I thought that perhaps she was ill and asked the teacher what was wrong. She said that Sarah belonged to a religion that did not celebrate Halloween and her parents should have kept her home for the day. What message did Sarah receive from this experience? What message did the other children learn? What are ways that we can respect all members in the classroom when we conduct celebrations?

(Continued)

Many programs do not celebrate holidays for several reasons. First, many teachers believe that since families have different religious and cultural beliefs about what holidays to celebrate and the appropriate way to celebrate or not celebrate, the celebrations are best done in the child's home or church. Second, since children are typically exposed to an extensive amount of holiday celebration outside the classroom, many teachers feel it is not necessary to also celebrate within the classroom. Holiday periods can be very stressful for both children and families. The early childhood setting may be the only setting where normal routines and activities are occurring. Third, teachers are also often concerned about whether "holiday curriculum" is the best use of children's learning time. Instead, these programs may celebrate the end of a long-term project with a culminating event, or celebrate an author's birthday (such as Dr. Seuss) after studying the author.

Early Childhood Programs as a Culture. While it is critical that the school reflect the cultures of children, families, and community, the school itself also forms a unique community and culture. The school not only translates culture but also creates the "culture of childhood," helping all to appreciate and value this time (Rinaldi, 2001, p. 53). The culture of childhood is formed partially by the adult's view of children and childhood. For example, if adults view childhood as a time of wonder, joy, and exploration, then they will set up experiences and environments where this is a focus. This will affect the way children experience and remember their childhood. The school culture, like all cultures, is influenced by and influences those who participate within it.

Being Responsive to Children with Special Needs. Children who have special needs are often, although not always, at special risk. They are more vulnerable to academic failure, due to both the disability and the lack of support and services to be successful. They might also experience a lack of social success, including peer rejection (Odom, Zercher, Li, Marquart, Sandall, & Brown, 2006) and being a more frequent target of bullies than their peers who are nondisabled (Sveinsson & Morris, 2006). Additionally, frustrated teachers sometimes increase the child's difficulties through reacting inappropriately to challenging behaviors.

It is critical that the teacher establish a warm, nurturing, respectful relationship with the child who has special needs and his family. The teacher will also need to help other children accept the child with special needs. You might help the other children understand the child's disability through discussions, reading books, and allowing children to try special equipment the child uses. If children have questions, you will want to offer the child who is disabled the opportunity to determine how to answer the questions. The child may choose to answer the question himself, choose to tell the other child that he does not wish to answer the question, or choose to refer the question to you to answer. You will also want to make sure your environment reflects children with disabilities (for example, dolls with disabilities and assistive devices in the dramatic play area, pictures in the room that include children with disabilities, and books that show children with disabilities).

To help children relate positively with those who have special needs, you might invite guest speakers with disabilities to visit your classroom. As a classroom teacher, I invited Jason, a neighborhood man who was paraplegic, to visit my program. The children had many questions. "What happened?" "Do your legs hurt?" "Can you walk?" "How do you get out of the wheelchair?" "Can you do a wheelie?" They were especially interested in how Jason drove. He showed them the brake and gas pedal on the steering column and gave them rides on the wheelchair lift. After the initial visit, Jason became a frequent volunteer, enriching all our lives.

In providing for successful inclusion of children with special needs, the teacher would use the following as steps. Many children with special needs can be served simply through providing step one. Each step becomes increasingly intensive but is needed by fewer children.

1. Provide a developmentally appropriate program.
2. Modify the curriculum through altering the schedule, environment, or materials; simplifying activities; providing special equipment or materials; or providing additional peer or adult support.
3. Embed opportunities to meet the child's goals within ongoing activities and experiences.
4. Provide child-focused strategies such as set-aside time to work individually with the child.

FIGURE 2.2 Building Blocks for Inclusion

Source: Based on Building Blocks for Teaching Preschoolers with Special Needs, *by S. R. Randall and I. S. Schwartz, 2002, East Peoria, IL: Paul H. Brookes Publishing Company.*

The Building Blocks Model. In addition to establishing positive relationships, it may be necessary to make modifications to help the child with a disability to be successful. Sandall and Schwartz (2002) have developed a successful model called Building Blocks (see Figure 2.2) that can help teachers with a process for inclusion. This process is effective whether the child has challenging behaviors, a specific disability, or an undiagnosed special need. The foundation of the model is a "high quality early childhood program," one that they define as having "engaging interactions, a responsive and predictable environment, many opportunities for learning, teaching that is matched to the child and activity, developmentally appropriate materials, activities, and interactions, safe and hygienic practices, and appropriate levels of child guidance" (Sandall and Schwartz, 2002, p. 11). This base is necessary for all children, regardless of whether they have special needs. It is crucial, because without it other interventions will not be effective.

If the child is not successful within the classroom even with this solid early childhood base, the teacher moves to the next block, curriculum modification. This is any modification that allows the child to participate fully in the classroom. For example, you might alter the schedule, environment, or materials; simplify activities; provide special equipment; or provide additional peer or adult support. To determine the modifications, it is important to observe the child so that you can clearly define the difficulties. Parents, previous teachers, and specialists often know what modifications have been successful in the past to alleviate issues. At times, it will also be necessary to brainstorm and experiment with different solutions. For example, Daniel, who had cerebral palsy, was unable to hold a paintbrush. Torrence, his teacher, first tried placing a pencil grip on the brush. However, this did not work. He then put a foam curler around the paintbrush for Daniel to try. With a happy grin, Daniel said, "I can do it."

If the child is still having difficulties after curriculum modifications are made, you will move to the next level of support called "embedded learning opportunities" (Sandall & Schwartz, 2002, p. 12). These short teaching episodes occur as part of regular classroom activities and routines.

If the embedded learning opportunities are not successful, you will move to the final building block, providing "explicit, child-focused instructional strategies" (Sandall & Schwartz, 2002, p. 13). These are more systematic, frequent, and carefully planned than embedded learning opportunities. While the other interventions occur within the normal class activities, these may require specific set-aside time on the part of the teacher and child. Throughout the book, we will be looking at meeting the needs of children with disabilities by using the Building Blocks model.

The CSEFEL Pyramid Model. The Center on the Social Emotional Foundations for Early Learning (CSEFEL) has established a model to support children's social competence and to decrease challenging behaviors (Fox et al., 2003). This model is similar to

FIGURE 2.3
CSEFEL Pyramid Model

In meeting children's social emotional needs, the teacher would use the following steps. Most children can be served through the beginning steps. Each step becomes increasingly intensive but is needed by fewer chidren.

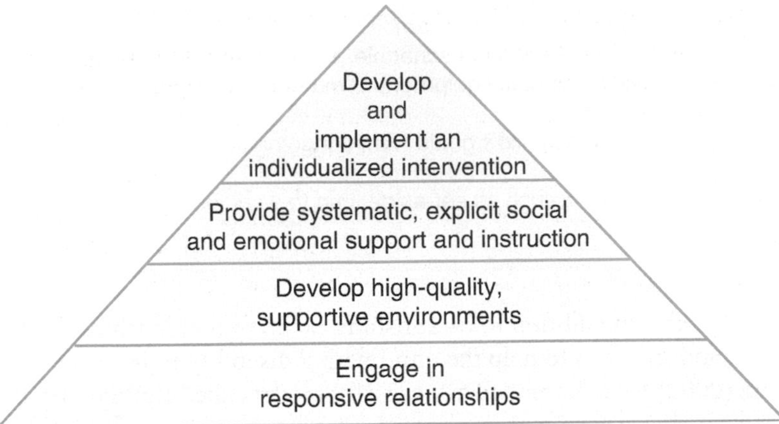

the Building Blocks model in that the foundation (the first two layers) is based upon providing responsive care and a supportive environment. The next layer of the pyramid is to provide explicit instruction to assist children in the development of social emotional skills. For example, children learn social emotional skills through playing games with a feeling faces cube, listening and responding to scripted stories, and learning techniques such as the Turtle Technique to cope with emotions. They learn how to solve problems using solution kits. See the CSEFEL website for access to these materials. These three levels are provided to all children. Only 4% of children will typically need the final level (Sugai et al., 2000). For these children, an intensive, individualized approach is developed that includes a behavioral support plan. The support plan is based upon the belief that the behavior works for the child providing either something they need or desire or something that they wish to avoid. See Figure 2.3 for a model. While CSEFEL is designed for infants, toddlers, and preschoolers, there are programs for elementary school (Positive Behavioral Intervention and Support) and special education (Response to Intervention) that use a similar model of tiered support. In each of these models an individualized, assessment based, problem-solving approach is used for the final tier. Each of these models uses some type of behavior support plan.

Watch the video to learn more about the CSEFEL Pyramid. Which specific strategies are used to support children's social emotional learning?

https://www.youtube.com/channel/UCQ2-KgUHhixii64uOQFEZUQ

Developing Behavior Support Plans. In the CSEFEL model the development of a support plan begins by conducting a functional assessment where the team members gather data through reviewing records, interviews, and observations of the child's behavior. Special attention is paid to the behavior, the triggers (what occurs before the behavior), the consequences (what happens after the behavior), the function of the behavior, the effectiveness of the behavior, and previous interventions. After collecting the data, the team develops a hypothesis statement that includes the triggers, the behavior description, the responses that allow the behavior to continue, and the purpose of the behavior. Next it is time to develop the plan. This includes examining ways to prevent the behavior, teaching replacement skills, and exploring the ways that the teachers can respond so they are not reinforcing the challenging behavior. The plan is then implemented and evaluated.

Being Responsive to Children in Poverty. Children in poverty are another group who are particularly vulnerable, and as such need the highest quality early childhood program. Yet, research indicates that when there is a high concentration of poverty in a program, the teachers are less sensitive and the quality of instruction is poorer (Pianta, Howes, Burchinal, Bryant, Clifford, Early, & Barbarin, 2005).

Child poverty continues to rise in the United States. Forty-nine percent of young children in the United States now live in low-income families. Children of color and those who are immigrants are disproportionately represented in this number. For example, 70% of American Indian, 67% of Hispanic, and 70% of Black children are low income, while 35% of White children are low income (Addy, Engelhardt, & Skinner, 2013).

Poverty is a risk for children, exposing them to stressors including inadequate and unstable housing, unsafe neighborhoods, and deficient prenatal and ongoing health care (Bowman, 2006; Ramsey, 2003). Studies have found that cortisol levels, a method of measuring stress, are elevated in children with lower socioeconomic status (SES) (National Scientific Council on the Developing Child, 2004b). As we learned earlier in this chapter, prolonged or frequent stress in young children can negatively affect the architecture of the brain. Unfortunately, early childhood programs sometimes add to children's stress. This can occur when there is a mismatch between the child's home and school culture, if there are conflicts between the child and the teacher, or when activities and environments are set up that allow children to fail (Bowman, 2006).

Children who are from low-income families are also at greater risk for developmental and behavioral problems, particularly if there are other risk factors as well (such as inadequate parenting, substance abuse or violence in the home, or disabilities) (Bowman, 2006). For example, research continues to show that children from low-income families begin school way behind their middle- or upper-income peers in reading and math, and that this gap is typically not narrowed as the child progresses through school. Unfortunately, this gap between children who live in low-income families and those in upper-income families is now 30% to 40% wider than it was 25 years ago (Reardon, 2011).

As teachers, we have limited control over society's inequities. However, there are things that we can do to assist children in poverty. First, we can assist children to develop resiliency. Resilient children overcome adversity to reach their full potential. Research has shown that resilient children show four common traits. They are socially competent, good at problem solving, have a sense of autonomy or **self-efficacy** (a person's belief about her competence in a given situation), and they have a sense of purpose (Bernard, 2004). In this chapter, we discuss ways to help children develop these strengths. While our goal is for all children to develop these strengths, this is especially important for children who are growing up with adversity in their lives.

Second, we can develop respectful, responsive relationships with low-income children and their families. As teachers, we can:

- Develop high expectations that challenge children but still allow them to experience success (Espinosa, 2010).
- Help ensure that our classrooms and curriculum represent children of all income levels. For example, a study of homes might include a discussion about homeless shelters.
- Reflect upon our program policies and requests from the perspective of a low-income family. For example, is it reasonable to ask families to donate money for their child to go on the class field trip, to provide a T-shirt for tie-dyeing, to provide a gift for an exchange, or to transport their child to attend Early Head Start (a program specifically designed for low-income children and their families)?
- Provide needed services within our programs whenever possible (school breakfasts, after-school care, transportation, access to social services).
- Learn about community services and, when appropriate, refer families for needed assistance.
- Be conscious of parent work schedules, transportation, and childcare needs when setting up family events.

- Advocate for equal educational opportunities for children who are low income. In areas where there is a high concentration of poverty, it is more likely that the budget per pupil is less, educational facilities and educational materials are inadequate, and that teachers are paid less and are more likely to be unlicensed. The turnover of teachers, student/teacher ratios, and class sizes are likely to be higher than if the children were in a school with more economically advantaged peers (Gorski, 2008). Children who may need the most support often receive the least.
- Examine our own biases and cultural lens and make sure that our biases do not negatively affect the child. It is sometimes difficult for those who have financial security to understand the profound effect of poverty (Ramsey, 2003).

Amelia, a child in my classroom, often came to class smelling bad with unwashed hair and dirty clothes. Unfortunately, this affected her interactions with her peers and even with the adults in the classroom. Even though I visited with the mother about Amelia's grooming, there was no change. I presumed that the mother was deliberately ignoring Amelia's needs. However, 2 weeks later when I went on a home visit, I found the sewer in the house backed up and the water turned off. The sewer smell seeped into the clothing and furnishings in the house. The family hauled all the water they used up a steep hill in buckets, making water for bathing or washing clothes a luxury. Even though the family had talked to the property owner repeatedly, he refused to fix the water or sewer, saying he was "planning to tear the house down and was not willing to put any money into it." The family, who lacked a deposit to move elsewhere, felt they had no other options but to stay in the inadequate housing. I found that my assumptions were biased and inaccurate. Due to my own upbringing and past experiences, I had not pursued why Amelia was dirty. Instead, I assumed the family did not care about her. Through the home visit, I learned the reason for the grooming issues and was able to refer the family (with their permission) to an agency that could assist them. With the agency's help, they were able to move into different housing and Amelia's grooming immediately changed.

To make children feel that they belong in our classrooms, we must form an attachment to every child. This begins with unconditional, positive regard for each child and family, and the establishment of a warm, respectful relationship. To demonstrate respect for children and families, we need to understand their values, beliefs, and culture and use this knowledge to create effective environments. We must make special efforts to meet the needs of those children who are most vulnerable, children who are from a nondominant culture, children who have disabilities, and children from low-income families. We will continue to examine ways that we can meet the needs of vulnerable children throughout the textbook.

Helping Children Achieve Mastery

When a child's needs are met, they develop the attitude that "the world will treat me well, my needs will be met in the future, and I have some control over my environment." However, when no one responds to children's needs they give up the expectation that they will get what they need, and "lose confidence in themselves and their abilities" (Bowman, 2006, p. 53).

When I was a houseparent for children who had been abused and neglected, a caseworker brought a 9-month-old baby to us with a very severe, infected burn on his little toe. Although he had to be in excruciating pain, he did not cry or show any emotion. Eventually, the toe needed to be amputated. He learned to walk and run. However, in the time he was with us, even if he was hurt, he never learned to cry. His early experiences had taught him that crying did no good; he could not expect others to meet his needs.

In early childhood settings, we would expect never to see this extreme type of abuse. However, meeting children's needs for attention can sometimes be difficult when you are caring for many children. If adults leave children to cry when they need us, they too will learn that the world is a harsh place, where no one will meet their needs. Some adults believe that if they always respond quickly to a child's cries, that the child will become "spoiled." However, research shows that this is not the case. Children whose cries are quickly responded to as infants display greater empathy and better self-regulation as they get older (Narvaez & Gleason, 2013).

We must also help children to achieve mastery and develop **self-efficacy** (a person's belief about her competence in a given situation). A wide body of research indicates that a person's self-efficacy strongly influences her performance and motivation (Bandura & Locke, 2003). For example, a mega-analysis (a review of several research studies) showed that 11% to 18% of a child's academic performance is due to his self-efficacy (Cohen, 1988; Schunk, 1989). Children with higher levels of self-efficacy are more motivated to try tasks and show increased persistence in completing tasks. So how can we promote self-efficacy? Here are several ways:

- Provide challenges in a variety of domains—climbing to the very top of the climber and ringing the bell, matching the numerals with a number of objects, or reading a picture book.
- Whenever possible, use individual and small-group activities rather than large-group activities. Individualized and small-group activities are more likely to meet children's current level of development, since teachers are able to scaffold each child's learning more effectively.
- Provide materials at increasing difficulties so that children can see their skills improving. Sandra provides math games with colored dots demonstrating the level of difficulty. Children in her room are excited when they can successfully complete the activity at the next level.
- Teach children skills they need to be successful. For example, demonstrate how to hold scissors correctly, how to use a specific art tool, or how to tag or point to items when you count them.
- Provide choices of activities to meet all children's interests and developmental levels.
- Assist children in setting and meeting individual goals. Even very young children have goals, as demonstrated by a baby learning to crawl. You can assist children to verbalize their goals or, for very young children, verbalize the goal for them, making the goal more visible.
- Recognize when children have met their own personal goals ("I know that you had a goal to climb the climbing wall all by yourself. You did it.").
- Avoid group competition. Instead, encourage children to master their own goals. Group competition can discourage children. As a result, they may avoid the activity. Without practice, their skills continue to fall behind their peers.

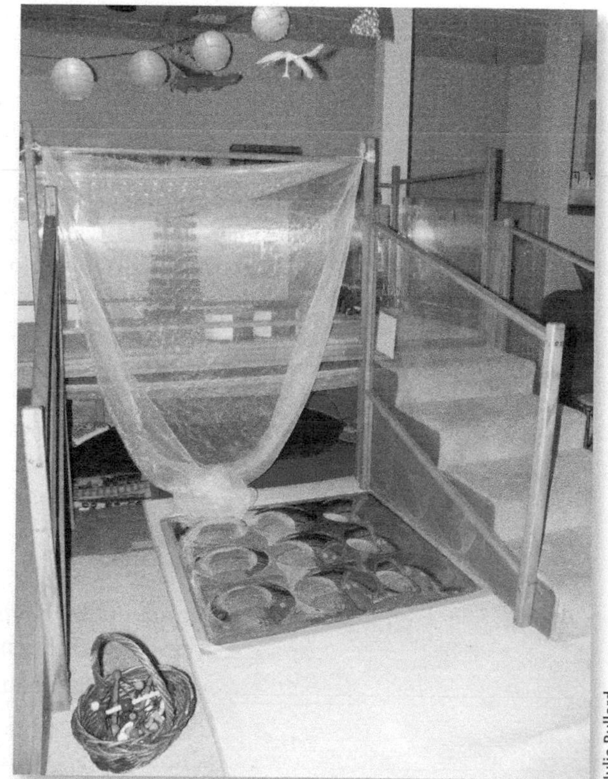

Julie Bullard

This infant loft provides a variety of challenges to meet the different developmental needs of infants. When children climb the steps or crawl under the loft, they find new exciting activities.

Table 2.3 Examples of Praise and Encouragement

Praise	Encouragement
Good job.	This is the first time you've completed the entire puzzle. I bet you feel proud.
I like the way you cleaned up.	You are working very hard putting away all the blocks.
Great artwork.	I see that you put a lot of detail in your picture, like adding all the branches on the tree. That must have taken a long time.

- Continue to improve your own self-efficacy. A teacher's self-efficacy, or his belief in his ability to teach, affects his interactions with children and the way he designs learning experiences. This in turn affects children's academic performance (Bandura, 1993).
- Make encouraging remarks. Encouraging statements reflect the child's effort, provide very specific information, encourage the child's judgment on his work rather than your own, and often lead to further interaction. Encouragement can boost children's self-confidence, persistence, and acceptance of their own and other's efforts. In contrast, praise tends to be more generic, focusing on the completed product and on the adult's judgment about the product. Praise may lead children to feel "conditional acceptance" (Gartrell, 2011, p. 265). Instead of developing intrinsic or internal satisfaction with what one has done, frequent praise can make children dependent on external acknowledgement making them think they are only worthwhile when someone else states they are. Table 2.3 provides examples of praise and encouragement.

Responsive care is the foundation in assisting children to experience a sense of mastery. We must also cultivate self-efficacy by providing challenging activities that children can successfully master, giving skill and goal-setting support, and encouraging children's efforts.

Assisting Children to Become Independent

Being independent allows the child to have individual power and autonomy (Brendtro et al., 2002). The amount of independence adults expect from children is culturally based (Day, 2006). Therefore, it is important to consult with parents in determining the goals for independence in the classroom. There are many ways that the teacher can encourage independence. These include the following:

- Setting up the environment to encourage independence (materials available and accessible, children taught how to use materials, and dependable routines).
- Allowing children to do what they can for themselves and to make decisions they are capable of making.
- With assistance from children, establishing clear and consistent guidelines or rules. When rules are clear and consistent, children are able to be more independent and self-regulating (Riley et al., 2008). When they assist in creating the rules, they feel more ownership and therefore will respect the rule more (Gartrell, 2011). The guidelines or rules should be worded in a positive way,

letting children know what to do rather than what not to do. However, beware of creating too many rules. Wien (2004) worked with a group of childcare centers in establishing rules. The programs agreed that all rules had to pass the following test: did the behavior harm the child, other children, or property? If not, the rule was not needed. Using these criteria, teachers discarded many rules, such as restricting the number of children in a learning center and forbidding toys from home. As the teachers discarded the rules, the setting was less stressful, quieter, and calmer; teachers spent less time monitoring and more time interacting; and the children became more independent and exercised more control over their own behavior (Wien, 2004).

- Allowing children to make choices and learn from the results. At some point, children will be required to make decisions that can have life-altering consequences. Providing children opportunities to make developmentally appropriate choices allows them to be independent and gives them experiences in making choices.

Allowing children to develop culturally appropriate independence and autonomy assists children to feel powerful and experience inner discipline.

Assisting Children to Display Generosity

The spirit of generosity reflects the ability to be caring, empathetic, and willing to share time and possessions with others. However, to demonstrate caring and empathy, we must be able to recognize and manage our feelings, control our behavior, and use **prosocial** skills to interact with others. Children who develop these skills enhance their ability to relate to others. Research also shows that learning these skills enhances children's later academic and behavioral functioning (Nix, Bierman, Domitrovich, & Gill, 2014).

Helping Children to Recognize and Control Their Own Feelings. Helping children to control their emotions begins by setting up a developmentally appropriate environment and schedule, thus reducing frustration. We need to create an environment that provides many options (spaces for physical activity and areas for quiet relaxation; spaces for being in groups but also spaces for being alone; a range of challenging, interesting activities; and enough materials so that all children are engaged). To support children, we need a schedule that alternates quiet and active activities and allows time for restful relaxation, but does not require children to stay on mats when they are unable to sleep. The schedule needs to limit large-group activities, instead focusing on individual and small-group activities.

We also need to help children learn skills. We should begin with the premise that all feelings are legitimate. It is often tempting for adults to try to tell children they should feel differently. However, this only masks the child's feelings. One of the skills young children need to learn is to identify their emotions. You can assist them through:

- Labeling their feelings ("You look excited that your mama is coming").
- Using feeling words to describe your own emotions ("I feel worried when the water is spilled all over the floor because I'm afraid someone will slip and get hurt").
- Interpreting the feelings of others for the child ("Rainey looks sad because you took her toy") (Riley et al., 2008).

Learning to identify and use words to describe feelings is one way that children learn to manage emotions. You can also assist children in finding other ways to deal with intense emotions. Different techniques might work better for different problems. In addition, some children respond more favorably to some techniques than to others. Marie-Élise,

FIGURE 2.4
Calming Techniques

When I am upset, I can:
- Work it out by hammering nails into the stump or squeezing squish balls
- Talk it over with a friend or the listening doll
- Act it out with the doll house or puppets
- Breathe it out by taking five deep breaths
- Draw about it or write about it

When I am too excited, I can:
- Listen to music
- Play in the water table
- Read quietly in the alone box
- Do yoga in the physical center
- Use the sand tray to make a design

a teacher at Pinewood kindergarten, developed a poster to remind children of different calming techniques (see Figure 2.4).

Lisa, a teacher of toddler children, has a poster that shows children expressing different emotions. When children are unable to verbalize their feelings, they are sometimes able to point to the way that they are feeling. Julie, who teaches preschool, makes a "dial a feeling" wheel for each child, which allows Julie to know immediately if there are children who might need some additional attention.

As you get to know individual children, you will learn what techniques are most helpful for each of them, and you can then help remind them of strategies that have been successful for them in the past.

Helping Children to Manage Their Behavior. If we want children to interact positively with others, we need to help them manage their behavior. However, we need to make sure the techniques we are using are consistent with the respectful way that we want the children to interact with others. For example, if we want children to talk to each other respectfully, then we need to use a respectful tone and words ourselves even when we are frustrated. Listed next are some positive guidance techniques that can be effective in managing behavior and are at the same time respectful of the child.

Active or Reflective Listening. When using active listening, the adult reiterates what the child has said. When actively listening, you refrain from giving advice. Instead, you simply repeat what the child has said, paraphrase the message, or reflect the feeling behind the statement. If reflecting the child's feeling, use a tentative voice to avoid sounding like a mind reader. For example, Jamaar says, "I'm not going to circle." Using a questioning tone, you state, "You really don't like circle?" Jamaar then explains that Andre won't sit by him, and that Andre says he isn't his best friend anymore and he can't come play at his house. By using reflective listening in this case, you were able to unveil Jamaar's real issue. Active listening encourages further conversation, validates the child, and helps the child to clarify his thoughts and feelings, often resulting in the child solving his own problem. Additionally, just discussing a problem or issue can often be therapeutic.

I Messages. You use an "I message" to express your own feelings about children's behavior. An "I message" typically contains a word describing how you feel, the specific behavior that caused you to feel this way, and how the behavior affected you. "I feel worried when blocks get thrown because I'm afraid someone will get hurt." Both adults and children are usually less defensive when they hear an "I message" rather than a "you message."

Natural Consequences. These consequences occur with no intervention from you. For example, a child who goes outside without mittens in the winter may get cold hands. Natural consequences allow children to learn from their behavior and the accompanying results. They are a very effective technique that teachers can use when the consequence is not harmful or dangerous for the child or others. In addition, for natural consequences to be effective, you must be able to accept the results. For example, unwashed paintbrushes will get hard and unusable. However, you may feel that this natural consequence is not appropriate for the program or other children in the classroom. Therefore, you would not want to use the natural consequence in this case.

Logical Consequences. These consequences clearly relate to the behavior, but do not occur naturally. For example, if you rip a book, you need to fix it. If you hurt someone's feelings, you need to figure out ways to make them feel better.

Redirection and Substitution. This technique may involve distracting a very young child with a more appropriate activity. For example, a baby is crawling toward the electrical outlet and you give him a ball to play with. When redirecting an older toddler or child, the teacher provides an acceptable substitution for the behavior (Marion, 2007). For example, if a three-year-old child is climbing on a shelf, you might redirect her to the climber if it appears the child's goal is to climb. If the child's goal is to reach something that is out of reach, you might substitute a safer way to obtain the material.

Problem Solving or Conflict Resolution. Problem solving or conflict resolution involves assisting the child or children to solve a problem using the following steps:

1. Define the problem—Use active listening and I messages to determine the underlying issue.
2. Explore alternatives—Brainstorm all possible solutions. It is important to accept all solutions and to write them down or digitally record them for later analysis.
3. Choose a solution—Go through your brainstormed list of solutions. If anyone has any objections to an alternative, then cross the alternative off. Choose a solution that is mutually agreed upon. This may be a combination of the initial brainstormed alternatives.
4. Obtain a commitment from everyone who is involved—Agree who is responsible for implementing the solution, when it will be implemented, and how it will be implemented.
5. Set up a time to discuss how the solution worked.

Watch the video to learn more about conflict resolution. How did the teacher assist the children to solve the conflict?

Initially, children need a lot of practice and support to use this method. However, once children learn the technique they will be able to handle more problems independently and will also have acquired a lifelong skill.

We can help children to manage their behavior by using these respectful techniques. We are also modeling effective techniques that they can use in interactions with others.

Assisting Children to Develop Prosocial Skills. In the early childhood years, children are developing skills for getting along with others. We help children develop these skills through having clear goals for our classroom, modeling, taking advantage of teachable moments to coach children, and through intentionally designing activities.

Establish Prosocial Goals. Two overarching rules for the prosocial classroom are 1) we treat everyone with respect and 2) we live peacefully with each other.

Julie Bullard

Children ages 3–6 effectively use the peace table at Curious Minds to resolve conflicts.

In addition to not physically or verbally hurting or bullying someone else, respect involves being friendly to others. Gartrell (2011) emphasizes that there is a difference between friendliness and being friends. Children need to have the right to choose their friends. However, they need to be friendly to all members of the class. The class can determine what being friendly means in their classroom through having in-depth discussions.

To live peacefully with each other, children need to learn to solve conflicts. To learn conflict resolution skills children need both modeling and direct teaching. It is also helpful to have a special place to go to work on the conflict if it cannot be immediately resolved. Many programs have established a peace table or peace rug. For example, Curious Minds Early Childhood Center has a peace table. The teacher posted the different steps to resolving a conflict (listen to each other, brainstorm ideas to solve the problem, choose a solution, and try the solution out). She provided a book with pictures and words to remind children of possible solutions. Puppets are also available, since some children find it easier to express themselves through the puppet. Even three-year-olds at Curious Minds successfully use the table and the steps to resolve conflicts. In other classrooms, teachers provide solution kits for children. These picture cue cards provide children options such as ignore, get a teacher, or say please.

When the conflict affects most of the class members, you might have a problem-solving circle. Anyone in the classroom can call a meeting. The teacher or child begins the meeting by describing the situation that needs to be solved. Then the class uses the conflict resolution steps to solve the issue (Gartrell, 2011).

Model Prosocial Skills. As a model for prosocial living, we must develop a positive relationship with each child in our care. As stressed by Bowman (2006), "Just as children must interact verbally with adults in order to get language, they have to interact emotionally and socially to develop relationships" (Bowman, 2006, p. 53). Positive adult relationships help children develop insights into others' thoughts and feelings and help them learn to positively interact with others. This sets the stage for current and future relationships. We can help make modeling even more powerful when we make our actions explicit, verbalizing what we are doing and thinking. For example, when Carletta was crying, her teacher said, "I wonder what would help Carletta feel better?" "Maybe she would like a hug, I'll ask her."

Watch the video to see a teacher using a teachable moment to coach the children on social skills. How does the teacher support the child in trying a variety of solutions?

https://www.youtube.com/watch?v=95wDHWOLFZ0

Use the Teachable Moment to Coach Children on Prosocial Skills. For example, this might be encouraging toddlers to "Use gentle touches" as they play with the baby. You might provide specific words a child might use. "Terrence, you can say, 'Stop, give back my truck.'" An important role of the teacher in the early childhood years is to assist children to successfully join a group of children they wish to play with and to maintain the play. Begin by observing children's strategies that are unsuccessful and assist them to learn successful techniques (see Chapter 7). The teacher should also notice socially appropriate behavior and encourage it. For example, "Rosie and Tanya, I see you are sharing the truck."

Intentionally Design Activities to Help Children Learn Prosocial Skills. In addition to modeling and taking advantage of teachable moments, you will need to intentionally design activities to encourage prosocial skills and to assist children in understanding others' perspectives. You might do this through

- reading books about feelings or solving social dilemmas or where children see something from a new point of view,
- playing games where children identify other's emotions, and
- enacting and discussing real and hypothetical situations. One way to do this is to develop a dilemma and have the children determine the ending. You might use role-playing, puppets, dolls, or play figures to tell the story (Gartrell, 2011). Some classrooms have designated characters that always tell these types of stories. You might create a dilemma or a social story around a situation you have observed in the classroom. For example, Maria developed the following story based on a classroom incident. She told the story using puppets and a shiny red car as a prop. "One day the children came to school and there was a brand new shiny toy car in the block area. Tim could not wait to play with it. All morning he waited. Finally, Bruce set the car down. But before Tim could reach it, Mark picked the car up. Tim went to Mark and grabbed the car. He had waited a long time and thought the car should be his." The children and Maria then discussed the feelings of Mark and Tim and discussed what each child might do. Research shows that these types of stories decrease challenging behaviors and increase prosocial skills (McNelly & Smith, 2013).

Assist Children to Become Culturally Competent. We have discussed the importance of the teacher being culturally competent. It is also important that we help children to develop cultural competence. We need to help children to be knowledgeable, comfortable, and respectful of people from varying cultural backgrounds so that they can engage in effective interactions and reject unfair treatment of others (Kostelnik et al., 2012). You can help children to become more socially competent by reading books and sharing music from other cultures, by creating opportunities for children to interact with people who are different from themselves (for example, diverse guest speakers, volunteers, and field trips), and by providing diversity materials (books, games, clothing, posters, and artifacts) in the classroom. Additionally, look for ways of embedding diversity in each topic you study. It is also extremely important to discuss hurtful comments and biased statements and to immediately address them if they occur. Children need to learn how to recognize such statements and how to respond when they hear them.

Prosocial skills are necessary for children to make friends and to succeed in the world. In addition, they help to ensure that our classroom will be a welcoming place for all.

How the Physical Environment Supports the Circle of Courage

The physical environment presents an immediate message of either belonging or exclusion. It can provide opportunities for success and mastery, or failure and boring repetition. It can provide an arrangement of space and materials so that children can be independent, or it can be set up where teachers are the "material brokers." It can provide spaces and activities for developing community, or be so noisy, crowded, and chaotic that this is impossible.

The well-designed physical environment can support the Circle of Courage, helping children to develop a sense of belonging, mastery, independence, and generosity. When designed as the "third teacher" the environment is also less stressful for both adults and children, allowing teachers to spend more time in positive interactions with children.

Check Your Understanding 2.4
Click here to gauge your understanding of section concepts.

Chapter Quiz 2

Click here to gauge your understanding of chapter concepts.

Throughout this book, we will be examining ways to provide a physical environment that supports the Circle of Courage.

We can establish a positive social environment that leads to courage rather than discouragement through supporting the Circle of Courage in our classrooms. When we make decisions about individual children, create changes in our environment, or adopt new curriculums, we can ask, "Will this assist the children to develop a sense of belonging, mastery, independence, and generosity?" When we reflect upon our interactions, we can ask, "Am I interacting with children in a way that lets them know they belong, they can achieve, they can make independent choices, and they can have and be a friend?" In establishing a Circle of Courage classroom, these and similar questions become our compass.

Sample Application Activities

1. Watch additional videos and read articles on childhood stress at The Center on the Developing Child website.
2. Observe in a classroom. Find evidence where the teacher or children are demonstrating the Circle of Courage: spirit of belonging, mastery, independence, and generosity. How skilled is the teacher in the classroom you are observing in using coaching to teach children prosocial skills?
3. Think about your own culture. How has your culture influenced your values (e.g., what constitutes mealtime—is it different on weekends, and what is everyone's role in preparation, serving, and cleaning up) and beliefs (e.g., the role of children, the role of adults, how people should express emotions, and your goals)?
4. Think about institutional racism. What are examples you have witnessed or experienced?
5. View a list of children's books, scripted stories, and activities to support social-emotional development by visiting the following Center on the Social Emotional Foundations for Early Learning website. This site also includes modules and video clips on social-emotional development for teachers. Choose one activity that you will implement with children.
6. Order a free book and the video, Starting Small, from the Southern Poverty Law Center. The video shows an example of a peace table for young children. Search for Starting Small Teaching Tolerance.
7. Choose a diversity topic and create a list of books to use as part of the topic by going to the Cooperative Children's Book Center website (multicultural books) and the Understanding Prejudice website (all types of diversity).
8. Use the environmental assessment (Figure 2.5) to evaluate the social-emotional environment of a classroom.

The teacher develops a warm, nurturing relationship with each child in the classroom through

- ❑ treating every child with respect and responding quickly to his needs.
- ❑ observing and responding to children's verbal and nonverbal cues.
- ❑ spending quality time alone with each child.
- ❑ advocating for ongoing sustained relationships between children and caregivers.

The teacher creates a welcoming caring community by

- ❑ developing an inclusive physical and social environment.
- ❑ expecting friendliness between children.
- ❑ assuring that all staff, children, and families represent classroom materials.
- ❑ providing activities to help children get to know each other and to bond together as a cohesive group.
- ❑ allowing time for children to systematically share with each other.
- ❑ providing time for children to work in informal and formal small groups.
- ❑ setting up the classroom environment to encourage children to work together.
- ❑ being realistic about sharing, and providing duplicates of popular materials and toys and enough interesting materials that all children are engaged.
- ❑ developing activities where children work together to complete a goal.
- ❑ developing a unique sense of place in the program.

The teacher provides materials that reflect the diversity within the program and exposes children to diversity they might not regularly experience. Materials

- ❑ expose children to many forms of diversity (such as race, ethnicity, family structure, age, disabilities, gender, occupations).
- ❑ portray the child's culture and all cultures in a positive, authentic, and realistic light.
- ❑ are integrated into the environment and curriculum, rather than being used only occasionally or in an isolated way.
- ❑ challenge all forms of stereotypes, such as only men or only women can have certain careers, or because you are from a particular race, you have a specific talent.
- ❑ emphasize individual differences and the diversity within large groups.

The teacher assists children to learn about and manage feelings through

- ❑ setting up an environment that reduces frustration (spaces for physical activity and quiet relaxation; spaces for being in groups but also spaces for being alone; a range of challenging, interesting activities; and enough materials so that all children are engaged).
- ❑ developing a schedule that reduces frustration (such as allowing time for restful relaxation but not requiring children to stay on mats when they are unable to sleep).
- ❑ labeling childrens' feelings.
- ❑ using feeling words to describe her own emotions.
- ❑ interpreting the feelings of others for the child.
- ❑ providing activities that help children to identify feelings.
- ❑ providing activities such as woodworking and puppetry to help children handle strong emotions.
- ❑ using positive child guidance (active listening, I messages, natural and logical consequences, redirection, and conflict resolution).

The teacher assists children to develop pro-social skills through

- ❑ establishing pro-social goals.
- ❑ modeling.
- ❑ coaching children on pro-social skills (providing words, and helping with group entry and play skills).
- ❑ teaching children conflict resolution skills.
- ❑ noticing and encouraging pro-social skills.
- ❑ intentionally designing activities to help children learn pro-social skills.
- ❑ assisting children to become culturally competent.
- ❑ immediately addressing hurtful and biased statements.

FIGURE 2.5 Environmental Assessment: The Emotionally Supportive, Equitable Environment

Chapter 3

Establishing a Context for Learning

Designing Schedules, Transitions, and Routines

Learning Outcomes

After you have read this chapter, you will be prepared to:

- Design an effective schedule
- Develop effective transitions
- Plan effective routines

Julie Bullard

Sophia was a new teacher who wanted to make sure that the children in her class were well-prepared for kindergarten. The children began the day with a half-hour large-group time, which Sophia used to emphasize a concept for the day. For example, she taught one letter a week. During group time, children would sing a song about the letter and think of items that began with that letter. Next, the children had selective choice. Sophia divided the children into groups and assigned them to a learning center. Every 15 minutes a bell rang and children moved to the next center. After selective choice, it was small-group time. Again, children were assigned to a group and rotated through three tables, each containing a small-group activity. After group time the children went to the gym for exercises, ate lunch, and then went home.

Designing Effective Schedules

In the opening vignette, Sophia is using a rigid production schedule where time is viewed as a limited resource that must be strictly controlled by the teacher. In this view of scheduling, it is not the needs of the individual children but the clock that takes precedence, with both teachers and children rushing throughout the day (Wien, 1996, 2004). Many teachers believe that short periods for play cause children to be more occupied, thus creating less boredom. However, research indicates the opposite is true. Short play periods result in less in-depth play and more onlooker and unoccupied play (Christie & Wardle, 1992; Tegano & Burdette, 1991). As stated by Doris Fromberg, a well-known early childhood professor and author, "Scholarship takes time" (Fromberg, 2002, p. 70). Only with adequate time will children be able to engage in cooperative play such as negotiating roles, acting out a plot, or building a complicated block structure. Play may be negatively affected by limiting the overall center time and also by rotating children through centers.

Apply Your Knowledge In addition to limiting opportunities for in-depth play, how could assigning children to centers and rotating them every 15 minutes negatively affect their learning?

Daily schedules are necessary to provide consistency and psychological stability, and to allow children to know what is expected. When children become familiar with the routines, they become less anxious, freeing their attention for higher order learning (Bowman, Donovan, & Burns, 2001). They can predict what comes next, allowing them to feel more competent, to build self-control, and to learn emotional and behavioral regulation (Butterfield, 2002). This is most likely why research shows that children have lower cortisol levels when there are firm but flexible schedules (Sajaniemi et al., 2014). Effective daily schedules are also a proactive discipline technique.

It is important to base schedules on early childhood philosophy. Early childhood philosophy dictates that children have extended blocks of time to engage in active exploration (Copple & Bredekamp, 2009). Research indicates that when there are frequent scheduling changes, children's internal motivation to complete tasks is decreased, their attention spans are reduced, and they show increased dependency on the teacher (Gareau & Kennedy, 1991). In contrast, large blocks of time allow children the time needed to plan and implement activities. Children increase their attention span as they are engaged in meaningful learning. They also learn to manage their own time rather than relying on the teacher. Additionally, large blocks of time reduce transitions, allowing more time for learning.

By planning large blocks of time that are predictable from day to day, children and staff can have the security of knowing what comes next and what behavior is expected during this time. However, the schedule should be used as a guide rather than as a rigid time schedule so that children's needs and interests can be honored.

Outdoor time was just ending at Inquiring Minds Child Care when the children noticed a flock of birds had landed on a nearby tree. The children were very interested in these unique migrating birds. Instead of rushing inside, the teacher and children observed the birds, discussing the colors, size, beak, tail feathers, and feet. One of the teachers went inside to collect the digital camera and the sketchbooks. Children made sketches of the birds and took digital pictures. When they went inside, the children and teachers were able to use their sketches, digital pictures, and the bird guidebook to determine the type of birds they had seen.

Because this teacher believed in the teachable moment and using the schedule as a guide rather than as a rigid framework, the children had a unique learning opportunity. **Teachable moments** are spontaneous educational opportunities, usually based on an unplanned experience or question. To manage a classroom effectively, we must plan daily schedules that include large blocks of time for active engagement. We must then use this schedule as a guide, allowing for teachable moments. What other criteria must we consider in planning an effective schedule?

Tips for Planning Effective Schedules

Planning the optimum schedule is a time-consuming process that requires the teacher to consider multiple and sometimes conflicting needs and criteria. The teacher must consider early childhood philosophy, philosophy of the program, the needs of the children, the wishes of parents, and the criteria for effective scheduling, such as alternating quiet and active activities. We will examine each of these areas.

Reflect Early Childhood Philosophy. Early childhood philosophy, informed by our current knowledge about child development, stresses that teachers need to allow children to learn through a play-based experiential process, to make choices among different activities, and to engage in integrated in-depth curriculum (Copple & Bredekamp, 2009). Teachers who understand the philosophies of early childhood education and theories of child development, and who are striving to put these understandings into practice, would usually be uncomfortable seeing separate times for each subject area (such as 30 minutes for science, followed by 30 minutes for social studies). Instead, in a developmentally appropriate setting, children will learn these subjects through using learning centers and participating in integrated projects.

In Nauala's kindergarten class, children were studying grasshoppers. Grasshoppers had invaded nearby fields and were a topic of interest to the children. Children developed a list of questions about grasshoppers and sought answers through observation, experimentation, reading, and visiting with experts. For example, they read factual and fictional stories about grasshoppers, developed and tested hypotheses about what grasshoppers ate, measured how far grasshoppers jumped, and visited multiple sites to determine where grasshoppers preferred to live. They also talked to farmers and examined the effect of grasshoppers on the crops, wrote their own book about grasshoppers, made diagrams and models of grasshoppers, and created artistic renditions of grasshoppers. Literacy, social studies, science, math, and creative art were all integrated into this project.

Reflect Program and Individual Philosophy. Program philosophy also affects scheduling. For example, HighScope uses a method called "plan, do, and review" (Hohmann & Weikart, 2002). Each of these components will be evident in the schedule for a program that follows the HighScope model. For example, the schedule might show that children spend 10 to 15 minutes in small groups making plans for what they will do during center time. The children will then have 45 to 60 minutes to use the centers and implement their plan (children might also engage in unplanned activities). Following this, they will spend 10 to 15 minutes in small groups reviewing and reflecting upon their learning.

Respect Children's Needs (Attention Span, Varying Levels of Development, and Differing Interests). The younger the children are, the more individualized their schedules will be. For example, in an infant room children need to eat and sleep on their own schedule (Copple & Bredekamp, 2009). As children get older, they will be able to eat and sleep at more predictable times. However, even for toddlers and preschoolers, it is important to individualize these routines when necessary. For example, you might have crackers to snack on if a child is very hungry or have a quiet place where a child can take a morning nap if she is tired.

Many teachers are flexible in following the schedule, allowing children's interests to determine when to move to the next phase of the day. For example, if the children are all highly engaged in using learning centers, they might extend this time.

Include Scheduled Times. There are parts of the day over which the teacher has limited personal control, such as use of the gym or playground. This varies depending upon the program. In some programs, outdoor time is scheduled so that several classrooms are not on the playground at once. In most programs, lunch is delivered at a specific time. It is essential to begin developing your schedule by listing these predetermined scheduled times. However, it is also important that the program day not be so interspersed with rigid scheduled times that having large blocks of time is compromised. If children's needs are being negatively affected by these set times, it is important to problem solve ways to meet the children's needs in your classroom while still meeting the needs of the entire program.

Provide a Balance of Child-Initiated and Adult-Initiated Activities. During **child-initiated** times, children make choices among many different activities. This allows children to choose activities that are at their appropriate developmental level and that are interesting and relevant to them. For example, it is center time at the Learning Garden Preschool. Two children are in the art center. One child is drawing a picture of the vase of flowers sitting on the art table. She has not only helped to grow the flowers, but has also just helped the teacher to pick them. Another child is creating a card for her sister who has just come home from the hospital. Although both children are drawing, they are more deeply engaged because the activities are personally meaningful to them. During this time, children can also choose to participate in activities alone or with others.

The schedule will also need to provide time for **adult-initiated** activities. For example, scheduled small- and large-group times are typically initiated by the teacher. Adult-initiated activities might also occur during center time. For example, during center time at the Learning Garden, one of the teachers was sitting with a small group of five children and providing guided exploration with clay. The group of children were following the teacher's suggestion that they try to "pull legs" from their chunk of earth clay. This activity choice helped the children to learn an important clay skill (Topal, 1983). Adult-initiated activities are important for children who are preschoolers or older. In a study of 125 classrooms, children in programs with a more balanced approach to child-initiated and adult-initiated activities, referred to by the authors as structured-balanced classrooms had greater learning gains in literacy. However, even in these classrooms children still spent one-third of their day in center time (Fuligni, Howes, Huang, Hong, & Lara-Cinisomo, 2012).

Julie Bullard

This photo, courtesy of Opal School of the Portland Children's Museum, provides an invitation to draw. The fresh flowers and magnifying glass allow for close observation and provide inspiration.

Provide a Balance of Individual, Small-Group, and Large-Group Activities. The younger the child, the more time they will spend in individual activities. As children become toddlers, the teacher might begin to provide some group activities that children can voluntarily attend. Preschool schedules and elementary schedules typically include large-group time. For children to learn they must be engaged in the activity or experience, meaning that they must be paying attention. Research shows that children are less engaged in large-group activities than in center time activities or small-group activities (Booren, Downer, & Vitiello, 2012). The length of time children are in large groups also affects their attention with longer group times resulting in reduced attention (DiCarlo, Pierce, Baumgartner, Harris, & Ota, 2012). Regardless of age, children in the early childhood years should spend most of their time in individual and small-group activities.

Alternate Quiet Activities with Active Activities. **Quiet activities** are those that have little physical movement (e.g., naptime, story time, or lunchtime). **Active activities** might include outdoor time or gym time. It is important that we alternate quiet and active activities, particularly when they are teacher-directed and when children are required to participate. For example, children who sit through a morning circle, then sit through a small-group literacy activity, and then sit during morning snack may become restless and inattentive. When participating in learning centers, teachers typically allow children to move freely and choose their own level of activity. In most classrooms, centers include quiet as well as more active activities.

Allow Adequate Time for Routines (Resting, Mealtime, Tooth Brushing, Clean-Up Time). Routine times can be learning experiences for young children if enough time is allowed for children to fully benefit from the activity. For example, contrast the two approaches to lunchtime at ABC Child Care Center and Spirit at Play.

At ABC Child Care, children go through a lunch line, where the adults prepare the children's plates. The children then sit quietly and eat. Teachers feel that it is important for children to finish eating quickly so that they can move on to learning experiences. Therefore, they have implemented a "no talking" policy. Teachers spend most of the lunch period reminding children to "eat, not talk." As the teachers rush through the routines, they not only hinder learning opportunities but also treat the children disrespectfully.

At Spirit at Play, teachers realize that mealtime provides a perfect opportunity to engage in meaningful learning and in-depth conversations. On any given day, you might hear lively discussions about the food they are eating ("Can we grow lettuce in a pot in the window or does it have to be planted outside?"), the activities that they completed in the morning ("How can we get the block tower to reach above our heads without crashing?"), anticipated events ("I wonder what we will see when we walk to the beach?"), and joys or concerns ("Where will daddy live if he doesn't live with us?"). Children eat family style, getting their own food. This allows children to learn self-help skills, reflect upon what foods they like and dislike, determine proper proportions, and learn about sharing with others. Teachers eat with children, modeling social skills. The teachers also use the mealtime as an opportunity to increase knowledge and skills, for example, pointing out that the oranges are cut into fourths as a way of assisting children with math skills and vocabulary. The children and teachers at Spirit at Play are all familiar with the mealtime routine and expectations. The mealtime at Spirit at Play provides a rich learning experience that is positive for both the teachers and children. Further, the teachers have modeled a respectful way of interacting with others.

Teaching children the classroom routines can be time-consuming, particularly when children first begin a program. However, research reveals that teachers who spend more time teaching routines at the beginning of the school year have children who are more engaged in learning activities and need less assistance later in the year (Bohn, Roehrig, & Pressley, 2004).

Plan Transition Times. A study of classrooms in 11 states, found that children spend 22% of their program time in transitions, making it vitally important that these times are learning experiences (Early et al., 2005, 2013). This is more likely to occur when the schedule allows unrushed time for transitions. Detailed information about how to plan effective transition times is included later in this chapter.

In addition, you will want to minimize the number of transition times whenever possible. One way to do this is to incorporate small-group time and special activities into center time. For example, some programs have children individually prepare and eat their snack during center time, eliminating the need for large-group transitions to and from snack.

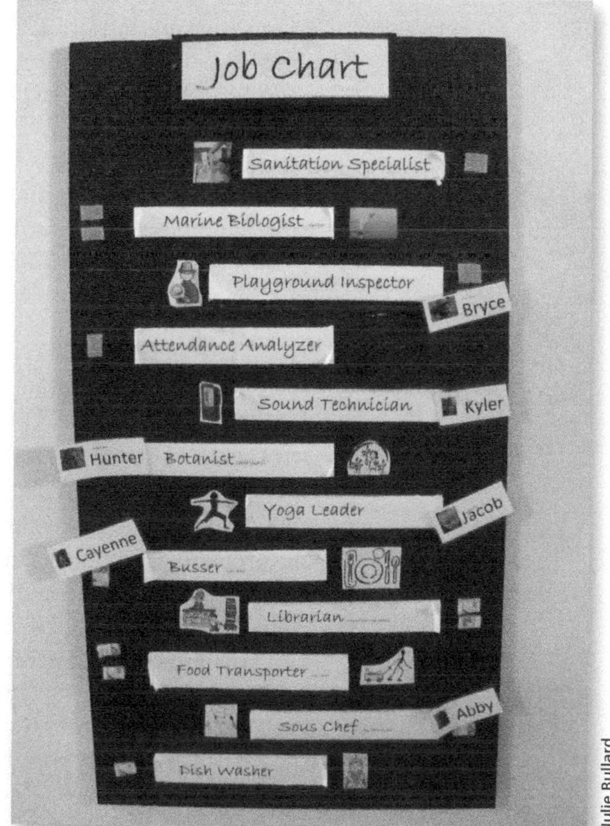

Julie Bullard

Classroom jobs are a routine that assist children to learn responsibility, experience a sense of accomplishment, and feel ownership for the classroom. Notice the interesting sounding jobs on this chart.

Include a Daily Time to Be Outdoors. Outdoor time is linked to improvements in academic skills and performance, concentration, attitudes and behavior, social skills and relationships, and physical skills (Gill, 2014). During outdoor time, children have the opportunity to participate in activities often not present in the indoor environment. Outdoor time allows for boisterous play, loud voices, and large motor engagement. In addition to exercise, the outdoors provides other health benefits including less concentrated infectious disease organisms and exposure to sunlight, which allows children to produce Vitamin D (American Academy of Pediatrics, American Public Health Association, & National Resource Center for Health and Safety in Child Care and Early Education, 2011). Outdoor play also allows children to be involved firsthand with nature and to experience the many aspects of weather. Many programs further enhance children's learning by developing their outside environment into an outdoor classroom containing a variety of learning centers. Children need to be outdoors every day, unless it would be a health risk to do so (American Academy of Pediatrics et al., 2011). In determining if it is safe to play outside, pay attention to National Weather Reports and the air quality index (AQI). It is important to have alternate plans when children cannot go outside. See Chapter 16 for a variety of indoor large motor ideas.

Include Extended Center Time for Engaging in In-Depth Learning. Learning center time should be a minimum of one hour to allow for deep involvement in play (Copple & Bredekamp, 2009, p. 153). This time period, alternately called work-time, self-selection, project time, free choice, or activity time in different programs, is an opportunity for children to participate in individual and small-group learning. During this time, children choose between the many available learning centers. These centers will vary depending upon the age group of the child, but often include dramatic play, blocks and construction, art, music, sensory, literacy, math, science, and manipulative centers. In addition, special small-group activities are often included during this time period, such as cooking projects, special art activities, and activities that support ongoing project work.

Children in a rural program were completing a project on tractors. After an in-depth study that included a field trip to an implement dealer, the children decided to create their own tractor. Each day during center time, several children worked on constructing a tractor from a large refrigerator box. Often they revisited a video they had taken of the tractors on their field trip, reviewed sketches they had made of tractors, consulted books and posters, and had lively discussions as they gained a more in-depth understanding of tractors.

Large blocks for center time allow children to make a variety of decisions, learn to plan and manage their time, and work at their own pace. During this time, children can choose whether to work individually or in small groups, and whether to engage in quiet or more active activities. They can also control the tempo of their work, determine how long to spend on an activity, and decide whom to interact with. In many programs, these large blocks of time also allow for some spontaneity. For example, a teacher and a small group of children might take a trip to a nearby library when children need additional information for a project.

Research reveals that children are more positively engaged in tasks and interact more with their peers during center time than when they are in more teacher directed activities (Vitiello et al., 2012). Research shows that this finding is true for special populations as well. For example, English Language Learners interacted more and used English more frequently during center time, allowing more opportunities to build language skills (Markova-Lama, 2013). Children who have autism showed similar results (Reszka, Odom, & Hume, 2012).

Include a Developmentally Appropriate Whole-Group Time (Preschool and Early Elementary). The younger the children are, the shorter the group time should be and the more choice children should have in whether or not they participate in the group. Group times can include participating in music and drama activities, storytelling, puppetry, or interactive story reading. Group times are also used to introduce new centers, discuss the day's events, share learning, review teacher's and children's joys and concerns, and discuss classroom situations and brainstorm solutions. Since group times are short, there is typically only time to focus on one or two of these activities.

In planning group times, the first thing that the teacher needs to do is to consider the goals for the activity. Next, she needs to determine whether these goals can be best met using a large-group activity. As might be expected, children are more off-task in large groups than in small groups (Rimm-Kaufman, La Paro, Downer, & Pianta, 2005; McWilliam, Scarborough, & Kim, 2003). See Figure 3.1 to learn about effective whole-group times.

Katie, a teacher at Northern Head Start, read a book to the children each day during large-group time. She wanted to introduce the children to different literature and

Research shows that children are more inattentive during whole-group activities than when involved in other classroom structures. So what types of activities increase attentiveness in children during whole-group times? DiCarlo, Pierce, Baumgartner, Harris, and Ota (2012) examined large-group times in 39 classrooms in 31 different programs. Large-group times averaged 22 minutes, with longer group times leading to more inattentiveness. The researchers found, in order of importance, that children are more attentive in whole-group time when teachers:

- ❑ acknowledge the children's contributions to the discussion;
- ❑ provide relevant materials to each of the children;
- ❑ relate whole-group activities to other classroom activities that the children have been doing;
- ❑ address multiple objectives, which may increase complexity;
- ❑ provide enough space so that children can freely move;
- ❑ have one teacher lead the group, while another manages the group; and
- ❑ use the time for modeling materials.

FIGURE 3.1 Research-Based Information on How to Increase Children's Attention During Whole-Group Times

to teach pre-reading skills such as prediction and phonological awareness. However, when Katie reflected upon her group time she realized that she spent much of her time managing the group, interrupting the book to ask children to sit quietly. When she asked questions some of the children answered quickly and others rarely seemed to respond. Children also complained about not being able to see the book. Katie decided to reexamine this time and try a variety of strategies. First, she divided the class into small groups so that each child would be able to have more opportunities to see and interact with the book by asking and responding to questions. She also carefully chose books to read aloud, making sure that they were age-appropriate quality books with pictures that were large enough to be seen by the children. She tried to make her stories more interesting by using a dramatic voice, bringing story props, and occasionally telling the story with puppets. Katie also strived to more actively involve the children in the stories by reading stories the children could dramatize, encouraging children to repeat phrases as she read predictable books, and asking children relevant questions as she read the book (What do you think will happen next? Why do you think he did that? What else could he have done?). These changes resulted in children being much more attentive during story time.

Watch the video to see an example of a large group time. How did providing relevant materials assist in making the children be more engaged?

Determine Needs for a Small-Group, Teacher-Directed Time. While small-group activities are often incorporated into center time, many programs also include a separate time for small groups. During this time, teachers set up many different types of learning experiences. These include project planning and implementation, math and science activities, small-group reading activities, or writing in journals. In some programs, small groups may also be child-led. For example, in the Helena Public School Montessori 1st–3rd grade classroom, a child-led circle focusing on joys and concerns is held each day. If someone introduces a concern, the child leads the group in problem-solving solutions.

Meet the Needs of Families. When developing schedules, it is important to consider the needs of the families in your program. For example, do most of the children eat breakfast before they arrive? If many of the children typically eat breakfast before they arrive, you might want to consider a breakfast bar. Children who have not had breakfast can help themselves to a bowl of cereal and a piece of fruit rather than having everyone sit down for breakfast. If parents and children need to spend extended time in the car commuting after child care, you might want to plan your schedule so that the child has had an opportunity to participate in active activities before leaving.

Make the Schedule Visible. Schedules are typically posted so that children, teachers, families, and volunteers can anticipate the next event. For younger children, the schedule is often displayed in picture form. See the picture at the beginning of the chapter for an example of a picture schedule.

Regularly Analyze the Schedule. Teachers need to regularly assess the schedule to ensure that it is meeting the needs of children, families, and teachers. The schedule is not an end in itself, but instead is designed to meet children's needs and to allow program goals to occur.

Establishing an effective schedule provides a framework that allows a community of learners to engage in rich learning opportunities. Each teacher is a decision maker in developing a schedule based upon the needs and unique characteristics of the children, staff, and families, and the philosophy of the program. However, in developing schedules it is sometimes helpful to examine what others have done. Following are sample daily schedules.

Sample Daily Schedules

Each of the following sample schedules is designed for a different age group. In addition, each of the schedules varies based upon the detail they provide and the terms they use for common activities during the day (center time, selective choice).

Sample Infant Schedule. In designing the infant schedule, it is important to understand parental everyday routines so that you can provide continuity and meet the cultural needs of the children. Shonkoff and Phillips, in *From Neurons to Neighborhoods* (2000), discuss behavioral inheritances, stating that they are "embodied in the 'scripts' that characterize everyday routines for such common activities as sleeping, feeding, and playing" (Shonkoff and Phillips, 2000, p. 867). For example, are infants rocked to sleep or do they fall asleep on their own? How independent are infants expected to be? It is important that parents and teachers work closely to meet infants' and toddlers' needs (Butterfield, 2002).

In planning for infants, individual schedules are followed where children engage in self-initiated activities. However, during the day each child needs to have the opportunity to:

- Have undivided adult attention and interaction during routine times such as feeding and diapering. This time provides a prime opportunity to engage in individualized and meaningful communication.
- Be read to.
- Listen to music.
- Engage in floor time.
- Have one-on-one interaction with a teacher around individualized learning goals.
- Explore materials in the classroom.
- Engage in gross motor activities both indoors and outdoors.

During arrival and departure time, teachers and parents share news about the child and written communication sheets regarding the child's sleep, eating, and diaper changes. Special instructions and daily anecdotes are also discussed and often written on communication sheets.

Sample Toddler Schedule. Toddlers have developed more self-regulation in comparison with infants and can therefore have a more group-oriented rather than individualized schedule. Since children at this age are seeking greater independence, more time needs to be planned for individualized transitions. For example, toddlers may take a long time putting on a coat or shoes. The schedule also needs to allow ample time to explore and discover.

7:45 Arrival—Special table time activities and books. Individualized handwashing.

8:30 Breakfast—Children who are hungry eat breakfast family style. As children finish eating, they wash their hands and go to centers.

9:00 Center time—Choice of dramatic play, art, music, manipulative, blocks and construction, sensory, gross motor, and book nook. Teacher-planned special activities (art, literacy, music, project). Diaper checks and changes.

10:00 Clean up and transition outdoors.

10:20 Outdoors—Gross motor activities and interaction with the natural environment.

11:10 Transition indoors—Wash hands for lunch, sing songs.

11:30 Lunch—Children and a teacher sit in small groups sharing food and conversation. As children finish lunch they wash hands, brush teeth, and have their diaper changed.

12:15 Naps—Children look at books or listen to teachers telling stories until they fall asleep.

2:15 As children wake, they have their diaper changed, eat a snack, and engage in quiet center time activities (books, manipulatives, media, art).

3:10 Clean up and transition outdoors.

3:30 Outdoor—Gross motor activities and interaction with the natural environment.

4:00 Transition indoors.

4:15 Centers—Choice of dramatic play, art, music, manipulative, blocks and construction, sensory, gross motor, and book nook, plus teacher-planned special activities (music, movement, creative drama), and diaper checks (in warm weather, teachers set up outdoor centers and this time is spent outside).

5:30 Departure.

Sample Preschool Schedule. You will note that in this schedule snack time is included as part of the center activities. This technique allows children to eat when they are hungry and can free up time for other activities. You will also note that not all children are required to lie down on a mat. Instead, quiet time for non-nappers involves participating in quiet activities. It is important that you plan naptime based upon the need of the child and family. Some families request that their child have a nap so that they will have more time together as a family in the evening.

A playground is adjacent to this classroom. In the afternoon, children have the choice of using the outdoor or indoor learning centers.

7:45 Arrival—Children and parents sign in. Work jobs (individualized and small-group tabletop activities). Individualized handwashing.

8:30 Breakfast—Children and teachers eat family style; conversation, social skills, and self-help skills are stressed. As children finish breakfast they go to the circle area to dictate stories, write, or draw in their individual journals.

9:10 News and views small group—Children are divided into two groups. Teachers share information about new materials, centers, and activities for the day.

Two children each day share journals. Children and teachers make plans for activities and projects.

9:30 Transition to outdoors—Children are individually released from the circle using self-concept boosting activities (description of the child, photo of child engaged in an activity or with a special person, happygram describing something the child did the day before, etc.). Time is allowed for toileting, gathering materials for outdoor play, and putting on coats.

9:50 Outdoors—Choice of outdoor centers (climbing, balancing, swinging, art, music, woodworking, Zen garden, sand and water, gardening, dramatic play) or participating in teacher-planned special activities. In bad weather, gross motor activities are set up indoors.

10:30 Gross motor transition—Children use gross motor skills to enter the building (hop, skip, crawl through tunnel). Children put coats away, wash hands, use toilet, and so on.

10:40 Center time—Children choose from literacy, math, manipulative, sensory, science, dramatic play, block and construction, woodworking, music, and creative art centers or teacher-directed individual and small-group activities. Snacks are available for children who are hungry.

11:40 Clean up—As children complete clean up they go to small-group story areas and look at books.

11:50 Small-group story—Teachers read books to small groups of children.

12:10 Concept transition—Children are released individually to wash hands using a concept-based transition (addresses, full names, colors, patterns, etc.).

12:15 Lunch—Children and teachers eat family style with an emphasis on conversation, social skills, and self-help skills.

12:45 As children complete lunch they brush their teeth, wash their hands and face, and get out their mats.

1:00 Quiet time/naptime—Children lie down on cots and listen to stories told by the teacher or look at books. Non-nappers go to a separate area and have quiet alone time for half an hour during which time they look at books, draw, or write in journals or complete other quiet activities.

2:00 Indoor and outdoor learning centers—As children awake or finish quiet time they can participate in indoor or outdoor learning centers. During this time, children also prepare their own individual snack by following simple picture recipe cards.

4:30 Clean up and movement—Children put away materials in indoor and outdoor centers and assist in cleaning the center for the day. Each child is assigned a chore (e.g., watering plants, cleaning paint containers, emptying the water table, putting balls away, etc.). As children finish cleaning, they join a circle where one teacher is leading the group in movement activities.

5:00 Closing circle—Children and teachers meet in small groups to share joys and concerns. Children dictate daily news. The teacher writes the news on chart paper and displays it for parents to see.

5:15 Departure.

Sample Kindergarten Schedule. The teacher in this program has posted the state standards that children are meeting as they engage in each of the learning centers. Since the school district emphasizes literacy and math, these are infused within each learning center. Additionally, there are teacher-directed times that focus on these subjects.

8:45 Opening circle—Self-concept activity and daily announcements (new centers, activities planned for the day, news from home).

9:05 Work stations—Children participate in literacy and mathematically infused learning centers—literacy, math, cognitive manipulative, science, dramatic play, block and construction, woodworking, music, and creative art, plus teacher-directed individual and small-group activities.

10:15 Transition—Clean up and wash hands to prepare for snack.

10:30 Snack—Children and teacher eat in small groups; informal conversation is encouraged.

10:45 Physical skills—Large motor and movement activities (indoor or outdoor movement centers, teacher-led activities).

11:10 Circle time—Introduction and synthesis of learning center activities (e.g., review of the characteristics of items that sank or floated in the science center).

11:30 Small-group activities—Children engage in small-group, teacher-directed learning activities focused on math, science, and social studies.

11:55 Transition to lunch.

12:00 Lunch and outdoor time—As soon as children finish lunch they go to the playground where they use gross motor equipment or participate in dramatic play or teacher-organized or child-initiated games.

1:05 Transition indoors.

1:15 Literacy activities—Children read books, write in journals, participate in author's circles, and engage in teacher-led literacy activities.

1:45 Work stations—Children participate in literacy and mathematically infused learning centers—literacy, math, cognitive manipulative, science, dramatic play, block and construction, woodworking, music, creative art, plus teacher-directed, individual and small-group activities.

2:30 Clean up—As soon as children finish cleaning up, they go to the circle area and complete a quick daily evaluation (mark on a sheet of paper the favorite thing they did that day, fill in a circle indicating how well they got along with friends, and indicate what activities they completed at centers).

2:45 Closing circle—Summarize and evaluate the day.

3:00 Departure.

Sample First- Through Third-Grade Schedule. This classroom emphasizes the project approach to learning. During the afternoon, students conduct research on their project using the many centers and integrating the different subject areas. For example, this group is currently studying our bodies. They have many questions about the skeletal system and body organs. In the art center, they are using different materials to construct a body; in the science center, they are examining X-rays and identifying different bones using research books; in the manipulative center, children are dissecting an owl pellet, finding bones that they hope to reconstruct; and several children are writing a research book on what they are learning about their bodies.

8:15–8:45 Morning meeting (morning messages, group sharing, community-building activity, daily announcements, and planning).

8:45–9:45 Literacy workshops and centers.

Reading—Mini lessons, reading conferences, independent and partner reading, author's chair.

Writing—Mini lesson, author's chair, writing conference, prompted writing.

Centers—Games (spelling and word games), listening center, writing center, book center, computer center.

9:45–10:00 Clean up centers—prepare to go outside or to the gym.

10:00–10:30 Outdoor time or gym.

10:30–11:15 Math skill groups.

11:15–11:40 Read aloud—chapter book.

11:45–12:30 Lunch and recess.

12:30–1:00 Individual or buddy reading.

1:00–3:00 Projects, centers, special guests.

Centers—literacy, manipulative, math, dramatic play, construction, science, art, music, puppetry, special project center.

3:10 Closing meeting—self-reflection on day, joys, and concerns.

3:25 Dismissal.

Check Your Understanding 3.1
Click here to gauge your understanding of section concepts.

You will note that in some of the previous samples, the teacher has noted her transition times and transition activities on the schedule. Well-planned transitions help bring closure to an activity and move children smoothly to the next part of the day. As the preschool example illustrates, these can also be learning times if well-designed. The next section will discuss how to plan for effective transitions.

Designing Effective Transitions

Nicole carefully planned her morning activities with the group of three-year-old children that she was teaching. Although she normally planned carefully, today she had planned with extra deliberation because she was being observed by her early childhood college professor. Her morning had gone perfectly. Nicole and the children were completing a project on caterpillars, and during free time the children were involved in many activities relating to the project that Nicole had planned. During circle time, the children all listened attentively when she read The Very Hungry Caterpillar *by Eric Carle. The children even helped to tell the story as she read. Then everything fell apart. After circle when she told the children it was time to wash up for lunch, they all jumped up and began a stampede for the sink to wash their hands. Before she knew it, three children had been pushed on the way to the sink (one of the children was on the floor and two other children were crying). There were several children all trying to wash their hands at once who were shouting at each other. The college professor had to stop observing to help restore order.*

Transition times, the process of changing from one activity to another, can provide opportunities for learning. They can be meaningful ways to organize one's day. However, research shows that children are less engaged, have more conflict, and are less self-reliant during transitions than in other parts of the day (Booren, Downer, & Vitiello, 2012, Vitiello, Booren, Downer, & Williford, 2012). Children are expected to listen to the teacher's instructions, end one activity, follow multiple-step directions, and begin another activity all while filtering out distractions from peers. If not well-planned, transition times may involve children congregating in one spot and waiting with nothing to do. These times can be difficult for all children. But, for children with disabilities such as attention deficit hyperactivity disorder (ADHD), characterized by difficulties with attention, impulsivity, and hyperactivity, the reduced structure and multiple demands during transition times can make coping extremely difficult (Buck, 1999). This is all complicated further by the fact that during transition times, teachers are often multitasking, trying to assist children to move through the various stages of the transition while also facilitating the next activity. Like Nicole, many early childhood practitioners fail to plan for transitions, making the transition process even more difficult (Sainato, 1990).

Effective transition times are particularly important when one considers that a typical program in early childhood can include 12 to 15 transition times (Rogers, 1988). Research from pre-K programs in 11 states show that transitions account for 22% of the child's day. Meal and snack time account for another 11% of the day. While transition and routine times can be educational, 88% of the time they were not in these 652 programs (Early et al., 2013).

Well-planned transition times not only decrease frustration and behavior problems, but can also turn wasted time into educational opportunities, allowing both adults and children to feel competent. How do we plan effective transition times?

Tips for Effective Transition Times

Following are several techniques that can help make transition times effective and educational.

Determine if It Is Necessary to Have a Transition Time. Could you reduce the number of times that children need to make transitions by rearranging your schedule? In many cases, activities can be incorporated into center time. For example, instead of children all engaging in a group art activity, the special art project could be available throughout center time. This creates fewer transition times and smaller group sizes, and allows the child to choose when to participate.

Visualize How the Transition Would Look if It Was Successful. What would the children be doing? What would the teacher be doing? After you have done this, develop a concrete plan to achieve what you visualize (Buck, 1999). For example, Nicole, the teacher in the previous scenario, must plan a transition time for children to wash their hands. She must also think about what the children will do after they wash their hands. Will they go directly to the lunch table? Will they sit wherever they wish or will they sit in designated spots? If they go directly to the table, can they begin to eat immediately or must they wait until everyone is seated?

Place Transition Times on the Daily Schedule and on the Daily Plan. This acknowledges the importance of these times and is more likely to result in the time being planned. It is important to realize that transitions take time. Rushing through transition times can cause stress for children and adults while diminishing the opportunities for learning that can occur during these times (Greenman & Stonehouse, 1996). However, you also want to avoid prolonging transition times. For example, you would not want to sing an entire song for each child as you release them from circle.

Predetermine the Roles and Responsibilities of Each Adult During Transition Times. For example, Nicole could ask her assistant to be by the sink. She could then release the children individually or in small groups to wash their hands.

Reduce the Waiting Time That Often Accompanies Transition Times. In addition to wasting valuable time and increasing the likelihood of behavior problems, requiring children to wait with nothing to do is disrespectful. As stated by Davidson (1982), "Adults who often make children wait for them or the group, or who otherwise waste children's time convey a basic lack of respect for children which may well have a detrimental effect on the way that children view themselves" (Davidson 1982, p. 16). Additionally, teachers may inadvertently punish children who conform to their expectations by making them wait until all the children are finished before beginning an activity. Avoid waiting time by having everything ready for an activity before the children begin. Move children in small groups rather than large groups. For example, as soon as some of the children are ready, they go outside with a teacher rather than waiting for the large group to be ready.

Use Any Wait Time During Transition Times Wisely and Effectively. If children must wait, it is important to provide transition activities. For example, you might sing songs, play language games, tell a story, complete finger plays, clap patterns, write or draw in journals, exercise, or perform creative movement activities. Jeareal, a preschool teacher, plays a game called "what it is, and what it isn't" when there is waiting time. Using any object, children list what it is and then what it is not. For example, a pencil might be pointed, round, red. It is not a pen, stick, or elephant. Some beginning teachers make a list of ideas to use while waiting that they post on the wall or keep in their pocket so they are always prepared.

Make Transitions Predictable. Some teachers have a specific song they play for cleaning up, or they might say the same chant every time they transition inside from the playground. These routines provide stability and add an opportunity for rituals that are enjoyable for the teacher and children (Greenman, 2006).

Give a Warning Before the Start of a Transition Time. For example, "In five minutes, we will be cleaning up so that we can go outside." As adults, we would be insulted and likely resistant if a friend were to say, "You need to stop what you are doing and put everything away because we are going outside now." Giving a warning demonstrates that we have respect for children and their work. The time between the warning and the transition allows children to bring closure to the task they are engaged in and to begin planning for the next event. This often results in children being more cooperative. Whenever possible, it is helpful to allow children to complete the task they are involved in before they transition to the next activity.

State or Review Expectations Before the Transition Time Begins. In addition to giving children verbal instructions, some teachers have directions in pictures showing the children performing each of the tasks during the transition. This technique has been used effectively with children who are hard of hearing or who have autism. It is important that the expectations are necessary and developmentally appropriate. For example, some teachers require children to sit quietly before they are released from circle. Although this may be the traditional way that circle releases have occurred in the program, teachers need to ask themselves if there is a reason this is important. For many children, sitting quietly is very difficult and not developmentally appropriate.

Engage in Active Supervision During Transition Time. Researchers have found that those teachers who engage in the active supervision skills of scanning, moving, and interacting increase appropriate behavior (Colvin, Sugai, Good, & Lee, 1997). Scanning involves looking frequently around the room and noticing children's behaviors. Moving involves walking in unpredictable patterns, using proximity to control and reinforce behavior. Interacting includes modeling, conversing with children, reinforcing behavior, and reminding children of expectations when needed (McIntosh, Herman, Sanford, McGraw, & Florence, 2004). Since transition times can be difficult for children, it is important for every teacher in the room to be actively engaged in assisting and supervising children. It is best if materials needed for the next activity are set up before the transition time begins.

If Needed, Adapt the Transition Time Expectations for Children with Special Needs. Children with disabilities may need extra assistance during transition time.

Sean, a four-year-old child with ADHD, had difficulty with the transition time from outside to inside. Moving from the playground to the classroom involved walking down a steep flight of steps. Sean, who was extremely hyperactive and anxious to get inside, had on more than one occasion accidentally pushed the child in front of him. The teachers, after brainstorming options, decided to have Sean come into the classroom before the other children. Not wanting to make Sean feel like he was being punished, they decided to let Sean be the lunch helper. Sean was excited to perform this role.

There are many strategies that assist children with special needs to effectively negotiate transition times. The most important, as illustrated in the example, is to problem solve solutions based upon the specific need of the child. Some children may need additional time to complete the transition, fewer multiple-step directions, a picture card showing the sequence of the transition, or a student buddy.

Make Transition Times Educational. Transition activities can be made educational in a variety of ways. For example, you can release children from circle through emphasizing a new skill they are learning, such as recognizing their first and last name, colors of clothing, or addresses. Children can improve listening skills, vocabulary, and observation skills when they try to guess which classmate the teacher is describing. Physical skills can be enhanced as children kick an imaginary ball as they move from the playground to the classroom. Creativity and problem solving can be emphasized when teachers ask children to find their own unique way to move down the hall.

Helpful Hints for Different Types of Transitions

Some daily transition times present especially difficult challenges. Following are some of these along with ideas to help make these transition times run smoothly.

From Home to Program. This is often a difficult transition time for several reasons. The transition not only involves the child and teacher, but also may involve the parent, making it unclear who is responsible for the child during this time. The teacher's time is often divided between welcoming families and children and attending to children who are already present. Both the child and the parent might be grieving the need to be apart. Given next are some helpful hints:

- Have a teacher designated to assist children and families during this transition time.
- Encourage parents to stay at the program until they and their child feel comfortable parting. You might have special books that families can read to children especially for this time.
- After the parent leaves, support the child until he becomes engaged in an activity. You might support a toddler by holding the child, walking to the door or a window, and waving good-bye to the parent. Some programs have low "good-bye windows" at the infant and toddler level that they can crawl to and look out. A preschooler might be helped by giving them a choice of activities.
- Have engaging activities immediately available for the child. These activities should take a minimum of teacher attention and be highly desirable to the children. For example, some teachers have a clay table with a variety of tools. Others have a basket of books, a set of puzzles and games, or work jobs (individual fine motor and cognitive activities) that are used only at this time of the day.

Julie Bullard

Children at the Renaissance School of Arts and Sciences are eager to arrive each morning to read the notes that fairies have left for them in the mailbox.

- Accommodate children who have especially difficult times with transitions by allowing them to bring a security item from home. This assists them in bridging their two worlds. You can also provide individual family photo albums or family taped stories that children can look at or listen to when their parents leave.
- Provide assurance to families who leave their distraught child by sending a text with a photo showing a happily engaged child.

Moving from Place to Place in a Group. It is difficult for children to move in a group. The temptation is to get there quickly by running ahead of the teacher. Teachers can assist children by giving them something specific to do as they walk:

- Play follow the leader.
- Walk in different ways—like a rag doll, stiff legged, on toes, or heel to toe.
- Move like different animals or forms of transportation (car, plane, bus).
- Practice different gross motor skills like hopping, jumping, or skipping.
- Find certain landmarks or items along the path.
- Sing a song while marching to the beat.

Moving from Indoors to Outdoors. In cold climates, preparing to go outside can involve putting on hats, coats, boots, mittens, and snow pants. Rainy climates can also necessitate dressing in a variety of gear. In many programs, all the children are preparing to go outside at once, resulting in crowded conditions. Because children have different skill levels and clothing that varies (for example, rain pants that pull on versus rain pants that zip), they are ready to go outside at different times. Therefore, this transition is more effective when:

- Children get ready to go outside individually or in small groups.
- Children who are ready earlier help other children who might need assistance in zipping a coat or pulling on boots.
- Children go outside with one of the teachers as soon as a small group is ready. If the indoor and outdoor environments are connected, a teacher can be posted outside and children can go out individually.

Transitioning to Naptime. In setting up the naptime transition and routine, you will first want to make sure you have realistic expectations. See Figure 3.2 for research on naps. Children should not be required to lie on their mats for long periods of time (more than half an hour) when they are not asleep. Instead, non-sleepers can relax by participating in quiet activities. For children who do nap, set the stage for napping by helping children to relax through the following activities:

- Prepare the room by playing relaxing music and dimming the lights.
- Have children move to mats in a slow way such as pretending to be turtles, snails, or toys that are winding down.

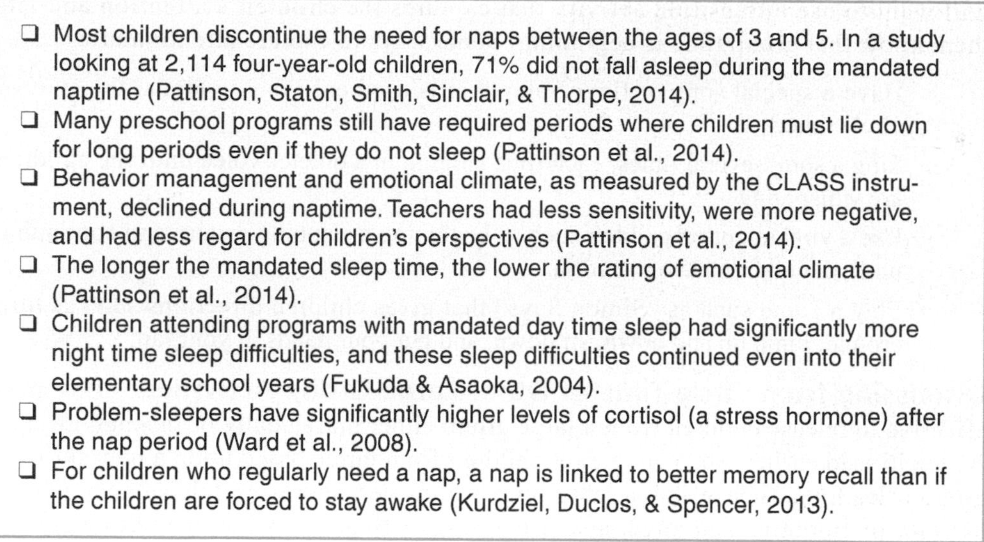

- Most children discontinue the need for naps between the ages of 3 and 5. In a study looking at 2,114 four-year-old children, 71% did not fall asleep during the mandated naptime (Pattinson, Staton, Smith, Sinclair, & Thorpe, 2014).
- Many preschool programs still have required periods where children must lie down for long periods even if they do not sleep (Pattinson et al., 2014).
- Behavior management and emotional climate, as measured by the CLASS instrument, declined during naptime. Teachers had less sensitivity, were more negative, and had less regard for children's perspectives (Pattinson et al., 2014).
- The longer the mandated sleep time, the lower the rating of emotional climate (Pattinson et al., 2014).
- Children attending programs with mandated day time sleep had significantly more night time sleep difficulties, and these sleep difficulties continued even into their elementary school years (Fukuda & Asaoka, 2004).
- Problem-sleepers have significantly higher levels of cortisol (a stress hormone) after the nap period (Ward et al., 2008).
- For children who regularly need a nap, a nap is linked to better memory recall than if the children are forced to stay awake (Kurdziel, Duclos, & Spencer, 2013).

FIGURE 3.2
What Does Research Say About Naps?

- Once on the mats, help children engage in progressive relaxation exercises such as being a rag doll, limp noodle, or melting ice cube (Pica, 2004); participate in guided imagery such as being a cloud floating in the sky or a stream flowing through the mountains; or partake in deep-breathing techniques such as pretending to blow up a balloon.
- Give children back rubs.
- Tell stories, read books, or let children look at books as they prepare to sleep.
- Use a special transition routine. For example, a sleepy-time puppet can be brought out each day to tell the children a special story as they lie on their cots.

Watch the video to see a naptime routine. How well does this routine reflect the naptime research found in Figure 3.1?

By teaching children relaxation skills and modeling the establishment of a relaxing atmosphere, we can help provide a more pleasant transition for children and adults. In addition, we are teaching children a lifelong skill.

- **From Clean-Up to Circle Time.** Cleaning up can be an overwhelming job, particularly if children have not been cleaning up as they have been playing. To aid in this transition, you can:
- Have a routine with chants or songs to signal the beginning of clean up.
- Give a small group of children a specific area to clean; often, these are the children last playing in the area.
- Increase cooperation by giving choices of what to pick up within the area: "Would you like to pick up the large blocks or the small blocks?"
- Make clean up a game, "You be the bulldozer and push the blocks to the shelves, and I'll put the blocks on the shelf."
- Play an energizing song that children dance and move to while cleaning up. This not only accomplishes the task, but also encourages physical movement.
- Have an activity available as soon as children complete their cleaning such as listening to and following an activity CD or looking at books. It is important to plan activities that children can easily become involved with as they join the group. For this reason, most teachers avoid reading stories during this time.

Capturing Children's Attention at the Beginning of a Group Activity. Once all the children have gathered for circle time, or any other group activity, you

Watch the video to see how a teacher captures the children's attention. How does this activity help prepare the children for the group activity?

will want to use a transition activity that captures the children's attention and lets them know that group time is beginning. Some ways to capture attention are:

- Have a special song or finger-play that is used each day to signal the start of circle time.
- Sing a song several times, each time singing in a quieter voice until the children are whispering.
- Use a viral attention grabber such as beginning a clapping pattern and continuing until all children have joined in.
- Play a game such as "Simon Says" that gives children directions such as turn around, jump up and down, sit down, and put your hands in your lap.

Dismissing from Circle Time or Other Large-Group Activities. It is most effective to release children from a large group either individually or in small groups. As mentioned earlier, you can release children from circle based upon a new skill the group is learning, such as initial letter sounds of names, addresses, telephone numbers, or color of clothing. You might also use a song or finger-play that includes a child's name as a way of releasing children such as "Willoughby Wallaby Woo." A descriptive element might also be used. For example, "Everyone who has buckles on their shoes can go and wash their hands for lunch" or "Everyone with brown eyes can go to get their coats on."

School to Home. Leaving the program might be difficult for some children, particularly those who have a difficult time with change. Children are often engaged in an activity when parents arrive and may be reluctant to discontinue it. Often children have not received a warning that they will be leaving. Additionally, parents, teachers, and children are all tired at the end of the day.

Just as children might bring a transition object from home to ease entry into the program, a transition object from the center might ease the exit. For example, children might check a book out from the center that the parent will read to them at home. Teachers can also make a conscientious effort to warn children that their parents are coming soon. If children are in the middle of an activity, such as eating a snack or finishing an art project, and the parent is unable to wait, the teacher might want to send the unfinished snack or art project home to be completed.

Check Your Understanding 3.2
Click here to gauge your understanding of section concepts.

Through carefully planned transitions, teachers can reduce stress and behavioral issues, limit wasted time, and increase learning opportunities. Children can learn independence and inner control, learn to use time wisely, and acquire the skills needed to make successful transitions throughout their schooling careers and life.

We will next examine routines. We'll explore the difference and similarities between transition times and routines and discuss how to establish effective routines.

Designing Effective Routines

As mentioned earlier, transition times are the times that occur between activities. **Routines** are a predetermined sequence of consistent actions that are regularly followed—a script for a way to act. Like well-planned transitions, routines can assist the classroom to run more smoothly and allow everyone to know what to expect. They provide predictability, stability, and security for children. In addition, well-established routines provide order and structure to a classroom and result in less behavioral issues (Kostelnik et al., 2012). Routines also provide the framework so that children can learn social skills such as independence, self-control, and socially acceptable behavior. Because routines "become part of the fabric of the classroom through their repeated use" they can also be powerful avenues for interaction and learning (Ritchhart, Palmer, Church, & Tishman, 2006).

Types of Routines

In early childhood, we have three main types of routines:

1. Organization or housekeeping—keep the classroom safe, healthy, and functioning smoothly.
2. Interaction—govern the way that we function with each other.
3. Learning—assist to organize learning or learning processes.

To help illustrate each of these types of routines we'll examine the arrival of four-year-old Kayla and her mother, Trista, at Curious Minds Early Care and Education Center. When Kayla enters the program, she begins with a housekeeping routine. She removes her coat and mittens and places the mittens in the sleeves of her coat. She hangs the coat on a designated hook that is labeled with her name. Next, she washes her hands, carefully following a sequence of steps that are posted above the bathroom sink. This housekeeping routine assists in keeping Kayla and her classmates healthy. Kayla and Trista then sign into the program. While Trista signs the attendance form, Kayla removes her laminated name card and a blank strip of paper. She carefully writes her name while looking at the name card strip. She places her signed strip in the in-box. This is a learning routine that encourages Kayla to practice writing her name and to use literacy for an authentic purpose. Trista then reads Kayla the daily poster where the teacher has described what the children will be doing that day. As she reads, she points to each word (a learning routine). When Trista is ready to leave, she and Kayla engage in an interaction routine that they have repeated many times. Trista assists Kayla to find a toy, gives her a kiss, and tells her she will see her at the end of the day. Kayla waves to her mother as she leaves the room.

Using Interaction and Learning Routines

Although many programs use organizational or housekeeping routines, they may not realize the power of interaction or learning routines. A group of researchers from Project Zero at Harvard have been exploring and conducting research on thinking routines (Ritchhart, Palmer, Church, & Tishman, 2006). The purpose of thinking routines is to assist children to learn thinking skills and dispositions and to make thinking visible to children, peers, teachers, and families. Making thinking visible allows children to become more engaged in thinking and to learn from each other. It assists teachers to have a better understanding of children's reasoning, understanding, and misconceptions. When thinking routines were implemented with preschool children, researchers found that children and teachers developed a culture of thinking and that thinking skills and dispositions were enhanced (Salmon, 2008).

One thinking routine that has been used successfully with young children is the See/Think/Wonder routine, where children answer the following questions: What do

Julie Bullard

This aesthetic sign-in area is welcoming for Kayla and contains the materials she needs to complete her morning routine.

Watch the video to learn more about thinking routines. What are the advantages of using thinking routines?

https://www.youtube.com/watch?v=kATy9HnXoYY

you see? What do you think about that? What does it make you wonder? For example, children at Best Beginnings were starting a unit on bugs. The teacher brought in a ladybug and the children used the See/Think/Wonder routine, beginning with carefully observing and describing the ladybug, discussing what they thought about their observations, and then generating further questions that they would explore. Teachers might also use this routine when they examine a piece of artwork.

Teaching Routines to Children

It takes time to learn routines. Research on effective teachers reveals that they teach children routines through a variety of methods (Leinhardt, Weidman, & Hammond, 1987). This includes the teacher explaining the importance of the routine, intentionally teaching the routine, and consistently following the routine. Effective teachers also use modeling, practice, reinforcement, and visual prompts. They may pair children who do not know a routine with a child who does. The teacher focuses on routines when new children enter the classroom until the routines are well-established.

Sharing Routines with Families

Check Your Understanding 3.3

Click here to gauge your understanding of section concepts.

Especially when working with infants and toddlers, it is important that families and teachers share the routines that are used. Many routines, such as feeding and sleeping routines, are specific to a family and are culturally based. When routines are used from one setting to another they can provide consistency and security for children. For example, since the time that Ember was born her parents placed her in a swaddle when she showed signs of being tired, dimmed the lights, and sang her a special song. She began to associate this routine with sleep. When she entered a home child care at four months of age, her parents explained the routine to the caregiver and gave her a recording of the song they sang. When the caregiver followed the routine, it helped Ember in her transition to child care.

Click here to gauge your understanding of chapter concepts.

Effective schedules, transitions, and routines provide the context for learning. When they are appropriately planned, everyone knows what to expect, chaos is diminished, and learning is enhanced. As stated by Greenman (2006), "Avoiding a rigid order that chokes or constricts or a too loose order that frightens or intoxicates generally requires a thoughtful and complete analysis of how all the program structural elements interact" (Greenman, 2006, p. 56).

Sample Application Activities

- Examine each of the schedules in this chapter. Note that each has a different amount of detail. Determine the degree of detail that you would use in designing a schedule.
- Develop a schedule for an infant/toddler, preschool, or early elementary classroom. Use the schedule critique in Figure 3.3 to assess your schedule.
- Develop a list of finger-plays, songs, and activities that you can use for transitions. Combine your ideas with your classmates and create a booklet of transition ideas.
- Visit an early childhood program. Use the transition critique found in Figure 3.3 to assess at least one transition.

FIGURE 3.3 Environmental Assessment: Schedules, Transitions, and Routines

Schedules

- ❑ Is there a consistent daily schedule that is adjusted as needed to provide for teachable moments and special activities?
- ❑ Is the schedule developmentally appropriate for the age group? For example, individualized schedules for infants, no required group times for young toddlers?
- ❑ Is the schedule consistent with the program philosophy?
- ❑ Is a schedule posted for both children and adults to follow?
- ❑ Are quiet and active activities alternated?
- ❑ Is there a developmentally appropriate balance of large-group, small-group, and individual activities?
- ❑ Does the schedule provide a balance of child-initiated and adult-initiated activities?
- ❑ Does the child have at least one hour of center time each day?
- ❑ Is there an outdoor time scheduled each day (or a gym time for bad weather)?
- ❑ Are routine times included in the schedule?
- ❑ Is the schedule explained in enough detail that you can understand what children are expected to do during this time period?

Transitions

- ❑ Are times for transitions listed on the schedule and the lesson plans?
- ❑ Is there evidence that the transitions are planned?
- ❑ Is there a limited amount of waiting time during transitions?
- ❑ If waiting time is necessary, are children engaged in a meaningful activity?
- ❑ Are transition times used to increase children's knowledge and skills?
- ❑ Are children given enough time to make transitions so that they are not rushed?
- ❑ Are children given advance notice that a transition will be occurring?

Routines

- ❑ Are there enough routines so that the program flows smoothly?
- ❑ Are there a variety of types of routines—organization, interaction, and learning?
- ❑ Do all the adults and children in the classroom know and follow the routines?

- Increasing the learning that occurs during transitions and routines could have a profound effect on children's learning over the course of a year, especially considering that transitions and routines consume nearly a third of the child's time. Choose a curriculum area such as dance, music, drama, math, or literacy and think about the way that you could incorporate this area into transitions and routines.
- Think about the routines that you use in your daily life. What are the advantages of the routines that you use?
- Learn more about thinking routines by visiting the Visible Thinking website.

Chapter 4

Planning a Play-Based Curriculum

Learning Outcomes

After you have read this chapter, you will be prepared to:

- Explain what early childhood curriculum is and the reasons why teachers write curriculum plans
- Describe the eight steps in developing effective curriculum
- Develop a plan for learning

Julie Bullard

Tom is a teacher at Little Tykes Academy. His program has just decided to seek NAEYC Accreditation. As the teachers review the criteria, they discover that they need a written curriculum. Would the program be better to just purchase a prepared curriculum rather than develop their own? Although many programs use purchased curriculum, this curriculum must often be modified to meet the needs of a particular group of children. As stated by the NAEYC, "Strong, effective early childhood curricula do not come out of a box or a teacher-proof manual" (NAEYC, 2009, p. 16). Developing curriculum is challenging. Teachers must ground their curriculum in a research-based understanding of child development and learning. In addition, it is critical that teachers know the children in their care, since each child constructs their own knowledge based upon their preferred learning styles, interests, family culture, and past background knowledge and experiences. The curriculum also needs to align with the program's and families' philosophy and values.

The teachers decide to meet weekly to collaboratively develop their written curriculum framework.

In this chapter we will explore curriculum design for the early childhood classroom. We will begin by defining curriculum and discussing the need for a written curriculum. We will then examine the steps to curriculum planning, including the steps in designing a learning plan for young children. How does this relate to early childhood learning environments? One of the most effective ways to deliver curriculum for young children is through the learning environment. The curriculum and the learning environment have a symbiotic relationship. The learning environment is enhanced and can become richer when teachers intentionally design the environment to meet curricular goals. In turn, curriculum goals are accomplished as children interact within rich environments. An effective environment not only supports the delivery of the curriculum but also supports the assessment process. For example, an effective learning environment allows teachers to gather authentic assessment data. When the learning environment is well-designed, it also allows the teacher to have the time to invest in the assessment process.

What Is Curriculum?

Curriculum is an educational plan that guides the teacher in:

- knowing what knowledge and skills to emphasize,
- the learning experiences that will be used in helping children achieve these objectives,
- how these learning experiences will be organized, and
- the assessment methods that will be used to determine if children have gained the intended knowledge and skills.

The NAEYC and the National Association of Early Childhood Specialists in State Departments of Education stress that it is important to "implement curriculum that is thoughtfully planned, challenging, engaging, developmentally appropriate, culturally and linguistically responsive, comprehensive, and likely to promote positive outcomes for all young children" (NAEYC & NAECS/SDE, 2003, p. 2).

Why a Written Curriculum?

As Tom and the other teachers at Little Tykes Academy discovered, a written curriculum has several advantages. First, it allows a program to be more intentional about what they are teaching. As a result, it is more likely that the curriculum will be thoughtfully designed and coherent, contain all curriculum content areas, be aligned with learning standards, and meet the individualized needs and interests of individual children. Second, the process of developing a written curriculum allows others, including families, to be involved in the creation of the curriculum. Tom and the other teachers formed a curriculum committee that included families. Third, after it is developed, a written curriculum is a tool that can be shared with others. It allows all stakeholders to know about, examine, and critique the curriculum. Little Tykes shared their curriculum with prospective families and with the school districts that the children transitioned into.

Check Your Understanding 4.1

Click here to gauge your understanding of section concepts.

Written curriculums vary in the amount of detail that they provide. For example, many programs develop a **curriculum framework**, a curriculum structure that includes learning guidelines, examples of types of learning experiences, and a description of instructional and assessment methods used. Then the classroom teacher develops the detailed learning plans.

Steps in Long-Term Curriculum Planning

There are many steps to effective curriculum design. Curriculum development is a complex task where each design step includes gathering information and making multiple decisions. Please see Figure 4.1 for a graphic of the steps teachers take to develop long-term curriculum. In the next section, we will examine each of these steps.

1. Develop Long-Term Curriculum Outcomes

What are **outcomes**? They are the "vision for the desired results of the curriculum" that provide a "destination without a road map" (Solomon, 2003, p. 89). National and state standards, outcomes, and learning guidelines are typically very general (Solomon, 2003). As when you take a long trip, there are many midpoints to reach your destination and many different ways to get there. Your curriculum provides the road map to assist children to reach the outcomes. Some examples of long-term outcomes are:

- Children will demonstrate the ability to regulate their behavior and emotions in a developmentally appropriate way.
- Children will understand and use increasingly diverse and complex vocabulary.

FIGURE 4.1 Steps in Long-Term Curriculum Development

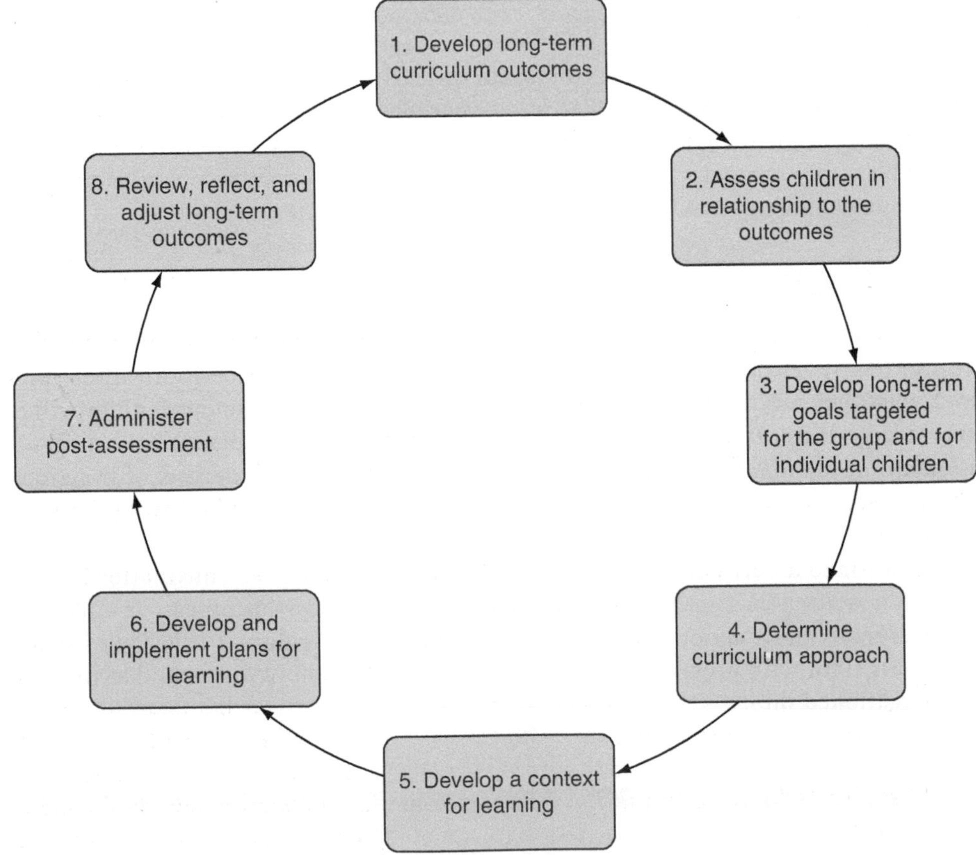

In developing long-term outcomes, you will want to consider the following:

- Program philosophy and goals
- Family and community beliefs and values
- State and national standards
- The development of a well-rounded curriculum

In this section, we will cover each of these in more depth.

Program Curriculum Philosophy and Goals. Your curriculum needs to align with your program and individual philosophy of learning. Your philosophy dictates what you believe regarding the purpose of education, what is important to learn, the role of the teacher, the role of the student, what constitutes learning, the best methods to achieve learning, and the best way to determine if learning has occurred. There is a long history in early childhood of subscribing to the **constructivist philosophy**. Constructivists believe that children are not just empty vessels waiting to be filled with knowledge, but instead that children actively construct their knowledge through their interactions with materials and others. Each learner is viewed as a unique individual with their own needs, interests, background knowledge, and cultural experiences and beliefs that affect their learning. Constructivists view the teacher as a facilitator who promotes active, social learning. Jean Piaget and Lev Vygotsky are two theorists who promoted the constructivist philosophy.

In addition to a curriculum philosophy, many programs have other outcomes that they believe are important. These often help to form the identity of the program. For example, programs might emphasize a particular curricular area such as literacy or the arts, or they might use a particular approach such as the Reggio Emilia or HighScope approach. This will influence your outcomes.

Family and Community Beliefs and Values. In addition to considering the program's philosophy and goals, we must also consider the values and beliefs of families and the community. What are the values that the community holds? For example, Brenda lives in a community that is attempting to become more eco-friendly. Some of the initiatives in the community are eco-friendly housing, an emphasis on gardening and farmer's markets, city composting and recycling, and open green spaces. As Brenda determines goals for her program, she will want to consider goals that align with and support these community values.

National and State Standards. National and state standards give guidance about expected knowledge and skills for different age groups. At this time, nearly all states have standards or outcomes for children beginning with infants and going through high school. Standards are developed to assure equality in education and to provide accountability. They are typically created by experts within the field and go through extensive comment periods and reviews, adding to their credibility. Standards can provide useful guidance to teachers.

However, there have been concerns about the standards movement. At times standards might not be developmentally appropriate for young children. Additionally, standards often drive the curriculum. When standards are developed for only some of the curricular areas or domains, there is a tendency to view these as more important than areas or domains that are not addressed. Assessments are frequently based on achieving these standards. Additionally, the assessment results may result in high stake consequences for children, teachers, and schools. For example, the No Child Left Behind Act initially required elementary education standards and assessments that addressed reading and math. In many programs, this resulted in little

Julie Bullard

This sunflower project involved many different curriculum areas, including science, literacy, and art.

emphasis being placed on science, social science, the arts, and physical skills, with the majority of the school day being spent on reading and math. In some states, whether children were promoted to the next grade level or teachers retained their jobs or received pay raises was based upon a single assessment of these two areas.

You will need to find out which standards your program uses for guidance. These could include your state's Early Learning Standards, the Head Start Child Development and Early Learning Framework, the Common Core State Standards, content area national standards, or your state department of education standards. You will want to use the standards for guidance, while ensuring that they are developmentally appropriate and you have a well-rounded curriculum.

A Well-Rounded Curriculum That Includes All Domains and Curricular Areas. You will also want to assure that your curriculum is comprehensive. It is important that your curriculum address the following areas:

- Language and literacy
- The arts: music, creative movement, dance, drama, and visual arts
- Mathematics, science, and technology
- Physical activity, physical education, health, and safety
- Social studies
- Social and emotional development
- Approaches to learning such as learning dispositions and skills

1. Develop long-term curriculum outcomes
2. Assess children in relationship to the outcomes
3. Develop long-term goals targeted for the group and for individual children
4. Determine curriculum approach
5. Develop a context for learning
6. Develop and implement plans for learning
7. Administer post-assessment
8. Review, reflect, and adjust long-term outcomes

Steps in Long-Term Curriculum Development

2. Assess Children in Relationship to Outcomes

Often a program will choose a formal, in-depth assessment instrument to periodically assess children's knowledge and skills. Teachers can use formal, in-depth assessments to identify children's needs, determine progress, determine curricular and individual goals, provide concrete information to share with families, and evaluate the effectiveness of learning experiences. It is critical that you choose an instrument designed for your intended use. For example, a standardized screening instrument is used to determine if children are meeting developmental milestones. Children who are not are referred for further assessment. These developmental screening instruments are not designed for curriculum development.

You will want to ensure that the assessment instrument you choose is developmentally and culturally appropriate; comprehensive; based on accurate, significant developmental trajectories; and aligned with your philosophy, curriculum, and outcomes. You will also want to examine how the assessment information is gathered. For example, some assessments only allow a teacher to give children credit for an indicator if they demonstrate it in the testing situation. However, young children are not always good at performing on command. In addition, they make rapid growth during the early years. Therefore, it is important that the assessment instrument allows children to demonstrate their learning over time and in multiple ways. For example, Tanya had completed an assessment on Michael and found he was unable to draw a circle. However, later she observed him draw a circle as he was drawing a self-portrait in the art area. Tanya went back to Michael's assessment and gave him credit for this skill.

3. Develop Long-Term Goals Targeted for the Group and for Individual Children

Group Long-Term Goals. The results of your assessments will help you to determine long-term goals. Long-term goals are generally broader than the objectives or outcomes found on a daily or weekly lesson plan. The weekly or daily objective or outcomes are specific and designed to help children to accomplish these long-term goals. Long-term goals provide a focus. For example, Catherine completed an assessment on the four-year-old children in her class and found that most of the children reached developmental milestones for body movement such as running, balancing on one foot, and climbing stairs using alternate feet. However, they struggled with object manipulation such as catching a ball and riding a tricycle. While Catherine's curriculum will include both body movement and object manipulation, she will want to have a specific focus on object manipulation since the children are not meeting developmental milestones in this area. These long-term skills and concepts will be learned over time, often in small steps. The curriculum for different ages will often over lap, with children getting multiple opportunities to gain ever increasing skills.

When writing long term goals you will want to focus on what the children will accomplish rather than what you will be doing. For example, Catherine would want to state, "Children will reach developmental milestones in object movement" rather than "I will provide more outdoor physical activities for the children in my classroom."

Individual Long-Term Goals. Individual long-term goals are often developed in collaboration with families. Children in the early elementary grades may also be included as part of the goal-setting meeting. Typically, the teacher will share the assessment results with the family during this meeting. For example, when Catherine shared assessment results with Erin's family they were concerned that his fine motor skills were below age level. They said that they lived in a small house and that Erin had three younger siblings. It was difficult to find a place at home where Erin could write, draw, or play with small manipulatives. They wanted this to be a goal that he worked on at school.

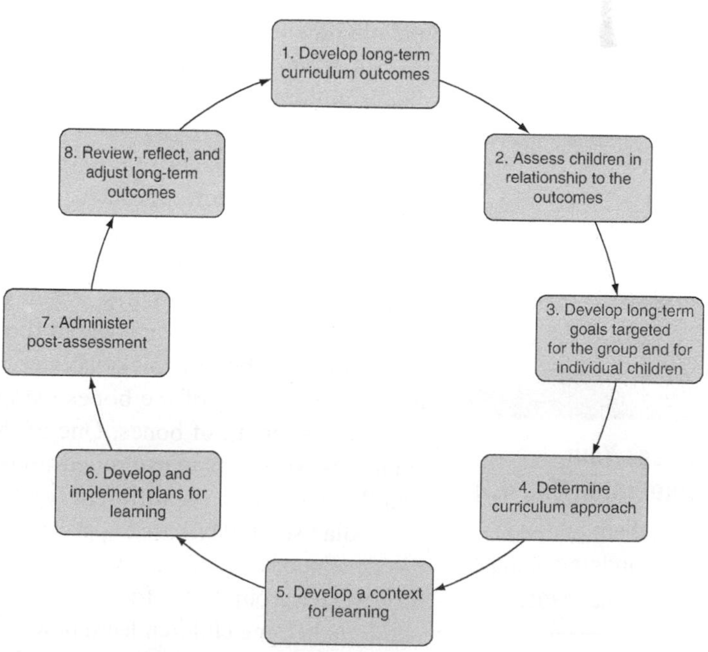

Steps in Long-Term Curriculum Development

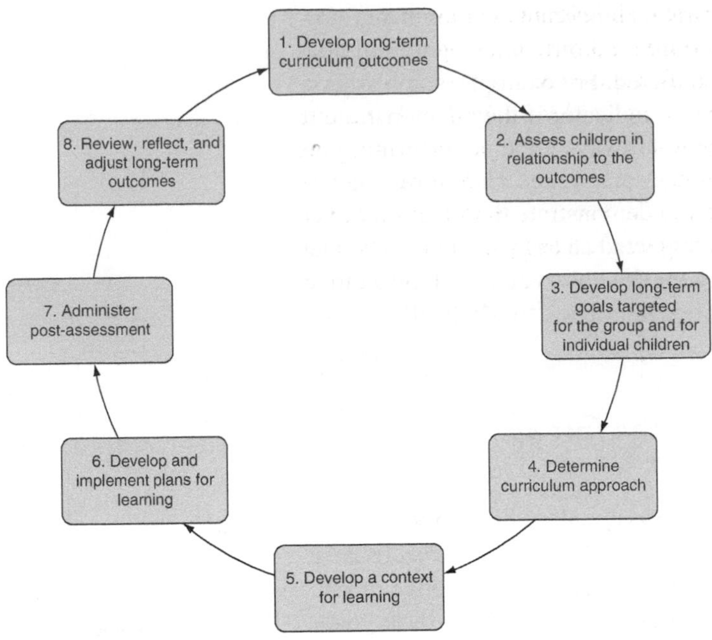

Steps in Long-Term Curriculum Development

4. Determine Curriculum Approach

There are many different approaches to curriculum development. The curriculum approach you choose is based on your philosophy. As mentioned earlier, most early childhood programs subscribe to the constructivist philosophy. Many curriculum approaches are consistent with the constructivist philosophy. For example, some teachers develop integrated lessons around an early learning guideline or outcome. Other teachers use themes or units, projects, or a play-based approach. Each of these approaches uses an integrated curriculum. Many programs use a combination of these approaches, combining a play-based approach with integrated lessons, themes, or projects. Let's examine how these might look in action.

Belinda is in a toddler classroom. Each week when she plans her daily learning plans, she chooses some specific early learning guidelines to focus on. For example, today she is focusing on helping children identify feelings using an integrated lesson. She reads the children a short book on feelings, and then she and the children sing, "If you're happy and you know it, clap your hands." Later she puts cards showing different facial expressions on a table with two mirrors so that children can practice making the different facial expressions in the mirrors.

Tessa is a teacher in a kindergarten classroom that uses a theme-based approach. Since it is the beginning of the year, she and the other kindergarten teachers are beginning with a "Getting to Know You" theme for the first two weeks of school. Tessa has planned many different experiences for the children, such as creating all-about-me posters, completing self-portraits, describing favorite things at circle time, and reading books and singing songs relating to similarities and differences. On the first day of class Tessa takes a group photo that she makes into a puzzle and adds to the manipulative area. She places children's name cards and many books about "me" in the literacy center such as *The Foot Book* by Dr. Seuss.

Cathy is a teacher in a multigrade preschool classroom who uses the project approach. The project approach topic is based on children's interests, with children's questions being a focus of the study. Children engage in investigations to answer their questions, make field site visits, consult with visiting experts, and represent their knowledge in many different ways. When Cathy broke her arm, the children became very interested in bones. They answered the question "What do different bones look like?" by examining fish bones, chicken bones, cow bones, and a model of a human skeleton. They tested the strength of the bones using different types of tools to answer their question about the strength of bones. One of the activities that they completed to determine how skeletons work was to use rolled-up paper to develop a standing skeleton. They also visited the hospital to see different types of X-rays and machines and to interview a doctor.

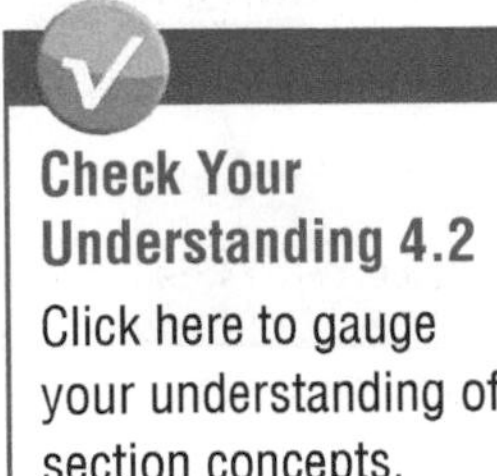

Check Your Understanding 4.2
Click here to gauge your understanding of section concepts.

Alia uses a play-based approach with the four-year-old children in her classroom. She has developed a "rich" environment containing an abundance of challenging, interesting materials. Her group times focus on introducing new materials, providing challenges for the children, helping children learn new skills they will need in a center, providing background information, sharing of children's work produced in learning centers, discussing with children what they have learned, and helping children to synthesize their learning. For example, when Alia was setting up a center on magnifying glasses, she gave each child a magnifying glass and they went outside for their group time. They each took a small section of the grassy outdoor area and observed using the magnifying glass. They also collected items to bring into their science table. As time went on Alia added different strengths and types of magnifying glasses, as well as different types of materials to examine with the glasses. She had another circle where the children discussed what they had learned. For example, several children had discovered that just because a magnifying glass is bigger does not mean it is more powerful.

Throughout this book, we will be learning more about establishing the environment and developing a play-based approach. We will also learn how to develop "rich" environments to support other curriculum approaches.

5. Develop a Context for Learning

How do you manage your time to allow learning to occur? Let's examine two teachers' approaches to establishing a context for learning.

Meagan carefully plans her circle times and teacher-led, large- and small-group times. She uses the time that children participate in centers to prepare, only interacting with children to manage conflicts. Although Meagan would state that she believes in the value of child-initiated activities, her actions demonstrate that she truly values only teacher-directed activities.

Rebecca views each part of the children's day as a learning opportunity. She carefully plans routines, learning centers, outdoor time, and group times. During center time, she either observes children or interacts with them, building relationships and facilitating learning.

Rebecca's approach is more consistent with an early childhood constructivist philosophy. The emphasis is on children constructing their knowledge, with the teacher establishing an environment, planning experiences, and interacting with children in ways that assist this process. Since children are continually constructing their knowledge, every part of the day and all experiences are viewed as learning opportunities. Both teacher-directed time and child-initiated time are viewed as important. As we learned in Chapter 3, we need to carefully structure our schedule and transitions to match the early childhood philosophy and to provide optimum learning opportunities.

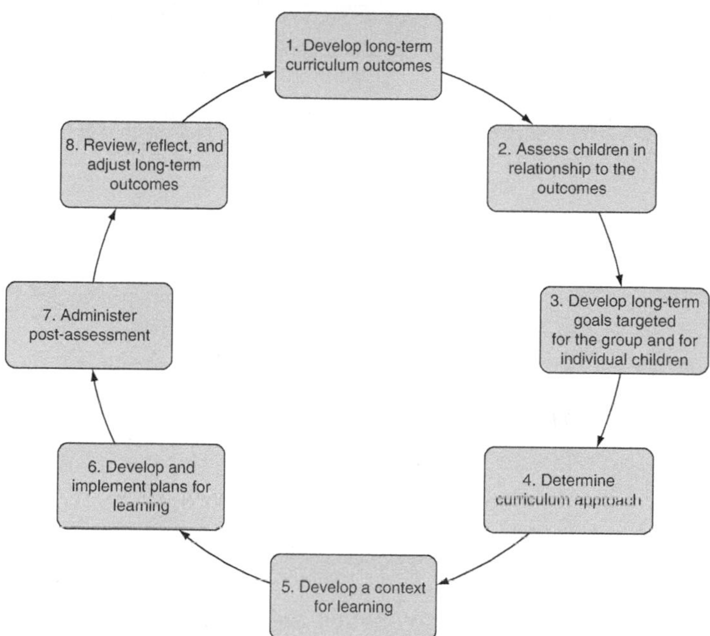

Steps in Long-Term Curriculum Development

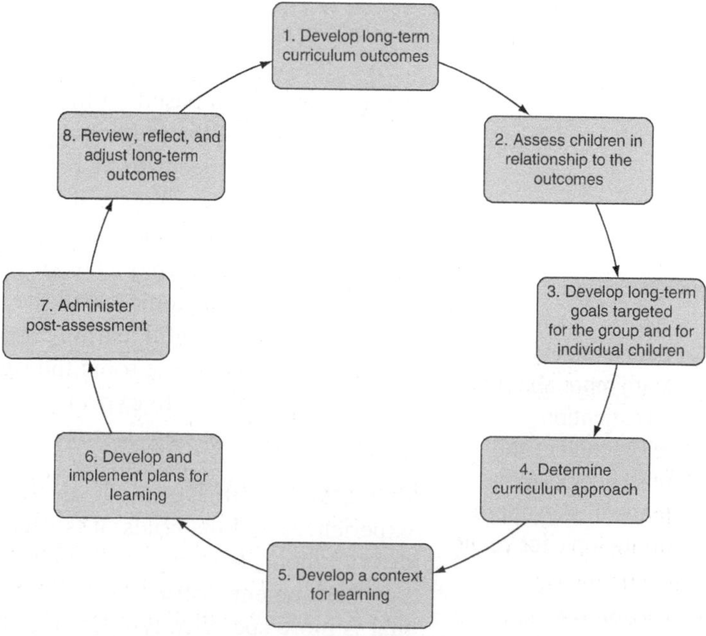

Steps in Long-Term Curriculum Development

6. Develop and Implement Plans for Learning

Plans for learning are guides that teachers use to determine what specific activities and

FIGURE 4.2
Steps for Developing Plans for Learning

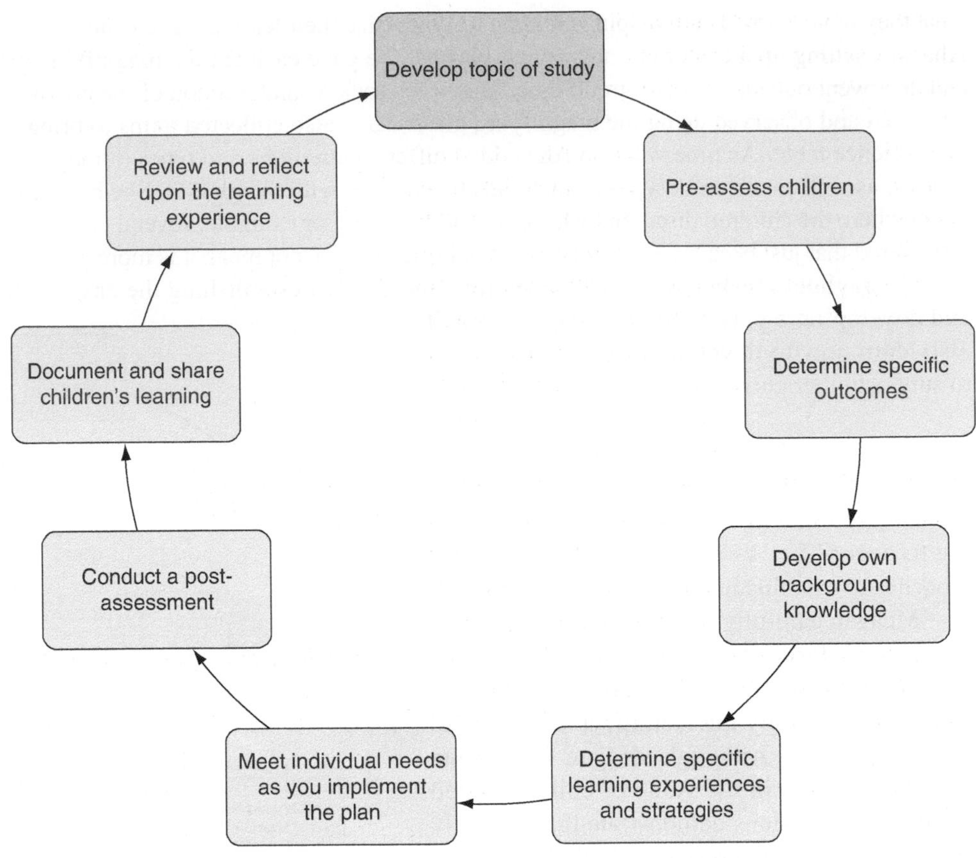

environmental changes they will implement each day. As students or as beginning teachers, you will typically develop plans that are very detailed. As one repeats this planning cycle, much of the planning becomes more automatic and may require less detailed written plans. See Figure 4.2 to see the steps in developing a plan for learning.

Develop Topic of Study. Depending on your curriculum approach, you might plan a topic for one lesson, or a day, a week, or even a year's focus. For example, if you are using an approach based on integrated lessons, you might have a specific topic for one lesson. If you use the project approach, you might have a long-term topic of study. The topic you choose needs to be based on children's interests, their development, and your long-term outcomes. You will want to carefully choose your topic based upon a sound rationale. Does the topic lend itself to hands-on learning? Is the topic developmentally appropriate? What prerequisite knowledge and skills will the children need to have to be successful with this topic? Will the topic be engaging to most of the children? Will the topic lead to meaningful learning about the topic as well as address standards in different curriculum areas? Is the topic the right size to allow for in-depth study? For example, it would be unrealistic to expect young children to understand the concept of living and nonliving after one brief lesson.

Watch the video to learn more about an investigation of balls with toddlers and preschoolers. What made this an appropriate topic for young children?

https://www.youtube.com/watch?v=rZ3ynCkQufk

Pre-assess Children. To design engaging and developmentally appropriate learning experiences and materials, it is necessary to continually assess and document children's development, learning, and interests. Although you will have results from a formalized assessment instrument, you will also want to conduct a pre-assessment of children that is more specifically related to the topic of study. This will help you to build on the children's prior learning and experiences and to discover children's preconceptions and misconceptions. For example, the picture featured in the opening of the chapter shows children's knowledge about chickens before they began their chicken project. Children are continually constructing and changing their knowledge base. As part of this process they often develop naïve explanations about phenomena and relationships that are based upon their experiences. It is helpful to understand the typical misconceptions for the age group you are working with. This can be a starting point in understanding the children in your group. For example, it is common that children believe that someone who is taller is older, or that all silver-colored items are attracted to a magnet. However, you will also want to understand children's individual theories and ideas. You can discover this by having children explain their theories or having them draw or create models of their theories. For example, during a project at Reggio Emilia, children visited a fountain. Teachers wanted to discover their theories about how the water got into the fountain. They placed a transparency of the fountain on an overhead projector, taped a piece of paper under the fountain, and had children draw their ideas. They also interviewed children about their drawings asking them to explain their thinking. Through this process, the teacher not only learned more about each child's thinking but the drawings and the questioning also helped the child to think more deeply.

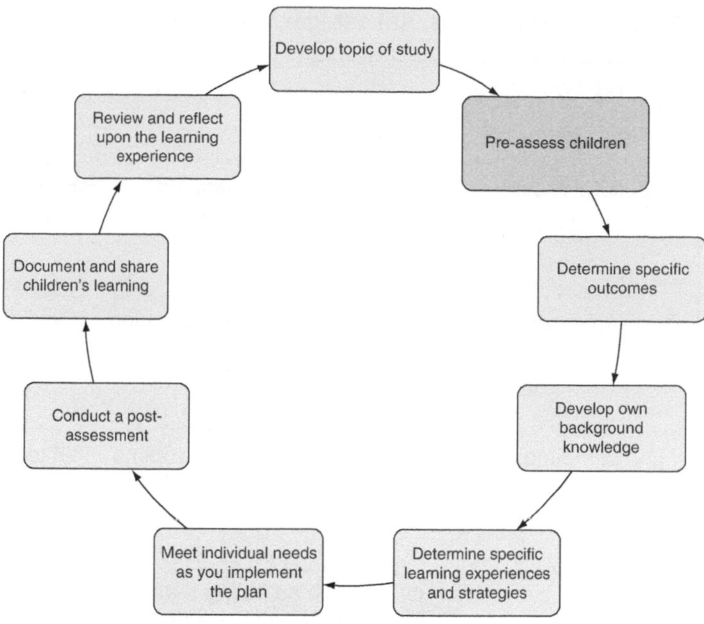

Steps for Developing Plans for Learning

In addition to the pre-assessment, you will assess children at the end of the experience to see if they have met the outcomes. If the learning experience is occurring over time, you will also be assessing during the experience to ensure that you are on the right track. This is often referred to as **formative assessment**. This will help you to create "a trail of evidence" of what the children have learned. There are many assessment tools you can use, each having its own strengths and limitations. Table 4.1 provides information on several different types of assessments. To be effective, teachers must be intentional about the information they wish to collect and have a plan for how they will collect the information.

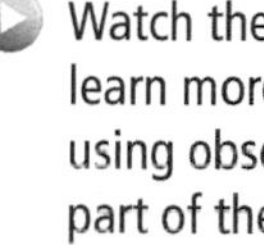
Watch the video to learn more about using observation as part of the assessment process. How are the observations used in the curriculum process?

https://www.youtube.com/watch?v=t1Xtr3RKjGc

Diana uses a play-based curriculum. She has developed a variety of work jobs focused on children's math skills that she has placed in the math center. She has also developed a checklist that includes the skills the children are learning. When a child demonstrates a skill (such as counting by rote to ten and matching numerals with the correct number of objects), it is recorded on the list. Diana uses this information both as a pre-assessment, allowing her to know what new work jobs need to be created to challenge the children, and also as a post-assessment, letting her know what skills children have mastered.

Diana hangs clipboards in each center so they can easily record anecdotal records. At the end of the week, she cuts the anecdotal records apart and places them in individual children's files. At times, she places a tape recorder in a center. She then listens to the tape and/or has volunteers transcribe the tape. This information provides valuable insight into children's thoughts, language, and social skills. Diana also assesses children informally as she interacts with them. For example, she asks questions that help her to analyze the child's knowledge and thinking. When a roly poly bug was in the classroom, she asked a child why he thought the bug had a hard shell and how the roly poly was similar and different from the ants in the ant farm. During a walk outside, she asked a child why she thought the grass was green.

Table 4.1 Descriptions, Advantages, and Disadvantages of Different Types of Assessment Techniques

Type of Assessment	Description	Advantages	Disadvantages
Anecdotal records	Short descriptive detailed narrative about a specific event	Flexible, open ended	Time consuming, may be difficult to determine group needs without careful analysis
Running record	Sequential narrative spanning a longer period of time than an anecdotal record	Flexible, open ended	Time consuming, may be difficult to determine group needs without careful analysis
Time sampling	Observation of what happens during a given period of time often using tallies.	Objective, can observe several children simultaneously	Closed ended, lacks behavioral and contextual detail
Event sampling	Observation of a specific event such as hitting that includes the antecedent, behavior, and consequence	Can reveal patterns such as triggers, this information can be used to design an effective intervention strategy	Time consuming, may be difficult to capture antecedent events
Checklist	A list of behaviors or traits that the teacher checks off	Easy to use, time efficient, can be used to examine entire group	Closed ended, lacks behavioral and contextual detail
Frequency counts	A tally of each time a behavior occurs	Can document change over time. Effective in determining if interventions or other changes have produced results	Closed ended, lacks behavioral and contextual detail
Analyzed work samples	Tape and video recordings, photos, and artifacts (e.g., Venn diagrams, KWHL charts, webs, handwriting samples) that show children's current work and thinking	Authentic, can be used to show both progress and accomplishments	May be difficult to determine individual or group needs without careful analysis Analysis can be time consuming

Children are also active participants in documenting their own learning, using recording sheets, tape recorders, and digital cameras. They complete recording sheets by writing, drawing, or circling answers. For example, in a sink and float center, Diana includes a sheet that has a picture of each item the child is testing. Children circle the items they think will float, then they test each item, and then go back and correct their predictions. Children record themselves reading, telling a story, singing, or playing a musical instrument. A digital camera is available for children to take pictures of block structures, sand creations, and pattern block designs. Children also use the camera to show the process of their work over time. For example, children created a car from a cardboard box. They took several pictures showing the various steps.

Some teachers, particularly in kindergarten through third-grade classrooms, require that children visit certain centers or complete some mandatory center activities each week. The children are often given a checklist of required activities. The tracking sheets that document the completion of the activities then become one more piece of assessment evidence.

Table 4.2 Sabrina's KWHL Chart on Insects

What I Know	What I Want to Know	How I Will Find Out	What I Learned
There are many insects.	Are spiders insects?	Look at a bunch of spiders.	
They all have eight legs.	What happens if a poisonous insect bites you?	Look in a book.	
Some insects bite.	How long do they live?	Ask insect scientist.	
Some insects fly and some crawl.	How far can they fly?	Look in a book.	
	What do they do in the winter?	Ask my dad.	

Sabrina is a first-grader. When she finishes her investigation, she will fill out the "What I Learned "section.

Throughout this book, we will be examining ways of assessing individual children's learning as well as assessing different learning environments. Here, we will examine three different types of artifacts or work samples that one might use for pre-assessment, ongoing, or post-assessments/KWHL charts, Venn diagrams, and webs.

KWHL Charts. **KWHL** (what we know, what we want to know, how we will find out, and what we learned) charts are used to elicit children's prior knowledge, determine their questions, plan ways to answer their questions, and allow them to reflect upon their learning. Teachers can also use this information for curriculum planning. For example, Tamia, a first-grade teacher, was planning a study of insects. She used the KWHL to determine the children's current knowledge and questions, so that she could design relevant experiences for them. See Table 4.2 for the KWHL that one of the children, Sabrina, created.

Apply Your Knowledge You will note from Sabrina's KWHL chart that she has a misconception about insects. What materials might you add to the science center that will assist her to clear up her misunderstanding and answer her questions?

Venn Diagrams. A **Venn diagram** typically consists of two or three overlapping circles that are used to classify and compare attributes. Nissa teaches children to use Venn diagrams in classifying materials. For example, she used a Venn diagram to have children predict which items would sink or float. In the intersecting area of the circles were items that would sink and float. See the example in Figure 4.3.

Webs. Webbing is a way of organizing and structuring ideas and information. We can **web** to capture children's knowledge and ideas, to identify misconceptions, to document and organize children's questions, and to record children's learning. Webbing can also be used for creating a tentative curriculum plan and for documenting what has been accomplished. See Figure 4.4 for an example of a tentative curriculum web based on a group of children's question: "How do chickens have babies?"

In creating a web, one writes the topic in the center of a sheet of paper and then creates subtopics around the topic. Ideas or activities continue to web outward. Individual children, groups of children, or the teacher can complete the webs.

FIGURE 4.3 Children's Float and Sink Predictions on a Venn Diagram

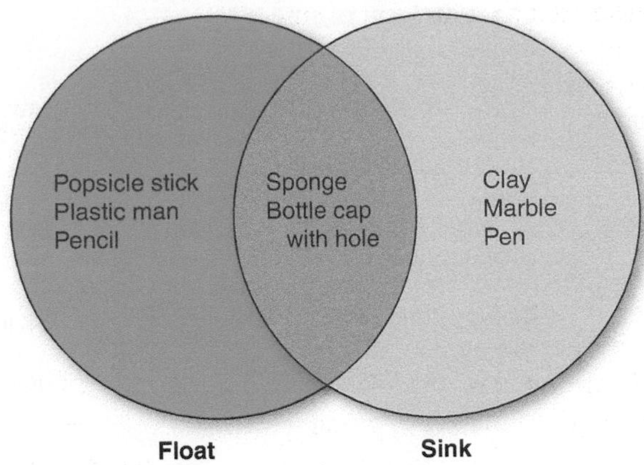

FIGURE 4.4 Curriculum Web

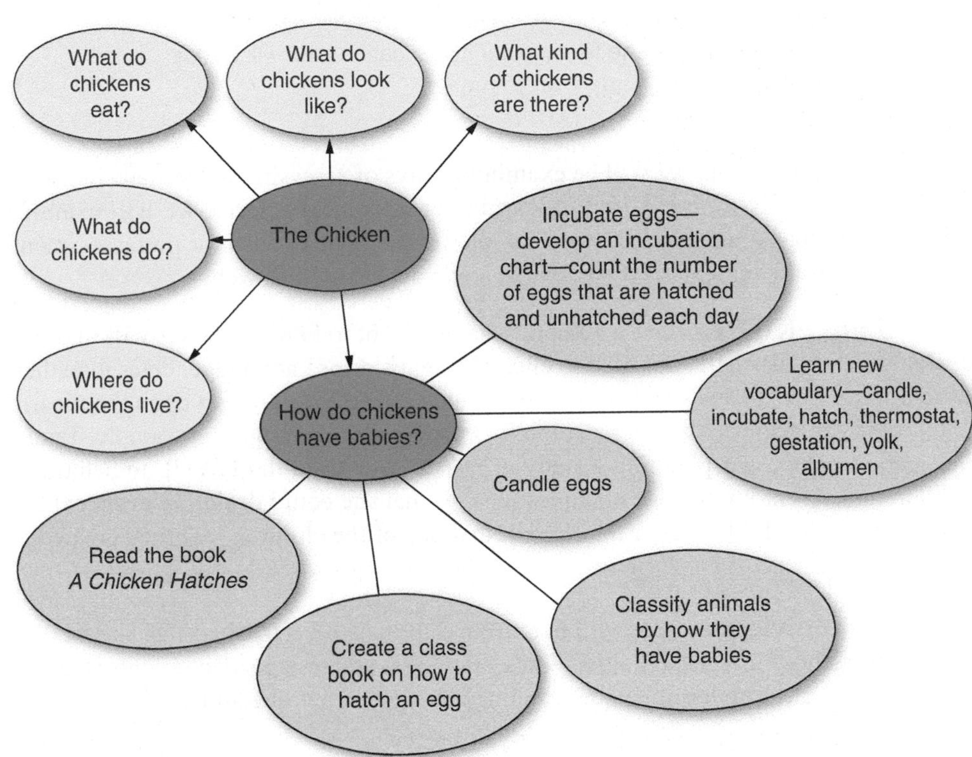

Determine Specific Outcomes. After you have completed your pre-assessment, it is time to develop outcomes. Developing outcomes helps teachers to be intentional about what they want children to gain from an experience. You will want to create **SMART outcomes**. There are many different variations of SMART outcomes, we will use the following: **S**pecific, **M**eaningful, **A**ppropriate, **R**elevant, and **T**imely.

Specific. Your outcome needs to be specific enough that you can tell at the end of the experience if children have met the outcome. For example, "Children will learn to count" is not specific enough, while "The children will be able to count four objects and tell how many" is specific. Just as when you wrote goals, you will want to list what the child will learn rather than what you will teach. For example, you would not say, "I will teach the children to count to four."

Meaningful. Your outcomes need to be worthwhile and have significant developmental and educational content. You will want your outcomes to tie to past lessons, promote big ideas, and to relate to standards. For example, Tina was working with 4-year-old children on making repeating patterns using seashells by placing one clamshell and then two sand dollars on a table. She reminded the children that they also clapped patterns during circle time. Patterns are a "big idea." There are patterns found in nature, language, art, music, and math. Patterns are one of the items that are addressed both in national math standards and in Tina's state early learning guidelines. Learning to identify and create patterns is a meaningful outcome for young children.

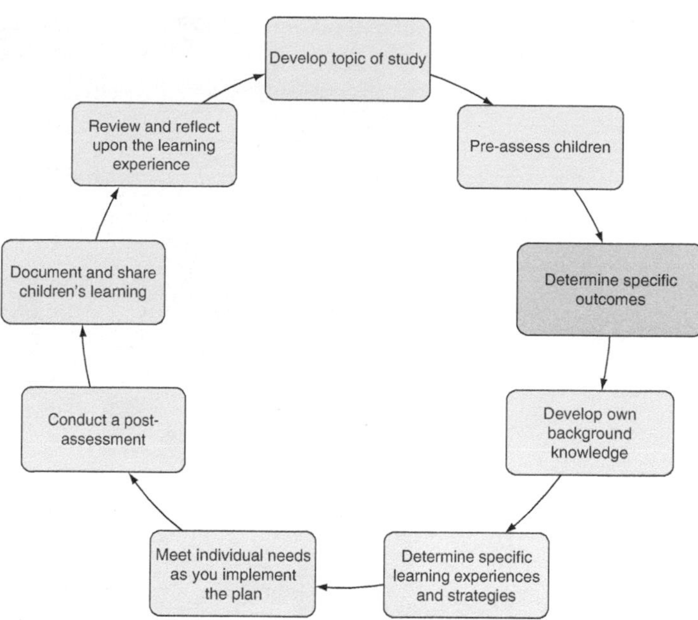

Steps for Developing Plans for Learning

Appropriate. You will need to assure that your outcomes are developmentally, individually, and culturally appropriate. Are the children in your group able to understand the concepts or skills? Does the outcome build from the children's strengths? Are the outcomes challenging enough or do children already understand this concept? Your pre-assessment will assist you in knowing if the outcomes are appropriate. You will also need to consider that what is developmentally appropriate for one child may not be for another. For example, Tina adapted the activity with patterns for individual children. Terrence struggled with the concept, so she showed him a less complex pattern that alternated a clamshell and sand dollar.

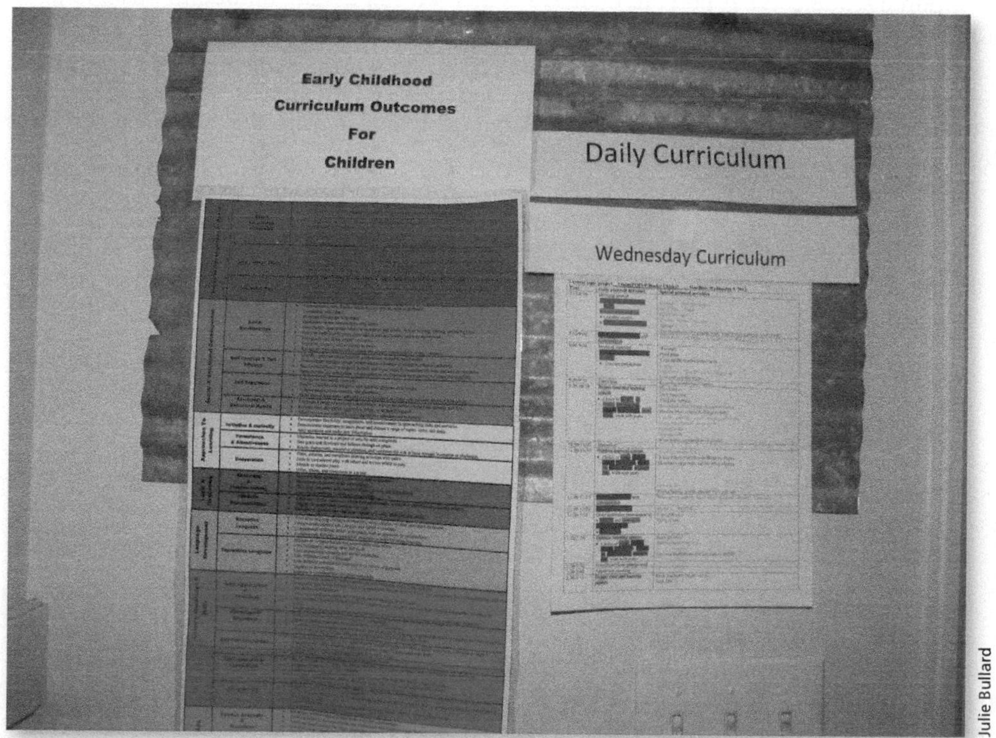

The outcomes at Curious Minds: Early Care and Education Center are color coded. The daily curriculum is also color coded so that families and staff can easily see what outcomes are being stressed.

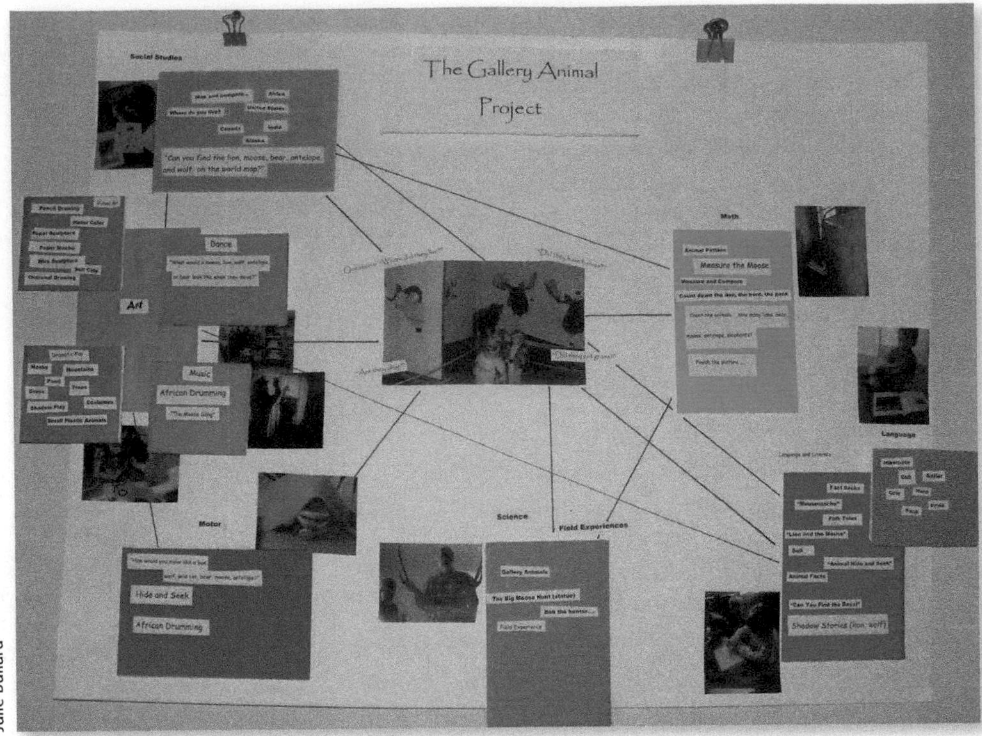

Julie Bullard

The project web on gallery animals is also color coded to show which outcomes are being addressed.

Relevant. Are the outcomes relevant to children's lives? Are they realistic? Do they relate to children's interests? If not, are there ways that we can assist children to become interested? For example, Tina chose seashells to pattern as a way of building interest in the activity. Since she and the children live near the ocean, the seashells are relevant to their lives.

Timely. Is this an opportune time for this outcome considering the season, geographic location, resources, and staffing?

Apply Your Knowledge Jeff decided to develop a unit on guinea pigs, since the children had just acquired this classroom pet. Two of the outcomes that Jeff developed for his unit on guinea pigs were:

1. Children will conduct a simple experiment with the guinea pig, and at the conclusion will describe the steps in the scientific process.
2. Children will describe several similarities between what the guinea pig needs to live and what they need to live, including air, food, water, and an appropriate habitat.

Were Jeff's outcomes SMART outcomes?

Develop Own Background Knowledge. Once you determine a topic, it is important to research the topic to ensure that you have accurate, current, and in-depth information. As part of this review, you will want to think about vocabulary you might introduce to children and open-ended questions you might ask. You might also develop a sheet that contains background information, vocabulary, and open-ended questions that can be shared with others.

Before Jeff began his unit on guinea pigs, he learned as much information as he could about them. For example, a guinea pig has open rooted front teeth that are constantly growing. They need something to chew on to keep their teeth trimmed. Guinea pigs originally came from South America. They are rodents, not pigs. He developed a background sheet that he posted for the other adults in the classroom. This allowed Jeff and the other adults to offer accurate information, extend the children's engagement with the guinea pig, assist children's understanding, and individualize the experience for children. For example, when some of the children became very interested in the teeth of the guinea pig, the adults had the background knowledge to describe the differences between the rodent's teeth and their teeth. One of the new vocabulary words that Jeff introduced to the children was "cavy," another name for the guinea pig.

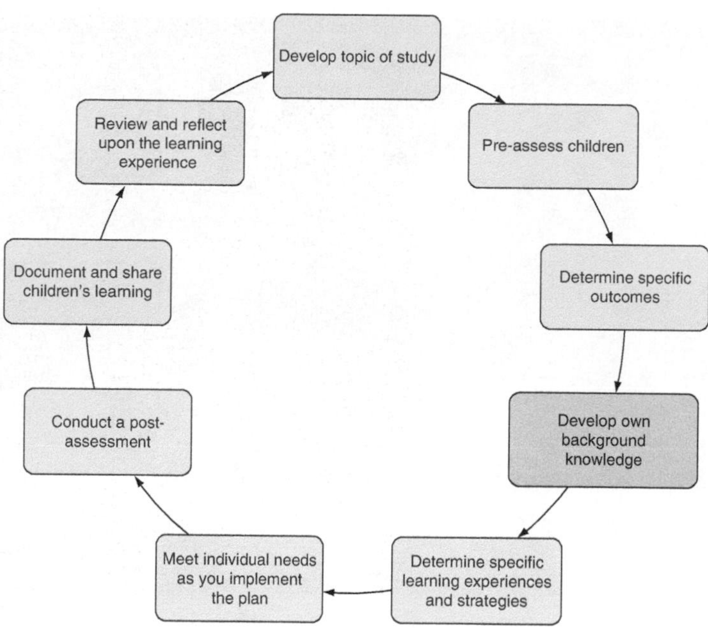

Steps for Developing Plans for Learning

Determine Specific Learning Experiences and Strategies. You may wonder why the term *learning strategy* is used rather than teaching strategy. Although teaching strategy is a term that is frequently used, by using the term *learning strategy* we are reminded that we are focusing on what children are learning rather than on what we as teachers are teaching. There are many appropriate methods you might use when planning learning experiences for young children. These may be child-initiated or teacher-directed. Because young children learn through play, you will want to ensure that you have an environment that provides the opportunity to read books, listen to stories, write stories, role play, build, dance, create art and music, listen to music, engage in scientific inquiry, conduct an experiment, practice math skills, complete puzzles, investigate materials, play games, or use technology.

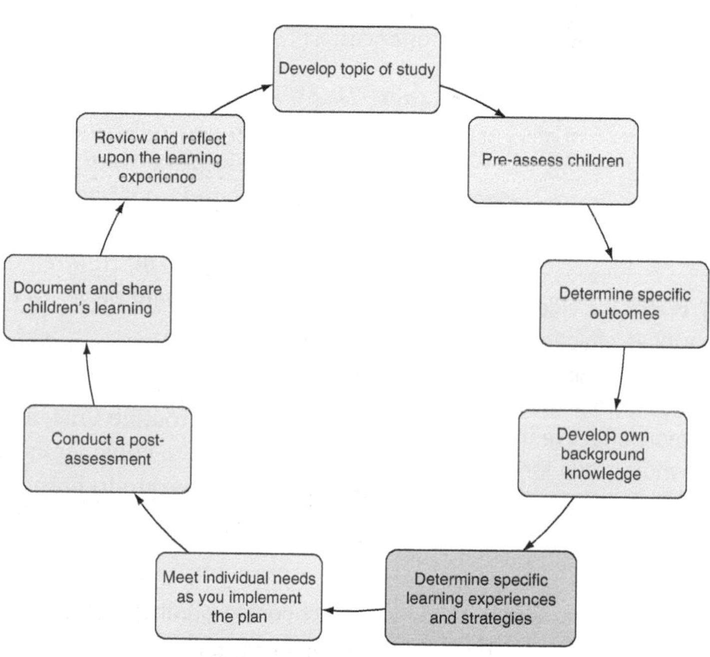

Steps for Developing Plans for Learning

Jeff added several items to the environment to enhance the unit on guinea pigs, including:

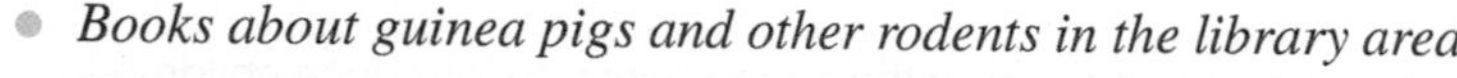

- *Books about guinea pigs and other rodents in the library area*
- *Short video clips about guinea pigs and guinea pig–shaped journals in the science area*
- *Different pictures of guinea pigs in the art area, including photos and realistic and abstract drawings and paintings*

The children used these different materials to learn more about guinea pigs during center time.

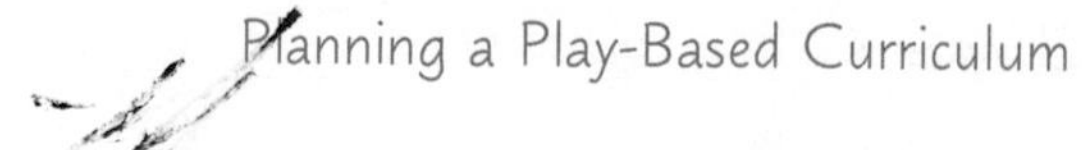

Julie Bullard

One of the activities that children participated in as they completed the gallery animal project was to create masks of their adopted animals. They used their masks for a variety of different role-playing experiences.

While play is usually child-initiated (see Chapter 1 to learn more about play), there are also many learning strategies that might be teacher-led or teacher-initiated. These include asking thought-provoking questions, providing information, engaging in reciprocal interactions, giving a mini-lecture, posing a problem to solve or offering a challenge, assisting children to reflect on their own or other's work, making thinking visible through such things as KWHL charts, showing a video clip, leading a brainstorming session, facilitating discussions, providing demonstrations, modeling, leading a field trip, providing a puppet show, reading a story, or overseeing a guided practice, inquiry, experiment, or simulation. Regardless of whether the experience is child-initiated or teacher-directed, the child needs to be actively engaged rather than a passive recipient.

When the guinea pig first arrived, Jeff modeled how to hold the guinea pig. He also demonstrated how to clean the guinea pig's cage. This then became one of the classroom jobs. After researching what guinea pigs need, the children and Jeff constructed a habitat for the guinea pig. They created a Venn diagram that showed the similarities and differences between what guinea pigs need in their environment and what humans need in theirs. They also created a KWHL chart. This prompted a trip to the pet store to learn more about guinea pigs and to examine and compare different rodents. The children and Jeff also conducted an experiment to determine what the guinea pig would prefer to eat.

Watch the video to see an effective small-group activity. Why was a small group more effective than a whole group for this activity?

The learning format might be individual, small-group, or large-group. See Figure 4.5 to learn more about when to use each type of group. The learning might occur during a learning center time, routine time, a planned group time, or an impromptu teachable moment. You will want to consider carefully the type of activity and the attention span of the children in your group to help you determine the proper format. No one method is best for all outcomes and topics.

FIGURE 4.5
When to Use a Small Group Versus a Whole Group

When choosing whether to use a whole group versus a small group consider the:

- ❑ Number of adults
- ❑ Amount of materials
- ❑ Available space
- ❑ Temperament of children
- ❑ Ability to provide active engagement
- ❑ Content

Whole-group times are often used to share the day's events, to introduce children to new materials, and for movement, drama, and music activities.
Small groups are often used for discussions, differentiated instruction, and for reading stories. Small groups allow more individualized interaction, chances for questioning, and less waiting. This often results in greater learning. For example, interactive book reading in a small-group results in children having higher levels of comprehension than when they are in a large group (Morrow & Smith, 1990).

Jeff decided to discuss experiments with the children during a large-group circle. He began by bringing the guinea pig to circle time, and the children and Jeff discussed what they would like to know about the guinea pig. Then they discussed ways they could find answers to their questions. One question the children had was what the guinea pig would prefer to eat, and they decided to conduct an experiment to determine which food their guinea pig would like best. During center time, some of the children and Jeff researched foods that were safe to feed the guinea pig. The next day the small group shared their findings with the large group, and after a lively discussion, the children decided what foods they would use for their experiment (dandelion greens, carrots, and guinea pig food pellets). Jeff chose the large-group format as a way of developing interest in the experiment and as a way to share information about experiments with the entire group. However, he used small groups for the actual experiment. Jeff and the children conducted the same experiment over several days with a different small group conducting the experiment each day. The group set up the experiment, recorded their observations, and briefly shared what they had learned during circle time. Jeff posted a chart showing each day's result. The small group allowed each of the children to have more hands on involvement with the process.

Jeff provides an exemplary example of engaging children in teacher planned whole-group and small-group activities, as well as using the environment to learn about the topic. See Figure 4.6 to see other ways that you might enrich your environment to support your learning topic.

Meet Individual Needs as You Implement the Plan. When you implement the plan, you will need to meet the needs of all the learners. For example, Peter is a child in Jeff's class who has been identified as being gifted. As a way of challenging Peter, Jeff asked him to design the chart to collect their data. To do this, Peter examined other data charts and had to think about which format would be best for his classmates. Jeff also asked Peter to design a picture chart of the different steps in the scientific process that would assist the other children to understand the process. Again, Peter needed to think about this in relationship to his classmate's understanding. These activities challenged Peter academically and socially.

Even when plans are developmentally appropriate and well-designed, they do not always work. For example, Sarah, an aid in Jeff's classroom, had planned an excellent circle time activity, but then the fire truck went by the window blowing its sirens. She abandoned her plan and she and the children went to the window to determine what was happening. After the fire truck was gone, the children were still excited. They wanted to talk about the fire truck and where it was going. Sarah and the children discussed the causes of fire and the role of the fire fighters.

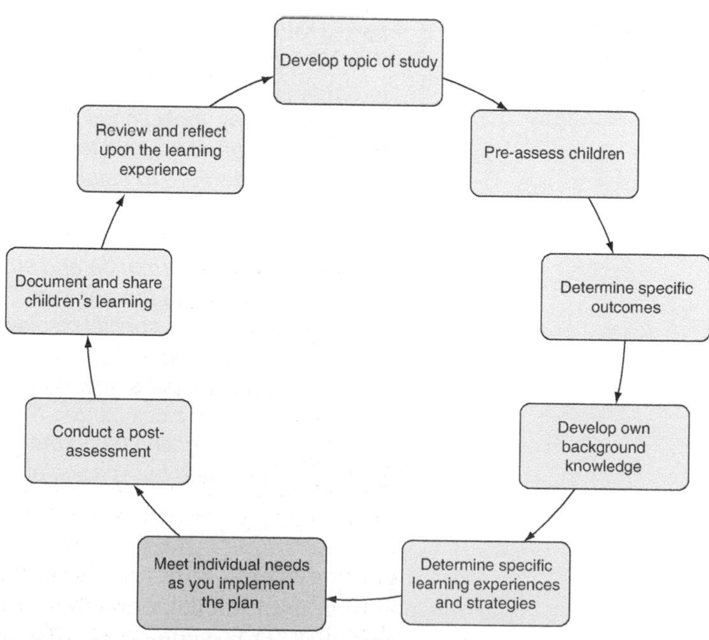

Steps for Developing Plans for Learning

Conduct a Post-assessment. At the end of the experience, you will want to conduct a post-assessment to determine if children have achieved the outcomes. There are many ways that you might do this, such as informal checks (ongoing questioning and probing), written product (written story, poem, letter), oral product (audio of a dramatic play episode, a song,

FIGURE 4.6 Enriching your Learning Environment to Support a Topic of Study

When supporting a topic of study, teachers can add materials to one center, several centers, or create a new center. In some cases, teachers feel they must add materials to every center when they change to a new topic. However, this is not necessary. Instead, determine what materials will assist children to learn about the topic and where these materials might logically be placed. See the following examples of how two teachers used the environment to support their topics of study.

Toddlers at Early Head Start had discovered bugs outside in the play yard and had become very interested in them. Emma, their teacher, brought some of the insects inside and placed them in a magnifying jar in the science center for temporary viewing. The children and Emma also created habitats for some of the different kinds of bugs they caught, allowing the insects to be on display for longer periods of time. These were also placed in the area along with magnifying glasses. Emma also created a book containing pictures of insects found in the local area. Some of these were pictures she took herself, as children pointed out bugs on their walks or in the play yard. Collection items such as jars, nets, and a turbo vacuum bug catcher were also housed in this area.

Emma also added books on bugs and insect puppets to the reading area and an insect matching game and plastic bugs to the manipulative center. Because the children were very interested in pretending to be bugs, she also added bug costumes to the dramatic play center. She had purchased these inexpensively after Halloween. By changing the science center and adding materials to other existing centers, Emma was able to support the children's interest in insects.

However, sometimes, because of the nature of the project or the materials, a separate center is established.

Tessa, a teacher in a multi-age preschool classroom, lived in a community that had been plagued with forest fires. Recently, several houses had been evacuated and many families were being housed in a temporary shelter in the city hall. Many of the children had witnessed a helicopter filling a bucket with water from a nearby pond and flying with it. Children in Tessa's class were very worried and had many questions about the fire, the firefighters, and what happens if you have to leave your home. The teachers decided to make this the focus of their project and began to make a list of questions that the children wanted to investigate. Since many of the questions focused on how the fire was fought, Tessa called the local ranger district to see what materials and tours might be available. She was told that the children could see a wild-land firefighting engine, tour a helicopter, and visit with a member of the helitack crew. In addition, a retired firefighter was willing to demonstrate the clothing, tools, and fire shelters that were being used. They could also let the children try some food from meals ready to eat (MREs). At the conclusion of the visit, the firefighter lent the program several props to display, including clothing, canteens, some tools, a fire tent, and MREs. Tessa wanted children to be able to look at the materials; however, they were not suitable for play. She decided to establish a special firefighting display and information center. The center included the authentic forest fighting equipment and tools, books on forest fires, pictures of the fire from the local newspaper, pictures of the city hall shelter, and a computer with information and streaming video on forest fires in their area. The children's questions and the answers they had discovered were also posted in this area.

In addition to this special display and information center, Tessa added materials to several existing centers. For example, she added firefighter and family finger puppets and a shoebox puppet stage to the literacy center. Model helicopters and fire trucks were added to the block center. The children and Tessa changed the dramatic play center into a firefighting camp that contained a dispatch center with a telephone and radios, clothing and backpacks, and firefighting tools created by the children.

a group discussion, or a child telling a story), visual product (drawing, web, collage, painting, map, model, computer graphic, diagram, diorama), self-assessment, performance task, observation (checklist, anecdotal record), interview, or having children apply their knowledge to a new situation or setting. With older children, you might give a quiz. Some teachers model quizzes after popular games such as *Jeopardy*.

Jeff could use several different assessment methods to determine whether the children could describe the steps in the scientific process. He decided to have the children draw the steps. This would allow him to assess each individual child's understanding. In addition, he chose this assessment method because it would not be too time consuming to administer.

Document and Share Children's Learning. It is important that we document what children have accomplished and learned. This allows us to share this information with children, families, colleagues, administrators, and the general public. The way that you share this will depend upon the type of experience and the depth of the plan. For long-term plans, you might document children's learning through documentation panels or books, videos, power points, displays of artifacts, or children's presentations. You might share this information in children's portfolios, at family-teacher conferences or home visits, or at special events. For shorter range plans you might share the documentation information either verbally or in writing as families pick up children, or in happy grams and update notices that are sent home to families.

Jeff placed the information in the children's portfolios as evidence of their knowledge about the scientific process. This was one of the artifacts he shared with families when they met for family–teacher conferences.

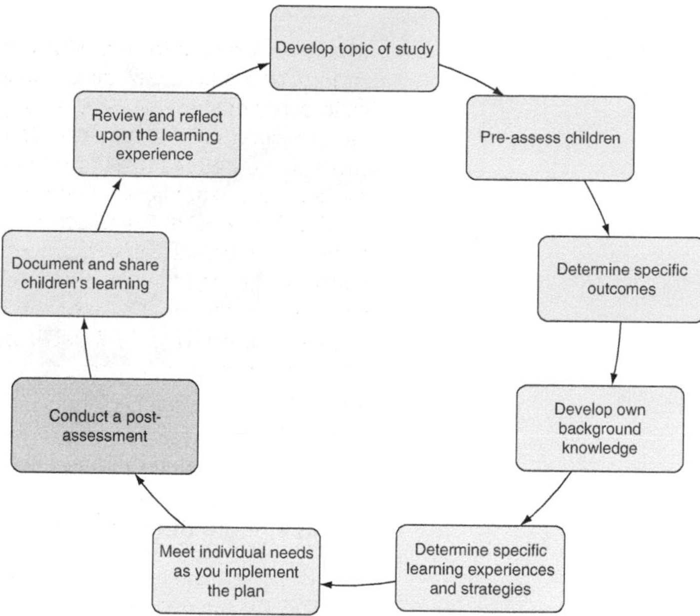

Steps for Developing Plans for Learning

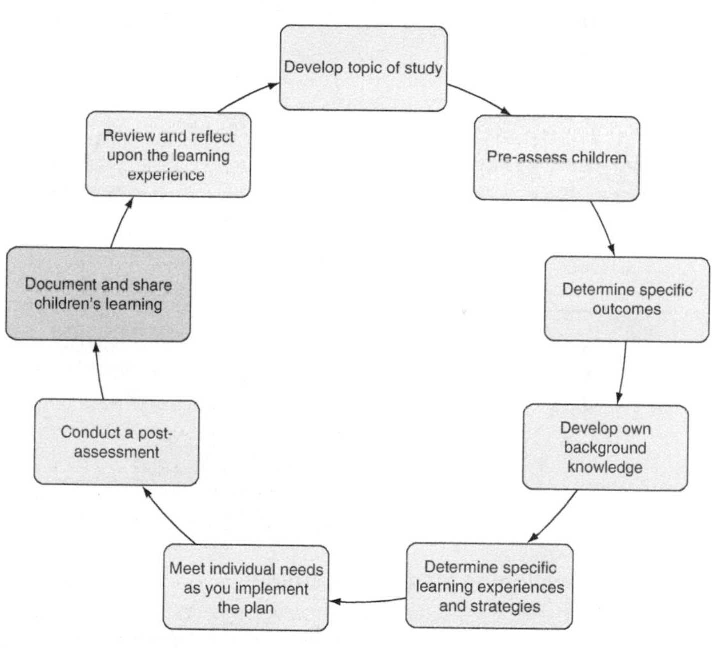

Steps for Developing Plans for Learning

Review and Reflect upon the Learning Experience. At the end of the learning experience, you will want to review and reflect upon what the children learned and on your own skills and learning. Reflection is a valuable way to critique our teaching and to discover ways that we can improve. It can also help us to become more mindful of our teaching and the impact of our teaching on children. When reflecting upon what the children learned, you might ask yourself the following questions: What specifically did the children learn? Did all the children meet the outcomes? How did I modify the learning experience so that all the children were successful? What are the children still struggling to understand or do in relationship to this experience? Was the learning that occurred relevant and meaningful? How did I connect this learning to what the children previously learned? Do the children have unresolved misconceptions? What are the next steps in the children's learning? What were unintended or unanticipated outcomes?

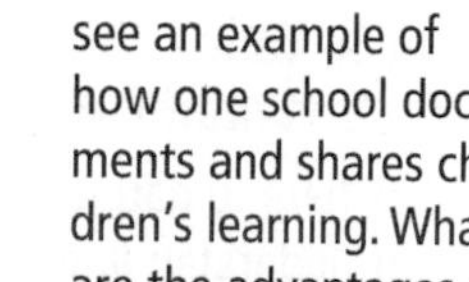

Watch the video to see an example of how one school documents and shares children's learning. What are the advantages of this evening for the children, families, and school?

Julie Bullard

One way that the gallery animal project was documented was through a documentation board that showed several of the children with the masks they had created. With the mask was a photo of the animal that they were creating.

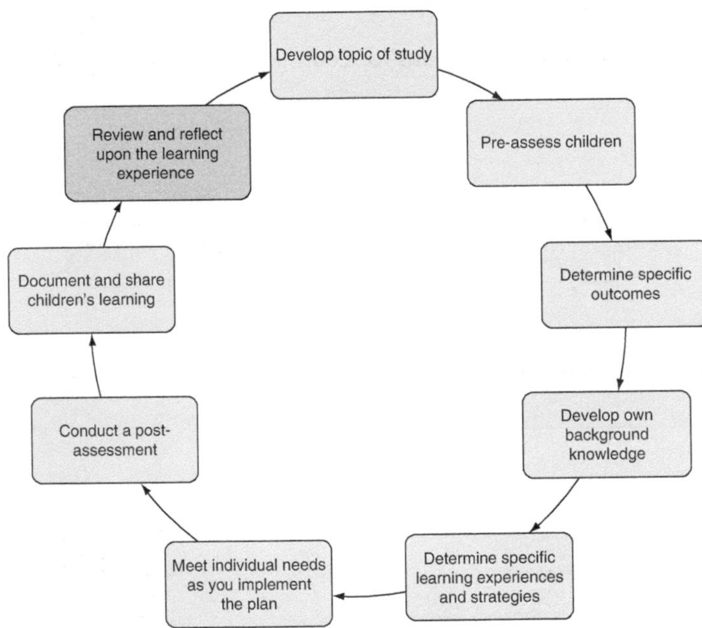

Steps for Developing Plans for Learning

In reviewing and reflecting on your own skills and learning, you might ask yourself the following questions: What did I learn? Did I feel adequately prepared? Were my goals SMART? Did I sufficiently probe the children's background knowledge and skills? Did I allow sufficient time, have the needed resources, and provide enough different opportunities for the children to learn? Were the learning experiences and strategies developmentally appropriate and effective? Did I meet the learning styles, developmental needs, and interests of the children? Did I build on the children's background knowledge and strengths? How would I change this experience if I could begin again? Did the children enjoy the experience? Did I enjoy the experience?

Emily was excited because today she had the opportunity to implement a learning plan. Last week when Emily was at the lab school, the children had been finding bugs in the playground. She decided that she would plan a circle time activity to teach the children more about bugs. Emily ran into the library and grabbed a book on bugs. She decided she would read the children a story and then have them draw a picture of their favorite bug.

For her initial attention getter, Emily led the children in performing the actions and singing "The Eensey, Weensey Spider." All the children were engaged. However, she hadn't even been reading the book for 15 minutes when children began to wrestle with their friends and ask to leave the circle. Emily gave up on finishing the book and had the children go to the table to draw a picture of a bug. She was disappointed when the children made a few quick lines on their papers and left. She knew that they were capable of more.

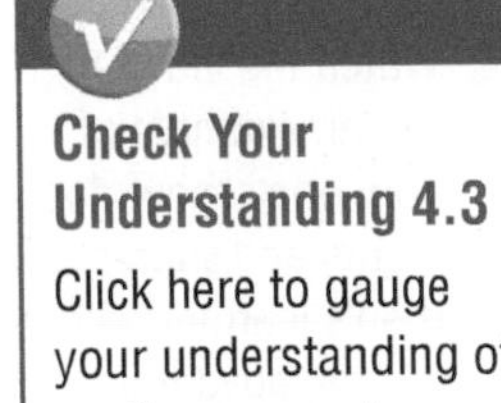

Check Your Understanding 4.3

Click here to gauge your understanding of section concepts.

Later that day Emily met with her college professor to discuss her learning plan. Emily said she was disheartened that the children hadn't been engaged. The professor asked her several open-ended questions such as: "What specifically did you hope that the children would learn?" "What do you know about the attention span of 3- to 5-year-old children?" "What makes a book a good choice for young children?" "What activities have you observed in the classroom where children were highly engaged?" Emily reflected on each of these questions and realized that the book she had chosen was developmentally inappropriate for the children, and that her expectations regarding their attention span was unrealistic. She also realized that the children were most engaged when they were in centers or small groups, involved in hands-on activities, and when they were given a choice of participating.

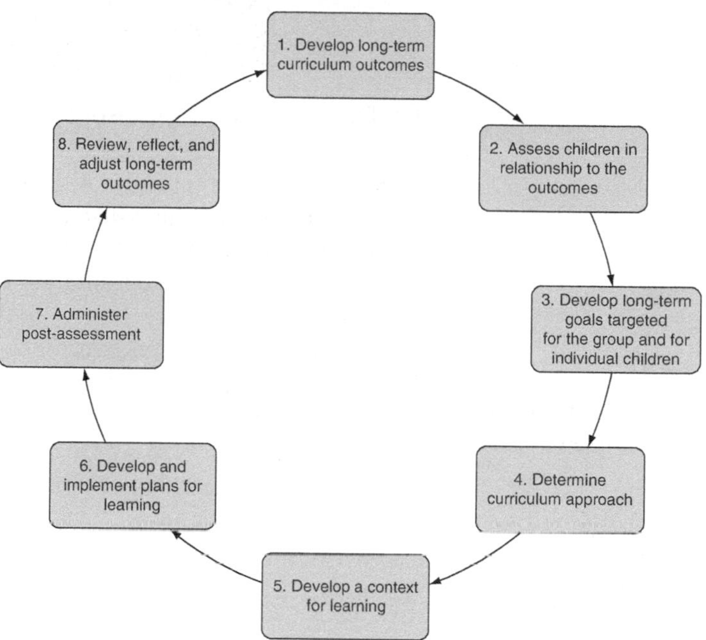

Steps in Long-Term Curriculum Development

When Emily planned and implemented her next activity, she used this knowledge. She involved the children in collecting bugs and asked them if they would like to build a habitat for the bugs. Several children were interested in participating. This time she had carefully chosen a high-quality book that discussed bug habitats in an age-appropriate way. The small group of children was highly engaged with the book and had many questions. Using materials that Emily had lined up ahead of time, they then developed a bug habitat. Emily placed informational books, magnifying glasses, and paper and colored pencils near the bug habitat. She noticed several children looking at the bugs. She asked if they would like to draw the bugs. This time they carefully drew what they were observing.

7. Administer Post-Assessments

Over time, individual learning experiences combine to help children meet long-term goals. Just as you assess to assure that you are meeting the outcomes for each learning experience, you will want to assess to make sure children are meeting their long-term goals. Most programs conduct in-depth assessments two or three times per year.

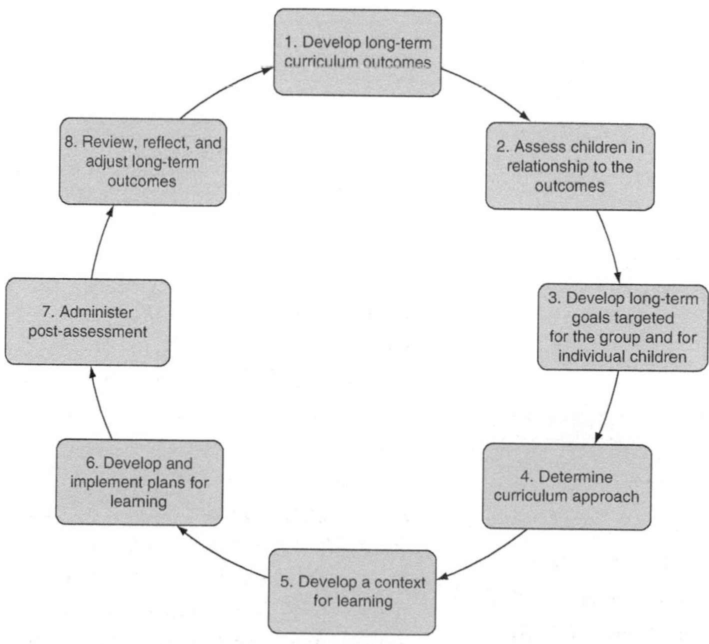

Steps in Long-Term Curriculum Development

8. Review, Reflect, and Adjust Outcomes

After you have completed your assessments, you will want to review and reflect upon your long-term curriculum outcomes, goals for children, children's learning, assessment tools, curriculum approach, context for learning, and

learning plans. You will often review and reflect upon your long-term planning as a part of a classroom or program team. At the conclusion of your reflection, the team will develop new long-term outcomes and the cycle will begin again.

Chapter Quiz 4

Click here to gauge your understanding of chapter concepts.

The knowledge, skills, and dispositions acquired in the early years form the foundation for all later learning. It is rewarding to be part of this process—to see children engaged, excited, challenged, and meeting or exceeding comprehensive learning outcomes. Well-planned learning experiences are the first step in providing this solid foundation.

Sample Application Activities

1. Determine your philosophy of learning. Compare your philosophy to others in your class.
2. Visit an early childhood program and review their learning plans. Can you tell from the learning plans what the philosophy and values are of the teacher, program, and community?
3. Compare and contrast different types of assessments. Do they meet the criteria included in this chapter?
4. Interview a teacher or director about the development of children's long-term goals.
5. Complete and implement a learning plan (see Figure 4.7 for a sample learning plan form).
6. Interview several families who have young children to see what goals they have for their children.
7. Examine the learning outcomes pertaining to the age, program, and state where you wish to teach or are teaching.

FIGURE 4.7
Sample Learning Plan

Plan (Complete This Portion Before You Implement)

Topic—Provide a rationale for why you chose this topic. Include how this plan relates to children's interests and why this topic is developmentally appropriate.

Pre-assessment—What are children's prior knowledge and skills in relationship to this plan? How did you or will you find out?

Outcomes—List specific SMART child outcomes.

Learning plan description—Describe the activity/activities, including specific learning experiences and strategies. Also include the learning formats such as small-group activities, large-group activities, or changes to the learning environment.

Individualizing—How will you ensure that all children's needs are met?

Post-assessment—What assessment method will you use to determine if the child outcomes were met?

Implement the Plan and Conduct the Post-Assessment

Describe any changes that you made to your plan. Describe the post-assessment results.

Document and Share the Children's Learning

Describe how you documented and shared the children's learning.

Review and Reflect

On children's learning—What happened when you conducted your learning plan? What specifically did the children learn? Did all the children achieve the child outcomes? Provide specific information. How did you modify the learning experience so that all the children were successful? What are the children still struggling to understand or do in relationship to this experience? Do the children have unresolved misconceptions? What are the next steps in the children's learning?

On your learning—What did you learn through completing this learning plan? How did you develop your own background knowledge? Did you sufficiently probe the children's background knowledge and skills? Did you allow sufficient time, have the needed resources, and provide enough different opportunities for the children to learn? Were the learning experiences and strategies developmentally appropriate and effective? Did you meet the learning styles, developmental needs, and interests of the children? Did you build on the children's background knowledge and strengths? How would you change this experience if you could begin again?

Planning a Play-Ba 96

Chapter 5

Arranging an Effective Environment

Learning Outcomes

After you have read this chapter, you will be prepared to:

- Describe what makes a high-quality learning center
- Develop effective room arrangements and floor plans for different age groups
- Discuss appropriate bathrooms, diaper-changing stations, and sleeping areas
- Describe appropriate furniture and storage

Julie Bullard

A consultant was asked to visit a grade K–3 (multigrade) classroom to assist Dana, the teacher, with children who Dana described as "out of control." As the consultant entered the room, she found numerous items hanging from the ceiling. All the walls in the classroom were plastered with

posters, children's work, written rules, transcribed stories, and a variety of store-purchased signs. The children sat in desks in the center of the room. On the outskirts of the room were shelves that were overflowing with material. Stacks of books filled much of the remaining floor space.

During worktime, children worked individually or in small groups using the materials off the shelves while other children met in small groups with the teacher. Children often interrupted the teacher because they could not find the materials they were looking for. Some of the children became distracted by the activities of the other children. This necessitated the teacher leaving the group she was working with to help these children get back on task.

Dana was surprised when the consultant suggested that changing the classroom environment might meet her goal of allowing children to work effectively in individual and small groups while also providing a solution to the out-of-control behavior.

Guidelines for Creating a Room with Learning Centers

Our classroom environment either promotes or distracts from our learning goals, encouraging or discouraging success for all children. The environment also affects children's stress levels. A study of six-year-old children found that the greatest influence on children's **cortisol** (a stress hormone) levels in early childhood programs was the environment. Research shows that it had more effect than the individual characteristics or the demographics of the child. Unstructured environments that did not support learning led to the highest cortisol levels (Sajaniemi et al., 2014). Another study of preschool children found similar results; children in higher quality settings had lower cortisol levels than children in lower quality settings (Sajaniemi et al., 2011).

Learning Centers Reflect Early Childhood Beliefs. To promote learning and reduce stress, the environment needs to reflect early childhood beliefs and theories about how children learn. Do you believe in children working cooperatively in small groups? Do you believe in the teacher as a facilitator of learning? Do you believe in meeting children's individual learning styles and needs? Do you believe in children being highly engaged with learning materials? Do you believe in children having choices? Do you believe in children learning through hands-on activities? Do you believe that learning should be active and child-centered? When these questions were posed to Dana, like most early childhood educators, she immediately answered "yes," making her a perfect candidate for the learning center approach. Dana reorganized her classroom and materials into several learning centers and removed materials no longer needed. The centers allowed small groups of children to work together without interruption. Barriers between centers helped the children to concentrate. Children were also more easily able to locate materials and so they could work independently.

What Is a Learning Center? A learning center is a self-contained area with a variety of hands-on materials organized around a curriculum area or topic. Learning centers are also referred to as interest centers, learning stations, workstations, or activity areas. Because learning centers are so consistent with early childhood philosophy, most early childhood teachers choose this method of arranging their rooms. Well-designed learning centers respect children's learning styles and interests and allow them choices, thereby fostering their self-esteem and decision-making abilities (Rushton, 2001). Research reveals that when teachers give children choices of activities, especially those with emotional or behavioral difficulties, they are more self-directed, have less disruptive behavior, and are more engaged in tasks (Dunlap et al., 1994; Vitiello et al., 2012).

Each learning center helps students develop unique content knowledge, skills, and dispositions while promoting different social skills and work habits. For example, the dramatic play and block centers may encourage cooperative play, while the science center may encourage individual investigation.

A high-quality learning center is planned with a purpose in mind. It is inviting and aesthetically pleasing, containing an abundance of developmentally appropriate, relevant, interesting, and interactive materials. Learning centers that are high quality are planned to encourage independent use by children. We will discuss each of these criteria in more depth.

Clearly Establish Goals Based on Children's Backgrounds, Interests, Development, and State and National Standards

What are the goals for the learning center? What specific skills, knowledge, and dispositions do you want to promote through this learning center? In determining goals, you will want to examine program, state, and national standards and early learning guidelines. It will also be important to examine children's background knowledge and interests to develop environments that are relevant and developmentally appropriate.

Supply the Center with an Abundance of Interesting, Interactive Materials

Having an abundance of interesting, interactive materials creates a resource-rich environment. In resource-rich environments, children are more engaged in independent learning activities (Moore, 2002).

Provide the Right Amount of Materials. There must be a balance of clutter and abundance. If the shelves have too many materials, children may have a difficult time making choices or locating the materials they want. However, if there are too few materials, children have limited choices and may waste time waiting for materials to become available. The lack of resources can also result in increased conflict among children. Additionally, children's ability to reach their full potential may be hindered. For example, 100 unit blocks are recommended for each child using the block center at one time (Phelps, 2012). With an abundance of blocks, several children can work at once creating elaborate block structures. Running out of blocks before a structure is completed can stymie the child's creativity, attention span, and problem solving. Eventually children in these classrooms learn to build quick, less complicated structures.

Determining the exact quantity of materials requires close observation of the children in your group. If children are waiting for toys or fighting over toys, this may indicate that there are not enough materials or that duplicates of popular materials are needed. This is especially important for toddlers who are often engaged in parallel play, using identical play materials (Legendre, 2003). If children are wandering rather than engaging in play, there may be too few materials available or children may be overwhelmed because there are too many choices.

Watch the video to learn more about supplying an abundance of materials. How did the materials enhance the children's learning?

Be Cautious About Reducing Materials for the Wrong Reasons. Sometimes teachers reduce the number of materials so that children can clean up the area more quickly. However, it is important to reflect upon your goals. Is your goal to create an optimum learning environment? Then you would not want to reduce materials simply to decrease the time needed to clean the center.

Other teachers may eliminate any toys that children fight over. However, this results in fewer toys, which often increases rather than decreases fighting behavior. Teachers might instead add duplicate toys.

Provide Variety. Children also need variety in materials and room design. Too little variety leads to boredom. However, if the environment is too complex children experience cognitive fatigue, and learning and competency is compromised. According to Maxwell (2007), an expert in environmental design, children need the opportunity to recover from cognitive fatigue through activities that do not require focused attention, such as sitting and watching fish or birds (Maxwell, 2007, p. 232).

Create a Range of Challenges. One way to create a range of challenges is to use open-ended materials. **Open-ended materials** meet the needs of a range of developmental levels, maintain the interest of children for a longer period of time, and invite creativity and deeper thought than closed-ended materials. For example, when a jar of old buttons was placed on a manipulative shelf in a kindergarten classroom, children became very interested. They postulated about where the different buttons came from, discussed which buttons they liked best, classified (or sorted) the buttons in multiple ways, seriated the buttons (arranging them from largest to smallest), and counted the buttons. When providing **close-ended materials**, such as puzzles, include many different levels to meet individual needs. Also, make sure the materials are self-correcting. For example, a teacher created a matching sound game by placing different ingredients (buttons, sand, and paper clips) in film canisters. He then placed a sticker of each item on the bottom of its canister. As a result, children could check to see what item was in the container and see if they had paired the sound jars correctly.

Maximize Affordances. When planning, ensure that you maximize the **affordances**, the opportunities to learn. For example, affordances are increased when you add a drawing pad, journal, magnifying glasses, and books to the butterfly hatching garden center. Color coding a keyboard and music so that children can play a song, increases the affordances of a keyboard. When adding a new activity, think about how the children will use the materials and what additional materials you could add to enhance the learning.

At times children and teachers may create a display of materials to inspire children or to emphasize a particular concept. For example, a teacher of toddlers created a display of yellow items to emphasize the color. However, it is important that most displays and materials contain interactive components. Young children learn best when engaged in hands-on activities (Copple & Bredekamp, 2009).

Assure Materials Are Safe and Healthy

Safe. To keep children safe, you will want to make sure that materials and equipment are age appropriate and developmentally appropriate for the group. For example, all materials for infants, for toddlers, and for children who are still mouthing toys need to be choke resistant. Toys and materials also need to be lead free and nontoxic. One must also examine toys to make sure that they cannot lead to strangulation. In addition, all materials need to meet the standards of the Consumer Product Safety Commission (CPSC).

A daily safety check and maintenance are critical to keep equipment and the child's environment safe.

Healthy. Cleaning and sanitation play critical roles in preventing disease in early childhood programs. To keep children healthy, you will want to wash toys and dress-up clothes weekly and whenever soiled. When children put toys in their mouths, the toys need to be sanitized before being used again. Playcare, a program serving infants and toddlers, has established systems to make sanitizing toys easier. They hang several mesh bags on walls throughout the play area to collect any mouthed toys. At the end of the day, they dip the bags of toys into bleach water and hang them to dry. Any surface with bodily fluids, including diaper-changing tables, needs to be cleaned and sanitized immediately. It is essential to wear gloves when touching bodily fluids that contain or may contain blood to prevent the possibility of spreading AIDS or other blood-borne diseases. Having gloves conveniently located throughout the classroom and any other areas used by children is necessary to ensure this occurs.

Ensure Materials Are Developmentally Appropriate

Materials need to be developmentally appropriate for the children in the classroom. They need to be challenging, but not so difficult that children cannot be successful. If materials are too easy, children become bored. On the other hand, if the materials are too challenging, children become anxious (White, 2004). When materials are slightly above the child's current level of functioning, they can act as a scaffold to assist children to reach the next level of development (Maxwell, 2007; Vygotsky, 1986). Children gain knowledge, skills, and confidence when they successfully negotiate challenges.

Choose Materials That Foster Active Learning. High-quality materials encourage children's exploration, promote active hands-on participation, and challenge and stimulate their thinking. They enable children to learn through their senses. Many materials also promote socialization and interaction with others.

When choosing toys or materials be cautious about those that need extensive assistance from an adult. This can be a sign that the toy is not developmentally appropriate. For example, some toys such as a spinner top (advertised as being for children three months and older) must be operated by an adult while the child is a passive observer. Instead, choose toys that are responsive to a child's actions (Copple & Bredekamp, 2009). Also, make sure that the size, weight, choice of materials, and concepts are developmentally appropriate. For example, some board books have advanced concepts such as alphabet letters. By the time the child is developmentally ready to identify letters, they would no longer need or want board books. Likewise, many rattles designed for young infants are too heavy for infants to hold.

Choose Toys That Are Flexible. What do Hot Wheel cars, paint and easels, tinker toys, magnatiles, wooden vehicles and traffic signs, and Duplo blocks have in common? They are all winners in the TILPANI Toy Study. Researchers observe children using the toys to determine which toys are best at promoting thinking, problem solving, cooperation, social interaction, creativity, imagination, and verbalization (Osborn, 2014). These characteristics are also indicators of a toy's flexibility. How long a child plays with a toy and whether he can use it in multiple ways are other indicators of a toy's flexibility. Flexible toys and materials typically appeal to children at a variety of age levels. As such, they are a good investment for an early childhood program. For example, toddlers, preschoolers, and elementary children can all use paint and easels.

Ensure Materials Are Authentic, Durable, and Aesthetic

Choose authentic items and materials when possible since they are often more interesting, meaningful, durable, and functional. Consider a real hammer versus a plastic hammer. The real hammer is more effective in pounding a nail into wood. It may be more meaningful to the children, especially if they have seen family members using hammers. Think about the difference between a real flower and an artificial one. Although artificial flowers can look very realistic, they do not provide the smell or textural quality of the real flower. You cannot observe the differences between the flower petals or the slow decay as the flower ages. Your learning is diminished. In buying materials, you will also want to consider how the material will age with hard use. Wood typically ages beautifully, while plastic gets scruffy.

Ensure Materials Are Culturally Relevant

Johnson et al. (2005), in discussing culturally relevant materials, state that many classroom materials are culturally neutral, such as balls, blocks, and math manipulatives. They emphasize, "Efforts to make such materials relevant to specific groups of children are humorous at best and potentially counterproductive" (p. 234).

However, many materials are not culturally neutral. It is critical that books, posters, play people, dramatic play props, puzzles, and other materials that reflect cultures be inclusive. These materials need to reflect the diversity within the program. In addition, we want to expose children to diversity they might not regularly experience (Wardle & Cruz-Janzen, 2004). In evaluating toys and materials for diversity, consider the following (Johnson et al., 2005):

- Materials should expose children to many forms of diversity (e.g., race, ethnicity, family structure, and disabilities). Teachers need to integrate the materials into the environment and curriculum, rather than using them only occasionally or in an isolated way.
- Materials need to portray the child's culture and all cultures in a positive, authentic, and realistic light. For example, you would not want to portray American Indians as only living in tepees and wearing headdresses, since this is not an accurate portrayal either historically or currently for many American Indians.
- Materials should never convey that one group is better than another group. Not seeing diversity can marginalize some groups of children and make them feel that they are not important and can cause children who are represented to feel superior (Derman-Sparks & Edwards, 2010).
- Materials need to challenge all forms of stereotypes, such as only men or only women can have certain careers, or because you are from a particular race, you have a specific talent.
- Materials need to emphasize individual differences and the diversity within large groups. Just because you belong to a specific group (female, male, African American, Caucasian, Asian American, etc.) does not mean that you think, act, or have the same talents as every other member of the group. Many children are multiracial and multiethnic. It is important to have materials that reflect this group as well.

In ensuring that you are being culturally relevant, it is also important to consider the children's experiences and geographic background, as the following story illustrates.

A teacher in a small rural area in the northwest was changing her dramatic play area. After looking through activity books, she decided to create a circus, complete with tumbling mats, balls to juggle, a hoop to jump through, circus clothing to wear, clown face paint, stuffed circus animals, cages for the animals, and a canopy for the circus tent. However, none of the children had ever been to a circus. Since they had no idea what to do with the materials, they rarely used the center. After reflecting on why the children were not using the center, the teacher decided to establish a center that would be more relevant to the children. After thoughtful contemplation, she decided on a fishing center. Her community contained blue ribbon trout streams, drawing anglers from all over the country. One of the children's parents was a fishing guide, and many of the children had gone fishing with their parents. All the children had seen people standing by the river fly-fishing or floating down the river dragging a fishing line. The fishing center contained a rubber raft surrounded by a blue plastic tarp (the water), paddles, life jackets, children's fishing poles, paper fish, a fishing net, a tackle box containing lures with the hooks removed, waders, a fishing vest, a cooler, and a campfire ring and frying pan (for cooking fish). Because the center was relevant, children spent many weeks engaged in this center.

Throughout this book, you will find examples of ways teachers have made their environments culturally relevant.

Julie Bullard

Child-created kaleidoscopes are displayed in an attractive way, showing the importance of the children's work.

Reflect the Goals and Philosophy of the Program

Whenever you buy books, materials, or software you need to think about whether the values being presented are congruent with the program's values. For example, at Nature Way Preschool, children are taught to treasure all living things. Providing the Ant Smasher app would be contrary to these values, even if the program had other worthwhile benefits.

Display Materials in an Inviting and Aesthetically Pleasing Way

What do you want children to notice? An engaging display can invite us to become involved. It catches our eye, provokes our interest, and entices us to look and to touch. In speaking about arranging the Reggio Emilia environment, Lella Gandini stresses that when materials are arranged attractively in transparent containers, items that are typically discarded like seeds, dried flowers, buttons, and scraps of colored paper all look like precious things (Bartlett, 1993, p. 32). The way materials are displayed shows the value or importance we place on them, and by extension the importance we place on children's learning.

Design the Center for Independent Use

For children to be able to use learning centers independently, materials need to be accessible and organized. Children also need to know how to use the materials. To be accessible, materials are placed within children's reach and located in the center where they are used. This typically means that materials are stored on accessible, open shelves and organized and labeled so that children can easily locate them and return them to the proper place when they are done. Teachers can label shelves with digital photos, pictures out of a supply catalog, an outline of the item, and/or a word designating the item. Collections of items might be placed in baskets and labeled by categories of materials, for example, zoo animals or farm animals.

If children are going to use materials independently, they also need to know how to use the center and the materials appropriately. One way to accomplish this is to introduce materials. In some classrooms, the teacher introduces materials to individual children as they are ready to use them. Typically, children in these classrooms are allowed to use the materials only after they have been introduced. In other classrooms, teachers introduce the materials to children during group time. Introductions allow the teacher to build interest in the materials, while establishing ground rules for use. For example, in introducing the fishing center, the teacher built interest by showing the children a short video clip of some people fishing. She then let the children preview each of the new materials and discussed how the materials should be used. For example, she demonstrated how to use the paddles while emphasizing the need to keep the paddles in "the water." At times, it will also be necessary to remind children of the rules as they use the materials.

Another way to assist children in using centers independently is to create task cards using words or pictures or both. A digital pen can also be used to record audio directions. For example, children in a kindergarten classroom made clay boats as part of a sink and float center. They designed their clay boats and then tested them to see how many pennies they would hold. See Figure 5.1 for an example of a picture task card. Children recorded their data and continued to try to design boats that could hold more pennies. They then discussed the similarities and differences between the boats, determining the characteristics that allowed the boats to hold more weight.

Teachers need to carefully think about and design each individual center. They also must consider the entire room arrangement. Are there common criteria that teachers must consider in arranging classrooms regardless of age? What learning centers should be placed next to each other? Are some arrangements of space more effective than others? We'll examine these questions next.

Check Your Understanding 5.1

Click here to gauge your understanding of section concepts.

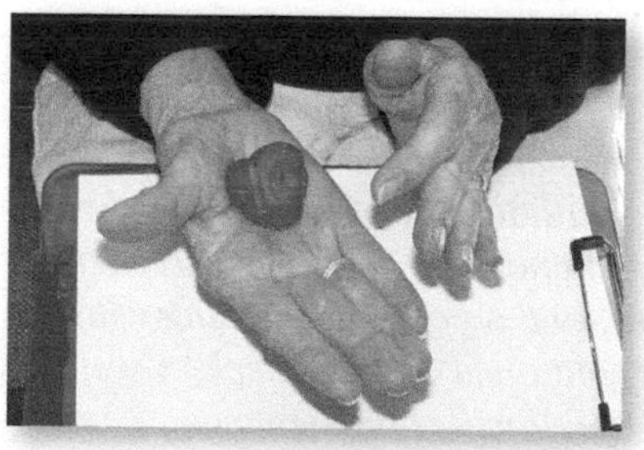
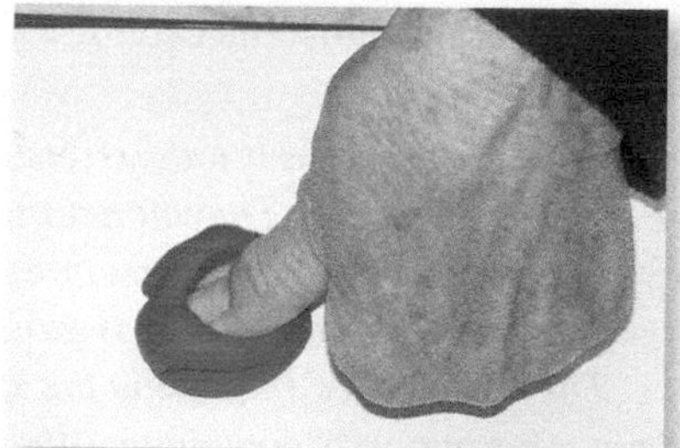
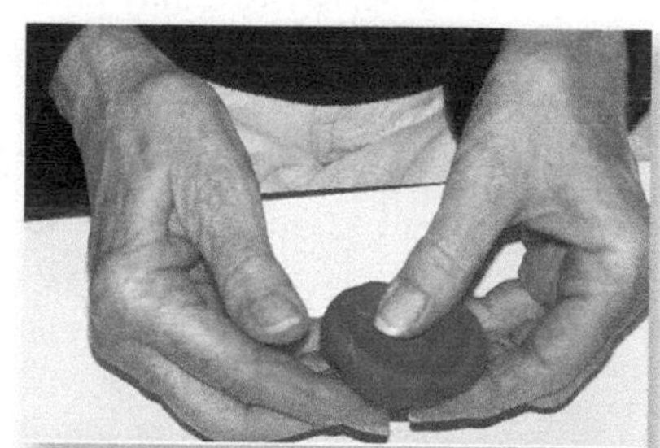

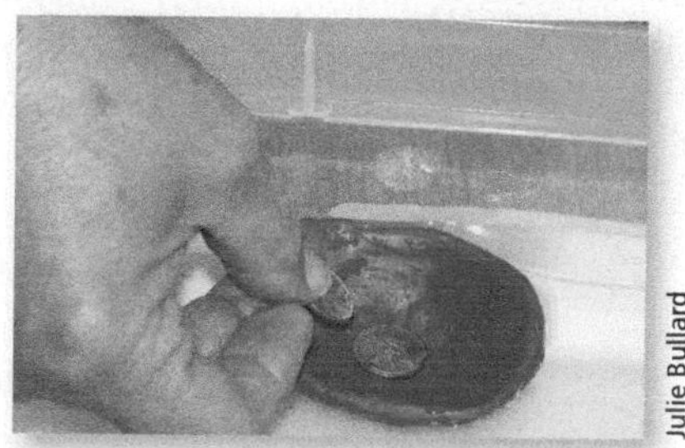

Julie Bullard

FIGURE 5.1 Make a Clay Boat

Guidelines for Developing Effective Room Arrangements and Floor Plans

There are some guidelines that apply to all early childhood room arrangements (infants, toddlers, preschool, and early elementary). These include providing boundaries between centers, establishing clear traffic paths, and grouping similar centers. Other common characteristics that need to be considered for all age groups include establishing an effective entry space, providing places to gather as a group, providing retreat or alone areas, and providing a variety of centers.

Develop Effective Entry Spaces

Entry spaces have a variety of purposes. When well-designed, they provide a positive first impression and a welcoming, inviting transition for:

- Families and children to observe what is happening in the classroom. For example, there may be windows between the pathways and the classroom (Reinisch & Parnell, 2006).
- Children to make a gradual transition to the classroom (there may be a place for children and families to read books before entering the classroom).
- Informational displays and documentation of children's learning. For example, some programs have daily pages. These pages capture daily experiences in the classroom (Reinisch & Parnell, 2006). Other programs have digital picture frames with short videos and digital photos that capture daily occurrences. These are conversational starters between families and children and families and teachers. They can also help families and visitors understand how the everyday experiences within the classroom contribute to children's ongoing learning.
- Daily interaction between families and staff.
- Conveying important messages about the program.
- Providing an enticing element to attract children and make them excited about coming to the program.

Entries into programs vary; some children enter long institutional halls while other children may enter directly into their classroom. Regardless of the entry point, the entry area conveys a message. Programs need to think carefully about what message they want to portray.

At Aware Early Head Start, an infant/toddler program, teachers analyzed their entryway for the message it was conveying. They noted that the bulletin board was covered with required notices, such as worker's compensation flyers, mandatory child abuse reporting requirements, parental notification of illness guidelines, and a poster discussing what to do in case of lice. They also noted that while the space contained a child check-in system, there was no avenue for two-way communication between families and teachers.

Through their analysis, the staff realized the entry created an institutional, rule-bound, and rather frightening feeling (this is a place where you might get sick or injured). The teachers made several changes. They first removed all items from the bulletin board, replacing them with children's photos and matted children's artwork. They added a basket of books and a bench where families could read to their children as they were entering and leaving the program. To create a mechanism for reciprocal written dialogue, they provided a two-way communication book. A joys and concerns box was also added, so that families could have the option of sharing information anonymously. Since one of the families was Spanish-speaking, teachers wrote all information in both English and Spanish. To make the area appealing to the infants and toddlers, the teachers added

Julie Bullard

This entry is beautiful. It is also practical, providing individual cubbies and places for children to sit to put on or remove boots.

a variety of different types of mirrors at the children's eye level. The entry now conveys an entirely different message than before, letting families and children know, "You belong here and your input in valued."

There are many other ways to make your entry welcoming. The Diana School, a preschool in Reggio Emilia, Italy, features a disguise closet in their entryway. The closet is full of interesting costumes that allow children to change their appearance before entering the classroom. As one child stated, "You get in like one person and come out like another" (Bondavalli, Mori, & Vecchi, 1993). Messages on ceilings, mirrors than open like books, and photos of children engaged in recent activities are some of the other ways that the Diana School provides a message that children are valued (Bartlett, 1993).

Provide Well-Established Boundaries Between Centers

To be effective, centers need a well-defined area with boundaries that still allow children to see the options available to them (Olds, 1989). Boundaries provide both physical and emotional security for children. Research indicates that children in well-defined areas are more deeply engaged in their activities and are more task-oriented. They display more appropriate behavior, positive interaction, and cooperation, and they engage in more exploration (Abbas & Othman, 2010; Moore et al., 1994; Zimmons, 1997). Probably because children are more engaged in both activities and positive peer interactions, teachers are less controlling and spend their time in more active involvement with children when areas are well defined (Moore, 1986). Both child engagement and teacher involvement are linked to enhanced learning outcomes for children.

Teachers can create boundaries from low bookshelves or furniture. Some programs hang old doors or windows from the ceiling over the shelving to create more room division. Sheer curtains or strips of fabric hung from ceilings, or low dividers made from fabric, colored Plexiglas, lattice, or pegboard are other ways to create boundaries. Whenever

Julie Bullard

This wall creates a unique boundary in the Mentor Graphics Child Development Center art studio. Children assisted in designing and creating the cobb wall using a mixture of clay, sand, straw, soil, and water.

possible, the dividers should be portable, allowing flexibility to change the room arrangement as children's interests change.

Teachers can also use different colored rugs or masking tape to create boundaries, or hang fabric or parachutes from the ceiling to create a separate area. However, these are not as effective since they do not provide protection from visual stimulation.

Plan Coherent Circulation or Traffic Paths

Effective traffic paths can assist with the flow through the room, reducing conflicts and interruptions of children engaged in activities. For example, a traffic path through a block area is likely to lead to block structures getting knocked down resulting in conflict, frustration, and the need to begin the building again. In planning your classroom, think about how children will navigate through the room. If designed effectively, the path can lead to greater discovery. However, if designed poorly it can lead to confusion. Have you ever gone into a department store that is divided into a confusing maze of departments? It can be frustrating and rather frightening if you feel trapped and unable to find your way out. We want to develop our classroom so that it makes logical sense to the young child and does not appear to be a confusing maze. In addition to being logical, to be safe the path needs to provide an unobstructed access to a door or fire escape and be wide enough to accommodate children, including children in wheelchairs. Avoid long or circular paths. Children look at environments for the affordances they provide. Long and circular paths afford the opportunity to run (White, 2004).

Provide a Variety of Learning Centers

The number and type of learning centers will vary based on the ages of the children, the space in the room, and the interests of the children and staff. For example, in addition to the typical centers found in preschool classrooms (literacy, dramatic play, creative art, music, manipulative, sensory, computer, science, math, and blocks), many programs will provide special centers. These might include carpentry, cooking, games, sewing, or research centers. Some of these centers, such as the sewing center, might be portable and brought out only during certain times of the day.

Strategically Group the Centers

In planning the arrangement of learning centers, it is important to consider the fixed features in the room, whether activities in the center are quiet or noisy, and how materials in adjacent centers might be used to enrich play.

Fixed or permanent physical features include windows, electrical outlets, sinks, and floor coverings. Consider these features when choosing the most feasible locations for each learning center. For example, the art center needs a sink and an easily cleanable floor surface. Natural lighting is important for close work, so the art area and reading area might be best near windows. Shelves that house materials and the workspace for using the materials need to be located close to each other. When they are not, children are less likely to use the materials (Maxwell, 2007).

To allow children to effectively concentrate and engage in conversation, centers need to be grouped according to whether they are quiet or active areas. Typically, the literacy, art, computer, science, math, manipulative, and sensory centers are considered quiet areas. These centers should be located in the most protected part of the room, usually away from doors. The music, block, dramatic play, gross motor, and woodworking centers are considered active or noisier centers and can be grouped near each other.

A final consideration in grouping areas is to think about which learning centers can be used in a reciprocal way to create opportunities for more enriched play. These centers can be placed adjacent to each other. For example, teachers in a toddler center moved the block and dramatic play areas next to each other. One of the children made a platform with the large blocks. Another child, who was in the dramatic play center wearing a fire hat, saw the platform and said "fire truck." She brought another fire hat to the block area and both children sat on the block platform making fire truck noises. It is unlikely that this scenario would have occurred if the dramatic play and block areas were not adjacent.

Provide Places to Gather as a Group

Classrooms for toddlers, preschoolers, and early elementary children need to have a place where children and the teacher can gather as a group. Because classrooms are often small, it is important that this space be multipurpose. Belinda, a teacher of preschool children, uses the music and dance center for her group area. Unless the instruments are being used for the group activity, she reduces distractions by covering the shelves housing the musical instruments with a sheet.

Develop Retreat Areas or Places to Be Alone

"At times all children feel an acute need for privacy" (Lowry, 1993, p. 58). Yet adults in early childhood programs often do not respect this need (Readdick, 1993). Readdick states, "In many instances the only provisions for solitary pursuits are the bathroom stall and the time-out chair" (Readdick, 1993, p. 60).

Solitary retreats provide children the opportunity to think and dream, engage in uninterrupted concentration, regain control of emotions, and unwind after intense periods of interaction. In examining early childhood centers with and without alone spaces, researchers found that when there were no places to retreat, children interacted less with peers, engaged in more wandering behavior, and were more hostile and aggressive (Sheehan & Day, 1975). Research also indicates that having places to be alone or retreat from the group are linked to later enhanced cognitive development (Moore, 2002). Too much stimulation can negatively affect optimal development (Lowry, 1993). Although it is tempting for teachers in crowded environments to eliminate alone areas as a way of saving space, when children are in a more dense situation, there is an even greater need to be alone.

Alone spaces need to be situated in a quiet space away from popular activities (Maxwell, 2007). They also need to be enclosed. Studies indicate that when

Julie Bullard

This inviting space is a retreat area for children. Note that this is the same location as shown in the opening photo for this chapter. The staff at Helen Gordon Child Development Center redesigned the space with a new group of children.

children are given a choice of a more open or closed area, they choose the more enclosed area (Lowry, 1993). "The essential feature … lies in the encapsulations of a relatively small amount of space into which a child can enter and experience variable degrees of sensory discontinuity from the larger surrounding environment" (Gramza, 1970, p. 177).

Since children have little control over leaving an environment to seek solitude, it is crucial that adults develop areas within the classroom where solitude can be found. There are many ways to create retreat areas. What you choose will depend upon what the children in your group find calming and relaxing:

- Put a basket of books next to a pillow-filled bathtub.
- Place a small tent in the room and include puzzles or drawing materials.
- Create an enclosed art area with clay and tools for one child.
- Develop a quiet "office" by cutting the side out of a refrigerator box and adding a desk and writing materials.
- Create a magical space by decorating a refrigerator box with shimmery gold paper, adding a sheer gold curtain for a door, painting the inside of the box black, and adding a flashlight and glow-in-the-dark chalk or an individual light table with translucent items.
- Provide a box or triangle mirrored enclosure with items to explore.
- Suspend a hula hoop from the ceiling and attach sheer curtains reaching to the floor; add a tape player and tapes.

Alone areas can also be created under stairs, a loft, a desk, or a counter; in a closet with the door removed; with cable spools with some of the slats removed; or in a tunnel. If you have children in your room with Aspergers, autism, or ADHD, you might consider adding a weighted blanket or vest to your retreat area, since deep pressure can assist children with sensory issues to feel calmer.

Ensure You have Enough Space in Each Center

Carefully plan the space each learning center requires. When a popular center is too small, crowding within the center can occur. Some teachers control this by having a sign-in system for each center. For example, to use a center, children might hang their nametag on a hook by the center. When all the hooks are full, there is no more room in the center. Limiting required accessories is another way to control numbers. For example, only two goggles may be available at the woodworking table or four aprons at the water table. Children realize that when these props are in use, then they need to find another place to play. It is imperative that children have several choices for play spaces. As a rule of thumb, you will want one-third more spaces in centers than there are children in the classroom. It's also important to analyze each of your centers for usage patterns. If there are centers not being used increase their appeal. This provides more learning opportunities and decreases density in other centers. You might also need to adjust the size of the center.

Julie Bullard

As part of a study on recycling, the children and the teacher created this alone area from reused gallon milk containers.

Use Space for Multiple Purposes

For example, children might only use an area of the room for group time, naptime, lunch, or certain projects. In a large room, this might still allow enough space for the children to use the rest of the day. However, in most classrooms, it is important to use the entire room during the majority of the day, creating areas in the classroom that are multiuse.

Sample Room Arrangements

When planning room arrangements, consider the physical features of the room, the size of the furniture and equipment, the developmental levels of the children, the learning centers that you wish to include, and the guidelines listed previously for planning effective room arrangements. Because of these many variables, each room arrangement is unique. However, the following examples can provide ideas for room arrangement.

Infants

When planning a room arrangement for infants, there are several things to consider. These include providing a comfortable, pleasant location for mothers to nurse their babies; enough room for individual cribs or baskets in a quiet area; a diaper-changing area with a sink large enough to bathe a child and an adjacent counter to hold supplies; convenient storage for strollers; and easy access to food preparation. Because infants spend much of their time on the floor, you must plan for a "plopping place" that allows adults to sit with several infants at once. This needs to be accompanied by comfortable places for adults to sit on or near the floor such as stacking back seats, canvas sling chairs, or stadium seats (Olds, 2001, p. 305).

Because infants are developing gross motor skills, they need space and a variety of surface levels to practice on such as a carpeted riser or a 2–4-foot-high loft (Olds, 2001). Ramps and steps provide additional climbing opportunities. Infants need an open area to play with balls, and push and pull toys. Low, secure shelves containing manipulatives such as baskets of rattles, activity boxes, dump and fill items, cause and effect toys, puzzles, musical items, and safe household items also need to be available. A book area containing sturdy books and a cozy place to sit are also important in the infant environment (Copple & Bredekamp, 2009). See Figure 5.2 for an example of an infant room arrangement.

Toddlers

Toddlers are still mastering movement, and so, like infants, they need room for gross motor activities and uneven surfaces to practice climbing up and down. Platforms for this age group can be 36 inches off the floor (Olds, 2001, p. 312). The toddler room will need to include a diaper-changing table with steps to provide independence and to protect adults' backs as well as small low toilets. It is also important to have storage for small cots, strollers, and car seats. Centers that are typically found in toddler rooms include dramatic play, creative art, literacy (reading, writing, and listening), music, sensory, manipulative, and a block and construction center. Learning centers for this age group should not be totally enclosed. When children are able to see the teacher, they use more of the room (Legendre, 1999). There also needs to be a place where toddlers can gather as a group and spaces where they can retreat and be alone. Figure 5.3 shows an example of a toddler room arrangement.

Preschool

The preschool classroom needs to provide for children's physical needs, different learning formats, and a variety of learning centers. Because children of this age have longer attention spans, they are able to engage in projects over an extended period. Revisiting

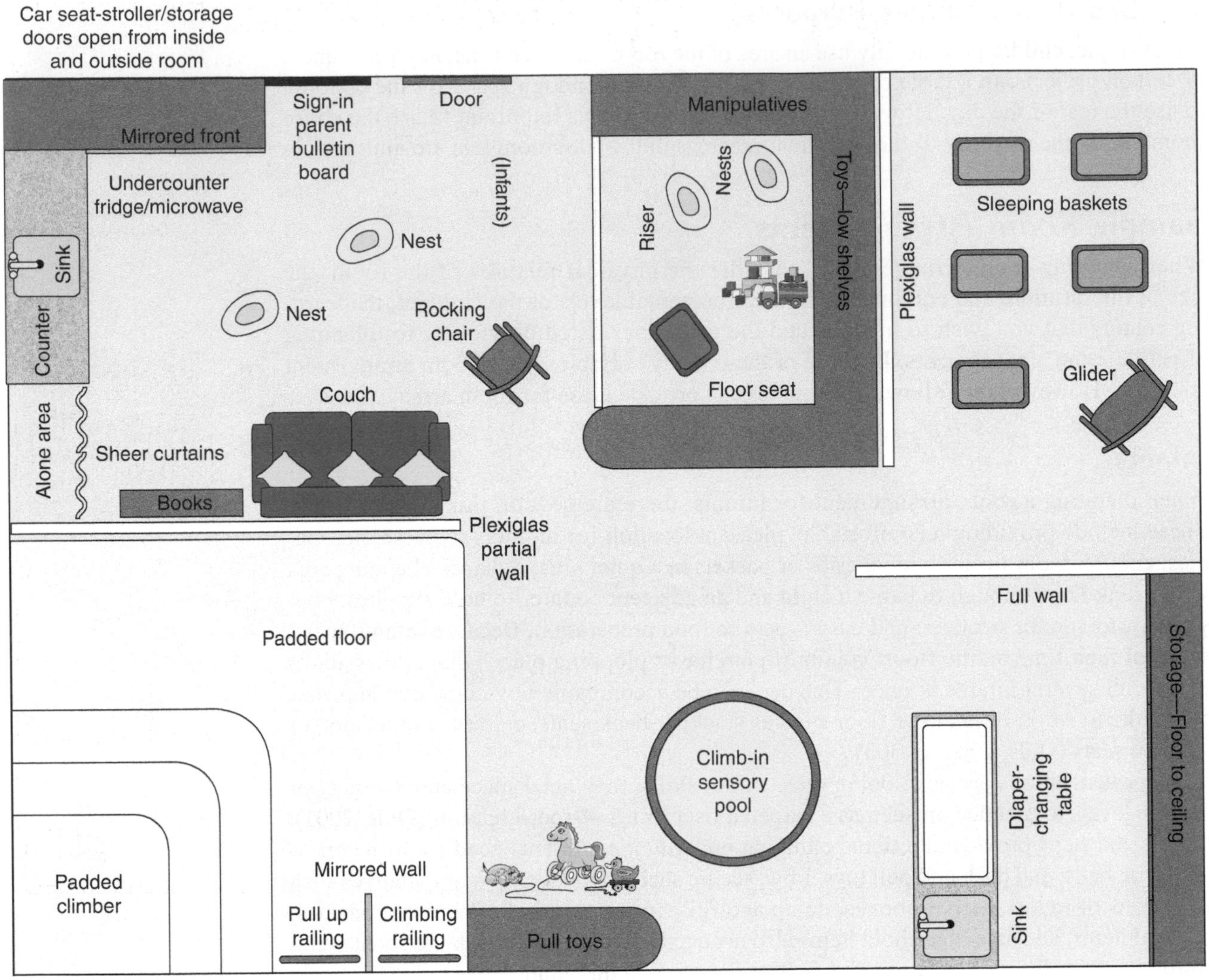

Car seat-stroller/storage doors open from inside and outside room
Mirrored front
Sign-in parent bulletin board
Door
(Infants)
Manipulatives
Nests
Riser
Toys—low shelves
Plexiglas wall
Sleeping baskets
Undercounter fridge/microwave
Sink
Counter
Nest
Nest
Rocking chair
Floor seat
Glider
Couch
Alone area
Sheer curtains
Books
Plexiglas partial wall
Full wall
Padded floor
Storage—Floor to ceiling
Climb-in sensory pool
Diaper-changing table
Padded climber
Mirrored wall
Pull up railing
Climbing railing
Pull toys
Sink

FIGURE 5.2 Infant Room Arrangement

Check Your Understanding 5.2
Click here to gauge your understanding of section concepts.

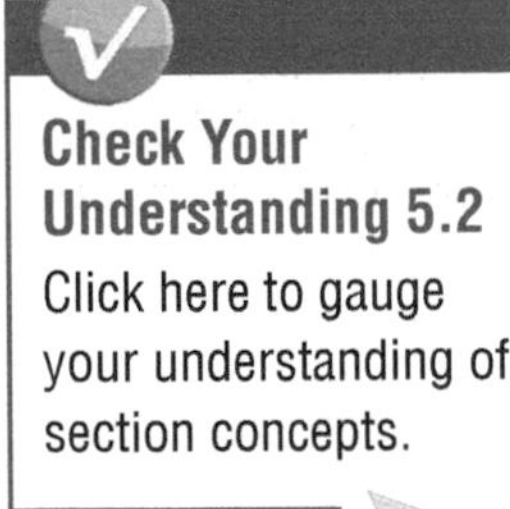

their work assists them to develop more in-depth knowledge and skills. Therefore, it is important to provide enough room to both engage in and store ongoing projects.

Some children at this age take naps, while most do not. Therefore, the room designer needs to consider the needs of both sleepers and non-sleepers. Bathrooms and drinking fountains are also important in preschool rooms; letting children be independent while still allowing adult supervision.

To accommodate different learning formats, there needs to be a large group gathering space, several small group areas, and individual retreat spaces. At a minimum, learning centers in preschool classrooms include dramatic play, creative art, literacy (reading, writing, and listening), music, sensory, manipulative, science, math, and a block and construction center. Technology is infused throughout the centers. Figure 5.4 shows one preschool room arrangement.

K–3 Classrooms

In the past, many grade K–3 classrooms contained desks in straight rows. However, recognition of the importance of cooperative and active learning has caused many teachers to rethink this arrangement. In a study of 294 grade K–5 classrooms, 76% used a small-group

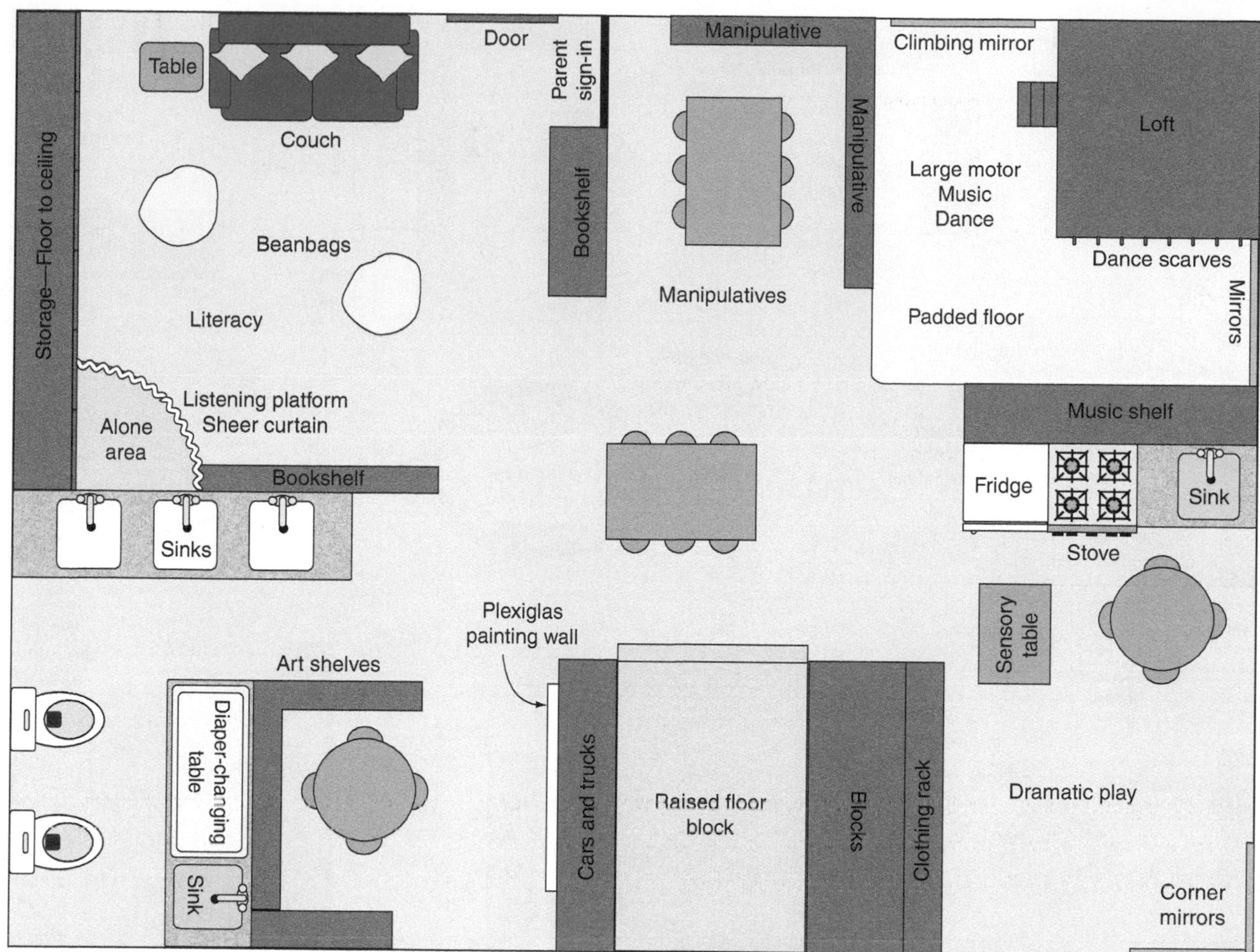

FIGURE 5.3 Toddler Room Arrangement

cluster design in their classrooms. In another study, 94% of teachers surveyed also used this design (Patton, Snell, Knight, & Gerken, 2001). Classrooms are affected by the prevailing philosophy of the school and the teacher. A recent impact has been the 21st-century education movement. How can we assist children to thrive in a future work setting where they will likely spend much of their time collaborating on interdisciplinary teams, working on projects with others from around the world, dealing with enormous amounts of sometimes conflicting data and information, and working with continually evolving technology (Helm, Turckes, & Hinton, 2010)? To be able to do this, children need to learn to think and work creatively with others, implement innovations, effectively communicate and collaborate, engage in critical thinking and problem solving, master core subjects, and gain information, media, and technology skills (The Partnership for 21st Century Skills, 2009). So how can we set up classrooms to accomplish this?

Watch the video to learn more about preschool environments. What are the strengths of this preschool environment?

In planning K–3 classrooms to meet these needs, include a large gathering space with projectors and whiteboards, places for independent and small group work, a variety of types of seating, large tables to work on projects, places to showcase and to store 2D and 3D works in progress, and flexible and reconfigurable space with furniture that is easy to move. In a well-designed classroom, the following centers are available where children can engage in **agency**, autonomy, active inquiry, interactive projects, and solve real-world problems; literacy (reading, writing, listening), social studies and project work, math manipulative, dramatic play, creative art and music studios, a science

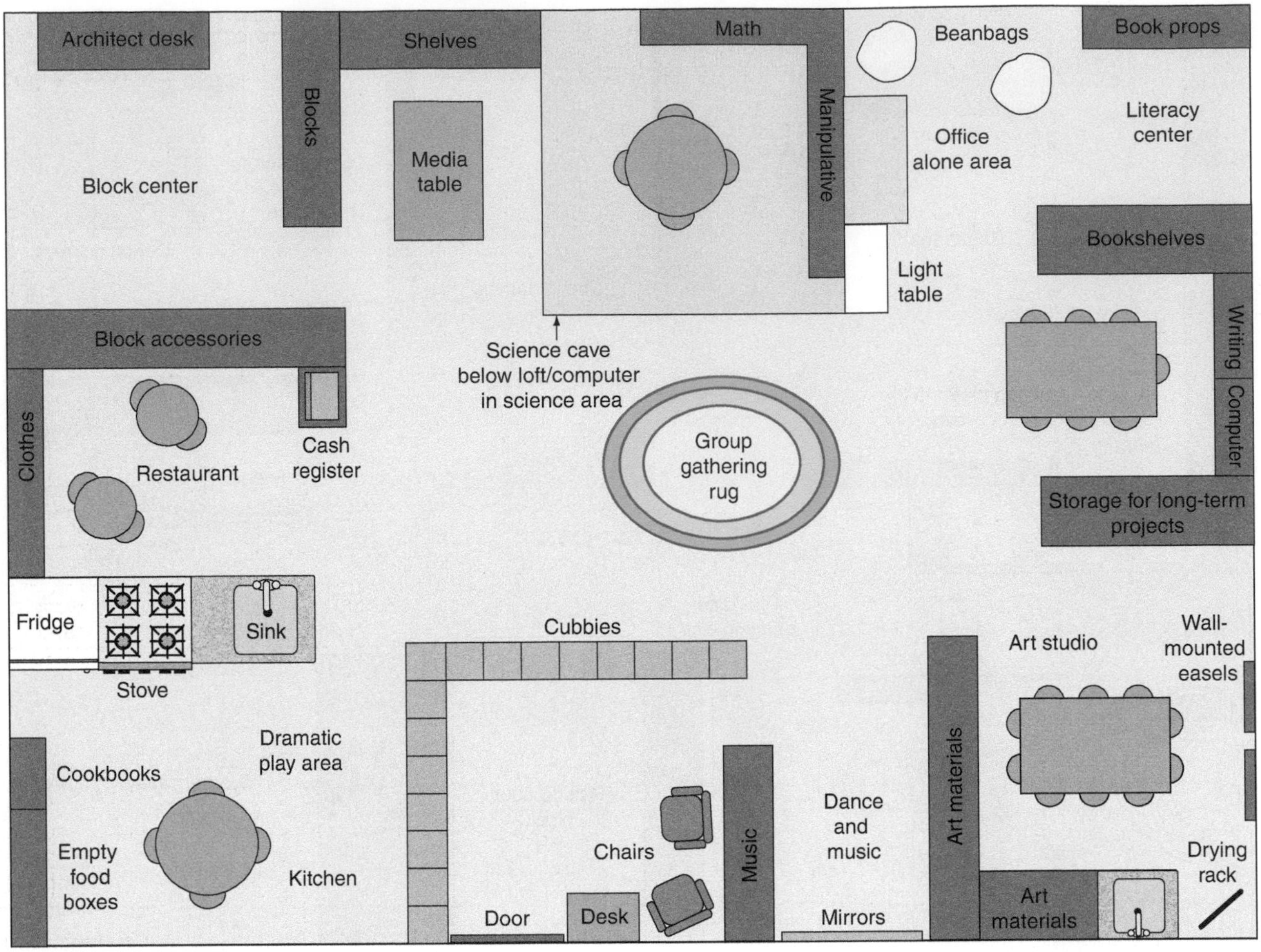

FIGURE 5.4 Preschool Room Arrangement

> Watch the video to see a 5–7-year-old-classroom at Opal School in Portland, Oregon. How does the arrangement of space and displays enhance the children's learning?
>
> https://www.youtube.com/watch?v=TsQwvGycL0I

lab, and an engineering and construction center. Technology is infused throughout the centers. To reduce time away from learning, a bathroom and drinking fountain in the classroom is helpful. See Figure 5.5 for an example of a K–3 classroom.

When we design environments, we must consider the arrangement of space within the classroom. It is also important to think about the spaces we use for routine care, including bathrooms, diaper-changing stations, and sleeping areas. In a well-designed environment, no space is ignored.

Bathrooms, Diaper-Changing Stations, and Sleeping Areas

Bathrooms, diaper-changing stations, and sleeping areas may be located in the classroom or in a separate space. In designing these often-overlooked areas, consider the amount of time that children and adults spend in these environments. They need to be functional, safe, healthy, and aesthetic.

Healthy, Aesthetically Pleasing Bathrooms

Bathrooms in early childhood settings, designed for functionality and ease of cleaning, often include harsh lighting, cold, hard surfaces, rule-oriented posters, and unpleasant smells. However, bathrooms can be aesthetic, provide an opportunity for learning, and still

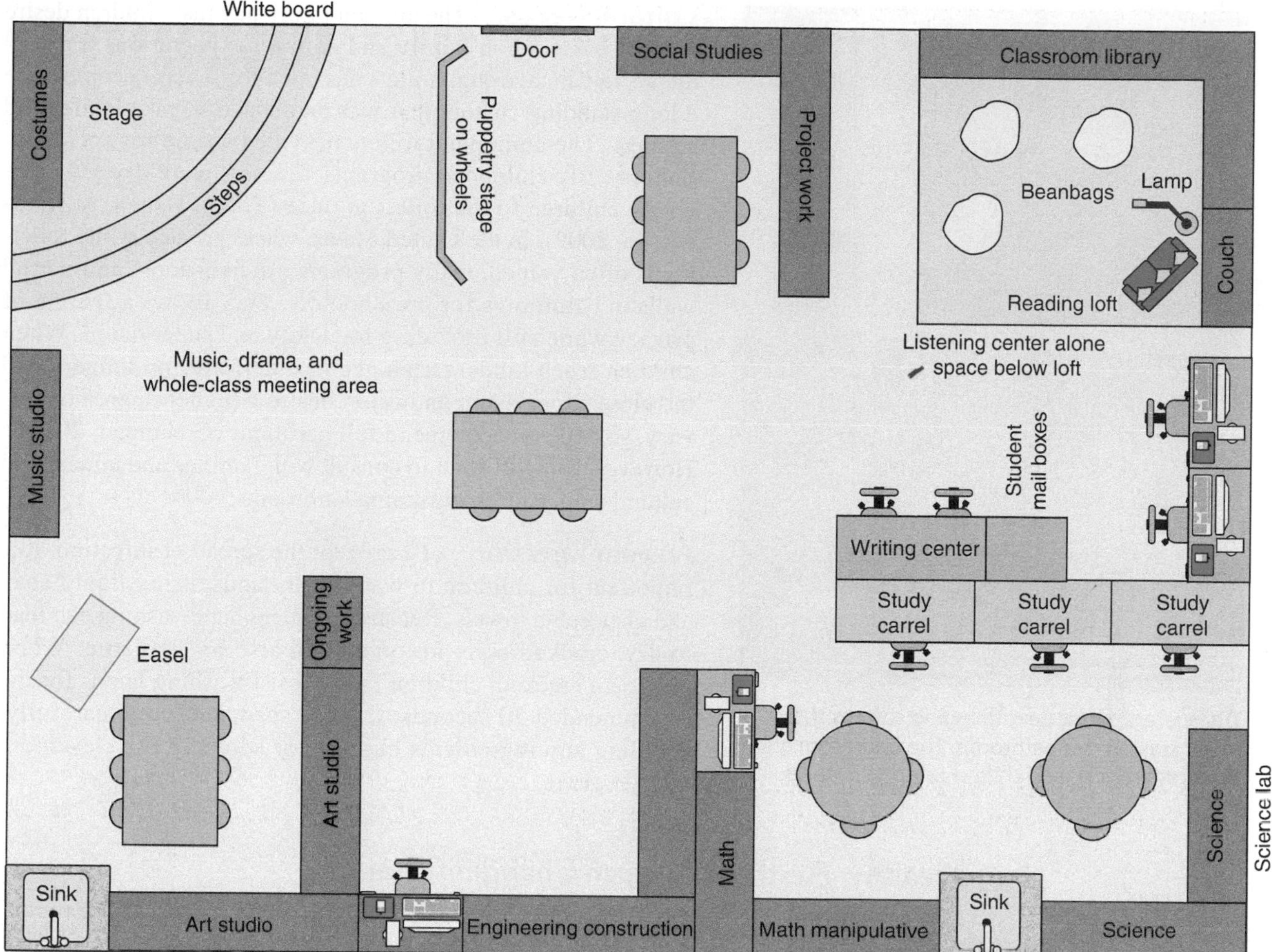

FIGURE 5.5 K–3 Room Arrangement

meet health and safety codes. As stated by Greenman (2005a), "It is important to keep in mind the concept of the primal importance of the bathroom experience to young children, as we determine the aesthetics and functionality of bathrooms" (p. 194).

Aesthetics. In Reggio Emilia preschools, bathrooms have different shaped mirrors; plants; hanging sculptures; transparent, colored mobiles; collages; and complicated pipe structure that children can use for experiments (Bartlett, 1993, p. 31). At Mentor Graphics Child Development Center, small bubble-shaped fish bowls with betta fish hang on the walls behind the toilets. Serenity School features full-length windows that look into a small, enclosed garden surrounded by a high fence. Discovery Preschool uses clear plumbing pipes below the sink so that children can see what happens to the water when it drains. To increase learning, some programs have interesting posters on the walls that children examine as they use the toilet. See an example in "Create Your Own Poster."

Location. Ideally, bathrooms are located in the classroom. This allows children who are developmentally ready to care for their own personal needs. In programs where bathrooms are located outside the room, adults must often accompany children to the bathroom, which affects the time adults have to interact with children in other ways. You can assist children to be independent by providing color or picture codes for the hot faucet and cold faucet, and by posting pictures of the proper handwashing procedures.

Julie Bullard

Transparent fabric beautifies and softens the metal stalls in this bathroom. The bathroom also features artwork and child-created sculptures.

Cultural Needs. The amount of privacy that children desire is often based upon family and cultural expectations. For example, in China, trough toilets designed for several people were a long-standing custom that was duplicated in early childhood settings. The communal toilets provided a time for socialization. In early childhood programs, teachers were likely to take all the children to the toilets at once (Tobin, Hsueh, & Karaawawa, 2009). In the United States, where privacy while toileting is often valued, many programs use half-doors and partial walls in bathrooms for preschoolers. This allows a feeling of privacy while still providing for safety and supervision. When children reach kindergarten age or older, they no longer need the close supervision and often desire a higher degree of privacy, so experts recommend full partitions (Greenman, 2005a). However, you will want to consult with families and understand cultural values when designing bathrooms.

Prevent Infection. To prevent the spread of infection, it is important for children to wash their hands, using liquid soap and disposable towels. Because frequent handwashing can lead to dry, cracked skin, lotion should also be available. When hands are cracked, children might resist washing hands for the recommended 20 seconds. Choose soap and lotion carefully, avoiding any ingredients children or adults in the classroom are allergic to.

Healthy, Aesthetic Diaper-Changing Stations

Diaper changing is a frequent, important part of the care routine in infant/toddler rooms. This space needs to be functional and sanitary. Since so much time is spent in this environment, it will be beneficial to the staff and children if it is also aesthetically pleasing.

Design for Tranquility. The routine of changing diapers provides the ideal opportunity for a tranquil, personal one-on-one time between the adult and child. To allow for relaxed time and to ensure safety, adults should not have their back to the other children while changing diapers (Greenman, 2005a). If this is absolutely necessary, mirrors can be strategically placed to see the rest of the room.

Julie Bullard

At Middle Creek Montessori, this wash center, located in the bathroom, provides children many learning experiences.

Reduce Injuries. To reduce the risk of back strain, which is the leading cause of worker's compensation claims for childcare providers (Pardee, 2005, p. 23), the height of the diaper-changing area needs to be comfortable for the adult. Another way to reduce back strain and to provide for toddler independence is to provide steps to the diaper-changing table.

Eliminate Germs. Diaper-changing tables can be a breeding paradise for germs. Therefore, it is important to use proper diaper-changing procedures. Having a sink near the table and having everything prepared before beginning the diaper-changing can also reduce germs. Each child needs his/her own

Create Your Own Poster

Julie Bullard

Young children are fascinated with toilets. When you post this poster on the bathroom wall, you provide an interesting item to engage them. Additionally, children, like adults, become familiar with a certain way of doing things and then view this as the "correct" or "right" way. By exposing children to differences, in this case differences in toilets, you can assist them to expand their worldview.

Directions

1. Gather photos. These were taken by the author. However, you can also ask families for photos or find non-copyrighted photos on the Internet.
2. Use a program to create a poster. This poster was created with the free program Pixlr. It includes a poster template.
3. Print your poster on a wide-format printer or have it printed at a copy shop.
4. Either laminate the poster or cover the poster with clear contact paper.

Variation

Once you learn to make posters, you can make a variety of types such as shoes from around the world, different types of houses, ways of carrying babies, or types of eating utensils. Each of these assist children in understanding that there are many different ways to accomplish our normal routines and ways of living.

separate supplies to reduce cross-contamination. There should be a separate diaper-changing facility and sink for each group of children (Aronson, 1999).

Provide for Safety. It is also important to be continually aware of safety. To reduce the danger of falls there should be a lip on the changing table and the adult should always keep one hand on the child. Experts state we should not use safety straps because they harbor germs and can provide a false sense of security.

TIP

If space in the bathroom is an issue in a home childcare environment, a removable diaper-changing table that is placed above the tub can be a solution.

Remember Aesthetics. Like bathrooms, diaper-changing areas can be safe and healthy and still provide an interesting, aesthetic environment. Mirrors on the ceiling and beside the changing table can allow children to look at themselves and see what the adult is doing. Mobiles, pictures, photos, or skylights can provide interesting viewing and points for discussion. Exhaust fans or open windows for ventilation can keep the

FIGURE 5.6
Diaper-Changing Station

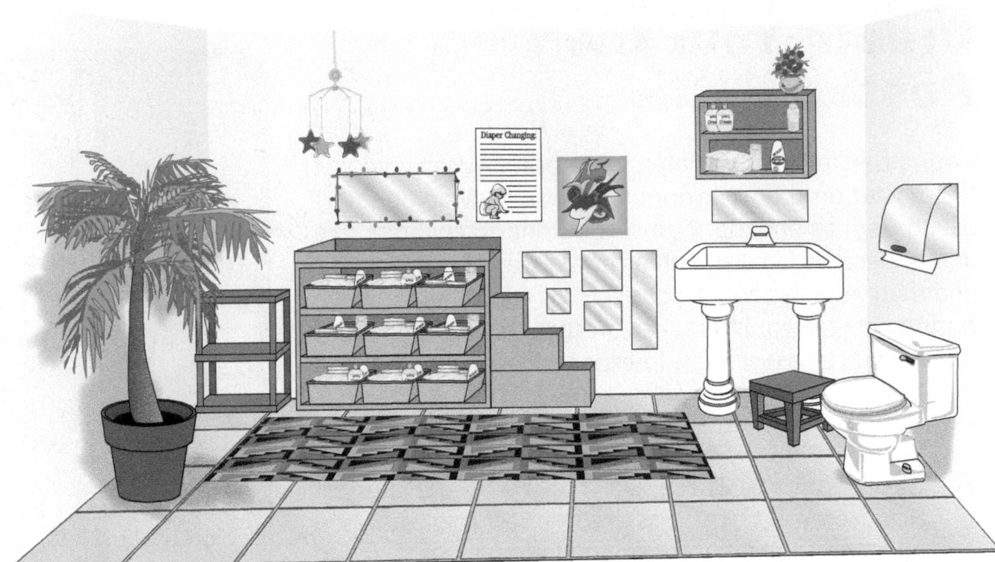

Check Your Understanding 5.3

Click here to gauge your understanding of section concepts.

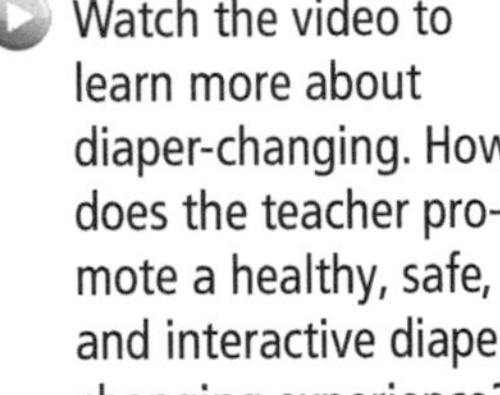

Watch the video to learn more about diaper-changing. How does the teacher promote a healthy, safe, and interactive diaper changing experience?

environment more pleasant smelling. Some programs even install disposal chutes to the outside of the building. Tina, a teacher of infants, improves the ambiance in her environment by adding fresh bouquets of flowers (donated by a local floral shop) to the diaper-changing area. See Figure 5.6 for an illustration of a diaper-changing area.

Healthy Napping and Sleeping Areas

Sleeping environments can be challenging in early childhood settings, since they need to be arranged to provide for the differing sleeping needs of children. It is disrespectful, agonizing, and developmentally inappropriate to require children who are not sleeping to lay quietly for more than a few minutes. While separate napping rooms are ideal, many programs do not have this luxury. Unless there is abundant space, it is generally better to use program space for multipurposes. If the classroom has to be used for napping, you might place the children that are most likely to sleep in one area of the room. Non-sleepers might lie down for a short period of time and look at books and then use the classroom's quiet centers. To provide additional quiet activities, Lisa, a teacher of preschoolers, has a special box of books and materials that she only brings out at this time of day. Angelo provides individual manipulative and cognitive activities for children to work on during quiet time. Dim lights, drawn shades, quiet music, and backrubs can help to relax both sleepers and nonsleepers. If needed, lamps can be used to give additional light for those working on quiet activities.

To provide for children's health and safety needs while sleeping, the cots need to be placed at least three feet apart. Storage for bedding can be difficult, since bedding cannot be shared by children or stored so that one child's bedding touches the bedding of other children (American Academy of Pediatrics et al., 2011). Some programs accomplish this by storing bedding in pillowcases and then placing them in children's individual cubbies.

Because infants and young toddlers sleep on their own schedule, it is important to have a sleeping area within the classroom. This allows children to be visually supervised as they sleep. Babies must be put to sleep on their backs to help prevent sudden infant death syndrome (SIDS). SIDS is the leading cause of death in babies that are 1 to 12 months of age (Center for Disease Control and Prevention, 2012). Firm mattresses and an uncluttered sleeping area (no soft bedding, bumper pads, stuffed animals) are also important in decreasing suffocation risks. When children are able to roll over on their own, it is not necessary to reposition them if they roll onto their stomach.

It is crucial that health and safety rules be followed. It is also important to develop an environment that is conducive to sleep.

Tracey, who worked in an Early Head Start Center, wanted to change the hard lines, harsh lights, and bright white walls that gave the napping area an institutional feel. She painted the room a pale blue with fluffy white clouds on the ceilings and draped a soft cloth over the florescent lights (after first checking with the fire marshal). Some of the cribs were no longer being used, and these were removed to create additional space. She then had room to add a rocking chair to the area. A sound machine that played calming ocean and other environmental sounds was also added.

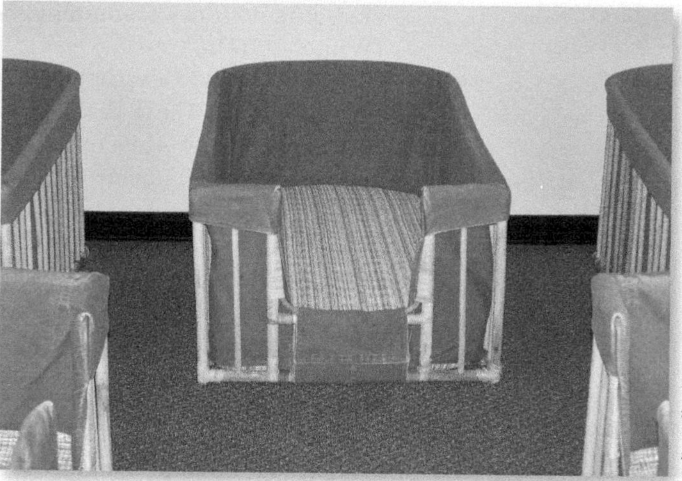

Julie Bullard

Specially designed sleeping baskets at Helen Gordon Child Development Center allow babies the freedom to crawl out when they awaken. Adults are always located in close proximity.

In designing your classroom floor plan, you will want to consider how best to provide for children's sleeping, diaper-changing, and toileting needs. In addition to developing the floor plan, teachers must also consider furniture and dividers. The floor plan and furniture play a reciprocal role. For example, the size of the furniture and the type of dividers affect the room layout.

Furniture and Storage

Furnishings reflect the program's values and can either support or impede the program's philosophy and curriculum. For example, in most programs infants are placed in cribs to sleep. When they wake, they must wait for the adult to remove them. However, some programs, wanting to allow infants greater independence and control, are using baskets instead. The baskets sit on the floor and have an entryway at the end that allows the infant to crawl in and out. This allows children the freedom and independence to crawl out of the basket when they wake up. The baskets are aesthetic and also save space. Furniture needs to provide for learning opportunities and be ergonomic, comfortable, safe, and aesthetically pleasing.

Provide for Learning Opportunities

To provide for optimal learning, the environment must accommodate a variety of learning styles. This includes having an array of seating and learning arrangements. There should be places for children to sit alone, to sit with peers, and to share with a teacher. Providing cozy, comfortable stuffed chairs, couches, beanbag chairs, hammocks, rocking chairs, window seats, wooden chairs and tables, and stadium chairs allows children and teachers to find areas that are conducive to their current activity and comfortable for them. For example, in one third-grade classroom some children remain in their desks, others get out mats and lay on the floor, and still others sit in beanbag chairs during silent sustained reading. One child reads best when rocking in the rocking chair. Recognizing the importance of classroom design in meeting the individual learning styles of students, one New York school district mandated that all teachers provide a variety of learning and seating spaces (Burke & Burke-Samide, 2004).

Ensure Furniture Is Ergonomic and Comfortable for All Who Inhabit the Space

Furniture needs to be **ergonomic**—designed for comfort and efficiency, and to meet the user's physical needs. For example, research reveals that when furniture is child size, it is not only ergonomic, but children engage in more extended, complex play (White, 2004).

In addition to a variety of seating options, most classrooms have a set of chairs (one for each child). These chairs need to be adjustable to allow for differences in children's size, with shallow seats that slant back. McDougal (2006) argues that the plastic chairs and desks found in many elementary classrooms are not only uncomfortable and ergonomically incorrect but are also designed for short-term use. He states, "Between the age of 5 and 16, children will spend around 16,000 hours sitting on a chair intended for short term occasional use" (McDougal, 2006, p. 49). He further challenges readers to consider whether they would be willing to swap their office chair for a plastic chair often found in schoolrooms and to do this without reducing performance.

Children should be able to touch the ground with their feet when they are sitting in chairs. Because many classrooms will have children that are different sizes, it is important that chairs in the classroom reflect this. Tables should be waist high and designed so that chairs will fit easily under them with plenty of room for the children's legs. It is important for teachers to also consider the needs of children who have physical disabilities when purchasing and using furniture. For example, can tables accommodate a wheelchair, or does inappropriate furniture cause the child in the wheelchair to be excluded from the group? The classroom also needs to have comfortable places for adults to sit, with adult seating throughout the room.

Make Certain Furniture Is Safe

In addition to being ergonomic, furniture must be safe. To prevent accidental tipping, shelves and furniture must be stable. Rounded corners on furniture help prevent injury if children fall. Because the furniture needs to be sanitized frequently, the surface must be designed to withstand sanitizing solutions. Also, consider the glare from the surface and the amount of contrast between work surfaces and reading materials. High contrast can cause eye strain (Waldecker, 2005, p. 2).

Ensure Furniture Is Aesthetically Pleasing

Furniture either contributes to or detracts from the aesthetics in the classroom. The condition of the furniture, the type of material, the color and texture, the way it reflects light, and the furniture lines all contribute to aesthetics. Furniture should be in good condition. If not, you might consider a slipcover for a couch or chair or a tablecloth to cover a shelf or table.

Shelving is a visible, important element in classrooms, providing a backdrop for materials that are placed on them. It is important to avoid bright primary colors that compete with the materials (Pardee, 2005, p. 22). Instead, consider using light wood shelving or shelves painted white or a very pale color. Shelving and tables can either reflect or absorb light. "Selecting furniture with lighter surfaces, for example, creates ambient light, accentuating incoming natural light and brightening the room" (Waldecker, 2005, p. 2).

The choice of materials for shelving and tables can also affect aesthetics. While plastic will often get dingy with age, wood ages gracefully (Olds, 2001). Some programs incorporate old wooden furniture (often purchased at garage sales) into their classrooms, combining functionality with unique lines and characteristics. For example, one program uses a beautiful rolltop desk as a sign-in area. The multiple cubicles in the desk serve as parent mailboxes.

Furnishing a classroom is a long-term investment. For example, it is estimated that it will cost between $14,000 and $19,500 to furnish a preschool classroom for 20 children. In addition, $125 to $150 per child should be budgeted each year for toys, books, and materials (Pardee, 2005, p. 26). To protect our investment, we must have adequate storage for the materials that are not currently in use.

Provide Effective Storage

Appropriate storage can help to reduce clutter, save time, make materials accessible, enhance the rotation of toys and equipment, and maximize the use of resources. Because storage is so important, a minimum of 10% of the square footage of a program should be devoted to storage (Greenman, 2005a). Several different types of storage are necessary in an early childhood program, including child accessible storage, personal storage, and teacher storage.

These stools made from tree trunks add a unique type of seating, while adding to the aesthetics of the room.

Child-Accessible Storage. Child-accessible storage space is needed for toys and materials that are currently being used by the children. To meet this need, storage is often provided on low, open shelves that are located throughout the classroom. It is hard for children to obtain materials independently and to determine choices when materials are placed in stacks or left in boxes. For this reason, it is more effective to place materials in labeled baskets or containers. The type of container you choose affects the aesthetics of the room. While primary-colored containers can add to visual clutter, wood, wicker, and fabric can add interest, warmth, and textural richness (Greenman, 2005a, p. 213).

Personal Storage. Children and teachers also need personal storage. Cubbies or low coat hooks and baskets often provide for this need. Personal storage acknowledges that each person is important in the room, while safeguarding private materials and possessions. To ensure that children do not have access to purses or coats where adults might store personal medication, the personal space for teachers and volunteers should be in a locked room or in locked cubbies.

Teacher Storage. The final type of storage is typically off-limits to children. It includes storage for toys, materials, and supplies needed for replenishment and rotation, to meet individual needs, and to provide for impromptu learning opportunities; teacher supplies and materials; and cooking, cleaning, and medical supplies. This storage is often in closed cupboards or closets. Open cupboards are frequently hung with curtains to clearly differentiate the storage as off-limits and to reduce the appearance of clutter. To save space, many programs place teacher storage cupboards high on the wall. This leaves the bottom portion of the wall available for classroom use. While much of the storage will be unlocked, potentially dangerous materials such as cleaning supplies and medications need to be in locked cabinets.

Planning for Storage

In planning for storage, consider the amount of access needed and who will need the access. You will want your storage to be well organized and in close proximity to where the material will be used. Since it is often difficult to have enough storage, you will need to think creatively about storage spaces and options.

Accessibility. Carefully consider whether you want the materials to be child-accessible. For example, do you want children to access extra art materials to assist in replenishing an area, or do you only want teachers to do this? Child-accessible materials need to be within the child's reach. If the materials are teacher materials only, it is important to have this clearly distinguished. Also, consider how often the materials will be used. Items infrequently used, bulk items, or items shared with other classrooms can be stored outside of classrooms, freeing up classroom storage space for more immediate needs.

Close to Intended Use. To allow for easy access, the storage of materials should be close to their intended use. For example, one program wanted to make sure that they took needed science supplies on discovery walks. However, this usually did not occur because the materials were on shelves in the teacher's supply room. The teachers decided to create a science bag that they hung on a hook by the door. The bag included magnifying glasses, a tape measure, plastic bags to gather specimens, clay to make casts of objects such as tree trunks, field guides, paper and pencils, and so forth. Because the science bags were readily accessible, the teachers and children remembered to take them each time they went for a walk. These tools for investigation greatly enhanced children's learning.

Well-Organized. Having a specific place for each item and labeling shelves, containers, or bags helps to organize space. Disorganized storage can be costly in terms of staff time, program quality, and money. Staff may spend an inordinate amount of time finding materials, become discouraged and purchase new supplies, or just not bother to rotate toys or replenish needed materials when storage areas are disorganized.

Check Your Understanding 5.4

Click here to gauge your understanding of section concepts.

All Available Spaces and Storage Options Effectively Used. Because most programs have limited storage, it is important to take full advantage of all the storage that is available. For example, you might store materials under cribs, lofts, tables, or window seats. You can also use backs of doors or cabinets for storage. Some teachers create a storage area by cordoning off a corner of the room with a curtain or screen.

You can create inexpensive storage units by wiring together milk crates or creating a shelving unit with a PVC frame and wooden shelves. Some teachers use labeled, sturdy boxes covered with fabric or contact paper for infrequently used materials. They place the boxes on high classroom shelves or stack them in the classroom. Space might be saved by placing some materials in labeled plastic bags (for example, collage materials), reducing the space taken by containers.

Chapter Quiz 5

Click here to gauge your understanding of chapter concepts.

High-quality learning centers and room arrangements; comfortable, functional furniture; and appropriate storage all contribute to an effective environment. Effective environments enhance relationships and support program goals, leading to increased learning, independence, and competence in children. Furthermore, the organized, aesthetic, well-designed environment provides a comfortable, joyful place to learn and work.

Sample Application Activities

1. Develop or redesign a learning center to meet the criteria found in this chapter.
2. Use the Environmental Assessment found in Figure 5.7 to assess the learning centers and room arrangements of several early childhood programs.
3. Develop an action plan for at least one of the classrooms you assessed, detailing what changes you would make to meet the criteria.
4. Develop a floor plan for your ideal classroom. You can find a free room-planning guide at Environments Inc.
5. Design a plan for an aesthetic, yet healthy, early childhood bathroom or diaper-changing area.
6. Investigate storage options. When developing the floor plan for your ideal classroom, describe the type of storage you would provide and provide a rationale for why you chose this option.
7. Visit a store selling secondhand furniture. How could the furniture be modified for use in an early childhood classroom? What would be the advantages and disadvantages of doing so?

FIGURE 5.7 Environmental Assessment: Learning Centers and Room Arrangement

Learning Centers

- ❑ Is the purpose of the center evident?
- ❑ Is the center inviting and aesthetically pleasing?
- ❑ Is there an abundance of materials—enough so that children do not have to wait and so that children can engage in exploration and deep learning?
- ❑ Are materials developmentally appropriate, providing challenges but not being so difficult that children become frustrated?
- ❑ Are there materials for a wide range of developmental levels?
- ❑ Is there an abundance of open-ended materials?
- ❑ If the materials are close ended, are they self-correcting?
- ❑ Do the materials reflect cultural diversity?
  Are there materials that reflect the lives of children with disabilities?
- ❑ Are materials anti-biased?
- ❑ Are materials located in the centers where they are used?
- ❑ Are materials readily available and within reach of the children?
- ❑ Are materials well organized?
- ❑ Are shelves labeled so that children can easily find items and know where to put them away?
- ❑ Do children know how to use the materials?

Room Arrangement

- ❑ Do the centers have well-established boundaries?
- ❑ Are centers the size needed to accommodate the number of children and the activity occurring in the center?
- ❑ Is every area of the room being effectively utilized?
- ❑ Are the boundaries movable so they can be changed as needed?
- ❑ Are traffic paths wide enough to accommodate a child in a wheelchair?
- ❑ Do traffic paths allow clear access to a door or fire escape?
- ❑ Is the arrangement of centers transparent to children and adults, so they can easily navigate the space?
- ❑ Is the room arranged to prevent long or circular paths that encourage running?
- ❑ Are centers placed to take the best advantage of physical characteristics of the room (outlets, lighting, sinks, flooring, etc.)?
- ❑ Are centers grouped according to whether they are quiet or active?
- ❑ Are centers that might combine to contribute to more in-depth play adjacent to each other?
- ❑ Is the entry space welcoming for parents, children, and staff?
- ❑ Does the entryway provide an effective transition area into the program?
- ❑ Are there places in the room to gather comfortably in small and large groups?
- ❑ Are there places to be alone?
- ❑ Are there a variety of clearly designated learning centers?
- ❑ Is there a space for personal belongings?
- ❑ Can the space be adapted to meet childrens' special needs?
- ❑ Did the teacher invite and use input from children to design the space?
- ❑ Can teachers and children easily modify the environment to allow more space in some areas?

CHAPTER 6

Design Considerations

Learning Outcomes

After you have read this chapter, you will be prepared to:

- Describe how to achieve an aesthetically pleasing, homelike environment
- Explain how design elements help to achieve design outcomes
- Describe how to use ceilings, walls, and floors as effective design palettes
- Discuss how to improve air quality, reduce pesticides, decrease crowding, and limit noise, and describe why this is necessary

Julie Bullard

Imagine two environments. One environment is a coffee shop. It has many different forms of lighting, the rich smell of coffee, quiet music playing in the background, small tables for two to four people to visit, plants, local artists' paintings displayed on the walls, and a bookshelf with games and magazines.

The other environment is a large department store during a huge sale. The store is crowded with shoppers and shopping carts. Shelves contain items packed from floor to ceiling. The local radio station is playing music with an occasional interjection from the store loudspeaker promoting store ads.

Environments such as the two just described evoke emotions and establish a mood. The environment also affects productivity and sends a message regarding the value we place on those that use the environment. Did you know that businesses, realizing the importance of the environment, spend billions of dollars a year to create just the right ambiance or mood? Additionally, research since the 1920s has established a link between the environment and employee productivity (Young, Green, Roehrich-Patrick, Joseph, & Gibson, 2003). However, in early childhood we don't always consider research when designing the environment. Since children and teachers often spend 8 to 10 hours a day in an early childhood environment, we need to intentionally design this setting, using research to assist us.

Through manipulating design elements (color, light, texture, shape, form, and space) and design principles (balance, rhythm, proportion, and scale), we can create stimulating early childhood environments that are also harmonious (Read, 2003, p. 233). Conducive facilities benefit children, families, and staff. For example, research suggests that facility improvement can improve staff retention as much as increases in pay (Buckley, Schneider, & Shang, 2004). Research also shows that children in better designed facilities have increased achievement, better behavior, increased self-esteem and pro-social behavior, and a sense of pride (Young et al., 2003). The school can also be a source of pride for the community.

In this chapter we will examine desired design outcomes (homelike, aesthetically pleasing), design elements (natural items, softness, color, texture, lighting, focal points), design palettes (ceilings, walls, floors and different surface levels), and special design considerations (air quality, pesticides, density, noise). You might wonder how you as a teacher can influence some of these variables. A large study conducted in the UK found that environmental design explained 51% of the variability in children's learning and that 73% of this was at the class level, much of which the teacher controls (Barrett, Zhang, Moffat, & Kobbacy, 2013). It is critical that we understand design principles so that we can create environments that are conducive for learning and that show value for the children and teachers who use the environment.

Desired Design Outcomes

What kind of ambiance should early childhood programs try to achieve? Two outcomes that early childhood design experts frequently mention are a homelike environment and an aesthetically pleasing design.

Homelike Environment

Many experts recommend that early childhood teachers strive to create a homelike ambiance (Butin, 2000; Curtis & Carter, 2005; Olds, 2001; Torelli, 2002; Trancik & Evans, 1995). However, in practice this is often not the case. Instead, early childhood environments often look like a commercial for a school supply catalog, filled with hard, plastic items and primary colors. It is difficult to discern the influence of the children or the communities in which they live (Curtis and Carter, 2005). Gandini (1984), known for her work with the Reggio Emilia schools, states, "Even though we may value individuality in children and adults, we rarely build environments which have personality" (p. 17).

Homelike environments have personality. They help to establish a sense of belonging, easing the transition between home and school. Individualized environments, personalized for the inhabitants, also lead to **place identity**. When one has place identity,

Julie Bullard

This horse swing reflects the place identity of this rural community, which frequently hosts rodeos.

one has a greater sense of belonging and ownership over the environment, leading to increased self-esteem and happiness (Fisher, 2006). Following is a list of characteristics to consider in developing a homelike environment:

- Welcoming
- Divided into usable space for different functions
- Includes private places to escape
- Includes places for people to gather together
- Provides comfortable furniture and different types of seating
- Contains different types of lighting
- Filled with real, functional items (dishes, pottery, pots and pans, tools)
- Filled with images of the inhabitants through photos and mirrors
- Includes living things (plants, flowers, animals)
- Contains softness (rugs, throw pillows, wall hangings, curtains, tablecloths, soft furniture)
- Provides richness of texture and color without being overwhelming
- Provides attention to detail
- Contains beauty
- Reflects the values and culture and ethnicity of inhabitants
- Reflects the surrounding social and cultural community and geographic location
- Contains objects that have personal meaning, such as framed art and collections of natural items (seashells, rocks)
- Is personalized by the inhabitants

The ability to personalize the environment creates a sense of belonging and control. There are several ways this can be achieved in an early childhood setting. Teachers can add open-ended materials that children can use to create a unique space. For example, children can use large pieces of fabric to create a tent, instantly transforming the environment. Items that children have collected or brought from home can be displayed. Children can also help choose what is placed on the walls or change some aspects of the environment such as seating arrangements or lighting. "Allowing a child to personalize the environment encourages them to claim ownership, form attachments and become familiar with their surroundings" (Trancik & Evans, 1995, p. 52).

Aesthetically Pleasing Design

To create an aesthetically pleasing, harmonious environment, one must not only think of each of the design elements in isolation but also think of them in unison. As stated by Olds (1989), "To design for aesthetic richness, the building's or room's elements (floors, walls, ceilings, horizontal and vertical supports, objects, forms, and architectural details) all should be conceived of as interactive surfaces to be sculpted, painted, draped, and molded much the way artists sculpt, paint, and mold wood, clay, canvas, fibers and colors" (p. 8). In the aesthetic environment, teachers design each of these elements to create beauty and harmony.

The well-designed environment is clutter-free and is thoughtfully organized with attention given to details (Bartlett, 1993). To accomplish this requires constant vigilance. For example, at Mentor Graphics Child Development Center, the teachers "tidy up" and "reset" the room several times a day to keep the environment clutter-free, organized, and inviting. The director states that she can look in a classroom and tell immediately if there are problems based upon the way the environment looks. The types of materials and the way that materials are displayed also contribute to the aesthetics of the room. At Community School in Spokane, Washington, the teachers and children view materials as "treasures." When something is a "treasure," we display it beautifully and care for it respectfully.

In addition, the program is filled with "sensory delights." Olds describes these as "pleasant aromas; delightful sounds; interesting colors, plants and live moving creatures (fish, pets); changing light and shadows; and wonderfully varied tactile experiences" (Olds, 2001, p. 303).

Julie Bullard

This tea chest provided inspiration for a way to display children's art materials. A photo on the lid of the box assists children to know where to return items and adds to the aesthetics of the display.

Finding Inspiration

Think about places you enjoy being. This might be a natural or manmade environment. What elements make this space special? As you are designing your classroom, you might seek inspiration from your favorite settings or other early childhood programs. You might also seek inspiration by looking through books or magazines, watching design programs on television, or visiting art galleries. As you visit different settings, such as churches, government buildings, office buildings, motels, and restaurants, think about the space. What is the purpose of this space? Is it functional? Is it aesthetic? What elements contribute to the design of this space? Also, look for items that spark your imagination. This could be a piece of fabric, a new lighting element, material from a home improvement store, or an item from a secondhand store. For example, Tenille found a beautiful silver box with an intricate locking mechanism that she knew would fascinate children. This inspired her to create a display of fascinating boxes filled with different treasures.

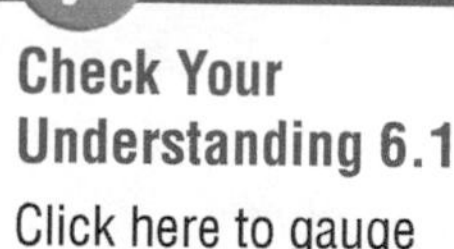

Check Your Understanding 6.1

Click here to gauge your understanding of section concepts.

Design Elements

Elements of design that are important to consider in early childhood environments are natural items, softness, texture, color, lighting, and focal points. When planned carefully, these elements can help to establish an aesthetically pleasing, homelike environment.

Natural Items

"Incorporating natural elements inside the four walls of your classroom can effortlessly transport children into a world of beauty. Not only does nature provide an infinite supply of sensory experiences that can be integrated into all learning domains, it conveys a sense of calmness and tranquility for both children and adults" (Deviney, Duncan, Harris, Rody, & Rosenberry, 2010, p. 51). Natural items provide variety within sameness. For instance, even if you have a basket of the same type of pinecones, there will be natural variations among them, providing opportunities for close observation. Natural materials are also alluring for children and provide a connection with the earth. A frequent question that I am asked about aesthetic environments is how programs on limited budgets can afford to make their environments beautiful. One solution is to use natural items since they are typically free or very low cost.

Watch the video to learn more about using natural items in early childhood environments. In what ways could these materials enhance the children's learning?

https://www.youtube.com/watch?v=k0mKfgeFTns

Marietta wanted materials that the three-year-old children in her classroom could sort. Instead of buying plastic teddy bear counters, she collected seedpods from many different types of trees in the area. Not only did this create an opportunity for children to classify, but they also learned about the trees in their area.

Softness

One thing that clearly distinguishes an institutional environment from a home environment is softness. Although softness is often eliminated in early childhood programs due to the desire to have an antiseptic environment, softness is important in creating an environment that is cozy, comfortable, and homelike. Softness is also critical in reducing noise levels and reverberation. Children can experience softness through upholstered furniture, pillows, beanbag chairs, covered mattresses on the floor, and throw rugs. Teachers can also create the appearance of softness by adding tablecloths, curtains, drapes, canopies, and wall hangings.

Julie Bullard

Soft furniture, pillows, a plant, a wall hanging, and a lamp all assist in providing homelike ambiance in this reading area. Note that basil is used instead of a houseplant, creating fragrance while also being safe to eat.

Texture

Although our skin is the largest body organ, touch is the most ignored sense in planning early childhood environments (Olds, 1989, p. 10). According to Olds (1989), texture contributes more to overall ambiance than any other design element.

Anyone who has the irresistible desire to touch a rich velvet drape, run their hand along a bumpy brick wall, or feel a cold marble countertop knows the sensory pleasure derived from textures. Textures in classrooms cause light to reflect differently, creating interest. They provide for a more complex environment, creating opportunities for children to compare, contrast, and experiment (Olds, 2001). Textures also contribute to a more homelike environment and can help reflect the lives and cultures of children. On a practical note, textures help to control sound and to create space definition. Providing a variety of textures is important because each person experiences perceptions differently. The environment needs to be rich in a variety of tactile stimuli, allowing each person to have his or her needs met (Ceppi & Zini, 1998).

Textures can be incorporated through more permanent design features, such as adding different floor, ceiling, and wall surfaces. These can include a variety of materials such as brick, wood, metal, glass, ceramic tile, rubber, and bumpy plaster designs. You can also add different textures to environments through furniture, drapes, canopies, pillows, wall hangings, tablecloths, baskets, sensory tables, and play materials, and by creating texture walls. Children's three-dimensional artwork can also add to the textural landscape (Reinisch & Parnell, 2006). Even everyday items used in a different way can add new tactile experiences.

Leigh Ann, a teacher in an Early Head Start infant room, placed a rubber bath mat below the sink to prevent slipping. One day one of the infants pulled back the edge and found the bumpy suction cups on the underside of the mat. She became fascinated, touching the suction cups with her hands, arms, legs, and feet. Soon several children gathered around, experimenting with the bath mat. Seeing the children's interest, Leigh Ann developed a texture crawl, taping together items with different textures such as velvet, bubble wrap, corduroy, and burlap.

Color

Like texture, you can use color in the classroom to create a differentiated space. Color can also be used to emphasize the physical features of a room, to create an illusion of more or less space, and to make a room more attractive. Color affects the luminosity in the room by reflecting or absorbing light. There is also evidence that color evokes moods. However, it appears that this is culturally based rather than biologically based (Ceppi & Zini, 1998), and that it is not only the color but also the value and saturation that influence emotions (Manav, 2007). Perhaps this is why, after examining 200 studies of school environments, Higgens, Hall, Wall, Woolner, and McCaughey (2005) came to the conclusion that there "is conflicting evidence, but forceful opinions on the effects of colour" (Higgens, Hall, Wall, Woolner, & McCaughey, 2005, p. 22), with studies producing inconsistent results.

In determining the best color to paint an environment, you should consider whether you want the space to look larger or smaller. Dark colors will make a space look smaller. If ceilings are high, you might want to paint them darker to make them appear lower. If the room is long and narrow, you can make the distant wall appear nearer by painting it a darker color.

Many design artists and early childhood specialists recommend using visually demanding bright colors only for accents (Olds, 2001; Torelli & Durrett, 2000). Bright colors on shelves and furniture can cause overstimulation, especially when we consider all the color that will be added to the environment by the toys, materials, items on the walls, and even the children's clothing. Instead, experts recommend that neutral colors be used, with learning centers being painted different but harmonious colors to differentiate the space (Olds, 2001). The neutral background allows the emphasis to be placed upon the toys, materials, and inhabitants of the space. In *Children, Spaces, and Relations*, Ceppi and Zini (1998) emphasize that the walls should be a basic background, allowing those using the space to exercise their own creativity in applying a "second skin" (Ceppi & Zini, 1998, p. 63). Varieties and ranges of colors in materials can then add needed complexity, variety, and richness to the environment. This gives children the opportunity to learn about, compare, contrast, and experiment with color. This philosophy is in opposition to the often-found practice of using bright primary color schemes or pastel nursery themes that are based upon a

simplified viewpoint of children (Ceppi & Zini, 1998). However, all considerations of color should be thought about in relationship to contemporary and cultural beliefs, since the early childhood setting needs to reflect the society it resides within rather than be an isolated entity.

Lighting

Lighting affects the aesthetics of the room as well as the visual acuity and mental health of the occupants. "Creating good lighting is not just a matter of having 'enough' lighting.... Good lighting is ultimately a matter of achieving a desired look and feel. Light can shape our moods. It can soothe the mind and invigorate the body. Light, in all its manifestations, has the power to not only illustrate what we see, but influence how we see it, even to make it beautiful" (Karre, 2003, p. 5).

Windows not only provide light but also allow access to the world outside, creating a "spirit of place" (Olds, 2001). Children can observe nature and the elements and feel like they are part of the community surrounding the classroom. The room can feel larger when one can view the outside. If windows are strategically located, children can see what is occurring in the building before they enter, helping them to build anticipation and ease the transition. Unlike artificial light, natural light from windows is dynamic, changing throughout the day. To help reduce glare, it is best for natural light to come from at least two directions (GSA, 2003).

Learning may also be enhanced with natural lighting. Researchers claim that natural lighting can improve achievement by 20% or more (Earthman, 2004; Heschong Mahone Group, 2003). Poor lighting, on the other hand, can cause headaches, eye strain, and fatigue, negatively affecting learning (Higgens et al., 2005).

However, it is typically not practical to rely totally on natural light. When natural light is not possible, full-spectrum lights are recommended (GSA, 2003). Some researchers indicate that full-spectrum lights result in better physical health (Graves, 1985; Hathaway, Hargreaves, Thompson, & Novitsky, 1992). However, other researchers claim that these benefits have not been proven (NLPIP, 2005).

It is also recommended that classrooms have a variety of different types of lighting (track, pendant, recessed, dimmer controlled, lamps, hanging lights, rope lights) to create "a distinctive atmosphere" in different areas of the room (Torelli, 2002). By using different types of lighting in different areas of the room, we can create a "tapestry of light and dark areas" with "pools of light" that draw people together (Olds, 2001, p. 191).

Different types of lighting accommodate different environmental needs. Dimmer-controlled lighting for sleeping areas allows low light when children are napping while still allowing supervision. Different types of lighting also allow children to have some control over their environment. For example, a lamp with a three-way bulb in the reading area allows children to adjust the degree of lighting according to their needs.

Julie Bullard

This infant area at Mentor Graphics Child Development Center includes natural light as well as an interesting light fixture made from netting and icicle light strands. Also notice the softness in the area.

To get the best advantage of your lighting, you should paint ceilings and walls with a high light reflectance value (LRV) paint. High LRV can lead to a 25% reduction in needed lighting fixtures (Fielding, 2006). Mirrored ceiling tiles can also achieve this effect.

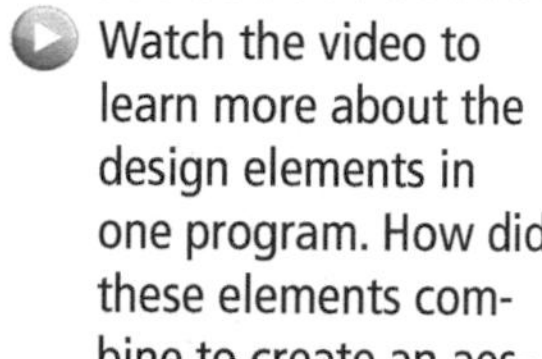

Watch the video to learn more about the design elements in one program. How did these elements combine to create an aesthetic environment?

https://www.youtube.com/watch?v=kQdAU7Dm9A0

Focal Points

Focal points create an emphasis that draws your interest to an object or area, making the space feel less disorganized. A focal point may be an architectural feature such as a window, a special piece of furniture, a piece of artwork or photo, an interesting rug or piece of colorful fabric, an interactive component, or a display (Deviney et al., 2010). You might also use color or lighting to create focal points. For example, at Mentor Graphic Child Development Center, each area of the room has a unique light. When a chandelier over the dramatic play table is turned on, this area becomes a focal point. Some programs establish "invitations" as a focal point. They set up a changing interactive display that serves as a focal point and an invitation to explore and learn. For example, at Opal School teachers set out several vases, each containing a different type of flower. The color and beauty of the display immediately draw your attention as you enter the room. However, the teachers did not leave this as something to only look at; instead, they added a few sets of watercolors, paper, and brushes around the flowers to encourage deeper interaction.

Check Your Understanding 6.2

Click here to gauge your understanding of section concepts.

Natural items, softness, texture, color, lighting, and focal points are design elements that can contribute to a more homelike, aesthetic environment. We'll next examine design palettes.

Design Palettes

Just as an artist uses a palette to draw or paint on, the early childhood teacher and children use the ceilings, walls, and floors as the design palette for the classroom.

Ceilings

Ceiling height provides a sense of your significance within the environment, helps to establish the type of activity expected, and affects noise reverberation. Perhaps you have entered a cathedral or courtroom with very high ceilings. In this environment, you may feel small and insignificant. For this reason, some researchers suggest that ceiling height be lowered for children's spaces, to promote security and self-esteem (Moore et al., 1994; Weinstein, 1987).

Ceilings less than 8 feet high suggest quieter types of play and greater intimacy (Moore et al., 1994; Olds, 2001). In one study, researchers found that children engaged in more cooperative behavior when ceiling heights were lowered (Read, Sugawara, & Brandt, 1999). Higher ceilings promote active play. However, they also introduce more formality (Moore et al., 1994; Olds, 2001). Creating varied ceiling heights in a classroom can create interest, accommodate different learning activities, and help reduce noise reverberation (Olds, 2001).

Some teachers reduce high ceilings through hanging canopies or draping fabric from the ceiling. Other teachers lower ceilings by horizontally suspending large sheets of foam panels or sheets of lattice. Notice how a frame is hung over the area in the opening photo of this chapter. Hanging door or window frames is another way that ceilings may be made to feel lower. The illusion of a lower ceiling can also be created by hanging kites, banners, or branches. In determining what items to hang, it is important to consider visual clutter.

Walls

Walls can be solid or transparent, be partial or reach to the ceiling. Transparent walls help to block sound while enhancing light. They also keep children from entering an area while still allowing visual access. Programs may place transparent walls or windows between classrooms, between the kitchen and classroom, or into halls. Infant/toddler classrooms frequently place transparent partial walls between the classroom and the diaper-changing area.

Backdrop for Displays. Walls also form the backdrops for displays. In the article Aesthetic Codes in Early Childhood Classrooms, Tarr (2001) discusses the typical early childhood environment. She describes the walls as "a visual bombardment of images" (Tarr, 2001, p. 1) plagued with primary colors and simplified, flat figures that are cartoonish or of greeting card quality. Children's work in these environments is often displayed on brightly colored backgrounds with commercially made borders. Other walls are crowded with items such as large calendars, weather charts, ABCs, and number lines. Rather than reflecting the culture and society, this is an environment that would only be found in a school or childcare setting. Tarr (2004), in another article, discusses how this type of environment can silence children. "The mass of commercial stereotyped images silence the actual lived experiences of those individuals learning together. An overload of commercial materials leaves little room for work created by the children—another kind of silencing. Finally, children are muffled when what is displayed does not accurately reflect who they are in terms of gender, culture, and ethnicity but rather in stereotyped ways" (Tarr, 2004, p. 3). Olds (2001) also emphasizes the need to avoid stereotyped images, specifically mentioning Disney, television, and fairy tale characters. She states that they "tend to be 'Cutesy' and are often used to make a place appear child-oriented when everything else is not" (Olds, 2001, p. 248).

Purpose of Displays. When planning how to use wall space, teachers must think about the purpose of the display. Displays can provide an impetus for imagination and creativity, expose children to beauty, spark interest in a topic, and become interactive learning materials. Most important, walls form the backdrop for children's work and photos. Displays tell children that they are valued learners who belong in this environment or that they are not (Cheryan, Aiegler, Plaut, & Meltzoff, 2014).

Provide Inspiration. Pictures can provide inspiration, thereby promoting children's learning. For example, when Tessa placed pictures of different famous architectural buildings on the wall in the block center, children in her preschool classroom went from creating basic wooden constructions to creating elaborate block structures. Mrs. Sampson hung a selection of flower paintings by Georgia O'Keeffe, exposing children to a beautiful display and also providing inspiration. As a result, the kindergarten children began painting flower pictures. The children's artwork was also used to create a display.

Allow for Vertical Learning Surfaces. Walls and bulletin boards can become interactive displays or "vertical learning environments" (Readdick & Bartlett, 1995). For example, Lisa a teacher in a toddler program used two posters of children showing a variety of different emotions to create an activity. She made a matching game by cutting up one of the posters and adding Velcro. In an elementary school, a teacher used the bulletin board to create a display titled "100 Ways to Use a Plastic Bag." As children thought of new ideas, they wrote them on cards that they added to the board.

Display Children's Work. And, of course, walls are used to display children's work. It is important to display children's products respectfully, with the primary focus on the creation itself. You must be careful not to overpower the child's creation with the border and background (Tarr, 2004). In some preschools and elementary schools, each child is given an individual space on the classroom wall to display his choice of work. This allows children to choose what they want to highlight, while allowing them to learn about design and experiment with creating attractive displays. The Learning and Belonging (LAB) preschool uses a different approach. Rather than hanging up all the children's artwork, they have three frames hung on their bulletin board. Children's artwork rotates through these frames. The teachers believe that displaying all the children's work at once, even when the work is individualized, diminishes the work of each individual child. The three focus pictures contain varying media and subjects, highlighting the uniqueness of each child's work.

Provide Images of Children, Families, and Staff. Walls should also contain photos of current children, families, and staff. Photos demonstrate the importance we place on each of these groups, provide documentation, allow for revisiting and reflection on experiences, and provide an avenue to learn about each other.

Photos can be included in a variety of ways. Pictures of current children participating in relevant activities may be hung in the different learning centers. Instead of purchased posters, current children's pictures can be used to illustrate handwashing steps or the daily schedule. Photos of the artist may be displayed with the child's artwork. One program makes a family quilt each year that displays pictures of the children and their families. Parents and children choose photos to include. These often contain the family pet, favorite places, and their homes. Many programs provide framed photos and short biographic sketches of the teachers in the program to help families identify and get to know staff better.

Pictures for children should be hung at their eye level. For example, very low bulletin boards covered with Plexiglas can contain pictures at the eye level of infants and toddlers. The Plexiglas protects the pictures while allowing children the opportunity for a close look.

Avoid Visual Bombardment. It is also important to avoid having too many items on the walls. When the walls are crowded with materials, even if they are appropriate items, it can create a visual sensory bombardment. Research on kindergarten children show that this can decrease engagement, increase time off task, and result in fewer learning gains (Fisher, Godwin, & Seltman, 2014). Additionally, children may have trouble finding pertinent information when the walls are cluttered. Items that are intended for the children need to be hung at their eye level. If hung too high, materials add to visual clutter while serving no useful purpose.

Walls in early childhood programs have the potential to become overcrowded because of the multiple users, such as teachers, assistants, children, and administrators. To help decide what is placed on walls, it is helpful to develop a set of guiding principles. See Figure 6.1 to see guiding principles created by one program.

FIGURE 6.1 Guiding Principles for Wall Usage

The Learning and Belonging (LAB) preschool at the University of Montana have developed guiding principles for materials placed on the wall. They must be:

- authentic-materials are considered more authentic if they are related to the children in the group or the activities that they are engaged in. For example, a photo of a current child building a block structure is considered more authentic than a picture from a book.
- have a defendable purpose—a sound rationale for why this needs to be on the wall.
- provide a balance of form and function–is the space worth the function it will provide. For example, large birthday calendars are often found on early childhood walls. The form or space occupied by the large display might not be an appropriate balance. Instead, there could be a special class birthday book, with a page for each child containing a current picture, baby picture, birth date, and a list or picture of some favorite things.
- be current—reflect the current children and adults in the group.

Floors and Different Surface Levels

Flooring Materials. A variety of flooring materials provides children the opportunity to learn through comparing and contrasting. For example, how fast will a toy truck roll on a rug versus a wooden floor? Floor surfaces can be flat or inclined, rough or smooth (Trancik & Evans, 1995, p. 49). They can be made from a variety of materials. While in the past wall-to-wall carpeting was a popular flooring choice, many programs today are installing linoleum, tile, or wood floors. Teachers then add area rugs where soft surfaces are desired. Throw rugs of different types of materials add variety to the setting and can reflect the culture of the community (bamboo mats, braided rugs, hand-woven rugs, cotton rag rugs, or Oriental rugs). Rugs allow for more flexibility in arranging space, are easier to clean, and are more eco-healthy than wall-to-wall carpeting. The Eco-Healthy Child Care endorsement, developed in Oregon, includes elimination of wall-to-wall carpeting as one of their criteria (Children's Environmental Health Network, 2010). In installing wall-to-wall carpeting, toxic glues and adhesives are used. It is more difficult to clean carpets than a hard surface, which allows the build-up of pesticides and other materials that are carried on children's and adults' shoes. Carpets can also harbor allergens, including mold and mildew.

Experts recommend that floors be neutral colors (Ceppi & Zini, 1998). Torelli (2002) urges programs to avoid teaching rugs such as ABC rugs or number rugs because they add to the visual clutter.

Varied Surface Levels. Different surface levels can help to differentiate space, reduce noise levels, add interest to the room, create intimate areas, allow a new view, increase usable space, provide gross motor activity, and help children to feel powerful. You can create different surface levels using lofts, risers and stages, platforms, and recessed areas. Each of these allows for a variety of possibilities. For example, lofts can be equipped with rope ladders, stairs, fire poles, knotted ropes to climb, ramps and slides, ball rolls (like a marble roll), and buckets and pulleys to transport items into the loft.

Lofts can also be used for a variety of purposes. In one elementary classroom, children and the teacher developed a constitution regarding loft usage and rules. The loft became a mini-library, a performing stage, a place for private conferences, a puppet stage, and an area for small-group work at various times throughout the year (George, 1995). In another classroom, each child receives the use of the loft for one week. During this week, the child decorates the loft and chooses how the loft is used. In a K–3 multigrade classroom, the loft became a space ship, with instruments created by the children. Both creating the spaceship and engaging in dramatic play within the spaceship reinforced the information they were learning in their space unit. One preschool program built small lofts by modifying bunk beds. These cozy lofts, which increase the space in the small classroom, are just the right size for one or two children. When planning lofts, examine your state's licensing regulations and make sure you comply with safety standards of the American Society for Testing and Materials (ASTM).

Julie Bullard

A puppet stage in the bottom of the loft and a reading area above provide an appealing literacy environment to these kindergarten children.

Our ceilings, walls, and floors become our design palettes, allowing us to personalize our classroom space. However, remember that these are not the central focus, but are the backdrop for children's play, materials, and displays. What are other criteria we need to consider when we design classrooms? We must also make sure that our rooms are healthy and safe. We will examine this next.

Check Your Understanding 6.3
Click here to gauge your understanding of section concepts.

Special Design Considerations

As we design our early childhood programs, it is also important that we plan for emotional and physical health and safety. In this section, we will examine how we design environments to improve air quality, reduce pesticides, decrease density, and control noise. Why is this important?

1. Both teachers and children deserve to be in environments that are healthy and safe, where they do not become sick due to building conditions.
2. As there is increasing pressure to increase learning and raise achievement scores, it is wise to look at how the environment affects this. Many recent studies reveal a link between these building conditions and children's achievement and attendance even after controlling for other variables (21st Century School Fund, 2009). For example, research indicates that when children are in better facilities they score 5–17 points higher on standardized achievement tests (Young et al., 2003, p. vii). Placing children in the best environment versus the worse environment could impact their progress as much as an additional year of schooling (Barrett, Zhang, Moffat, & Kobbacy, 2013).
3. Teacher satisfaction and retention are also affected by building conditions. In one multicity study, 30% of teachers in schools they rate C or lower were considering leaving the teaching profession. This increased to 40% for those teaches who have experienced health issues as a result of the building conditions (Schneider, 2003).
4. Many early childhood programs have poor quality facilities. For example, over half of all U.S. public schools need money to bring them up to a good condition. Children from lower income backgrounds are more likely to be in inadequate buildings (Cheryan, Ziegler, Plaut, & Meltzoff, 2014).

In this section we will examine indoor air quality, pesticides, crowding, and noise levels.

Improving Air Quality

When we think about designing environments, we must consider indoor air quality (IAQ). Poor IAQ is listed as one of the top five environmental risks. Indoor air pollutants are often up to 100 times higher than those found outside (EPA, 2009). Schools and childcare programs pose a special risk due to having a greater concentration of people per square foot and the tendency to be housed in older buildings. The EPA states that one-half of our nation's 115,000 schools have problems linked to indoor air quality. Children who are from racial minority groups and/or from families who are low income are disproportionately affected by poor air quality since they often are in home and school environments with high levels of both indoor and outdoor pollutants (Schneider, 2002).

Impact of Poor Air Quality. Poor air quality can cause and contribute to both long-term and short-term health problems, increased absenteeism, and poorer student performance (EPA, 2009; Mendell & Heath, 2005). Because children breathe more air per body weight than adults, they are often more adversely affected (Kennedy, 2001). Poor air quality can also cause upper respiratory infections, nausea, dizziness, headaches, fatigue, allergic reactions, and irritated eyes, nose, and throat (EPA, 2009; Schneider, 2002). It also contributes to asthma, resulting in American children missing 14.4 million days of school a year (ALA, 2014; Schneider, 2002). As might be expected, indoor air quality is linked to children's test scores.

Improving Air Quality. How can we design our classrooms and buildings to improve air quality in early childhood settings?

- Reduce harmful **contaminants** by using "green" building materials, cleaning supplies, and grooming products and by eliminating carpets.
- Keep humidity between 40% and 70%. High humidity causes mold, contributing to poor indoor air quality and allergic reactions, while low humidity reduces children's natural mucus, one of their lines of defense against illness.
- Ensure adequate ventilation either by opening windows or through ventilation systems. In one study of 100 classrooms, 87 had below the recommended levels of ventilation. The study revealed an association between classroom ventilation rates and students' academic achievement. For every unit increase in the ventilation rate, nearly 3% more students pass the math and reading achievement tests (Haverinen-Shaughnessy, Moschandreas, & Shaughnessy, 2011).

Watch the video to learn more about indoor air quality. How does air quality affect achievement?

https://www.youtube.com/watch?v=8QxdcORr-1M

Reducing Pesticides

As we create our environmental designs, we must also consider ways to reduce the use of **pesticides**. Like air quality, pesticides are listed as one of the top five environmental threats to children (Mott, 1997).

Impact of Pesticide Exposure. Pesticide exposure can cause coughs, shortness of breath, nausea, vomiting, headaches, and eye irritation (NIOSH, 2007, p. 1). There is also concern about long-term damage. For example, chlorpyrifos, the most investigated ingredient in insecticides, is known to destroy neurons, affect the migration of neural cells, and reduce the connections among brain cells. This is especially alarming because even small changes in brain architecture can cause problems in learning, attention, and emotional control (National Scientific Council on the Developing Child, 2006, p. 4). If children are exposed to pesticides, they are also more prone to have cancer, neurodevelopment impairment, immune dysfunction, and reproductive problems in adulthood (National Research Council, 1993; NIOSH, 2007).

Methods of Exposure. Children are exposed to pesticides through inhaling contaminated air, by eating or drinking contaminated food, by skin absorption from handling contaminated materials, and from contamination on the child's hands that comes in contact with the mouth (Wilson, Chuang, Lyu, Menton, & Morgan, 2003). Pesticides can also be tracked in on shoes and deposited on floors and carpets in early childhood settings. This is especially harmful for young children who play on the floor and breathe the dust that is contaminated or have hand-to-mouth contact.

Watch the video to learn more about integrated pest management. Why is it important to be able to identify pests?

https://www.youtube.com/watch?v=6TSJaDtqAeY

Reducing Pesticide Exposure. What can you do? There are several steps that can be taken to reduce children's exposure to both pests and pesticides in schools and childcare settings. While it is important to control pests because they may inflict painful bites, spread disease, and cause allergic reactions, many programs are accomplishing this through implementing integrated pest management (IPM). See Figure 6.2 to learn more about IPM.

To prevent pesticides from entering classrooms on shoes, some programs place rugs at outside doors and encourage everyone entering to wipe their shoes. In many programs

FIGURE 6.2
Integrated Pest Management

Integrated pest management (IPM) uses the following progressive steps. In many cases, it is not necessary to move beyond step one.

1. Identify pests and try to eliminate them through prevention.
   a. Block their access to the building by placing screens on all the windows and plugging all holes where pests might enter.
   b. Eliminate pests' access to food, water, and shelter by removing crumbs and emptying all garbage cans regularly.
2. Use nonchemical methods such as traps or power washing.
3. Use the least toxic chemical available, and use targeted spot treatments rather than whole-building treatments or treatments based on a predetermined schedule.

teachers and children remove shoes when they are in the classroom. This is especially critical in infant and toddler classrooms.

Decreasing Crowding or Density

Another aspect that you will want to consider in designing environments is **density**. While air quality and pesticide exposure affect physical health, high density can affect both physical and emotional health.

Impact of High Density. Density levels or the number of children per square foot of space can have profound effects upon children and adults. High density levels increase aggression and destructive behavior in some children, while leading to withdrawal in other children (Kantrowitz & Evans, 2004; Maxwell, 1996). Additionally, research shows that children in high-density classrooms engage in more solitary play, have fewer positive social interactions, display shorter attention spans, and have lower levels of achievement (Evans, 2001; Kantrowitz & Evans, 2004; Legrendre, 2003; Maxwell, 2003). High density levels can also increase stress. For example, one study found that when toddlers had less than 54 square feet each for play, their cortisol levels (a stress hormone) increased (Legendre, 2003). This is especially worrisome since frequent or extended periods of stress are linked to developmental problems (Shonkoff & Phillips, 2000).

Crowding can be especially detrimental for children with special needs, for example children who have ADHD or anxiety (Kantrowitz & Evans, 2004; Loo & Kennelly, 1979). The behavioral effects of high density in early childhood programs are magnified when children also experience crowding in homes (Maxwell, 1996).

Although many state standards require 35 square feet per child, many design experts recommend a minimum of 50 square feet (White & Stoecklin, 2003). For example, the GSA National Standards for Child Care Facilities, the United States Department of Defense, the Head Start Technical Assistance Centers, and the Easter Seal Child Development Centers all recommend 45 to 50 square feet per child.

Reducing Density. It is important to begin with an adequate sized space. It is also important to carefully design the space you have.

- Free space through removing unnecessary furniture and using smaller furniture.
- Provide adult storage options that do not take floor space such as high enclosed shelves.
- Divide your group and have half of the children in outdoor centers, while the other half are in indoor centers.
- Ensure all learning centers are being used.

- Add a loft.
- Use all available spaces such as halls and closets (after doors are removed).
- Make sure that spaces are multipurpose (the cubby room is also a center).

Impact of Low Density. While high density is often the concern in early childhood programs, low density can also be an issue, causing more onlooking behavior and less interaction between children (Smith & Connolly, 1986). Programs experiencing reduced interaction due to a large space may want to block off sections of the room to increase the density.

Limiting Noise

Like high density, excessive noise can have physical and emotional ramifications. Although it is difficult, it is important that we reduce noise in early childhood facilities. Noise level is affected by both the background noise and the reverberation in the room. Noise may come from equipment such as projectors in the classroom, heating and air-conditioning units, malfunctioning fluorescent lights, and adjacent indoor and outdoor spaces. Hard surfaces, walls that do not reach the ceiling, and high ceilings also contribute to noise (Maxwell & Evans, 1999). In addition, because children and furniture are close to the floor in early childhood classrooms, 50% of a room's volume is empty. This allows noise to travel unimpeded and increases reverberation (Olds, 2001, p. 182). However, while noise can come from outside sources, the major source of noise is the children themselves (Shield & Dockrell, 2003). Several studies have found that even when children are engaged in quiet activities, the noise level in classrooms is typically high enough to interfere with speech development, understanding of language, and letter/number recognition (Kryter, 1985; Maxwell & Evans, 2000; Shield & Dockrell, 2003).

Impact of Noise. There is growing concern about children's exposure to noise, with 25% of 8- to 10-year-olds in the United States exhibiting some hearing loss (Kilgore, 2005). While many teachers realize that high noise levels can cause hearing loss, there is also a need to regulate lower levels of noise. Lower levels of noise can negatively affect memory, attention, use of language, and academic achievement, especially reading and speech development (Evans & Maxwell, 1997; Maxwell & Evans, 1999, 2000). For example, children in quieter preschool classrooms have higher attentional levels and higher levels of language skills, and they perform better on language tests (Maxwell & Evans, 2000). Exposure to noisy environments also leads to elevated stress levels and increased blood pressure (American Academy of Pediatrics et al., 2011; Evans, Hygge, & Bullinger, 1995).

While noise levels impact all learners, they pose a greater threat to those learners with visual, hearing, or central nervous system disabilities (Doctoroff, 2001). For example, hearing aids may amplify all noises, including background noises, making it more difficult to hear relevant speech in a noisy room.

Noise and **reverberation** have a greater impact on younger children's listening comprehension and speech perception than on older children or adults (Klatte, Lachmann, & Meis, 2010). These findings are especially troublesome when one considers the rapid pace of learning in the early childhood years.

Noise also affects teachers, causing additional emotional and physical stress and affecting relationships. Due to being in noisier environments, both childcare and elementary teachers have a higher incidence of voice disorders than colleagues in other professions (Sala, Laine, Simberg, Pentti, & Suonpää, 2001; Teisler & Oberdorster, 2008). High noise levels can also impact psychosocial well-being in teachers. Teachers in classrooms with higher levels of noise display increased withdrawal and disruptions in personal relationships (Grebennikov & Wiggins, 2006).

Noise Reduction. To reduce negative impacts, at least 80% of the time, noise levels need to be below 35 decibels. This is the level where a person can be clearly understood in a normal conversation without raising her voice level (American Academy of Pediatrics et al., 2011).

To reduce noise:

- Incorporate soft elements into the room like area rugs, pillows, and curtains.
- Keep equipment in good repair, and only use equipment when necessary.
- Add ceiling materials that absorb sound such as acoustical ceiling tiles or ceiling hangings.
- Cover walls and backs of bookcases with rough, soft, or porous surfaces like acoustical panels, cork board, textured wall hangings, divider drapes, or carpet.
- Decrease reverberation by using partitions, different ceiling heights, lofts, and climbers.
- Provide earphones for music devices and computers.
- Reconsider background music: Instead of reducing noise, it may increase noise as children and teachers talk over it.
- Teach children to use the right voice level for the occasion. For example, use a visual noise meter with a dial for no voices, buddy voices (only heard by the person next to me), table voices (heard at a table full of children), and classroom voices (heard across the room).
- Model using a low voice. When teachers speak quietly, children often do so as well

Check Your Understanding 6.4

Click here to gauge your understanding of section concepts.

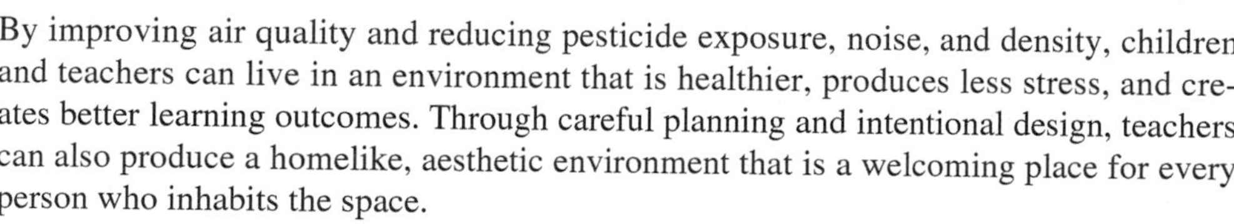

TIP

While acoustical tiles can be expensive, teachers can make their own soundproofing panels by covering fiberboard with eggshell foam and then adding fabric (Wien, Coates, Keating, & Bigelow, 2005).

By improving air quality and reducing pesticide exposure, noise, and density, children and teachers can live in an environment that is healthier, produces less stress, and creates better learning outcomes. Through careful planning and intentional design, teachers can also produce a homelike, aesthetic environment that is a welcoming place for every person who inhabits the space.

Chapter Quiz 6

Click here to gauge your understanding of chapter concepts.

Sample Application Activities

1. Examine a variety of pictures from architectural magazines. What mood does each environment evoke? Compare your reactions to other pictures. Determine what specific characteristics of the environment create the mood you are experiencing.
2. Review the YouTube video from Bambini Creativi, a Reggio-inspired preschool in Kansas City, Missouri, to critique the design elements that they are using in their center.

FIGURE 6.3
Environmental Assessment: Design Considerations

- ❑ Is the environment homelike?
  - ❍ welcoming
  - ❍ divided into usable space for different functions
  - ❍ includes private places to escape
  - ❍ includes places for people to gather together
  - ❍ provides comfortable furniture and different types of seating
  - ❍ filled with real, functional items (dishes, pottery, pots and pans, tools)
  - ❍ contains objects that have personal meaning such as framed art and collections of natural items (seashells, rocks)
  - ❍ filled with images of the inhabitants through photos and mirrors
  - ❍ includes living things; plants, flowers, animals
- ❑ Is the environment aesthetic?
  - ❍ beautiful
  - ❍ clutter free
  - ❍ sensory rich
  - ❍ thoughtfully organized
  - ❍ attention given to detail
- ❑ Does the environment reflect the inhabitants of the program (lives, families, culture, ethnicity, geographic location, interests)?
- ❑ Are there ways that children can personalize the environment?
- ❑ Is there an abundance of natural lighting coming from at least two directions?
- ❑ Are distinctive atmospheres created through different types of lighting (track, pendant, recessed, dimmer controlled, lamps)?
- ❑ Are natural items incorporated into the environment?
- ❑ Does the environment contain a variety of soft elements?
- ❑ Are a variety of textures found in the room?
- ❑ Are neutral or pale colors used for most walls and shelving?
- ❑ Are there focal points in the environment?
- ❑ Do the walls contain a few carefully chosen items, or is there a visual bombardment of images?
- ❑ Are materials on the wall authentic and related to the current group of children?
- ❑ Is there a defendable purpose and a balance of form and function for each of the items that are on the wall?
- ❑ Are there different surface levels in the classroom (lofts, risers)?
- ❑ Is the flooring a neutral color?
- ❑ Is there a variety of flooring surfaces?
- ❑ Does the program use integrated pest management?
- ❑ Does the program use practices that enhance indoor air quality?
- ❑ Is there a minimum of 50 square feet of space per child in the classroom?
- ❑ Is all the available space being used (unless there is low density)?
- ❑ Are children distributed evenly throughout the space during center time?
- ❑ Can individuals be clearly heard and understood in a normal conversation without raising their voices?

3. Visit an early childhood environment and analyze the environment using the environmental design checklist found in Figure 6.3.
4. Develop a list of criteria that will govern what is placed on the walls of your current or future early childhood program.
5. Brainstorm a list of interactive bulletin board ideas for children of different ages.
6. Visit an early childhood classroom and pay special attention to the noise level. What steps is the teacher taking to reduce the noise level? What additional steps could she take?
7. Learn more about reducing noise level by visiting the Quiet Classrooms website.

8. To learn more about design, visit the National Clearinghouse for Educational Facilities.
9. Investigate one of the following websites to learn more about environmental issues affecting children and strategies to ensure our environments are healthy:
   - Oregon's Eco-Healthy Child Care
   - EPA Indoor Air Quality in Schools
   - National Resource Center for Health and Safety in Child Care
   - Early Education National School IPM
10. Examine the air quality and pesticide regulations in your early childhood state licensing standards.

CHAPTER 7

Developing Dramatic Play Centers

Learning Outcomes

After you have read this chapter, you will be prepared to:

- Describe the development of play skills
- Discuss how the dramatic play center enhances children's development
- Design effective indoor and outdoor dramatic play centers
- Explain how to design dramatic play centers for different age groups
- Describe multiple ways that teachers facilitate learning in the dramatic play center

Julie Bullard

Christine Ferguson, a teacher of kindergarten children, took her class to visit a pet store. The store manager gave the children a tour of the store, discussing the different pets. The children helped to feed the pets and observed their different habitats, behaviors, and eating habits. In many cases, this would have concluded the visit. However, Christine had asked the store manager to show the children different aspects of a pet store employee's job, especially as it related to literacy. The store manager showed the children the store signs, labels, coupons, price tags, and the pet books they sold in the store. She described and demonstrated how the cash register worked and showed how she wrote receipts for the customer.

At the conclusion of the visit, she gave the children a variety of items (blank store signs, flyers, coupons, store sacks) so they could create their own classroom pet store. After the visit, the children helped to design a pet store in their dramatic play center. The children played in the center for several weeks, reenacting what they had seen in the pet store and extending it with their own ideas (Ferguson & McNulty, 2006).

This story illustrates several elements needed for creating a successful dramatic play center. The children shared a common first hand experience when they visited the pet shop. The visit allowed them to learn about pet stores and also about the work of the pet store employee. This shared experience helped children in developing the "scripts" they used in their sociodramatic play. Group dialogue and discussion during subsequent circle times extended their group knowledge about pets. Interest in the pet store was extended by having the children actually design the sociodramatic center. An abundance of props supported the children's play and also reminded them of different aspects of the pet store employee's role (e.g., making signs).

Dramatic play allows children to "become representers of their experiences" and also to create new imaginative realities (Brown, Sutterby, & Thornton, 2001, p. 1). This highly motivating activity has been linked to social, emotional, cognitive, and physical growth (Calabrese, 2003).

Development of Play Skills

Children's dramatic play ability is enhanced as their development allows them to use symbolic representation and to engage in cooperative play with others. Very young children under the age of two often need realistic objects for pretending. However, around the age of two they begin to use less realistic objects where an item might be a symbolic representation for something else (a block may be used for a telephone). By the age of three, most children are capable of pretending with imaginary objects and events even when props are not present (Elias & Berk, 2002).

The amount of social interaction in play also changes. Infants typically engage in **solitary play**, where they play alone. Between the ages of one and two, children begin to demonstrate reciprocal imitation during play (Shonkoff & Phillips, 2000). This is referred to as **parallel play**. They will imitate another child and then will build upon what the other child is doing, expanding their repertoire for acting out roles. For example, Paul and Samantha were cooking. Paul used a large spoon to stir the pretend mixture in his pot. Samantha imitated Paul with her own pot and spoon. She then got a small plate and used the spoon to put some mixture on the plate. Paul imitated Samantha by dishing the pretend mixture onto his plate. Toddler play is often characterized by repetitive activity, where children re-enact the same scene repeatedly. As children gain play experience they might begin **associative play**, where they begin to interact with others and share similar activities but do not engage in a single common endeavor.

During the preschool years, the number of players often expands (Frost, Wortham, & Reifel, 2012) and dramatic play becomes a cooperative activity where players work together to carry out a predefined theme (Smilansky & Shefatya, 1990). This is referred to as **cooperative play** or **sociodramatic play**. For play to be considered sociodramatic, several components must be present. The child must (a) engage in role-playing (pretends to be another person, animal, or object); (b) make believe with actions and objects;

(c) have verbal and social interaction with at least one other person to coordinate roles and plot; and (d) have a play theme that persists for 10 minutes or more (Smilansky & Shefatya, 1990). We once thought of these as stages of play. However, researchers now state that children may use multiple types of social interaction during one play episode depending upon play partners and length of play (Frost, Wortham, & Reifel, 2012).

Check Your Understanding 7.1

Click here to gauge your understanding of section concepts.

There are also cognitive categories of play. The categories of play vary depending upon the theorist. Smilansky (1968), who is well-known for her categorization of play that is based upon the work of Piaget, includes the following categories: **functional play** (repetitious play to learn about the physical characteristic of objects), **constructive play** (play that results in creating a structure or object), **sociodramatic play** (symbolic play), and **games with rules** (play based upon acceptance of agreed upon rules). Knowing the social and cognitive category of play that children are engaged in can assist you in providing an effective environment and props. In the next section, we will examine why sociodramatic play is important.

How the Dramatic Play Center Enhances Children's Development

"In the Vygotskian tradition, dramatic play is accorded a special place in the development of young children" (Bodrova, Leong, Hensen, & Henninger, 1999, p. 1). As stated by Vygotsky, "In play the child is always behaving beyond his age, above his usual everyday behavior; in play he is, as it were, a head above himself" (Vygotsky, 1978, p. 74). Play scaffolds or supports learning, providing the optimal context for development (Bodrova et al., 1999, p. 1). Dramatic play allows children to practice skills they learned in real-life situations, to assimilate information, and to try to make sense of it. While engaging in sociodramatic play, children gain literacy, self-regulatory, cognitive, social, emotional, and creative skills. These benefits are enhanced when children participate in mature dramatic play creating an imaginary situation, using language to create pretend scenarios, forming explicit roles and implicit rules, and enacting play for an extended time frame (Leong & Bodrova, 2012). For example, a recent study of children in 18 Head Start classrooms found that children's peer play increased over time and that higher levels of peer play in Head Start were linked to higher kindergarten school competence (Eggum-Wilkens et al., 2014).

Literacy Development

Sociodramatic play is an especially powerful medium for supporting literacy development. Play promotes oral language, as children become "storytellers of pretend events" (Brown et al., 2001). During sociodramatic play, children must negotiate play scripts and roles with their peers. They must also determine the meaning of props. In addition, they act out the role using different voices, inflections, and rich verbal exchanges (Elias & Berk, 2002). In this age of curriculum standards and accountability, some teachers and programs are adopting more teacher-directed activities to promote language skills. However, research indicates that this may be the wrong approach. A review of research suggests that narrative development (the ability to tell and comprehend stories) is enhanced by pretend play (Lillard et al., 2013). Additionally, when children participate in sociodramatic play, they use more elaborate narratives than when they are engaged in a more teacher-directed storytelling activity (Kim, 1999).

Watch the video on a kindergarten dramatic play center. How does the teacher encourage literacy in this center?

https://www.youtube.com/watch?v=PCOBKuwzDZU&list=PLg-YvqRj12PSpURfHZ2eBMu8DQMpr-9iW

Dramatic play also is important in reading and writing. To read or write, children must understand that the written word is a symbolic representation of an object or idea. Often, the first place that children encounter and understand symbolic representation is during dramatic play, when children use an item to stand for something else. In addition to this, dramatic play in an enriched environment allows children to practice writing and reading in an authentic, highly motivating context. For example, children playing restaurant might read menus, signs, and cookbooks. They might write orders, signs, recipes, and menus. As stated by Vivian Paley (2004), "fantasy play is the glue that holds together all other pursuits, including the teaching of reading and writing" (p. 8). Research shows a literacy-rich environment can increase the amount and range of children's literacy behaviours, knowledge of writing, and recognition of print (Christie & Roskos, 2009).

Julie Bullard

This child-created dramatic play area contains a child-decorated sign; an eating area complete with a tablecloth, flowers, and menus; and a waiting area complete with magazines to read. What does this area tell you about the children's concept of a restaurant?

Self-Regulation and Cognitive Development

Sociodramatic play may be especially important in the development of self-regulation, particularly for children who are impulsive (Elias & Berk, 2002). As discussed in Chapter 2, self-regulation is the ability to control one's emotions, actions, and thinking (Riley, San Juan, Klinkner, & Ramminger, 2008, p. 65). Self-regulation assists us in regulating our social and cognitive processes, allowing us to develop goals, make plans to achieve them, monitor our learning, implement our ideas and plans, and use reflection. According to Vygotsky (1978), dramatic play is the ideal arena for learning self-regulation, because it is a highly motivating activity to practice rule-bound behavior. In addition, the imaginary situation helps children to separate their thoughts and behaviors from what is going on around them and to use their internal ideas to guide their behavior. During dramatic play, children use self-regulation to keep the play script going, to be flexible with others, and to control themselves. Children also use more **private speech** (using self-talk to control behavior) while engaged in dramatic play than when playing in other classroom centers (Krafft & Berk, 1998). Private speech is associated with self-regulation.

Watch the video about Vygotsky and play.

https://www.youtube.com/watch?v=bulTeiHu8ME

In addition to the development of self-regulatory skills, dramatic play allows children authentic opportunities to use many other cognitive skills. For example, one study that examined the dramatic play of 18-month-old to four-year-old children found that they used a variety of everyday mathematics skills while playing. These skills included using spatial awareness, classification, fractions ("half for you and half for me"), counting, simple addition and subtraction, patterns, and geometrical knowledge (Lee, 2007). Dramatic play, like art and writing, is a way that children represent their knowledge.

Play appears to be circular, meaning that those who are intellectually competent participate in more advanced play. Advanced play leads to greater intellectual competence, creativity, and problem solving (Trawick-Smith, 2014).

Social Development

Dramatic play allows children to practice social skills and to "gain culturally valued competencies" (Elias & Berk, 2002, p. 219). Researchers have found that children participate in more complex social interactions in dramatic play than in other centers in

Julie Bullard

Note the diverse array of breads (matzo, French bread, croissants, pita, bagels, pretzels, braided). Also, examine the way that this grocery center is organized.

the classroom (Petrakos & Howe, 1996). While playing in this area, children negotiate roles, take turns, and resolve interpersonal relationships. Through their negotiations and discussions, they begin to understand their own and others' family and cultural beliefs, practices, and values. For example, Tina and Sylvia were role-playing cooking and eating a meal. Tina said, "Let's pretend the bookcase is a TV." Sylvia was confused about why they needed a television for their meal. This exchange led to a discussion about the differences in mealtime at their two homes. As illustrated by this example, "children bring to the play experience their cultural background and lifestyle as sources of information" (Kostelnik et al., 2012, p. 199). During dramatic play, children also take on the roles of others, allowing them to gain an understanding of the role, experience another's perspective, develop empathy, and engage in rehearsal for life.

Emotional Development

Dramatic play can act as a cathartic release (a way to discharge emotion). It also allows children to act out fears and traumatic events in a safe environment. Through play, children have the power to control what happens and to change the endings if they wish. They can practice solving dilemmas and use play as a form of communication. For example, they can "use toys to say things they cannot verbalize, to do things they would otherwise feel uncomfortable doing, and to express feelings and emotions they might be reprimanded for expressing in other contexts" (Brown et al., 2001).

Creative Development

Through dramatic play, children practice skills needed for creativity. For example, children use their imagination for fantasy and make believe. The quality of the child's pretend play is also linked to the child's ability to use **divergent thinking** (generate multiple ideas), which is another aspect of creativity (Russ, Robins, & Christiano, 1999). While using the dramatic play center, children also use drama skills such as developing scripts and assuming roles. They imitate others' mannerisms, language, and behavior, and often use materials and props in creative ways.

Check Your Understanding 7.2

Click here to gauge your understanding of section concepts.

Dramatic play provides rich opportunities for children to develop literacy, cognitive, self-regulation, social, emotional, and creative skills. As Christine in our opening scenario demonstrated, we can enhance children's dramatic play by establishing an effective dramatic play center.

Designing Effective Indoor and Outdoor Dramatic Play Centers

Although children participate in dramatic play even with few props, we can enrich their experiences with thoughtfully designed environments. To assist children in achieving optimal development, the dramatic play needs to be available on a daily basis. Teachers must also effectively arrange and supply the center to provide rich experiences.

Designing Effective Indoor Dramatic Play Centers

An effective indoor dramatic play center has the following characteristics:

- A well-defined area such as a separated corner of the room. Some experts suggest a special entry to the play area such as an arch to set it apart from other classroom centers (Pardee, 2005). You might also think about the ceiling height. Research shows that children participate in more cooperative play when the ceiling height is lower (Read, Sugawara, & Brandt, 1999). Some teachers use cloth drapes in the dramatic play area to lower ceilings and to further define the play space.
- Sufficient space for at least four to six children to play.
- Located next to the block area to increase the interaction between the two centers. For example, children at Bright Beginnings took a bus ride as part of a transportation unit. Marlis, the teacher, placed bus driver uniforms and hats in the dramatic play center. The children donned the hats and uniforms and decided they needed a bus. They went to the block area, used the large hollow blocks to create the bus, and then commenced to role-play.
- Familiar and authentic items that allow children to represent their experiences. For example, in Reggio Emilia centers children use the same pottery and dishware that they would find in their homes. The dramatic play center also contains real food that would be found in kitchens, such as dried beans and pasta in different shapes (Gandini, 1984, p. 19; see controversy about using food for play on p. 267). Adding materials that children can use for "cooking" can often enhance their play. At Birge Nest, an infant/toddler classroom, the teachers moved the sandbox into the dramatic play area. They also added play dough. The children's play included more social interaction, was more in-depth, and lasted for a longer period of time after these items were added. Several children who had previously not played in this area began to participate.
- Materials that reflect all the members of the classroom—children with disabilities, from all types of family groupings, and from all ethnic and cultural backgrounds. It is also important to ensure that both boys' and girls' interests are promoted through the center theme and materials.
- Materials that represent many cultures (even those that are not in the classroom). One way to include different cultural materials is to ask families in the classroom to donate items they are not using. For example, when one teacher asked families to bring in materials, she received a bamboo steamer and a Chinese tea set from one family. You might also receive donations from ethnic restaurants and stores. It is important to represent many cultures. "When teachers fail to include a wide variety of multicultural and nonsexist props in their dramatic play areas, they unconsciously reinforce monocultural ideas about how a business or home setting is 'supposed' to look" (Boutte, Scoy, & Hendley, 1996, p. 34).
- Clothing or pieces of fabric for children to create their own clothing. Clothing helps children "step into the role" (Bafile, 2004). Pieces of fabric allow children to create the clothing or prop that they need (a cape, sarong, turban, doll blanket, sling, tablecloth, tent). Some programs worry about clothing because of the possibility of spreading head lice. However, the CDC states that head lice are typically spread by direct head-to-head contact and it is uncommon for lice to be spread through clothing or personal items (CDC, 2013). As a precaution, many programs do eliminate clothing in the dramatic play center during a lice outbreak.
- Full-length mirrors so children can see themselves.
- A variety of props to support rich play opportunities. Props often suggest play themes; for example, a stethoscope in a doctor's kit will encourage listening to

each other's heartbeats. While less realistic toys or props result in more varied play, the play is often shorter in duration (Pellegrini, 1985). Real items are often sturdier and less expensive, and might do more than their play counterparts (Bafile, 2004). For example, when real stethoscopes rather than play stethoscopes were used, children had the opportunity to actually listen to each other's heartbeats. See Figure 7.1 for props that can be added to a home living center.

TIP

If you use life-sized baby dolls, you can supply the doll with an inexpensive wardrobe by using secondhand newborn baby clothes. You might obtain newborn baby clothing at thrift stores or garage sales, or through donations.

Julie Bullard

The tablemat, centerpiece, rug, baskets, curtains, and draped fabric all combine to make this an aesthetic dramatic play environment. The saying on the wall and the masks invite children to try on a new identity in this aesthetic dramatic play center.

- Duplicates of props (shopping carts, doll strollers) so children can participate in parallel play. This is particularly important for younger children.
- Authentic math props. In a home living area, you might find a calendar on the wall, watches in the jewelry box, clocks, receipt books, calculators, cell phones, and food items that are sorted and classified in the cupboard.
- Authentic and appropriate literacy props. In a home living area, you might add cookbooks in the kitchen area; notepads, pens, and a telephone book by the telephone; magazines by the child-size couch; recipe cards with pictures and words and blank recipe cards for children to create their own recipes; grocery list paper; store coupons; and empty checkbooks.
- Loose parts so children can develop what they need. For example, rug samples, blankets, boxes, and boards can become magic carpets, forts, or doghouses with some imagination.
- Ways to make clothing and prop choices available and organized. For example, you might include hooks or hangers for clothing, a labeled basket or hat rack for hats, coat racks for displaying purses, and a jewelry box for jewelry. Baby clothes and props can be placed in a chest of drawers with picture and word labels. Outlines made from contact paper can be placed in the cupboard so children know where dishes and pots and pans belong. As children put items away, not only does the area stay neat, but children are also practicing one-to-one correspondence and classification.
- Needed equipment such as a stove, fridge, sink, cupboard, tables, and chairs. While wooden equipment is more expensive than plastic, it is typically more aesthetic and durable. You will want to ensure that the equipment is the proper size for the age group.

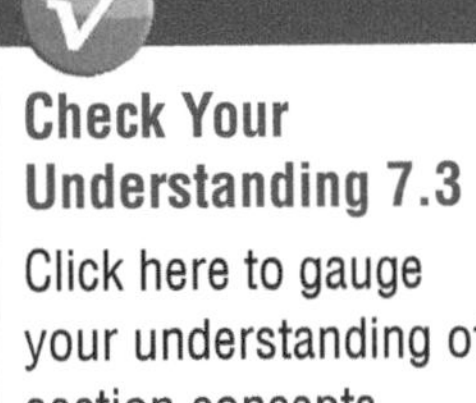

Check Your Understanding 7.3

Click here to gauge your understanding of section concepts.

FIGURE 7.1
Teresa's Home Living Center

At the beginning of the school year, many teachers establish a home living center in the dramatic play area. Teresa, a teacher of preschool children, sent a note to parents before the school year and began asking them for empty food boxes, clothing, baby items, utensils, pictures, magazines, and other items that would represent their culture. With the parents' assistance, Teresa began the year by providing dramatic play props representing the cultures in her classroom. This allowed the children to participate in dramatic play using some familiar props and introduced them to their classmates' cultures. When the children started school, they were excited to find items in the classroom that they had in their homes and were proud to show other children how to use the materials. As children became familiar with these materials, Teresa slowly began introducing and adding materials from cultures that were not represented in the classroom. She also drew on the children's background knowledge and elicited their ideas to help plan materials to add to the area. For example, when one of the boys in her room suggested that they needed materials for pets, several other children agreed. So pet props were added to the area. Following is a list of materials that Teresa had in her dramatic play center:

- ❑ Child-size furniture, including tables and chairs, cozy chair, couch, rocking chair, stove, fridge, sink, cupboard, closet, chest of drawers, and hat rack
- ❑ Child-sized broom, mop, and dustpan
- ❑ Sponge, dishtowels, and potholder by the play sink
- ❑ Mirrors (hand mirrors, full-length mirrors, and wall mirrors)
- ❑ Multicultural dolls, doll bed and doll basket, doll clothes (unisex), diapers, receiving blankets, doll toys, empty powder and shampoo containers, adaptive doll equipment, strollers, front baby packs, and baby slings
- ❑ Dress-up clothes for boys and girls, including clothing, shoes, and boots; two pairs of traditional Chinese children's shoes and a dragon pattern suit donated by a parent; used cowboy boots and cowboy hats from a family; and colorful sarapes donated by another family
- ❑ Jewelry boxes containing necklaces, earrings, rings, bracelets, eyeglasses, and sunglasses
- ❑ Briefcase, purse, billfold, keys, diaper bag, lunch box, tool belt, and suitcase
- ❑ Two real, nonworking phones with the children's names and phone numbers in a recipe file next to it
- ❑ Pets and pet props (water dish, dog bones, dog toys, and an empty container of dog food)
- ❑ Pots, pans, dishes, and utensils (small cast iron frying pan, wok, bamboo tongs, tortilla press, tortilla warmer, mortar and pestle, Mexican wood molinillo [chocolate stirrer], Chinese tea set, forks and spoons, chopsticks, and Chinese soup spoons)
- ❑ Play food and empty food containers (parents brought in empty cans, boxes, and spice containers, providing cultural variation)
- ❑ Placemats and tablecloths with real flowers (donated each week from a flower shop)
- ❑ Adaptive equipment (crutches and a wheelchair lent by a local business)
- ❑ Literacy props (Chinese, English, and Spanish newspapers and magazines; different ethnic cookbooks; and a phonebook and notepad near the phones)
- ❑ Clock hanging on the wall with a paper clock below it so that children could set the paper clock to match the real clock
- ❑ A separate sitting room with child-sized couches and chairs, a CD player, a magazine rack, plants, reading glasses, a table, a lamp, and a beautiful rug that a parent brought back from China when she visited her family

By involving the families, Teresa was able to set up a rich dramatic play area that was culturally relevant to the children in her classroom.

- An aesthetic environment. In our home environments, many of us strive to create an aesthetic environment that reflects our individual style. Many early childhood programs also strive to create aesthetic dramatic play areas using beautiful

Outdoor dramatic play is encouraged through providing props and materials. This golf cart is just the right size for children.

materials (copper pots and pans, china dishes, vases of flowers, plants, tablecloths, rugs, fabric, and throw pillows).

- Is dynamic, being changed or added to as needed to sustain rich play opportunities.

Designing Effective Outdoor Dramatic Play Centers

Dramatic play is often ignored when planning playgrounds (Brown et al., 2001). While dramatic play takes place on playgrounds even when specific places are not established, an encapsulated site increases the length and the depth of children's play (Frost, Wortham, & Reifel, 2012).

There are many potential dramatic play areas, including a lean-to, playhouse, grotto, platform, and even vehicles such as golf carts or old rowboats. Children can also help to create their own play sites. For example, children and adults can build snow caves, straw houses, sandbag houses, and forts. They can plant climbing peas or sunflowers to create an enclosed area. Creating huts and enclosures out of living willow is another way to create an enclosed dramatic play space.

Outdoor dramatic play can be enriched with natural materials found on the playground such as flowers, dirt, leaves, branches, and water. When natural materials are available, children often use the materials to maintain play episodes (Brown et al., 2001). Loose parts (boards, tarps, and blankets) can also extend play opportunities.

Special Considerations for Different Ages

Throughout the chapter, we have been focusing primarily on preschool children. While much of the information also applies to infants, toddlers, and school-aged children, this section will explore these age groups in more depth.

Dramatic Play for Infants and Toddlers

Infants are toy oriented. As children become toddlers, they become more people oriented (Leong & Bodrova, 2012). Children's early pretending is context driven and suggested by the objects that are available in the environment. To enhance their ability to make-believe, it is important that children have a range of materials that support pretending.

As with older children, toddlers practice adult roles as they play. As soon as children begin to walk, they need a dedicated area for dramatic play. It is important to have familiar centers (home living) and realistic props (pots and pans, baby dolls). Because sharing is difficult for infants and toddlers, it is crucial that there be duplicates of popular items. Duplicate items will also allow children to copy each other as they participate in parallel pretend play.

Many of the items that Teresa included in her home living center would be appropriate for infants and toddlers. However, in planning for this age group you will want to consider their development. Dress-up clothing and baby doll clothing need to be easy to get on and off with Velcro, large buttons, or elastic so that children can be successful. Jewelry and other materials need to be large enough to prevent a choking hazard. Also, consider children's interests in making your plans. Many toddlers enjoy pushing items, so baby buggies are popular. They enjoy equipment with knobs that actually turn and doors that open, so it is important that play equipment provides these options.

At this age, adults are often play partners or mentors. This is an important way that infant–teacher relationships are formed and enhanced (Jung, 2013). As such, adults might model play dialogue and use of props, make suggestions, encourage the child, and provide words for what the child is doing. The effective teacher matches the child's pace and allows the child to be the play leader when possible.

Dramatic Play for K–3rd Grade Children

As children become school-aged, they continue to participate in sociodramatic play. As with younger children, sociodramatic play can enhance children's literacy, self-regulation, and cognitive, social, emotional, and creative development. See Table 7.1 to examine how dramatic play can assist children to meet the Common Core Standards.

Table 7.1 Meeting Common Core Standards Through Dramatic Play

Sample Common Core Standards	How Dramatic Play Can Assist Children to Meet the Common Core Standards
Vocabulary acquisition and use With guidance and support from adults, explore word relationships and nuances in word meanings. a. Sort common objects into categories (e.g., shapes, foods) to gain a sense of the concepts the categories represent. c. Identify real-life connections between words and their use (e.g., note places at school that are *colorful*).	**Vocabulary acquisition and use** As children use a well-designed dramatic play center, they are categorizing different items such as play food, dishes, and clothing. As teachers make changes to the dramatic play center, children have the opportunity to have hands-on experience with new items and their use, assisting with vocabulary acquisition and use.
Comprehension and collaboration Participate in collaborative conversations with diverse partners about (kindergarten, grade 1, grade 2) topics and texts with peers and adults in small and larger groups. a. Follow agreed-upon rules for discussions. b. Continue a conversation through multiple exchanges. c. Ask questions to clear up any confusion about the topics and texts under discussion.	**Comprehension and collaboration** As children are using the dramatic play center, they are involved in a highly motivating activity that is reliant on collaborative conversations to negotiate play scripts and roles and to keep the script going.
Text types and purposes Write narratives in which they recount two or more appropriately sequenced events, include some details regarding what happened, use temporal words to signal event order, and provide some sense of closure. **Production and distribution of writing** With guidance and support from adults, children focus on a topic, respond to questions and suggestions from peers, and add details to strengthen writing as needed. With guidance and support from adults, children use a variety of digital tools to produce and publish writing.	**Text types and purposes, production and distribution of writing** In many 1st–3rd grade classrooms, children develop written narratives or stories to act out. As children get other children to act out their story, they receive authentic feedback about what works in the story and what does not, what makes sense to the audience and what does not, and what is missing in the story.

Source: © Copyright 2010. National Governors Association Center for Best Practices and Council of Chief State School Officers. All rights reserved.

Create Your Own Fairy Garden

Julie Bullard

Fairy gardens allow children to exercise their imagination and creativity, while engaging in microworld dramatic play. This fairy garden is unique because it combines mini versions of children along with the fairies, so that the children can become part of the story. Children can help to create the fairies, collect natural items, make accessories, and construct their garden.

Directions

1. Draw or have the children in your class draw fairies on cardstock-weight paper.
2. Take full-body photos of each of the children in the classroom and run the photos off on photo paper, making the photos a size comparable to the fairies.
3. Laminate the front only of each of the fairies and the children's photos.
4. Cut out the fairies and the children's photos.
5. Using craft glue, attach a wooden cabinet maker's biscuit to the back of each fairy and photo, with half of the biscuit below the subject's feet. You can buy the biscuits at hardware stores or home centers.
6. Fill a dish with at least two inches of sand. When the fairies and children are poked in the sand, they will be able to stand.
7. Collect natural items to create your fairy scene. You can sort the items into bowls or baskets and make them readily available so that children can easily re-create scenes. Provide mirrors or Mylar for water features.

Dramatic play can also support social study units. The study of historical events can come alive as children have the opportunity to dress up, use props, create props, and assume the role of someone from another time period.

As children reach school age organized games with rules become important and their sociodramatic play often changes to reflect this focus. I once witnessed children in an after-school program spend the entire hour of center time negotiating their play script. Fortunately, at this age they are also able to keep their scripts going over a longer period of time (Kostelnik et al., 2012). These children continued to organize their script over the next several days, eventually enacting it.

Check Your Understanding 7.4
Click here to gauge your understanding of section concepts.

While children in kindergarten will typically have a traditional dramatic play center, this may be replaced by a stage with clothing and props or by microworlds (such as a fairy garden) as children get older. On the stage or in their microworlds, children can create and reenact stories, movies, and their own narratives.

Teachers' Facilitation of Learning in the Dramatic Play Center

To promote high-quality dramatic play, teachers need to support children in creating play plans, maintaining play roles, using props in symbolic ways, using role speech, and developing the play scenario. Teachers can do this by planning effective centers; providing rich, shared experiences; building and maintaining excitement and interest in dramatic play; and facilitating children's play skills.

Provide Rich, Shared Experiences

A shared background of experiences can enrich children's dramatic play (Bodrova & Leong, 2007; Smilansky & Shefatya, 1990). Often this is accomplished through a field trip. Bodrova and Leong (2007) suggest that the adults you are visiting model the "actions, words, and social interactions" associated with the role (Bodrova & Leong, 2007, p. 148). They also recommend that several different roles be modeled to allow children to play out the script. It is important that children see people performing their roles and that the tour guide at the location is prepped for the age of the group of children you are bringing. It might be helpful to give the person a sense of what the children are interested in, questions they may have, and the depth of their current understanding. For example, if visiting a grocery store, it is important to see the variety of vegetables and also to see the produce manager unpacking the vegetables, cleaning them, setting up the display, creating signs, and describing how to sell the produce to an interested customer. You might help children remember the trip and the roles people play by having each person wear a distinctive article of clothing that represents what he or she does. For example, one classroom took a trip to a grocery store. The florist wore brightly colored gloves to keep thorns from poking her. The baker wore a tall baker's hat to keep flour out of his hair. The butcher wore an apron. The teacher then placed these props in the dramatic play center to remind children of the different roles at the grocery store. Children can also learn about roles from guest speakers, puppet shows, stories, and short videos.

Julie Bullard

This stage provides a backdrop for the fairy tales this group of children have been reenacting.

You might also use Vivian Paley's (2010) method of storytelling and story acting to help children to appreciate their own and others' stories. In this method, children dictate stories to the teacher with the teacher asking clarifying questions as she records. The children then dramatize their stories with children in the classroom taking on different roles from the story. As children engage in telling and dramatizing each other's stories, they collaborate and make sense of their world. As the YouTube videos written by a child illustrate, dramatized children's stories can also be made available to a wide audience. When we dramatize children's stories, we show that we value their storytelling. Writing down or recording children's stories also gives teachers the opportunity to reflect, question, discuss, and make meaning of children's play.

Julie Bullard

This center, designed by the teacher and the children after visiting a veterinary clinic, includes stuffed animals, a file for each animal, a cash register, phone, prescription pads, clothing, and veterinary props.

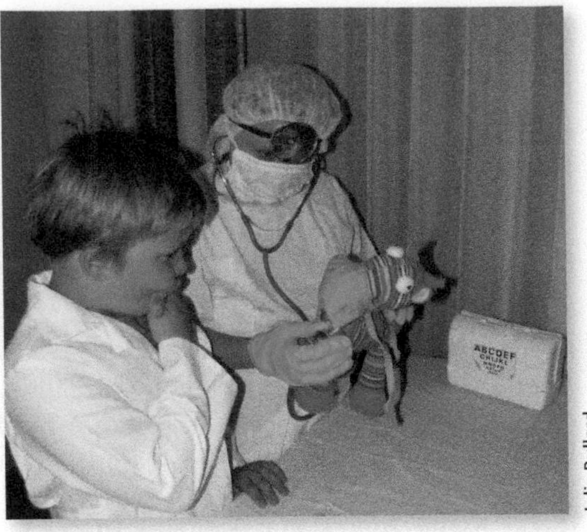

Julie Bullard

As illustrated in this picture, the veterinary center allows children to experiment with new roles.

Plan Centers That Encourage Active Engagement

When planning the dramatic play center, teachers must think about children's play opportunities. Each time you change the center or add new materials to the center, ask yourself the following questions:

- What will the children do in the center?
- What roles can be carried out?
- How do the props support the roles?
- Are the children knowledgeable about the roles?

Changes in the center need to lead to active engagement for children. For example, a student teacher spent many hours creating a dramatic play backdrop that included a fireplace, each brick having been drawn by hand. Much to the disappointment of the teacher, the children had no way of interacting with the backdrop, so they did not play in the area.

Build Excitement

Teachers can build children's excitement and interest in the center in many ways. For example, the teachers in the beginning scenario had children help to construct the center. In another program, the teacher built excitement in a grocery store by first setting out the grocery bags full of store items. Then she put out a sign stating "Grand Opening." On the opening day, a ceremony was held that included a ribbon cutting and free samples (Rybczynski & Troy, 1995, p. 9).

Keep Interest Alive Through Providing a Dynamic Center

The effective dramatic play center is rarely static. Instead it is dynamic, changing to meet children's interests and expand their learning. While the teacher is an observer who builds on children's interests by adding props and changing the center as needed, she also may at times be a protagonist. For example, the teacher who developed the grocery store kept children's interest alive by adding new store specials each week and continuing to

FIGURE 7.2
Dramatic Play Center Possibilities

Stores
Pet store
Farmers' market
Bakery
Flower shop
Grocery store
Shoe store
Music store
Restaurant
Pizza parlor
Clothing store

Community services
Bank
Post office
Hair salon
Repair shop
Garage or mechanic's shop
Gas station
Office
School
Fire station
Library
Theatre
Farm
Horse stable

Medical Services
Hospital
Doctor's office
Dentist
Optometrist
Veterinarian

Transportation
Airport
Bus or train station

Activities
Skiing
Camping
Fishing camp
Fitness center
Dance studio
Skating rink
Beach (add tide pool with small wading pool)
Boating

Teachers can enrich centers through shining a scene on the wall using an overhead projector. For example, Dabria was changing her center into a train station. She shone a picture of a local train station on the wall. Transparencies of photos can be created using color copying machines or colored printers. Make sure you buy transparency film that is designed especially for the machine that you are using.

provide free food samples along with picture recipes to create the food (something that would happen in a real store).

It is important to carefully observe children's play to determine when to add props or change the center. If children do not seem interested in dramatic play even with the addition of new props, it is time to change the center. Changing the center allows children to experiment with new roles, explore new scenarios, and use additional vocabulary. The change may also spark interest in children who have not previously used the center. For ideas on possibilities for the dramatic play center, see Figure 7.2.

Watch the video on how one preschool teacher involved children in planning the dramatic play center. What techniques did she use?

Children can assist in planning changes to the dramatic play center. For example, they can brainstorm the types of play centers and props. As illustrated in the opening scenario, children can help to collect and make the props and physically arrange the center. This level of involvement can assist in building interest, provide additional materials and props, and help children to think about and share their knowledge in relationship to the proposed center.

TIP

If you are removing the house center, it is helpful to have a dollhouse with furniture and props so that children can still act out events in their lives.

Develop Prop Boxes

Many programs develop prop boxes. The advantage of prop boxes is that they save time, volunteers can help create them, and classrooms can share them. Often when teachers share them, they pool their resources so the prop boxes have a greater quantity and variety of props than one teacher alone would have access to. In some areas, organizations such as local childcare associations, NAEYC chapters, or museums create prop boxes that members can check out.

Prop boxes can be used in different ways. Often they are used for teacher convenience, as the starting point for changing the dramatic play center. However, Amanda lets the children use the prop boxes, having a variety of prop boxes on shelves for children in her afterschool program to choose from. Carrie, a pre-K teacher, fully develops the dramatic play center following the children's lead, but adds two or three related prop boxes to the center that children can use to enrich their play.

When creating prop boxes, it is helpful to begin with similar-sized sturdy boxes or totes for easy stacking and storing. To obtain the needed materials, you can send out a list to parents, go to inexpensive stores (secondhand, dollar), and go to the stores or community services that are being represented.

To be effective, prop boxes need to be developmentally appropriate and relevant to the group of children using them. They need to contain authentic props whenever possible, enough materials for a small group of children, and literacy materials (Barbour, Desjean-Perrotta, & Rojas, 2002). Prop boxes also need to be nonsexist and contain multicultural materials.

Provide Adequate Time for Dramatic Play

There needs to be adequate daily center time for dramatic play. Developing the scenario, choosing and negotiating roles, and selecting props are a time-consuming process. Children also need time to allow scenarios to evolve and change (Leong & Bodrova, 2012). For older children, this process usually takes place even before the children actually participate in dramatic play. The amount of time needed will vary depending upon the age of the children. However, for preschool and kindergarten children, a minimum of one hour for center activities is necessary to allow for this type of in-depth play (Copple & Bredekamp, 2009).

Introduce Materials and Teach Mini Lessons as Needed

It is helpful to introduce materials and teach mini lessons to support children's play. For example, you might introduce and model the use of a prop, especially one that the children might not be familiar with. You might also introduce unfamiliar literacy materials such as checkbooks. When teachers introduce and make suggestions about literacy props, children engage in a greater quantity and a greater variety of literacy activities (Morrow, 1990). Mini lessons about joining and sustaining play are also helpful. For example, you might give a puppet show where one puppet wants to join in the dramatic play and tries a variety of unsuccessful and successful approaches.

Another way to introduce or enhance play is to provide a **QR code** that links to a short video. For example, a child might use a tablet computer to scan a code showing a video of someone using a sushi roll mat.

Extend Play Through Assisting Children to Develop a Play Plan

With younger children, you might extend children's play by being the play partner, but as children begin to play cooperatively with peers, it is important for children to determine and enact their own storyline (Calabrese, 2003). Unless it is absolutely necessary, you should not redirect the play. "Redirection gives control of the learning situation to the teacher, not the student; thus, the situation loses some of the motivational power of play" (Rybczynski & Troy, 1995, p. 10).

Instead of being a play partner, you might assist preschool and early elementary children to deepen and extend their play through a play plan (Leong & Bodrova, 2012). Children using play plans spend more time participating in mature dramatic play, recall more details of their play, and argue and fight less while playing (Bodrova & Leong, 1998, 2007).

To produce a play plan the child writes or draws what he plans to do during the dramatic play period, including the imaginary situation and the roles. The teacher can ask open-ended questions to help children think more deeply about the roles and about the story line, as well as suggesting new roles. She can also remind children about their previous script and help them to extend it. Children reflect upon their dramatic play at the end of the play session, determining if they want to continue the script the next day. It is also important that they review the plan immediately before beginning the play, helping them to recall their previous ideas. Although play plans are often first initiated by the teacher, children typically adopt the idea of play plans and begin to use them independently not only in dramatic play but in other areas of the classroom as well (Bodrova & Leong, 1998, 2007).

Assist Children to Develop More Mature Play Through Scaffolding

In addition to setting up an effective dramatic play center, giving children needed background knowledge, providing adequate time, introducing materials, and helping children develop play plans, teachers can assist children to develop mature play through temporarily entering the play to model different roles, the symbolic use of props, and role speech. Role speech includes using the vocabulary and intonation associated with the role. The teacher can also scaffold learning by asking children questions that can help continue the story line or play scenario (Leong & Bodrova, 2012).

Assist Individual Children to Join Play

Teachers play an important role when they teach children successful strategies for joining play. To be effective in helping children to join play, teachers must first understand the play-entry strategies successful children use. Successful peer entry begins with the child participating in low-risk behavior (low risk of being rejected). This includes observing the other children at play and engaging in parallel play. The child then moves to high-risk behavior (risk of rejection higher), such as asking a question or suggesting a role that he might play. If granted entry into play, the successful child causes minimal disruption to the group (Beilinson & Olswang, 2003). It is important to observe the child who is unsuccessful in peer entry to determine the area of difficulty. Then you can teach the child the needed strategy to be successful. In addition to teaching these strategies, the teacher might:

- Interpret the child's behavior to the group, "Josie is cooking spaghetti just like you."
- Assist by suggesting a role to the group that the child might fill, "Perhaps Josie could be the big sister." Once children have entered into a play scenario, they may reject a new child wanting to enter the play because of the cognitive challenge of determining a role for the child (Kostelnik et al., 2012).
- Give the child a highly valued prop to help ease the entry (Beilinson & Olswang, 2003).

Assist Individual Children to Sustain Dramatic Play Episodes

After children gain entry to the dramatic play, they must be able to sustain the play. To assist children having difficulty sustaining play, observe and document their play to

determine what specifically is causing them problems. Does the child not understand her role or how to use a prop? Does he not want to play the role he has been assigned or not understand the play script? There are many ways that adults can thoughtfully intervene in children's play, including the following. From least to most intrusive, these are:

- Visually looking on and offering assistance only if needed.
- Using nondirective statements to describe what the child is doing, such as "You are feeding the baby because the baby is hungry."
- Asking questions such as "What will you do next?"
- Giving directive statements such as "Now you can help to set the table for dinner."
- Entering the play for a short time to demonstrate a prop or role (Levy, Wolfgang, & Koorland, 1992, p. 250).

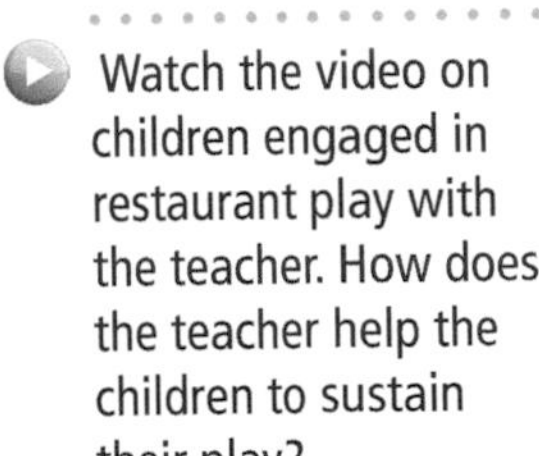
Watch the video on children engaged in restaurant play with the teacher. How does the teacher help the children to sustain their play?

When adults provide experiences for children, create special dramatic play areas based on these experiences, and then observe children's play providing individualized support for children who need it, the frequency and complexity of play are increased (Smilansky, 1968). This method also enhances language development, social skills, and achievement (Frost, Wortham, & Reifel, 2012).

Enrich the Dramatic Play by Incorporating Materials from Other Centers

Incorporating materials created in other learning centers allows children to make new props, use their products for an authentic purpose, and integrate skills learned in other areas with dramatic play. For example, children's artwork can be framed to decorate the walls in the dramatic play area. Children can use the writing center to create signs, checkbooks, and blank tablets, or the art center to create wallets, jewelry, and crowns. Clothing and pillows can be created in the sewing center, while small stools can be built in the woodworking area. Each of these props can enrich the dramatic play center. In addition, creating props can help children to develop an interest in this area.

Julie Bullard

Children in early elementary grades at Renaissance School of Arts and Sciences designed and created fairy wings, wands, and head gear. Dramatic play can become enriched when children develop their own props.

Facilitate Children Acting Out Their Fears

"Through play, children can explore stressful experiences in a safe environment, helping children understand and gain some control over them" (Huffman, 2006, p. 3). Teachers can facilitate children acting out their concerns and fears by learning as much as they can about the children in their classrooms and any stressful situations they might be facing. The teacher can then provide the needed props to assist the child in role-playing the event. For example, if the child is having a medical procedure, you can learn as much as you can about it and add books, pictures, props, medical clothing, and medical materials to the center. For toddlers, it might be helpful if the adult takes the role of the child and models coping strategies.

Another strategy is to ask open-ended questions as the child plays with the props. For example, if the toddler is role-playing the doll going to the hospital, the adult can ask how the doll feels and ask the child to describe ways that we might make the doll feel better, thereby understanding how the child wishes to be comforted (Huffman, 2006).

Older children are often able to enact scenes without adult intervention. However, sometimes the teacher needs to take the time to understand what the children are trying to accomplish through their play before negating it with rules. One day in Nancy's Head Start class, the children began to move all the furniture to another part of the classroom. When Nancy asked the children about this, they stated that they were being evicted. If Nancy had stated the rule "All furniture stays in the housekeeping area," she would never have understood the need of the children to reenact the scene that so many of them had experienced. The children role-played this scene over several days, each time moving everything from one area to another. Finally, they asked to permanently move the dramatic play center to the new area of the classroom, and after they did the eviction play ended.

Apply Your Knowledge At times, children may play out life experiences that are foreign to you or that you are uncomfortable with. Brainstorm a list of possible dramatic play topics that would fall in this category. How can you validate children's experiences and their lives in situations such as these?

Meet the Needs of All Learners

Supporting Children from All Cultures. It is important to represent each child's culture in the dramatic play area. The dramatic play area also offers the opportunity to teach children about cultures that are not represented in the room. While many programs now have multicultural dolls, it is important to think of multiculturalism in relationship to all aspects of the dramatic play center. For example, when planning a home living center we can include doll props, cooking utensils, eating utensils, dishes, clothing, hats, shoes, books, pictures, fabric, food containers, and print representing different cultures. When introducing unfamiliar items to children, it is important to weave the familiar and the unfamiliar together. Whenever possible, let the children see the object being authentically used. For example, before you introduce a tortilla press, you might invite a guest to demonstrate how to make tortillas and then eat them for snack. Visiting ethnic sections of a grocery store and ethnic restaurants are other ways to gain experiences. Family members can also be a great resource for such enrichment. Pictures on the wall can also help children to learn about different forms of dress, food, eating utensils, and ways of cooking food.

Julie Bullard

This dramatic play shelf includes real kitchen items, a cookbook, and a child-made clock. When families were asked to donate cultural items, one family donated a rice steamer, another a camping espresso maker, and a third family donated a variety of dried beans.

In our eagerness to add multicultural props, we must also be cautious about not inadvertently teaching children misconceptions and stereotypes. These misconceptions can occur if we teach children that everyone from the same culture has the same beliefs, lives in the same style of housing, or wears the same type of clothing. Customs within the

same culture often differ based on personal beliefs, age, income level, and geographic area of the country.

Misconceptions can also occur when we place an emphasis on traditional rather than modern life. For example, when we add a kimono to the dramatic play center we need to help children understand that most Japanese wear western clothing in public. However, the kimono might be worn at home or on special occasions.

> **TIP**
>
> When buying multicultural dolls, make sure that they have not only various skin tones but also different facial features and a variety of hair and eye colors. Include both male and female dolls.

Supporting Children with Disabilities. To support children with disabilities it is important that the center be accessible, that materials reflect the children who are disabled, and that the children receive the coaching and support they need to successfully interact with peers. To be accessible, the child not only needs to be able to enter the center but also must be able to reach and use the materials. Accommodations will vary depending upon the child's needs. For example, if a child needs to lean against the toy stove to play with it, it is important that the stove be anchored securely so it will not tip. If the child has difficulty picking up the kitchen utensils, a foam hair curler might be inserted over the handle to provide a better gripping surface.

Children with disabilities also need to see themselves reflected in the materials and props in the dramatic play center. Assistive devices such as hearing aids, wheelchairs, and glasses can be available for dramatic play. You can also provide assistive devices for children to use as they play with dolls.

Children with disabilities may engage in more solitary and less cooperative play at the same age as their peers (Hestenes & Carroll, 2000). While children with mild disabilities tend to go through the same stages of play as their peers, they make the transitions from one stage to the next at a later age (Guralnik & Hammond, 1999).

How can we assist children with disabilities to interact with their peers? Some experts advocate script rehearsal, where the teacher participates in a play scenario, coaching the child as they interact. The adult uses direct teaching, models a script, uses script words, and finally prompts the child to act out the role using the script words she has learned. After the child is successful in interacting with the adult, another child is invited into the play session. Finally, the child joins the regular playgroup. After preschool children participated in this intervention, their solitary play was reduced from 49% to 6%, and group play increased from 14% to 61% (Neeley, Neeley, Justen, & Tipton-Sumner, 2001).

Observe and Document Individual Children's Learning

Assessing and documenting children's play in the dramatic play center can help you understand their level of play, play interests, common scripts, and ability to interact with others. You can also observe many other skills in this area (language, math, science, emotional, social, self-regulatory, and creative). You might use anecdotal records, running records, and artifacts such as their play plans, video recordings, or audio recordings to assess children's learning in this area. Some questions you might ask while observing are:

- What type of play does the child typically engage in—social category (solitary, parallel, associative, or cooperative) and cognitive category (functional, constructive, sociodramatic, games with rules)?

- Is the child able to successfully enter a dramatic play situation with others? What strategies do they use?
- Whom does the child prefer to play with?
- Can the child make a play plan?
- Does the child role-play, pretending to be another person, animal, or object?
- Does the child make believe with actions? If yes, give an example.
- Does the child make believe with objects? If yes, give an example.
- Does the child create make-believe situations? If yes, give an example.
- Does the child verbally interact with at least one other person? If yes, describe the interaction.
- Does the child interact with others to coordinate the roles and the plot? If yes, give an example.
- Can the child maintain the play script for 10 minutes or more?
- Does the child use role speech?
- What type of literacy behaviors does the child demonstrate?
- What stories does the child tell?
- What types of mathematical skills does the child use in the dramatic play area?
- What scripts does the child enact?
- What role does the child prefer?
- Is the child a leader or follower in developing and maintaining the play script?
- Is the child able to successfully use different props in the center?
- Can the child negotiate successfully with others?

Manage Challenges in the Dramatic Play Center: Superhero and War Play

Should superhero and war play be banned? Teachers are often uncomfortable with this type of play, being concerned about safety, the limiting nature of the play, and what children are learning by enacting violent scenes. However, it often does not work to ban gun and superhero play, because this type of play allows children to feel powerful and to face their fears. Many children have a strong need for this. Superhero play can also encourage friendships and help children to establish their identity (Frost, Wortham, & Reifel, 2012). Additionally, when teachers try to ban this type of play, children may become deceptive, hiding their play or declaring that the play is not superhero or gun play (Levin, 2003). Furthermore, banning the behavior does not give the children the opportunity to work through their issues (NAEYC, 2006).

If you are uncomfortable with the play that is occurring, but still want to meet children's needs to feel powerful and face their fears, you can do the following:

- Promote imaginative play rather than imitative play by observing the children and helping them to expand on their play script (NAEYC, 2006). Since superhero play or war play often has a very limited storyline, it might also be helpful to have children write or draw a play plan to expand their play.
- Redirect children to accompanying play behaviors. For example, several children were playing pirates pretending to have sword fights. The teacher suggested they problem solve other ways they could escape from the boat. The children also became involved in making costumes, boats, and hideouts.

- Focus on the helping behaviors of superheroes (such as making a list of the ways that Batman helps other people). Cathy Jackson, a Head Start teacher, had a group of children in her class who were very interested in being superheroes. They created superhero costumes, and after studying what superheroes did decided that they needed to perform superhero activities. Cathy visited with people in the neighborhood who needed something accomplished. They would then call the classroom and let the children know that superheroes were needed. The children would all don their costumes and proceed to perform the feat.
- Focus on real-life heroes, fairy tales, and folk tales to give children alternative powerful figures to act out.
- Help children to understand the difference between real and imaginary characters and behaviors.
- Provide additional outlets for facing and describing fears, including drawing and writing. Also, provide ways for dealing with an abundance of high energy, including plenty of outdoor time and opportunities for indoor physical activities (tumbling, pounding nails into a tree stump).
- Provide additional ways for children to feel powerful, for example through the accomplishment of physical feats and challenges.

Check Your Understanding 7.5

Click here to gauge your understanding of section concepts.

Click here to gauge your understanding of chapter concepts.

It is also important to guarantee the physical and emotional safety of all children in the group. One way of accomplishing this is by having the children help to establish rules surrounding this type of play, such as "Only play with those who want to play" and "Superhero play occurs only in a certain area" (NAEYC, 2006).

Through dramatic play, children can enact and transform reality, while increasing their cognitive, social, literacy, self-regulatory, creative, and emotional skills. When teachers design rich dramatic play areas and scaffold children's learning, the quality and quantity of dramatic play increase, leading to increased learning across the curriculum.

Sample Application Activities

1. Observe an individual child and assess what type of play he or she is demonstrating. Examine both social and cognitive categories.
2. Observe children entering a sociodramatic play episode that is already in progress. What skills do the different children use in entering the play?
3. Write a parent newsletter explaining how play assists children in the development of a variety of skills.
4. Visit an early childhood program and evaluate their dramatic play area using the environmental assessment found in Figure 7.3.
5. Choose a theme or topic and brainstorm a list of props. Think of the dramatic play area. What would you do to make sure it represents different cultures?
6. Brainstorm a list of different kitchen utensils, dishes, and cooking pots that could give children experience with different cultures.
7. Design a dramatic play center for a first-grade classroom. Describe how it would differ from a preschool dramatic play center.
8. Develop a prop box that would be relevant to children in your community.
9. Observe a teacher during center time. Describe how she is facilitating children's play.

FIGURE 7.3 Environmental Assessment: Dramatic Play Center

- ❑ Is the dramatic play center in a well-defined area such as a separated corner of the classroom or outdoors in a "cave," boat, den, or playhouse?
- ❑ Is sufficient space provided for at least four to six children to play?
- ❑ If the center is indoors, is it located next to the block area to increase interaction?
- ❑ Are there familiar and authentic items that allow children to represent their experiences?
- ❑ Are there materials that represent all members of the classroom—boys and girls, cultural materials, assistive devices, different family groupings?
- ❑ Are materials included that introduce children to many cultures and family groupings (even those that are not represented in the classroom)?
- ❑ Is the dramatic play center aesthetic?
- ❑ Is there clothing or pieces of fabric for children to create their own clothing?
- ❑ Are there full-length mirrors?
- ❑ Are there a variety of props to support rich play opportunities?
- ❑ Are there duplicates of props so children can participate in parallel play?
- ❑ Are authentic and appropriate math props included?
- ❑ Are authentic and appropriate literacy props included?
- ❑ Does the center include some loose parts so children can develop what they need?
- ❑ Are clothing and prop choices readily available and organized?
- ❑ Is there needed equipment, such as a toy stove for a home living center?
- ❑ Is the dramatic play center dynamic, being changed or added to as needed to sustain rich play opportunities?

Chapter 8

Developing Manipulative and Sensory Centers

Learning Outcomes

After you have read this chapter, you will be prepared to:

- Describe how the manipulative center enhances children's development
- Design an effective manipulative center
- Discuss how manipulative activities vary based upon the children's age and development
- Describe multiple ways that teachers facilitate learning in the manipulative center
- Design an effective sensory center
- Describe multiple ways that teachers facilitate learning in the sensory center
- Discuss how to design outdoor sensory and manipulative experiences and centers

Julie Bullard

Armelia, a teacher in an Early Head Start center, noticed that the infants in her room were very interested in textures. Wanting to give the children a whole-body sensory experience, she put a small rubber blow-up boat in the classroom and placed a variety of pieces of cloth inside, including cotton, velveteen, satin, burlap, nylon, and chiffon. At the end of each day, Armelia washed and dried the fabric to have it clean for the next day. The babies climbed into the boat and crawled on the material, laid on the fabric, and even sometimes fell asleep in the "textured nest." They also used their developing manipulative skills to pick up the fabric, place it over their heads, and rub it between their thumbs and fingers. The babies seemed to develop their own fabric preferences, digging the desired cloths out of the pile. As the year progressed, Armelia changed the materials in the boat to meet the children's new interests. For example, the children became intrigued with the suction soap dish when they found it on the floor one day. Armelia responded by putting suctioned bath mats (suctions facing up) into the boat. She also placed other suction items (suction balls, suction soap dishes) for child experimentation into the boat. Through the sensory boat, the infants were able to develop sensory, manipulative, gross motor, fine motor, and cognitive skills.

The Manipulative Center: Enhancing Children's Development

The manipulative center includes materials to develop children's **fine motor skills**. Fine motor skills consist of coordinating movements in the fingers, hands, and arms (Trawick-Smith, 2014, p. 223). This calls for strength, dexterity, and control in finger, hand, and arm movement. Fine motor skills are necessary for writing, drawing, assembling puzzles, and performing self-help skills like eating with utensils, buttoning, zipping, tying shoes, and using tools. They are influenced by perception, the nervous system, cognition, motivation to accomplish a task, and environmental support (Feldman, 2012).

Stages of Fine Motor Development

Children make incredible strides in fine motor skills in the early childhood years. Quinell, who is four months old, is picking up things with her entire hand. By eight months, like 50% of other children her age, she is able to use the **pincer grasp** (using her finger and thumb to pick up an item) (Feldman, 2012, p. 125). Her strength, dexterity, and control will continue to develop as her neurological and physical system matures. However, she will also need experiences to gain fine motor skills. Throughout the early childhood years, Quinell, like most children, will develop the needed manipulative skills through involvement in purposeful, self-chosen activities, using a variety of tools and objects (Exner, 1992). With practice, the use of tools becomes automatic. For example, controlling a pencil becomes automatic for most children as they grow older, allowing them to concentrate on other aspects of the writing process (Rosenblum et al., 2003).

As we plan developmentally appropriate experiences, it is important to remember that motor skills typically develop from the head downward (**cephalocaudal trend**) and from the middle of the body out (**proximodistal trend**). For example, the child gains control of the arm, the hand, and then the fingers (McDevitt & Ormrod, 2013).

Why Fine Motor Skills Are Important

Children who have difficulty with fine motor skills are more likely to be dependent on others, experience trouble with school tasks, get teased by classmates, and have a poor self-concept (Losse, Henderson, Elliman, Hall, & Knight, 1991; Wehrmann, Chiv, Reid, & Sinclair, 2006). Teachers often view these children more negatively, wrongfully believing the child's messy paper is because of carelessness or laziness (Rosenblum, Weiss, & Parush, 2003). Children with poor fine motor skills may engage in avoidance behaviors, reinforcing others' beliefs that they are unmotivated (Thorne, 2006). Additionally, writing is a way of demonstrating knowledge in all subject areas. Poor fine motor skills can interfere with the writing process since children are concentrating on the physical skill of making letters rather than on creating ideas and expressing them (Stevenson & Just, 2014).

The early childhood years set the stage for children's future success. For example, children who have neat handwriting receive higher grades on their work even when the content is very similar and the handwriting is not supposed to influence the scoring. In one study, scorers received training to try to reduce this bias. However, even with training there was evident scorer bias toward more neatly written papers (Sweedler-Brown, 1992).

Since technology is now so readily available and so many children struggle with handwriting, you might wonder if handwriting is still an important skill. In a recent study, researchers compared two groups of preschool children; one group practiced learning letters through visual means and the other group practiced letter recognition through writing. **Neuroimaging** showed more brain activity for the group that wrote the letters (James, 2010). In another study, more areas of the brain were activated when writing rather than typing (James & Atwood, 2009).

Still other research reveals a strong link between fine motor skills and later reading and math achievement (Grissmer, Grimm, Aiyer, Marrah, & Steele, 2010). Brain imaging shows that areas of the brain needed for math, reading, and other cognitive functions are activated when children engage in fine motor skills. This suggests that there may be an underlying neural network used for both fine motor and cognitive skills. Since these skills appear to be strongly linked throughout childhood, to improve future reading and math performance we may want to not only work on cognitive skills in the early childhood years but also enhance fine motor skills (Davis, Pitchford, & Limback, 2011; Grissmer, Grimm, Aiyer, Marrah, & Steele, 2010).

In addition to the link with cognitive skills, so much time is spent in fine motor activities during preschool and elementary school that children who have fine motor difficulties are at an extreme disadvantage (see Table 8.1). Think of the time that you engage in fine motor activities each day. How is your life impacted by your skill level in this area?

How the Manipulative Center Enhances Children's Development

The well-planned manipulative area can be a rich source for learning. Children use fine motor and perceptual skills, practice motor planning and execution, and engage in eye-hand coordination in this center. Most of the materials found in the manipulative area also enhance cognitive skills. In addition, children increase their attention span and self-discipline as they participate in these activities. For example, children often continue to work until they complete an entire puzzle or match all the lids to the jars. They experience

Table 8.1 Children's Age and Percentage of Time Spent in All Fine Motor Tasks and Only Paper-and-Pencil Tasks

Children's Age	Percentage of Time Engaged in Fine Motor Tasks	Percentage of Fine Motor Time Devoted to Pencil-and-Paper Tasks
Head Start (preschool)	37%	10%
Kindergarten	46%	42%
Elementary	30% to 60%	85%

Sources: Marr, Cermak, Cohm, and Henderson, 2003; McHale and Cermak, 1992; and Rosenblum, Weiss, and Parush, 2003.

a sense of satisfaction as they complete a challenge for the first time (matching all the nuts and bolts). While many activities in this area are designed to be accomplished alone, some are designed for two or more children (floor puzzles, games). These activities help children learn to work cooperatively with others and to develop skills of turn-taking.

So what can we do in the early childhood years to enhance children's fine motor skills? This chapter will review environments, materials, and teacher interactions that can assist all children to develop these needed abilities.

Check Your Understanding 8.1
Click here to gauge your understanding of section concepts.

Designing an Effective Manipulative Center

Children develop fine motor skills in many areas of the early childhood classroom (literacy, block, math, science, cooking, and art centers). However, most early childhood programs also include a designated manipulative center where the primary purpose is the development of fine motor and self-help skills.

It is important for the teacher to focus on the skills to be developed and to carefully choose materials that will enhance these skills. In one study, researchers presented kindergarten children with more than 50 manipulative activities to use as one option during center time. The researchers chose materials that were self-corrective and attractive and that focused on the pincer grasp. For example, in one activity children used a spoon to move "diamonds" from a beautiful bowl to a decorated egg carton that had a blue velvet pillow glued inside each compartment. The activities were introduced either by the teacher or by a tape recording. The children in the control group also had opportunities to use manipulative activities and spent the same amount of time as the experimental group engaged in these activities. However, in spite of this, the children in the experimental group outperformed the children in the control group in an authentic fine motor task. This study underscores the need for thoughtful planning and for introducing each activity (Rule & Stewart, 2002, p. 10).

Important Criteria in Designing the Manipulative Center

Some important criteria in developing the manipulative center include providing:

- A quiet, uninterrupted area for children to work.
- An area that is well lit, preferably with natural light.
- Low, open, and labeled shelves to hold materials. Many teachers label shelves and trays with pictures and words. This allows children to practice literacy skills and enables them to return materials to a designated space.
- Trays or baskets to hold all the materials needed for each discrete activity. Children need to be able to easily see their choices. Trays can help children to define the workspace when using the table. If using baskets to hold materials, you might use carpet squares or place mats for defining the child's workspace.
- Storage for additional materials. Since materials for fine motor skills need to be rotated frequently to meet the developmental needs and interests of children, it is important for teachers to have accessible, convenient storage. Classroom storage also allows teachers to meet the immediate needs of an individual child or small group of children.
- Horizontal surfaces including tables, chairs, and floor space (for completing large floor puzzles).
- Vertical surfaces. Occupational therapists stress the importance of using vertical surfaces such as white boards, flannel board, or magnet boards hung on walls or placed on easels. Vertical surfaces naturally cause children to properly position their wrist and to use thumb opposition. Working on a vertical surface also assists

Julie Bullard

Attractive containers filled with colored water entice children to practice pouring.

with wrist extension, which supports the balanced use of hand muscles and aids in shoulder and arm muscle development (Benbow, 1990; Myers, 1992). As stated by Myers (1992), "Switching activities from a horizontal to a vertical orientation can transform an ordinary or mediocre activity into a powerful tool for encouraging fine-motor skill development" (Myers, 1992, p. 48).

- Attractive materials. In both the Reggio Emilia and the Montessori approaches, the importance of using beautiful materials is stressed. The following quote describes the Montessori philosophy: "Look for the most attractive materials that you can find and afford. Design activities that will draw the child's interest and create a prepared environment that is harmonious and beautiful. If possible, avoid using plastic pitchers, bowls, trays, and other materials.... Children respond to the beauty of wood, glass, silver, brass, and similar natural materials" (Seldin & Wolff, 2007). (See Chapter 1 for more information about the Montessori and Reggio approaches.)
- Enticing materials that are interesting to the range of children in the group. Tina noticed that Terrance, a boy who struggled with fine motor control, very rarely used the manipulative center. However, Terrance was always the first to notice a bug in the play yard or classroom. Tina capitalized on this interest by adding several plastic bugs, small bug houses, and different-sized spoons for picking up and moving the bugs into the bug houses. When Tina introduced the bugs, she stated that they were pretending that these bugs were very fragile and should only be carefully lifted with a spoon. Terrance was fascinated with the new activity, telling the names of each type of bug to his classmates as he carefully categorized the bugs into the bug houses.
- Diverse materials that are developmentally appropriate and that meet individual children's needs. The teacher needs to understand the developmental sequence of fine motor skills, activities that help enhance development, and the specific developmental skills of the children in her group to design a developmentally appropriate manipulative center. Since there will be children at a variety of levels, it is important that the center include some open-ended activities, such as a variety of nuts to sort into trays or waffle blocks to build with. A variety of complexity levels should be made available for closed-ended activities. For example, the diamonds activity described earlier would be easier with a larger spoon. Having more than one size of spoon allows children to be successful while providing them the opportunity to increase the challenge, as they are ready.
- Enough developmentally appropriate materials to provide four to six children with several choices each.
- High-quality tools such as scissors. To reduce frustration and encourage scissor practice, scissors should be sharp and should cut paper easily. The holes should be small, just the right size for the thumb and finger (Myers, 1992). Both right- and left-handed scissors need to be available and labeled in an obvious way. It is important that children be taught safety rules when using scissors. For example, Amy, a teacher of three-year-old children, has the following rules for scissors: "Only use scissors at the art table," "Always sit when you use scissors," and "Scissors are for cutting paper or other art materials." Tessa, who teaches four-year-old children, includes these rules: "Scissors need to be held down and away from you when you are carrying them" and "You always use walking feet when you are carrying scissors."

Appropriate Materials for the Manipulative Area

When you plan materials for the manipulative area, it is important to consider the different manipulative skills young children are learning. These include the development of the pincer grasp, strength in grasp, bilateral coordination, eye–hand coordination, wrist swivel, wrist stability, finger dexterity, and development of the hand arches. In this chapter, materials are listed under each of these skills. While the materials primarily address the skill under which they are listed, they may assist with other manipulative skills as well. For example, stringing beads develops bilateral coordination, but it also develops eye–hand coordination and the pincer grasp.

Materials to Develop the Pincer Grasp. Learning to use the pincer grasp is a critical fine motor skill. When children use the pincer grasp, it is important that the web space, or the space formed by holding the thumb and finger together, be rounded. This allows the child to hold a pencil or other tool in a way that is less tiring for the hand. The pincer grasp can be developed by materials such as:

- A sieve with colored toothpicks for inserting through the holes (using colored toothpicks allows children to classify by color if they wish).
- Colorforms or stickers to place on paper.
- Eyedroppers to move water from one container to another.
- Tweezers, tongs, or spoons to move glass marbles, beads, shells, or pinecones from one place to another.
- Hair clips or barrettes and a doll with long hair.
- Wooden chopsticks that are tied together at the top with a rubber band to pick up pompoms.
- A Lite Brite.
- Pins to push into a piece of paper with a cork board underneath to punch out a design of choice.
- Buckles to open and close and shoes to tie (at Bright Beginnings Preschool, an actual shoe is nailed to the wall for children to lace and tie).
- A sunflower with tweezers to remove the seeds.
- A rubber band ball for removing and adding rubber bands.

Materials to Strengthen Grasping and Squeezing. Following are some materials to enhance grasping and squeezing:

- A plant sprayer and colored paper so that children can spray a design on paper.
- A paper punch, many different types of paper, and a beautiful container to hold the punches (the punches can be used for other activities).
- A turkey baster and cotton balls (the child can blow the cotton ball across the table with the baster).
- Squeeze toys, such as toys whose eyes bulge when squeezed.

Julie Bullard

Children practice the pincer grasp as they move the flat glass marbles.

- Clothespins that are used to attach items to a clothesline (the clothesline can be placed on the wall of the manipulative area).
- Sponges and basters. In a Montessori program, the manipulative shelves included a tray furnished with a baster, a pitcher of colored water, and two glasses. Children pour the water into one of the glasses and use the baster to move the water to the other glass. Another tray includes a pitcher of water, two small bowls, and a sponge. The child pours the water from the pitcher into one dish and then uses the sponge to move the water from that dish to another one.
- A nutcracker with nuts to crack (nuts can later be eaten for snack).
- A garlic press with water soaked small sponges to squeeze in the press

Materials to Strengthen Bilateral Coordination. **Bilateral coordination** involves using both hands together or using one hand for one thing while using the other for something else (holding paper with one hand while cutting with the other). Following are manipulative materials that enhance bilateral coordination:

- Cotton balls to pull apart (these can then be used to glue onto a picture or to make a project).
- Pop beads to put together and pull apart.
- Newspaper for tearing (the newspaper can be used for collages, papier mâché, or other art projects).
- Beautiful small coin purses to unzip and find the treasure.
- Small building materials such as Legos and waffle blocks.
- Beads to string into necklaces.
- A stapler and paper.
- Lacing cards.
- Cards that show a clapping rhythm for children to imitate.
- A child's shirt to practice buttoning (Joanne, a preschool teacher, took the shirt and placed it over a frame, making it easier to button).
- Paper for folding airplanes or origami.

Materials to Strengthen Eye–Hand Coordination. **Eye–hand coordination** refers to focusing and coordinating eye movement and the processing of visual input to control and direct the hands to accomplish desired tasks (Johansson, Westling, Bäckström, & Flanagan, 2001). Some materials that encourage eye–hand coordination are:

- Poker chips and a covered potato chip can with a slit in the lid for inserting the chips.
- Golf tees, with clay or Styrofoam to pound the golf tees into.
- Nails and a wood stump to hammer nails into.
- A variety of items to pour (water, aquarium gravel) and dishes to pour them into.
- A wire strainer, pebbles, and two dishes for transferring the pebbles from one dish to another.
- Peas to shell (these can later be used for lunch or snack).
- Nesting dolls to stack together.
- Games such as Pick Up Sticks, Barrel of Monkeys, Operation, Bedbugs, and Don't Spill the Beans.

Design Your Own Puzzle

Julie Bullard

Creating puzzles with pictures that are interesting and familiar to children, such as this family picture, provides an enticement for children to complete puzzles and creates an element of delight. The number of puzzle pieces can be determined based upon the child's age and development. Puzzles can be created of individual children, groups of children in your program, or of children and their families. They can also be created to accompany topics of study, such as creating puzzles from farm animals that you took on a field trip.

Directions

1. Enlarge a photo or find a picture of interest to the children, such as a picture from a calendar. It works best if the picture is on cardstock-weight paper.
2. Use rubber cement to glue the photo or picture to foam board. Foam board works better than cardboard because it is thicker and easier for young children to use.
3. Find a puzzle template; many are available.
4. Tape the template over the top of the photo or picture.
5. Use a sharp X-Acto knife to cut through the template, picture, and foam board using the template as a guide.
6. Label the back of each puzzle piece with a color or figure. If several puzzles get mixed together, this will make it easy to sort the puzzle pieces.
7. If you wish to create an "element of surprise," place the puzzle in the manipulative area and let the children discover it.

- Small building materials such as one-inch blocks, Legos, tinker toys, gears, Lincoln Logs, bristle blocks, marble rolls, and erector sets.
- A variety of types of puzzles—5–12-piece puzzles for three-year-olds, 12–24-piece puzzles for four-year-olds, and 18–35-piece puzzles for five-year-olds (Maldonado, 2006).

Materials to Enhance Wrist Rotation. Wrist rotation includes being able to perform a twisting motion with the wrist. This is necessary for everyday activities such as opening doorknobs. Some materials that promote wrist rotation include:

- Lids and jars to match (provide a variety of different interesting jars and lids).
- Nuts and bolts to screw together.
- Padlocks and keys to open and close (provide several different padlocks).
- Screws, wood to screw them into, and screwdrivers.

Julie Bullard

The padlocks and keys develop wrist rotation. The different sizes also encourage seriation.

- Items to take apart (hair dryer, toaster, carburetor) with a screwdriver or nut remover.
- An Etch-a-Sketch.
- A flashlight for taking apart and reassembling.

Materials to Enhance Wrist Stability. Children's wrist stability is enhanced by using a vertical surface. There are many options for providing vertical surfaces. For example, you might create a magnetic board that has changing activities, such as magnetic letters, photos of children and their names to be matched, a set of magnetic gears that can be moved, or a magnetic marble roll. You might also attach pegboards, a Magna Doodle, or an Etch-a-Sketch to the wall using Velcro. Chalkboards, white boards, or easels can be mounted for drawing and writing. If there is not room on the walls, consider using tabletop easels to provide this experience.

> **TIP**
>
> You can create your own tabletop easel to increase children's opportunities with vertical surfaces by cutting diagonal cuts on two opposite sides of a box. Then tape cardboard to the open side.

Materials to Enhance Finger Dexterity or Moving Individual Fingers in Isolation. Children often develop **finger dexterity** while performing finger plays. To extend this activity to the manipulative area, you can add finger puppets (one for each finger) that the child can use to retell a familiar story, song, or finger play. For example, children might have frog finger puppets to use with the song "Five Little Speckled Frogs." You can learn the verse and tune for this song and for many others through searching for finger plays and children's songs on YouTube. Providing a typewriter for children ages four to eight can also allow children to develop finger dexterity, but only if they are using all of their fingers as they type.

Materials to Develop the Arches of the Hand (General Hand Development). There are several materials that are used in therapy to help develop the arches. These can also be used in an early childhood setting with preschool and K–3 children. These materials include:

- Small tongs or clothespins to pick up small objects, such as beads or cotton balls. Children can classify these objects into sorting trays.
- Small items (pennies, marbles, plastic bugs) with teacher-created cards. The card contains a picture of the type of item and the number of items to hold in your cupped hand. The child draws a card and completes that challenge.
- Games that include dice (the child shakes the dice in her cupped hands until she reaches a number spun on a dial).

- Sock puppets (the child can make the puppet "talk" by opening and closing her hand).
- Plastic packing bubbles to pop with the fingers and palm.
- Tomy Waterfuls (games where the top is filled with water and you move small objects by pushing a button) (Myers, 1992).

Julie Bullard

These strips are an invitation to practice cutting with scissors. An element of surprise is added by having children's faces on some of the strips.

Materials to Enhance Cutting. Cutting may occur in the art area, writing area, or manipulative area. Children typically progress through developmental stages in cutting. They are first able to cut play dough with a plastic knife or scissors, next snip paper into small pieces, then fringe paper, and finally cut lines (creating strips for paper chains or cutting out newspaper comic strips). At the next stage, children are able to cut out geometric shapes, turning the paper with their holding hand. It is easier for children to cut with high-quality scissors using paper that is card stock weight.

Check Your Understanding 8.2

Click here to gauge your understanding of section concepts.

Additional Considerations to Meet the Needs of All Age Groups

Infants and Toddlers

Some of the previously mentioned materials are appropriate for infants and toddlers, such as pop-together beads, large pegs and pegboards, and colorforms to place on and pull off surfaces. It is important to make sure that materials are not choking hazards. Infant manipulative materials may be in baskets on the floor with each basket containing groups of similar items. However, toddlers age two or older need a designated manipulative area (Texas Child Care, 2005). Some manipulative materials that are suitable for infants and toddlers include:

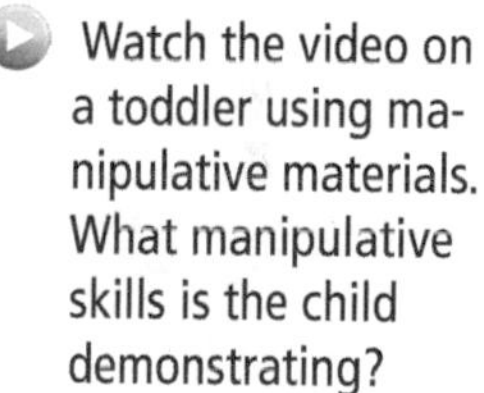

Watch the video on a toddler using manipulative materials. What manipulative skills is the child demonstrating?

- A basket of different types of rattles.
- An assortment of small boxes to open and close, each filled with a surprise (stuffed toy, unbreakable mirror glued inside, jewelry, shiny key chain).
- Nesting boxes, bowls, or butter tubs to stack.
- Pots and pans with lids to take off and on.

Large tongs with items to move.

- A decorated coffee can or hot chocolate can with a hole in the top with items that fit through the hole (the items can be changed when children lose interest in the current items).
- An empty tissue box with scarves to pull out.
- Simple puzzles—use 1–3-piece, knobbed puzzles for toddlers (Maldonado, 2006).
- Busy boxes.
- Duplos or other snap-together building blocks.

> **TIP**
>
> Many of the previous examples use everyday and found items instead of expensive store-bought items to develop manipulative skills. This helps families to understand that everyday items in their homes can be used for learning experiences.

Marlis, a teacher of infants, decorated a hot chocolate can. She cut a round hole in the plastic lid and placed an unstitched nylon mesh bath scrubby in the can. Children enjoyed pulling the nylon mesh out of the can and then stuffing it back in.

School Age (K–3rd Grade)

Teachers often abandon the manipulative center as children enter elementary school. However, it is important to continue to provide this center, particularly since 10% to 34% of children experience handwriting difficulties (Rosenblum et al., 2003). Manipulative materials can assist children in developing the skills they need for handwriting and other fine motor tasks. As you read earlier, this area will also help with cognitive development. Many of the activities listed previously are also appropriate for children in K–3 classrooms. However, as children mature they are ready for more complex and challenging activities. In addition, children of this age often like to play games with rules such as jacks or marbles. Some additional, more challenging materials include:

- Model building.
- Sewing (create costumes, clothing for dolls, pillows for dramatic play).
- Knitting.
- Weaving with a loom.
- Beading with small beads.
- Creating products with carpentry hand tools.
- Creating designs with nails.
- Making string art.
- Braiding.
- Using yo-yos and hacky sacks.
- Folding origami and paper airplanes.
- Playing games such as jacks and marbles or string games like Cat in a Cradle.
- Building with Legos or other small building toy sets that have motors and gears.
- Putting together puzzles.

Check Your Understanding 8.3
Click here to gauge your understanding of section concepts.

Teachers' Facilitation of Learning in the Manipulative Center

Some teachers believe that the manipulative center might be one area in the classroom where children can learn on their own without teacher intervention. However, research indicates that teacher presence in the manipulative area is associated with more engagement in both the center and the materials (Tomes, 1995). Some roles that teachers use to scaffold children's learning in this area are covered in the following sections.

Introduce New Materials

Teachers might introduce materials to children as a group or individually as a child demonstrates readiness. Introducing the materials assists children in knowing how to use them and also builds interest.

Lisa Bullard

Teachers kept the manipulative center interesting by adding mortars and pestles with rinsed eggshells. Children ground the shells, which were later sprinkled on the school garden.

Keep the Center Interesting

Teachers keep the center interesting by adding new materials and removing materials children are no longer using. It is important that children have the opportunity to master materials and tools before teachers remove them.

Provide Encouragement and Recognition

Teachers can provide encouragement and recognition of children in the manipulative area by noticing what they are doing, making encouraging remarks, discussing their progress with them, and documenting their learning. Many teachers also provide a place for children to display products created in the center. For example, Tessa helped children in her afterschool program create a mobile from some of the paper airplanes they had created.

Check Your Understanding 8.4
Click here to gauge your understanding of section concepts.

Provide Challenges

Many manipulative materials can be made more challenging. For example, if children have moved water from one cup to another using a baster, challenge them to move the water using an eyedropper, or to think of other ways they might move the water.

Teach Children the Correct Way to Use Tools

As children are developmentally ready, it is important to help them learn to use tools in the correct way. For example, to use scissors properly, the child should have the thumb and middle finger in the holes of the scissors and use the index finger to stabilize the scissors. While it is common that children hold the scissors with the thumb and index finger, this does not allow for the needed control. Proper scissor positioning and the opportunity to cut can enhance many areas of fine motor and hand development (Myers, 1992).

Provide Assistance to Children Who Are Struggling

Observe children. If they are struggling, it might be helpful to provide different tools or materials. For example, a child who is left-handed may be trying to cut with right-handed scissors. Providing left-handed scissors will allow the child to be successful. Another child may be unsuccessfully trying to cut tissue paper and becoming increasingly frustrated. If the child's goal is to cut, then providing a firmer paper will assist the child. If the child wants the tissue paper to be smaller, you could suggest tearing it.

Scaffold Children's Learning

There are several ways that teachers can scaffold children's learning. For example, a child may become frustrated when she is not able to complete a puzzle and might want you to complete it for her. Observe the child to determine what strategies she is currently using. This allows you to suggest other strategies she might try. For example, you might suggest she turn over each puzzle piece so it faces upright, find the outside edges first, look carefully at each piece, think about which puzzle pieces might be at the top of the puzzle, and look at the picture on the box.

Assist the Child with Proper Positioning

It is important to have proper body position for many fine motor activities. For example, it may be more difficult to cut effectively while leaning over to cut something placed on the floor than it is to sit at a table and cut at a waist-high level.

Encourage the Child to Cross the Midline

To cross the midline, the child must move a hand over the middle of the body. You can encourage children to do this by placing the activity on his dominant side with the container on the other side. Crossing the midline is an important task that children need to master in the early childhood years.

Choose the Correct Object Size

Children are more likely to use more advanced in-hand manipulation when using small-sized objects (1/2" to 1") (Exner, 1992). However, if you are working with infants and toddlers or any other children who mouth objects, you must make sure that any materials you are using will not pose a choking hazard.

Participate in Conversations with Children

The manipulative area provides an ideal opportunity to engage in reciprocal conversations with individual or small groups of children. Conversations might include discussion of the materials or strategies the child is using. In addition, as children sit and put puzzles together or build with Legos they often will initiate conversations unrelated to the materials at hand.

Meet the Needs of All Learners

Children with Disabilities. While there are many disabilities, such as cerebral palsy, that are classified as physical disabilities, many other disabilities are not primarily physical but often co-occur with perceptuomotor deficits. This includes **attention deficit hyperactive disorder (ADHD)**. In Nordic countries, a special diagnostic category recognizes this relationship: DAMP (deficits in attention, motor control, and perception) (Yochman, Ornoy, & Parush, 2006). Children with DAMP are slower and less accurate when performing fine motor tasks. The severity of the ADHD predicts the severity of fine motor skills. Other disabilities that often co-occur with poor fine motor control include Down's syndrome and fetal alcohol syndrome (Bruni, 1998).

According to Losse et al. (1991), who studied the long-term effects of children with motor difficulties, it is crucial that even children with minor motor problems receive intervention in the early childhood years. It is very important to intervene early, since perceptuomotor activities greatly influence children's current and future learning (Yochman et al., 2006). In addition, support is necessary so that children can be successful in many everyday activities such as dressing, tying shoes, and using a fork to eat. Instruction and practice can assist children to improve their skills (Bruni, 1998). Unfortunately, children often do not choose to engage in activities that are very difficult for them (Walsh, 2007). For example, kindergarten children who have difficulty with penmanship may avoid writing, thereby increasing the problem. Rather than having the child practice writing repeatedly, it is helpful to provide other activities that enhance fine motor control. These materials should appeal to the child's interest, so that he will choose to use them. Teachers should also provide appropriate materials so that the child can experience success. Providing needed assistance based on individualized observation is also important. For example, a child may have difficulty writing because he is not holding the paper with his nonwriting hand. After observing this, the teacher can model how to hold the paper while writing. Occupational therapy can also be an effective method for improving fine motor skills, especially when it includes teacher and family consultation and teacher training (Wehrmann et al., 2006). See Figure 8.1 to learn about other helpful strategies.

Children Who Come from Diverse Backgrounds. Children come to early childhood programs with vastly different experiences relating to fine motor skills. Children's interests and dispositions, resources available, and cultural values influence the amount of time children have devoted to this area. Since fine motor skills are so crucial in preschool and K–3 settings, it is important that teachers provide many opportunities for children who have less developed fine motor skills. Materials that reflect children's cultural backgrounds, especially items they see family members use, often have high appeal. For example, Puanani created an activity in her manipulative center in Hawaii with chopsticks, rice spoons, small seashells, and wooden sorting trays. Debbie, who has several children in her classroom whose parents are mechanics, added small engine parts for disassembling to her manipulative center. Both teachers found that children participated in manipulative activities more when these high-interest materials were available.

Children Who Are Left-Handed. Children who are left-handed face special challenges in a right-handed world, often struggling with fine motor tasks. Between 8% and 10% of children are left-handed. In one study, 90% of the children who were left-handed also had family members who were left-handed, suggesting a genetic link (Giagazoglou, Fotiadu, Angelopoulou, Tsikoulas, & Tsimaras, 2001). In the past,

FIGURE 8.1
Meeting Scott's (a child with ADHD) Needs

Scott was a six year-old child who had been diagnosed with ADHD and perceptual motor disabilities. His teacher first provided a variety of different types of pencil grips for Scott to experiment with. However, he continued to struggle with writing. Writing was tortuously slow, and full concentration was required to write each letter. At an Individual Education Program (IEP) meeting, there was discussion about the negative effect of the fine motor deficit on Scott's overall learning. The team (Scott's mother, teacher, special education teacher, and principal) decided on several modifications. They included:

- ❑ Providing extended time for written and fine motor tasks.
- ❑ Reducing the amount of fine motor tasks by allowing verbal and tape-recorded answers.
- ❑ Teaching Scott to type.
- ❑ Encouraging fine motor tasks that do not involve writing, such as model building.

drastic efforts such as tying the left hand behind the child's back were made to change the child's hand dominance. However, we now recognize that this is inappropriate. Instead, it is important to provide tools, such as scissors, that are designed for children who are left-handed and to teach children the proper ways to position tools and materials to be successful.

Observe and Document Children's Learning

Unlike other areas such as art and writing that might produce a product that is saved, the manipulative center often does not produce a permanent product. Therefore, it is even more important to note children's progress, struggles, and accomplishments through techniques such as photos, checklists, or anecdotal records. For example, Samantha documents the progress of children in her kindergarten class by creating a checklist of items in the manipulative area. She then checks off an item if she sees the child successfully complete it. For ease of use, the checklist is hung on a clipboard in the area. To protect confidentiality, Samantha places a paper listing the skills that children learn in the manipulative area on top of the list. This provides information for families and other visitors. Some questions you might want to consider in assessing and documenting children's learning include the following:

- Which hand does the child use?
- Does the child consistently use the dominant hand?
- Can the child use the pincer grasp?
- Is the web space rounded?
- Can the child effectively use both hands (bilateral coordination)?
- Can the child move individual fingers without the other fingers also moving?
- How does the child hold scissors?
- What is the child's skill level in cutting?
- Can the child effectively use the materials in the center (e.g., string beads, place nuts on bolts, put together puzzles, and pour without spilling)?
- What type of strategies does the child use when completing puzzles or other activities? For example, does the child use trial and error, or does he use more intentional methods?
- What is the child's attention span in using the manipulative materials?
- What type of materials does the child choose to use?
- What ideas do children have for using materials?

Manipulative skills are critical for children's current and future schooling success, as well as for their quality of life. We know that a child's fine motor skills are partially based on her development. However, children also must have appropriate experiences to develop to their full potential. Therefore, as early childhood teachers, we have the obligation to provide children with rich, abundant, developmental, relevant, and interesting fine motor materials and experiences.

The Sensory Center: Designing an Effective Center

Like the manipulative center, the **sensory** center provides children the opportunity to develop fine motor and cognitive skills. For example, the sensory center often provides opportunities to learn science and math skills. In addition, the sensory center "fosters curiosity, imagination, and experimentation" (Crosser, 1994, p. 28) and, since children often use the center with others, social skills and language are enhanced. From birth, children learn and explore their world through their senses (seeing, smelling, tasting, hearing, and tasting). Infants are born with most of their senses fully developed having used these senses prenatally. For example, a fetus will turn toward the source of a sound at five months (Woolfolk & Perry, 2015). The exception to this is vision. At birth, babies can only clearly see objects that are eight inches away. However, by six months, they have developed visual acuity levels similar to those of an adult.

The sensory center, sometimes called a sand and water area or media table, is also an area that is soothing, tension releasing, and open-ended, thereby making it failure proof for children (Koch, n.d.). Since the 1920s, when Margaret Lowenfeld introduced sand play, this area has been considered therapeutic. Sand, when combined with miniature people, animals, and houses, allows children to re-create and have control over their world (Stevens, 2004) and to role-play and work through their dilemmas. Through the play, the child can tell his story and express his feelings nonverbally. As a teacher observes the child, she has the opportunity to glimpse the child's inner thoughts. This is especially important with young children since they may not be able to express their feelings verbally. We will next examine ways to develop an effective center, interact with children in the center, and explore solutions to challenges in the sensory area.

Important Criteria in Designing the Sensory Center

The focus of the sensory center is often a water or media table. While there are advantages to store-bought media tables, including ease in draining, wheels for ease of moving, a lid to close the table when it is not in use, and a design that is the correct height for children, there are many options for creating other sensory play environments (Koch, n.d.). These include the following:

- A wading pool or blow-up boat for whole-body sensory experiences.
- Homemade water tables.
- Dishpans or plastic storage tubs.
- Baby bathtub.
- Cardboard box for dry sensory play.
- Serving tray for flubber, goop, or play dough (see Figure 8.2 for recipes).

Additional suggestions to create an effective sensory center include the following:

- Place the sensory table away from the wall so that children can access all sides of the table. Because children in the sensory center usually have their backs to the surrounding centers, it is not as necessary that the center be separated from the rest of the room by dividers.
- Provide low storage shelves on which to place baskets or tubs full of materials. A low pegboard on a nearby wall can also be helpful for hanging the clean-up tools and smocks. At North Idaho College Children's Center, teachers keep water play

Lisa Bullard

Even a bowl, a washcloth, and a small amount of water provide sensory play for Seamus.

FIGURE 8.2
Recipes for Sensory Exploration

Three sensory materials that are popular with children are flubber, goop, and play dough.

Flubber Recipe
Mixture 1
1⅓ cups very warm water
2 teaspoons Borax (can be found in the laundry section of a grocery store)
Stir mixture 1 until Borax is completely dissolved. Set aside.

Mixture 2
1½ cups very warm water
2 cups Elmer's glue
Liquid watercolor
Thoroughly blend mixture 2.
Pour mixture 1 into mixture 2, and mix with hands until fully combined. Flubber is created by a chemical reaction. Use vinegar to clean up flubber. It dissolves the mixture.

Goop Recipe
Add one box of cornstarch to 1½ cups of water. Add water to the cornstarch until semi-firm. If the mixture becomes too hard, add more water. You might want several boxes to provide enough mixture for a water table. You can also use this mixture in a cake pan or tray. To clean up goop from the floor, let it dry and then vacuum or sweep it up.

Play Dough Recipe
2 cups flour
1 cup salt
2 tablespoons alum
1 cup boiling water
2 tablespoons oil

Mix flour, salt, and alum in a large bowl. Make a dip in the center, and add the oil and water. Mix together, adding more flour if too sticky or more water if too firm. Many teachers add Kool-Aid to the dough for the scent and the color.

utensils close by hanging a large picture frame (with glass removed) horizontally above the media table. Utensils such as whisks and eggbeaters for water play hang from the frame.

- Place the sensory center near a sink so that it is easy to fill and empty the water table. It is helpful to be able to run a hose directly from the sink faucet to fill the table. Specially designed tables also allow one to screw a hose onto the drain for emptying it. Olds (2001) recommends that the table be permanently connected to a water source and plumbed into a drain for ease of cleaning.
- Provide an easy to clean floor. If you have carpet, you might consider duct taping a shower curtain or plastic runner under the table.
- Supply long-sleeved waterproof smocks that are easily accessible to children. These might be hung on hooks at the end of the water table or on a wall that is nearby.
- Include a battery-operated handheld vacuum, small broom and dustpan, and small sponge mops so that children can clean up the area when there is a spill or at the end of center time.
- Provide a variety of interesting props. Begin by having children explore the media without props. When children have fully explored the media, add props to sustain interest and to provide new opportunities for exploration and learning.

- Add literacy materials—contextual print and photographs can be used to label items in the area (to identify where the broom is kept or what is placed in the basket or tub). You can also add books to support the play of the children. For example, Mrs. Ames's kindergarten class visited a farm as part of a study on mammals. Many of the children had little previous exposure to farm life and were interested in re-creating, in the sandbox, what they had seen. Mrs. Ames added farm props along with books about farm life to expand their experience. Children used the books as a reference as they created their own farm.
- Provide a safe and healthy experience. To keep children safe and to prevent the spread of infectious diseases, it is important to observe the following precautions (American Academy of Pediatrics, American Public Health Association, National Resource Center for Health and Safety in Child Care and Early Education, 2011):
    - Empty water after each group of children is done playing.
    - Wash and sanitize the tub and the toys daily.
    - Ensure that children with cuts, scratches, and open sores do not use the table or that they wear disposable rubber gloves.
    - Make sure children wash their hands both before and after playing in the sensory table.
    - Be aware of children's allergies in your classroom and avoid any materials that the children might be allergic to.
    - Do not use materials that pose a choking hazard if working with younger children.
    - Clean up the floor when spills occur so that the floor is not slippery.
    - Supervise water play since young children can drown in small amounts of water.
    - Make sure that bleach is not added to the water.

While following these rules may seem daunting, many teachers involve the children in assisting with clean-up. For example, at Kid's World Preschool, children enjoy helping to fill and empty the water table. They also use child-sized cleaning tools to keep the floor clean and dry. Their teacher, Alexandria, has found that the time required to maintain the table is worth the effort.

Appropriate Materials for the Sensory Center

The sensory table can be filled with a variety of media. The most common are water, sand, dirt, and a combination of these. However, your imagination is the only boundary in thinking of other safe sensory materials with which to fill the table. Props add additional play and learning opportunities. While you might find many of these same materials in the science area, the primary purpose in this center is to provide sensory stimulation. However, as children explore the media, they will also be developing many different concepts.

Water. As children play in water, they gain therapeutic, social, physical, and cognitive benefits. They also have the opportunity to learn many scientific concepts, such as water flows when it is poured, water takes on many forms, water dissolves some materials, and water takes the form of the container it is in. Some materials float in water while other items sink. Some materials absorb water while others are water resistant. Water can be used for cleaning objects (Schwartz, 2007). Your goals for water play and the children's interests will help determine the materials that you will add. For example, you can add:

- Different herbs or other scents.
- Colored dye.
- Ping-pong balls, shells, and small plastic fish with tongs, aquarium nets, or scoops to pick them up with.
- Ice cubes with tongs.
- Bubbles mixture and materials for creating a variety of bubble-making wands.
- Soap flakes, eggbeaters, and hand whisks.
- Materials for sinking and floating experimentation (for example, children can collect a variety of seeds to see which will sink and float—coconuts, rose hips, nuts in shells) (Crosser, 1994).
- Corks, Styrofoam, and tinfoil to create boats.
- Sponges, wash cloths, and baby shampoo for washing dolls.
- A clothesline, clothespins, and doll clothes for washing the clothes and hanging them to dry.
- Plastic animals and toys.
- Play dishes, pots, and pans with dishrags, sponges, and a drying rack.
- Cars and trucks with a chamois for drying them.
- Ice blocks—allow children to choose a container to fill with water and freeze. These different sizes of ice blocks can be placed in the water table. Children can also freeze items in the ice such as small plastic animals, figures, bugs, or flowers.
- A block of ice with a squirt bottle of colored salt water, plastic knives, small rubber hammers, and safety goggles for creating ice sculptures.
- Basters, eyedroppers, ladles, spoons, pitchers, sponges, and water cans for moving water.
- Tubing, PVC pipe, accordion tubing, marble works, and funnels for developing more advanced means for moving water. You might want to suspend the funnel over the table to enhance interest and give children a starting point for their experimentation.
- Pumps such as bilge pumps, kerosene pumps, and pumps found in liquid soaps (Chalufour & Worth, 2005).
- Different sizes of containers and measuring cups for experimenting with conservation.
- Shiny plates and bowls to experiment with reflections.
- Water wheels (store-purchased or child-created).

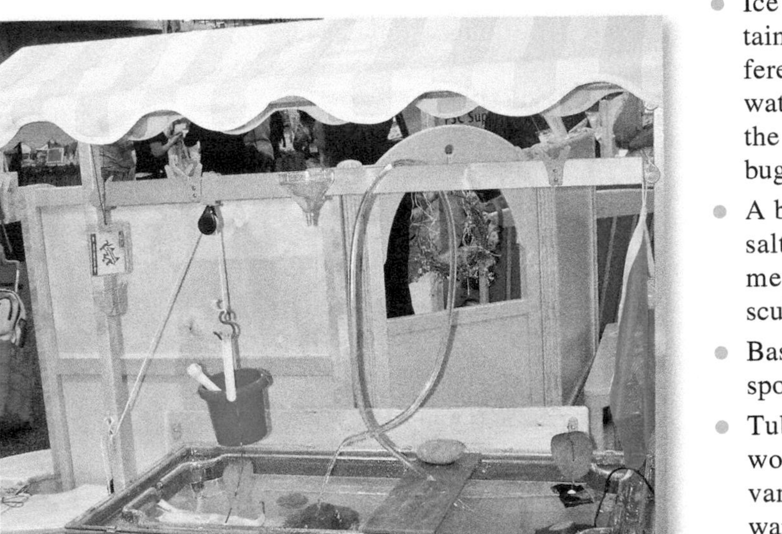
Julie Bullard

Leaves, twigs, and bark become boats in this water table. Note also how the cross bar on this water table creates many possibilities for using pulleys, funnels, and tubing to learn science concepts.

Children in Katie's classroom were very interested in experimenting with water flow. She moved the water table near a wall and placed a piece of metal between the wall and the table. She added items with magnets on the back that children could use for their water flow experimentation (funnels, water jugs that included spigots, and small pieces of rain gutter). She also added magnetic clips that children could use to hold cups or plastic containers. The children would place the water jug on the top of the metal backdrop, and then experiment with the arrangement of the other items. By opening the spigot on the water jug, they could observe how the water flowed through the objects.

Check Your Understanding 8.5
Click here to gauge your understanding of section concepts.

Sand. Sand is another natural material that is therapeutic and provides many learning opportunities. Following are some concepts that children can learn while playing with sand: Sand can be dry or wet. It absorbs water. Wet sand is heavier than dry sand. You can mold wet sand. Different types of sand have different textures. Objects can be hidden and found in sand (Schwarzt, 2007). You can add the following materials to enrich sand play:

- Small cars, dump trucks, and bulldozers.
- Magnets with hidden magnetic treasures to find in the sand (Hill & Berlfein, 2000).
- Sand wheels.
- Magnifying glasses to closely examine grains of sand (Hill & Berlfein, 2000).
- Small rakes and combs for creating designs.
- Sifters and funnels of different types.
- Shovels, scoops, and spoons.
- Play dishes, small empty food boxes, and egg cartons.

Children at Livingston Head Start visited the Museum of the Rockies to see the life-sized dinosaur exhibit. They also witnessed and were fascinated by the paleontologist who was painstakingly removing rock from around a bone. Later, their teacher, Cathy, hid bones encased in plaster of paris in the sand table. When children discovered them, they requested tools to remove the bones. Cathy provided toothbrushes and small plastic knives for the children.

Apply Your Knowledge Which of these materials would enhance science concepts? Which might be more therapeutic? Which would enhance math concepts?

Sand and Water. "Patting and poking, piling and smoothing, the children's eager hands turned the sand area into a fairyland of shapes" (Hill & Berlfein, 1977, p. 18). When water is combined with sand, children will spend more time engaged in play than when playing with sand alone (Herrington & Lesmeister, 2006). As they create, they will be learning about change, mass, and volume. To enhance play with sand and water, you can add the following:

- People, houses, and animals for creating a habitat.
- Stones, sticks, and other loose parts for expanding the habitat.
- Rocks and wood for making islands and bridges.
- Pie tins, muffin tins, and other smooth-sided containers to use as molds.

In addition to sand and water, there are many other tactile items that can be added to the sensory table. You will note that food items such as rice and beans are not included on the list. Many early childhood educators believe that using food for play is inappropriate when 20% of U.S. households with children have food insecurity (Coleman-Jensen, Nord, & Singh, 2013). See Figure 8.3 for many different nonfood ideas.

Teachers' Facilitation of Learning in the Sensory Center

As in all areas of the classroom, it is important that you, as the teacher, take cues from the children regarding your involvement with them in the sensory center. Sometimes involvement can be as unobtrusive as observing and recording children's play. At other times, you may join in the activity, particularly with very young children. It may be helpful to have a chair to sit on, so you are at the same level as the children. The following sections provide a variety of ways that teachers may be involved in the sensory center.

Develop Goals for the Center

Think about the sensory center's primary purpose for the individual children and the group of children in your classroom. The goals will help you to determine what types of material to place in the sensory center. For example, if your goal is to use the center as a therapeutic outlet, you will likely want small figures, houses, and animals. However, if your goal is to explore science concepts, you might add a variety of materials to explore a concept such as how to move water from one place to another.

Extend Children's Learning

Teachers can extend children's learning by adding relevant props and materials. For example, Jeremiah observed that the children were creating roads in the sand table. He added small wooden traffic signs from a toy train set along with some buildings. The children began to incorporate these into their play, expanding their learning.

FIGURE 8.3 Other Tactile Items That Can Be Added to the Sensory Table

Different media have unique attributes providing varied possibilities for children's sensory experiences. Some potential materials that can be added to the center include:

- ❑ snow (add gloves)
- ❑ dirt
- ❑ clean mud
- ❑ leaves
- ❑ cedar chips
- ❑ pine needles and boughs
- ❑ shredded paper or paper punches
- ❑ paper scraps
- ❑ sawdust
- ❑ goop
- ❑ cotton
- ❑ used dried coffee grounds
- ❑ scraps of different kinds of fabric
- ❑ aquarium or pea gravel
- ❑ seashells
- ❑ animal food or bedding (if studying a certain animal)
- ❑ Styrofoam peanuts
- ❑ flubber
- ❑ recycled items (plastic pieces, juice can lids, old CDs)

Create New Puzzlements

Children have the desire to make sense of their world (Piaget, 1954). Therefore, "puzzling, novel situations can promote learning" (Crosser, 1994, p. 28).

The toddlers in Corentine's classroom had been playing with cups, filling them with water and pouring the water into a bowl. Corentine added two new cups to the area. One had one hole punched in the bottom, and the other had three holes punched in the bottom. The toddlers were intrigued by the new cups. Aaron began to experiment to see if he could still scoop the water with one of the new cups and place it in the bowl. Alicia watched Aaron for a few minutes and then filled the cup that had three holes. Using it as a sieve, she held it above the bowl. Both Aaron and Alicia watched the water drain into the bowl. Aaron then began to fill the new found sieve with water from a cup that did not have holes.

Promote New Vocabulary Acquisition

Incorporating new vocabulary within conversations is an effective way to help children to learn new words. You can label tools (colander, sieve, funnel, eggbeater, ladle), processes (strain, flow), and characteristics of the media (coarse, grainy, gritty). Often positional words (above, below), words that express relationships (larger than, less than), and other mathematical terms (none, numerals) can also be stressed.

Ask Open-Ended Questions

Encourage children to problem-solve and predict what will happen by asking open-ended questions. For example, you might ask, "How many cups of water will it take to fill the container?" "Will both containers hold the same amount of water?" "How much cargo (small plastic boxes) do you think your boat will hold?" or "What are other materials you might use?"

Create Challenges

When children are interested and developmentally ready, you might create a challenge. For example, you might challenge children to create a boat, a bridge, or a water wheel.

Facilitate Prosocial Play

There are several ways that teachers can promote prosocial play in the sensory center. Teachers can help children to understand another child's point of view: "Terrence gets upset when you take the boat he is playing with." Modeling prosocial language is another way to encourage prosocial play: "Anita wonders if she can share the waterwheel with you." Encouraging children to work together on a project such as designing a bridge over their river can also help children to develop prosocial skills.

Create Limits and Simple Rules

Because of the limited space around the sensory table, too many children can limit play opportunities and may lead to aggression. Therefore, many teachers place limits on the number of children allowed at the table. If they find that more children want to use the area, they set up individual tubs on tables that are nearby. Some teachers help children to remember the limits by only providing four aprons and requiring that all children using the table wear an apron. Other rules for successful use of the center are typically developed with the children. For example, "The water and sand stay in the table."

Meet the Needs of All Learners

"Water play is developmentally appropriate regardless of the child's physical condition, mental condition, age, language, gender, culture, or exceptionality" (Crosser, 1994, p. 28). This is true for all sensory materials. However, make sure that the water table is the correct height for the children that are using it. Children usually stand when they are using a media table. But if you have a child in a wheelchair, the water table will need to be lower. Tennille built a stair step water table. One end was the right height for someone who was sitting, while the other end was the right height for a child who was standing. This allowed Natalie, who used a wheelchair, to access the water table. It also allowed other children the option of standing or sitting while using the table.

The sensory center is especially important for children who have **sensory integration dysfunction (SID)**, a neurological condition where children have difficulty receiving information from their senses. Children with this condition may be under or overly sensitive to sensory stimulation. This area allows the child who desperately seeks physical sensory stimulation to receive it. It can also be helpful to the child who is overly sensitive to stimulation. These children feel constantly bombarded by stimulation over which they have no control. In the sensory area, they are in control of the sensory input they receive. They also gain the therapeutic benefits of the play.

Observe and Document Individual Children's Learning

Observing and documenting children's learning in the sensory center assist teachers in learning about and documenting individual children's development. They also assist teachers to know what types of materials or experiences could be added to the center to meet individual children's needs. Some questions you might answer while observing in the sensory center include the following:

- What tactile activities does the child engage in?
- How does the child interact with the material? For example, does the child cautiously touch the media only with her fingertips, or does she use her whole hand and arm?
- What type of play is the child engaged in—unoccupied, onlooker, solitary, parallel, associative, or cooperative? (See Chapter 7 for definitions of each type.)
- What is the primary purpose of the play (social interaction, sensory, problem solving, reenacting a familiar scene, dramatic play)?
- What strategies does the child use to enter play with others?
- What type of scenarios does the child role-play?
- What type of issues is the child trying to resolve?
- How does the child react to the different media?
- What fine motor, problem-solving, math, and science skills is the child using?

Watch the video of a teacher interacting with toddlers as they play in the sensory table. How is the teacher enhancing the children's learning?

Manage Special Challenges in the Sensory Center

Families Who Do Not Want Their Children to Get Dirty. Some people believe that their parenting skills are being judged by the clothes that their children are wearing. Therefore, they send children to early childhood programs in their best clothes, warning children to stay clean. You can use several strategies in this situation. In some cases, providing information to the parents about the value of "messy" activities and asking them to send children to school in play clothes produces results. In other cases, providing smocks that totally cover the child's clothing is sufficient. In still other cases, children might change into play clothes after they reach the center.

Children Who Are Overly Sensitive to Stimulation or Concerned with Getting Their Hands Dirty. Some children who display sensory defensiveness (an intolerance of many normal sensory experiences) might not want to touch the media. Other children may not wish to get their hands dirty. In these cases, it is helpful to offer the child nonlatex gloves to wear when using the media. This allows the child to play with messy materials while respecting her personal needs. You might also provide props so the child can experience the play without actually touching the media. Modeling play with sensory materials might also provide encouragement for the child to use sensory media. However, it is important to never force a child to use the materials.

We have examined manipulative and sensory play indoors. The outdoors also provides a rich opportunity for manipulation and sensory opportunities. We will explore this topic next.

Check Your Understanding 8.6
Click here to gauge your understanding of section concepts.

Outdoor Manipulative and Sensory Play

Children gain abundant manipulative and sensory experiences outdoors. In a rich play space many opportunities are naturally available. As children pick up pinecones and place them in a basket, they use manipulative skills. They also have the opportunity to use sensory skills, as they observe and touch the rough surface of the pinecone and in some cases smell the pitch on the cone. Many programs specifically design their playgrounds for sensory experiences, such as providing wind chimes to hear, herbs to smell and taste, and of course water and sand to play with.

In designing your sand area, you will want to buy sand that is specifically labeled as safe for sandboxes since collected sand may contain toxic substances. You will also want to cover the sandbox when it is not in use to prevent contamination from animal feces. However, the sand needs an opportunity to dry to prevent the growth of mold and to keep bugs from breeding. Some programs cover their sand area with netting to prevent contamination but also allow the sand to dry. When possible, you will want to provide shade for the sand area.

Consider adding different types of materials to the sand and water area. This can influence who plays in the area and the types of play they engage in. Also, adding more materials increases the mental complexity of the play (Jarrett, French-Lees, N. Bulunuz, & M. Bulunuz, 2010). You might want to:

- Establish a car wash—add sponges, spray bottles, and chamois for children to wash bikes, trikes, and other riding toys (Crosser, 1994).
- Provide large paintbrushes and water so children can paint the side of buildings and sidewalks.
- Spray paint a sheet with colored water.
- Add gutters to the sand area—Sue Dinwiddie (1993) describes using rain gutters with preschool-age children. She states that three or four gutters cut into different lengths (5, 31/3, 71/2, and 21/2 feet) were sufficient for in-depth play. Children used the gutters to transport sand, water, mixtures of sand and water, vehicles, and balls. They experimented with slope and angles, different mixtures and solutions, and different ways of transporting the solutions.
- Add a variety of molds and props to the moist sand area for making sand castles. Molds can be made with any type of recycled, open container with smooth sides (yogurt containers, milk cartons with the tops cut off). Feathers, sticks, rocks, shells, and other natural materials can enhance creations. You might also want

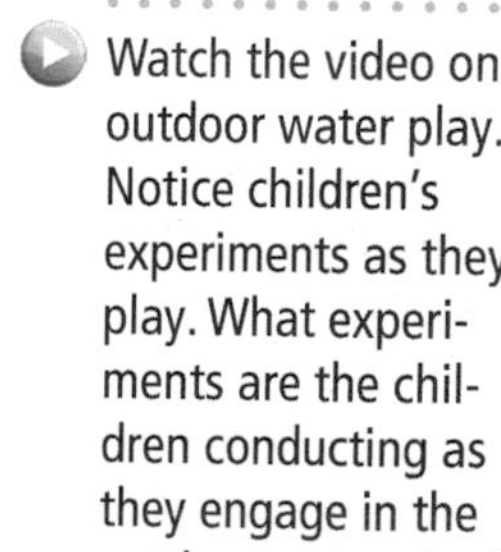

Julie Bullard

Sand play is enriched in this outdoor area through the addition of props. Pay special attention to how the props are stored.

to add signs or materials that children can use to create their own signs so that they can save their creations (West & Cox, 2001).

- Provide pails for collecting. As children collect and sort natural items such as small rocks, leaves, twigs, and seed pods, they use fine motor skills.
- Add shovels, buckets, and rakes for digging and moving sand.
- Provide trucks, cars, farm animals, and play figures. In one study, this increased the amount of constructive and pretend play (Jarrett et al., 2010).

Sand and water are basic elements of the earth that can soothe the soul while providing many learning opportunities. All age groups enjoy sensory play, from the youngest baby who is interacting with a sensory quilt to the 90-year-old grandmother walking barefoot on a sandy beach. In today's busy, fully scheduled world, children need the opportunity to experience messiness and open-ended materials.

In both the manipulative and the sensory centers, children can successfully engage in either individual or group play. A well-developed center gives children the opportunity to use fine motor skills, practice eye–hand coordination, enhance cognitive skills, and at times create imaginary worlds.

Check Your Understanding 8.7
Click here to gauge your understanding of section concepts.

Chapter Quiz 8
Click here to gauge your understanding of chapter concepts.

Sample Application Activities

1. Visit a thrift store and look for attractive, enticing materials that could be used in a manipulative center. If possible, buy the materials and create an activity using them.
2. You are designing a manipulative area for a 3–5-year-old classroom. List at least one material you will add for each of the different manipulative skills listed in the chapter.
3. Review the opening scenario. Make a list of additional sensory or manipulative materials the teacher might add to the boat for infants or toddlers.
4. Observe children using a manipulative center. What specific fine motor skills are they demonstrating? What additional materials could you add to further enhance these skills?
5. Create a sketch of an ideal sensory center for a group of toddlers. Make a list of materials and props that you would rotate through the center, keeping in mind that you would need to avoid materials that could be a choking hazard.
6. Experiment with different media. What words would you use to describe the materials? What other new vocabulary words could you introduce? What open-ended questions might you ask?
7. Review one of the following websites to gain additional information about topics in this chapter.
   a. Learn more about sensory integration at the Sensory Processing Disorder Foundation.
   b. Learn more about children's physical developmental milestones at the Learn the Signs: Act Early website.

8. Add different items to the sensory center. Observe whether the children's type of play changes based upon the items added.
9. Observe and document a child's learning as she uses the media table. Use the questions found in the chapter to guide your observation.
10. Brainstorm a list of sensory items that you could add to an outdoor play environment.
11. Assess a manipulative or sensory center using the environmental assessment found in Figure 8.4.

In assessing the manipulative center, consider the following. Does the center contain

- ❑ a quiet, uninterrupted area to work?
- ❑ an area that is well lighted, preferably with natural light?
- ❑ low, open, labeled shelves to hold materials?
- ❑ trays or baskets to hold all the materials needed for each discrete activity?
- ❑ enough materials to provide four to six children with several choices each?
- ❑ storage for additional materials?
- ❑ horizontal surfaces, including tables, chairs, and floor space?
- ❑ vertical surfaces?
- ❑ aesthetic materials?
- ❑ materials of high interest to the children?
- ❑ materials that meet the children's developmental needs?
- ❑ materials that develop the pincer grasp, grasping and squeezing, bilateral coordination, eye–hand coordination, wrist rotation, wrist stability, finger dexterity, and cutting?
- ❑ high-quality tools such as scissors?

In assessing the sensory center, consider the following. Does the center provide

- ❑ a sensory table placed so children can access all sides?
- ❑ storage for materials to use in the center?
- ❑ a nearby sink or other water source to easily fill and empty the table?
- ❑ an easy to clean floor?
- ❑ long-sleeved waterproof smocks that are easily accessible to children?
- ❑ child-sized cleaning implements?
- ❑ a variety of interesting props?
- ❑ a safe and healthy experience?
    - ○ Water is emptied after each group of children is done playing.
    - ○ The tub and toys are washed and sanitized daily.
    - ○ Children with cuts, scratches, and open sores do not use the table or they wear rubber gloves.
    - ○ Children and adults wash their hands both before and after playing in the sensory table.
    - ○ Materials that children in the classroom might be allergic to are avoided.
    - ○ Materials do not pose a choking hazard if younger children are in the classroom.
    - ○ Floor is cleaned when spills occur.
    - ○ Water is bleach free.
- ❑ literacy materials, including contextual print?

FIGURE 8.4 Environmental Assessment: Manipulative and Sensory Centers

CHAPTER 9

Developing Block and Building Centers

Learning Outcomes

After you have read this chapter, you will be prepared to:

- Describe the history and stages of block building
- Discuss multiple ways that the block and building center enhance children's development
- Demonstrate the ability to design effective block and building centers both indoors and outdoors
- Explain how to design block centers for different age groups
- Describe multiple ways that teachers facilitate learning in the block and building center

Julie Bullard

After attending a workshop on blocks, Adalina, a teacher of five-year-old children, became very motivated to develop a rich block environment for children in her classroom. Although she had always had a block area in the classroom, Adalina, like many teachers, approached it with a "laissez-faire" attitude (Bruce, 1992). In the past, she randomly cycled props through the center, she rarely interacted in the center, and she never went beyond individual discussions with a builder to enrich, extend, or discuss the learning that occurred in the block area.

Adalina began her block area transformation by closely observing the children to determine their stage of building. She also noted what they were building. She saw that many of the children were building houses and that some of the children were representing actual structures they had seen. To expand the children's background knowledge, Adalina invited an architect and a carpenter to the classroom. The architect showed the children a picture of the studio where she worked, blueprints she had designed, and photos of the houses made from the blueprints. The carpenter discussed how he used the blueprints and showed the children some of the tools he used. The children were fascinated.

Next, Adalina made changes to the environment. She added a small drafting table with a gooseneck light and different types of paper so children could develop their own blueprints. She laminated blueprints and hung them with Velcro on the wall so that children could move the blueprints closer to their building area. During circle time, Adalina and the children talked about different kinds of houses and realized that their blueprints were only for stick-built single-family dwellings. The children decided to create blueprints for other types of housing (a duplex, an apartment, and a trailer house). One of the children, who had attended a pow-wow the summer before, decided to create a blueprint for a tepee. Adalina added books and magazines on different types of houses to the block area. The children and Adalina spent several circle times examining, comparing, and discussing the blueprints children were developing. Several children began to draw blueprints and then produce the building they had drawn. They also spent significant time engaged in dramatic play with their blocks.

Adalina also enriched the block area with some of the tools that the carpenter had discussed, including a level and tape measure. Many of the children began measuring and comparing buildings. Adalina developed a graph where children could record their measurements.

The increased use of the block area caused Adalina to reexamine the block area rules, one of which was that all blocks needed to be put away at the end of center time. As children became more involved in in-depth building experiences, they often could not complete the projects in one day. Therefore, Adalina and the children decided to let the structures remain as long as they were actively being built or used. Paper and markers were added to the center so that children could create signs to label or to save their structures.

Additional props were added as needed, including linoleum and carpet samples, different sizes of Masonite (for roofs and floors), and pulleys (for building an elevator). Adalina and the children continued to closely observe buildings as they went for walks, creating a book of photos of surrounding structures. Parents also became involved, bringing in not only pictures of their own homes and places they worked, but also photos of houses they had seen on travels.

As a result of these changes, children engaged in more literacy, math, and science activities. Adalina also observed more cooperative building activity, and reluctant builders becoming involved with block building.

With the help of a child, blocks of wood come to life. "Blocks become airports or empires. Blocks become stadiums and skyscrapers, houses and hovels, castles and, today, even condominiums. Out of the imaginings of a child, blocks become everything! Lacking imagination, blocks revert to chunks of wood . . . waiting to become again" (Cody, 1989, p. 109). These open-ended materials provide a multidisciplinary curriculum where children of all developmental levels can engage in many skills simultaneously (O'Hara, Demarest, & Shaklee, 2005). As Adalina illustrated, with close observation and intentionality, teachers can greatly enrich and extend these learning opportunities.

History and Stages of Block Building

Block building has a rich history within early childhood. Friedrich Froebel (the father of kindergarten) is credited as being the first to use blocks as part of a systematic curriculum (Gura, 1993). Maria Montessori also used blocks as part of her materials. In both these cases, blocks were used in a prescribed way. For example, one set of Montessori blocks is designed as cubes that are to be placed in increasingly smaller sizes to create a tower (Provenzo & Brett, 1983).

In 1915, Caroline Pratt, desiring blocks that would allow children to have the freedom to design and build what they wished, developed the unit block. The unit blocks are designed mathematically (two smaller blocks equal a larger block). Unit blocks are still used in early childhood settings throughout the United States and in schools throughout the world (Cartwright, 1988).

Harriet Johnson, who worked with Caroline Pratt, studied the children's use of unit blocks. Based on this, study she developed stages of block building. Like the unit blocks, these stages are still used today to assess children's block-building skills.

- Stage 1—Prebuilding: In the prebuilding stage, children often experience blocks as a sensory material. They may physically examine the blocks, bang blocks together, taste the blocks, and fill containers with blocks and either dump them out or carry them around. This is an important stage, assisting children to learn about the weight and properties of blocks.
- Stage 2—Rows and Towers: In this stage, children build horizontal or vertical rows. As is characteristic of children this age, there is much repetition. As children first begin to build, they typically place the blocks directly in front of each other. Blocks are placed side-by-side in rows or stacked in towers. As children advance in this stage, they may make adjoining towers that are connected by a row of blocks. The children may use the row of blocks as roads. By age three, most children will be exhibiting this stage or beyond (Johnson, 1996; Reifel, 1984).
- Stage 3—Bridging: This stage refers to children placing two blocks close together and then balancing another block as a roof between the blocks (Johnson, 1996, p. 14).
- Stage 4—Enclosures: As the name implies, this stage involves enclosing a space. Most children will be building enclosures by age four (Johnson, 1996). At this stage, children will be able to clearly differentiate indoor and outdoor space as they build.
- Stage 5—Patterns: In this stage, children begin to use symmetry in their building, and decorative patterns may emerge.

- Stage 6—Naming of Structures and Early Representation: Children at this stage use all they have learned at previous stages. Unlike earlier stages, where children may name a structure due to an inquiry by an adult, children at this stage have an intention in mind as they begin to build. They also begin to use the building for dramatic play.
- Stage 7—Reproduction: Children in this stage actually reproduce buildings and structures they have seen. As in stage 6, children at this stage use their structures in dramatic play. By age seven, most children have progressed to the point that they can coordinate interior space with interior objects. They also can include exterior landmarks that are of appropriate scales and that portray relationships with the building (Reifel, 1984).

Watch the video of a group of boys building with blocks. What stage of block building are the boys displaying?

With ample opportunities to build, some children may progress through these stages quickly (especially stages two to five). They may also cycle back to earlier stages at times. Older children who have never had experience with blocks still proceed through each of the stages. However, they might advance through them even more quickly than younger children (Johnson, 1996).

The more time and experience the child has, the more complex the block play becomes (Hanline, Milton, & Phelps, 2001; Johnson, 1996). For example, children who have more experience tend to use more dimensions, building three-dimensional rather than one- or two-dimensional structures (Reifel, 1984).

Check Your Understanding 9.1

Click here to gauge your understanding of section concepts.

How the Block Center Enhances Children's Development

Block play provides rich opportunities. While children build with blocks they develop mathematical skills, use symbolic representation, practice science skills, make use of literacy, exhibit social-emotional skills, demonstrate aesthetic awareness, and practice geography.

Mathematical Skills

The block center may be one of the most important areas in the classroom for creating opportunities to experiment with quantity and number sense and to increase **spatial awareness** and knowledge of geometric concepts. These two math standards are often viewed as the most crucial for children in the early years (Clements & Sarama, 2000a).

There is a strong relationship between spatial skills and mathematics (Casey & Bobb, 2003). Block building enhances spatial skills. For example, research shows that children who perform well in preschool block building take more math classes (these are more likely to be honor classes), receive higher standardized math test scores, and have better math grades in middle and high school than children who were less competent preschool block builders. This is especially true for higher level math skills such as geometry. The correlation between block-building skills and higher performance in later mathematics is true even when considering gender, intelligence, and social class (Wolfgang, Stannard, & Jones, 2001).

Blocks provide children the opportunity to enhance spatial skills and geometric concepts (Piaget, 1967). According to Clements and Sarama (2000a, p. 82–83), some of the geometric concepts that children develop through block building are the ability to:

- "Recognize, name, build, draw, compare, and sort two and three dimensional shapes."
- "Describe attributes and parts of two and three dimensional shapes."

- "Investigate and predict the results of putting shapes together and taking them apart."
- "Describe, name, interpret, and apply ideas of relative position in space."
- "Describe, name, interpret, and apply ideas of direction and distance in navigating space."
- "Find and name locations with simple relationships, such as 'near to'."
- "Use coordinate systems, such as those in maps."

In addition, the National Council of Teachers of Mathematics (2000, p. 96) stresses that children can learn to recognize and apply **slides**, **flips**, and **turns**, and to recognize and create shapes that have **symmetry** as they play with blocks.

Children's spatial skills increase when they play with blocks, learn **spatial language** (such as above, below, and beside), and engage in spatial planning where they develop images of structures they plan to build (make a blueprint for their building). With experience and a higher level of thinking, children's understanding of shapes deepens. For example, they are able to relate a square to a rectangle. Most preschool children can accurately identify circles and squares. They identify triangles correctly 60% of the time and identify rectangles correctly 54% of the time, not always recognizing that rectangles need right angles. Children's ideas about shapes, while not always accurate, often stabilize by age six (Clements & Sarama, 2014). Surprisingly, little is learned about shapes from preschool to middle school. In their research, Clements and Sarama (2000c) found that the opportunities to learn are more important than developmental levels in children's knowledge of shapes.

Blocks can also increase children's knowledge of quantity and number sense (Chalufour, Hoisington, Moriarty, Winokur, & Worth, 2004). "Quantity or number sense may be as important to math development as phonemic awareness is to emergent literacy" (O'Hara et al., 2005, p. 4). For example, classifying, seriating, and using conservation in block and construction play relate to higher standardized achievement test scores in kindergarten and the first grade (Pasnak, Madden, Martin, Malabonga, & Holt, 1996; Pasnak, McCutchen, Holt, & Campbell, 1991).

In some programs, block building is dominated by boys. Because of the rich opportunities for mathematical as well as other learning, it is important to encourage girls as well as boys to use this area. Research shows that when girls have equal block-building opportunities, they are as competent as boys in block-building skills (Gura, 1993; Hanline et al., 2001; Ramani, Zippert, Schweitzer, & Pan, 2014).

In Brianna's classroom, the girls very rarely used the block area. Because several of the girls enjoyed playing in the dramatic play area, she added miniature props to the block area (people, furniture, dishes). She also made a point of inviting several of the girls to play with her in the area.

Symbolic Representation

By age three, most children represent symbolically with blocks (Reifel, 1984). In a study of four-year-old children, Cohen and Uhry found that all the builders used symbolism in their block building (Cohen & Uhry, 2011). For example, 74% of the children's buildings were based on real-world symbolism and 26% on imaginary worlds. According to Piaget (1962), symbolic representation is one of the most important cognitive achievements of the preoperational years. In the beginning stages of block building, children might first show symbolic representation as they use the block to represent another object such as a car or phone. As children become more proficient builders, they are able to intentionally represent their ideas and their concepts of different types of structures.

To do this they must attend to the differences and similarities between the structures and think about the purpose of the structure. As children represent their thinking, their ideas and concepts become visible to themselves and to others. This allows further discussion and engagement in understanding the concept. For example, Ricardo and Daniel were building stores. Ricardo said, "You didn't make a store, stores always have windows in the front. You don't have a window." Daniel answered, "It is a store. Not all stores have windows." Adelaida, their teacher, overheard the conversation. She and the boys discussed why stores might or might not have windows. They decided that they would look at stores as they traveled through the neighborhood to see if all the stores had windows.

Science Skills

Block play helps children learn about the properties of materials, stability, and balance (Chalufour et al., 2004). As children gain experience in building all kinds of structures, they learn what can or cannot be done with different types of material. "A child learns to work with a cause-and-effect approach and to predict the structural stress resulting from the forces of gravity interacting on various parts of a building" (Moffitt, 1996, p. 31). The block area also provides many opportunities to learn other scientific content. Children can learn about force and motion as they build roads and ramps and use them with toy vehicles. As children become more advanced builders, they may also learn about other simple machines such as pulleys or wheels and axles.

While children learn science and math process skills in many centers, blocks are a "medium that is particularly well adapted for children to use these processes" (Moffitt, 1996, p. 27). Skills such as questioning, problem solving, analyzing, reasoning, communicating, investigating, creating, and using representations can be practiced as children play with blocks (Chalufour et al., 2004).

Literacy Skills

The block area is a natural area for promoting literacy (Vygotsky, 1976). During block building, children practice many skills needed in reading. Research indicates that children, both with and without disabilities, who were better preschool block builders had higher reading abilities in elementary school (Hanline, Milton, & Phelps, 2010).

The block area, when enriched with literacy materials, gives children authentic opportunities to read and write for a purpose and to practice visual discrimination. Visual discrimination is needed to distinguish differences in letters and words (such as the difference between a *b* and a *d*). As children use blocks of different sizes and shapes, they use visual discrimination to create structures that are the same on both sides or display symmetry. Even as children are putting blocks away on shelves, they are practicing these skills (placing the triangle block on the shelf so that it matches the outline).

Since block building is often a cooperative activity, children have many authentic opportunities to use oral language. One study found that children produced more oral language and exhibited greater diversity in vocabulary in the block center than in the dramatic play area or a theme-based area (Isbell & Raines, 1991) Children also use language to explain their ideas, which is a crucial aspect in the development of thought (Bodrova & Leong, 2007).

Children in the block area practice fine motor and coordination skills as they build with blocks and as they carefully decorate and use their buildings. These are important skills in handwriting.

Finally, children have many authentic opportunities to practice reading and writing in the block area. However, this will only occur if the teacher is intentional in providing materials and in modeling and encouraging literacy activities. One study showed that

when the block area was enriched in a first-grade classroom, children increased the number of literacy behaviors. While children engaged in rich oral language before the block area was enriched, other literacy activities rarely occurred. When literacy materials such as stickers, paper, writing tools, books, pictures, posters, rulers, and sign-making materials were added to the block area, literacy activities dramatically increased. Further, when the teacher interacted with children in the block area, discussed what children were doing, introduced materials, and modeled the use of print during play, literacy activities exploded to more than 50 separate literacy incidents in one week (Pickett, 1998). Teachers in the study were careful not to direct play. Instead, they played alongside children, discussing ideas, asking questions when appropriate, and at times making suggestions. For example, the teacher suggested placing a sign on the store that a child was building so everyone would know what type of store it was. After this, several other children began to develop signs to identify their buildings.

Social-Emotional Skills

Block building allows children to develop relational skills, express and deal with emotions, and feel capable. While playing with blocks, children have the opportunity to negotiate, interact, and cooperate (Pickett, 1998). Blocks also provide children the opportunities to scaffold the learning for others (Vygotsky, 1978). In a study examining interactions during block building, Johnson-Pynn and Nisbet (2002) found that children as young as three spontaneously engage in peer tutoring. During peer tutoring, children most often give nonverbal cues such as demonstrating, modeling combinations of blocks, pointing, or selecting the correct block and handing it to the other child. When peers give verbal cues, they often ask the novice to look at some aspect of the block or building, discuss the shape or color, or describe the novice's actions. There was no difference found in the types of aid offered by older versus younger block-building experts.

Block building can also be an avenue for expressing and dealing with emotions. While block building, children can enact scenes and confront fears. They have the power to act out their feelings and even change endings if they choose.

Additionally, while playing with blocks, children develop a feeling of competence. Block building allows children to become the "physical master over their environment, which may in turn give them a greater sense of control, empowerment and self-confidence" (Miller, 2004).

Aesthetic Awareness

Block building is a form of transitory art. While building, children learn about balance, symmetry, shape, and design (MacDonald & Davis, 2001). They critique their own and others' buildings, developing artistic appreciation. As children build, they often add aesthetic details that are not needed for functionality alone. Block building also allows for individual creativity and novel thinking (O'Hara et al., 2005). Teachers can assist children to develop aesthetic awareness by providing materials that children can use to decorate their structures and by encouraging children to discuss and critique building details.

Watch the video to learn more about the value of block building. What is research demonstrating about the value of block play?

https://www.youtube.com/watch?v=zWS8OWWEtZQ

Geography Skills

As children create in the block area, they often build homes or other structures found in the community. Church and Miller (1990) discuss several ways that teachers can extend this learning to enhance geography skills, including:

- Going on neighborhood walks and having children document what they see through sketches and photographs.

- Facilitating discussions. For example, discussing similarities and differences in homes, different types of structures, and purposes of different types of structures.
- Displaying pictures and books of different kinds of homes, including pictures of the children's homes and homes in the neighborhood.

Children may also use blocks to develop models and maps of their classroom, school, and community. How do you develop a block-building center that will promote these skills? We will examine this question next.

Check Your Understanding 9.2
Click here to gauge your understanding of section concepts.

Designing an Effective Indoor and Outdoor Block Center

To develop an effective block center, you must provide an appropriate space with an adequate supply of blocks and accessories that are developmentally appropriate for the age group. These materials need to be stored in an accessible manner.

Designing Effective Indoor Block Centers

It is very important that the block area be large enough so that it can easily accommodate the number of children using the space. If building with unit blocks, each child will need 20 to 25 square feet of building space (Phelps, 2012). This allows children room to build elaborate structures. It will also reduce conflict and help prevent accidental structure destruction. Since it is recommended that preschoolers and elementary-aged children be allowed to save their structures, it is also important to consider this when planning your space.

To provide protection for the builders and structures, the block center needs to be in a semi-enclosed area protected from the traffic path. Many teachers develop a "no building zone" bordering the shelves. This allows children to get blocks off the shelves and return them without disrupting other builders. To be effective, the "no building zone" needs to be at least 2 feet wide or 4 feet wide if accommodating a wheelchair (MacDonald & Davis, 2001). The block area needs to be grouped with "noisy centers" and is best placed next to dramatic play to allow children to use dramatic play props while interacting in the block area.

The block center needs a stable building surface. A flat carpet or rug can provide a stable surface to build on while providing some protection from excessive noise as blocks fall. You might also provide individual building sites by cutting marine-grade plywood into 4-by-8 pieces (Phelps, 2012). This can help to define building space and keep structures more secure.

To provide a rich building experience, it is critical that there are enough blocks. The exact number of blocks needed will be based on the number of children in the block area at one time and the children's stage of block building. For example, you should plan on 100 unit blocks for each preschool child who will be using the block area at any one time. Children will often use 50 to 100 blocks for a structure. Kindergarten and elementary school children need 200 blocks per child (Phelps, 2012).

To make blocks easily accessible, they need to be stored on open shelves. The shelves should be labeled with an outline of the correct size block. Outlines can be painted on the shelf, made with contact paper, or

Julie Bullard

There is room for several block buildings in this large preschool block area. Note how children are using writing to save and label their buildings.

Julie Bullard

These blocks made from tree branches encourage children to create a magical space for fairies.

drawn with a marker. You can also add a label that gives the name of the block (unit, double unit).

Blocks need to be arranged on the shelves to illustrate the mathematical relationship. For example, a quadruple unit block on the bottom shelf, with the two double unit blocks arranged on the shelf above them, and four unit blocks on the shelf above that. For an illustration, see the photo at the beginning of the chapter. Additionally, when the longest blocks are placed on the bottom shelf, it is more stable, making it easier and safer for children to get the blocks on and off the shelf (MacDonald & Davis, 2001).

In addition to unit blocks, many programs add other types of blocks (foam, cardboard) to the area. This can increase the total number of blocks, allow children to experiment with different properties, and provide different building opportunities. Additionally, table blocks can be added to the block area or to the manipulative center such as interlocking, magnetic, wooden cube, waffle, or tree blocks. Similar to research found related to unit blocks, children who score high in Lego building in preschool are more likely to have higher math grades and better test scores, and take more advanced math classes in middle and high school (Wolfgang, Stannard, & Jones, 2003).

Watch the video to learn more about the Timpani toy study. Why were the magna tiles and train set chosen as the winners of the 2013 toy study?

https://www.youtube.com/watch?v=PvTxz__-7qw

Block accessories such as people and animals can enrich the block play. They are typically stored in baskets and bins on open shelves, and labeled with pictures and/or words. For example, there may be a basket of zoo animals and one of farm animals.

Choosing Appropriate Materials

Appropriate materials for the block area will be based upon the children's stage of block building and their interests. In addition to blocks, you will typically add block play accessories, motivational materials that provide ideas and information, and writing materials.

Block Play Accessories. Carefully observe, sketch, or take photos, and analyze children's work in the block area (Miller, 2004). This process will assist you in determining what accessories and materials to add to enrich the children's learning. Materials should be appropriate for the age group, authentic (found in an adult setting), and functional (practical and useful) (Neuman & Roskos, 1990).

To be practical and useful, the items need to be added when children are developmentally ready to use them and when the materials promote the children's current interests. For example, if children are creating towers and roads, you might add pictures of towers and roads, and toy vehicles. If children are making enclosures, you might add toy people (variety of ethnic groups as well as some people who have disabilities), furniture, animals, sign-making materials, and pictures of houses (Newburger & Vaughan, 2006). You might also add a variety of open-ended materials to be used for flooring, roofs, decorations, and for child-created accessories. If children are beginning to add doors and windows to their structures, you and the children might create some doors and windows from wood and transparency film that can become part of the props.

See Figures 9.1, 9.2, and 9.3 for suggestions of materials that might be added to the block area, based upon the children's interests and level of development. Children might visit local businesses to collect some of the samples, providing an opportunity to learn more about building while also obtaining materials to use in the program.

Open-Ended Materials to Enhance Block Play

- ❑ Pieces of wood and Masonite (samples of wallboard are an appropriate size)
- ❑ Cardboard tubes
- ❑ Empty cans
- ❑ Empty thread spools
- ❑ Linoleum and carpet samples
- ❑ Wallpaper samples
- ❑ Countertop samples
- ❑ Ceramic tiles
- ❑ Cone-shaped hats or cups
- ❑ Popsicle sticks
- ❑ Natural items—pinecones, rocks, boughs, trees, stones
- ❑ Aluminum foil
- ❑ Bottle caps
- ❑ Small boxes that can become buildings
- ❑ Clay (to keep signs up, to provide stability for fences made out of Popsicle sticks, to create people)
- ❑ Plastic tubing
- ❑ Hay (if children are creating farms)
- ❑ Sheer curtains
- ❑ Pieces of fabric
- ❑ Rain gutters (for making car ramps)
- ❑ Plastic berry containers
- ❑ Meat trays
- ❑ Packing peanuts
- ❑ Materials for connecting (tape, duct tape, string, rope, yarn, twine)

FIGURE 9.1
Open-Ended Materials to Enhance Block Play

Teacher-or Child-Created Materials to Enhance Block Play

- ❑ Child-created stained-glass windows—create by taking tissue paper and gluing to waxed paper using liquid starch. When the creation is dry, you can trace around each piece of tissue paper with a black marker if you wish. Cut the stained glass windows into desired shapes and laminate them for durability (MacDonald & Davis, 2001, p. 141).
- ❑ Doors and windows (often created with Popsicle sticks and transparency film)
- ❑ Current children's pictures pasted on cardboard, cut out, and laminated—use binder clips for the base so pictures will stand up
- ❑ Digital pictures of children or buildings on tubes or pieces of wood
- ❑ Signs
- ❑ Small twigs put into a cork base for trees
- ❑ Fences made from Popsicle sticks—by adding Velcro on the corners they can easily be assembled
- ❑ Newspaper or magazine pages rolled into skinny sticks
- ❑ Enlarged, laminated street maps
- ❑ Duct tape or felt road-ways
- ❑ Large laminated piece of paper with road mazes for matchbox cars

FIGURE 9.2
Teacher- or Child-Created Materials to Enhance Block Play

Purchased Materials to Enhance Block Play

- ❑ Vehicles (cars, boats, busses, trains)
- ❑ People (multiethnic, nonbiased)
- ❑ Dollhouse furniture
- ❑ Animals
- ❑ Traffic signs
- ❑ 1-inch blocks for decoration
- ❑ Landscaping materials (trees, bushes)
- ❑ Pulleys
- ❑ Electrical circuits, lights, switches (to create lighting for a town)
- ❑ Dress-up clothes (especially if children are in block-building stage 6 or 7)
- ❑ Measuring tapes, carpenter tape, yardstick
- ❑ Mirrors to explore symmetry and see different perspectives
- ❑ Graph paper to design buildings

FIGURE 9.3
Purchased Materials to Enhance Block Play

Motivational Materials to Provide Ideas and Information About Structures. Children's ideas for building come from a wide range of sources. Most often, these are from the curriculum theme, television, or peers (Reifel & Yeatman, 1991). You can provide additional ideas by supplying cards with pictures of structures, architectural magazines, travel magazines, art books of bridges and buildings, calendars that feature buildings, photo albums of local buildings, and books about structures and building.

Writing Materials. The reason children usually write in the block area is to designate ownership of their building, identify their buildings (for example, a bakery), and save structures (Stroud, 1995). In addition, children may make blueprints for structures they plan to build or sketches of completed structures. Teachers can add materials so that children can complete these tasks. These can include materials such as paper of various sizes, sticky notes, and adding-machine tape; markers, pencils, and crayons; masking tape and string to attach signs to buildings; and scissors.

In addition, teachers can add authentic literacy materials that architects and carpenters use in their work. These could include invoices, order forms, envelopes, house plans, blueprints, and pictures of roads, architectural features, and different kinds of buildings. Some teachers also add a block center journal. Children can sketch and write or dictate stories about their structures as a way of documenting their building experiences.

The teacher provides additional writing opportunities when she allows children to save structures from day to day. Children will often write signs letting others know that they wish to keep their building. When children have ample building time over a period of days, they often will add signs identifying their building, as well.

Designing Effective Outdoor Block and Building Centers

The outdoor area allows children the opportunity to build forts and interact in larger, even life-sized, structures. The microworld unit blocks give way to the life-sized world of large blocks (Cartwright, 1990, p. 41). In addition to all the skills gained by inside block building, outside building provides more opportunities for large motor development and often demands more cooperation to complete a structure.

Outdoor environments are perfect for building forts, an activity engaged in by children in all societies. Forts allow children to make and shape their world and to fulfill their need for independence, privacy, and self-sufficiency (Elkind, 2006, p. 10; Sobel, 1993). Forts can be built from a variety of materials such as large building blocks.

Large hollow blocks are frequently used as building materials outside, but can also be used indoors, if space permits. A basic building set typically includes blocks, long and short boards, and ramps. Large blocks provide the benefits of unit blocks. In addition, they allow children to build large structures that they can interact in using their whole body. Further, some activities, such as building ramps, can take on new dimensions with large blocks. Cartwright (1990) recommends a minimum of 20 blocks and 10 boards for a group of children if used indoors and 40 blocks and 20 boards for outdoors. She also recommends a 30 foot by 40 foot level space for building.

Props need to be proportional to the size of the block or the building. Accessories such as miniature sawhorses, wooden packing boxes, wood scraps, small ladders, and cloth or tarps can assist in creating forts and other structures. Dramatic play can be enhanced by adding hats, clothing, and props. Observation will help to determine the props that might be most helpful. For example, if children are creating vehicles, a steering wheel might be a useful prop. Many natural materials can also be used for outdoor building, as illustrated in the following story.

Kindergarten and first-grade children in one school were studying different types of housing. They took a field trip to several different homes, including a straw-bale house that was in the process of being constructed. After the visit, the children became excited about creating their own straw-bale house. They developed plans, talked to builders, contacted a farmer to supply the bales, and eventually built their house. Each day a group of preschool children walked by the playground and watched the development of the straw-bale house. They too wanted a straw-bale house in their playground. Again, the process was repeated. The preschool teacher was able to locate smaller bales of straw. However, it still took three or four children to lift each bale and much problem solving to determine how to get the straw bales to the top level. Both the preschool and early elementary children were proud of their accomplishment, showing their house to parents and visitors. The straw-bale houses were also used for an extended time in dramatic play.

Julie Bullard

This tepee frame at Spirit at Play allows children to create an enclosed structure using bark, logs, and branches. The structure is large enough that several children can play inside it.

There are many other open-ended materials that can be used for outdoor building. See Figure 9.4 for a list of ideas.

As with indoor building, it is important that the outdoor building space be located in an area with limited interference from other areas. For example, you don't want children building in the zone that is used for swinging or hauling materials through this zone to reach the building area. Just as it is important to have effective storage indoors, it is also important to have storage for blocks outdoors. Providing storage immediately adjacent to the outdoor building area saves time in accessing materials and cleaning them up. When it is inconvenient to retrieve materials, they may not be used. You might consider having a locking box to store materials rather than having to return materials to a storage shed that is located across the playground.

Outdoor block and building centers provides opportunities to use larger and often more natural materials. This provides a different building experience for children, encouraging cooperation and large motor development. The indoor and outdoor block centers complement each other, providing valuable learning opportunities for children when well designed and stocked with an abundance of appropriate materials.

Check Your Understanding 9.3

Click here to gauge your understanding of section concepts.

FIGURE 9.4 Open-Ended Materials and Accessories for Outdoor Building

Materials
- ❑ PVC pipe and joints
- ❑ pieces of wood or synthetic decking remnants
- ❑ willow poles
- ❑ stones
- ❑ logs, tree stumps, or tree cookies (slabs of trees)
- ❑ plastic milk crates or large empty popcorn cans
- ❑ straw bales
- ❑ foam noodles with slots cut into them to create giant Lincoln logs
- ❑ small filled sand bags
- ❑ wooden telephone wire spools
- ❑ wooden shipping crates

Accessories
- ❑ pieces of fabric, sheets, tarps, or blankets
- ❑ carpet squares
- ❑ heavy-duty cardboard cylinders
- ❑ hats
- ❑ license plates
- ❑ steering wheels
- ❑ large traffic signs
- ❑ large toy vehicles
- ❑ play dishes
- ❑ old headphones
- ❑ flashlights

Julie Bullard

This toddler block area at Mentor Graphics Child Development Center features unit blocks and many natural materials. The children adopted a tree in the forest and the two-by-four tree, the paper tree trunk on the wall, and the tree limbs, tree cookies, bark, and pine cones all help them to expand on this interest.

Special Considerations for Different Ages

Although most of what is discussed in the earlier sections also applies to infants, toddlers, and school-aged children, in this section we will examine some unique characteristics for these age groups.

Block Building for Infants and Young Toddlers

It is important to begin block building in infancy (Reifel, 1984). Infants and young toddlers should be provided a variety of blocks that are different sizes and types. For example, blocks that are similar sizes but made from different materials (sponge and wood) allow children to explore weight. For infants you might consider soft stacking blocks. These come in a variety of types including photo blocks, blocks with textures and mirrors, and blocks that make sounds. Phelps (2012) recommends using unit blocks with children as young as 18 months. You can buy dense foam unit blocks that are lighter and safer for infants and toddlers. Some other building blocks for this age group include cardboard blocks, large interlocking blocks such as DUPLOS, giant interlocking blocks, bristle cubes, and small wooden blocks such as alphabet blocks.

Infants and young toddlers also need many different-sized containers to put blocks into, assisting them to discover concepts of space and shape (Newburger & Vaughan, 2006). Since young toddlers enjoy moving materials from place to place, you can also provide small wagons or carts. Many of the accessories mentioned earlier would also be appropriate for infants and toddlers (cars, people, and animals).

Check Your Understanding 9.4

Click here to gauge your understanding of section concepts.

Block Building with K–3rd Grade Children

Blocks can be used for a variety of purposes in the K–3rd grade classroom. Playing with blocks can improve spatial and mathematic skills in the early elementary grades (Verdine, Golinkoff, Hirsh-Pasek, & Newcombe, 2014). Blocks can also be used for design and construction to enhance engineering skills, to study and create buildings and structures to enhance social studies, and to create and role-play to enhance drama skills. Children can also learn science concepts or experiment with technology as they use blocks.

While having unit blocks in elementary schools appeared to be declining, a resurgence at least in some areas of the country is occurring. For example, in New York City many private and charter schools have unit blocks in all the early grades (Spencer, 2011). In other areas of the country, children in kindergarten have a traditional block center. However, as children advance through the grades the block area may become merged with other centers such as the manipulative/game center or the science center. For example, in the manipulative/game center, you might include architectural unit blocks. These small wooden blocks contain architectural elements such as pillars and doors. You can supplement a basic set with additional sets such as baroque, Egyptian, or Middle Eastern blocks. As children build with these blocks you can assist them to explore big ideas such as architectural features, aesthetics, dimensions, and proportions (Wellhousen & Kieff, 2001). You might also include other small building sets such as Legos. Research shows a strong correlation between competence in Lego building and mathematics performance (Nath & Szücs, 2014). Children at this age are interested in creating their own designs as well as creating models by following the directions that accompany Legos or other building sets. They can also build and program interactive robots using Legos. In the science area, you can include materials that allow children to explore different scientific concepts as they build such as exploring gears and motors when building with Capselas or investigating solar energy as they build with K'NEX.

Providing an effective block center that is developmentally appropriate and rich in resources provides children with innumerable learning opportunities. This learning can be further enhanced through teacher facilitation. We will examine this next.

Teachers' Facilitation of Learning in the Block Center

Teachers can enhance the learning in the block area by providing background experiences, acknowledging builders, establishing rules that are conducive to building, interacting with individual and small groups of children as they play, and implementing group block talks, challenges, and provocations. It is important that the teacher also meet the needs of all learners. She must also regularly assess the center as well as observe and document individual children's learning.

Provide Experiences

Children often build and create what they know from experience. To provide these experiences, teachers can take children for walks, explore structures, and talk about building features (Reifel, 1984). You can also take children on field trips to visit different types of buildings. Like Adaline, who we met at the beginning of the chapter, you can invite guests such as carpenters and architects to visit the classroom.

Acknowledge Block Builders

Kuschner (1989), in an article titled "Put Your Name on Your Painting: But the Blocks Go Back on the Shelves," discusses the lack of visibility and acknowledgment that often occurs in the block area. For example, artwork is labeled and displayed in the classroom, admired, sent home to parents, and collected for portfolios. The work is permanent, and the owner is acknowledged. Block building, on the other hand, is often transitory. The teacher might make a quick comment, and the building is destroyed. There is not a sense of ownership or permanency. Permanency is important because it allows the opportunity for further reflection on one's work. When work is not publicly acknowledged, the message we may be sending to children and parents is that block building is not valued. We can assist block builders to gain visibility and acknowledgment by

- Photographing or sketching block structures.
- Displaying block structure photos and sketches.
- Sending block structure photos and sketches home to families.
- Including block structure sketches and photos in portfolios.
- Labeling structures with the builder's name. When a name is connected to something a child has done, it creates a sense of pride and a valuing of the activity (Kuschner, 1989).
- Encouraging the child to reflect upon and discuss the structure.
- Allowing block builders to keep their structure until they are finished building and using it.
- Encouraging children to write about their structure.

Establish Rules That Are Conducive to Building

It is important to establish rules that help children work successfully together. For example, "Structures are only destroyed by the builders" and "A structure remains standing until all the builders agree that it should be torn down." Many teachers also establish rules regarding safe ways to build high structures.

However, it is also important to evaluate the necessity of rules. For example, two rules that may interfere with block building are "Everything needs to be placed back on the shelf at the end of center time" and "All materials must remain in their respective centers." As mentioned previously, in-depth block building takes time, and if it is at all possible, structures should be allowed to remain standing until children are done using them. In the past, the block area was often used as a space for circle time. Many experts no longer recommend this practice since it interferes with keeping block structures.

Allowing children to bring items from other areas often enriches the children's play experience. For example, Heisner (2005) describes an observation where a child wanted to bring a chair from the housekeeping area to the block area. At first, the teacher told the child to return the chair, but later the teacher acquiesced. The child used the chair as a captain's command post, giving orders for building and directions on using the block-built spaceship. In this case, the chair was an important prop that conveyed the power of the captain's position.

Interact with Individual or Small Groups of Children as They Build

In a rich environment, children learn through their own explorations. They also learn from their peers both through observation and through peer teaching (Johnson-Pynn & Nisbet, 2002). However, scaffolding by an adult can increase these learning opportunities. Some of the ways that teachers interact with children during block play include the following:

- Listening to children's explanations about their buildings.
- Asking questions to help children think more deeply. By asking thoughtful questions, the teacher can assist children to reflect upon their building process. This can include discussing reasons the children used certain techniques, their building

intentions, the materials they used, the difficulty they had carrying out their plans, and the ideas they have for changing, modifying, and revising their building (Kuschner, 1989, p. 53). As children discuss and reflect upon their building, they think more deeply and may draw new conclusions.

- Naming the type of block being used (unit, double unit, half unit, etc.), which helps children recognize the mathematical relationships between the blocks. See Figure 9.5 for a sketch and name of each type of unit block.
- Using spatial and mathematical vocabulary as you discuss the process and structure (add, subtract, more, less, greater than, fewer, equal to, point, side, line, angle, surface, plane, symmetry). You might also use ordinal order (first, second, third), cardinal numbers (1, 2, 3), and names of shapes (triangle, square) to describe the structure. Children naturally use more spatial language when engaging in block play versus other types of play. However, research demonstrates that you can enhance this by discussing structures with them (Ferrara, Hirsh-Pasek, Newcombe, Golinkoff, & Lam, 2011).
- Increasing vocabulary related to building and structures through using new words when talking with children. The vocabulary the teacher stresses will vary depending upon the developmental level of the child. An infant and toddler may be learning basic words like roof, floor, window, and door. As children get older, they can learn more advanced architectural terms and features (arch, column, dome, dormer, eave, and gable) (Miller, 2004). School-aged children may be ready to go more in depth, learning words that more accurately describe each type of feature (round arch, triangular arch, and gothic arch). To help themselves remember to use enriched vocabulary, some teachers post vocabulary words on the wall in the block area.
- Providing correct information. Teachers often pass on their misconceptions to children. Some of these misconceptions are that all diamonds are squares, a square is not a rectangle, and a square cut in half always makes a triangle (Clements & Sarama, 2000b, p. 485a).
- Helping problem solve a building dilemma.
- Making suggestions when children appear to be "stuck."
- Sketching and photographing buildings.
- Helping measure buildings.
- Modeling interacting together to create a building.

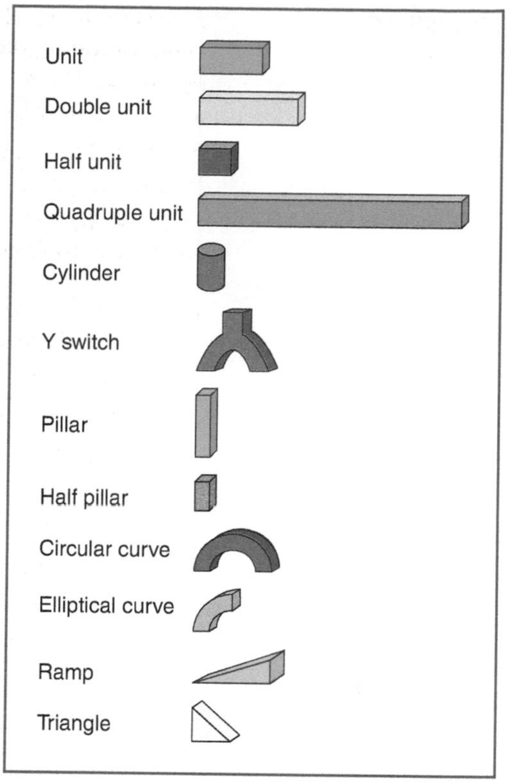

Unit
Double unit
Half unit
Quadruple unit
Cylinder
Y switch
Pillar
Half pillar
Circular curve
Elliptical curve
Ramp
Triangle

FIGURE 9.5
Unit Block Names and Sketches

When interacting with children, be careful that you do not take over the children's play, which can result in children spending less time in the play experience (Heisner, 2005).

Implement Group Block Talks

Group block talks can be used to motivate and provide inspiration, extend learning, and recognize block builders (Chalufour et al., 2004). Some ideas for group talks include the following:

- Show pictures of interesting buildings and discuss the architectural features.
- Provide information through guest speakers.

FIGURE 9.6 Children's Books Related to Building

Arches to Zigzags
An Architecture ABC by Michael Crosbie
Block City by Robert Louis Stevenson and Daniel Kirk
Building by Philip Wilkinson
Bridges Connect: A Building Block Book by Lee Sullivan Hill
Bridges: From My Side to Yours by Jan Adkins
Blocks by Jay Allen (board book)
Building by Elisha Cooper
Building a House by Bryon Barton
Building an Igloo by Ulli Stelzer
Building Big by David Macaulay
Changes, Changes by Pat Hutchins
Dreaming Up: A Celebration of Building by Christy Hale
Gargoyles, Girders, & Glass Houses by Bo Zaunders
How a House Is Built by Gail Gibbons
Homes by Fionna MacDonald
Jobs People Do: A Day in the Life of a Builder by Linda Hayward
The Lot at the End of My Block by Kevin Lewis
This House Is Made of Mud by Ken Buchanan
This Is My House by Arthur Dorros
Skyscrapers by Judith Dupre
Wonderful Houses Around the World by Yoshio Komatsu
If You Take a Mouse to School by Laura Numeroff
Albert's Alphabet by Leslie Tryon
Traditional classics such as *The Three Little Pigs* and their modern alternatives the *Three Little Wolves and the Big Bad Pig* by Eugene Trivizas

- Extend learning or motivate new building with books (see Figure 9.6). One teacher reads a story during circle time using the props (animals, people) found in the block-building center. She then places the props back in the block center along with the book. The result is increased dramatic play in the block area as well as increased time spent in block play (Heisner, 2005).
- Introduce new building materials.
- Make plans for block projects.
- Examine photos and sketches of children's current block building, and discuss design elements and what worked or didn't work.
- Conduct a walkabout where the group examines each other's block structures and discusses them (Chalufour & Worth, 2004).
- Facilitate a builder's circle (similar to a writer's circle) where a child shares his work with others, describing what he created, problems he faced, and his future plans.
- Discuss and problem solve building dilemmas (such as how to keep blocks from toppling when they reach a certain height).
- Use blocks to demonstrate or teach a lesson (science lessons on simple machines—lever, incline plane, wheel, and axle; math lessons on naming the blocks, carefully examining and discussing the shapes—their sides, points, and angles; and asking children to discover different combinations of blocks that equal the unit block) (Sprung, 2006).
- Use blocks for prediction and problem solving (such as what are all the possible combinations of blocks that would equal a unit block, or how many blocks would it take to cover a 2-feet area with blocks).
- Discuss and analyze block data (such as a graph showing the heights of the children's structures).

Watch the video to see an example of a block talk. How is the teacher facilitating the children's learning as they use the blocks?

https://www.youtube.com/watch?v=gsDY6qftzQk

Introduce Block Challenges and Provocations

Teachers can also create block challenges and provocations. While the challenges are often related to children's current block play, in some cases, particularly with older children, they might be new provocations created by the teacher. Challenges cultivate curiosity, create interest, help to improve children's block building skills, and may encourage reluctant builders to participate (Andrews, 1999; Casey & Bobb, 2003). Following are some examples of block challenges.

- Casey and Bobb (2003) describe posing mathematical problems that arise out of a character's adventure, such as those posed by *Sneeze Builds a Castle.* To assist Sneeze, children participate in mapmaking, build enclosures and archways, create a tower three levels high, and develop an entire castle complex.
- One kindergarten and first-grade classroom created structures from a book called *Block Building for Children* (Walker, 1995). Although children began with a plan shown in the book, they often changed, improved, and modified their block buildings. Children who had not used the center previously began to build with the blocks, particularly the girls (Andrews, 1999).
- One class read *Albert's Alphabet* and created each of the alphabet letters out of blocks. They took photos of the block-created letters and placed these on the wall in place of pictures of alphabet letters (Andrews, 1999).
- Chalufour and Worth (2004) describe challenging children to build a tower as high as possible using one kind of block.
- Many teachers have children use blocks to create maps of their school, neighborhood, town, or city. According to Clements and Sarama (2000a), even preschoolers as young as three can build and understand very simple maps. Mapmaking with blocks allows children to gain perspective as they examine their map from various points of view.
- Dreier (1996) describes a third-grade class that created a city out of blocks and then used it to enact community life. Each child created a building found in a city and then added accessories, including a miniature representation of himself or herself. The children used their block city to role-play city life. This created a need for more in-depth exploration and deeper understanding. As children "lived" in their block city, they became aware of the need for city services, taxation, group interdependence, and many other concepts.
- Other challenges involve asking children to devise ways to get people from the first floor to the second floor of a block building or to make their building accessible for someone in a wheelchair.

Meet the Needs of All Learners

It is important to consider children's levels of ability and their cultural and experiential backgrounds in planning the block environment. Hanline et al. (2001) compared the block building of children with and without disabilities (physical, speech, language, and autism). They found that children with disabilities progressed through the same block stages as children without disabilities, although at a significantly slower rate. However, for all children, both with and without disabilities, the time spent in block play was significantly related to growth in block building, block-building scores, and complexity of structures.

It is important that all children have the opportunity to build with blocks and that their needs be accommodated. Typically, this will involve problem-solving adaptations for each child. Following are some suggestions that might be a starting point for problem solving.

- Children who have visual impairments may be assisted by sandpaper or cardboard block outlines on shelves or by labeling shelves with braille. Children should be encouraged to use both hands to fully explore the blocks. Because children learn block skills by observing their peers, it is helpful to verbally describe other children's block building solutions or ask children to do so.
- Horizontal building might be most successful for children who have involuntary movement problems (Church & Miller, 1990).
- Children who are in wheelchairs may be able to be removed from their wheelchair for block building or they may need a wheelchair-accommodating table that they can build on.
- Experiment with a variety of different positions for children who have physical disabilities. For example, a child might be most comfortable propped on his stomach to build (Wellhousen & Kieff, 2001).

It is important that block accessories reflect diversity. For example, you might add vans that are marked as handicap accessible, handicap parking signs, seeing eye dogs, and figures using wheelchairs, mobility canes, hearing aids, and glasses (Wellhousen & Kieff, 2001, p. 163). You will also want to add people and accessories that reflect different racial and ethnic groups. It is important that all materials be closely examined to make sure they do not reflect gender or racial bias.

Children in all cultures use blocks or other construction materials (Wellhousen & Crowther, 2004). These materials differ based upon the culture and upon the building materials available. In developing culturally relevant environments, we need to include accessories and pictures from the children's culture. In a childcare center on a Montana American Indian reservation, the teachers added animal skins, natural building materials such as sticks and small stones, and materials to make small tepees to their block area. Children often made tepees with a floor of animal skins. In front of the tepee would be a fire ring made out of the stones. Since some people still lived in tepees and others used tepees during pow-wows, these accessories honored the children's culture and allowed them to portray their experiences.

We can also introduce children to new cultures through pictures, photos, books, and accessories. For example, when showing different structures, we can show a variety of dwellings, including straw huts, high-rise apartment buildings, trailer houses, and open-air houses.

Assess and Make Changes to the Area as Needed

It is important that we continually assess the block area to make sure that it is providing the needed materials to enhance children's development and provide for their interests. This will include carefully observing the stages of block development the children are displaying as well as examining what they are building.

Manage Special Challenges in the Block Center

To provide an effective block center, teachers must also overcome challenges as they arise. Three challenges that we will discuss are difficulty with cleaning up, children not using the center, and an insufficient number of blocks.

Cleaning Up. When children build elaborate structures using all the blocks on the shelf, putting blocks away can be time-consuming. In addition, because block structures may be developed by many children, no one wants to take ownership when it is time to pick up. Following are some strategies that might assist clean-up:

- Recognize that clean-up will take time. Fantastic learning experiences are worth the time it takes to clean up.

- Acknowledge the child's construction. Take a picture of the structure with the builders, label the construction with the builder's names, and discuss the construction with the child or children.
- Allow block structures to remain standing until they are no longer in use.
- If blocks must be put away, give an advance warning so builders can complete what they are working on.
- Make clean-up a game—create tickets showing a number and the type of blocks to pick up and have children draw tickets out of a basket. Have some children be bulldozers and push all the blocks to the shelf, have other children be cranes who lift the blocks onto the shelves and put them away. Use toy vehicles to move the blocks to the shelves.
- Model putting the blocks away and cleaning up by assisting children with this task.
- In some programs, the entire class helps to clean the block area. This technique provides all children the opportunity to handle the blocks, learn about the properties of blocks (weight and size), and experience mathematical ideas and classification.

Children Not Using the Block Center. If children are not using the block center, begin by assessing the block center to make sure that it is arranged properly and is designed around children's interests and needs. Also, consider whether there is enough time to devote to block building. Without enough time, it may seem to children that the time needed to clean up is not worth the effort to build. If the environment and schedule are conducive to block building and children are still not using the block center, you might consider the following strategies:

- Read books about block building.
- Invite guests who are builders.
- Take field trips to visit structures.
- Begin a "starter" building (Church & Miller, 1990).
- Sit in the block center; your presence will draw children to this area.
- Acknowledge block structures that children create.

An Insufficient Number of Blocks. A set of hardwood unit blocks will last longer than most items in your classroom. However, they are expensive. As this book went to press, unit blocks from Community Playthings, for example, were priced at $1,980 for 772 blocks. They are guaranteed against breakage or splintering and will last for many, many years. Some programs have special fund raising events for buying blocks. Others make their own blocks from white pine. Bakawa-Evanson, Oesterreich, and Ouverson (1995) state that you can make 77 blocks using one 8-foot-long 2 × 2 and two 8-foot-long 2 × 4s. Read their article for a detailed description on how to make your own unit blocks. You can also make a variety of other homemade blocks. These include creating blocks from:

- Milk cartons—To create these blocks, trim the tops of two milk cartons and slide them together facing each other.
- Boxes—Children can save and bring different size boxes from home. These can be painted or covered with contact paper. To make the boxes stronger, stuff them with shredded paper.
- Cans—Cover different sizes of cans with contact paper.
- Trees—Create blocks by cutting up sections of tree branches.
- Sponges—Use a variety of dense sponges as blocks. These can be covered with fabric.
- Pool noodles—Cut into three-inch pieces

Julie Bullard

Observe and Document Individual Children's Learning

Many developmental areas can be assessed while observing children in the block area. Following is a list of questions that you might use as a guide in assessing children's development in this area.

1. What stage of block building is the child engaged in (prebuilding, rows and towers, bridging, enclosures, patterns, early representation, reproduction)?
2. What are the child's interests? What is the child building? Does the child build the same thing repeatedly, or do his structures vary?
3. What problem-solving approaches does the child use (trial and error, asking others, observing others)?
4. How do children describe what they are doing (physical description of their building, problems they are encountering, their building intentions)?
5. How does the child interact with others (engage in solitary play, build parallel buildings, build cooperative structures)?
6. Does the child engage in peer tutoring (verbal or nonverbal)?
7. If another child is using materials desired by a child, how does the child obtain the materials? For example, does the child take the materials from another child, offer an exchange, verbally negotiate, or ask the teacher?
8. What math skills is the child demonstrating (classifying shapes, counting, putting shapes together to create another shape, describing and naming shapes, measuring, graphing, using mathematical equivalents; there is not a unit block available so the child uses two half-unit blocks in its place)?
9. What science skills is the child demonstrating (balance, symmetry, use of simple machines)?
10. What writing skills is the child demonstrating?
11. Does the child examine books, photos, sketches, or blueprints in designing his building?
12. Does the child sketch her building or create the building in another media after it is completed?
13. Does the child draw blueprints as a way of planning his building?
14. What vocabulary (spatial and architectural) does the child use?

There are many different tools you might use to assess children in the block area, including observation, checklists, recordings of children discussing their structures, anecdotal records, work samples, photographs, or videos.

The teacher plays a crucial role in the block area by establishing the conditions for learning—creating an effective block area that meets the needs of all learners, providing background experiences, establishing rules, and continually assessing the block area and the children's use of the area, making changes as needed. It is also critical that teachers enhance children's learning by encouraging and acknowledging them, interacting with them as they build, providing block talks and challenges, and assessing their skills.

"Blocks respond to children's need (to carry, to build, to balance, to imitate, to fantasize) and respects their uniqueness" (Cody, 1989, p. 111). With the help of the builder, inert pieces of wood come to life, allowing children to create a world of their choosing.

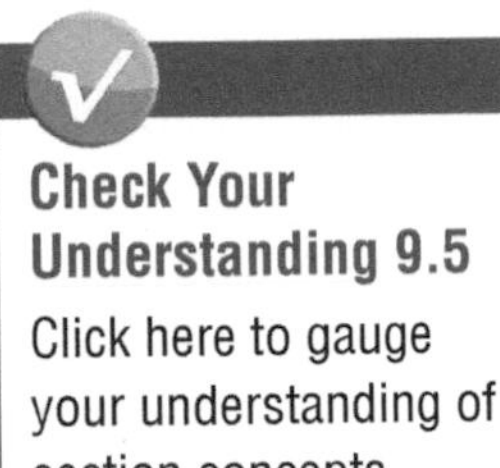

Check Your Understanding 9.5

Click here to gauge your understanding of section concepts.

While children are creating their worlds, they are engaging in math, science, and literacy. They are developing aesthetic awareness and social skills and expressing themselves emotionally. Through intentional environmental design and thoughtful interaction, the teacher expands children's learning opportunities.

? Chapter Quiz 9

Click here to gauge your understanding of chapter concepts.

Sample Application Activities

1. To learn more about blocks and their impact on learning, visit the Yale-New Haven Teachers Institute and search for Kids/Blocks/Learning.
2. Watch a 30-minute video on the value of blocks at Community Playthings.
3. Examine a block area to determine what accessories are available that would encourage literacy, math, and science.
4. Use a digital camera to photograph several classroom block areas. Analyze them by the standards described in the text.
5. Use the Environmental Assessment in Figure 9.7 to critique a block area.
6. Search Lego Robotics K–3rd grade to see how different schools provide this to students.
7. Get building ideas, activities, and challenges for 1st–3rd grade children, and gain background information by visiting the Building Big PBS website.
8. Visit an online school supply catalog such as Constructive Playthings to see the many types of soft blocks available for infants and toddlers.
9. Observe center time at an early childhood program. How are adults interacting with children? Are they expanding knowledge? Do you observe missed opportunities? Are adults too intrusive? How are children's block buildings being acknowledged?
10. Observe children while they are playing in the block area. Determine their stage of development and interests. What block accessories could the teacher add to assist their play?

- ❑ Is there a designated block area?
- ❑ Is there a stable surface to build the blocks on?
- ❑ Is the block area in the "noisy" area of the room?
- ❑ Is the block area situated so that it is not in a traffic area?
- ❑ Is there adequate room for children to build?
- ❑ Are unit blocks available (except for infants)?
- ❑ Are the blocks arranged mathematically on open shelves?
- ❑ Are the shelves labeled with block outlines?
- ❑ Are there enough blocks to create the structures that children wish to make (100 blocks per preschool child using the block center at one time and 200 blocks per elementary-aged child using the block center at one time)?
- ❑ Are accessories available (props, writing materials, motivational materials such as books and photos)?
- ❑ Do accessories support the stage of development and children's interests?
- ❑ Are there some open-ended materials so that children can create their own accessories (preschool and elementary)?
- ❑ Does the schedule allow enough time for children to engage in in-depth building?
- ❑ Over a course of time, are all children involved in the block area?
- ❑ Are pictures and accessories antibias?
- ❑ Do pictures and accessories portray a variety of different cultures?
- ❑ Do pictures and accessories reflect children who have disabilities?

FIGURE 9.7 Environmental Assessment: Block and Building Center

Chapter 10

Developing Literacy Centers

Learning Outcomes

After you have read this chapter, you will be prepared to:

- Describe the stages of literacy development
- Discuss multiple ways that the literacy center enhances children's development
- Demonstrate the ability to design effective literacy centers both indoors and outdoors
- Describe multiple ways that teachers facilitate learning in the literacy center

Julie Bullard

Evangeline noted that few children were using the reading area during center time. She discussed this concern with a coteacher, wondering if she should assign children to centers. Her coworker suggested that instead Evangeline consider ways of emphasizing this area and enticing children to want to read.

Evangeline began by analyzing the current exposure children had to books. Each day they read a story during a whole group circle. Reflecting upon this experience, Evangeline realized that much of the time was spent managing the group rather than emphasizing reading enjoyment. Because of the group's inattentiveness, she often read the story as quickly as possible, rarely pausing to ask questions or seek input from the children.

A pleasurable reading experience became Evangeline's first goal. She divided her circle activities into two groups, with the assistant taking half of the children. They pre-planned each story time, thinking about ways to engage the children. Typically when reading, they would pique children's interest by discussing the cover of the book, asking prediction questions, relating the content to the children's lives, and encouraging children to ask questions. At times, they became storytellers and dressed as a character in the story. At other times, they read audience participation books such as predictable books where children recited part of the story along with the teacher. They often brought in props that related to the story, such as flannel boards, stuffed animals, and puppets.

At the end of each story time, they placed the books and props in the reading area. Children began to look forward to story time and frequently read the modeled books and used the props in the reading area.

Language is a universal human trait that helps define us as human beings. Words, verbal and written, can transport us to real and imaginary worlds, assist us to convey and gain valuable information, capture our history and allow us to learn from the history of others, help us to solve problems, and provoke our emotions. Do you remember the joy of a favorite story? Have you ever become so lost in a book that you stayed up late at night to finish it? As a teacher, you can provide the club membership to this wonderful world of language and literacy.

Early literacy skills lay the foundation for current and later success in oral and written language and play a crucial role in learning content in other areas. Language involves a symbol system where a word (either oral or written) represents an object or idea. The ability to master these symbolic systems is critical, since the child's literacy skills at the end of the preschool years are predictive of later reading and academic success (Farran, Aydogan, Kang, & Lipsey, 2006; Scarborough, 2009). But, children begin school with a vast difference in the number of words in their vocabulary. For example, in one study the total number of words children heard before the age of four was 13 million for children who were from low-income homes versus 45 million for children from the highest economic group. Children who have low vocabularies often continue to struggle throughout their schooling (Hart & Risley, 1995). As children mature, this foundation affects their future careers and ability to function in a democratic society.

However, as an early childhood teacher you have the opportunity to help change this statistic by developing rich literacy environments and exposing children to descriptive language in the way that they learn best, in an authentic context. Research reveals that all children learn literacy skills best when they are in stimulating environments with sensitive adults who frequently scaffold their learning (Burchinal & Forestieri, 2011). In this chapter, we will explore how we establish these environments.

Stages of Literacy Development

Reading and writing acquisition is a developmental continuum that begins at birth (IRA/NAEYC, 1998, p. 5). From birth, children are primed to learn language, recognizing their parent's voices and preferring speech to other sounds. By the age of two months,

Table 10.1 Child's Age, Average Sentence Length, and Receptive Vocabulary

Child's Age	Average Sentence Length	Number of Vocabulary Words Understood
24 months	2–4 words	500–2,000 words
36 months	4–5 words	1,000–5,000 words
48 months	5–6 words	3,000–10,000 words
60 months	6 or more words	5,000–20,000 words

Sources: CDC Developmental Milestones, 2007; and Berger, 2009.

they can make a range of different meaningful noises such as cooing, laughing, and crying. One-year-old children are able to make sounds from their native language and often are speaking their first words. Beginning at about 18 months of age, after children learn their first 50 words, they go through what is referred to as a naming explosion. During this time, they gain 50 to 100 new words per month. Most of these beginning words are nouns (Berger, 2009). This growth in vocabulary is an important predictor of reading success (Harris, Golinkoff, & Hirsh-Pasek, 2011). Children's rapid growth in vocabulary and sentence length continues through the early childhood years. See Table 10.1 for average sentence length and vocabulary of children ages 24 to 60 months.

Julie Bullard

Note how intently Emera is filling the page with print.

Written language also progresses rapidly in the early years, proceeding through the following stages as children are motivated to communicate their ideas (MacDonald, 2006). Typically, as children move to more advanced stages of writing, they will begin to use the earlier stages of writing less and less. However, they are more likely to use lower levels of writing if the task is complex (Mayer, 2009). The stages of writing are:

- Random scribbles.
- Controlled scribbles—Children begin to use linear scribbles to represent print.
- Letter-like forms—Children begin to create mock letters with letter-like forms. They separate writing from drawing.
- Letter and symbol relationship—Children begin to write their names and copy words in their environment.
- **Invented spelling**—Children begin to write their own words, spelling them phonetically or according to the sounds of the speech. Words will often contain consonants but may not contain vowels. This is a meaningful, important phonemic process. It often occurs before children know the names of all the alphabet letters or have mastered **phonemic awareness** (Richgels, 2001; Roskos, Christie, & Richgels, 2003).
- Standard spelling—Children begin to use conventional spelling.

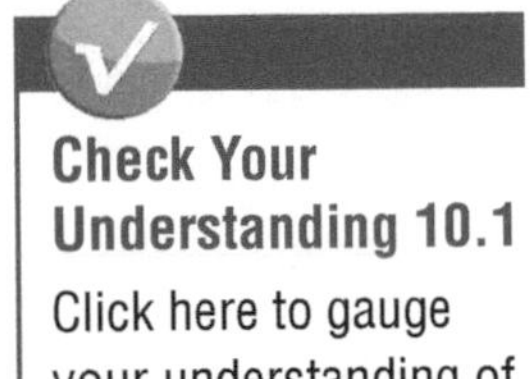

Check Your Understanding 10.1

Click here to gauge your understanding of section concepts.

See examples of each of these stages of writing in Figure 10.1.

FIGURE 10.1
Stages of Writing

Literacy skills (reading, writing, speaking, and listening) develop concurrently and continue to increase throughout the early childhood years. By the third grade, most children can read fluently using a range of word strategies, write expressively, edit their work, and use a rich and varied vocabulary (IRA/NAEYC, 1998).

How the Literacy Center Enhances Children's Development

In a well-developed literacy center, children get the opportunity to practice important skills needed to become effective speakers, listeners, readers, and writers.

Watch the video to learn more about children's writing. What types of writing experiences do these teachers provide for children?

https://www.youtube.com/watch?v=VTIsnGFQoU0&list=PLOi8GvrHbwFE9onAKpT84N0IhMP0gdcCL&index=4

Writing Skills

The ability to write letters and one's name in the preschool years is predictive of later literacy (National Early Literacy Panel, National Institute for Literacy, & National Center for Family Literacy, 2008). The well-developed literacy center includes materials needed to practice this skill. In addition, writing is often incorporated in other centers in the classroom.

Oral Language

Speech is a crucial tool in expressing oneself. Oral language is also considered a building block or foundation for reading and writing (Searfoss, Readence, & Mallette, 2001). Through oral language, children gain essential background knowledge, experience language sounds that lead to **phonological awareness**, learn new vocabulary, and learn about the uses and **conventions** of language (Halle, Calkins, Berry, & Johnson, 2003, p. 2).

Listening Skills

Children spend 65% to 90% of their time listening while in school settings (Gilbert, 2004, p. 20). However, of all the language arts, teachers place the least emphasis on helping children develop listening skills (Smith, 2003; Timm & Schroeder, 2000), causing some to call it the "forgotten language art" (Tompkins, 2005). A well-developed literacy center can help develop these important skills.

Print Awareness

Print awareness allows a child to understand the organization of print and that print carries meaning. This includes concepts of print such as the distinction between a letter, word, sentence, or paragraph. Also included is that print has a direction (left to right, top to bottom in the English language) and occurs in a particular order (beginning, middle, and end in a story). Another important component of print awareness is that print can be used for a variety of purposes. For example, print can be used to give directions and information, to provide pleasure, and to communicate with others (Searfoss et al., 2001).

Phonological and Phonemic Awareness

"The term **phonological awareness** refers to a general appreciation of the sounds of speech as distinct from their meaning" (Snow, Burns, & Griffin, 1998, p. 51). This includes learning that oral language is composed of sounds that can be **segmented** (divided) and blended. Children usually begin this process with learning about rhyming, then sentence segmenting, syllable segmenting and blending, **onsets** (initial word sounds) and **rime** (middle and ending word sounds), and finally individual **phonemes** (smallest unit of sound) (Chard & Dickson, 1999). Phonological skills are linked to a child's later ability to decode words, spell, and comprehend text (Pelatti, Piasta, Justice, & O'Connell, 2014).

Alphabetic Principle

The **alphabetic principle** is the understanding that there is a relationship between letters and sounds and that words have a structure made of sounds and sound patterns (Epstein, 2014). Alphabetic knowledge and phonemic awareness are important in learning to decode words (National Early Literacy Panel, National Institute for Literacy, & National Center for Family Literacy, 2008).

Positive Attitude Toward Reading

To become proficient in using literacy, children must have a positive attitude toward reading and writing. Positive attitudes increase motivation to read and write. As children engage in additional practice, they typically become more proficient. Children who like to read have often had an abundance of positive experiences being read to. They view reading and writing as pleasurable and something that they are successful at. For example, children who are in early elementary school become more successful readers when they are able to choose their own texts, spend most of their allocated literacy time actually reading rather than working on reading skills, and when they read texts that are matched to their ability level (Allington, 2011). To persist at reading, children need to experience a 90% to 95% rate of success (Neuman, Copple, & Bredekamp, 2000).

Enhancement of Other Curricular Areas

In addition to learning specific literacy skills in the literacy center, children also have the opportunity to:

- Increase knowledge in all curriculum areas. As children are exposed to a variety of texts, they gain academic vocabulary and concepts that are crucial for their success in different curriculum areas. For example, research indicates that when teachers read science-focused texts to young children, there is a significant difference in children's scientific content and vocabulary (Anderson & Fenty, 2013).
- Learn about new worlds, both real and imaginary. Through books, children can learn about others and gain cultural knowledge.
- Cope more effectively with difficulties. Stories can help children realize that others have had similar experiences. Books can provide information on coping strategies and answer questions that children might have. They can also act as a springboard to open dialogue about a difficult situation. In addition to stories, you might have children draw or write about their feelings. Tessa begins each day with "emotional literacy." Children draw or write about their emotions and experiences. For example, one child was happy because she got a new puppy. Another child was sad because he missed a grandfather who died.
- Improve social interactions. Children learn literacy skills through social interaction. However, social skills are enhanced by increased language skills.
- Be entertained and experience enjoyment.

Through using an effective literacy center, children gain skills in literacy and other curricular areas. But how does one design an effective center?

Check Your Understanding 10.2

Click here to gauge your understanding of section concepts.

Watch the video to learn more about early literacy. What are the five predictors that the video lists as being important for early literacy?

https://www.youtube.com/watch?v=HqlmgAd3vyg

Designing an Effective Literacy Center

A rich, effective literacy center provides a comfortable, enticing place for children to engage in reading, storytelling, listening, writing, and manipulating and playing with letters and words. Each of these different activities may be included within one center or divided into smaller centers such as reading, writing, and listening areas. If they are divided into separate centers, they should be placed in close proximity to each other, since activities in one area of literacy often provide inspiration for other areas. Additionally, literacy will be incorporated throughout all other learning centers in the environment. For the sake of clarity in this chapter, we will examine each of these areas separately.

Watch the video to learn more about creating a print-rich environment. What are the many different ways that the environment supports children in gaining literacy skills?

Designing an Effective Reading Area

To design an effective reading area the teacher must think about the appropriate placement of the center; the size of the center; how to create an enticing, inviting environment; and what books and props to include in the center.

Placed in a Quiet, Well-Lit Area of the Room. Since reading is often a quiet activity, the center should be located in the quiet area of the room. It is important to have adequate lighting in this area. Having a three-way light bulb allows children to adjust the lighting according to their needs.

Clearly Defined. The literacy center may be in a loft, on a riser, or divided from the rest of the room by bookshelves and dividers. A clearly defined, separated area reduces distractions and encourages more in-depth experiences.

Julie Bullard

This blow-up bathtub provides a comfortable, private spot for this toddler to look at books.

Large Enough Area to Accommodate Five to Six Children. In planning the reading center, you need to consider the number of children that might be using the center at any point in time. Morrow, Freitag, and Gambrell (2009), well-known literacy experts, recommend that the center should accommodate a minimum of five or six children. In addition, there should be at least one very private, quiet place to read. A small blow-up boat filled with pillows, a treehouse reached by climbing a ladder, or a special seat for reading such as a rocking chair or a recliner can all become special individual reading spaces. I once had a classroom with a bathtub filled with pillows that was just right for an individual reader. Ecole, a Head Start teacher, created a reading hut by laying a shelf on its side.

Julie Bullard

This couch is a comfortable space for children and adults to read together. Families and children can also watch the digital picture frame and reflect upon the activities that have occurred in the program.

Comfortable and Aesthetic. The area needs relaxing places to sit (pillows, beanbag chairs, hammocks, backrests, or sofas). Soft lighting, rugs, and interesting displays also make the center more inviting.

Enticing. There are many ways to make the reading area enticing, such as adding book-related displays (posters advertising books, book covers), objects that go with highlighted books (a display of seashells if highlighting books about the ocean), a large stuffed animal to read to or cuddle up with, photos of children reading books, or an interesting entry into the book area. You might also involve the children in naming the reading area and in designing and building a special entry into the area.

Engaging. The reading center needs to provide opportunities for active reading and storytelling involvement (Reutzel & Morrow, 2007, p. 38). Roskos and Christie, two early literacy experts, stress that story reenactments should occur after most class read-alouds assisting children with reading comprehension (Roskos & Christie, 2011). The props used for the reenactments can then be placed in the literacy center. Storybook props can assist children to actively engage with the literature. Following are some examples:

- Flannel boards—Children can retell a story using a flannel board and flannel board figures. You can create your own flannel board stories by making color duplicates of figures in storybooks, laminating them, and adding a backing of sandpaper, Velcro, or felt (you will want to make sure to check with the publisher or copyright holder) (Jalongo, 2003). Magnetic boards and figures can also be used.

- Roll movies—To make a roll movie, you can use shelving paper or any other paper that comes on a roll. Unroll the paper and draw or glue pictures to the paper. Cut out the front of a box making a hole that is a little larger than the width of the paper. Cut circular holes on both the top and the bottom of each side of the box. Place dowels through the holes to wind the paper on. The dowel should extend at least 4 inches on each side of the box. To play the roll movie, turn the top dowel. Children can use the roll movie to tell the story.
- Puppets—Provide finger puppets, a storytelling glove puppet, hand puppets, stick puppets, or masks that relate to a particular story for story retelling (see Chapter 14 for more information).
- Storytelling props that relate to a specific story—For example, if you were reading or telling the story *Stone Soup* by Jon Muth, you might use a large pot and plastic vegetables as props. Hats might be added to go along with *Caps for Sale* by Esphyr Slobodkina. A mitten and small plastic animals could be props for *The Mitten* by Jan Brett.
- Special clothing—A storytelling apron, costume, or hat can be used to designate a person as a storyteller. This is especially effective if the teacher uses the special clothing when she tells a story. As stated by Vivian Paley (2004), "the stories I so eagerly read to the children were not the only or even the primary source of stories in the classroom. The children were, in fact, natural-born storytellers who created literature as easily as I turned the pages of a book" (p. 16). Recorded children's stories can be transcribed and placed into the reading center for additional literacy opportunities.
- Stuffed animals related to the books—For example, you might add a stuffed Curious George monkey to go with the *Curious George* books.
- An overhead projector with pictures or figures from a highlighted book that children can use to tell the story.

In Terri's kindergarten classroom, children assist in determining the props that go with the stories. Children think about what props would work best for a particular book and then create or collect the props. For example, one child created finger puppets to use in reading or telling the story, *The Very Grouchy Ladybug* by Eric Carle. Another child created a flannel board story to use with Charles Shaw's book, *It Looked Like Spilled Milk*. If the props are small, Terri keeps them in a plastic bag that she attaches to the back of the book by using binder clips. She displays large props in many different ways. For example, Terri places the plastic vegetables and the *Stone Soup* book in the pot and displays it on a shelf. She uses a child-size coat rack to display the hats for *Caps for Sale*. The book is placed in front of the rack. Terri alternates these larger book props to save space and to keep children's interest.

Well Stocked with Quality Books. An abundance of high-quality books is the cornerstone of the reading area.

- The reading area needs to contain five to eight books per child (Morrow, 2012; Morrow, Freitag, & Gambrell, 2009; Reutzel & Morrow, 2007).
- Featured books need to be displayed with their fronts showing. Display options include bookshelves designed for this purpose, revolving wire racks, or open shelves with rain gutters used to support the books. Highlighted books might relate to the current theme or project or to an author's study.

Julie Bullard

Organized baskets of books provide additional reading opportunities.

- Additional books can be organized in baskets or on shelves by genre, topic, picture books, easy to read, and so forth. For children who are beginning to read text, multiple copies of popular books encourage children to read together (Morrow, 2012). Amanda, a teacher of preschool children, codes books with a colored dot that matches a label on the shelf to make it easier to put the books away. Children's magazines and newspapers can also be included for additional reading material. Although experts stress the importance of having a large number of books per child, this often does not occur. In a national survey of more than 300 child-care centers, Neuman, Celano, Greco, and Shue (2001) found that there was an average of only one to two books per child and that most of these were of poor quality. It is critical that we remedy this situation if we want children to gain literacy skills.
- Books should be of high quality. Every year more than 20,000 children's books are published in the United States (Bogart & Blixrud, 2011). Since you will have an opportunity to expose children to very few of these books, you will want to choose the very highest quality literature that you can locate. To find high-quality books, you can:
  - Choose those that have won awards (the Database of Award-Winning Children's Literature).
  - Choose from a recommended list of books; Association for Library Services to Children (ALSC) is one organization that prepares recommended reading lists.
  - Use the criteria listed in Figure 10.2 to choose your own books.

Check Your Understanding 10.3

Click here to gauge your understanding of section concepts.

Books and Props Rotated. Books need to be rotated to meet the needs of the children in the group and to expose children to new literature. Morrow (2012) recommends introducing and rotating at least 25 new books every two weeks. While this seems like a lot of books, teachers find innovative ways to obtain books, including borrowing books from libraries, buying second hand books, creating wish lists for donated books, hosting book drives, and having book sales. In many cases, teachers receive free books for the classroom based upon the books sold. Additionally, there are several programs for schools serving low-income children such as First Book and the Literacy Empowerment Foundation that provide books free or at a very low cost.

Responsive to the Needs and Interests of the Children. To be responsive to the needs and interests of the children, you will need books at a variety of different levels of difficulty that cover topics and genres of interest to your group, and that are written in the home languages of the children. In most settings, you will need difficulty levels representing three to four age or grade levels (Morrow, Freitag, & Gambrell, 2009). For example, in a four- and five-year-old classroom, you might have children who are beginning to read and need easy-to-read books, others who are just learning about reading who will be assisted by predictable books, and still other children who have had extremely limited exposure to books and are still learning about book-handling conventions.

FIGURE 10.2
Criteria for Choosing High-Quality Books

All books used in early childhood settings should meet the following criteria (Jalongo, 2003; Sawyer, 2004):

- ❑ Interesting and enjoyable
- ❑ Developmentally appropriate for the audience (appropriate topic, length, amount of text on each page, print style, and print size). The location of print should help children to understand that reading in English proceeds from left to right and top to bottom.
- ❑ Literary value (credible, consistent, realistic characters; descriptive, "rich" language; interesting, engaging, well-developed plot)
- ❑ Quality illustrations and photographs (award-winning artwork, well integrated with the text, demonstrates attention to detail, mood in artwork complements story, allows the child to "tell" the story from the pictures)
- ❑ Free from stereotypes (authentically portrays diversity; does not promote stereotypical views of gender, culture, or families)
- ❑ Cultural books need to be authentic and the author needs to have the authority to speak for the group or at least some members of the group (Sipe, 2011).
- ❑ Appealing to you as an adult (if you enjoy the book, you are more likely to demonstrate this joy as you read the book)
- ❑ Quality binding and paper that will last through many readings

Nonfiction Books Should Meet These Additional Criteria
Nonfiction books should provide accurate information that is written with the developmental level of the child in mind. If the child is going to use the book as a resource, it is important that it is easy to locate information in the text.

A wide range of topics and genres need to be included to meet the interests of all the children in the group and to expose children to a variety of different types of literature. For example, the Common Core State Standards state that children in K–5 should be reading stories, dramas, poetry, nonfiction, and historic, scientific, and technical texts from different cultures and time periods (National Governors' Association, & Council of Chief State School Officers, 2010). In addition to picture storybooks, informational books, fairy tales, wordless books, predictable books, poetry, and realistic literature, you might also want to include some less traditional books such as joke books and cookbooks in early childhood classrooms (Morrow, 2012). Digital books are another popular option with children. See Figure 10.3 for more information about choosing quality e-books.

In the early childhood years, all books need to contain pictures. Since different sizes of books appeal to different children, you might include very small books to big books. Big books might be housed on a stand with a special pointer such as a "magic wand" to use when reading the book. Walls in the area can also provide reading opportunities. Poems, finger plays, songs, and **rebus stories** (stories containing pictures for some of the words) can be placed on the walls.

Julie Bullard

Child-created books should also be available in the literacy area. Here Shauna sits in the author's chair reading her book to her peers.

Representative of a Variety of Cultures. "Good multicultural children's books challenge stereotypes,

FIGURE 10.3 Integrating Technology: E-Books

E-books have been found to provide similar benefits as an adult reading a print book to a child. Studies have shown that e-books can improve children's vocabulary, comprehension, phonological awareness, and word recognition (Neumann & Neumann, 2014). As with printed books, learning is enhanced when facilitated by an adult (Hoffman, 2013).

A high-quality e-book:

- ❑ meets the criteria of high-quality literature.
- ❑ meets the developmental needs and interests of the child.
- ❑ is linked to the curriculum.
- ❑ scaffolds children's learning.
- ❑ allows text to be highlighted as it is read.
- ❑ allows children to turn pages.
- ❑ provides different language options.
- ❑ allows the child the option of having a recording of the book read to them or reading the book to themselves.
- ❑ allows additional options such as recording your own stories to go with pictures. For example, *Pat the Bunny* allows children to record their voice and also insert their photo.
- ❑ allows for interactivity. For example, the child might be able to hear the actual sounds of an animal in an animal book when they touch the animal. However, the effects need to be consistent with and integral to the story or they can become distracting.
- ❑ has clear navigation and instructions.

You can find evaluations of digital textbooks from different sources including Digital Storytime or the Texas Computer Education Association (under Learn on their website). You can also find a variety of well-known fiction books in e-book format such as the *Curious George* and *Dr. Seuss* books and informational e-books such as *The Smithsonian Backyard Series*. The Smithsonian e-books are a series of books with wonderful illustrations, professional narration, and factual content.

provide a realistic glimpse into the lives of diverse groups of people, help children learn to recognize unfairness, and provide models for challenging inequity" (Anti-Defamation League, 2003). It is important that the cultures of the children in the classroom are represented in the literature that is chosen. It is also important to expose children to other cultures and ways of life so that we don't create bias by omission. "If literature is a mirror that reflects human life, then all children who read or are read to need to see themselves reflected as part of humanity. If they are not, or if their reflections are distorted and ridiculous, there is the danger that they will absorb negative messages about themselves and people like them. Those who see only themselves or who are exposed to errors and misrepresentations are miseducated into a false sense of superiority, and the harm is doubly done" (Bishop, 1992, p. 43). Books should also represent all kinds of families. The way that stories are told also needs to be respectful and appropriate to the culture's practices and beliefs. For example, some American Indian stories are only told during certain seasons.

You will also want books written in the children's home languages. In addition to paper books, you might consider adding some digital books where children can hear familiar stories read in several different languages. Another digital option is One Globe Kids. You can visit children from around the world and hear their stories either online or through an app. For example, real children tell you about their daily lives, what they do for fun, what they eat, and about where they live.

The furniture, props, fabric, and rugs in the literacy center can also represent different cultural backgrounds. For example, some American Indian tribes used willow backrests. These are very comfortable seating options for the reading area. Storing books in locally woven baskets and providing a rug woven by a local artisan are other ways to introduce culture.

Designing an effective reading area that is supplied with high-quality books can encourage children to read. Many teachers also encourage reading by creating a check-out system so children can take a favorite book home to read to younger siblings or their parents.

It is also important to create a print rich environment by having functional print throughout the classroom. This can include written directions, written schedules, labels for parts of the room and for materials, written morning messages, and signs (exit). Functional print should be written in English and in other languages spoken by the children in the classroom.

TIP

Create a book repair kit or book hospital so that children can mend damaged books. The kit can include clear packing tape, glue sticks, erasers, and scissors. You will need to teach children the basics of repair. Some teachers have this as one of the children's classroom jobs.

Including Literacy Manipulatives

Literacy manipulatives may be included within the reading, writing, listening, or manipulative areas. You might also have a separate center. Materials need to be rotated to keep children's interests. When designing the area or rotating materials it is important to make sure that developmentally appropriate materials from each category (oral skills, alphabetic awareness, phonemic awareness, and materials to enhance knowledge of words) are included in the classroom.

Oral Skills Materials. Verbal skills can be enhanced by using a variety of manipulatives including:

- Picture cards—The child turns over a card and describes the object to another person to see if he can guess what is being described. Alternatively, the person who cannot see the card might ask questions about the picture.
- Feeley box—A feeley box is a closed box with a hole in it large enough for a child to insert her hand. Children describe the characteristics and identify the items in the box by feeling them. The items can be changed frequently to create new opportunities for description.
- Play microphones—Microphones encourage children to be weather or news reporters.
- Recording devices—There are a variety of small recording devices that encourage children to record a short message and hear it played back (e.g., YakBaks or digital pens).

Alphabetic Awareness Materials. Matching and manipulating letters help children to begin to recognize differences between letters. With the assistance of an adult or a more competent peer, children can also begin to learn the letter names. Some materials that enhance children's knowledge of the alphabet include:

- Different types of letters (magnetic, wood, foam, sandpaper, letter molds, letter stamp sets).
- Matching games (such as lowercase and capital letter puzzle match).
- ABC puzzles (each individual letter should be a separate puzzle piece).

- Letter activities (such as letter beads to match and string, letters to lace around, letter cookie cutters with play dough, Wikki Stix so that children can create letters, magazines to cut out letters).

Lyhn produced letter-matching games by using her computer to create alphabets in different fonts. She printed these on card stock and cut the letters apart. She placed the letters in an intricately carved box that enticed the children to sort them.

Phonemic Awareness Materials. Awareness of phonemes can be enhanced through a variety of manipulative materials, including the following:

- Lotto games of rhyming words or words that begin with the same sound.
- Syllable clapping cards—The child draws a picture card from a basket and claps the number of syllables in the word. The child then turns the card over to see if he is correct. The back of the card contains a numeral indicating the correct number of claps.
- Word cards to sort by beginning sounds, vowel sounds, and the number of letters (Owocki, 2005).
- Small objects to sort by the beginning sound.
- Literacy phonics cubes—One cube might contain beginning consonants, and the other might contain word endings. The child rolls the two dice and creates a word.

Materials to Enhance the Knowledge of Words. The following manipulative materials will assist children when they are ready to begin identifying words.

- Letter beads to string into words or letter tiles to create words.
- Puzzles with words and matching pictures—Puzzles can be created by teachers or bought from supply catalogs.
- Word cards (might be from the word wall) to identify and sort by prefixes, suffixes, and root words.
- Paper fish with words written on them and a fishing pole with a magnet to fish for the words (the fish have a paper clip to attract the magnet). After children identify the word, they can look at the pictures on the back of the fish to see if they were correct.
- Board games such as Spill and Spell, Boggle Jr., Scrabble Jr., Memory, Pictionary, or teacher-produced games such as the Letter Beans—These can be created by putting lima beans with letters written on them in a plastic egg. Children shake the egg, spill the beans out, and spell as many words as they can (Jalongo, 2003).
- Sentence strips, word tiles, or magnetic words on a cookie sheet to make sentences.
- Cloze stories (cloze stories leave blank spaces for some of the words)—There are often word cards the child can use to insert into the story. Sometimes several different words would be appropriate. For example, At the ______ (zoo, farm) we saw a ______ (pig, cow, tiger, lion).

Julie Bullard

These reading manipulatives located in a K–2nd grade classroom encourage children to learn about words and sentence structure.

Materials to Enhance Comprehension. Felt board stories and puppets that can be used to retell stories can assist children to develop comprehension skills.

Apply Your Knowledge At what age are children beginning to recognize words? What words would you expect children to recognize first?

Designing an Effective Writing Area

All preschool and elementary classrooms need to have a writing area. This center may also be called an author's spot (Morrow, Freitag, & Gambrell, 2009) or a print production center (Searfoss et al., 2001). The following items are important to include in this area:

- Table and chairs for several children to sit and write.
- Author's chair (a special chair where children sit to share their work with others)—In addition to using the chair informally, children might sit in the chair to share their work during circle time. The author's chair may be especially effective because young children often learn about the processes and purposes of writing through interacting with their peers (Mayer, 2009).
- Assortment of writing materials (pencils, pens, markers, crayons)—Special writing materials might be added occasionally to encourage writing (gel pens, feather pens, pens that talk, pens that light up, pens with bobbles on the top).
- Variety of materials to write on (paper in a variety of types, colors, and sizes, lined and unlined, paper for making roll movies, envelopes, postcards, stationary, rolls of adding machine paper)—To provide variety you can add unusual items to write on such as bark.
- Transitory writing surfaces (such as a tray of sand, magic slates, white boards, plastic bags filled with colored hair gel).
- Computer with installed writing software and a printer so children can print their stories. There are many effective apps for writing including Book Creator by Red Jumper Studio or the free StoryKit by the ICDL Foundation, which allow children to create and easily share their books. Being able to use digital tools to produce and publish writing is one of the standards found in the CCSS (National Governors' Association, & Council of Chief State School Officers, 2010).
- Children's journals.
- Blank books—Blank blue exam books or teacher-created books (books can be cut into shapes to suggest writing about a certain topic). See the "Create Your Own Blank Book" box to see another example.
- Book-making supplies so children can create their own books—These include different types of paper, materials for covers (fabric, wallpaper samples, construction paper), and materials to hold the books together (staples, yarn, hole punch, wide arm stapler, brads).
- Clipboards for writing and drawing in other areas of the classroom.
- Alphabet strips or cards (since children's ability to quickly focus their eyes from near to far vision is still developing, it is easier for young children to use print that is located closer to them rather than an alphabet that is posted on the wall).

Create Your Own Blank Book

A beautiful blank book is an invitation to the budding author or artist. When filled with their creations it becomes a cherished treasure. Creating your own books is inexpensive and allows you the flexibility to create books that will appeal to different children. You can make books of varied sizes, with different types of paper, and with interesting covers.

Julie Bullard

Directions

- Fold several sheets of paper in half.
- Sew a seam on the fold using hand stitching or a sewing machine.
- Cut two pieces of cardboard a little larger than your paper after it is folded.
- Choose a cover material for your book (fabric, wallpaper samples, craft paper, contact paper, bark). The cover material needs to be two inches wider than your paper when it is unfolded.
- Lay the two pieces of cardboard on your cover with a slight gap in the middle to create a spine.
- Fold the corners of your cover over the cardboard as shown in the photo and glue them to the cardboard.
- Fold each side of the cover to the cardboard and glue them down.
- Place the paper inside the cover.
- Glue the first last sheet of the paper to the front and back cover. This will cover the seams.

Variations

- Teach children how to create the books.
- Instead of sewing the book, punch holes through the cover and the pages and tie them with yarn.
- Create books of different sizes.

- Sample words and letters:
  - Words to trace or use as models—Teachers at the Early Childhood Learning Center place an index card containing a word and a picture illustrating the word into a plastic bag and organize the words by topics using a round metal ring to hold each collection of words together.
  - Word walls (see Figure 10.4 for more information).
  - A book of writing samples containing a list, poem, story, letter, and thank-you note.
  - Individual word banks—Index cards with words written on them that the child has written or dictated (store them in index card boxes or plastic bags) (Morrow, 2012). Alternatively, children can write words on sticky notes and insert them into their own personal dictionary.
  - Picture dictionaries, both commercial and child-made.

FIGURE 10.4
Word Walls

Word walls are organized collections of words that are displayed for children to use. Words walls might be:

- ❑ related to the current unit, project, or theme
- ❑ high-frequency words
- ❑ commonly misspelled words
- ❑ words chosen for word analysis such as rhyming families
- ❑ "interesting words" that are chosen by children

To Create an Effective Word Wall, You Can Do the Following

- ❑ Place the alphabet on the wall and organize the words under the proper letter.
- ❑ Make the words large enough and post them low enough so they can easily be seen.
- ❑ Add photos or illustrations next to the word.
- ❑ Only add about five new words per week and move older words to word banks (Kieff, 2004).
- ❑ Color code by parts of speech (e.g., red for adjectives) for older children.
- ❑ Create the word walls so they can be manipulated by children (match words with pictures on a magnetic board, match letters of the word).
- ❑ Increase usage by engaging children in interactive word wall activities (clapping syllables, finding words that rhyme) child is going to use the book as a resource, it is important that it is easy to locate information in the text.

- Pictures and photos to stimulate writing or to use in child-created books.
- Folders for children to store their own writing and a filing system for easy retrieval of the file.
- Ways of sharing writing with others such as bulletin boards for displaying writing, mailboxes, or message boards. Children's written dictations and stories can be placed in the reading area as another way to share.
- Special highlighted activities to promote learning and to keep children interested and motivated to write.
- Labeled shelving for holding writing materials.
- Labeled containers for organizing and storing paper (stacking trays), journals, individual children's writing files, and pencils, crayons, markers, and other writing implements (cans, glasses).

Julie Bullard

This aesthetic writing area allows children to concentrate as they compose.

Special Activities in the Writing Area.

Preschool and early elementary-aged children might complete many special activities in the writing center. In choosing special activities, teachers need to consider the children's interests and developmental levels. Often the special activities are presented during group time, and then the materials are placed in the writing center for children to use during center time. With modifications, most of the activities listed are appropriate for pre-K–3rd grade. For example, while a preschool child might create a "Feelings Book" by drawing and labeling pictures, a third-grade child might write and illustrate poems or short descriptive essays about feelings. Some ideas for special activities include the following:

- Write an individual or class book about ourselves (All About Me Book, What I Can Do Book, Feelings Book, My Wishes Book).
- Write a factual book on a topic that has been studied.
- Make an individual or class alphabet book (pre-K–K)—The teacher should provide a variety of alphabet books to use as models. High-quality alphabet books have one letter per page, pictures that children recognize, and an interesting story (Beaty, 2013). You might also provide stickers and pictures for creating the books. One kindergarten class made a very personalized alphabet book by forming their bodies into alphabet letters. The teacher took photos and the children used these to create their book. Another classroom made an alphabet book by finding and creating letters from objects found in nature and then taking photos of them.
- Create a book modeled after a published storybook, poem, or song. Children can use the published storybooks for inspiration and as starting points for creating their own similar stories (e.g., *Willoughby Wallaby Woo*, a poem by Dennis Lee; *Mr. Brown Can Moo! Can You?* by Dr. Seuss; *Are You My Mother?* by P. D. Eastman; and *Brown Bear, Brown Bear, What Do You See?* by Eric Carle).
- Make a pictionary (a picture dictionary).
- Create a book of **environmental print** (print such as signs, food wrappers, and other print found in the environment).
- Create an environmental print bulletin board.
- Write a rebus story (a story where some of the words are pictures) using stickers or a computer program such as Kid Pix or Kid Works Deluxe.
- Write daily news reports of classroom happenings to share with parents (this is often one of the rotating, assigned children's jobs).
- Write greeting cards to parents and to sick classmates.
- Write thank-you notes to class guests or field trip hosts.
- Create invitations to an event being held at the school.
- Create announcements of different classroom events (hamster had babies, child lost his first tooth).
- Make a class newspaper containing pictures and script from class members.
- Create an ad for a favorite book.
- Develop a roll story with a friend.
- Draw a comic strip.
- E-mail parents or pen pals.
- Take a classroom poll.

For children in kindergarten through third grade, you might include a help board in the writing center. The board often includes the following (Diller, 2003):

- A list of ideas for writing.
- Models of different forms of writing (list, letter, poem, instructions, story).
- A list of where to go for help (word wall, friend, pictionary, teacher).

Julie Bullard

Children draw items out of the story box and use these as prompts to create stories. Directions are available so the adults in the room, including volunteers, will know how to assist children.

To promote writing at home, some teachers provide a writer's briefcase that can be checked out. The briefcase contains paper, writing implements, and ideas and inspirations for writing (Jalongo, 2003).

Designing an Effective Listening Area

A listening center is one important way to encourage and enhance listening skills. Following are materials and criteria to consider in establishing the listening center:

- Provide a media player with multiple headphones. If children are not yet reading, it is helpful to label the on and off button so children can operate the machine independently.
- Provide a variety of stories, finger plays, music, and listening games. Provide some of these in different languages. One way to provide additional languages is to have children listen to stories on the computer. Many children's stories have options for changing the language. You can also ask families to record favorite stories in their home language.
- Provide comfortable listening places such as beanbag chairs or pillows.
- Label media so that children can easily locate what they are looking for.
- Keep books, props, and media stored together in a plastic bag or basket.
- Encourage active listening by having children do the following:
    - Listen to activity songs and do the actions as they are sung.
    - Read along in a book and turn the pages when indicated. Providing multiple copies of books allows several children to actively follow along.
    - Act out the story using puppets, flannel board figures, or other props. You might create figures to match the story by cutting out pictures from the dust jacket or by photocopying pictures from the book, laminating the figure, and making a stand from Styrofoam to create standing paper dolls.
    - Use story sequence cards to display the part of the story that is being read.
    - Identify different sounds (such as household sounds) on a recording by putting pictures of the items producing the sound in the correct order. Children can turn the cards over to check the numbering to see if they are correct.
    - Listen to a story and discuss it afterward with a friend who has listened to the same story. If teachers create their own recordings, they can embed questions in with the text. The children play and stop the recording and discuss the question with his or her partner.
    - Have children listen for particular types of word in a story and perform an action when they hear the word. For example, when listening to *The Grouchy Ladybug* by Eric Carle, the children could form a circle with their hands each time they hear "o'clock." These types of listening activities would be introduced during a group reading and then the recording along with verbal directions would be placed in the listening center.
    - Play listening games such as Simon Says. Children can play the game with each other or listen to a recording.
    - Respond to a story by drawing a picture or writing about it.
- Provide ways for each child to record his or her own stories or create stories to go with their pictures. For example, the Sago Mini Doodlecast app allows you to record your story as you draw.

- Encourage children to develop interview questions and interview others either face-to-face or through digital means. There are many examples of even young children using Skype and similar programs to visit digitally with others.

TIP

Create your own recordings using a digital recording pen such as the Franklin Any-Book Reader. You place a specially designed sticker on a page of any book and record. When the child touches the sticker with the pen, they hear your recording. The stickers can also be removed and re-recorded.

Special Considerations for Infants and Toddlers

To promote infant and toddler literacy, adults need to provide a comfortable environment rich with books, pictures, language, and experiences.

Comfortable, Cozy Place to Read. The environment needs to provide comfortable and cozy places for reading and interacting. For example, an infant/toddler reading area needs to include comfortable places for adults and more than one baby to snuggle and read (love seats, a baby crib mattress placed against a wall, a hammock). There should also be places for toddlers to read on their own. This might be an individual reading place, such as a decorated appliance box. A low canopy or children's tent can also provide an intimate reading space. A small swimming pool or fishing boat with a sheepskin rug or pillows are other options for a comfortable reading area. As with reading areas for older children, this area should be in a quiet, contained space.

Books Within Reach of Children. Books need to be within children's reach. Providers can prop books on the floor for very young infants. They can place books on very low bookshelves or in plastic see-through pockets attached to the wall for mobile infants and toddlers.

A Variety of High-Quality, Durable Books. The book area for infants and toddlers should contain a variety of different books, with several books per child. Books for infants and young toddlers are often cloth, plastic, or board books. Although they are sometimes difficult to find, it is important to provide high-quality books. The content should be relevant to the lives of the children and appropriate for the age group. They should be either wordless or contain a simple text with few words. Since children are trying to learn about and make sense of the world, it is important that illustrations are realistic (no pink elephants). The size of the book should be small enough to manipulate by little hands and durable enough to handle some rough exploration. Magazines such as ***BabyBook*** and store catalogs featuring many pictures might also be included.

It is also important to provide personalized books. s can make these using small photo albums or plastic sandwich bags that are hooked together on a ring. Books can be created about class happenings, families, pets, or common words the child knows. Books of individual children participating in different activities can also be interesting for children. Individual books can also help children deal with sadness and loneliness. Seamus, a young toddler, had a father who lived in another state. To help with the separation, his grandmother created a book of Seamus and his father doing a variety of activities together (flying a kite, taking a walk, riding in the stroller, throwing rocks, sleeping) called *Daddy and Me*. She wrote a simple story to accompany the pictures that Seamus enjoyed hearing repeatedly. Teachers can also create individualized group books. Lisa, a teacher of toddlers, created a book based upon *Brown Bear, Brown Bear, What Do You See?* She used children's names and photos (Zinnia, Zinnia what do you see? I see Terrance looking at me).

Even very young infants are interested in looking at pictures in books.

Additional Literacy Materials. In addition to books, it is helpful to provide laminated picture cards or postcards that children can carry around, manipulate, or match to the actual object (Miller, 2005). These can be placed in a small basket or can be attached to a wall with Velcro. Another way to use walls for infant/toddler literacy is to mount pictures behind a sheet of cardboard with doors that open to reveal a picture underneath. Pictures can also be taped on the floor. Very young infants can have pictures propped around them to look at. For example, soft fabric blocks can be created that contain a plastic viewing window. You can also purchase these from toy companies such as Discovery Toys.

Although it is unusual to find a separate writing area in infant/toddler environments, even very young children learn from making marks on paper. Therefore, it is important that paper and a variety of writing implements be available somewhere in the environment.

Watch the video to see how a teacher uses the time spent in routine care to enhance the child's language. Which techniques does she use?

Rich, Abundant Language. It is crucial that infants and toddlers hear an abundance of language. From birth, adults need to read and sing to children. Adults should use language to describe what the child is doing, to name objects and feelings, and to describe what the adult is doing. Since many hours with very young children are consumed in routine care such as feeding and diapering, it is very important that adults take this opportunity to visit with children. Describing to children what you are going to do as you diaper them or move them from place to place is also a way of showing respect for the child. Adults also need to respond to all efforts the child makes to communicate, responding to children's coos, engaging in conversational give and take, and expanding and extending children's speech as they begin to use words.

Rich literacy experiences are not confined only to the indoors. Next we will examine ways to enhance the outdoor play space to encourage literacy.

Literacy in the Outdoors

The outdoor playground can provide many authentic opportunities for integrating literacy. For example, in the Little Explorers playground, the following are available:

- Signs label each playground zone.
- Each type of plant, shrub, and tree is labeled with its name and photo.
- A chalkboard is hung inside the playhouse with a bucket of colored chalk nearby.
- A basket of books sits beside the porch swing.
- Along the bike path are stop signs, yield signs, and arrows indicating the direction of travel.
- Clipboards, paper, and a variety of pencils and crayons are available for writing or making sketches.
- Guidebooks for identifying bugs and birds are accessible.

Julie Bullard

This rolling book cart is brought outdoors each day to provide for literacy. This aesthetic area allows one to easily read to an individual or a group.

All the materials are organized and stored in a locked cupboard that is opened when the children are outdoors. Providing the storage saves teachers' time and helps to ensure that the materials are available on a daily basis.

Events in the outdoors can also enhance oral language.

One day the children at Kid College arrived to find that the basement of their center had flooded, and rainwater continued to flow into the building. Some of the children began to experiment with ways of stopping the water from entering. As they worked, they discussed and debated many different options. Sherri, a five-year-old, watched the efforts for a while and then became a news announcer describing the flood and the efforts to stop it. When Sherri ran out of ideas for continuing the narrative, her teacher suggested that she interview others about the flood. Sherri continued as a news announcer for nearly an hour.

Outdoor events such as the flood at Kid College, finding a worm, seeing a bird visit the bird feeder, or finding the first flower in bloom are experiences that most children want to exuberantly share with others. Outdoor activities also encourage social interaction and language as children swing, climb, run, and play together.

Establishing an environment, both indoors and outdoors that encourages literacy is critical. Teacher involvement in the literacy center is also critical since children need language models, language partners, and more competent peers and adults to scaffold their learning. We will examine this next.

Teachers' Facilitation of Learning in the Literacy Center

Large-scale research studies indicate that the language and literacy exposure that children receive in early childhood classrooms is highly variable between classrooms and even within classrooms. As you might predict, the more opportunities for learning, the greater skill level of the children. For example, the amount of teacher interaction with children is related to children's language and literacy skills (Pelatti et al., 2014). In the next section, we will explore the many ways that the teacher facilitates literacy.

Provide Opportunities for Children to Gain Background Knowledge

"Reading involves comprehending written texts. What children bring to a text influences the understandings they take away and the use they make of what is read" (Strickland & Riley-Ayers, 2006, p. 3). To increase vocabulary and background knowledge, children need an abundance of concrete, varied experiences with people, places, and things. They also need the opportunity to play and engage in sustained in-depth learning experiences (Neuman, 2010).

Expand Children's Language

Teachers can increase children's vocabulary acquisition by adding information to what the child has said ("See the ball." "Yes, it is a very big blue ball.").

Intentionally Use Rich Language and New Vocabulary Words

There is a strong relationship between the child's vocabulary and his reading achievement and comprehension (Strickland & Riley-Ayers, 2006). It is important to not only use common words but also include rare or sophisticated vocabulary that goes beyond the 8,500 most common words when you are talking with children (Dollins, 2014; Harris et al., 2011; Strickland & Riley-Ayers, 2006). Children need multiple opportunities to hear a new word used in context before they learn it (Justice, 2004). They are most likely to learn vocabulary during natural interactions when something they are interested in is being discussed (Harris et al., 2011). While intentional vocabulary development is crucial in developing desired literacy outcomes, research indicates that teachers in early childhood settings often do not use rich vocabulary (Girolametto, Hoaken, Weitzman, & van Leishout, 2000). Since teachers often have multiple focuses as they interact with children, it is sometimes difficult to think about rich vocabulary during the actual time of interaction. Therefore, teachers need to be intentional and pre-plan new vocabulary words they want to use with children. Some programs post vocabulary words on the walls that they wish to stress, so all adults remember to use them. These words might relate to a new center, or material, or to a topic that is being introduced.

Model Active Listening

To actively listen, you must give the child your full attention. We do this by being at the child's eye level; making appropriate eye contact; not interrupting or changing the subject; giving verbal and nonverbal feedback; focusing on the message, the underlying meaning, or the emotion being conveyed; showing our understanding by reflecting what the child has said; and asking open-ended relevant questions (Jalongo, 2008). Teachers must provide the needed time to listen to children. Although this is sometimes difficult for teachers to do, especially with children who stutter or are hard to understand, it is critical. Teachers sometimes want to assist the child by guessing what the child is trying to say. However, effective teachers allow children to finish their own sentences rather than interrupting and finishing sentences for them.

Ask Appropriate, Open-Ended Questions

Open-ended questions increase children's language since they usually take more than a one-word answer, tend to increase dialogue, and often ask for thoughts, opinions, or feelings. Open-ended questions often begin with how, why, what, when, or where. In classrooms, 80% of teacher interactions are task-oriented (instructions, giving information, providing corrections). When teachers do ask questions, only 7% to 12% are open-ended (Jalongo, 2008; Wittmer & Honig, 1991). Since asking open-ended questions does not come naturally to many teachers, it is necessary to intentionally plan questions to ask. It is also important to actively listen to children's responses. To revisit information on open-ended questions, see Chapter 1.

Support Peer Interactions and Discussions

In social contexts, children learn new words and get an opportunity to use the words they know. In the literacy center, teachers might support peer interactions by encouraging buddy reading, placing two or three chairs at the computer, and encouraging activities that children co-produce (such as producing a puppet show or jointly writing a rebus story).

Read Books to Children

"The single most important activity for building the understandings and skills essential for reading success appears to be reading aloud to children" (IRA/NAEYC, 1998, p. 5). A meta-analysis of 99 research studies found that exposure to storybooks accounts for 10% to 12% of the difference in children's language skills and 8% of the difference in children's basic reading skills (Mol & Bus, 2011). Exposure to books is related to children's vocabulary acquisition, oral language skills, reading skills, and reading comprehension skills. One study found that even listening to a story twice, allowed elementary children to learn new words (Brabham, Buskist, Henderson, Paleologos, & Baugh, 2012). Reading to children also enhances children's listening skills and their motivation to read.

Center time is an ideal time to read aloud to individual and very small groups of children. This time allows an intimacy between the children and teacher and the opportunity to interact with the book in a way that is often not found in larger groups. Interactive reading is critical to obtain the maximum learning experience (Morrow & Gambrell, 2001). It is "the talk that surrounds the reading that gives it power, helping children to bridge what is in the story and their own lives" (IRA/NAEYC, 1998, p. 5). Interactive reading occurs before you read the book (building interest, asking for predictions, discussing and introducing the topic, and relating the book and topic to children's experiences). It occurs during book reading (asking open-ended and prediction questions, asking children to share personal experiences that relate to the book, and encouraging children to ask questions and make comments). It is also important to have discussions after reading the book (reflecting upon, discussing, and responding to the book's plot and characters; for example, you might ask, "What would you have done?"). Some teachers have children respond to the book through writing in their journals, drawing a picture, or completing an activity related to the story.

Teachers also scaffold children's literacy learning as they read. For example, they might teach new vocabulary, print conventions, phonological awareness, print recognition, and book concepts. However, it is important to do this is a thoughtful manner so you do not negatively affect the flow of the story (Roskos, Christie, & Richgels, 2003). Davey Hagland, a preschool teacher, has a child-sized, stuffed wizard who helps introduce new words before a story. The word wizard is enchanting to the children, who pay special attention whenever he is involved. After words are introduced, they are added to the word wall in the writing center.

Teachers should pre-read books they plan to read aloud, read the book with expression, set the stage, and show enjoyment for the book and the reading experience. See Figure 10.5 for a model on interactive ways to read books to children.

Develop Interest in Books

Teachers help children develop interest in reading by providing an engaging, enticing literacy center. As the opening scenario illustrated, children also become interested in books when there are interesting, pleasurable story times. If possible, it is helpful to read to small rather than large groups. This allows the child more opportunities to actively engage with the text, which enhances learning and prevents boredom and misbehavior. Teachers can also tailor the book and the interaction to meet the needs and interests of the children participating.

Dialogic Reading is an evidence-based, interactive reading model that has been found to increase children's oral language skills (What Works Clearinghouse, 2010). The teacher begins by carefully choosing a book that is appealing and developmentally appropriate and that allows rich opportunities for alphabetic knowledge, comprehension, concepts about print, and dialogic reading. When implementing dialogic reading, teachers use different types of prompts with an acronym of CROWD:

- ❑ Completion: asking children to complete a fill in the blank sentence related to the story
- ❑ Recall: asking questions related to the key elements in the story
- ❑ Open-ended questions: asking questions related to the story or pictures
- ❑ "Wh" questions: asking who, what, where, and why questions
- ❑ Distancing: relating story to children's lives

The teacher also scaffolds children's learning through a process called PEER:

- ❑ Prompt: one of the above prompts is asked
- ❑ Evaluation: the teacher evaluates the child's response
- ❑ Expansion: the teacher expands on the child's response
- ❑ Repetition: the teacher repeats the prompt

FIGURE 10.5
Dialogic Reading

Convert Words to Text

Teachers can help children understand the conversion of words to text by recording and then transcribing children's oral storytelling, putting children's favorite songs and finger plays into writing, writing down children's individually dictated sentences and stories, and creating class experience stories. Experience stories, as the name suggests, often occur after the children have had a shared experience. After a conversation about the experience, the children will create a story about the experience to share with others. Many teachers are also using interactive writing activities, where the child and the teacher "share the pen." Children, based upon their development, might write beginning letters, words, or sentences as part of the group story writing experience (Hall, 2014).

Model the Use of Reading, Writing, and Storytelling Props

During the day, teachers have many opportunities to model reading and writing. At times, it might be helpful to verbally state what you are modeling. "Oh I see that the glue bottles are almost empty. I'm going to write glue on my shopping list, so that I remember to buy it."

The use of props also needs to be modeled so that children will understand how they can be used. If the teacher does not model the use of the props, children often will either ignore the props or use them inappropriately.

Offer Individual and Group Instruction for Reading and Writing

Teachers support children's reading and writing by offering individual and group instruction as needed. Most early childhood experts agree that we need a balanced approach to reading instruction where the teacher provides small- and large-group instruction on new concepts and skills combined with opportunities to play in literacy-rich environments. Play allows children to put the instruction to practical use (Roskos & Christie, 2011). While it is beyond the scope of this book to provide in-depth information on group reading instruction, it is important to remember that instruction needs to be delivered in developmentally appropriate ways. As teachers are becoming more concerned about meeting standards, some are beginning to use direct instruction such as DISTAR, Reading Mastery, and Language for Learning. These are typically delivered as whole group instruction techniques that are prescribed, fast-paced, and teacher-directed, with teacher reinforcement or correction for the appropriate response. The What Works Clearinghouse that evaluates research, based on scientific evidence, has found that these programs have no discernible effect on preschool or kindergarten age children's oral language, print knowledge, or cognition (What Works Clearinghouse, 2007).

Instead, it is most effective when practice relates to children's interests and level of development. For example, Sarah's kindergarten class had visited the fire station. When they returned, she and the children engaged in an interactive writing activity, working together to create a shared story about their experience. On another day she used this opportunity to teach children about the conventions of thank-you notes during small group time using the thinking, writing, and publishing process (Pilonieta, Shue, & Kissel, 2014). During center time, Sam was writing an individual thank-you card. He wanted to know how to spell "firefighter." Sarah showed him how to find the word on the word wall. Sam then wrote the word in his own individual word bank. You can see in this example that Sarah had intentionally designed a small group activity to help children learn a new skill. She also extended this learning by provided thank-you cards, word walls, and individual word banks so that children could practice this skill during center time.

It is also important to model and encourage specific skills that children need such as the correct way to form a letter, talking with the children about the strokes and the directions to draw the stroke. Encouraging proper pencil grip and paper placement is also important. For example, correct pencil grip and paper placement assists children to write more legibly and effectively (it is not as tiring for the hand). You should encourage children to hold the paper with their other hand as they write and to use the correct slant for their papers so that they are keeping their wrist straight. If the child is left-handed, the left corner of his paper should slant upward.

Meet the Needs of All Learners

We need to meet the needs of all learners in our classroom by providing a wide range of developmentally appropriate literacy materials and activities. In this section, we will address two groups of children that research indicates are at special risk in the area of English literacy: children who are learning English as a second language and children who are from low-income backgrounds.

Supporting Children Who Are Learning English as a Second Language. Thirty-two percent of all children in the United States live in households where a language other than English is spoken (Child Trends Databank, 2014). As a starting point, teachers should view the second language as additive (adding to the child's first language), rather than in a negative light. Research studies provide evidence that rather than being a disadvantage, there are cognitive benefits to young children learning more than one language (Adesope, Lavin, Thompson, & Ungerleider, 2010). The development of a strong base in the child's first language assists him in acquiring a second language by providing background knowledge, vocabulary, and concepts about print. In addition, "children's identities and senses of self are inextricably linked to the language they speak and the culture to which they have been socialized" (Genesee, Paradis, & Crago, 2004, p. 33). For these reasons, teachers should never attempt to replace the child's home language with the second language. It is also important to understand that the child's culture will influence not only the language that is spoken but the way that language is used. For example, culture may influence the amount of language that is spoken, the purposes for which language is used, the way directions are given, the types of questions that are asked, and what is considered socially appropriate communication (Okagaki & Diamond, 2009).

To support children and their relationship to their families and culture, we need to continue to support children in learning and maintaining their home language and make sure the school environment includes literacy materials that represent the home language (IRA/NAEYC, 1998, p. 6). We can ask families and community members to bring objects from their culture, ask families and community members to tell stories or sing songs in their language and record them, and provide authentic children's literature reflecting the culture and experiences of children in the group. If at all possible, we should speak at least some words from the child's home language or find others who can do so. "The earliest interactions between a child and the significant others around him communicate to the child what types of language are valued" (Espinosa, 2006, p. 40). Using children's native language shows respect for the child and his culture, helps the child to gain knowledge and feel pride, helps to establish parental rapport, and encourages family involvement (Lucas & Katz, 1994).

We also need to assist the child to learn English. It is important to use gestures, manipulatives, and visual aids to assist children to grasp the words we are saying. See Figure 10.6 for strategies for working with dual language learners. According to second language acquisition theory, children go through stages as they learn and use a second language. For example, children might understand hundreds of words in a second language before they begin to speak the language. Additionally, it is much easier and faster to learn social language, the language we use every day, than it is to learn academic language. Academic language includes technical terms, longer words and sentences, and the topics are often more complex, unfamiliar, and abstract (Tompkins, 201, p. 12). Experts state that it takes four to seven years for children to become proficient in using academic language (Child Trends Databank, 2014). Finally, it is normal that children will code switch, using both languages in the same conversation. This is often purposeful. Children as young as three will code switch when interacting with different language speakers. They also tend to use the grammar rules of the language that they are speaking (Sandhofer & Uchikoshi, 2013).

- Stage 1: Silent/Receptive—During this stage, children may not speak. However, they may understand up to 500 words and will respond nonverbally.
- Stage II: Early Production—Children in the early production stage have developed around 1,000 words that they can understand and use. They often speak in one- or two-word sentences at this stage.
- Stage III: Speech Emergence—Children at this stage speak in short phrases and sentences using approximately 3,000 words.
- Stage IV: Intermediate Language Proficiency—At this stage, children can use 6,000 words and speak in complex sentences.
- Stage V: Advanced Language Proficiency—To acquire advanced proficiency can take 5 to 7 years. Children at this stage are able to use grammar and vocabulary similar to those of same-age native speakers (Reed & Railsback, 2003, pp. 15–17).

Watch the video to learn more about English language learners. Which strategies do the teachers suggest using to support a child learning a new language?

https://www.youtube.com/watch?v=09PrmLppQ1A&list=PLyizHCAockpoWzLf4kDaq3BirJXl5mEpR

Supporting Children from Families with Low Socioeconomic Status. Statistically, children who live in low socioeconomic (SES) households have lower vocabularies, fewer literacy skills such as recognizing alphabet letters and writing their names, and poorer background knowledge when entering kindergarten than their higher income peers (Neuman, 2006). This is especially troubling since those children who begin with poor skills often do not catch up. For example, in a classic study, Juel (1988) discovered that if a child is a poor reader at the end of grade one, there is an 88% chance that the child will still be a poor reader at the end of grade four.

So what causes this knowledge gap? It appears to be experience with words. Statistically, research indicates that the accumulated experience with words is much lower for children who are low income (13 million for four-year-old children who are low income, versus 45 million for four-year-old children from the highest economic

FIGURE 10.6
Strategies for Working with Dual-Language Learners

Communicating with the Child

- ❑ Keep messages short for children when they are first learning a new language.
- ❑ Speak slowly and clearly.
- ❑ Provide wait time.
- ❑ Engage in meaningful conversations, listening respectfully, asking questions, and expanding and extending children's speech.
- ❑ Use body gestures and pointing.
- ❑ Select key vocabulary to concentrate on and intentionally use the vocabulary throughout the day. Research indicates that the quality of the teacher's language predicts the English language learner's expressive and receptive language. Expressive and receptive language predicts a child's phonological awareness and math skills (Sonnenschein, Thompson, Metzger, & Baker, 2013).

Group Times

- ❑ Use small groups and individual interactions versus large groups.
- ❑ Before reading a story, summarize the story in the child's home language.
- ❑ Read the story, several times in the child's home language, or if you don't speak the language use an e-book on the read mode.
- ❑ Check frequently for understanding such as head nods or thumbs up.
- ❑ Provide visual aids such as pictures, photos, and real objects.

Classroom

- ❑ Provide books that include stories, pictures, and the language of the child's home culture. One free source for digital books is the International Children's Digital Library. Digital books from many cultures are easily searchable by type of book and by country.
- ❑ Provide a listening library with stories in English and children's home languages: e-books often will have multiple languages.
- ❑ Invite guests who speak the language to the classroom such as storytellers and family members.
- ❑ Encourage, but do not force, children to talk using puppets, microphones, dramatic play, photos, and wordless books. Also provide ways that children can record themselves.
- ❑ Use hands-on learning.
- ❑ Have predictable routines and use a picture schedule.
- ❑ Involve families by sending home materials in the home language and providing book packs that include the book in the home language with an audio in English. One source of bilingual books is Bilingual Books for Kids (Wessels & Tranin, 2014).

group). Not surprisingly, the majority of words that children use are part of the parents' vocabulary. In addition the size of the vocabulary also parallels that of the parents (Hart & Risley, 1995). A recent study found that differences in vocabulary are evident as early as 18 months. By 24 months there is a six-month lag between children in low-income families and high-income families in processing speed, the speed in which a child understands a familiar word. Processing speed is associated with language development and cognitive skills (Fernald, Marchman, & Weisleder, 2013).

Children who are low income also often have disparate print opportunities. They may lack opportunities to read books because there are often fewer books in the home, public libraries in the area are often open fewer hours, and many school libraries are closed (Neuman, 2006). Statistically, low-income children are read to less before entering kindergarten than their middle-class peers (25 hours versus 1,000 hours) (Adams, 1990).

Many low-income parents also have fewer economic and emotional resources for enhancing background knowledge and literacy development. For example, children who are low income have fewer opportunities for high-quality child care, lessons, camps, and outside activities. Parents are also more likely to experience depression and have concerns that affect the quality of interaction with their children (Neuman, 2006).

Early childhood programs need to provide children with literacy opportunities that will enhance their skills. This includes hearing high-quality books, increasing background knowledge through many experiences, engaging in rich conversations, and hearing many vocabulary words. Some programs help to ensure that children have more opportunities to be read to by having "foster grandparents" or other volunteers come into the program during center time to read to children.

To produce better results for children who are low income it is also necessary to encourage families to talk with and engage in reading and storytelling with their children. Providing book and writing briefcase checkout programs is especially important in low-income neighborhoods. Programs may also be available to provide free books for children. A meta-analysis of research studies revealed increased literacy skills, reading ability, and reading motivation when low income children are given books (Lindsay, 2010).

Observe and Document Individual Children's Learning

Children's literacy learning can be assessed in a variety of ways, including observation, anecdotal records, analysis of written and oral samples, and vocabulary and reading inventories. Teachers and children might create individual literacy albums or portfolios that contain writing samples, recordings of children reading and telling stories, lists of books that the child has read or listened to, and transcripts of a conversation as a way of documenting their achievements. Children often assist in choosing artifacts to include and reflect upon why they want this particular entry to be included. These reflections can also become part of the literacy album or portfolio.

Teachers can gain an extraordinary amount of knowledge about children through careful observation. Following are some questions that can guide you in observing children in the literacy center.

- Does the child know how to handle a book (turns pages one at a time, starts at the beginning of the book, holds the book right side up)?
- Does the child look at or read books voluntarily?
- Does the child listen attentively when being read to individually, in a small group, and in a large group?
- Does the child demonstrate the ability to comprehend stories (can retell a story, can add information, can answer open-ended questions, is able to talk about the story and make predictions)?
- Is the child able to name alphabet letters? Which ones?
- Does the child demonstrate concepts about print (English is read from left to right and top to bottom)?
- Can the child identify words (sight words, environmental print, frequently used words, own name and names of friends)?
- Can the child read a book (telling story from the pictures, memorizing the book, reading some words in the story, reading all the words in the book)?
- Is the child able to tell or retell a story (story told in sequential order, story involves characters, setting, problem to be solved, plot, resolution)?
- Does the child demonstrate phonemic awareness?

- Is the child able to clap the number of syllables in a word?
- Can the child give examples of rhyming words?
- Does the child scribble, draw, or write voluntarily?
- Can the child record her ideas through pictures and words?
- What book genre is favored by the child?
- What writing conventions does the child use (left to right, top to bottom, space between words, capital letters at the beginning of a sentence, uses punctuation)?
- What stage of spelling is the child in?
- Does the child engage in conversations (takes turns, uses appropriate eye contact, initiates conversations, responds to others' initiations)?

Check Your Understanding 10.4

Click here to gauge your understanding of section concepts.

TIP

Some teachers provide a system so that children can keep track of which books they have read or have had read to them. For younger children, individual picture charts can help them to document the books they have read. These charts then become part of the child's literacy portfolio.

Click here to gauge your understanding of chapter concepts.

Teachers are critical in designing effective literacy environments and then scaffolding children's learning as they interact in these environments. Early childhood teachers can set the stage for children's lifelong love of reading and writing.

Effective literacy centers allow children to use reading, writing, and listening for authentic purposes; to interact with others; and to make sense of the written word that surrounds them (Searfoss et al., 2001). In the literacy center, teachers can introduce the magic of books, share the power of language, and lay the foundation for future success.

Sample Application Activities

1. Visit the website Look Who's Talking: All About Language Development to learn more about children's language development. Observe a child, does the child show typical language development?
2. Learn more about the importance of early childhood literacy by visiting the NAEYC Early Childhood Literacy website.
3. Critique an early childhood literacy environment using the environmental assessment found in Figure 10.7. What could be added to make the environment richer?
4. Critique a random sample of five books found in the early childhood environment. Do they meet the standards for high-quality literature found in Figure 10.2?
5. Record yourself reading a book to children. Critique yourself using the information found in Figure 10.5.
6. Record yourself having a conversation with children. Analyze what type of questions (open or closed) you asked and how often you expanded or extended the child's speech.
7. Make a list of environmental print found in an early childhood learning environment.
8. Assist a child to create a book using ideas from this chapter. Place the book in the reading center when it is completed.

FIGURE 10.7 Environmental Assessment: Literacy Center

Reading, writing, listening, and literacy manipulatives may be combined in one center or may be in separate centers.

Reading Area

- ❑ Is the literacy center in a quiet, well-lit area of the room?
- ❑ Is the literacy center clearly defined (in a loft, separated from the rest of the room by bookshelves)?
- ❑ Is the center a large enough area to accommodate five to six children (Morrow, 2001)?
- ❑ Is the center comfortable and aesthetic?
- ❑ Is the area enticing (book-related displays, objects to go with highlighted books, interesting entry)?
- ❑ Is the center engaging, providing props and materials for active reading and storytelling involvement (Reutzel & Morrow, 2007, p. 38)?
- ❑ Is the center well stocked with five to eight quality books per child?
- ❑ Are books in good condition (no torn pages or missing covers)?
- ❑ Are featured books displayed with their fronts showing?
- ❑ Are additional books organized on shelves or baskets?
- ❑ Are books high quality (quality illustrations, award-winning authors, interesting stories)?
  Are new books and props added on a regular basis?
- ❑ Are the books responsive to the needs and interests of the children in the group (variety of difficulty levels, range of topics and genres, in languages spoken by the children)?
  Are the books representative of a variety of cultures and families?
- ❑ Are there developmentally appropriate literacy manipulatives that promote oral skills, alphabetic awareness, phonemic awareness, and knowledge of words?

Writing Area

- ❑ Is there a table and chairs for several children to sit and write?
- ❑ Is an author's chair available?
- ❑ Is there an assortment of writing implements?
- ❑ Is there a variety of materials to write on, including transitory writing surfaces?
- ❑ Are there labeled shelves and containers for organizing writing materials?
- ❑ Is there a computer with installed writing software and a printer so children can print their own stories?
  Are there journals or blank books available?
- ❑ Are book-making supplies available?
- ❑ Are there clipboards for writing or drawing in other areas?
- ❑ Are there models for children to use in their writing (such as alphabet strips or cards, word walls, writing samples, picture dictionaries)?
- ❑ Is there a system for children to store and easily retrieve their writing?
- ❑ Is there evidence in the room that children are sharing their writing with others (mailboxes, message boards, bulletin boards with experience stories, child-created stories in the reading area)?
  Are there special highlighted activities to promote learning and to keep children interested and motivated to write?

Listening Center

- ❑ Is there a CD player with multiple headphones?
- ❑ Are there a variety of stories, activity tapes, finger plays, music, and listening games (in English and the children's native language) for children to listen to?
- ❑ Is there a comfortable listening place such as beanbag chairs or pillows?
- ❑ Are CDs labeled so that children can easily locate them?
- ❑ Are there props and materials for active listening?
- ❑ Are the CDs and props stored together in a plastic bag or basket?
- ❑ Are there blank CDs so each child can record her own stories?

Literacy in Other Centers

- ❑ Is there print throughout the room?
- ❑ Are there books in several classroom centers?
- ❑ Are there writing materials in several classroom centers?

Chapter 11

Developing Science Centers

Learning Outcomes

After you have read this chapter, you will be prepared to:

- Describe how children learn scientific concepts and the ways that the science center enhances this development
- Demonstrate the ability to design effective science centers both indoors and outdoors
- Create learning center activities that are developmentally appropriate and that assist children in meeting science standards
- Explain how to design science centers and activities for different ages
- Describe multiple ways that teachers facilitate learning in the science center

Julie Bullard

One day several children in Kelly's class of three- to six-year-olds found caterpillars on the playground. After examining them, Kelly and the children decided that they would like to find out more about caterpillars. They began their research by studying caterpillar habitats. Kelly and the children observed where the caterpillars lived in their playground, looked through books, and invited an expert on insects to visit. They then developed habitats for the caterpillars and placed them in the science center. A child found cocoons in his yard and these were also added to the science center. Kelly added journals to the center so that children could draw and record their theories and their findings. For example, children drew their theories on metamorphosis, drew their observations of the different stages, and drew sketches of moths and butterflies based on observation. Through discussions and by examining the pictures children drew, Kelly could see what current ideas and misconceptions the children held. This helped her to plan relevant experiences. Kelly also added a life-cycle seriation game, a self-correcting classification game featuring insects and noninsects, and fiction and nonfiction resource books to the science center.

Kelly carefully thought about the concepts she hoped children would develop as part of this study. She chose two "big concepts" to stress: (1) basic needs of living things and (2) life cycles. She developed a list of facts specifically related to insects and butterflies that she posted in the center, so that she and other adults in the classroom could share the information with children as they were interacting and discussing the insects in the science center. Two interesting facts she discovered were that insects comprise about 53% of animal life in the world (Danoff-Burg, 2003, p. 33) and that 90% of bugs go through metamorphosis. She also made a list of vocabulary words that she wanted to stress (chrysalis, cocoon, larva, metamorphosis, pupae, egg, silk, thorax, abdomen, caterpillar, and entomology) and posted these in the center. She and other adults intentionally used these words both in individual discussions with children and during group times.

At the beginning of the project, Kelly and the children made a KWHL chart about butterflies and moths (what I know, what I want to know, how I will find out, and what I learned). This helped to activate children's prior knowledge and reveal their questions. It also served as documentation of learning at the completion of the project. The children and Kelly frequently revisited their questions during group time to see what questions had been answered and to add new questions. Some of their questions included, "Do all caterpillars make the same kind of butterfly?" "Do all caterpillars turn into butterflies?" and "What does the pupa eat?" Whenever possible, they found out their answers through experimentation. For example, they observed the caterpillars they had found in their yard to see if they all spun cocoons. They experimented with what the pupa ate by offering them a variety of different types of food. In addition to revisiting their questions during group times, Kelly used this time to read books about insects that she then placed in the science center. Children developed plans for their experiments and discussed new things they had discovered while interacting in the science center. Kelly also used group times to focus on the life cycles and basic needs of living things. They discussed their own basic needs as well as the needs of the butterflies. Each of these group times served to reinforce the children's hands-on learning in the science center.

By the end of the study, children were actively using several of the vocabulary words in their discussions. They were able to discuss habitat requirements for butterflies and compare them to their own needs. They were

able to sequence the life-cycle seriation game and describe metamorphosis. They also knew several facts about butterflies and moths: butterflies are insects, and insects have six legs, an outside skeleton, three parts to their body, and a pair of antennae. Children also discovered through careful observation that butterflies have an elongated knob on the end of their antennae and moths do not. Through this center and the accompanying activities, children learned science process skills, concepts, and content.

Apply Your Knowledge If you were Kelly, how would you further develop children's knowledge of living things and life cycles?

Science curriculum began to appear in American schools in the late 1800s. However, in the past 60 years there has been an increased interest in science due to international competition and the increased needs of the workforce.

In 1957, when the Soviet Union launched Sputnik, it was the first country to launch a satellite into space. This event created a flurry of interest in science curriculum in the United States. Curriculum interest and reform have also been prompted due to ongoing concern about how American children fare in international science and math comparisons. For example, children in Japan and China are approximately one year ahead of middle-class American children. American middle-class children are one year ahead of American low-income children (Prentice Starkey in National Research Council, 2005).

There has also been an increased interest due to the need for a scientifically literate workforce. As stated by the Glenn Commission, "At the daybreak of this new century and millennium ... the future well-being of our nation and people depends not just on how well we educate our children generally, but on how well we educate them in mathematics and science specifically" (Glenn, 2000, p. 4).

The increased interest in science has also prompted an interest in science in the early years. Children are scientists who are naturally curious and biologically primed to learn about the world around them (French, 2004). For this reason, the early years are recognized as "years of promise" in the area of science (Carnegie Task Force, 1996). Children use the information they gain through their everyday experiences to make sense of the world and to develop theories about how the world works, whether accurate or inaccurate. In this chapter, we will examine children's development in the area of science, how science supports other curriculum areas, and how we can design and facilitate effective science learning through centers. We will begin by examining how children develop scientific concepts.

Development of Scientific Concepts and How the Science Center Enhances This Development

Development of Scientific Concepts

The development of scientific concepts is crucial to the understanding and use of scientific knowledge. **Concepts** help children organize information, acting as building blocks for learning. Concepts help children with cognitive tasks such as "identifying objects in the world, forming analogies, making inferences that extend knowledge beyond what is known, and conveying core elements of a theory" (Gelman, 1999, p. 51). Researchers have written more than 7,000 journal articles during the past 30 years about children's development of scientific concepts (Gelman, 1999, p. 50). This research has challenged previous thinking about children's concept development. The following themes have been identified (Gelman, 1999, p. 50; Gelman & Frazier, 2012):

- Concepts are tools that have powerful implications for children's reasoning—both positive and negative.
- Children's early concepts are not necessarily concrete or perceptually based. Even preschool children are capable of reasoning about nonobvious, subtle, and abstract concepts.
- Children's concepts are not uniform across content areas, across individuals, or across tasks.
- Conceptual understanding change with experiences and from learning from others. As children gain more experience, especially when facilitated by a skilled adult, their conceptual understanding becomes more sophisticated and focused.
- Children's concepts reflect their emerging "theories" about the world. To the extent that children's theories are inaccurate, their conceptions are also biased.

As we develop science centers, we need to understand children's current theories. There are many ways that you might do this. For example, you might write observations of what children are doing, have children draw their theories, ask children to make predictions, or listen to children's theories and ask them clarification questions, such as "Why do you think round items always sink?" We also need to help children link what they are learning to larger concepts. Conceptual understanding is enhanced when we provide depth over breadth.

How the Science Center Enhances Children's Development

"The cognitive skills in mathematics and science displayed by young children are not only the roots of later literacy in those areas, they are the building blocks in the development of the capacity to comprehend complex relationships and reason about those relationships" (National Research Council, 2005, p. 4). Science provides the context for learning language, literacy, and math. Through science, children learn skills that transfer to other curriculum areas. For example, they improve their ability to observe, problem solve, collect and organize data, and create hypotheses and test them. They add to their vocabulary and learn to communicate information. They develop concepts about the world around them. As they engage in science, children often use math and literacy skills in authentic ways. For example, children in Kelly's classroom used math skills as they counted the number of butterflies that hatched each day and created a graph of what the pupa liked to eat. They used literacy skills as they learned new vocabulary, wrote stories about the butterflies, discussed information with their peers, read fiction and nonfiction books about insects, and created a class metamorphosis book. What specific content and skills should children learn in the early childhood years? The New Generation Science Standards (NGSS) stress that children need to learn content (the disciplines core ideas), **scientific and engineering practices** (previously referred to as process skills), and **crosscutting concepts** (NGSS Lead States, 2013). Ideally, these are taught and learned concurrently.

The practice skills children need to learn are defined for K–12th grade children by the NGSS. Children need to ask questions, define problems, develop and use models, plan and implement investigations, analyze and interpret data, use mathematical thinking, construct explanations, design solutions, defend position based on evidence, and obtain, evaluate, and communicate information (NGSS Lead States, 2013).

The process for young children often begins with noticing, wondering, and exploring. After children have had experiences with the materials or phenomena, they are ready to engage in the inquiry process (Chalufour & Worth, 2012).

- Ask a question.
- Plan a way to answer the question.
- Predict what will happen (form a hypothesis).
- Conduct investigations and observe the results.
- Develop an explanation or conclusion.
- Communicate information and your findings to others (tell someone, dictate or write, draw, or make a chart).

The basis of scientific inquiry is asking questions. You will need to guide children, helping them to choose questions that they are capable of answering through inquiry. For example, in one classroom, children's observation of snails led to several questions, including how snails have babies, how snails move, and how snails get into their shells. The teacher chose to help the children explore the question of how snails move because it allowed for direct investigation (Worth, 2010).

While inquiry process steps are well established, appropriate science content is limitless and it is not clear what content is critical or important in the early years (National Research Council, 2005). Instead, we might think about the important criteria for choosing a science topic to study. Worth (2010), a renowned expert on early childhood science, states that topics should be chosen that:

- Allow for direct exploration and engagement.
- Include important scientific concepts.
- Are developmentally appropriate, engaging to children and adults, and allow for multiple opportunities to explore the concept in in-depth ways over an extended time (NSTA, 2014).
- Provide for both physical and life science over the course of a program year.

It is also critical that teachers link what is studied to big ideas or crosscutting concepts. Crosscutting concepts are patterns; cause and effect; scale, proportion, and quantity; systems and system models; energy and matter; structure and function; and stability and change. These tie science and engineering together, but are also relevant for many other subjects. For example, let's examine patterns. Children's understanding grows in complexity as children proceed throughout their schooling. In the early years children begin to notice patterns, describe them, and use them as evidence. By the time that children are in the 8th grade, they should be able to recognize the relationship between microscopic and atomic-level structure and macroscopic patterns, identify patterns in the rate of change, use patterns to identify cause and effect, and use charts and graphs to identify patterns in data (NGSS Lead States, 2013). These crosscutting concepts aid children in making connections and in learning core content, scientific practices, and scientific vocabulary. How do we design environments that will support this kind of learning? We will examine this next.

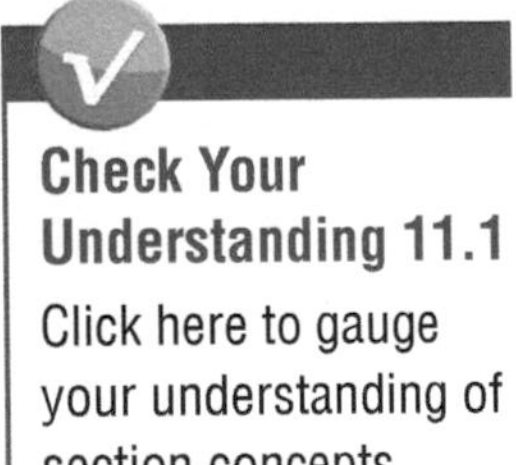

Check Your Understanding 11.1
Click here to gauge your understanding of section concepts.

Designing Effective Indoor and Outdoor Science Centers

Purpose of the Science Center

While science can occur throughout the classroom, it is important to provide a focus on science by having a science center. In the science center, children can spend intensive time observing, predicting, experimenting, using scientific tools, practicing processes, and learning content. However, research indicates that in preschool classrooms there are few planned or spontaneous science activities (Brenneman, Stevenson-Boyd, & Frede, 2009; Greenfield et al., 2009; Nayfeld, Brenneman, & Gelman, 2011). In one study, only 50% of the early childhood classrooms had a science center (Tu, 2006). Tu found that even when science centers did exist, teachers spent little time in them.

Types of Science Centers

Science centers may focus on a current theme or project or be isolated from other current curriculum. They may be organized in different ways.

- Some teachers develop science boxes that are available throughout the year. Each box contains materials around a different topic and children have the choice of choosing from many different activities. For example, Sherwood (2005) develops ABC science shoeboxes. Each box is created for an individual or a small group. For example, Sherwood's (2005) "A" box contains materials (eyedroppers, water cup, materials to test for absorption, and a record sheet for drawing results) on the concept of absorption, "B" contains a variety of toys emphasizing the concept of balance, and "M" contains magnet activities. The Next Generation Science Standards (NGSS Lead States, 2013) stress the need for depth over breadth of topics covered. The approach described earlier exposes children to a variety of science activities. It also may be a way to allow children to follow up on previously introduced activities or centers. However, it may be difficult to provide the needed depth for optimum learning when there are so many concepts to focus on.
- Science centers can also focus on inquiry, where children are encouraged to focus on a question or questions to answer. After a local oil spill that coated birds' feathers in oil, teachers and children in one school explored the following questions: "What happens to a duck feather when it is coated with oil?" and "What will remove the oil from a bird's feather?" Duck feathers (some that were coated in oil) and a tub of water were placed in the center. The center also contained a variety of tools and substances to remove the oil (brainstormed by the teacher and children). Children kept track of their experiments with a picture chart where they circled any item that cleaned the oil and crossed out any item that did not. Like scientists, as children engage in these in-depth inquiries they use scientific practice skills (developing and testing hypotheses and communicating results) while answering their questions. When the inquiry is relevant to children, these centers can be highly motivating, building upon children's natural curiosity. The teacher in this approach to centers will often introduce the inquiry at a large- or small-group circle and then place the materials in the science center for children to use during center time.
- A science center can also be a discovery center (Charlesworth & Lind, 2010) where children, instead of pursuing an answer to a specific question, might be exploring scientific concepts. A discovery center will often have less specific outcomes than an inquiry center. For example, at a preschool center children were completing a long-term project on cars. The science center contained a variety of car parts that children could examine, explore, disassemble, and reassemble. The teacher helped children to explore the concept of how tools help us as they tried to disassemble parts with and without

tools and using different types of tools. The children also explored pulleys and gears.

- Science centers can also contain inquiry tools that children can use throughout the classroom. For example, children might use measuring tools to determine if the plants growing by the window grow faster than the plants that do not have natural light. They might be building structures in the block area and using the pulley to design an elevator that will carry items from one floor to the next.

Establishing the Indoor Science Center

Regardless of the type of center you choose to create, it is important that the center:

- Is an enclosed space in the quiet area of the classroom, allowing for uninterrupted work and concentration.
- Is large enough to accommodate several children and the teacher.
- Is near a sink, since many activities require water for experiments and cleanup.
- Is near a window, since many explorations need natural light.
- Provides an organized, labeled science table and shelving to highlight and store materials.
- Provides adequate work space, often a table and chairs, since many times children will need to spread out materials housed on the science table or shelf to complete them.
- Contains a bulletin board for posting science information and findings.
- Is designed to encourage cooperation and communication between learners (providing materials, seating, and space for small groups of children to work).
- Is enticing. Kelly provides lab coats to make the science center more interesting to the children in her room. Rene uses visors with "scientist" written on them to designate the number of children in the center and to assist children in assuming the scientist's role. Some teachers develop an enticing science enclosure such as a tent or cave for a science lab. Many teachers introduce the center to the group at circle time, building interest through a teaser.
- Allows for individual differences by providing open-ended material or a variety of tasks at different levels.
- Allows children to use the center independently through ensuring that all needed materials are available and within the children's reach, materials are arranged in a logical order or sequence, and there is a clearly designated place for each item. If there are directions for completing an activity, they are provided through pictures, written, recorded, or introduced at circle time.
- Encourages children to represent their knowledge (paper, graph paper, tape recorders, journals, recording sheets, clipboards, pencils, and markers).
- Contains resource materials such as books, posters, videos, and a computer. See Figure 11.1 for books related to science topics discussed in this chapter.
- Contains any inquiry tools such as magnifying glasses, microscopes, eyedroppers, pulleys, scales, and specimen bags that are needed to complete activities in the center.
- Includes science content background sheets and a list of vocabulary to be stressed so adults can scaffold children's learning. The background sheets should also include the crosscutting concepts being stressed.

FIGURE 11.1 Children's Books Related to the Science Topics Discussed in This Chapter

Science tools
I use science tools, Hicks (2011)
You can use a magnifying glass, Blevins, W. (2003)

Liquids
Does it absorb or repel liquids, Hughes (2014)

Bubbles
Pop: A book about bubbles, Bradley (2001)
Bubbles float: Bubbles pop, Weakland (2011)
How to make bubbles, Shores (2011)

Float and sink
What floats? What sinks? A look at density, Boothroyd, J. (2011)
Fun with water and bubbles, Gold-Dworkin, H. (2000)
Does it sink or float, Hughes (2014)

Moving water
Water as a liquid, Frost (2000)
Raindrops, Brimner (1999)

Moving objects
Roll, slope, and slide: a book about ramps, Dahl (2006)
Move it! Motion, forces and you, Mason (2005)
Push and pull, Murphey (2002)

Magnets
A look at magnets, Alpert, B. (2012)
Discover magnets, Vogel, J. (2015)

Shadows
What makes a shadow? Bulla, C. R. (2008)
Guess whose shadow? Swinburne (1999)

Rocks
Rocks and soil, Kay (2011)
Rocks and minerals, Squire (2002)
Fossils, Squire (2002)
Everybody needs a rock, Baylor, B. (1999)
The scoop on soils (a free book from GLOBE.gov)
Nature close up junior: Soils, Pascoe, E. (2005)

Water and ice
Melting and freezing, Greathouse, L. E. (2011)
Freezing and melting, Nelson (2003)

Animals
Animalium, Broom, J., & Scott, K. (2014)
Animals that make me say wow! (National Wildlife Federation): Secret hideaways, infrasonic hearing, bubble gills, and more, Cusick (2014)
Beneath the sun, Stewart (2014)
The facts about habitats, Hunter, R. (2007)

Plants
Next time you see a maple seed, Morgan (2014)
The tiny seed, Carle, E. (2015)
Seed, sprout, pumpkin pie, Esbaum (2009)
Apples for everyone: Picture the seasons, Esbaum (2009)

Engineering
Engineers solve problems, Miller & Sikkens (2014)
Engineering the ABC'S: How engineers shape our world, Novak, P. O. B. (2010)

Worms
Wiggling worms at work, Pfeffer (2004)
Wonderful worms, Glaser, L. (2001)
An earthworm's life, Himmelman (2001)

Choosing Materials and Activities for the Science Center

To effectively meet children's needs and help them to acquire scientific knowledge, skills, and dispositions, we need to choose materials and activities for our science center that meet the following criteria:

- Designed for action rather than just for looking (Charlesworth & Lind, 2012). Young children learn through active engagement with materials and ideas. For example, in the butterfly center Kelly provided journals for sketching the butterflies' transformations, graphs to record the number of days in each stage of metamorphosis, and magnifying glasses for closer examination of the pupae and butterflies. If she had not provided these materials, children would have had limited engagement other than just looking at the butterflies. As stated by

Julie Bullard

This science center, filled with child- and teacher-collected natural items, is made more enticing by the burlap curtains over the mirror and the tree branches hanging over the center. A basket of different strengths of magnifying glasses helps children in their exploration of the materials.

Greenman, "A creative science area is more laboratory than museum" (Greenman, 2005a, p. 269).

- Relevant to the children in the classroom. The emphasis in science centers for this age needs to be on things that children can actually touch and feel. For example, in Hawaii this might include tide pools, oceans, volcanoes, rain, local flowers, and native insects. Children are curious about the world outside the classroom that affects their immediate lives. As they have relevant experiences with the world surrounding them, it allows for the joy of discovery and active experimentation.
- Built upon current knowledge, background, and previous activities so that it is developmentally appropriate for the group of children using the center.
- Encourage "what would happen if" statements (Charlesworth & Lind, 2012). One way of encouraging this is to provide open-ended, enticing materials that allow for different variations so that children can extend their experiments. For example, if experimenting with connected tubes to create a marble roll activity, the child should be able to take the tubes apart and assemble them in different ways. Different weights or sizes of marbles can also be provided for more variability. Other types of tubing can also increase the amount of variation.
- Provide the needed materials so that children can test their hypotheses and try out their ideas. This may include using a variety of inquiry tools such as magnifying glasses of different types, microscope, Petri dishes, scales, eyedroppers, pulleys, tweezers, twine, clay for imprints, specimen bags and boxes, and nets.
- Encourage scientific practices by providing ways of recording ideas and plans, materials for close observation, and ways of reflecting what the child has learned.
- Expose children to specific content related to the topic being studied.
- Tie into bigger overriding concepts. For example, in studying any topic relating to biology, some big ideas that can be stressed are life cycles and living versus nonliving. Even one- and two-year-old children are "adept at concept acquisition." This helps them to organize information and prevents the world from being a chaotic place (Gelman, 1999, p. 50).

Perhaps because so many early childhood teachers are uncomfortable with science, science centers are often lacking or not fully developed in early childhood settings. It is important when developing a science center to make sure that it provides tools, resources, and materials needed for active engagement and for documenting learning. Children need time for in-depth exploration. It is unnecessary and counterproductive to change the center each week. In fact, the NSTA Position Statement for Early Childhood Science Education stresses that children need sustained engagement with the same ideas over weeks, months, and years (NSTA, 2014, p. 3). However, teachers should continue to add materials and make changes to the center to answer new questions emerging from the children.

Establishing Science Centers Outdoors

An outdoor sorting table encourages children to collect and classify materials.

Outdoors is the perfect place for engaging, hands-on science learning. As children interact in the outdoors, they learn science content and concepts. They also learn to appreciate our world and are therefore more apt to want to sustain it. Outdoors children can:

- Explore wind with kites, pinwheels, windsocks, wind ribbons, paper airplanes, and feathers.
- Learn about plants by gardening (see Chapter 17 for more information).
- Develop and maintain compost and recycling bins.
- Observe bugs and animals in their natural habitats.
- Create elaborate water systems using the garden hose and PVC pipe.
- Conduct simple experiments. For example, if you have ants in your playground children might take a plate and divide it into several sections, placing a different potential food item in each section (sugar, grass, bird seed, crumbs of bread, a larger slice of bread) (Williams, Rockwell, & Sherwood, 1987). Which foods are the ants attracted to?
- Learn what birds prefer eating by setting up a variety of types of bird feeders.
- Observe the weather and record information at a weather station. You can examine the temperature, the type of day (sunny, cloudy, rainy, snowy), the type of clouds, the amount of wind. The Kid Weather app provides information and allows you to record this information digitally.
- Observe and discuss the indicators of seasonal change.
- Take walks to examine and identify the different plants and trees in your area. A free app called Leafsnap helps you to identify plants and trees and provides a wealth of information.
- Encourage children to create collections of natural items through providing access to natural environments, time to collect and to interact with the items, and space to store the collections. In one study over 80% of adults had collections of natural items as children. Collectors scored higher in their connection to nature as adults than non-collectors (Leckies & Beerey, 2013).

Watch the video to see how one school incorporates gardening into their curriculum. What science skills are children learning through the garden?

https://www.youtube.com/watch?v=5i25_8u91Wo

Teachers can support outdoor science learning by providing the tools and resource materials needed to fully explore the topic. Some teachers create science inquiry bags or totes that can be taken outside with them. These contain reference books or laminated sheets for identifying birds and bugs, measuring tools, various magnifying glasses, insect nets, jars and sacks for collecting specimens, and clipboards and paper for documenting information. After the center is established, you will need to determine appropriate activities for the science center. We will explore this next.

Check Your Understanding 11.2

Click here to gauge your understanding of section concepts.

Meeting Standards Through Science Center Activities

In this section, we will examine some possible science center materials and activities for preschool and early elementary grades in the areas of science tools, physical science, life science, earth and space science, and engineering. We will examine the concepts that the activities and materials promote, the standards that are being addressed by the materials and activities, and when applicable some common misconceptions that children might hold. The standards will be divided into two parts, *A Framework for K–12 Science Education: Practices, Crosscutting Concepts, and Core Ideas* (National Research Council, 2012) applies to K–3rd grade. This framework provides the basis for the Next Generation Science Standards. State Early Learning Standards guide the work of preschool teachers and vary from state to state. The pre-K standards listed are based on the expertise of two well-known early childhood science educators and publishers. The following centers are typically introduced to the children during a small- or large-group activity. Children then complete the explorations during center time.

Using Science Tools

The big science idea or central concept in studying science tools is that "tools such as thermometers, magnifiers, rulers, or balances often give more information about things than can be obtained by just observing things without their help" (American Association for the Advancement of Science, 1993, p. 10).

For example, Kendis and her class of kindergarten children studied magnification. During the study, children:

- Compared different strengths of magnifying glasses.
- Compared different types of magnifying glasses to determine which were easier to use for different purposes.
- Explored different types of machines that magnify (overhead projector, telescope, binoculars).
- Explored water drop magnifiers by placing waxed paper over a newspaper and adding different sizes of drops over the letters.

In addition to containing the different magnification tools, the science center contained books on magnification, interesting small items to examine with the magnifying glasses (a collection of coins, different kinds of bugs, and an assortment of rocks), graphs for recording results, and prediction charts. Kendis also prepared a fact sheet on magnification and a list of vocabulary words relating to magnification. She posted these along with the overriding concept on the wall in the center. Kendis scaffolded children's learning at the center by listening carefully to their theories. The children believed that the larger the magnifying glass, the more powerful it was. They had found that to be true by examining the magnifying glasses in the center. To dispell this misconception, Kendis introduced some new, even larger (but weaker) magnifying glasses. By continuing their exploration, the children found that their theory was not accurate. Through this activity, the children learned about tools and magnification, engaged in scientific practices (making and testing predictions), and used literacy (read books) and math skills (developed graphs).

Physical Science Standards

Physical science is the study of nonliving things. For early-elementary-aged children, the core ideas as defined in *A Framework for K–12 Science Education* are:

- Matter and its interactions.
- Motion and stability: Forces and interactions.

- Energy.
- Waves and their applications in technologies for information transfer (National Research Council, 2012.)

Standards for preschool children include the study of the following:

- Properties of solids and the properties of liquids.
- Position and motion of objects.
- Properties and characteristics of sounds and light (Worth & Grollman, 2003).

Physical Science Learning Center Activities

Some sample activities for science centers that allow children to gain an understanding of physical science include liquids, bubbles, float and sink, movement, magnets, and shadows.

Liquids. Two important concepts that children can learn relating to liquids are that (1) liquids have different properties that can be described, and (2) liquids take the shape of the container they are in. To help children explore liquids, teachers might provide pictures or written task cards and materials so that children can do the following:

- Place drops of dish soap, oil, honey, water, corn syrup, and vinegar onto paper towels or coffee filters to examine the absorbency of different liquids. Have children first predict which liquid will produce the largest circle on the paper towel.
- Drop a liquid onto different materials (cloth, newspaper, waxed paper, aluminum foil, and construction paper) to see the absorbency of different surfaces.
- Look at the drops with a magnifying glass.
- Make the largest drop possible (children can use straws, basters, and eyedroppers).
- Make the smallest possible drop that can still be seen, using toothpicks.
- Add water to the different liquids to see what happens. Will the water mix with the other liquid?
- Drop food coloring into the different kinds of liquids.
- Put water and oil in a bottle to examine density (vegetable oil floats because it is less dense than water; corn syrup sinks because it is more dense than water). Will the other liquids float or sink? What will happen if colored salt water is added to plain water?
- Classify several different kinds of liquids in jars by fluidity, which is how easy the substance flows.
- Discuss the characteristics of a liquid.
- Sort objects by whether they are liquid or solid.

Bubbles. A bubble is a film of liquid surrounding a gas or air pocket. Two concepts that children can learn about bubbles are that (1) bubbles have air inside them and (2) air takes up space. Some bubble activities that children could complete in the science center to help them understand these concepts include the following:

- Have children predict which objects will make bubbles by dividing objects into things that will make bubbles and things that will not make bubbles. Provide a variety of objects that might be used to make bubbles, such as strawberry baskets, slotted spoons, sieves, funnels, wire bent into a closed circle, and wire bent into an open circle. Also provide laminated sorting sheets labeled with pictures and words for children to use in sorting the objects into those that will make bubbles and those that will not. Children can then test each item to see if their predictions were correct.

- Hold up the bubbles to the light to determine what colors can be seen.
- Make a pile of bubbles by using a straw to blow into the bubble mixture. Task cards might ask children to see what shapes are in the bubbles and to look at just one of the bubbles to see how many flat sides there are.
- Experiment to find out if different types of objects produce different shapes of bubbles (provide a variety of objects with holes in them such as sieves, square bubble blowers, tea strainers, funnels, and strawberry baskets).
- Create a bubble maker (provide wire, straws, and string).
- Experiment with different bubble solutions (using different types of detergent, adding sugar to the bubble solution, adding glycerin to the bubble solution, adding white corn syrup to the bubble solution) to determine which makes the longest lasting bubble.

You will want to encourage children to record their experiments and write or draw what they did, dictate their findings to an adult, or share their findings at circle time.

Float and Sink. Floating and sinking combine the study of liquids with the study of solids. One of the "big ideas" for floating and sinking is that solids have properties. One of these is whether they sink or float in water. The teacher might introduce activities or challenges during group time, or she might draw or write challenges on task cards for children to follow. These can be explored over a period of days or even weeks. For example, you might challenge the children by asking them to do the following activities and answer the following questions.

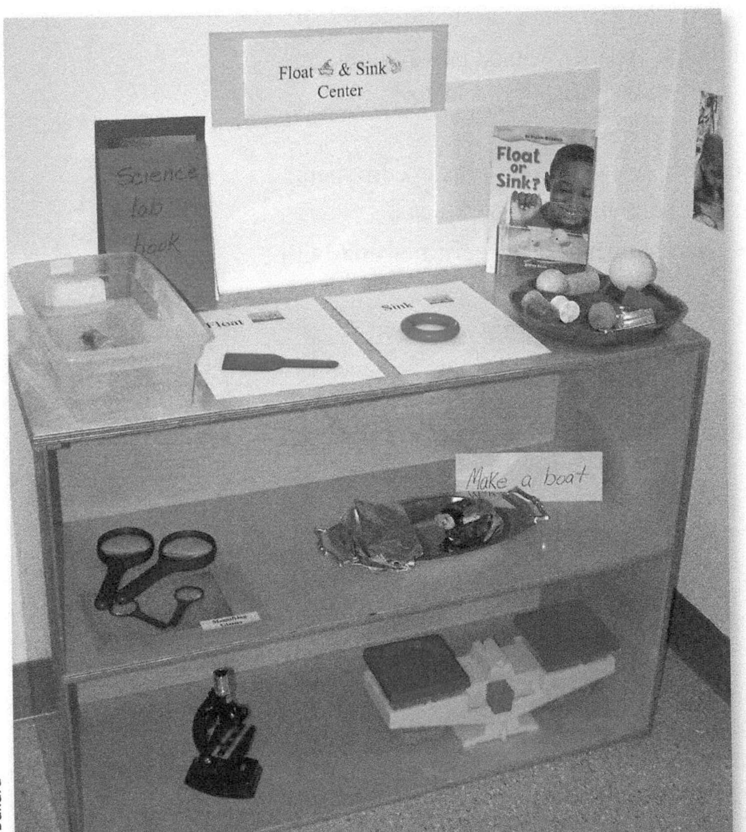

Julie Bullard

This float-and-sink center contains items for experimentation as well as a lab book for recording results. Laminated sorting sheets encourage children to make predictions before they experiment with the objects.

- Predict which objects will float and which will sink. Provide a variety of items, including items that are similar but different weights, such as a ping-pong ball and a golf ball. Also, provide laminated sheets with pictures and words for sink and float that the children can use for their predictions.
- Put the objects in the water to see if the predictions are correct.
- What are the similarities in the objects that sink? What are the similarities in the objects that float?
- Will a plastic film canister float? Does it float if you fill it with water? Does it float if you fill it with clay?
- Make a boat out of clay that will float. How many pennies can the boat hold?

- Make a boat out of tinfoil the same size as the clay boat. How many pennies can the boat hold?
- Redesign the boats so that they can hold more pennies.
- Can you make a straw sink?
- Predict which baby food lid will sink first. Provide baby food lids with different sizes and patterns of holes.
- Design an object that will float for one minute and then sink.

Some common misconceptions that children have in regard to buoyancy is that objects float because they are lighter than water, they sink because they are heavier than water, wood floats and metal sinks, and all objects containing air float (Operation Physics, 1998). Buoyancy is determined by density, which is the mass divided by volume. If the item weighs more than the water it displaces, it will sink. As teachers, it is important that we understand these misconceptions, so that we can avoid reinforcing them when we work with children. We need to assess children's understanding and scaffold their learning as needed. For example, we might want to include materials that help children to see that their misconceptions are not accurate (for example, a metal boat).

Movement. Some concepts that children learn about movement include, the following: there are different ways to make something move, there are ways to change the way that something is moving, things move in different ways and at different speeds, objects naturally fall toward the earth unless something is holding them up, and tools make work easier by altering the way the work is done (AAAS, 1993).

Moving Water. One way that children can learn about these concepts is by moving colored water. Provide children with clear containers, basters, squeeze and spray bottles, eyedroppers, pumps, siphons, funnels, tubing, and plastic connectors. Allow them to discover ways to move the water. In the beginning, it might be helpful to provide some examples to spark interest and provide some early success. As children experiment with the water, they will also be learning that water flows down unless it is acted upon.

Moving Objects. One way to move objects is by using ramps. Children can create their own ramps using lengths of rain gutter, cove molding, or pool noodles cut lengthwise. They can experiment with different slants, ramp designs, rolling materials, targets, and ramp surfaces (DeVries & Sales, 2011). As children are using ramps, they can learn important concepts such as that the characteristic of the object will determine whether the object rolls, slides, or stays put. The amount of force will also help determine whether an object moves and how fast is moves. The center can be enhanced with the Sid the Science Kid—Sid's Slide to the Side app.

Magnets. Two of the "big ideas" for magnets are that "magnets can be used to make things move without being touched" and that "forces can act at a distance with no perceivable substance in between" (AAAS, 1993, p. 94). Children can also learn specific information about magnets, such as magnets attract some things and not others, magnets vary in strength, and magnets can be a helpful tool. Explore magnetism with preschool and early-elementary-aged children by completing the following activities and asking them the following questions.

- Explore a variety of items (screws, paper, buttons, aluminum foil, pennies, paper clips, rubber bands, scissors, eraser, dime, and bottle cap), predicting and then testing theories about what is attracted to the magnet.
- Make a rule about the objects the magnet attracts.

Create Your Own Ball Rolls

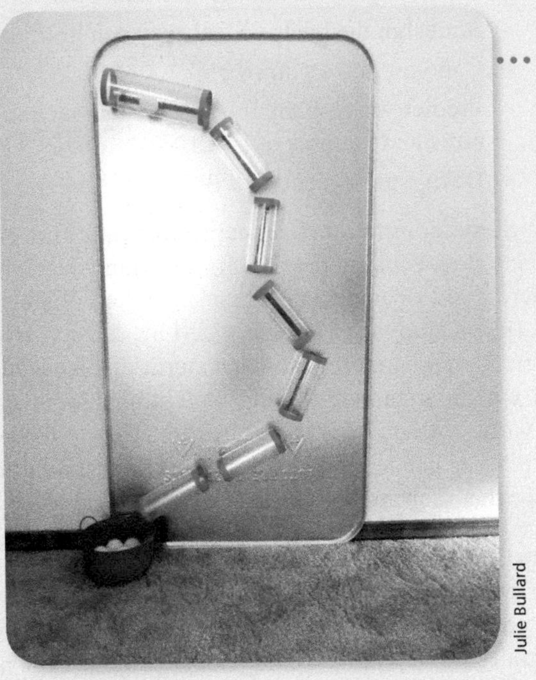

Julie Bullard

As children experiment with the placement of these ball rolls, they will use problem-solving skills and experiment with slope, speed, and properties of objects.

Directions

- Cut off each end of plastic water bottles to create several tubes.
- Place tape around the cut end of the bottle, folding half of the tape on the inside of the bottle and half of the tape on the outside of the bottle.
- Use a hot glue gun to glue the magnetic tape lengthwise onto the bottle.
- Place bottles on a magnetic surface, such as a metal automotive drip pan, metal door, or refrigerator.
- Allow children to experiment with arranging the ball rolls in different ways.
- Provide ping-pong balls for the ball rolls.
- As children become more proficient, you can add additional sizes of water bottles, plastic tubes, and funnels.

Variations

If you are using a metal automotive drip pan, you could bring the ball rolls outside and use it with water.

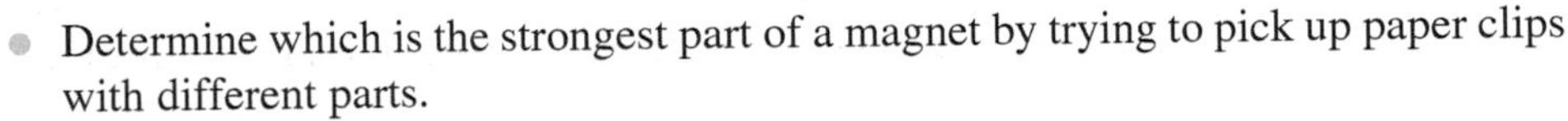

- Determine which is the strongest part of a magnet by trying to pick up paper clips with different parts.
- Experiment with different magnets (bar, horseshoe, ring, or rod) to see which is strongest. How many linked paper clips will each magnet pick up? Record results.
- Move metal shavings with a magnet. How far away can you be and still move the shavings?
- Will a magnet move a paper clip that is in water? Will it move a paper clip through a layer of cloth, through a piece of paper, or through a piece of wood? Complete a recording sheet. Circle the smiling face if yes, the magnet can move the paper clip, and a frowning face for no, the magnet cannot move the paper clip. Teachers can design the sheet by either drawing or taking a picture of someone conducting each experiment. For example, take a picture of a paper clip that is on top of a red piece of cloth with a magnet underneath. Place a smiling face and a frowning face beside each picture, so the child can circle the correct one.
- Find things in the classroom that are attracted to the magnet. Draw a picture of each thing you find.

- Experiment with toys that are magnetic (magnetic building blocks, magnetic sculpture, magnetic marbles, or a Magna Doodle toy). Teachers can also create their own toys with magnets. For example, attach a magnet to the bottom of a toy duck and place the duck in a shallow pan of water. The children can move the duck around in the water. Tie a magnet to a small tow truck and let the children tow the steel cars.

When choosing materials or activities to explore magnetism, it is important not to reinforce misconceptions. Common misconceptions that children have regarding magnets are that all metals are attracted to magnets, all silver-colored items are attracted to magnets, all magnets are made of iron, and large magnets are stronger than small magnets (Operation Physics, 1998, p. 7). For example, Cora had placed magnets and a variety of materials in the science center. As she observed children using the center, she discovered that they had developed a hypothesis and, after testing their hypothesis, had concluded that shiny materials are attracted to the magnets. Cora then added some shiny objects to the center that were not attracted to magnets. This allowed children to reexamine their hypothesis. She also added a book that provided information about magnetism. Teachers can help children look up information when they have questions that they cannot answer. However, as this case illustrates, it is important that the teacher is knowledgeable enough about the topic to recognize children's misunderstandings.

Shadows. Some concepts that children can learn about shadows are that they are created when light is blocked by an object, when the direction of the light changes the shape of the shadow moves, and the size of the shadow is affected by the distance between the object and the light.

- Experiment with different light sources such as flashlights, overhead projectors, and the sun.
- Provide a variety of transparent, translucent, and opaque objects on an overhead projector so children can see which creates a shadow.
- Engage in different types of shadow play such as shadow puppetry, dancing with your shadow, playing shadow tag, and participating in shadow treasure hunts
- Draw around and measure the size and position of outdoor shadows at different times of day.
- Create challenges such as "How can you make a shadow larger, smaller, disappear? How can you change the way that your shadow looks? What objects will make a shadow? Can an object have more than one shadow at the same time?".

Life Science Standards

Life science is the study of living organisms and their relationship to each other and their environment. For children in the early elementary grades, the core ideas, as defined in *A Framework for K–12 Science Education,* are:

- From molecules to organisms: Structures and processes.
- Ecosystems: Interactions, energy, and dynamic.
- Heredity: Inheritance and variation of traits.
- Biological evolution: Unity and diversity (National Research Council, 2012).

Worth and Grollman (2003) have defined life science goals for the preschool years as being:

- Physical characteristics of living things.
- Basic needs of living things.

- Simple behaviors.
- Life cycles.
- Recognizing variation and diversity in living things.
- Relationship between living things and their environments.
- People (Worth & Grollman, 2003, pp. 26–29).

Life Science Learning Center Activities

Animals. In addition to the life science standards listed earlier, concepts for studying animals include "All animals have offspring, usually with two parents involved" and "Animals have features that help them live in different environments" (AAAS, 1993, p. 102). "People need water, food, air, waste removal, and particular range of temperatures in their environments, just as other animals do" (AAAS, 1993, p. 128).

Too often class animals are relegated to the top of a shelf or corner of a room with children displaying little interest. One year when I was teaching preschool, we bought gerbils for our classroom. The children named the gerbils, and each day one of the children was responsible for feeding the gerbils. However, other than that, no one paid much attention to the class pets. The gerbils were master escape artists. One night when they escaped, they fell in the fish tank and drowned. The children discovered them in the morning, and for the first time displayed a lot of interest in the gerbils. In reflecting upon this experience, I became aware that I had assumed that simply placing the animals in the classroom would create science opportunities. However, I had done nothing to promote this.

While classroom pets can serve different purposes (some animals might provide a therapeutic outlet), for pets or animal visitors to provide science opportunities teachers need to think about the science learning they are trying to promote. For example, teachers can help children to learn about a habitat by having children study and design the habitat for the class pet or visitor. To tie this to a "big idea," teachers and children can discuss what other creatures need the same type of habitat. What are some things that all animals need as part of their habitat? What are unique characteristics that help animals live in different habitats?

Julie Bullard

In this center, children and teachers are hatching eggs. The center is made more engaging through a hatching countdown chart, photos of the chicken that produced the eggs, a bag where children add new facts that they have learned, an ostrich and emu egg, and a child-created book on the class trip to visit the chickens, ostrich, and emu.

Teachers can encourage focused observations of the animal or insect through asking questions, providing recording materials, and including tools in the center. For example, Meiying and the children in her class had just returned from the pet store with a dozen crickets. They developed a KWHL chart listing their current knowledge and questions. The children had many questions that they were interested in investigating: "What makes the cricket chirp? How does the cricket move? How do they make the chirping sound? Where do they spend their time while in the cage? What are their antennas like? Are they the same as the bumblebee that we studied earlier?" These questions helped to guide children's investigations. Having books and resource materials available assisted the children in finding answers to their questions when they could not be answered through direct observation. Meiying also showed the children a cricket cage that she used as a child in China. The children were fascinated and became interested in building their own cages. She also told them about the cricket songs, stories, and beliefs from her native land, increasing their interest and cultural knowledge.

Because of their abundance and relatively short lives, insects such as crickets, butterflies, and mealy worms are interesting to study. They are ideal for studies of life cycles and biological change.

Another way that children can be engaged with classroom animals and insects is to conduct simple experiments. For example, they might provide different types of foods to determine which ones the animal or insect eats. Children could provide different types of bedding materials to see which a hamster prefers. Or they might create a house without windows and one with windows to see which one a cricket goes into.

Watch the video to see a group of children and a teacher exploring tadpoles. What questions does the teacher ask to help the children think more deeply?

Plants. Some concepts for studying plants include that organisms have needs that must be met by the environment, organisms have life cycles, and plants and animals affect each other. Specific information that children might learn about seeds and plants include the following: seeds differ in appearance (size, shape, color, texture); each seed grows into a specific kind of plant; seeds grow into flowers, shrubs, trees, fruit, and other kinds of food; and some plants come from seeds, and others come from roots and stems (Lind, 2005, p. 212). Following are some activities that could be placed in a science center that would allow children to explore seeds and plants:

- Sort, classify, and identify a collection of seeds.
- Examine a variety of kinds of fruits and vegetables. Find their seeds (cucumber, ear of corn, green beans, nuts, apricots, apples, oranges).
- Remove seeds from a variety of different types of pods such as peas or sunflowers.
- Conduct experiments such as planting seeds in different types of soil, placing plants in different light or heat conditions, or planting seeds at different depths and seeing how long it takes them to grow. While these activities will often be completed as a small-group activity, the experiments can then be placed in the science center for children to observe, sketch, and graph data.
- Examine the root structures of plants by planting a seed between two pieces of Plexiglas or in glass jars, or by sprouting beans in plastic bags.
- Collect, closely examine, identify, and sketch common plants found in the local area. The children and teacher might collect a variety of plants from their homes and then place them in the center with magnifying glasses, sketch books, and identification cards. Teachers might want to create their own identification cards containing the picture and name of each plant that is in the center. This will be easier for children to use than a guide book, since it contains only the plants that are present and shows

Julie Bullard

In this center, children are experimenting with growing plants and keeping track of results in their journals. A KWL (what we know, what we want to know, what we learned) helps to keep track of children's questions and learning.

pictures of them in their present form. Guide books can also be present for children to look through.

- Grow a dish garden by cutting off the top inch of carrots or beets. Keep the tops in a dish with water. Keep track of the results by carefully observing and keeping records in a journal.
- Grow plants to eat such as herbs and lettuce.

Earth and Space Science Standards

Earth and space science is the study of the earth, the climate, the solar system, and the universe. The National Research Council (2012) in *A Framework for K–12 Science Education* identifies the core ideas for early elementary grades for earth and space science as being:

- Earth's place in the universe.
- Earth's systems.
- Earth and human activity.

Worth and Grollman (2003) have identified earth and space standards for preschool children as being:

- Properties of earth materials.
- Weather and climate.
- Pattern of movement and change of the moon and the sun (Worth & Grollman, 2003, p. 144).

One of the big ideas in earth science is that humans and the environment impact each other.

Earth and Space Science Learning Center Activities

In this section, we will examine soil, rocks, and water and ice. Another common topic of study in this area is the examination of seasons.

Soil. Some concepts in studying soil are that soils can be classified based on color, texture, and consistency; that soils can retain water and help plants survive; and that animals, plants, and humans can cause changes to soil (Lind, 2005, p. 240). There are several center activities that children can complete to learn about soils.

- Collect a soil sample and examine what is in the soil (insects, rocks, leaves, trash, leaves).
- Visually examine different types of soil with a magnifying glass, classify the soils, and see if any items in the soil are attracted to magnets. To make the activity more interesting, each child can bring a soil specimen from his own backyard.
- Children can add one cup of water to a jar of each of the different types of soil. The soil will separate into layers. Encourage children to first predict what they think will happen. After they have added water, encourage children to draw the layers in their journals.
- Let the children experiment with the different mixtures (clay, humus, and sand with small amounts of water added to them). Encourage children to share their observations. For example, the clay can be formed into a ball and humus will clump slightly.

- Plant the same type of flower in different soils. Does the plant grow differently based on the type of soil?
- Create soil through composting. For example, at Curious Minds the children created a worm bed. They began by adding red worms to a plastic box (with holes in the bottom for drainage and ventilation) that contained torn up newspaper. Over the newspaper they added some soil. After about a week, the children began to feed the worms fruit and vegetable scraps from their lunches. They learned that they could feed their two pounds of worms about one pound of food every 24 hours.

Rocks. Some concepts relating to rocks are that rocks are formed in different ways, rocks are nonliving things, and rocks can be classified based on common characteristics (Lind, 2005, p. 240). You can begin your rock study by helping children to closely examine a favorite rock, providing magnifying glasses, paper, and colored pencils so that children can draw a detailed picture. You can assist children with examination of their favorite rock by asking questions regarding the colors; whether the rock has air holes, layers, or fossils; the strength of the rock (does it crumble or break easily); and the texture (size of the bits) (Trundle, Miller, & Krissek, 2013).

In the science center, you can provide a variety of different types of rocks for children to classify by size, color, and hardness, whether they are layered or not layered, whether they are magnetic, or whether they sink or float. You will want to provide tools for testing and examining the rocks, including a scale, magnifying glasses, sorting trays, magnets, water for determining whether they sink or float, and nails and pennies to scratch the rock (notice the rock center and the different tools included in the photo at the beginning of this chapter). It will also be important to provide data charts to record information and resource books for identifying the rocks.

Nathan's class began a study of rocks when the children became interested in the huge decorative rocks that the contractors moved in next to their school. The children collected rocks and brought rocks from home to classify. During circle times, Nathan introduced the different tests that could be conducted on the rocks. Materials for the tests and the rocks were placed in the science learning center. Children kept records of the tests using a picture table that Nathan had prepared. When the children had spent extensive time exploring and sorting the rocks, Nathan introduced information on the classification of rocks into sedimentary, metamorphic, and igneous. He showed how the tests helped to determine what kinds of rocks they had in the classroom.

Apply Your Knowledge What age of children do you think Nathan was working with? Would rocks be an appropriate topic for other early childhood age groups? If so, what modifications in the activities should be made?

Water and Ice. An important concept that early childhood children need to learn concerning water and ice is that "Water can be a liquid or a solid and can go back and forth from one form to the other. If water is turned to ice and then the ice is allowed to melt, the amount of water is the same as it was before freezing" (AAAS, 1993, p. 67). Some learning center activities involving ice include:

- Experiment with different ways to make colored ice melt faster. Provide tools such as hammers to crack the ice, containers of water, squirt bottle filled with salt water, a hair dryer, and other tools that the children think of. The color will assist in keeping track of the different experiments that are occurring. Make sure that you stress scientific practices such as prediction before you begin.

- Examine the ice with a magnifying glass.
- Encourage children to place ice in different areas of the room to see which will melt the fastest.
- Have children design containers to preserve the ice without putting it in the refrigerator or freezer. Provide a variety of different materials that the children have brainstormed.

Engineering Standards

The National Research Council (2012) in *A Framework for K–12 Science Education* identify the core ideas in the early childhood years for engineering as being:

- Engineering design.
- Links among engineering, technology, science, and society.

Engineering Learning Center Activities

Why is it important to include engineering for young children? There are many reasons. Children have a natural interest in the way that things work and often engage in design activities. Engineering introduces children to the idea that there are systematic ways to solve a design problem. Without this, children generally use a "try and see" approach. However, research shows that when children use an engineering design process, their understanding improves and they become better at planning and critiquing future experiments (Lindeman, Jabot, & Berkley, 2013). Teaching children the engineering design process helps establish basic knowledge that is a building block for the future. Engineering integrates many other subjects, such as math and literacy, and enhances creative and original thinking. As with professional engineers, the process often involves collaboration (Dunn & Larson, 1990).

Children are continually designing (building a fort, developing a ramp to make their car go further, or creating a boat). However, the design process helps children to learn a more systematic way to design. The design process includes investigation, invention, implementation, and evaluation. In the investigation phase children determine the problem, generate ideas about the design, and investigate resources, materials, and tools. During the invention phase, children continue to plan and weigh alternatives. They draw or verbally describe their design and develop a prototype. The implementation phase allows children to test and modify their design. During evaluation, both the process and product are evaluated. The evaluation will be based upon criteria that has emerged throughout the process (Dunn & Larson, 1990).

For example, preschool children at Curious Minds were interested in building a jeep (the problem). They wanted the jeep to hold at least two children and to actually move (the criteria). They began by examining actual jeeps, pictures of jeeps, and diagrams of jeeps. They looked for potential materials they could use in creating a jeep (investigation). After this, they drew plans for a jeep. They decided to build the body of the jeep out of wood. The program had a woodworking center and the children had already been actively engaged in building. They measured, sawed, and nailed the body. A parent donated wheels and a steering wheel. The children faced the challenge of how to connect the axel to the jeep. They experimented with a variety of different options. Eventually, they sought help from the maintenance men on the college campus where they were located. With their help, they were able to attach the axel to the jeep allowing the jeep to roll. When the children attached a rope to the jeep, they were able to pull each other. They had developed their prototype (invention). They now experimented with the jeep, pulling each other around the campus. As they experimented, they continued to make adjustments such as lengthening the rope they used to pull the jeep (implementation). As part of the evaluation process they decided that they needed lights, and the design cycle began again.

This is a picture of the jeep that the preschool children at Curious Minds created.

As this example illustrates, design projects can be initiated by the children. The teacher can also create design challenges, such as building a simple machine out of Legos, designing a musical instrument that makes sound, making a windmill, creating a bridge, or designing a self-propelled boat. Programming robots is another way to help children learn about design and can be combined with other design projects such as creating a bridge that the robot can walk over and programming the robot to do so.

Over time, it is important to expose children to the different areas in science (physical science, life science, earth and space science, and engineering). We have examined a variety of learning center activities for preschool and early-elementary-age children that can meet standards in these different areas. Is it also important to have a science center for infants and toddlers? What science concepts are infants and toddlers learning?

Check Your Understanding 11.3

Click here to gauge your understanding of section concepts.

Special Considerations for Different Age Groups

Science for Infants and Toddlers

From birth, children actively investigate their environment using observation and their senses to develop theories about how the world works. As stated by Greenman, Stonehouse, and Schweikert (2007), "first they observe, followed by endless trial and error and experimentation with everything in their world" (Greenman, Stonehouse, and Schweikert, 2007, p. 271). As infants become toddlers, they refine their observation and experimentation skills. While infant and toddler programs often do not have a specific science center, materials that help children learn science concepts are incorporated into other classroom centers. The important science concepts that children are exploring in this age group are:

- Using their senses to explore the physical properties of materials.
- Becoming aware of cause and effect ("If I turn this switch the light will come on").
- Recognizing real and not real (a live animal versus a stuffed toy animal, a real rock versus a plastic replica of a rock).
- Making simple classifications (Miller, 2004, p. 25).

To learn concepts, children need to have hands-on experiences. This is particularly true for infants and toddlers.

Many years ago, I was a houseparent for children who were abused and neglected. One day a social worker brought a two-year-old child, named Jay, to live with us. Jay loved horses. He played with toy horses, we read horse books repeatedly, and he only wanted to wear the horse print pajamas. The county fair was coming to town, and I was excited to take Jay to see the horses. However, when we went he was very afraid. He didn't know that horses were big, that they made loud noises, or that they had a smell. He came home and never again asked to read a horse book, to wear the pajamas with horses, or to play with the toy horses.

As illustrated in the vignette, hands-on experience is necessary to gain complete and accurate knowledge. Infants and toddlers are dependent upon us to provide materials and experiences. Some materials for hands-on science explorations with infants and toddlers include:

- Natural materials to explore, group, and classify—leaves, pinecones, rocks, feathers, seashells, water, dirt, snow, ice, wet and dry sand, mud, bark, and tree stumps. You will also want to include props to help with the explorations such as sand wheels, scoops, sifters, shovels, buckets, and spray bottles.
- Living things such as dogs, cats, worms, and bugs, along with their food and the materials used to care for them.
- Items to explore how things move—ball rolls, toy cars, tubes, and ramps.
- Baskets of materials to compare and contrast, such as balls that are rough and smooth, hard and soft, and of different weights.
- Cause-and-effect materials such as chime balls, pop-up toys, music boxes, activity boxes, and pulleys with items attached. It is important that the children are able to create the effect themselves so they can link their action to the effect.

Infants and toddlers are learning about the people, animals, and plants in their environments, including how each should be treated. One teacher of toddlers adds pots of herbs to her classroom. She calls these "petting plants." Children can carefully touch the plants and smell the fresh herbs on their hands. Since children are often still mouthing items, herbs are especially suitable.

As a teacher of infants and toddlers, it is very important to observe children's interests and actions while they are using materials and to provide materials and experiences that expand their opportunities. For example, Ember was banging items on the floor. Her teacher observed Ember experimenting with sound and gave her a basket of items that made different sounds to extend her learning.

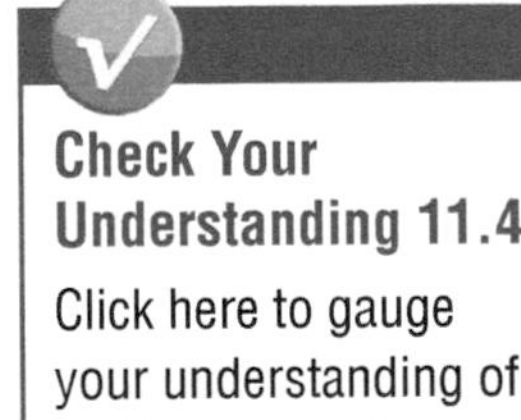

Check Your Understanding 11.4
Click here to gauge your understanding of section concepts.

Science for K–3rd Grade Children

The **NGSS** requires a conceptual shift for many early elementary teachers. The standards call for the active engagement in scientific practices (referred to previously as process skills or inquiry), an emphasis on crosscutting concepts, and a greater focus on fewer essential core ideas (a limited set of core knowledge) so that children can explore these in more depth. The standards are designed to provide coherence between grades resulting in children's growth in conceptual understanding. Each grade level includes a few focuses for study. For example, one of the expectations of kindergarten children is that they understand what is needed for plants and animals to survive and how the place they live affects this (NGSS Lead States, 2013). The learning centers on animals and plants described earlier could assist children to learn this. While the standards describe outcomes, they do not dictate how children achieve these outcomes. For example, they do not state what animals or plants are studied or what activities to use to assist children to gain this competency. However, they do stress that activities should allow for in-depth learning and hands-on engagement.

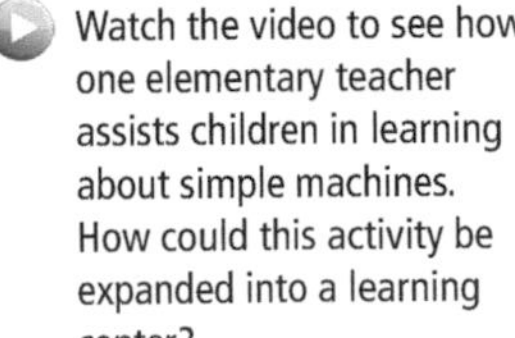

Watch the video to see how one elementary teacher assists children in learning about simple machines. How could this activity be expanded into a learning center?

How do teachers know which science activities to choose for their group of children? What is the role of the teacher as children use the materials? We will examine these questions next.

Teachers' Facilitation of Learning in the Science Center

To promote children's scientific knowledge, teachers must establish an effective science center and determine the activities and materials for the center. It is also crucial that we interact with children before, during, and after they use the center. Interacting with children has a significant effect on children's science learning and the way they use materials (Heath & Heath, 1982; Iatridis, 1984; Nayfeld, Brenneman, & Gelman, 2011). Following are some of the important roles that teachers have in promoting science through a center approach.

Determine Concepts to Be Taught and Provide Time for Children to Build and Refine Prior Concepts

"Concepts are building blocks of knowledge: they allow people to organize and categorize information" (Lind, 1999). The NGSS list seven crosscutting concepts, which are

- patterns,
- cause and effect,
- scale, proportion and quantity,
- systems and system models,
- energy and matter,
- structure and function, and
- stability and change (NGSS Lead States, 2013).

The concepts to emphasize and way to teach these concepts will be based upon children's interests, development, national and state standards, and the surrounding environment. You will want to go in-depth allowing children to revisit experiences using photos, video, and discussion. Children also need many opportunities to explore concepts in different ways and adults who assist them in seeing how these are connected. For example, in learning about patterns you might explore weather, seasons, and animals (patterns needed for survival).

Be cautious of ideas listed in activity books that might not be related to science concepts. For example, one time-honored activity often listed in activity books is creating a volcano by mixing soda and vinegar. While this activity could be used to teach about chemical reactions, when we use it as a volcano activity we may be inadvertently teaching misinformation. Are volcanoes caused by chemical reactions?

Choose Developmentally Appropriate Concepts and Activities

It is critical that we consider children's developmental understandings in planning science activities. They must be able to have at least an elementary understanding of the scientific explanation underlying the activity. If not, they come to view science as magic and their scientific learning is insecure. Although children may not have full understandings of some concepts until they are older, such as the scientific concepts behind ramps, they can develop practical mental relationships. For example, they can learn that the surface of a ramp influences how far a play car will travel (DeVries & Sales, 2011). Teachers also need to carefully choose activities that allow children to engage in experimentation.

Determine Children's Current Knowledge and Theories

Children have preconceived notions that may or may not be accurate (Miller, 2004). To determine children's current knowledge, theories, and misconceptions, you might have children explain their version of a phenomenon. Bonita does this by having children complete a KWHL chart. Jeri has each child draw his or her theories. Other teachers find out children's misconceptions through careful questioning. It is not helpful to tell children their theories are incorrect. However, as we've seen in previous examples in this chapter, understanding children's misconceptions allows the teacher to provide experiences where children can test their theories. While misconceptions can be resistant to change, providing "hands-on" experience that allows children to learn other explanations is extremely helpful.

Introduce Materials and Develop Interest

Studies have shown that even when well-developed science centers are available, they are rarely used by children. However, introducing the materials in the science center and developing interest through a circle time activity significantly increase the number of children using the center, the amount of time they spend in the center, and the learning that occurs (Nayfeld, Brenneman, & Gelman, 2011).

> Diego was introducing a sink and float center to the children. First, he took a round ball of clay and asked the children if they thought it would float or sink. After the predictions, he dropped the clay in water to see what happened. The children described their theories about why the clay sank. He next built a clay boat. Again, he asked the children to predict whether it would sink or float and to discuss why they thought so. After the predictions, he told children they could find out what would happen by experimenting in the science center. Nearly all the children in the class voluntarily visited the center.

Assist Children to Develop a Mental Structure

Children can build upon mental structures as they learn new information or observe phenomena (Gelman & Brenneman, 2004; National Research Council, 2005). "Once a mental structure is in place … children are much more likely both to notice new data that fit with what they have already learned and to store data in such a way that they can build on it in the future. Conversely, when children lack a mental structure for organizing particular domains of knowledge, the significance of new data is not evident to them and they must either construct a new structure to accommodate it or fail to benefit from it" (Gelman, 2005, p. 6). To assist children to develop mental structures and to add to existing structures, we can link new knowledge to previous schemas, mental structures, and big ideas. For example, what we know about a cat can be linked to what we know about other animals. When we have developed a schema about animals and are introduced to a new animal, even one that we have never met, we know that it can breathe, eat, reproduce, and move by itself (Gelman & Brenneman, 2004, p. 3).

Teach Children Scientific Vocabulary

Language and science concepts go hand in hand. We should not diminish the importance of vocabulary, since children learn words at a rapid rate and vocabulary is directly tied to concept development (Gelman & Brenneman, 2004). You must intentionally plan and teach both science content and process vocabulary. You can use the words within context, read stories that contain the vocabulary words, and have circle time discussions about the words. Posting the list of vocabulary words that you want to stress in the science center can help you and other adults remember to emphasize these words.

Provide Background Knowledge

To effectively help children develop background knowledge on the topic being studied, we need background information ourselves. Without background knowledge, we are unable to take full advantage of teachable moments, such as when a child asks why the leaves are falling. In addition, we might not recognize children's misconceptions or we might inadvertently teach misconceptions ourselves. We can gain knowledge by seeking professional development opportunities. We can also improve our knowledge one topic at a time by researching the topic the class is currently investigating. Likewise, it is helpful to experiment with new materials yourself

When we have background knowledge on the topic, we can share this information with children and enhance their learning. We might share information during individual conversations with children, with a group of children at circle time, or when children ask questions.

Ask Open-Ended Questions

When asking questions, we must be careful not to act like a quiz show host. The goal in questioning is to have a two-way, in-depth conversation. The purpose of asking questions should be to understand children's current level of thinking and to help them, through careful questioning, to think more deeply about a topic or theory. You can also use questions as a way to provide new challenges and provocations. For example, you might ask, "Why do you think that happened?" "How can you test out that idea?" or "What do you think would happen if . . . ?"

Encourage Children to Reflect Upon Their Learning

Through reflecting and communicating, children learn to recall information, generalize what they have learned, analyze their findings, and solve problems (Klein et al., 2000). Many teachers encourage children to systematically reflect upon their learning during small group times.

Encourage and Model Curiosity, Inquiry, and Enjoyment of Science

Unfortunately, many adults have had poor experiences in relationship to science education. We need to be careful not to pass this dislike of the subject on to children. Children are naturally curious. When we capitalize on this curiosity, we can develop science centers that children will enjoy, and perhaps we can learn to enjoy science ourselves. We can also model questioning, which is at the root of inquiry.

Implement Formal Science Talks for Preschool and Elementary-Aged Children

In a busy classroom day, teachers might wonder why it is necessary to have formal science talks. Formal science talks can provide opportunities for deeper scientific learning by building interest, teaching skills, aiding reflection, and emphasizing scientific practices, vocabulary, and concepts. Although in the past teachers often used this time to demonstrate experiments, there are many other more successful ways to enhance children's learning. For example, let's examine the ways that Cassandra used formal science talks as part of a study of worms. The study began when children discovered worms on the playground and became interested in learning more about them. Cassandra bought worms and placed them in an aquarium. Cassandra conducted the following activities during the many worm focused group talks to assist the children in learning science practices, skills, and content:

- Established ground rules for respectfully treating living things (how to handle the worms so they did not get hurt—explaining that earth worms die if they dry out).
- Took advantage of group synergy to develop questions (what do we know about worms, what do we want to know, and how can we find out).
- Chose which questions to investigate (how do worms move, what do worms eat, what do worms' tunnels look like, do worms like the dark or light, and do earthworms like wet soil, dry soil, or moist soil).
- Discussed and developed a plan to answer each of the questions.
- Taught children the skills they needed to be successful (how to record their findings, how to create a worm viewer, and criteria for an earthworm habitat).
- Focused on concepts or big ideas she wished to stress (what do living things need to survive, and the difference between living and nonliving).
- Provided additional information through inviting a guest speaker (an expert on worm composting).
- Introduced scientific vocabulary (experiment, habitat, burrow, humus, and invertebrate).
- Assisted children to share predictions, theories, and ideas.
- Solved problems (until the aquarium was covered with black paper the children were unable to see the worms or their tunnels—the teacher and the children decided to ask their worm expert what to do).
- Provided opportunities for the children to share and reflect on their documentation (the children shared their science journals, data tables, photos, models, drawings, and emergent writing with each other).
- Assisted children to retell the steps they took in the different experiments.
- Assisted children to draw conclusions. As one of the children discussed her conclusion another child challenged her. The discussion helped both children to learn.

Watch the video to observe a teacher exploring how animals move with children. How would you continue this lesson in your science learning center?

Meet the Needs of All Learners

It is important that all children have access and encouragement to learn science in the early childhood years. The early childhood years provide the foundation for later science learning. By becoming scientifically literate, we can better understand the world. Scientific reasoning can help us to make better decisions. In addition, science can be an equalizer or a gatekeeper for later success. Historically, research shows that girls, children of color, children with disabilities, and children who are poor "have been excluded from the science pipeline to higher education and the science/math related jobs of the future" (Sprung & Froschl, 2006, p. 7). For example, men hold 74% of science and engineering jobs in the United States. Even when women are employed in these fields, they generally are paid less than men. White men and women account for 73% of the science and engineering jobs and tend to be paid more than their minority peers (National Science Foundation, 2011).

How do the data apply to the early childhood years? According to many researchers, if we want to change these statistics and provide science equity to all groups, we must begin in the early childhood years (Sprung & Froschl, 2006). However, large-scale studies reveal that school readiness in science continues to lag behind other curricular areas (Greenfield et al., 2009). What are steps we can take to help all children succeed in science? We can do the following:

- Use inquiry-based science. "Inquiry-based science is a wonderful way to level the playing field for all students. Students who are less verbal or English Language Learners can shine in a hands-on environment; students with disabilities can utilize the problem-solving skills they hone through everyday living; and girls can engage in cooperative learning, a style that research shows works well for them" (Sprung & Froschl, 2006, p. 8).
- Make sure to include books and posters in the science center that show underrepresented groups engaged in science.
- Invite guest speakers who are from underrepresented groups.
- Honor what children know and bring to the classroom. Five-year-old Jeramiah had never traveled outside a 20-mile radius from home. He'd never been to a lake, mountain, zoo, science center, water park, or museum. However, his grandfather and grandmother had taught him about all the native plants (their names, which you could eat, and how they could be used for medicine) and animals on the reservation where he lived. His teacher began the year with a study of plants and encouraged Jeramiah and his family to share their knowledge.
- Provide open-ended materials in the science center to meet all developmental levels.
- Provide pictorial directions in the science center. If you include written directions, include the primary languages of all the children in the classroom.
- Most important, we must believe that all children can be successful in learning science.

Observe and Document Individual Children's Learning

Assess Interests. As mentioned previously, it is important for teachers to assess children's interests so they can plan experiences that are relevant to them. Teachers can do this by interviewing children, listening to their questions, or observing how they spend their time. Some teachers ask parents about their children's interests. At the beginning of a new school year in a toddler program, teachers gave parents a plastic bag and asked them to place an object, drawing, or photo of something their child was interested in into the bag. When the bags were returned, the majority contained rocks. Teachers were then able to begin the year with a relevant topic—rocks.

Assess Prior Knowledge. Once a topic is determined, children's prior knowledge and theories need to be assessed. This can be done by asking open-ended questions and recording the results. For example, Kelly began her butterfly center by asking what children knew about butterflies. Throughout the discussion, she continued to ask open-ended questions, finding out children's theories about how butterflies get their food, how they have young, and so forth. Answers can be recorded in a list, a web, or a KWHL. Gallenstein (2005) recommends using concept maps with preschool and early-elementary-aged children. A concept map is similar to a web but often uses words to show the relationship between items. Gallenstein recommends using actual objects or pictures of objects and arrows with words for the early childhood years. For example, in developing a concept map of the five senses, she begins with a picture of a child with arrows pointing to each sense. She then has the children place a plastic mouth, ear, eye, nose, and hand where they believe they belong. Next, she adds items or pictures of items to taste, smell, hear, see, and touch. Again, the children place them where they believe they belong. Finally, the children describe what they have done and how the objects relate to each other. Gallenstein uses this information in planning curriculum.

Check Your Understanding 11.5

Click here to gauge your understanding of section concepts.

Assess Learning. Artifacts such as drawings, constructions, writing, photographs, graphs, tables, and record sheets are important in documenting children's ongoing learning about the science topic. Their verbal descriptions can continue to be a rich source of information about their changing ideas and theories. If a web was initially created, a post-web can show growth in children's knowledge. Likewise, completing the "what I learned" on a KWHL chart can indicate increased competence.

As teachers engage in ongoing assessment of children's learning, they use this information to plan sequential learning activities and to add relevant materials to the science center.

Click here to gauge your understanding of chapter concepts.

Teachers play a critical role in developing science centers and interacting with children to help them develop competence in science. Children are naturally curious. From birth, they are continually forming hypotheses and testing them. By providing rich experiences, we can capitalize on this interest and assist all children to learn scientific processes and knowledge that will become the building blocks for future success in science.

Sample Application Activities

1. Observe children during center time to see what science activities they are engaged in.
2. Critique a science center using the science environmental assessment found in Figure 11.2.
3. Develop a science center using the criteria discussed in this chapter. Make sure you introduce your center.
4. Get ideas from these free science curriculums: *Inspiring Children's Spirit of Stewardship: A Toolkit for Early Childhood Programs; Quest for Less,* a recycling curriculum for K–8; *Science Discovery: A Hands-On Discovery Science Curriculum for Preschool and Kindergarten*; or GLOBE.gov for free books and earth science learning plans.
5. Learn more about using ramps and pathways with children at the University of Northern Iowa ramps and pathways website.
6. Observe an infant or young toddler interacting with materials. What theory is the child testing? What questions do they have? What materials or experiences could you provide to assist the child in furthering testing his ideas? Since infants cannot tell you their questions, you will have to make assumptions based upon careful observation.
7. Develop a booklet of science fact sheets for common early childhood topics.
8. Brainstorm a list of science vocabulary words for different common science topics.
9. Learn more about the Next Generation National Science Standards and your state's Early Learning Standards.
10. To improve your science background knowledge, view free science videos at the Annenberg Media website. For example, see "Essential Science for Teachers: Earth and Space Science."

- ❑ Is the science center in an enclosed quiet area of the classroom?
- ❑ Is the science center large enough to accommodate several children?
- ❑ Is the center designed to encourage cooperation and communication (Charlesworth & Lind, 2007)?
- ❑ Does the center allow for uninterrupted work?
- ❑ Is the center near a sink, if possible?
- ❑ Is there adequate work space?
- ❑ Does the center contain organized, labeled shelving to store materials?
- ❑ Does the center contain a bulletin board or other surface for posting information and findings?
- ❑ Is there adequate lighting in the center?
- ❑ Is the center near a window, if at all possible?
- ❑ Is the center enticing and inviting?
- ❑ Is the center designed for action rather than just for looking (Charlesworth & Lind, 2007)?
- ❑ Does the center encourage children to develop "What would happen if" statements?
- ❑ Does the center stress process skills by providing materials needed to perform these tasks?
- ❑ Does the center stress specific content related to the topic being studied?
- ❑ Does the center tie into larger overriding concepts or "big ideas"?
- ❑ Over a period of time does the center contain materials focusing on life science, physical science, earth and space science, and engineering?
- ❑ Does the center build upon current children's curiosity, interests, knowledge, background, and previous activities?
- ❑ Does the center allow for individual differences by providing open-ended material or a variety of tasks at different levels?
- ❑ Does the center allow children to use the center independently?
  - ❍ Directions for the center are provided in pictures, written, tape recorded, or introduced at circle time.
  - ❍ All needed materials are available.
  - ❍ Materials are arranged in a logical order or sequence.
  - ❍ There is a clearly designated place for each item.
  - ❍ Materials are within the children's reach.
- ❑ Does the center encourage children to represent their knowledge (paper, graph paper, tape recorders, journals, recording sheets, clipboards, pencils, and markers)?
- ❑ Does the center contain resource materials (books, posters, videos, computer)?
- ❑ Does the center contain inquiry tools (magnifying glasses of different types, microscope, Petri dishes, scales, eyedroppers, pulleys, tweezers, twine, clay for imprints, specimen bags and boxes, and nets) that are needed to complete activities in the center?

FIGURE 11.2 Environmental Assessment: Science Center

Chapter 12

Developing Math Centers

Learning Outcomes

After you have read this chapter, you will be prepared to:

- Discuss multiple ways that the math center enhances children's development
- Demonstrate the ability to design effective math learning centers both indoors and outdoors
- Create learning center activities that are developmentally appropriate and that assist children in meeting math standards
- Explain how to design math centers and activities for different ages
- Describe multiple ways that teachers facilitate learning in the math center

Julie Bullard

Juanita, a teacher at Brighter Future Preschool, was eager to implement what she learned at a preschool math workshop. However, the presenter had stressed that you must begin by observing the skill level and interests of the children in your room. Therefore, Juanita developed a checklist of mathematical skills based on the math standards and then carefully observed the children to determine their current level of mathematical knowledge and understanding. While observing, she noted that few boys used the math center. Instead, they spent all their free time playing with the cars in the block center. Following the observations, she began to enrich her environment. For example, since many of the children were learning to classify, she placed several items in the math area including small cars, beautiful small colored rocks, and pinecones to sort. To pique the boys' interest she also added wrenches to seriate (arrange from large to small). She created a game where children matched cars and garages based on a numeral and the correct number of dots. Juanita was pleased to discover that the children, including several of the boys, became more engaged in using math manipulatives.

Math manipulatives, the heart of the math center, have a rich and ongoing history in early childhood. In the 19th century, Froebel, considered the father of kindergarten, developed mathematical manipulatives or "gifts" for young children. This emphasis on using math manipulatives continues to be best practice in the 21st century.

Children in a developmentally appropriate classroom have numerous opportunities to learn mathematical skills and concepts as they play with materials. For example, children learn many geometry skills while they play with blocks (see Chapter 9 for more information). As children cook or play in the media table, they often practice measuring skills. Materials in the manipulative center encourage the use of one-to-one correspondence and counting. However, experts recommend that preschool and elementary classrooms have a designated math center. Having a separate math center encourages teachers to place an intentional focus on this area. Research indicates that there is a lack of attention to math in the early childhood years, and when math is included it is typically integrated into other areas. However, children learn math best when math is the primary focus (Bowman, Donovan, & Burns, 2001; National Research Council, 2009). A separate math center also makes the emphasis on math evident to staff, families, and children.

How the Math Center Enhances Children's Development

Development of Math Skills

Children first learn math content and process skills informally. From infancy, they use mathematics in everyday activities and to solve problems. As stated by Vygotsky (1978), "children's learning begins long before they enter school ... they have had to deal with operations of division, addition, subtraction, and the determination of size. Consequently, children have their own preschool arithmetic, which only myopic psychologists could ignore" (Vygotsky, 1978, p. 84). Ginsburg, an expert on early childhood mathematics, when discussing the similarities between young children and research mathematicians states, "Both young children and mathematicians ask and think about deep questions, invent solutions, apply mathematics to solve real problems, and play with mathematics. Clearly then, one of our goals should be to encourage and foster young children's *current* mathematical activities" (Ginsburg, 2006, p. 158). Children use math to help make sense of the world. They construct their knowledge as they reason actively (Kamii, 2003). Teachers need to build upon this natural interest, providing children with in-depth opportunities and time to use math materials and ideas (NAEYC/NCTM, 2010). They also need to plan activities and use every available opportunity to encourage children to reason (Kamii, 2003).

Watch the video to learn more about the importance of math. Why is it important for young children to learn about math?

https://www.youtube.com/watch?v=EYaLrPNtD8I

However, while children intuitively use math to solve problems, according to Piaget, the only way that they can learn **social-arbitrary knowledge** is from adults or more competent peers. Social-arbitrary knowledge consists of "arbitrary truths agreed upon by convention and rules agreed upon by coordination of points of view" (DeVries & Kohlberg, 1987, p. 21). For example, in math the names of the numbers, signs, and shapes are examples of social-arbitrary knowledge. Teachers must support children's learning as they use mathematical materials, helping them learn social-arbitrary knowledge.

Learning Math Standards

While interacting in a well-developed math center, children have the opportunity to learn about the mathematical standards as defined by the National Council of Teachers of Mathematics (NCTM). These are numbers and operations, geometry, measurement, algebra, and data analysis. Although the early childhood teacher needs to provide experiences relating to each of these standards, the primary emphasis for pre-K through second-grade children is numbers and operations, geometry, and the measurement standards.

In addition, children in the early childhood years need to develop math process skills, including problem solving, reasoning, communicating, connecting, and representing (NCTM, 2000). These process skills transcend mathematics, involving lifelong skills that children need to be successful in all areas of their lives. For example, in early childhood classrooms we can find many examples where children need to use problem-solving skills (planning a fair way to share a toy with a friend, determining a way to keep a tower of blocks from falling, or keeping a pool of water from sinking into the sand). We will explore each of these math processes in more depth.

Learning Math Processes

Problem Solving. Common steps for problem solving involve understanding the problem, making a plan for solving the problem, implementing the plan, and reflecting to see if the solution works or the answer makes sense. Problem solving entails not only learning and practicing these steps, but also acquiring dispositions to problem solve. "An effective problem solver perseveres, focuses his attention, tests his hypotheses, takes reasonable risks, remains flexible, tries alternatives, and exhibits self regulation" (Copley, 2010, p. 31).

Reasoning. When children reason, they "draw logical conclusions, apply logical classification skills, explain their thinking, justify their problem solutions and processes, apply patterns and relationships to arrive at solutions, and make sense out of mathematics and science" (Charlesworth, 2005, p. 142).

Communicating. Children share their mathematical ideas in a variety of ways. They may communicate verbally explaining their thinking or nonverbally (charts, tallies, and drawings). Even very young children display their mathematical knowledge (holding up two fingers when asked their age).

Connecting. "The most important connection for early childhood mathematics development is between the intuitive, informal mathematics that students have learned through their own experience and the mathematics they are learning in school" (NCTM, 2000, p. 132). As discussed earlier, children naturally use math to solve problems they encounter in their natural world. Unfortunately, as children begin school and use formal mathematics, they often begin to view math as a set of rules and procedures rather than as a way of solving everyday problems. Teachers can help children to avoid this by using familiar manipulative materials to teach math, making children's natural mathematics visible by using math vocabulary to describe their activities, and using examples from children's experiences when introducing a math concept.

Representing. Representing assists children in organizing, recording, and sharing information and ideas (NCTM, 2000). Children might use fingers, make tallies, create diagrams, produce graphs, make maps, or draw pictures to represent their knowledge (Copley, 2010).

Additional Specific Math Reasoning Processes. In addition to these general processes, children should develop the ability to **unitize**, **decompose and compose**, relate and order, and to look for patterns and structures and organize information (Fuson, Clements, & Beckmann, 2010, p. 65).

Other Curriculum Areas

The math center also supports other curriculum areas. Surprisingly, a large research study that included groups of children from the United States, Canada, and the United Kingdom found that children's pre-K math skills are a more accurate prediction of their later reading skills than their pre-K reading skills are (Duncan et al., 2007). When children engage in more math they increase their oral language including vocabulary, grammatical complexity, and ability to make inferences (Sarama, Lange, Clements, & Wolfe, 2012). Literacy is enhanced as children discuss their mathematical ideas, read math-related books, and write numerals. In addition, math, music, and literacy all use symbols. For example, a numeral represents a certain group of objects, a note is a symbol for a certain sound, and the word *flower* is a symbol for an actual flower.

Since there are many similarities in math and science process skills, as children learn process skills in math, they also strengthen their ability to use science process skills. There are many daily opportunities for children to think, reason, problem solve, and use math to solve issues. For example, children often use math as they determine a fair way to divide materials.

When developing the math center, it is important to consider the appropriate math standards. Equally important is helping children use the math process skills as they use the materials. For example, Carmen was enjoying sorting rocks into groups by color. Juanita pointed out that Carmen was classifying the rocks (tied mathematical language to an informal math activity). She asked Carmen how she was grouping the rocks (stressed mathematical communication). When Carmen had completed the classification, Juanita asked her if she could think of other ways that she might classify the rocks (encouraged problem solving). As you develop your math center, also think about how you can enhance other curriculum areas.

Check Your Understanding 12.1

Click here to gauge your understanding of section concepts.

Designing an Effective Math Center

The math center provides children the opportunity to independently use manipulatives that will assist them in developing their natural math skills. The center also houses tools, such as measuring devices, which might be used as resources in other centers. For example, Sofia and Carlos used a yardstick from the math center to measure their "tall block skyscraper."

Designing an Effective Indoor Math Center

An effective math center contains the following:

- A clearly designated space in the quiet area of the room.
- A large work area that allows children to explore the math manipulatives.
- A rich variety of developmental math manipulatives relating to the different math standards (numbers and operations, measurement, geometry, algebra, and data analysis).

FIGURE 12.1 Books That Support Mathematical Learning

A Million Fish-More or Less by Patricia C. McKissack
Bat Jamboree by Kathi Appelt
Chimp Math: Learning about Time from a Baby Chimpanzee by Ann Whitehead Nagda and Cindy Bickel
Cones, Cylinders, and Cubes by Tana Hoban
Dots, Spots, Speckles, and Stripes by Tana Hoban
Exactly the Opposite by Tana Hoban
Five Creatures by Emily Jenkins
Grandfather Tangs Story by Ann Tompert
Growing Patterns: Fibonacci Numbers in Nature by Sarah C. Campbell
Guess How Much I Love You by Sam McBratney
How Big Is a Foot? by Rolf Myller
I Spy Two Eyes: Numbers in Art by Lucy Micklethwait
Jack the Builder by Stuart Murphy
Mouse Count by Ellen Stoll Walsh
100 Hungry Ants by Elinor J. Pinczes
One Tortoise, Ten Wallabies: A Wildlife Counting Book by Jakki Wood
Over in the Meadow by Ezra Jack Keats
Shapes, Shapes, Shapes by Tana Hoban
10 Bears in My Bed by Stan Mack
Ten Black Dots Board Book by Donald Crews
The Foot Book by Dr. Seuss
The Grouchy Ladybug by Eric Carle
The Icky Bug Counting Book by Jerry Pallotta
The Very Hungry Caterpillar by Eric Carle
The Wildlife 123: A Nature Counting Book by Jan Thornhill
Tiger Math: Learning to Graph from a Baby Tiger by Ann Whitehead Nagda and Cindy Bickel

- Organized shelves with a clearly designated place for each item.
- Aesthetically pleasing containers that allow children to see what is available and that keep all needed materials together.
- A place to display completed and in-progress work such as a bulletin board, the top of a shelf for three-dimensional work, and a three-ring binder for sketches and photos of work.
- Books that support math (see Figure 12.1).

Choosing Appropriate Activities and Materials for the Math Center

In addition to carefully planning the placement and layout of the math center, it is important to choose appropriate math materials. Appropriate materials allow for active manipulation, have a clearly defined mathematical purpose, are based on assessments of children's knowledge and skills, and are either open-ended or self-correcting. Materials need to be rotated to meet the developmental needs and interests of the children. In the following sections, we will explore each of these criteria in more depth.

Provide for Active Manipulation of Concrete Materials. Children must have abundant opportunities to learn through active manipulation of concrete materials before using abstract ideas. Children can often memorize information, but will not understand unless they have had experiences with concrete objects. For example, when my son Christopher was a second grader, he exclaimed proudly at supper one evening that four cups make a quart and that four quarts make a gallon. However, later in the meal when I asked him about the size of the gallon milk carton on the table, I was met by a puzzled stare.

Julie Bullard

Individual trays containing all the needed manipulative materials for each math activity are attractive and easy to carry to the table. Color-coded dots help children to know the difficulty level of the math activity.

Have a Clearly Defined Mathematical Purpose or Goal. It is important that teachers are familiar with national and state standards and use this knowledge when choosing materials. At Bright Beginnings, teachers post an index card on the shelf next to each math manipulative. The index card includes the standard, the purpose of the material, how teachers can scaffold learning, and how to assess the learning. At first, the teachers felt that preparing cards might be too much work. However, they found that it helped them to be more intentional in choosing materials. It also provided helpful information for other teachers and volunteers.

Provide Materials That Are Either Open-Ended or Self-Correcting. Children can correctly complete open-ended materials in many ways. There are many right answers. For example, Amanda provided children with a variety of buttons to classify. Children could classify these by the number of holes in the button, color, shape, or material the button was made from. Any of these ways would be correct. A closed-ended activity, however, has a right answer. For example, if you have a puzzle where children place numbers 1 to 10 in order, there is only one correct answer. This is an appropriate activity for children who are developmentally ready for this step. For example, many four-year-olds will be beginning to learn numerals and their order. How can you make it self-correcting? One way would be to make it into a puzzle so the child would know immediately whether the numerals were in the correct order. Why does this matter? Let's look at the experience that one child, Joan, has in the math center. Joan plays with the number line every day. However, it is not self-correcting. Each day she places the numbers in this order 1, 2, 4, 3, 5. Teachers are supervising and assisting many children during center time and therefore do not notice this error. Each time she incorrectly completes the activity, it reinforces her misconception. Besides creating a puzzle, there are many other ways to make materials self-correcting. For example, Jeri observes

Julie Bullard

This is an example of a self-correcting material. The right number of pumpkins will completely cover but not extend beyond the ribbon.

Check Your Understanding 12.2
Click here to gauge your understanding of section concepts.

that children in her classroom are ready to match a number of items to the correct numeral. She takes a round pizza cardboard and divides it into six sections, placing one dot in one section, two in another, and so on. She then takes wooden clothespins and writes numerals on them. The children are to clip the correct clothespin to the right area on the pizza cardboard. Jeri can color code the clothespins and dots (very obvious) or she can color code just the back side of the pizza circle. For example, all dots on the front are blue, but the clothespins are different colors. The yellow clothespin has a numeral 1 on it. Children turn the game over when it is complete and look to see if the yellow clothespin is by the yellow dot.

Choose Materials Based on Assessment of Children's Mathematical Skills and Knowledge. Open-ended materials will meet a variety of developmental levels. However, since children can only successfully complete closed-ended materials in one way, it is even more crucial that the material matches the child's skill level. Just as we would not give children who were completing 10-piece puzzles a 50-piece puzzle, we should not give children who are learning one-to-one correspondence a number line to complete. Even if you have a single age level in the classroom, you will have children at many different developmental levels. Some teachers code closed-ended math and manipulative materials so that children know which materials to choose. For example, Cindy a kindergarten teacher places dots on the math manipulatives to demonstrate difficulty.

Relate Materials to Children's Interests. While many items can be used for counting, sorting, patterning, and classifying, as the opening scenario illustrates, children are more likely to use the materials if they relate to their interests. Lucia found that several of the children in her classroom rarely used the math center. Lately several of these children had been very interested in the butterflies that were on the playground. Lucia added butterfly photos to classify, plastic butterflies to use for counting and patterning, and a math board game that featured butterflies. After adding these materials, she found that this group of children became interested in using the center.

Rotate Materials to Meet Children's Changing Developmental Needs and Interests. Many programs make one of two errors. Either teachers never rotate materials, or they have a rotation pattern but change materials without consideration of children's developmental readiness or interests. Instead, changes in the math center need to be made based upon the observation and assessment of the children's skills and interests. If children are still using materials, you will generally want to leave the materials in the center. Allowing children opportunities for repetition encourages concept formation. Appropriate materials meet children's developmental needs and interests. They also provide opportunities to meet national and state standards and early learning guidelines.

Designing an Effective Outdoor Math Center

The outdoors also provides many opportunities for authentic math experiences. These can be enriched by incorporating math materials into the environment. For example, provide:

- Measuring cups and containers of all sizes for the sand and water area and dramatic play area.
- An easily accessible measurement tool kit. When materials are readily available, it encourages both teachers and children to use them. For example, children at Tiny Tots found a worm and got out the tape measure to measure it. They had a small journal in the tool kit where they recorded the length of the different worms they found. This was the longest worm found up to this time, causing great excitement.

- A built-in measuring tape on the jumping pit or a climbing structure.
- Graphs for collecting data (number of birds or type of birds visiting a bird feeder or how many times you need to fill the bird feeder each week). These can be created by painting a grid on a metal cooking sheet and using magnets as the markers.
- An outdoor weather station with a windsock, rain gauge, thermometer, sundial, and cloud cards. One of the children's rotating jobs can be to check, record, and share information from the weather station. Provide a journal in a sealed plastic bag where children can record their findings.
- Games that involve numbers such as throwing beanbags at numerals.
- Activities such as having children bury treasure and create a treasure map, photograph patterns, participate in a shape scavenger hunt, follow directional words as moving through an obstacle course, and play Simon Says that includes mathematical terms and concepts (jump three times, make a triangle with your body).

To meet children's mathematical needs, we need to have a rich mathematical environment with intentionally chosen materials that meet both the children's interests and needs and the standards. How do we choose materials that will accomplish this? We will investigate this question next.

Meeting Standards Through Math Center Materials and Activities

As discussed earlier, NCTM has identified five mathematical standards for pre-K through second grade. Additionally, they have established curriculum focal points for each grade level, including pre-K. The Common Core State Standards (CCSS) include standards beginning with kindergarten using a slightly different division of standards. For example, NCTM includes measurement and data analysis as two separate standards while the CCSS combines these into one standard. However, NCTM Curriculum Focal Points and the CCSS have similar degrees of rigor and are comparable in coherence and focus (Achieve, 2010). In this next section we will use the standards developed by NCTM since they include pre-K. We will examine possible learning center activities in relationship to each of these standards. The specific activities you choose will be based upon the developmental readiness and interests of the children in your classroom.

Materials and Activities to Support the Numbers and Operations Standard

Mathematicians consider the numbers and operations standard to be the most important of the standards for the early years (National Research Council, 2009). Operations include not only addition, subtraction, division, and multiplication, but also "counting, comparing, grouping, dividing, uniting, partitioning, and composing" (Clements, 2004, p. 17).

Counting. Children typically begin counting by memorizing the number words. This is often referred to as **rote counting**. Number words are more difficult than other words for children to learn due to their function as a grouping rather than an individual item. Numbers are also a concept rather than a noun (Mix, Huttenlocher, & Levine, 2002). Depending upon the environment, children may begin counting as early as the age of 2 (Clements, 2004). Counting out loud was the most frequent math activity cited by early childhood teachers in a large-scale study. While this is important, it is definitely not enough (Stipek, 2014).

Create Your Own Math Activity

Julie Bullard

These garages are an enticing math activity. Three developmental possibilities are shown. Initially, children might drive a car into each garage by matching the colored dots (example one). As children become more proficient with one-to-one correspondence, this task can become more difficult by adding a different number of dots to each car and the corresponding garage, allowing children to match the dots. Then numerals can be added to the garage, which are then matched to the dots on the cars (example two). Finally, numerals can be matched to words (example three).

Directions

1. Cover a milk carton with contact paper to create a garage.
2. Cut a door in the carton.
3. Write numerals (1–10), numeral words (one–ten), and dots (1–10) on bingo-colored disks with a permanent marker.
4. Add a Velcro circle to each garage and to each car. This allows you to easily change the colored disks to make the activity developmentally appropriate for the child or children using them.
5. Create your game based upon the developmental level of the children by placing a labeled colored disk on the Velcro on each car and garage. For example, for toddlers you might have children match colored dots, and for first graders you might match numerals with words.
6. Create a winding road out of felt, allowing children to practice manipulative skills as they drive their cars into the correct garages.
7. Make the task self-correcting by adding matching colored paper dots or symbols to the bottom of the car and the bottom of the garage.

Variations:

Begin with five cars and garages; as children become more proficient, you can add ten.

To count items successfully, children must know the number words. Next, they must understand **one-to-one correspondence**, or that there is one number word for each item they are counting. They must learn to keep track of items as they count them and to tag or count each item only once. It is often easier to do this if children move or touch each item they are counting. Finally, they must understand **cardinality**, that the final number that they count represents the number of all the items in the collection. This concept forms the basis for all future work with numbers and operations (Clements, 2004). When you assess children's understanding of numbers, it is important to look at each of these steps. By doing so, you can determine what skills the child will need to work on to progress to the next level. For example, Sabrina could count by rote to 10. She recognized small sets (up to four) without counting them. However, if the set was larger, she seemed unable to determine how many items there were. While observing Sabrina counting money in the dramatic play area, the teacher noted that Sabrina did not tag each coin as she counted it and therefore recounted several of the coins. The teacher demonstrated how to organize and tag the coins to count them.

One-to-One Correspondence. It is easier for children to use materials that are less abstract for one-to-one correspondence. Therefore, teachers should first provide real objects, then cutouts, then pictures, and finally symbols and patterns (Charlesworth, 2005). Following are several materials that you could place in the math center to assist in developing one-to-one correspondence.

- Outline game—Outline interesting items, and place the outline and the items in a box. Children can match each item to the correct outline.
- Match groups of items—For more advanced one-to-one correspondence, create matching games of items that go together (fork and spoon, nut and bolt, and mitten and hand).
- Pegs and pegboards—These come in a variety of sizes, so they can be chosen based upon the fine motor development of the children in the group.
- Jars and lids—Collect a variety of different types of jars with matching lids that children can put together.
- Cars and garages (see the create your own math activity)

Recognizing Numerals. Following are materials that you can add to the math center to help children recognize numerals.

- Objects with numerals, including calculators, adding machines, playing cards, magnetic numbers, and puzzles.
- Games where children match numerals. For example, use two old calendars that have similar-sized grids. Cut one apart and place magnetic tape on the back of each number. Attach the intact calendar to a cookie sheet or magnetic file cabinet. Children can match the appropriate number to the intact calendar. For another simple-to-create game, take a deck of cards and cut the top and bottom apart. By using a different type of cut for each card, the cards can be self-correcting.
- Sandpaper numerals. Add a blindfold that children can use if they wish. Children can feel the number and try to guess which numeral it is. Make sure to add dots to the other side of the card so children can check their answers.
- Play dough, clay, or wire for children to use to form numbers. You can add a spinner to add interest. The child spins the dial to determine which numeral to create.

Julie Bullard

The nests and eggs are enticing to the children at the Starting Small Preschool who have been studying birds.

- Numerals from burlap or other textured surface glued on a card. Children can place paper over the numeral and make a rubbing.
- Number sewing cards. You can cut plastic place mats into the shape of numerals and punch holes around the outside for an inexpensive option.
- Beanbag toss. Children throw a beanbag and then identify the numeral that the beanbag lands on. Include the numeral, number name, and dots to meet the developmental needs of more learners. When children have mastered the numerals, they can throw more than one time and add the results.

Check Your Understanding 12.3

Click here to gauge your understanding of section concepts.

Writing Numerals.

You can assist children to learn to write numerals by providing the following materials:

- Zip-lock plastic bags filled with hair gel or other items for a transitory writing slate. Children can write numerals and then erase them and start over.
- Laminated cards to trace or use as a model for writing numerals.
- Lined and unlined paper and different types of pencils and markers to use for writing numerals.
- Individual numeral books that children can create by writing a numeral on each page and materials such as stickers, stamps, pictures, or cutouts that they can use to complete their book.
- Old calendars with large squares that children can use to practice writing numerals.

Counting and Matching the Correct Number of Items to the Numeral.

There are many materials you can add to your center that allow children to practice identifying numerals and matching these to the correct number of objects. Following are a few suggestions:

Materials where children actively manipulate the objects they are matching to the numeral. For example, they might place golf tees into predrilled holes in a wooden numeral or the correct number of gems into a bowl.

Number games. When children are exposed to number games, they make significant gains in numeracy compared with children who do not have this opportunity (Young-Loveridge, 2004). Games should have an element of chance to keep them interesting and to prevent only the most skilled children from winning. Some appropriate games include Go Fish with a deck of cards, Math Bingo, Candy Land, Dominoes, Number Concentration, and Chutes and Ladders.

Number books. Researchers have found that using number books is also associated with larger gains in numeracy skills (Young-Loveridge, 2004). When you add counting books, make sure you also add props so that children can actively manipulate them as they read the book. For example, you might add flannel pieces or pretend pieces of fruit to manipulate when reading *The Very Hungry Caterpillar.*

Fishing game. Add string to a dowel with a magnet at the end. Create fish from cardboard and add a paper clip to their mouth. Write a numeral on the side of the fish. Children draw a card with a number of dots and then "catch" the fish with the correct numeral. To make it easier to find the correct fish, fish with larger numbers can be larger.

Adding to or Taking Away.

One experiment found that children as young as three can add and subtract sets up to 10 by first predicting and then counting (Zur & Gelman, 2004). It is helpful for children to use concrete objects or their fingers when they add and subtract. When numbers are less than five, using both hands is recommended if children are using their fingers for addition and subtraction (Fuson, Clements, & Beckmann, 2010). To assist children to add and subtract, provide the following materials:

- Objects from songs, finger plays, or books that stress addition or subtraction. Teachers can introduce these activities during circle time and then place the props in the math area for children to use. For example, if telling a story involving a baker who added ingredients to create different dishes, you could add both a baker's hat and flannelboard pieces to the math center (Zur & Gelman, 2004).

- Cuisenaire rods that children can use to create equal combinations (for example, two 5 cm rods equal one 10 cm rod). Cuisenaire rods are wooden, colored manipulative sticks, ranging in size from 1 to 10 cm that children can use for a variety of math activities. If you don't have access to Cuisenaire rods, you can create them using magnet sheets and printing the rods using correct colors and sizes. Children can use these on a cookie sheet.
- Addition and subtraction games. Play games with two dice. Children add the dice and move that many spaces on the game board.
- A money center. Based upon the children's developmental level, challenges can be created. For example, "How many different ways can you find to equal a nickel, a dime, a quarter, or a dollar?"

Julie Bullard

This attractive sand container entices children to practice writing numerals.

While numeracy is important, it is also very important that teachers focus on other math strands. Research reveals that early childhood teachers tend to focus primarily on numeracy and memorization. Instead, teachers should provide children with meaningful problem solving that includes this foundational knowledge with thinking skills (Hachey, 2013). We will explore these strands next.

Materials and Activities to Support the Geometry and Spatial Awareness Standard

Spatial skills are found to relate not only to geometry but also to other math strands (Verdine, Golinkoff, Hirsh-Pasek, & Newcombe, 2014). Children in the early childhood years are learning to name and describe shapes. They are also learning to transform shapes and describe spatial relationships. As children become familiar with shapes, they are able to form mental images (NCTM, 2000). When providing materials for geometry and spatial awareness, it is very important to be aware of children's common misconceptions. This is especially crucial for early childhood teachers, because concepts of two-dimensional shapes (whether right or wrong) become stable as early as age six (Clements, 2004). So what are the common misconceptions?

Clements and Sarama (2014) state that children can learn more about shapes if we discuss shapes and their attributes, provide a wide variety of different types of shapes, provide many varied types of activities, and introduce children to both examples and non-examples of shapes. For example, children are often introduced to only prototype shapes, such as an **equilateral triangle** (all sides are the same length), and often mistakenly believe that any triangle that does not display the same orientation or symmetry is not a triangle. To prevent this misconception, it is very important to give children a variety of examples of each type of shape (shapes that are different sizes and that have different orientations). When you are introducing triangles, include many types of triangles (acute, right, obtuse, and equilateral), but also include nontriangles (three-sided objects with a wavy line, or a three-sided object with an opening). It is also very important to discuss the defining properties of the shape such as the number of sides and angles (Verdine, Golinkoff, Hirsh-Pasek, & Newcombe, 2014).

Another common misconception occurs when teachers teach squares and rectangles separately instead of teaching that squares are a special type of rectangle. Rectangles are a type of parallelogram. Parallelograms are a specific form of a quadrilateral. Oberdorf and Taylor-Cox (1999) advise that we first introduce children to quadrilaterals by encouraging children to explore a variety of four-sided forms. Then have children classify these forms into different categories. Discussions should focus on sides and points. Given next are sample activities to enhance geometric thinking:

- Games—Create a "belongs and does not belong" game where children sort objects or cards by a certain attribute such as circle/not a circle. Other games that involve shapes include concentration with different types of shapes, shape bingo, or twister.
- Feeley box shape activity—Create a feeley box by cutting a hole in a heavy cardboard box and adding a sock cuff to the hole. Place differently shaped objects into the box. Children can draw a shape card and try to find an object in the feeley box that matches that shape.
- Picture shape cards and materials for children to use in creating shapes (clay, Tinker Toys, toothpicks, Plasticine, a geoboard). Varying the items used to create shapes enhances interest. Children draw a card and then create the shape using the materials.
- Legos, Unifix cubes, Cuisenaire rods, pattern blocks, tangrams, and parquetry blocks, along with graphics and diagrams for children to create pictures and objects. In addition to premade cards, at Burlington Little School preschool children take digital pictures of their unique designs. These are printed and placed in a three-ring binder allowing children to recreate their own and others' designs.
- Cards with designs, squared grid paper, and paper shapes so that children can copy a design on the grid (Fuson, Clements, & Beckmann, 2010).
- Puzzles—Studies have shown a direct relationship between experience with puzzles and the development of spatial skills (Verdine et al., 2014)
- Mirrors so that children can explore the **line of symmetry** (the line where both halves are the same).
- Folding Origami and paper airplanes (Verdine et al., 2014).

Materials and Activities to Support the Measurement Standard

Scores from the 2011 National Assessment of Educational Progress (NAEP) reveal that 4th graders score lower in measurement than in other areas of math (NAEP, 2011). Since the roots of learning measurement take place in the early years, it is important that we provide children measurement opportunities (Clements & Stephan, 2004).

In learning about measurement, children go through the following five stages. They:

- Learn that objects have measurement properties that can be described.
- Compare objects using measurement terminology (heavier, shorter, etc.).
- Determine a process and unit to use for measuring different types of items.
- Use standard units for measuring such as rulers and yardsticks.
- Create and use formulas (Copley, 2010, p. 119).

Measurement is a set of complex skills and concepts that completely develop over a period of many years (Clements & Stephan, 2004). Typically, children are not able to successfully use all measuring tools or create and use complex formulas until they are in the upper elementary grades. However, by grade 3 according to the Common Core State

Standards for Mathematics, children should be able to tell and write time; measure liquid volume and mass in grams; represent and interpret data by creating picture, bar, and line graphs; and measure and solve problems related to area and perimeter (National Governors' Association & Council of Chief State School Officers, 2010).

Research indicates that it is best if measurement activities begin with learning about length, developing concepts of "shorter," "longer," and "equal in length." Children should first explore the concept of length through making direct comparisons between objects—for example, deciding which string of pop-together beads is longer by holding them side by side. After children understand length, you can introduce other measurement attributes, including weight, volume, area, time, and temperature.

Comparing. Help children to learn about comparing properties of items and to use comparison vocabulary through the following materials:

- Items of different sizes to seriate, such as nesting dolls to order from smallest to largest.
- Weight canisters to match (these can be created by using black or gray film canisters and placing different items in them). Make these self-correcting by placing identical stickers on the bottom of the canisters that match.
- Several identical jars with different amounts of liquid so children can seriate the jars by volume.

Exploring Measuring Tools. When exploring measuring tools, children need to understand the concept of a measurement unit and learn techniques for accurate measurement, such as accurate alignment between two items and not leaving gaps between items that are being measured. In the past, it was considered best practice to avoid giving children standard measuring tools such as rulers until they were proficient at measuring using nonstandard measurement tools (measuring with feet, unifix cubes, or paper clips). Research now indicates that children benefit from using standard measurement tools at any age (Clements, 2004; Clements & Sarama, 2014). If you do use nonstandard measurement items, it is important to use only one type. For example, you would not want to use unifix cubes to measure one day and paper clips to measure the next day, since this may confuse children (Clements & Sarama, 2014). Following are materials that you can add to your math center to enhance measurement skills:

- A variety of measuring tools with several objects and ingredients to measure. For example, provide a household scale, a balance scale with weights, and a kitchen scale for measuring weight. Supply measuring cups, quart and gallon jugs, graduated cylinders, and measuring spoons for measuring liquids. Provide a tape measure, ruler, wheel measure, yardstick, and meter stick for measuring length. Make clocks and different types of timers available for exploring the measurement of time. It is important to fully explore each measurement tool before introducing other tools. When children become proficient with the various tools, they can experiment with which measurement tool works best for different objects.
- Pumpkins, gourds, or squash to measure (circumference, weight, length, and height). The vegetables can be measured both before and after cooking.
- Heavy strips of cardboard that children can use to make their own rulers.
- Balance scale and a series of oral, written, or pictorial challenges. As children become more proficient, they can create challenges for each other.
    - How many teddy bear counters weigh the same as one small unit block?
    - How many pennies does it take to equal the weight of one small toy car or one small doll?

  - Which weighs more—the toy boat or the toy car?
  - How many items can be found in the classroom that weigh the same as one penny?
- Variety of containers, measuring cups, and a bucket of sand. Add tall, thin containers as well as fat, short containers that have the same volume.
- A scale and several similar-sized balls (nerf ball, baseball, softball, and plastic ball) that weigh different amounts.
- Measuring box with a variety of measuring tools (tape measure, ruler, folding yardstick, meter stick) that children can use throughout the room when they wish to measure.
- "Beat the clock" games. Provide a timer and direction cards with pictures and words. For example, how many times can you hop before the timer runs out? How many screws and bolts can you put together in one minute?
- Mounted wall clock with a paper clock below it so that children can match the hands (Houle, 1984).
- Stopwatch for elementary-age children to use in determining how long it takes to complete common activities (tie your shoe or write your name).

TIP **Calendar Debate**

Although calendars are a time-honored tradition in early childhood programs, many early childhood professionals question whether they are developmentally appropriate. As stressed by Ethridge and King (2005), "The concept of time is ambiguous, socially constructed, and abstract" (p. 292). Preschool and kindergarten children have typically not acquired the developmental level to understand the calendar (Ethridge & King, 2005; Freeman & Swim, 2009). In fact, many are still grappling with the concept of today, yesterday, and tomorrow. Realizing this, some teachers use the calendar for patterning or counting activities. However, Beneke, Ostrosky, and Katz (2008) recommend that instead these math skills be taught in an individualized, meaningful context, such as through learning center activities. Time devoted to the calendar can instead be used more wisely in group "math talks." See the discussion of math talks in this chapter for more information.

Materials and Activities to Support the Patterns and Algebra Standard

Classifying. Before children can create patterns, they must be able to sort and classify. One of the goals for pre-K through second-grade children is to "sort, classify, and order objects by size, number, and other properties" (NCTM, 2000, p. 90). Teddy bear counters, for instance, allow children to classify by color or size. Contrast this to intellectual kits created by a long-time early childhood teacher, Eve Malo. These kits, created around a theme such as kitchen gadgets or office desk items, provide endless opportunities for classifying objects into sets. Additionally, children are often more interested in classifying objects such as kitchen items that they have seen adults using.

Children also need trays to sort sets into (muffin tins, deviled egg plates, egg cartons). To add interest and a sense of importance to the activity, teachers can use aesthetically pleasing sorting trays (wooden manacala trays, crystal relish dishes).

As children become more proficient in classifying objects, introduce the concept of Venn diagrams. Venn diagrams are used to identify common attributes between

shells	coins	nuts and bolts
rocks	bottle caps	discarded keys
seed pods	baby food	toy cars
pinecones	pouch caps	small toy animals
feathers	pom poms	picture cards
leaves	fabric samples	(e.g., where animals
beads	paint samples	live: water/land/both)
buttons	wallpaper samples	

FIGURE 12.2 Items to Sort, Classify, Count, and Pattern

different sets. Two or three overlapping circles can be created with plastic tubing, string, or inner tubes.

Patterning. Making patterns begins with understanding the unit (AB). Either the unit repeats (ABABAB) or grows (ABAABAAAB). Teachers designing pattern activities can plan color, shape, size, and spatial orientation patterns (Taylor-Cox, 2003). Some patterning materials for young children include the following:

- American Indian beads for duplicating or creating patterns (Sgarlotti, 2004). For a less expensive option, make pattern necklaces or bracelets out of pieces of colored straws cut into 1/4" segments.
- Manipulatives (seashells, unifix cubes, small blocks, or paper chains) and pattern cards.
- Stamps for creating patterns.

After children have mastered the recreation of a pattern and the creation of their own unique patterns, they are ready to describe or read their patterns, draw their patterns, and finally to record their patterns using numbers or letters. A variety of different items can be used for sorting, classifying, counting, and patterning. See Figure 12.2 for some ideas. You will want to choose the material based upon the children's interests and their level of development. Rotating the items can spark new interest and present new classifying and patterning challenges.

Materials and Activities to Support the Data Analysis Standard

In teaching graphing, it is important to begin by using physical objects. For example, all children wearing red stand on the floor graph. Then teachers should proceed to manipulatives, followed by picture graphs (an example of a picture graph is shown in Figure 12.3), then line plots, and finally bar graphs. According to the Common Core State Standards for Mathematics, second-grade children should be able to analyze data and create their own picture graphs, line plots, and bar graphs (National Governors' Association & Council of Chief State School Officers, 2010). Sample graphing materials for math learning centers include the following:

- Real objects for children to graph—For example, graph a collection of dolls on a floor graph. You can create floor graphs by using a tablecloth (use a flannel-backed tablecloth to prevent slipping on carpeted floor or place a nonslip rug pad under it for linoleum floors) and dividing it into columns with colorful tape.
- Small manipulative objects and ice cube trays for graphing.
- Pictures of children to use for graphing—Place a digital picture of each child on a juice can lid and provide a magnetic graph. Children can then use these for many different teacher- or child-initiated graphing activities, such as gender, hair color, or eye color, or who prefers dogs or cats.

FIGURE 12.3
Picture Graph

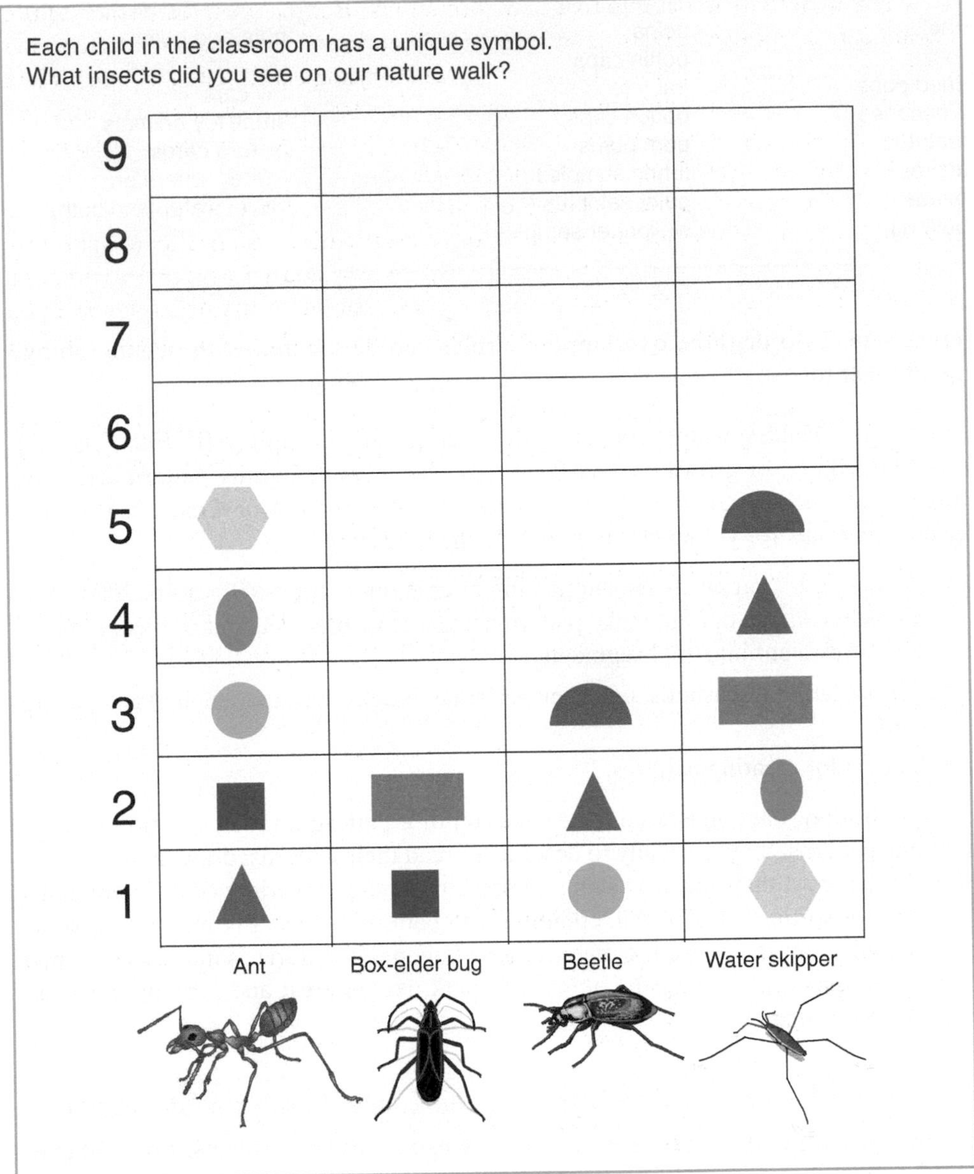

- Clothespins with each child's picture and name on a clothespin. Children can interview their classmates and clip the clothespin on a cardboard graph based upon the answer (Baratta-Lorton, 1972).
- Graph paper for children who are more proficient in graphing so they can create their own graphs.

Special Considerations for Different Ages

Mathematics for Infants and Toddlers

Infants appear primed to learn mathematics. Even from birth, infants are able to discriminate between small sets (one to three items). For example, when researchers repeatedly showed one-day-old infants sets with two items they became bored and looked away. However, when they were then shown sets with three items they became interested, demonstrating that they saw this set as different (Caulfield, 2000; Mix et al., 2002). Infants are also able to anticipate quantitative transformations (Berger, Tzur, & Posner, 2006; Mix et al., 2002). For example, if infants watch you place two items behind a screen and then see you place one more item behind the screen, they expect to see three items when the screen is removed. If there are two items or four items instead, they act surprised (Clements, 2004; Cooper, 1984). These studies help us to realize that infants have mathematical knowledge that we can expand upon as teachers.

Some of the activities mentioned previously in the chapter are appropriate for infants and toddlers. For example, many of the classification materials are appropriate as long as they do not pose a choking hazard. While you will typically not have a separate math center in infant and toddler classrooms, math manipulatives can be integrated into other centers. To assist children to learn early geometric skills, you can provide:

- A big and little center with a collection of big and little items to play with, compare, and contrast such as big and little balls, cars, dolls, and spaces (Isbell & Isbell, 2003).
- Small boxes and large boxes with items to fit inside.
- Heavy and light items to compare and contrast.
- A cardboard circle with a hole cut in the center and a variety of items for experimenting with size. Make sure that some items fit through the hole, while others do not.
- Shape-sorting toys. This is especially beneficial when the adult sits with the child and engages in shape naming (Verdine, Golinkoff, Hirsh-Pasek, & Newcombe, 2014).
- Nesting items such as measuring cups, bowls, or jar lids.
- Containers of various sizes to fill and dump.

To encourage matching and classification, you can provide:

- A basket of identical items such as gloves, hats, shoes, or boots for children to sort, match, and classify.
- Objects with opposing properties to sort (hard and soft or shiny and not shiny) (Miller, 2005).

To encourage one-to-one correspondence, you can provide:

- Large pegs and pegboards.
- Small stuffed animals with a compartmentalized shoe bag to store them in (Miller, 2005).
- A merry-go-round created by gluing spray can lids to a turntable. Provide small stuffed animals that children can place in each lid and give a ride (Miller, 2005).

Mathematics for K-3rd Grade Children

The Common Core State Standards, which have been adopted by most states, give guidance about **what** mathematics to teach at different grade levels. However, the standards do not tell teachers **how** to teach. Can learning centers assist children to meet the common core standards in math? Yes, learning centers can be ideal in helping children meet math standards since they permit individualization, provide experience and practice using concrete materials, let children go in-depth with learning, and allow children to solve real world problems.

By the time children begin kindergarten, 95% have mastered basic counting and shapes. However in a large-scale study, it was found that kindergarten teachers spent the

vast majority of their time on this math content. The amount of time spent on these skills was negatively associated with the children's math achievement (Engel, Claessens, & Finch, 2013). As with younger children, it is critical that teachers match their teaching to children's needs and interests. Additionally, teachers must individualize their teaching. One effective way to do this is through learning centers.

The Common Core State Standards call on teachers to go deep into content and to encourage children to solve real-world application problems. Learning center can provide this opportunity. However, it is important that the teacher is intentional about aligning the activities to the standards. For example, Anita, a 2nd-grade teacher, was working on a measurement unit with the children in her classroom focusing on the following Common Core Math Content standards. "Measure an object by selecting and using appropriate tools such as rulers, yardsticks, meter sticks, and measuring tapes. Estimate lengths using units of inches, feet, centimeters, and meters. Measure to determine how much longer one object is than another, expressing the length difference in terms of a standard length unit" (National Governors' Association & Council of Chief State School Officers, 2010). Anita has many centers throughout her classroom and allows at least an hour each day for children to use them. While children have free choice of centers, there are some mandatory activities they must complete each week. One mandatory activity was to complete one of the following measurement activities. In the math center, Anita created a measurement scavenger hunt for children where they chose different items in the room to measure, estimated the length, and then used the correct tool to see what the actual length was. In the woodworking center, children created something from their own design or followed a plan. However, again they needed to estimate the length and use the correct tool to measure the wood. Anita also created a game for the game/manipulative center called Measurement Mania. She found the directions at the Sunny Days at Second Grade website. Each of these activities provided children with experiences that would help them to achieve the common core measurement standards.

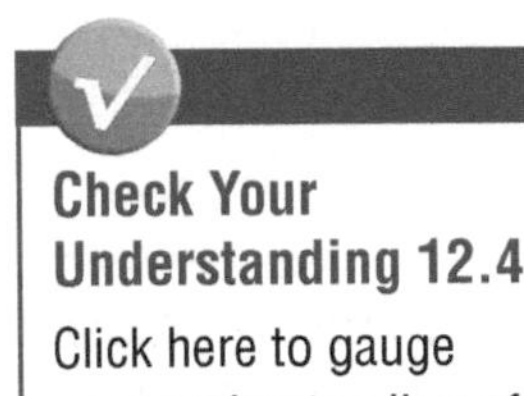
Check Your Understanding 12.4
Click here to gauge your understanding of section concepts.

Abundant, developmentally appropriate math activities and materials encourage children to gain needed skills in the math standards and processes. However, in addition to being the classroom designer, the teacher must interact with the children while they are using the materials to provide children optimal learning opportunities.

Teachers' Facilitation of Learning in the Math Center

While children do learn an extensive amount through play, "they can learn much more with artful guidance and challenging activities provided by their teachers" (Seo & Ginsburg, 2004, p. 103). A rich environment that promotes math play allows a teacher many opportunities to encourage math learning. Even without adult intervention, children participate in many math activities during play. For example, one study found that in a fifteen-minute period, 88% of the children engaged in some form of math activity. The amount of math used in play was similar across income levels and gender, suggesting that math concept formation is naturally embedded in play (Seo & Ginsburg, 2004). Imagine how this play is enhanced in a mathematically rich environment supported by a teacher who scaffolds learning.

To scaffold learning, teachers need to engage children in formal and informal math discussions. As teachers interact with children they can model mathematical language, ask questions to help children reason, suggest ideas for materials, ask children to communicate their thinking, build on children's intuitive knowledge connecting this to formal mathematics, and encourage children to solve problems. While children use the math materials, the teacher will also be assessing and documenting children's learning, making sure that the needs of all children are being met.

Engage Children in Formal, Preplanned Math Talks or Math Workshops

The National Council of Teachers of Mathematics calls upon early childhood teachers to actively introduce math concepts, methods, and language and to help children see connections between math and other subjects (NCTM, 2013). One way to accomplish this is through math talks. Math talks can be used to focus on mathematical content and concepts, introduce and build interest in materials, and share math learning. Research indicates that this type of targeted, focused math learning is critical (Fuson, Clements, & Beckmann, 2010).

Kristi, a Head Start teacher, discussed addition and subtraction while reading the book *No More Monkeys Jumping on the Bed.* She also introduced an activity where children matched plastic monkeys to numerals. After circle time, she placed the activity and the book in the math center. Because of the interest built during circle time, the majority of children chose to use the materials.

Marlis, a teacher of multi-age preschoolers, designated a "math talk" circle each day. The National Research Council recommends 20 to 30 minutes a day be devoted to math learning experiences (NRC, 2009). During "math talk" Marlis scaffolded children's learning through discussing and introducing math concepts. For example, for two weeks she introduced different patterning activities using materials from the math center. Each week she also had an estimation jar. The children would guess how many items were in the jar during choice times and then at the end of a week they would take the items out at circle time and count them.

Representing and communicating are two of the math process skills. Taurean encourages children in her kindergarten classroom to share their tallies, charts, diagrams, and drawings with the class during their "math talks" as a way of acknowledging and supporting these skills.

Engage Children in Informal Math Talk

The amount of teacher talk about math is significantly related to children's achievement in math, with those teachers who use the most math talk having children with the highest math skills at the end of the year (Klibanoff, Levine, Huttenlocher, Vasilyeva, & Hedges, 2006). Better outcomes are obtained when the teacher talk is focused on reciprocity, where "adults make overtures to children that are in tune with their current attentional focus, building on the children's activities, prior knowledge, and skill level" (National Research Council et al., 2001, p. 44). Informal math talk can be used to address the needs of individual or small groups of children and to assist in clarifying understanding. It assists children to **mathematize** their understanding.

Watch the video to see a teacher engaged in informal math talks. What are specific ways that the teacher enhanced this child's learning? https://www.youtube.com/watch?v=TLmm3U0eYX4&list=PLyizHCAockpoWzLf4kDaq3BirJXl5mEpR

Model Mathematical Language

"Although children exhibit many quantitative skills before they know the words for numbers or mathematical concepts, acquiring mathematical language opens the door to new ways of thinking and complex skills" (Mix et al., 2002, p. 135). For example, exposure to spatial language at a young age is related to children's spatial problem solving later (Pruden, Levine, & Huttelocher, 2011). Emphasize mathematical vocabulary by including directional words such as near, far, over, under, and above, names of shapes, and numeral names. Use mathematical terms such as more than, less than, fewer than, if-then, all-some, equal, none, sets, points, side, flip, turn, add, subtract, divide, and multiply to develop concepts and vocabulary (Copley, 2010). Daniel posted a list of math vocabulary words on the wall in the math center so that he would remember to use them with children.

> Watch the video to see a teacher and child discussing classification. What questions does the teacher ask to help the child with reasoning?

Ask Questions to Assist Children in Reasoning

"The use of questions and demonstrations can help draw out existing knowledge and build on it, contributing to a restructuring of the child's understanding" (National Research Council et al., 2001, p. 43). Ask questions that encourage children to reason and to think more deeply. Reasoning is one of the process skills emphasized by the NCTM. For example, you might ask, "I wonder what would happen if … ?" "How do you know … ?" "Can you show me another way to sort the objects?" "What other ways can you make the number 10?" or "Describe your pattern" (Copley, 2010).

Suggest Ideas for Materials

Carmella, a teacher of kindergarten children, observed two boys rolling cars down a ramp. They were discussing which car traveled the farthest. Because one of the cars had traveled straight and one had curved, they were having a difficult time deciding. Carmella took advantage of this teachable moment, suggesting that they measure the distance. The boys brought over the measuring tote and tried the different measuring tools to see which would work the best. They ultimately used the sewing tape and were able to answer their question. Carmella's suggestion allowed the children to use mathematical tools to solve a real-life problem.

Ask Children to Communicate Their Thinking

When children communicate their thoughts, they construct new meanings, think more deeply, and increase their math competence (Hofer, Farran, & Cummings, 2013). For example, research shows that when teachers ask children to justify their categorization of shapes they categorized them more accurately (Hannibal, 1999). It also allows the teacher to assess a child's understanding. Judy observed that Ella, who is four, had divided all the shiny buttons and a couple of flower buttons into one tray and all the other buttons into another. She presumed that Ella was dividing using "shiny" and "not shiny" and had made an error with the flower buttons. However, when she asked Ella to explain the grouping, Ella told her "pretty" and "not pretty." One way that teachers can assist children to talk as they think is to model this for children, such as "I wonder which of these pitchers will hold more water? How could I find out? I wonder if I could pour cups of water into each one?" (Edens & Potter, 2013).

Connect Children's Intuitive Math Knowledge and Formal Mathematics

"Play does not guarantee mathematical development, but it offers rich possibilities. Significant benefits are more likely when teachers follow up by engaging children in reflecting on and representing the mathematical ideas that have emerged in their play" (Ginsburg, 2006, p. 25). As children are engaged in using math in their play, it is important to label it as such, thus assisting children to make the connection between informal and formal mathematics. Additionally, you can record their work (photos, video, or transcriptions) and, after children have completed playing, you can show them the recordings and ask them to reflect upon what they were doing. This also allows you to point out the skills they were using in mathematical terms.

Encourage Children to Problem Solve

Teachers need to actively teach children steps to use in problem solving (to understand the problem, to make a plan to solve the problem, to implement it, and then to reflect to see if the plan worked). As discussed at the beginning of the chapter, this is one of the process skills emphasized by the NCTM. We also need to encourage the dispositions to problem solve and to try alternatives. For example, you might ask, "What else might you try?"

Assess and Document Individual Children's Learning

You will want to assess and document children's mathematical knowledge, skills, and dispositions to determine their progress and learning needs (NAEYC/NCTM, 2010). This allows you to plan activities and materials that will scaffold children to the next associated concept. Assessment and documentation can also assist you in reflecting upon your own effectiveness. Teachers can use many tools when assessing children's math skills. These include anecdotal records, checklists, an inventory of activities completed, work samples, and student interviews to determine children's thinking.

Janisa, a teacher of a multiage preschool classroom, developed math jobs for children. Each of these individualized, hands-on activities emphasized unique math skills. Janisa numbered each math job and created a chart with children's names and numbers so that anyone witnessing a child attempting or successfully completing the math job could annotate the chart. It was easy for Janisa to then transfer this information to the child's file. This information also helped Janisa to plan subsequent activities.

Meet the Needs of All Learners

The child's long-term academic success is built on the mathematical foundation that is established in the early childhood years. Interestingly, research shows that early math skills predict children's later success not only in math but also in reading (Grissmer et al., 2010). It is crucial that we meet the needs of all learners in our classrooms so they have an equitable opportunity for future success. Math equity is one of the principles that the NCTM has developed to guide math education (NCTM, 2000). The area where nonequity is especially pronounced in the early childhood years relates to socioeconomic status. Research indicates that children from middle and higher socioeconomic status have higher levels of math achievement than children from lower socioeconomic backgrounds even at a very early age (Klibanoff et al., 2006; National Research Council, 2009; Wang, Shen, & Brynes, 2013). The difference in math levels is one of degree. Children from lower socioeconomic backgrounds travel the same learning trajectory or course in regard to mathematical understandings and strategies as their higher income peers. However, they are delayed on this path. For example, "In a number knowledge test, low-income 5- to 6-year-olds performed much like middle-income 3- to 4-year-olds" (National Research Council et al., 2001, p. 81). This gap often has devastating effects, becoming more pronounced in preschool (National Research Council, 2009), elementary school (Denton & West, 2002), and continuing throughout high school (Braswell et al., 2001). Lack of math skills often contributes to students not attending or not persevering in college. For example, algebra is a "gatekeeper subject" for higher education (Taylor-Cox, 2003, p. 14). Those who do not have this skill are generally unable to acquire a college education.

Most likely, this gap is not related to intelligence, since research shows that nonverbal calculation skills are not related to socioeconomic status (Jordan, Levine, & Huttenlocher, 1994). Instead, the gap is probably related to opportunities to learn social-arbitrary knowledge. As stated earlier, children learn this knowledge from an adult or a more competent peer.

In addition, the kinds of materials used to learn math might be biased toward some groups. In one study, children in a third-world agricultural community who did not

attend school were compared with children in an urban area in the United States who did attend school. When the math task involved seeds and grain, the children in the agricultural community outperformed the children from the United States. However, when colored disks were used to perform the same tasks, the U.S. children did better (Lantz, 1979; National Research Council et al., 2001).

It is especially important that teachers assist children from low-income backgrounds to acquire math skills. Teaching children conventional knowledge and mathematical language, and providing a rich mathematical setting, are all important. It is also important to use familiar, interesting manipulatives.

In addition, it is vital to meet the needs of children at a variety of developmental levels. Caroline, a five-year-old girl with Down's syndrome, attended a Head Start center. Nancy, her teacher, was concerned about whether the materials in the different centers in the classroom met Caroline's learning needs. Using the Building Blocks model described in Chapter 2, Nancy began by first checking to make sure she was offering a high-quality program for all the children in the classroom. In examining the math center, she found that all the materials were closed-ended and would be appropriate for only a few of the children. Nancy developed several new activities for the math center that were open-ended, including many materials to sort, classify, pattern, and count. The center was now more appropriate for Caroline and her classmates. Since one of Caroline's goals was to match shapes, Nancy also added a shape-sorting ball to the center.

Check Your Understanding 12.5

Click here to gauge your understanding of section concepts.

Teachers need to provide opportunities for all children to gain the skills to be mathematically successful in numbers and operations, measurement, algebra, geometry, data analysis, and math processes. To do so, we must assess children's development and intentionally plan high-interest activities and interactions using developmentally appropriate materials that will challenge children to grow mathematically.

To function in society today it is crucial that all children gain knowledge and skills in math. The foundation for this learning begins in the early childhood years. Unfortunately, so do the inequities in learning opportunities. To prevent children's futures from being negatively impacted by this gatekeeper subject, we must provide all young children with rich experiences in math. One way we do this is by providing well-designed math centers that contain an abundance of developmentally appropriate math materials. As teachers, it is crucial that we interact with children as they use these materials to scaffold their learning.

Click here to gauge your understanding of chapter concepts.

Sample Application Activities

1. Observe children during center time to see what mathematical activities they are engaged in. How do the materials available assist in enhancing their developmental level?
2. Learn more about the standards by exploring the Early Learning Standards for your state, the Common Core State Standards for Mathematics, and the National Council of Teachers of Mathematics national math standards.
3. Read the NAEYC/NCTM Early Childhood Math Position Statement.
4. Critique a math center using the environmental assessment in Figure 12.4. What changes could be made to enhance the center?
5. Observe children outdoors, what activities are they participating in? What could be added to the playground to make these activities more mathematical?
6. Review this chapter, explore Pinterest, and brainstorm lists of inexpensive math manipulatives that you can create, scrounge, or purchase. Describe how you would use each of these materials to enhance children's mathematical knowledge and skills.

FIGURE 12.4 Environmental Assessment: Math Center

- ❑ Is there a clearly designated math area in the quiet area of the room?
- ❑ Does the center provide a variety of developmental math activities in each of the different math standards (numbers and operations, measurement, geometry, algebra, and data analysis)?
- ❑ Are shelves organized with a clearly designated place for each item?
- ❑ Does the center contain aesthetically pleasing containers that allow children to see what is available and keep all needed materials together?
- ❑ Is there a large space to work?
- ❑ Is there a place to display completed work such as a bulletin board, a three-ring binder for sketches and photos, and top of a shelf for three-dimensional work?
- ❑ Are materials or activities in the math center
  - ○ concrete materials that allow for active manipulation?
  - ○ based on a clearly defined purpose or goal?
  - ○ open-ended or self-correcting?
  - ○ based on assessment of the current group of children's skills and knowledge?
  - ○ related to children's interests?
  - ○ rotated to meet children's changing developmental needs and interests?
- ❑ Does the center contain books that stress mathematics?
- ❑ Are all needed materials available to complete activities (paper, pencils, graph paper)?

7. Develop some math games for the age you currently teach or plan to teach. Try to develop the game so it can be adapted to meet the changing development needs of children. For example, you might have different dice, some with dots and others with numerals.
8. Examine the Common Core State Standards for Mathematics, find a standard, and brainstorm materials that could be placed in a learning center to help children master the standard.
9. Record yourself in the math area or observe another teacher. How is the teacher facilitating children's learning? What math terminology is the teacher using? Are there examples of missed opportunities for facilitation?
10. View a video from *Teaching Math: A Video Library of K–4* at the Annenberg Learner website to see examples of ways to teach math.

CHAPTER 13

Developing Visual Art Centers

Learning Outcomes

After you have read this chapter, you will be prepared to:

- Describe the approaches to and stages of art development
- Discuss multiple ways that the art center enhances children's development
- Demonstrate the ability to design effective art centers both indoors and outdoors
- Choose art materials and activities that will assist children to meet art standards
- Describe multiple ways that teachers facilitate learning in the art center

Julie Bullard

It is National Arbor Day, and three early childhood programs nestled in the Rocky Mountains have responded by including activities focused on trees. At Kiddie World, the teacher has substituted pine boughs for paintbrushes at the easel. She has also added pinecones to the collage materials. At ABC Academy, the teacher is instructing small groups of children to follow her directions in drawing evergreen trees by overlapping a series of triangles. At the Nature Preschool, children are drawing their own evergreen trees. They first examine the tree growing outside their program by touching and smelling the needles, sap, and bark. They make casts of the bark and then use magnifying glasses to explore the bark, needles, and sap more intimately. Finally, they sit outside and make pencil sketches of the tree.

Visual arts are basic to humanity, existing in all cultures and dating back to prehistoric cave drawings. Art influences all aspects of our lives, including the design of our clothing, buildings, vehicles, and toys. Through the arts we decorate, communicate, and express ourselves aesthetically (Koster, 2015). Art is also a tool for thinking and inquiry, allowing children to "make their theories and ideas visible, take new perspectives, represent and explore emotions, and to study properties of the physical world" (Pelo, 2007, p. 110). As children create and share art, they also learn about others' perspectives and ideas.

Approaches to and Stages of Children's Art

Approaches to Art

In the opening scenario, the programs demonstrate three approaches to art: noninterventionist, production-oriented, and art as inquiry.

Noninterventionist Approach. The teacher at Kiddie World is using a noninterventionist approach to art. This might also be referred to as a process-oriented approach. In this approach, the teacher provides a variety of materials and encourages free exploration. Children are totally in charge of what they produce, with the process being the focus. The teacher views her primary role as providing encouragement and support for individuality. The belief underlying this approach is that children, given the right environment, will naturally develop artistic skills (Kindler, 1995). Exploration of art elements and media, often a preferred approach in early childhood, is an important goal for early childhood. However, teachers must be observant and know when to facilitate experiences in a more guided manner so that children are able to effectively use the arts as a tool for thinking, inquiry, and communication. Many artists contrast the noninterventionist approach to that used for verbal language, where adults model conversations, stimulate and challenge children, and present new language tasks. If adults were to take the same hands-off approach to learning language as some do to art, children would be extremely delayed in learning to talk.

Production-Oriented Approach. The teacher at ABC Academy is using the production-oriented approach (or product approach). In this approach, the children complete prescribed teacher-directed art projects. There is little room for individuality. The focus of the activity is on producing a product that is predetermined by the teacher. When children are presented with models to copy, they will often use this identical form extensively, stunting their further development. For example, in drawing trees they will use the triangle method that they have been taught. They do not need to examine trees, think about the branches on the trees, or decide how to represent this three-dimensional object in a two-dimensional form. Teachers who use this method might plan art around holidays, planning one-time activities with no continuity or developmental progression (Bresler, 1995). Because the production-oriented art approach stifles creativity as well as cognitive and artistic growth, it is considered developmentally inappropriate (Copple & Bredekamp, 2009).

Teachers may provide production-oriented art because of their discomfort with art methods and processes. Additionally, some teachers use this approach so that they have products to send home to parents. Many parents were raised in schools where crafts or patterned activities were sent home as art and so they expect that their child will also come home with these. We can improve our own and families' understanding of creative art through sponsoring art workshops and guest speakers at the program. Rather than sending home production-oriented art, we can show the progress in children's art at home visits or parent–teacher conferences. We can also attach notes to children's artwork explaining what children have learned. Some teachers have developed notes and have them ready to attach at the appropriate time. For example, Bonnie teaches children who are ages two through four. She has a note prepared when children first draw a tadpole person. "Today, Hope drew a tadpole person (a head with legs extending from it). People in all cultures and throughout history have drawn tadpole people as their first attempts to draw a person. This is an exciting step in Hope's development."

Art as Inquiry Approach. At the Nature Preschool, the teacher is using the inquiry approach to art. The art as inquiry approach involves active investigation. As children engage in art, they deepen their knowledge about art techniques as well as the art subject or topic. In this approach, art is viewed as a language to communicate thoughts, ideas, and feelings. The art is often related to an in-depth project with the children using art to express their knowledge. In the beginning stages, children still spend time exploring media and elements. However, teachers also scaffold children's learning by providing background experiences on the topic and through teaching art techniques. In this approach, children often revisit their artwork, allowing them to learn more about art, while deepening their knowledge of the world (Spodek, 2006). They will also revisit their ideas using multiple media. For example, in *To Make a Portrait of a Lion*, a video documenting a project at Reggio Emilia, children made field sketches of a lion statue, created paintings of the lion, and made the lion in clay.

Watch the video to see some art activities with young children. What approach to art is this teacher using?

The art approach that teachers promote is influenced by culture as well as individual preference and education. For example, in some cultures, children might receive instruction on art techniques at a younger age.

Stages of Art in the Early Childhood Years

Several experts have studied the stages of children's art. Perhaps the most famous has been Victor Lowenfeld. We will examine the stages that Lowenfeld and Brittain (1987) found in children's art, focusing on the early childhood years.

Scribble Stage. The scribble stage typically occurs before the age of four and is often considered to be primarily kinesthetic. Children do not preplan their artwork or begin with a subject in mind. This stage is further divided into three substages: random, controlled, and naming. During the random scribble stage, children use their whole arm and may even draw off the paper. When children enter the controlled scribble stage, they begin to use their wrist. This allows them to make smaller marks and have more control in placing lines on their paper. During the naming scribble stage, children make a variety of different lines and shapes. They also begin to name their scribbles. Often children will begin to draw and then decide the scribble looks like something. They will then add further detail to enhance the appearance.

Preschematic Stage. In the preschematic stage, which typically occurs between ages four and seven, visual ideas are developing. At the beginning of this stage, children will often draw tadpole people, characterized by a head with lines coming directly from it, representing legs and sometimes arms. Tadpole figures are found in children's artwork throughout the world and have been documented in children's drawings for more than 100 years (Lasky & Muderji, 1980). In the preschematic stage, children often use a larger size for those things that are most important, powerful, or impressive to them. For example, a child who is fearful of a dog may draw a dog that is very huge with disproportionately large teeth.

Schematic Stage. Children at the schematic stage, which typically occurs between the ages of seven and nine, have developed a schema for the way an object looks and may make the object the same each time they draw it. In this stage, children use baselines and skylines, and show beginning awareness of perspective. Many children will use "X-ray" drawings at this stage, drawing what they know rather than what they see. For example, they may draw clothes on a person but also draw the body underneath. Or, they may draw a person in profile but show both eyes. See Figure 13.1 to see an example of each stage of art.

Children who have rich art experiences continue to progress through additional art stages as they mature (dawning realism, pseudorealism).

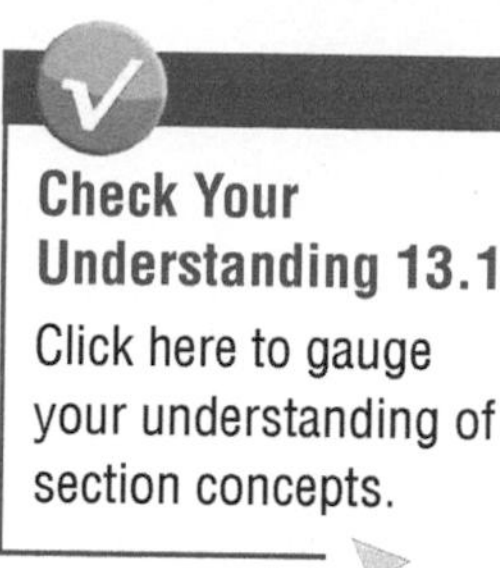

FIGURE 13.1 Stages of Art

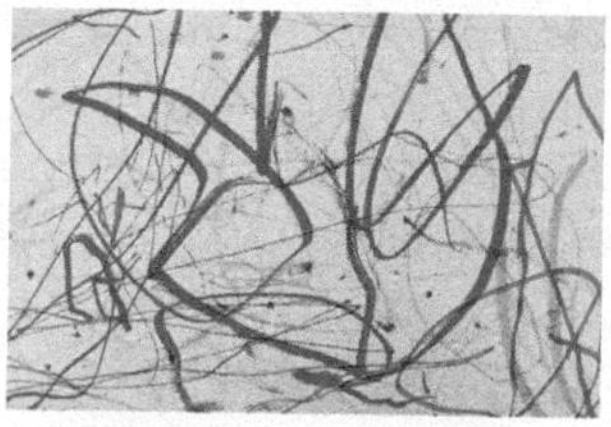	**Random Scribbling**—The child exhibited little control of the markers, drawing on the table as well as the paper.
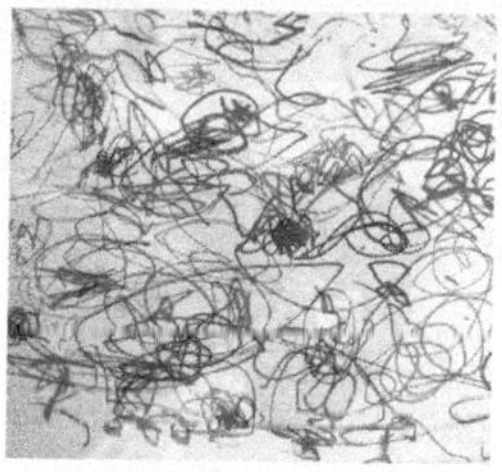	**Controlled Scribbling**—Note the better control and smaller marks.
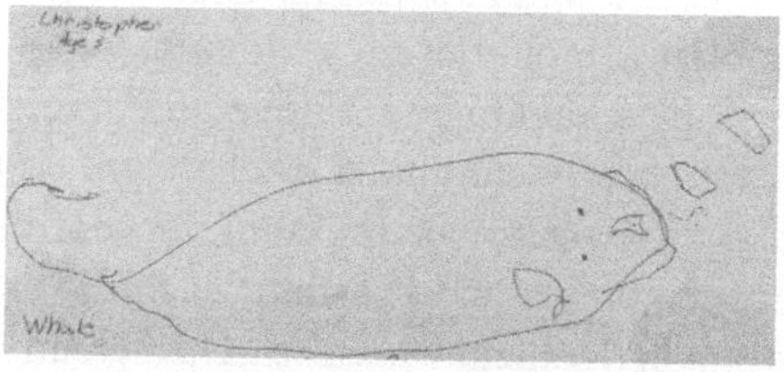	**Named Scribbling**—After drawing this picture Christopher stated, "Oh, it's a whale." Then he added the bubbles.
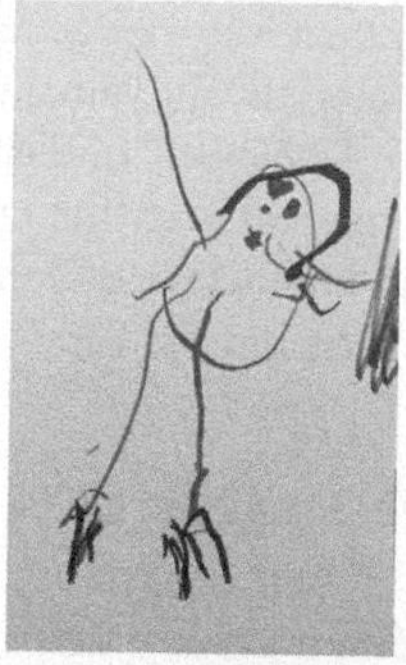	**Preschematic**—Note how the body and head are an oval with legs and arms attached.
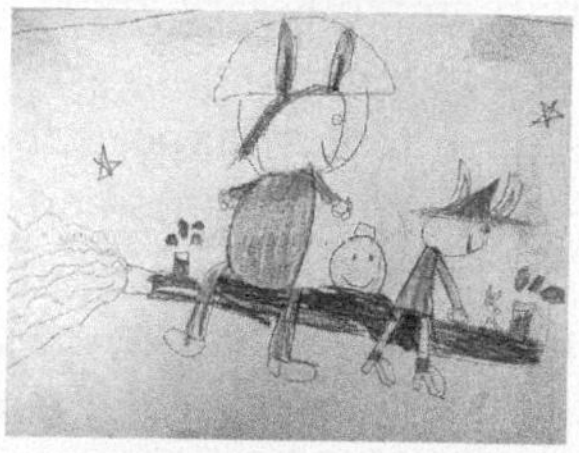	**Schematic**—Note the x-ray vision, showing both the hat and the ears underneath. The beginning of a profile is exhibited with one eye and one arm in the first figure. However, both legs are shown.

How the Art Center Enhances Children's Development

In many elementary schools, especially low-income schools, the arts are being cut (Armario, 2012). However, longitudinal studies show that children from low-income families who have high levels of art participation have better grades, test scores, high school and college graduation rates, and civic engagement than their peers who have low levels of art education (Catterall, Dumais, & Hampden-Thompson, 2012). When children participate in art they increase their artistic knowledge, skills, and creativity while enhancing emotional, social, cognitive, and physical development. They also are more likely to develop a "love of the arts" when they are exposed to art at a young age.

Artistic Development

Although most children will not choose to be professional artists when they become adults, they will nevertheless be surrounded by images. To be literate in today's world, one must be able to understand, analyze, and critique these images. Through early childhood art, children can increase observation skills, learn art techniques, begin to understand the relationship of art to culture and history, and learn to appreciate and enjoy images and art. They will also have the experience of joy that comes from creating unique products (West, 2006).

Although the arts are often the first subjects to be eliminated when there are school funding cuts, Hetland and Winner (2001) make the following important point: "Cultures are judged on the basis of their arts; and most cultures and most historical eras have not doubted the importance of studying the arts" (Hetland & Winner, 2001, p. 5).

Creative Development

Art enhances creativity, which is crucial for innovation and adaptation. Creative people have the ability to see multiple solutions to a problem, employ original thoughts, and use their imagination. As a field, art promotes these skills, encouraging unique and divergent responses and diverse ways of looking at things. Many early childhood teachers previously thought the best way to enhance creativity in the arts was to use the noninterventionist approach. However, we have now come to realize the power and possibilities in the art as inquiry approach. As stated by HMIE (2006), a group in Scotland who researched creativity,

> As pupils acquire experience, develop skills, and broaden their knowledge and understanding, they are able to use their increased control of materials, movements, media, and ideas to demonstrate a more mature level of creativity. Ironically, in contrast with the view that a climate of "anything goes" is conducive to creativity, the opposite is the case. Higher levels of creativity usually result from an interaction of considerable knowledge and skill with a willingness to innovate and experiment. (p. 3)

However, there is growing concern that creative thinking scores of children have decreased significantly. The Torrance Test of Creative Thinking (TTCT) measures creative thinking and has been administered to over 270,000 participants, beginning in the 1960s. Alarmingly, the tests reveal that there has been a steady decline in creativity scores since 1990, with the greatest drop in creativity in the K–3rd grade age range. The author states, "The results indicate younger children are tending to grow up more narrow-minded, less intellectually curious, and less open to new experiences" (Kim, 2011, p. 292). She speculates that this is due to overstructured schedules and a push for academics, resulting in less free play time.

Additionally, research reveals that **divergent thinking**, the ability to creatively generate multiple solutions or ideas, decreases as children progress through school. Land and Jarmin tested 1,600 children—first in preschool, then in elementary school, and finally in high school. When the group of children were tested as preschoolers, 98% were considered to be geniuses in divergent thinking. The test was repeated when the children were 8 to 10 years old, and only 32% of the children still reached the genius stage. When the children were tested as 14- and 15-year-olds, only 10% still tested in the genius range for divergent thinking. Preschoolers who once had the ability to think in divergent ways had lost this ability through their school years (Robinson, 2005). While thinking divergently is only one characteristic needed for creativity, it is critical, since the other characteristics of creative thinking are built upon this skill. It is crucial that we encourage divergent thinking in the arts, as well as in all curricular areas in the classroom.

 Watch the video to see an example of why conformity in art is discouraged. How did this teacher negatively affect the young boy's creativity?

https://www.youtube.com/watch?v=jamtKsgmP_I

According to Robinson and the National Advisory Committee on Creative and Cultural Education (1999), four characteristics are necessary for an activity to be defined as a creative process: thinking imaginatively; being purposeful; generating an original thought, idea, or product; and having this thought, idea, or product valuable in relationship to the task or objective. As we plan our art environments, we need to think about these characteristics. Children who have learned the artistic techniques needed to represent their ideas, and have the opportunity to explore topics and media in-depth, to revisit and add to their work, and to examine the same idea in different media, are more likely to embody these four characteristics.

Emotional Development

Art experiences can also assist children's emotional development. As children participate in art activities they gain self-confidence, feel pride in their work, and experience success. Art allows children to express strong emotions that they may have difficulty verbalizing. It may provide the child and others with insights into the child's thoughts and feelings, thus allowing for conversation and further discussion. For example, Gross and Clemens (2002) discuss how preschoolers in their class used drawings, paintings, and clay models to reenact the destruction of the twin towers in New York. Reenacting the scene was therapeutic for many children, allowing them to feel a sense of control, and opening up dialogue with the other children and adults in their lives.

Social Development

As children examine art from various artists in different time periods and diverse cultures, they have the opportunity to learn about and to appreciate similarities and differences. They come to understand that people have both similar and unique values.

In many classrooms, children also have the opportunity to collaborate with others on murals and other large art projects. Again, children learn about diverse views, practice negotiation, and have tangible proof of how their work, when combined with others, can create something beautiful.

Cognitive Development

Science and Math. Through art, children learn about the world, record thoughts and ideas, and enhance academic learning. "Artmaking is a form of inquiry and way of learning about oneself and the world" (Tarr, 1997, p. 2). For example, as a child observes a flower and then draws a sketch, he notices details he may not have considered before. Slight imperfections in the petals raise questions. What caused the holes in the petals? Why are some petals turning brown while others are not? He notes that the petal is a graduated color and must determine how he will portray this. When the child is done, he shares his work with others. "Through sharing and gaining others' perspectives, and then revisiting and revising their work, children move to new levels of awareness"

(Edwards & Springate, 1995, p. 1). Children use process skills in art that they also use in math and science. They pose and solve problems, organize thoughts, and reflect on their learning. They learn about properties of materials and experiment with cause and effect. Through art children see items from different vantage points and explore spatial concepts that are critical skills in geometry. Research confirms that studying visual arts is linked to enhanced geometric reasoning (Winner & Vincent-Lancrin, 2013).

Literacy. As with written language, the visual arts involve recording a thought or idea that then can be conveyed to someone else. For this reason, art is often considered the child's first written language (Koster, 2015). In addition, children's first writing efforts and storytelling are often related to the pictures they have drawn.

The arts can also enhance children's verbal language. Art can be a catalyst for rich dialogue among children and between the child and the teacher. Additionally the arts, like all fields of study, have a specific vocabulary that the child learns as she interacts with more knowledgeable peers or the teacher.

As children carefully study and discuss their art and the art of others, they are developing visual perception or 'visual thinking,' a cognitive process that takes images and gives them meaning" (Koster, 2005, p. 5). The child will also use these skills in reading.

Physical Development

Art develops large and small muscles and eye–hand coordination. Unlike prescribed writing or art exercises, creative art provides a motivating climate for children to practice and perfect motor control. Some teachers use production-oriented art as a way of promoting fine motor control. However, children are typically more passionate about their own creative art. Therefore, they are often more committed to the repeated practice that is needed to master the skills.

Check Your Understanding 13.2
Click here to gauge your understanding of section concepts.

As children participate in art they have opportunities to increase artistic skills, enhance creativity, and develop emotional, social, cognitive, and physical skills. However, for optimal development, the teacher must use the inquiry approach to art and must establish an environment that is conducive to learning. How does a teacher develop an art center that stresses the art as inquiry approach?

Designing an Effective Art Center

Designing Effective Indoor Art Centers

Art does not occur in only one area of the room; instead it is embedded throughout the environment. Children learn about art from picture books, pictures on the wall in other areas of the room, and the aesthetics of the room itself. However, it is also important to have a dedicated area where children can focus on producing and studying art. Art centers can be a separate room such as the *atelier* in the Reggio Emilia schools or they can be a center in the classroom. Whether a separate studio or a corner nook, art centers need to be places of inquiry and wonder. To provide this, we need a space with:

- Plenty of natural and artificial light.
- Easy clean-up with linoleum or tile floors, covered or easy-to-clean tables, and a close proximity to water.
- A quiet space that allows for focus and attention.
- Ample space so that children have room to create large projects and so that several children can work at a time.

- Space for drying creations and storing ongoing work. At the North Idaho College Children's Center, teachers have a trellis hanging horizontally from the ceiling over the art table. This creates a differentiated art space, and the top of the trellis is used as a drying rack.
- Space for displaying art creations (both two- and three-dimensional).
- An abundance of diverse materials. There may be a limited number of materials when children are first introduced to a medium. However, to allow for in-depth exploration and enhanced creativity, the range of materials should expand with the children's experiences.
- High-quality, authentic materials and tools in good working condition. Poor-quality tools inhibit children from expressing their talent. For example, trying to control the line of paint when the brush will not keep a point can frustrate children's efforts to create the picture they are envisioning. Clogged glue bottles or scissors that don't cut can also be very frustrating.
- Safe and nontoxic materials. Just because an art material is for sale does not mean it is safe or nontoxic. You can find certified product lists at the Art and Creative Materials Institute (ACMI), or you can look for the ACMI-certified nontoxic label. You can also request a Materials Safety Data Sheet from the manufacturer so that you can review the material yourself.
- Uncluttered, organized shelves so that children have easy access to materials.
- Aesthetically displayed materials that invite children to investigate and use the media. As we are teaching children about aesthetics, we need to model it in the environment. Materials can be displayed in baskets, transparent bowls, and in beautiful containers. You can organize materials by color palette. For example, color crayons or color pencils can be displayed in clear jars. Each jar can contain

Julie Bullard

In this art center, materials are displayed in baskets and glass and organized by color palette. Notice how the mirrors reflect the materials and add to the aesthetics of the center.

a different color with many hues represented. Mirrors can be used to reflect the materials in a different way.

- An abundance of reference materials and materials for inspiration. Especially when children are creating representational drawings, it is important to provide them with real-life objects, pictures, photos, and reference books to use as resources. Even adult artists, who have years of observational training and increased ability to remember detail, use references when creating pictures. In addition, reference materials provide opportunities for children to examine and appreciate art.
- Storage for replenishing supplies.

Designing Effective Outdoor Art Centers

The outdoor environment provides inspiration for artists, an abundance of natural materials that can be used to create art, and space for large and messy projects. The outdoors is also a wonderful place for permanent displays of children's art. Ideally, the outdoor art center is a permanent center, with ample storage for needed supplies. However, if this is not possible, a tote or bag can be used to transport needed materials outdoors. Following are some examples of outdoor art ideas:

Julie Bullard

This outdoor art center at Curious Minds: Early Care and Education Center is adjacent to the indoor art studio, allowing children to use either space. The adjustable art easel can accommodate either very small or very large pieces of paper.

- An easel placed under a tree can be used for quietly painting or drawing.
- A chalkboard with a bucket of colored chalk can be placed in the playhouse.
- A collage center can be created that is stocked with natural items (pinecones, twigs, dried berries, flower petals, seedpods, or nuts). Children can go on nature walks to replenish their supplies.
- A clay center can provide opportunities for making casts of trees, flowers, and pinecones as well as other clay creations.
- An outdoor loom stocked with natural materials (dried grasses, supple sticks) creates an invitation to weave.
- A sculpture center that includes a variety of similar items (bicycle parts, appliance parts, or different sizes and shapes of wood) provides opportunities for large sculptures.
- An art sack or tote that contains clipboards, paper, pencils, and markers encourages children to make representational drawings.
- Sand, ice, and snow can provide the media for transitory sculptures.

Check Your Understanding 13.3
Click here to gauge your understanding of section concepts.

Teachers can also display children's artwork to decorate the playground. For example, at Mentor Graphics Child Development Center, children working with an artist used strips of painted roofing paper to create three-dimensional art by weaving the strips through the fence. At the Helen Gordon Child Development Center, children created gigantic murals that were painted on a canvas and then covered with a polymer to protect them. Children and families at one program create and decorate stepping stones as a beginning of the year activity. The stepping stones are then used throughout the play yard as walkways and around trees and gardens.

Materials and Activities for the Art Center That Will Assist Children to Meet Art Standards

When developing your art center either indoors or outdoors, it is also important to consider art goals. The National Coalition for Core Art Standards includes four overarching anchor standards for all the art disciplines and for all students, regardless of age.

Appropriate Principles, Materials, and Activities for Meeting the Goal of Creating and Presenting Art

To meet the goals of creating and presenting art it is important to keep three important principles in mind. First, provide materials that can be transformed. Second, allow adequate time to explore each new art media, tools, or element. Third, encourage children to engage in in-depth artwork through revisiting. Keeping these in mind, you will want to plan the materials and experiences that you will provide. Art centers for young children will typically contain materials for drawing, painting, modeling, and creating sculptures and collages. Each of these media has different affordances, or differing physical properties and abilities to be transformed by a child's desire to represent an idea (Forman, 1994, p. 38).

Provide Art Materials That Can Be Transformed. As mentioned in the opening story, production-oriented or patterned art is developmentally inappropriate in early

	Artistic Process	Anchor Standards
Creating	Conceiving and developing new artistic ideas and work.	Generate and conceptualize artistic ideas and work. Organize and develop artistic ideas and work. Refine and complete artistic work.
Performing, presenting, and producing	**Performing:** Interpreting and presenting artistic ideas and work (dance, music, theatre). **Presenting**: Interpreting and sharing artistic work (visual arts). **Producing**: Realizing and presenting artistic ideas and work (media arts).	Select, analyze, and interpret artistic work for presentation. Develop and refine artistic techniques and work for presentation. Convey meaning through the presentation of artistic work.
Responding	Understanding and evaluating how the arts convey meaning.	Perceive and analyze artistic work. Interpret intent and meaning in artistic work. Apply criteria to evaluate artistic work.
Connecting	Relating artistic ideas and work with personal meaning and external context.	Synthesize and relate knowledge and personal experiences to make art. Relate artistic ideas and works with societal, cultural, and historical context to deepen understanding.

childhood. Patterned art tends to produce nearly identical looking products. In some cases, the teacher has precut much of the product and the child's role is to assemble the pieces. For example, children create snowmen by gluing teacher-made construction paper circles together.

Whenever you choose an art project, you should consider whether you are expanding or limiting creativity and the cognitive thought process. For example, many teachers have children make caterpillars out of egg cartons. While children are allowed to decorate the caterpillars any way they wish, is this the best way to encourage children to closely observe caterpillars, to think about how caterpillars look, to decide what media would be best to create the caterpillar, or to contemplate how to capture the fluffiness of the caterpillar? Epstein and Trimis (2002) urge us to choose art projects carefully. A good rule of thumb is to avoid art materials that are "cute or novel." Instead, choose art materials that can be transformed and used by the child to express an idea or feeling (Epstein & Trimis, 2002).

Allow Adequate Time to Explore Each New Media, Tool, or Element. When creating art, children first need the opportunity for in-depth experimentation with art media, tools, and elements. Teachers need to help children become competent in the use of art media so they can express ideas and thoughts in the way they intended. As mentioned earlier, when children are first introduced to a media or tool, it is important to begin with a limited number of materials, allowing children to explore and master them before gradually introducing more materials (Spodek, 2006). "We must be careful in our zeal to provide children with a variety of art materials and experiences, we do not short-change their time with each one" (Epstein & Trimis, 2002, p. 45). For example, Latoya, a teacher of three-year-olds, introduces children to tempera paint by giving them just one color. After children have thoroughly explored this color, she adds white paint so that children can create a range of tints of this color. Eventually she adds additional colors. As children become proficient, she also provides additional types of paper and brushes.

Encourage In-depth Artwork Through Revisiting. Art experiences need to be thoughtfully planned to encourage in-depth artwork. The practice in some programs of an art activity each day does not allow children the in-depth development of the skills they need to portray their thoughts and ideas adequately. Repetition with media, revisiting the same piece of art, and creating an idea in different media contribute to deeper learning and enhanced artistic outcomes.

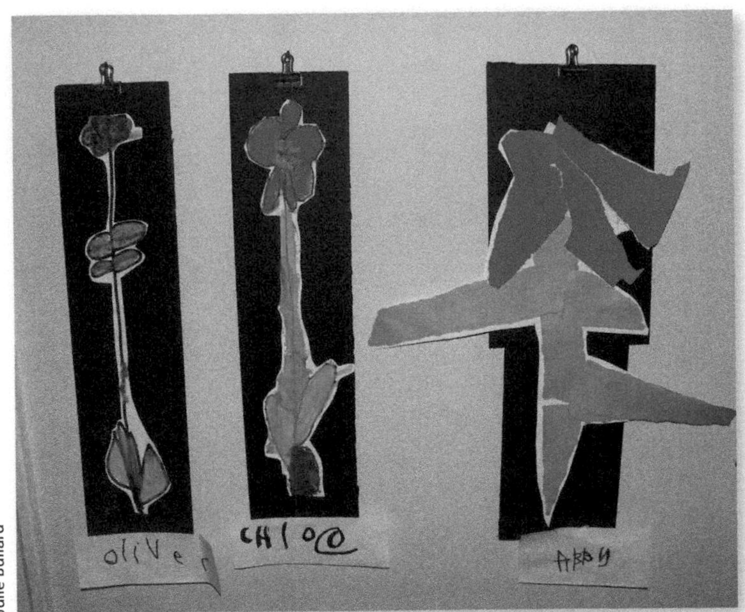

Julie Bullard

The children revisited their work and created their flower in different media, allowing these 3- and 4-year-old children to become more proficient with art materials while also revising their theories about flowers.

Revisit Media. To become proficient, children need many opportunities to use media over an extended period of time. This will allow children to move beyond exploration, which is the first phase when someone is introduced to a new media such as clay or watercolors.

Revisit Artwork. Just like professional artists, children need the opportunity to revisit their work. They also need the opportunity to determine when their art is complete. Artists often begin with a sketch, work on a number of pieces at once, revisit, and find ideas from a number of sources (Tarr, 1997). Most artists also name their work. Encouraging children to create names or titles for their creations helps them to reflect upon their art and is another way for children to revisit their work.

Revisit Ideas Using Different Media. Revisiting ideas through different media also helps children to reflect. When children use different media, they are challenged to think about the idea they are expressing in different ways. For example, a child might create a sketch of a caterpillar, then paint a picture of a caterpillar, and then create the caterpillar out of clay. Each media allows the child to represent his knowledge in a unique way and creates new questions and deeper thought. Todd was creating a caterpillar out of clay. He decided to use wire to represent the hairs on the caterpillar. This involved cutting the wire and placing each hair individually, causing him to focus on the hair. He had many questions. Does the hair grow straight up or does it curl slightly at the end? Are the hairs on all the caterpillars the same? Do they go in circles around the body or are they random? After closely observing the caterpillars for a length of time, he began to work. Forman (2006) suggests that to increase children's knowledge of their learning after they have created in different media, they should circle back and revisit their first drawing. "Children draw to learn as opposed to merely learn to draw. Children are revising their theories, not simply revising the accuracy of a copy" (Forman, 2006, p. 36).

Provide Materials and Activities for Drawing. Children gain inspiration for drawing from a variety of sources: observation, experiences, memory, and their imagination (Bartel, 2006). However, their drawings are more in-depth when they are observing rather than relying on memory (Colbert & Taunton, 1988). To assist children in observational drawings, it may be helpful to provide observational tools, such as magnifying glasses to observe fine details. A cardboard tube or a viewfinder can help to narrow the child's focus. Mirrors can also be a helpful tool, allowing children to see objects from a different view. Additionally, like artists, children need the real object, as well as representations of the object, for inspiration while drawing.

TIP

You can make your own viewfinder by cutting the center from an 8" square rigid piece of cardboard. Make the frame about 2" wide. This creates a 4" interior square. Children can hold the viewfinder at eye level and look through it or place it on a picture to narrow the viewpoint.

Esmeralda, like many teachers, begins each year with a study of self. In the art area, she provides photos of each child and his or her family. She also provides photos that focus on one facial feature, for example, a close-up photo of eyes, ears, or teeth for each child. Mirrors of different sizes are available throughout the art area. Magnifying glasses for close examination are also available. On the walls of the art area are framed pictures from famous artists: Gainsborough's The Blue Boy, *Durveger's* Alone, *and Cassatt's* Two Children Playing on a Beach. *A viewfinder is hung next to each reproduction to assist children in narrowing focus. She also provides a three-dimensional bust and a hardwood 12" manikin for children to study.*

The children make self-portraits beginning with sketches. Esmeralda adds skin tone paper and markers for the children to use if they wish. They then produce their portraits in paint and wire. Ultimately, the children make clay busts of themselves. They mix paints to match their skin tones and give each child's paint a creative, descriptive name (chocolate syrup, nutmeg, root beer float). They use these mixtures to paint their clay busts.

Esmeralda also adds a variety of costumes to the dramatic play area to help children extend the discovery of self. Children experiment with new identities through wearing the costumes—and often capture their transformations through their art.

Art centers for preschool and early-elementary-aged children should contain many types of drawing tools. Each tool has unique characteristics, allowing children to use them for different purposes. See Figure 13.2 for a description of the materials. At a minimum, the center should contain different types of pencils, markers, chalk, and crayons. These drawing materials are also typically available throughout the classroom to encourage writing, drawing, and sketching. For example, drawing materials and paper in the block area encourage the children to preplan their buildings and to document their buildings after they create them.

Provide Materials and Activities for Painting. Tempera, watercolor, acrylic, and finger paints are appropriate for preschool and early-elementary-aged children and should be available in the art center. See Figure 13.3 for a description of each of these types of paint. An easel set up in the art center with a variety of paint hues provides an appropriate surface while enticing children to paint. Rather than using a child's easel, the Helen Gordon Child Development Center uses an adult wooden adjustable easel finding that it is aesthetic and accommodating of both larger and smaller pieces of paper.

Even very young children can use tempera paint and an easel. For example, the Birge Nest room in Early Head Start, serving children from birth to age three, has an easel with several colors of paint that is continually available to children.

In many programs, children are encouraged to draw their pictures before painting them, allowing them to preplan their creations. The drawing may be made several days before or immediately before painting. Pencils and other drawing materials placed near the easel provide an invitation for children to draw before painting if they have not already done so.

You will want to give children many opportunities to explore paint. You might begin by exploring these questions. How does paint work on different types of surfaces?

FIGURE 13.2
Drawing Materials

Pencils. Pencils allow good control, produce precise lines, are clean to work with, and are readily available. Children can use drawing pencils, colored pencils, and pastel pencils.

Markers. Markers come in a wide variety of colors (skin tones, fluorescent, bold) and types (erasable, fabric, window). They allow smooth application, requiring little pressure. It is important to buy nonpermanent markers with a variety of different-sized tips. This allows children to use the markers for different purposes. For example, fine-tip markers are excellent for detailed work, while thick markers can be used for coloring in the child's creation.

Chalk. Chalk is inexpensive, blends easily, and can be used either wet or dry. A fixative helps the chalk to adhere to the paper and reduces chalk dust. Two solutions that work well as fixatives are liquid starch (equal part water and liquid starch) or sugar water (three tablespoons sugar to one cup of water) solutions. The child can either brush the solution on the paper or dip the chalk into the solution. Inexpensive chalkboards can be created by painting a piece of wood or the back of a cabinet with chalkboard paint.

Pastels, while more expensive, provide a vibrant color, do not rub off like chalk, and can still be blended. They do, however, crumble and break easily.

Crayons. Crayons are inexpensive, have a wide range of vibrant colors, and come in a variety of kinds (metallic, multicultural, fabric, scented, glitter, anti-roll). Unlike markers, changes in pressure influence the outcome of the drawing. This allows children to use different amounts of pressure to create depth and shading.

FIGURE 13.3
Types of Paint

Tempera Paints. Tempera paints are economical and come in a variety of colors, including metallic. You can buy tempera paints that are premixed, powdered, or in cakes. When buying the paint, choose a washable variety.

Finger Paints. Finger paints are a creamy, thick consistency that also come in a variety of colors. You can purchase special paints or use thick tempera paint in finger painting. You can also finger paint with lotion, cold cream, or a mixture of liquid starch and tempera paint.

Acrylic Paints. Acrylic paints are water soluble and produce bright vibrant colors. They are very adhesive and flexible, allowing the child to successfully apply the paint to many surfaces, including plastic, metal, canvas, and boards. For example, at the Opal School in Portland, Oregon, children created beautiful, transparent murals by painting pictures on a clear plastic shower curtain using acrylic paints.

Watercolor. Watercolor is transparent, dries quickly, and is water-based for easy cleanup. Watercolors come in a variety of forms, including watercolor pencils, watercolor cakes (both student and professional), liquid watercolors, and watercolors in tubes. Special watercolor paper (textured and designed to absorb water) is typically used with this media. Because the paper is expensive, you might encourage children to take smaller pieces if they plan to create small images.

What kind of lines can be produced with different size brushes? How can paint be made thicker (soap flakes), shiny (sugar), glittery (salt on wet paint), or gritty (sand)? What other substances can change the texture of the paint? What colors can be produced by mixing the paints? You can provide small clear glass or plastic containers for children to use for their experimentation. As children become more experienced, the teacher can also create mixing challenges such as trying to mix paint to match a paint chip. The mixed paints can be displayed in the art area and used for future paintings. The wide variety of hues in clear containers also adds an aesthetic element to the classroom.

When learning about the properties of watercolor paints, children can experiment with different size brushes, create shades by adding an increasing amount of water, and experiment with wet versus dry paper. Wet paper allows the paint to spread out and often creates a misty or hazy look (Romberg, 2002). As children become more familiar with the media, they may wish to produce special effects such as blotting with a sponge to create texture or overlaying colors (paint with one color, let the painting dry, and then paint over the picture with another color).

Providing a variety of paints allows children to experiment with the different properties of each. It also allows children to choose the most conducive paint for their specific purpose and surface. Many surfaces can be used for drawing and painting. See Figure 13.4 for a list of some possible surfaces.

It is critical to have quality brushes in a variety of sizes for children to paint with. The quality of the brush greatly influences the child's ability to manipulate the paints. If the child wishes to create a special effect, you might provide other items to paint with, including sticks, pastry brushes, feathers, sponges, small paint rollers, makeup brushes, toothbrushes, and vegetable brushes. For example, toothbrushes may be effective in creating a background for snow scenes.

Provide Materials and Activities for Collage. A collage, a composite of material or objects pasted onto a surface, can be two or three dimensional. Collage materials are often recycled or reclaimed items such as newspaper clippings, beads, buttons, wallpaper, fabric, and items from nature.

Collages may be created around a theme. For example, Sarah has children create "All about me" collages that include magazine pictures, drawings, and items representing

FIGURE 13.4
Surfaces to Draw and Paint On

Nearly any surface can be drawn or painted on, with one's imagination being the only limit. In addition to providing different types of surfaces, it is also important to provide different sizes of surfaces, since different sizes suggest different types of strokes. As a rule of thumb, the younger the children, the larger the surface will need to be for them to be successful. Some common surfaces are

- manila paper
- newsprint
- construction paper
- watercolor paper
- newspaper
- computer print-out paper
- large rolls of craft paper
- shiny papers to finger paint on such as butcher paper
- cellophane
- wax paper
- tissue paper
- wallpaper
- foam board
- gift wrap
- cardboard
- sandpaper
- bubble wrap
- foil
- fabric
- felt
- tree bark
- wood

For more transitory pictures, children can draw in sand or paint on tabletops. Transitory pictures can also be created using different items on a light table or overhead projector. The Children's Museum in Chicago provided children with a spray bottle of water, an abundance of cut and torn colored cellophane, and a Plexiglas easel. Children could create transitory pictures by spraying the Plexiglas with water and arranging the cellophane.

Julie Bullard

These natural collage materials become the focus of attention when they are displayed in the glass bowls. The mirror adds to the aesthetics on the display.

themselves. One child loved apple juice and added a small juice box to his collage. Another child included a clay model of a ladybug because she liked to collect bugs.

Infants can make collages by sticking items to clear contact paper. When the child is done, the teacher can place another piece of contact paper over the top of the picture, sealing the materials between the two layers.

Provide Materials and Activities for Sculpture. A sculpture is a three-dimensional figure. Like collages, they can be created from a variety of materials. Materials that are suitable for children include different sizes of wire, rolled-up newspaper, boxes, wood, papier-mâché, small appliance parts, and a variety of other recycled materials (see Figure 13.5 for ideas). You will also need the appropriate type of glue, tape, nails, and so forth to hold the sculpture together.

At the Mentor Graphics Child Development Center, children created bug sculptures following an in-depth study of insects. Children first drew their designs and then created the three-dimensional models using kitchen items such as forks, spoons, and colanders. After the bugs were completed, they were painted gold and were mounted to fence posts in the playground, becoming permanent art exhibits.

Provide Materials and Activities for Modeling. Many early childhood programs provide Play-Doh for children to use in modeling. While Play-Doh allows children to experiment with modeling, clay provides several benefits not found with Play-Doh. Clay is a natural material, coming from the earth. It allows for more detail than Play-Doh and holds its shape, allowing the artist to create upright sculptures. Some teachers are concerned that young children may be unable to use clay successfully. However, in the book *Poking, Pinching, and Pretending*, Smith and Goldhaber (2004) demonstrate that even toddlers can successfully use this media. If you want a material for modeling that is nondrying, you might consider Plasticine.

In introducing clay, let the children first experiment without using tools. For example, the teacher might sit with the children during center time and provide exploratory exercises to help children discover ways to change the shape of the clay. This might include using hands to change the surface of the clay (handprints, fingerprints), poking holes in the clay, squeezing the clay into tall shapes, breaking clay into pieces, and constructing balls, coils, and slabs (Topal, 2006). Children can also add water to the clay, experimenting with the different effects. Make sure you wedge (knead) the clay to mix it well before giving it to the children.

Julie Bullard

Notice that the clay mini studio provides children with tools that they can use to create their own three-dimensional designs. Clay boards help define space and make clean-up easier. They also allow a child to more easily move their design so that it can be stored and revisited later.

In many classrooms, children are given cookie cutters to use with clay or Play-Doh. However, Koster (2015), an early childhood art educator and author, equates this to giving children dittoes for drawing or coloring. Using cookie cutters often inhibits children from using the clay to develop three-dimensional models. It can also give children the impression that they are not capable of producing the items on their own. Instead, after you have introduced the clay, you can give the children cutting materials such as pizza cutters and plastic knives, rolling pins, ice cream scoops, cheese graters, and items to make impressions such as potato mashers. Or, you can introduce children to the tools that potters use. For example, you might introduce

FIGURE 13.5
Reusable Materials for Art Activities

Reusable resource centers are becoming popular throughout the United States and Europe. Businesses and individuals donate discarded materials, saving disposal fees while allowing the materials to be reinvented as resources for classrooms. For more information on reusable resource centers, visit the Reusable Resources Association at reusableresources.org. Some programs are beginning their own resource centers, making the materials available to their staff and the community.

Some examples of reusable materials include

glass beads	wood	CDs
pipes	fabric—netting, velvet, upholstery	shredded paper
sockets	Mylar	Styrofoam
ceramic pieces	wire	craft sticks
paper	yarn	cotton balls
cardboard	foam	buttons
leather		wire
rubber		

Natural items might also be used in collages and sculptures:

rocks	dried flowers	nuts
stones	shells	twigs
seedpods	leaves	wood shavings

Julie Bullard

At Mentor Graphics Child Development Center, children are creating a group weaving using a chicken wire base. Ribbons for weaving are easily accessible from a nearby rack.

carving spatulas and scoring and scribing tools. As children become more proficient with the clay, you might want to introduce the idea of a wire armature or framework to provide stability for their vertical sculptures (Wien, Keating, Comeau, & Bigelow, 2012).

In addition to providing an art medium, clay provides a rich sensory experience. Clay also encourages experimentation and revisiting. As long as it is still soft, clay sculptures can easily be changed, added to, or reinvented.

Provide Appropriate Art Tools and Paper. In addition to providing drawing, painting, collage, sculpture, and modeling materials, you will also want to stock your art center with some basic materials and tools. Besides quality paintbrushes and clay tools, you will want:

- Other basic tools (tape, stapler, hole punch, rulers, paper clips, glue and paste, and high-quality right- and left-handed scissors). Choose appropriate tools based upon the children's developmental level and their interests.
- Smocks to protect children's clothing, freeing them to focus on their artwork rather than worrying about keeping their clothes clean.
- A variety of types of paper (see Figure 13.1).

The art center or studio for preschool and early-elementary-aged children needs to be well stocked with a variety of drawing, painting, collage, sculpture, and modeling materials that are aesthetically displayed. A variety of tools and types of paper will also be necessary. In addition, you might include materials for special projects such as printing, weaving, puppet-making, mask-making, beading, and jewelry-making.

Appropriate Materials and Activities for the Goal of Responding and Connecting to Art

Children need many opportunities to meet the art anchor standards of responding and connecting. This section will examine how the art center can assist in accomplishing these goals.

Art appreciation has a long history in the United States, having been first introduced in American elementary schools in the 1880s (Kerlavage, 1995). Today we know that even toddlers exhibit the ability to make aesthetic choices, often showing preferences for specific colors and textures (Danko-McGhee & Shaffer, 2003). Generally, young children tend to prefer bright, saturated colors, pictures that have a familiar subject (either abstract or realistic), and simple compositions (Epstein & Trimis, 2002).

Without adult guidance, children tend to focus on the subject matter when discussing a work of art (Epstein & Trimis, 2002). However, when supported through open-ended questions, children can be guided to consider multiple aspects of a picture.

Most early childhood art centers focus on art production. However, you can add many materials to your art center and throughout your classroom that also introduce children to famous works of art and art appreciation. Often these will relate to the topics, media, or subjects that the children are exploring in their art production. You can accomplish this by doing the following:

- Display art from the community (weaving, pottery, quilts, and jewelry).
- Over time provide a variety of art from different cultural groups and time periods featuring different art media and styles.
- Provide postcards featuring art to match and classify. At first children may match identical cards or sort cards by the subject matter. However, with the opportunity to explore different types of art and through adult guidance they can learn to sort by the media or the type of art (oil, collage, drawing, fresco or wet plaster, pastel, print, sculpture, acrylic, mobile, or drawing) or by the broad subject (abstract, cityscape, interior, landscape, portrait, seascape, or still life) (Koster, 2015).
- Provide books with famous art reproductions.
- Use calendars of art prints to create puzzles.
- Provide a peek-a-boo window over an art print. The peek-a-boo window piques curiosity and helps children to closely examine one small part of the picture.
- Create bulletin boards of art featuring opposing concepts (realist/abstract) (Schiller, 1995).
- Place a picture frame in the art area that allows children or teachers to feature pictures.
- Set up an inspirational display of nature as art. For example, place rocks or shells in an interesting design or arrange a beautiful bouquet of flowers.
- Create a masterpiece corner to highlight a featured piece of artwork (Koster, 2015).

Special Considerations and Materials for Infants and Toddlers

As soon as children begin to show interest, they are ready to begin drawing. For example, Dunst and Gorman (2009), examined 25 studies of infants' and toddlers' mark making and scribbling and found that even one-year-olds create marks. Infants' and toddlers' drawing was more complex and lasted for a longer duration if the writing material produced a more visual effect (markers, crayons, and digitalized computer pens), if the writing surface was slanted, and if a background of animals or people were used to draw on. As would be expected, the more opportunities the child had for drawing, the younger the child was when she moved into the preschematic stage of drawing. Beginning at the age of one, most children are also ready to make collages, paint, and model with clay or Play-Doh. By age two, most children are ready to explore printmaking, especially with body parts such as hands and feet (Koster, 2015).

One of the major art goals for children three and under is the exploration of media and tools. Toddlers need the opportunity to use paper and cardboard, clay, crayons and markers, and nontoxic paint. They can also begin to explore art elements, especially color (Gandini, 2006). If children have these opportunities as toddlers, they will be ready to use the media and tools to create representational and imaginative art when they are preschoolers. Since children this age may still be mouthing items, it is crucial that all materials are safe to ingest and do not pose a choking hazard.

At Helen Gordan Child Development center the teachers created a studio space for infants and toddlers. The studio space allows children to engage in in-depth investigation of an idea, concept, or material. Over the course of time this studio space has been used to explore paper, clay, painting, building, natural materials, sensory materials, dancing,

sound, and rocking. For example, the rocking studio included a rocking boat, a child-sized rocking chair, a rocking horse, and other items that rocked.

TIP

To prevent marker tops from being a choking hazard for infants and toddlers, place the tops upright into a plaster of Paris mixture. After the mixture has dried, children can simply place markers onto the ummovable tops. Teachers at Playcare created the marker holder in a golden cookie tin and added glitter to the plaster to make it more attractive.

Even very young children can participate in long-term art explorations. For example, infants and toddlers in Reggio Emilia participated in an exploration of white. Young infants explored a multisensory landscape of white materials, each having different tactile and visual qualities. Children could crawl on the materials, try to tear them, mouth them, pick them up, and try to look through them. The toddler's explorations of white began by focusing on the properties of a white paper napkin. They continued exploring a variety of white materials (wool, cotton, paper, paper towels, plastic, slick paper, corn paper, tissue paper, sheer fabric, satin, and more). After repeated opportunities to explore, each child made his own individual creations that were included in a large, beautifully displayed composition (Vecchi & Giudici, 2004).

Apply Your Knowledge Early childhood educators using the Reggio Emilia approach believe in introducing a variety of art materials to children at a young age. For example, in Reggio Emilia, toddlers use beautifully displayed drawing materials, earth clay, wire, natural collage materials, and glass containers filled with paints. However, some early childhood educators question the safety and appropriateness of these practices. How do these practices reflect the Reggio Emilia philosophy (see Chapter 1)? What would a teacher from Reggio Emilia say were the advantages of providing these materials to toddlers?

Special Considerations and Materials for School-Aged Children

Many elementary schools have art specialists. However, 88% of classroom teachers, understanding the value, also include art as part of their ongoing instruction (National Coalition for Core Arts Standards, 2014). The arts also play a prominent role in the Common Core State Standards for English Language Arts. A study examining this link discovered that of the 396 standards listed for reading, writing, and speaking and listening, 74 or 19% of these made direct reference to the arts. In the visual arts this includes standards on analyzing and interpreting images, creating images to tell a story, and using visuals when speaking (The College Board, 2012). For example, one of the common core writing standards for kindergarten states, "Use a combination of drawing, dictating, and writing to compose informative/explanatory texts in which they name what they are writing about and supply some information about the topic." A speaking and listening standard for second-grade children states, "Create audio recordings of stories or poems; add drawings or other visual displays to stories or recounts of experiences when appropriate to clarify ideas, thoughts, and feelings" (National Governors Association Center for Best Practices and Council of Chief State School Officers, 2010).

The study also makes a link between the arts and the Standards for Mathematical Practice stating that the creative practices of imagine, investigate, construct, and reflect underlie both. For example, one of the mathematical practice standards is to model with mathematics. To do so a child must imagine (form a mental image or concept), investigate (observe or study through exploration or examination), construct (make or form by combining parts or elements), and reflect (think deeply or carefully about) (The College Board, 2012, p. 65). This study reinforces the concept that while art has an intrinsic value of its own, it also plays an important role in other curricular areas.

In the next section, we will examine the teacher's role in exposing children to art. As the teacher exposes children to art and then guides them to look at multiple aspects of a picture, children's ability to meet the visual art standards of creating, presenting, responding, and connecting is enhanced.

Check Your Understanding 13.4
Click here to gauge your understanding of section concepts.

Teachers' Facilitation of Learning in the Art Center

The teacher is crucial in helping children gain optimal art skills, dispositions, and knowledge. She exposes children to different types of art, provides life experiences, discusses art with children, teaches children techniques, acknowledges the artist and his art, challenges children, and documents and assesses their learning. Through providing culturally relevant, developmentally appropriate materials and making modifications as needed, she also meets the needs of all learners.

Expose Children to Art and Art Elements

In literacy, we rarely question that it is essential that children see adults and older children modeling reading and writing. We also believe that children need abundant exposure to high-quality literature. The same is true for art. Children need artist models and abundant exposure to art from the masters. Invite artists, sculptors, and potters to visit your program. They can model creating art and describe problems encountered as they work (Tarr, 1997). The artists can also work directly with the children modeling teaching techniques, art techniques, and art language for teachers and children (Bisgaier, Samaras, & Russo, 2005). In some instances, artists may work on a cooperative project with children. You can also take children on field trips to art galleries and pottery studios.

Many children's books have wonderful illustrations, providing another opportunity to expose children to art. For example, Caldecott-award-winning books are chosen based on their illustrations. When reading a book to children, discuss the pictures. What media or special techniques are used? How are color, line, shape, and texture used? How do the illustrations add to the story? Provide the background on the artist. Compare the illustrations in the book to illustrations in previous books you have read or to current work the children are engaged in. For example, Ezra Jack Keats uses a paper collage technique. When reading *The Snowy Day*, Lakisha discussed with the children how they also had been using the collage technique in creating pictures. She asked the children how their collages and Keats's were similar and different. Lakisha used a Venn diagram as part of the discussion to help clarify and focus the conversation (see Chapter 4 for information on Venn diagrams). The diagram was also a way to create documentation of the dialogue.

In addition, it is helpful to provide activities that allow children to explore and learn about different art elements such as color and line. See an example in the "Create Your Own Color-Matching Wreath" box.

Display Works of Art

The experiences children initially have with art will influence their tastes and preferences for art throughout their lives. These preferences are often resistant to change (Gardner, 1991). Therefore, you will want to expose children to a variety of art. For example, introduce children to male and female artists from different cultures and time periods. Study

Create Your Own Color-Matching Wreath

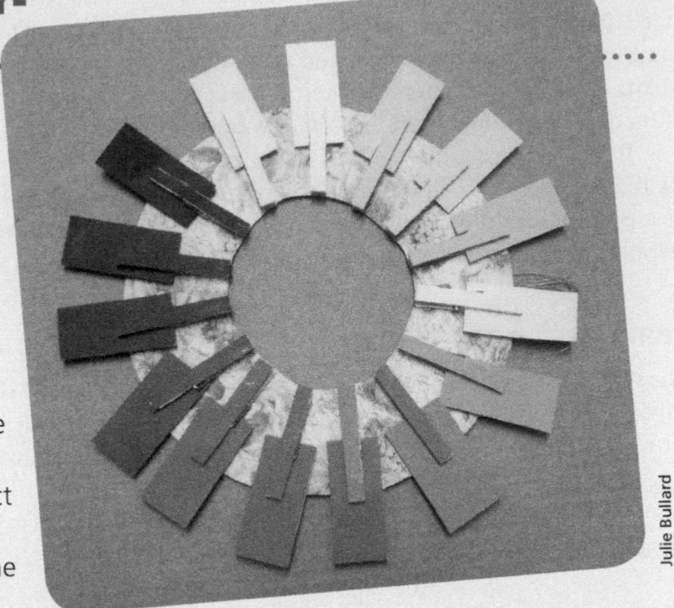

Julie Bullard

This color matching is designed so that children can match skin colors. You could use a similar approach for matching primary colors and shades or tints of one color. As children match colors, they are also using fine motor skills to squeeze the clothespins.

Directions

1. Begin with a cardboard circle. Cut out the center to create a wreath.
2. Cover the wreath with gift paper or contact paper.
3. Use a hot glue gun to glue clothespins to the wreath.
4. Obtain paint chips from a store that sells paints. Typically they will donate them to you.
5. Cut a piece of the paint chip the size of the clothespin. Use a hot glue gun to attach the paint chip to the wreath.
6. The remaining piece of the paint chip is used for matching.

Variations

The children could find the paint sample that matched their skin color and name the color. The children could mix paints to match their skin colors and then use this paint to paint a clothespin and piece of cardstock for a wreath.

art from the masters as well as local art. Pottery, weavings, and baskets from local artisians might be displayed or used throughout the environment. High-quality reproductions of the masters can be obtained from many sources. You can obtain inexpensive art from calendars, prints of great artists, art books, or magazines such as *The Smithsonian*. Koster (2012) recommends that you carefully choose art that helps children to understand the following:

- Art is made by people of all ages, in diverse geographic areas, and in different periods of time.
- Art can tell us about the lives of other people.
- Art is made from a variety of materials and in different styles, and is found throughout the environment (Koster, 2012, p. 171).

Discuss Art with Children

Talk to the children about the art that is displayed. Christine Mulcahey, a professor and art specialist at a lab school, says that you can begin by asking children what they see in the picture, how the artist made the picture appear as it did, and what they think the artist may have named the picture. You can then share the actual name of the picture and discuss this with the children (Mulcahey, 2009). You might also use a visible thinking routine (see Chapter 3) such as I see, I think, I wonder. During this routine, the children answer three questions about the art, "What do you see? What do you think about that? What does it make you wonder?"

You can also engage young children in art history. While art history is often reserved for older age levels, some art educators question this practice. Erickson (1995) researched second-grade students' understanding of art history by asking three questions: "How was life different back then? How would life back then have made a difference in the way the painting looked? What question would you ask to help better understand the painting?" She found that children attempted to make sense of the subject matter, difficulty, and skill of the painter, and made hypotheses about why artists may have painted the way they did.

Teachers can also help children learn more about art history by learning as much as they can about the art, the artist, and the historical time period so that they have information to share with the children. "Teachers do not have to become art historians overnight, just experts on one piece of artwork at a time" (Koster, 2005, p. 229). Some programs prepare a little informational card to go with a posted print, so that teachers and volunteers have the needed background knowledge.

Teachers can also engage children in art criticism or "provocative art dialogues" (Cole & Schaefer, 1990; Spodek, 2006). According to Spodek (2006), art criticism includes the following four stages:

- Description of the artwork—subject matter, elements, and medium.
- Analysis—relationship between the elements.
- Interpretation—ideas, feelings, and mood conveyed by the artwork.
- Judgment—based upon description, analysis, and interpretation.

By using questioning, you can guide even young children through this process (Epstein, 2005). In discussing the art, you can discuss art elements and ask children questions about the subject, the artist's intentions, and how the art was made. You can compare this art piece to other works of art. You can also ask children how the artwork makes them feel. Another technique is to encourage children to pick a spot in the painting and imagine they were there (Newton, 1995).

It is also important to discuss reasons people make art. For example, artists might be expressing an idea, illustrating a book, recording what they see, depicting an emotion, or exploring visual relationships (Tarr, 1997, p. 3).

Provide Life Experiences

"To create art, children must first have a feeling, thought, or experience they want to express. Without meaningful and individual experiences, children tend to draw stereotypical objects" (Epstein, 2005, p. 53). Rather than creating art activities that are isolated from the rest of the curriculum, teachers can tie art to other areas of learning.

Children at North Idaho College Children's Center were completing a project on flowers. Their study included a field trip to a greenhouse, visiting a field of wildflowers, interviewing gardeners, reading and looking at flower books, and ultimately creating their own flowerbed at the childcare centers. The children watered, fertilized, and cared for their flowers. They studied the flowers they grew, learning which ones lasted if they were picked and brought inside, which could be eaten, and which could be dried to form permanent bouquets. Using magnifying glasses, they carefully examined different types of petals, leaf patterns, and stamen. They also created their flowers in a variety of media, including representational drawings, paintings, and three-dimensional models in clay. As winter approached, and with it freezing weather, children decided they wanted to preserve their garden by creating a mural. They drew sketches, transferred their sketches to canvas, and then painted their creation with acrylic paint, creating a beautiful, vibrant, permanent rendition of their flowerbed. Because children had participated in a long-term project studying flowers, the mural captured their in-depth knowledge of the subject as well as their feelings and experiences with their garden.

Watch the video to learn more about scaffolding children's learning as they engage in art. Which techniques does the teacher use to scaffold the girl's learning?

Teach Techniques and Scaffold Learning

Early childhood practitioners must teach children the art techniques they need to be successful. For example, children need to know how to create a slip of water and clay to hold clay together or how to wet the paper when using watercolors. You can learn techniques yourself by taking a class or watching a video on YouTube. You might also invite an art partner to assist. Local art groups may volunteer to help teachers and children learn art techniques.

Learning to use proper techniques assists children to advance their artistic skill, thereby allowing them the ability to express their creativity. For example, when children were given guided opportunities to experiment with clay, they created more advanced human figures than did children who had not had this exposure (Grossman, 1980).

Acknowledge Learners

There are many ways that we can acknowledge children's creations. These include attractive classroom displays or art shows featuring children's work, referring to children as artists, and discussing children's art with them (Thompson, 2005).

Attractively displaying children's work surrounds them with beauty, provides affirmation for the artists letting them know that they and their work is important, extends project work, provides a window into children's thoughts and souls, and provides information to other children, parents, and administrators (Seefeldt & Waites, 2002).

Julie Bullard

This child created mural at Helen Gordon Child Development Center in Portland, Oregon, provides a vivid reminder of the children's work.

Make displays attractive and informational by doing the following:

- Frame the art with a mat, place it in a purchased frame, or create your own tagboard picture frame.
- Purchase several different sizes and colors of Plexiglas. Children's pictures can easily be taped to and removed from this surface.
- Use unusual backgrounds such as aluminum foil or newspaper, but only if it does not detract from the art.
- Include photos of children creating the art with their masterpiece.
- Include photos or still lifes that children were using for inspiration or references as they were drawing or painting along with their finished product.
- Include a written description or dictation from the child about the artwork when you display it.

Allowing children to determine what to display causes them to reflect upon their work. You can help children learn about displays by discussing their purpose, visiting exhibits, and making a list of criteria to consider when creating your own display (Clayton, 2002). Establishing a framing center in the classroom is another way to encourage children to be actively involved in creating the display. In addition to displaying children's art on bulletin boards, you might want to try one of the following:

- Create pedestals by stacking boxes or crates. Boxes can be arranged in numerous ways, including pyramids or stair steps or by stacking the same-size boxes on top of each other at different angles. Boxes and crates allow you to display art on all four sides and when stacked often provide room for three-dimensional displays. It might be necessary to weight the boxes to make them less likely to tip over.
- Use all available space. In small rooms, you may need to be creative. For example, consider using the backs of dividers for displays.
- Clip children's artwork to a clothesline hung across the wall or ceiling.
- Create a mobile out of coat hangers by taping them together to create a triangle or square. Children can clip their artwork to the hangers.
- Sew pockets on a clear shower curtain to display small works of art. These can be hung in a window or from the ceiling as a divider between centers.
- Create albums of children's work (include children's drawings, paintings, and photos of three-dimensional work).
- Use art as a permanent addition to the school. For example, children might make ceramic tables, sculptures, stepping stones, or placemats.

Watch the video to see an example of ways to display art. How does this display assist in acknowledging children's artistic development?

https://www.youtube.com/watch?v=tCCE_Szo2tQ&list=PLDCE28F176A432839&index=10

Discuss Children's Art

Another important way of acknowledging children is to talk to them about their creations. The discussion can also help children verbalize their intent and cause them to think more deeply about their art. Through the discussion, you can assess the child's understanding and learning and provide additional relevant information. "For dialogue to promote learning, it needs to be thoughtfully structured around a sequence of questions that invite reflection" (Burton, 2000, p. 330).

It is important to refrain from asking the child what the picture is or trying to guess what it is. Many of us have been in the embarrassing position of guessing incorrectly and disappointing a child. Also, avoid judgmental statements (beautiful, good job, nice painting). These are not helpful to the child and are often statements used by adults when they have not taken the time to examine the artwork carefully. In addition, children may be dissatisfied with the results and wonder about your judgment when you state the art is beautiful. Instead, there are several other ways you can discuss the work with the child.

- Ask the child to describe his work.
- Discuss the art elements; for example, line, color, shape, texture, form, pattern, and space (open area) (Tarr, 1997, p. 3). When you are describing the work, use correct art terms when it is developmentally appropriate: **tint** (white added), **shade** (black added), **primary color** (red, yellow, blue), **secondary color** (purple, green, orange), **hue** (color), **intensity** (brightness or dullness of color), or **symmetry** (same on both sides).
- Talk about the art subject (cityscape, landscape, portrait, abstract, or still life). What is the subject, and why was it chosen?
- Discuss the technique that was used. "How did you get the two pieces of clay to stick together?" "What colors did you combine to create the goldenrod color?"

Cathy Jackson

The children returned from spring break to find that the bulb they had planted had flowered. They were excited and motivated to draw their flower.

- Discuss the effort the child put into the work. "You've worked on your clay bear for the last three days. Each day I've noticed that you've added new details like the lines for the fur."
- Discuss the artistic decisions (Koster, 2015). "You decided to use only yellow items in your collage."
- Describe your own feelings when looking at the work. "When I see your picture of the ocean, it reminds me of when I was young and would pick up seashells with my grandfather."

Challenge Children

Teachers can challenge children to make sketches to capture memories, to draw ideas and theories, and to draw using different viewpoints. You can also encourage children to revisit their creations, exploring the media, the subject, or the current work of art in more depth. Additionally, teachers can challenge children to think about whether they have adequately portrayed their ideas and encourage them to continue to work on their art piece until they are personally satisfied with it.

Manage Special Challenges in the Art Area

Storage for Continuing Projects. Sometimes it can be difficult to locate space for children to store works in progress. Following are some suggestions:

- Have children work on trays or cardboard so that it is easier to move the creation to another location.
- For smaller three-dimensional art, use clear plastic boxes that can stack for storage.
- Store paintings and drawings on clotheslines. Several works by the same artist can be clipped together for later revisiting.
- Place crates containing artwork in progress on a large piece of plywood. Attach rope to each corner, and use a pulley system to raise and lower the storage as needed.
- Reconsider existing art display areas to see if you can redesign them for works in progress. For example, one teacher replaced her bulletin board with shadow boxes. This created a display area that could also be used for three-dimensional work in progress, without sacrificing wall or floor space. Shadow boxes can also be placed in windows.

Check Your Understanding 13.5
Click here to gauge your understanding of section concepts.

Using Food for Art Materials or Activities. *Developmentally Appropriate Practices* (Copple & Bredekamp, 2009) emphasizes that using food for art activities is inappropriate. The primary objection is wasting food when people are hungry. Since the value placed on a particular food varies among cultures, there is also the danger of offending people when a culturally valued food is used for play. Others assert that if teachers use food for art activities, it is difficult for children to make the distinction about when it is permissible to play with food and when it is not.

However, others state that food items provide a safe alternative to other art materials, are readily available, and may be less expensive than purchased art supplies.

They also argue that many purchased art items such as glue and Play-Doh contain food items (although these may be inedible residues) (Koster, 2015).

If you choose to use food items for art, it is important that you are sensitive to the children and families in your classroom. In many cases, nonfood items can be easily substituted.

Children Want You to Create for Them. If children ask you to draw for them, begin by trying to determine what underlying needs the children have. Do they need help with a specific technique? Do they want your attention? Are they having trouble determining how to begin their project? You will provide a different response depending upon each child's needs. For example, if the child does not know where to begin, you might offer suggestions or ask questions that will assist him. If he is drawing a person, you might suggest he begin with the head. You can then show him his face in a mirror, show him pictures, or discuss the facial features that can be added. In other cases, children might not understand the process. For example, they might be trying to paint at the easel and the paint runs because they are not wiping the brush after dipping it in the paint. In this case, it is important to teach children a more effective technique. Through careful analysis and problem solving, the teacher can alleviate many challenges.

Observe and Document Children's Art Processes and Products

There are many ways you can document children's artwork, such as keeping the actual artifact, taking photos of three-dimensional work, and saving children's renditions of the same subject over time or the same idea in multiple media. Having older children write a description of why they chose the subject, the art process they used, and the challenges they encountered can add additional information. Younger children can be interviewed about their art piece and recorded, or the information can be written by an adult. You might save children's artwork in portfolios, adding anecdotal records, photos of the child creating the work, and a description and analysis of the work. When observing and documenting children's work, consider the following questions:

- What ideas does the child express in her artwork? Is there a theme?
- What media does the child prefer using? Is the child able to use the media successfully?
- What art techniques does the child use?
- What was the purpose of this specific piece of artwork?
- Where did the idea for the art come from?
- How long did the child work on the art? Did he revisit his creation? What changes were made as a result of the revisiting?
- Did he produce the theme or idea in different media? How did the idea change when different media were used?
- What is the child's stage of art development?
- Is the child able to describe the art? Does the child use any art terminology in the description?
- What physical skills does the child demonstrate while completing her art (cutting on a line, using a pincer grasp)?

Assessing and documenting the child's art development provide information to share with the child and family. Teachers can also use this information for planning appropriate materials and activities.

FIGURE 13.6
Meeting a Young Child's Special Needs

> Thomas is a young child with cerebral palsy. He enjoys art but has difficulty grasping and controlling the materials. His parents, therapist, and teachers feel that Thomas will be successful with environmental support. They modify the art area by taping the paper to the table. They add foam from curlers to the crayons, pencils, paintbrushes, and glue sticks to make them easier to grasp. They also provide a rotary cutting tool that is easier to use than scissors. Although these adaptations were added to the center specifically for Thomas, children in the classroom are allowed to experiment with the adaptive tools if they are interested (West, 2006).

Meet the Needs of All Learners

Teachers need to make sure that the art center and materials reflect cultural diversity and meet the needs of learners with differing abilities. Art provides a wonderful opportunity to expose children to local culture, their own unique culture, and the culture of others. One preschool program, surrounded by sheep growers, brought in local culture by providing a variety of types of wool (wool that was unprocessed, carded, spun, and felted) for children to use in their art.

Tonisha, a teacher of first-grade children, invites families to share artwork they have created or collected. One family brought in tole painting they created and sold. Another family brought in a collection of quilts, telling children the stories of the different designs. Still another family shared a collection of American Indian art.

Displaying and discussing professional works of art from different cultures and by people with disabilities is still another way that children can learn about their own and others' cultures. Posting the picture of the artist with the work of art assists children to see this diversity.

Unfortunately, art activities can also perpetuate stereotypes. For example, some programs have children create totem poles when they study American Indians. This may cause children to think mistakenly that all American Indians created totem poles. Additionally, in some cultures the totem pole is sacred, and it is inappropriate for children to create one. Local artists or families from the culture being studied can often provide guidance on appropriate art activities.

We need to consider how to meet the needs of children with differing abilities, as well. See Figure 13.6 for an example of how one teacher met the needs of a young boy with cerebral palsy.

The teacher plays a crucial role in children's art development in a variety of ways. She provides an aesthetic, well-stocked art center and interacts with children while they use the center—discussing art history and criticism, teaching techniques, providing challenges, acknowledging children's work, and documenting their progress. The teacher provides background experiences and exposes children to art and artists.

Click here to gauge your understanding of chapter concepts.

In the art area, children participate in self-expression, create unique visual images of their ideas and thoughts, and engage in problem solving and inquiry. As children create and study art they take part in a universal language that breaks cultural barriers and transcends the changes of time.

Sample Application Activities

1. Imagine that the school board in your town is eliminating visual arts from the curriculum for K–3rd grade. Write a letter defending the value of art in the curriculum.
2. Learn more about children's art development by visiting the following websites.
   - Drawing Development in Children: Learning Design.
   - Web Archive of Children's Art at Indiana State University.
   - National Gallery of Australia (search for Childhood's Past to see art throughout the ages).

3. Collect children's artwork and classify them using the stages of art development.
4. Assess an art center using the environmental assessment checklist found in Figure 13.7.
5. Often we ask children to draw from memory. Choose an item, such as a flower, to draw from memory. Then draw the same item while examining a real object, a photo, or multiple illustrations. Compare your two pictures.
6. Experiment with different art media yourself. Become familiar with art techniques by taking a workshop or watching YouTube videos.
7. Choose one of the following websites that features art. Choose a piece of art that you would use with children. Describe why you chose this piece of art. Also, list questions you would ask children to help them explore art history.
   - Go to the Artnet website and search for an artist.
   - Go to Barewalls and search by artist or subject.
   - Visit the National Museum of the American Indian website and view their art collections.
   - Visit the Smithsonian Institution National Museum of African Art to view their collections.
   - Visit the Smithsonian Institution Freer and Sackler Gallerias and visit their collection of Asian art.
8. Learn about routines that assist children in exploring works of art at the Artful Thinking website. Choose one routine to use with children.
9. Design a plan for an attractive display of children's artwork. If possible, implement the plan.
10. Begin a collection of artwork (calendars, postcards, or magazine pictures).

❑ Does the art center contain plenty of natural and artificial light?
❑ Are the floor and tables easy to clean?
❑ Is the center located in close proximity to water?
❑ Is the center placed in a quiet space that allows for focus and attention?
❑ Does the center provide ample work space so that children have room to work on large projects and so that several children can work at the same time?
❑ Is there storage for ongoing work?
❑ Is there storage for replenishment of supplies?
❑ Are there low, uncluttered shelves so that children have easy access to materials?
❑ Is there an abundance of diverse materials for drawing, painting, modeling, collage, and sculpture?
❑ Are there high-quality, authentic materials and tools that are in good working condition?
❑ Are materials safe and labeled nontoxic?
❑ Are materials displayed aesthetically?
❑ Is there an abundance of reference materials on art and on the current topic being explored?
❑ Are there pictures and displays to provide inspiration?
Are there materials for art appreciation?
❑ Do materials encourage children to create their own artwork (no patterns, coloring pages, stencils, cookie cutters)?
❑ Is art displayed at the children's eye level, highlighting both their two- and three-dimensional work?
❑ Is the work of other artists (local artists, artists from other cultures, the masters) displayed?
❑ Is art displayed in an uncluttered and attractive way? For example, is the artwork framed or matted? Is a photo of the artist displayed with the work?

FIGURE 13.7 **Environmental Assessment: Art Center**

CHAPTER 14

Developing Music and Dance Centers

Learning Outcomes

After you have read this chapter, you will be prepared to:

- Describe the development of music and dance skills
- Discuss multiple ways that the music and dance center enhances children's development
- Demonstrate the ability to design effective music and dance centers both indoors and outdoors
- Create learning center materials and activities that are developmentally appropriate and that assist children in meeting music and dance standards
- Describe multiple ways that teachers facilitate learning in the music and dance center

Julie Bullard

In a small music and dance center, a plastic basket of various instruments sits on a shelf. Beside the instruments sits a tape player and a few children's tapes. A keyboard with a missing key sits on the floor. The children rarely use the center, which has remained the same all year. At a staff meeting, Martha, the teacher, wonders if she should remove the music center, allowing more room for the nearby dramatic play area. She says, "Since the children seem uninterested in music and dance, perhaps the space could be more wisely used."

Apply Your Knowledge Do you think the center should be removed? What are reasons other than disinterest that might inhibit the children from using this center? What are ways that the center could be enriched?

Music exerts a strong influence on us. Through music, we communicate powerful emotions, ideas, and thoughts. Throughout history, music has played an important role. For example, the early Greeks considered music to be the language of the gods (Carlton & Weikert, 1994). Music is significant in nearly all cultures, assisting in transmitting cultural beliefs, values, and heritage, and developing a culture's identity. Additionally, music is usually closely linked to our own personal histories. When we hear a particular song, it can bring us instantly back to the past, helping us remember other co-occurring events.

In early childhood settings, "music helps young children synthesize experiences, transition into new activities, calm down during naptime, share cultural traditions, and build self-esteem and a sense of community" (Shore & Strasser, 2006). Music also has academic benefits, such as boosting memory and improving spatial-perceptual development (Hetland & Winner, 2001; Sawyers & Hutson-Brandhagen, 2004). From the beginning of the early childhood education movement, Pestalozzi and Froebel advocated the study of music by young children (Fox, 2000).

For the young child, music and dance naturally occur together. Like music, dance exerts a powerful influence. "Dance embodies one of our most primal relationships to the universe. It is pre-verbal, beginning before words can be formed. It is innate in children before they possess command over language and is evoked when thoughts or emotions are too powerful for words to contain." (NDEO, 2015, p. 1).

Development of Music and Dance Skills

Children begin to experience elements of music even before birth. Did you know that the first interuterine sense to develop is hearing? By 26 weeks, fetuses will respond to sound stimulation with increased heartbeats (Federico, 2002). When infants are born, they will show preferences for not only their parents' voices but also songs that they heard in the final trimester of pregnancy (DeCasper & Spence, 1986; Shore & Strasser, 2006; Van de Carr & Lehrer, 1986). They will also respond differently to quiet and lively music (Koster, 2015). Beginning in infancy, caregivers around the world sing to children. These lullabies contain common characteristics, including simple melodies, a higher pitch, and a slower, more exaggerated rhythm than other songs. The rationale for singing to infants is supported by research. Children are more attentive to mothers when they are singing versus speaking (Trehub, 2001). Studies indicate that premature infants who listen to vocal music have less stress reactions, maintain more of their birth weight, and have shorter hospital stays than those babies who do not listen to music (Caine, 1991).

Infants have innate musical behaviors, including using music as a form of communication (Fox, 2000). They spontaneously create music, cooing, singing, and banging items to create rhythm. By seven months, infants can sing by matching or harmonizing to pitch 50% of the time. By 2½ years old, 75% of children sing spontaneous songs and 83% sing standard songs (Ries, 1982). By the age of six, most children can sing in an accurate key and are able to use an increased singing range. This range continues to expand during elementary school. The majority of studies show that boys and girls sing equally well (Flohr, 2004).

Children also develop in the area of keeping rhythm. At five months, infants will move to music and adjust their movement based on the tempo (Zentner & Eerola, 2010). By the age of three, 93% of children can keep a beat. However, this varies with the task. While 87% can clap hands to a beat and 67% can play an instrument to a beat, only 33% can march and clap to a beat. Fewer than half of four-year-olds can march and clap to a beat. Four-year-olds, however, can determine when rhythm beats are the same or different, while three-year-olds are not able to do this. By the time children are five years old, they can step and clap accurately to a beat and almost all of the children can also step and play an instrument to a beat (Frega, 1979). Four- and five-year-old children can improvise both simple and complex drum rhythms while keeping a steady beat (Whitcomb, 2010). The ability to keep rhythm also assists children with dance.

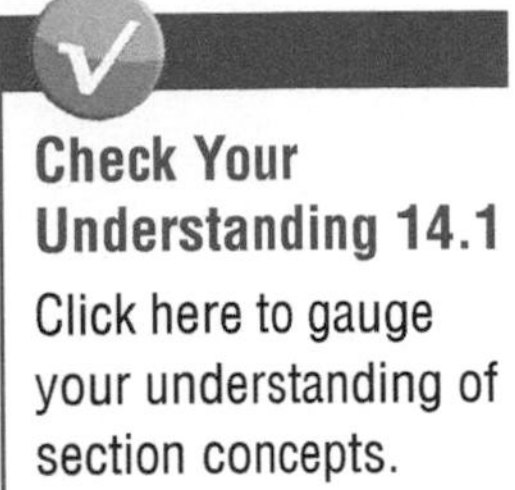

As children proceed through the early childhood years, they rapidly develop and refine the gross motor skills needed for dance. They move from sensorimotor movement to creating representational dance as a way to express their feelings and thoughts (The College Board, 2012, p. 14). Preschool and early elementary children continue to develop skills in balance, range of motion, strength, and coordination, all of which are enhanced through dance.

As children develop musical and dance skills, they also enhance many other areas of development. We will explore these next.

How the Music and Dance Center Enhances Children's Development

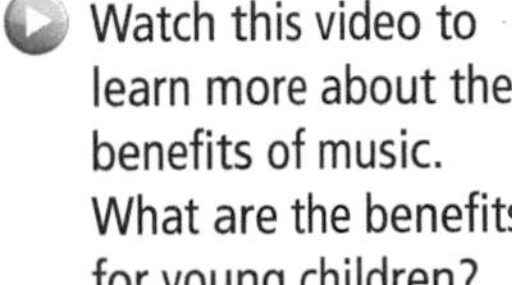

https://www.youtube.com/watch?v=ivxzHvk9M1w

Children develop musical and movement skills and appreciation as they interact in the music and dance center. While participating in these activities, children are also enhancing physical, language, social-emotional, and cognitive development. In today's world of high-stakes tests, many are using the arts' enhancement of cognitive development as a rationale for including music, dance, and visual arts in the curriculum. However, as stated by Hetland and Winner (2001), "The arts are a fundamentally important part of culture, and an education without them is an impoverished education leading to an impoverished society. Studying the arts should not have to be justified in terms of anything else. The arts are as important as the sciences: they are time-honored ways of learning, knowing, and expressing" (p. 5).

Music Skills and Appreciation

Even without adult intervention, children are natural, instinctive music makers. However, when we expose children to music through singing and playing instruments, they become more proficient and develop musical skills earlier (Kelley & Sutton-Smith, 1987).

When young children listen repeatedly to a style of music, they learn to prefer that music and these preferences become lifelong (Flohr, 2004; Peery & Peery, 1986). It is important, therefore, to expose children to music that broadens their repertoire. Learning to appreciate music from another culture or time period can open the door to further interest and learning.

Dance Skills and Appreciation

Children naturally move. However, this movement becomes dance when it "becomes structured and is performed with awareness" (NDEO, 2015, p. 1). With assistance from a teacher, children are exposed to elements of dance including space, time, and energy. They learn locomotor and non-locomotor ways to move their bodies. Since all cultures engage in some form of dance, dance is also an avenue to learn about their own and others' cultures (NDEO, 2015).

Cognitive Development

While the relationship between dance and cognitive development is just beginning to be explored (NDEO, 2015), many studies have found a correlation between music abilities and IQ, academic achievement, and academic performance (Shore & Strasser, 2006; Winner & Vincent-Lancrin, 2013). Music can aid in all areas of the child's development. A study of 106 preschool children found that those exposed to a systematic and integrated music program significantly increased their motor, cognitive, language, and social-emotional scores as assessed by the Preschool Evaluation Scale (McCarney, 1992). A recent study also found that children participating in music programs have better self-regulation. For example, they used effective techniques such as humming, singing, and private speech to regulate behavior (Winsler, Ducenne, & Koury, 2011).

Singing relevant songs can help children to learn science, math, and language concepts (Miche, 2002). History and geography can also be enhanced by examining the music of the time period or geographic area. Music can also assist with memorization. When items to be memorized are set to music, children remember them more readily (Sawyers & Hutson-Brandhagen, 2004).

Music is organized mathematically (Sawyers & Hutson-Brandhagen, 2004, p. 46). As children move to a beat or read music, they use one-to-one correspondence skills. As they recall a series of sounds or actions, such as when they sing the song "Head, Shoulders, Knees, and Toes," they gain seriation skills.

There is also a strong relationship between music and **spatial-temporal intelligence** (the ability to visualize and mentally manipulate spatial patterns). A review of 19 studies found this relationship was even stronger if children also learned music notation (Hetland & Winner, 2001). Other studies support these findings. When researchers assigned preschool children to computer lessons, piano lessons, singing lessons, or no lessons, those who received piano lessons showed a 34% increase in spatial-temporal intelligence while there was no change in children in the other groups (Shaw, 2003). Researchers found similar results in elementary-aged children (Schellenberg, 2004).

Although there were reports that children who listen to classical music at an early age show greater learning potential (sometimes referred to as the Mozart effect), this claim has been refuted (Shonkoff, Phillips & National Research Council (U.S.), 2000). Currently, there is no evidence to support a link between listening to music as an infant and brain size or school success (Hetland & Winner, 2001). However, one thing that we might learn from the study of music's effect on adults is that brain development appears to be related to active engagement with music (making music) rather than just passive listening to music (Fox, 2000).

Motor Development and Rhythm

As children create music, they improve fine and gross motor skills, coordination, and rhythm. Music also entices one to move and dance. Participating in movement or dance activities while listening to music enhances children's ability to sequence sound, recognize and respond to rhythm patterns, and discriminate melodies (Ferguson, 2005). As children dance to music, they increase coordination, flexibility, and motor skills. They develop body awareness and self-confidence.

When Curious Minds provided dance props in the music area, the children became more interested in using the center. They would often dance in front of the three full-length mirrors while rhythmically moving streamers or scarves. The children responded differently to sound and silence, fast and slow music, and different musical styles. The teachers at Curious Minds enhanced children's movement repertoire by describing what children were doing, making suggestions, and modeling movement.

Language Development

Like art, music and dance are forms of communication conveying mood, ideas, and concepts (Ohman-Rodriguez, 2005). As children listen to music, they hear differences in sounds, assisting them not only with music making, but also with speech (Miche, 2002). Music can also help children develop fluency (smoothness of speech), pronunciation, enunciation (speaking clearly), and vocabulary (Aquino, 1991). For example, children who are involved in music activities such as reproducing sound sequences, melody discrimination, and singing combined with motor activities and visual stimuli display a significant increase in vocabulary (Moyeda, Gomez, & Flores, 2006) and listening comprehension (Jordan-DeCarbo & Galliford, 2011). Another recent study of toddlers found that informal music play is linked to auditory discrimination and attention (Putkinen, Tervaniemi, & Huotilainen, 2013).

Social Development

Music and dance link children to their cultural heritage, assisting them to acquire cultural beliefs and values. Listening to music or watching different types of dances also exposes children to other times and cultures and provides the opportunity to gain appreciation for them. In addition, both music and dance promote social unity. For example, as children create music, they engage in a metaphorical experience, where different instruments combine to make a unique sound that no individual instrument could produce alone. Through this process, children learn that to make beautiful music, you must have unity and work together.

Emotional Development

From the time of Plato and Aristotle, music has also been viewed as therapeutic. Today more than 70 universities offer degrees in music therapy (Greata, 2006). Music helps to create and manipulate moods. It "has the ability to relax, give pleasure, irritate and deafen us, stimulate, excite, make us feel happier or sadder" (Federico, 2002, p. 534). With these mood changes also come physiological changes to our heartbeats, blood pressure, and breathing (Federico, 2002).

Dance improves self-confidence and provides an avenue for self-expression that is also considered therapeutic. For example, for over 50 years dance/movement therapy has explored the connection between the mind and body. Dancing can also improve children's social and emotional skills. A study of Head Start children found that those that were involved in a dance program had greater social competence and fewer behavioral issues (Lobo & Winsler, 2006).

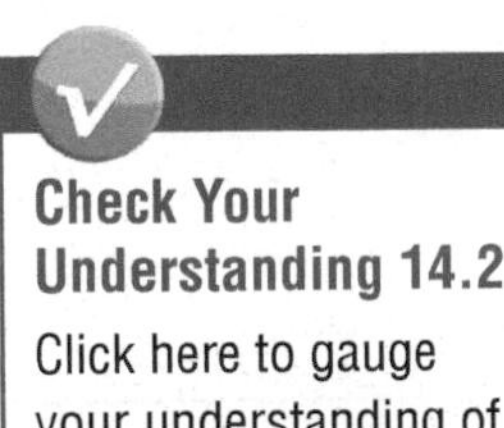
Check Your Understanding 14.2
Click here to gauge your understanding of section concepts.

As we have learned, through music children not only gain music skills and appreciation, but also enhance cognitive, motor and rhythm, language, social, and emotional development. While children and adults naturally engage in music, a well-planned center can enhance their development. What does a well-planned music center include?

Designing the Music and Dance Center

Indoor Music and Dance Center

The National Council of Music Teachers (NCMT) standards stress that "every pre-kindergarten and kindergarten needs to have a music center where children can access music materials and listen to music" (Music Educators National Conference, 1994). An effective music and dance center contains the following:

- An uncluttered area with ample space for dancing.
- Located away from quiet areas. Teachers should also attempt to reduce and absorb sound. This includes having earphones available for individually listening to music and providing sound-absorbing materials on the walls and ceilings of the music area.
- Mirrors so children can watch themselves dance.
- A variety of high-quality instruments (e.g., drums, rhythm sticks, finger cymbals, triangles, cymbals, gongs, jingle bells, resonator bells, step bells, xylophone-type instruments with removable bars, chorded zithers, fretted instruments, electronic keyboard instruments, and assorted instruments representing a variety of cultures; MENC, 1994). It is important that instruments are durable and that they have a high-quality sound.
- Dancing props such as streamers, lengths of fabric, and dress-up clothes.
- Instruments and dance props displayed so that children have easy access to them. They might be on labeled shelves, hung on hooks on the wall or on the back of a divider, or grouped in labeled baskets.
- Sound equipment (toddlers, preschool, elementary) and video equipment (preschool and elementary) that children can operate themselves (a CD player that has a green dot for start and a red dot for stop).
- A variety of exemplary music to use in listening and playing instruments, and for dancing and moving:
  - music from a variety of genres, cultures, and historical time periods.
  - high-quality, award-winning music. American Library Association's Notable Recordings, Parents' Choice Seal of Approval Audio Awards, National Parenting Publications Awards (NAPPA) program, and Grammy Awards for best musical albums for children all have lists of quality music. The Children's Music Web Awards (voted on by children) is another source for finding quality music.
- Books, posters, and other written and visual material relating to music and dance, including multicultural books.
- Written music, including music books, children's storybooks with music notation, and written music that

Julie Bullard

A preschool music and dance center.

children can play. For preschool and elementary-aged children, written music should be available with any pitched instrument (e.g., keyboard or xylophone).

- Materials such as paper, staff paper, note stickers, markers, and pencils so that children can write their own music and dance movements (preschool and early elementary).
- Computers and software for seeing dances, listening to music, creating and performing music and dance, playing musical games, and recording music. One way that you can do this is to create QR codes, children can use the codes with tablets to access music, games, and videos.
- Full development of each item in the center. For example, if including cultural instruments, label the instrument so that adults and children in the classroom can learn the name of the instrument. A recording or short video of a musician playing the instrument is also helpful.

Outdoor Music and Dance Center

The outdoors provides a unique musical and movement environment where there is less concern about noise, a larger space to move freely, and natural sounds. There are many ways to incorporate outdoor music. You can create a sound path, a music hut, a sound garden, or a soundscape with music interspersed throughout the playground. Rusty Keeler (2002), a playground designer, suggests hiding sound elements like wind chimes and different kinds of bells in trees, bushes, and flower and herb beds for the creation of ambient sounds. Children can also be encouraged to listen to natural sounds, like the sound of water in a fountain, birds in a tree, or wind rustling leaves. To assist with capturing sounds outside the fence, you can mount listening or traffic cones on the fence. Children can also experiment with sound through talk tubes that they can use to throw their voices. These tubes are designed in a U shape and can be buried on the playground or installed overhead.

Dance props and indoor instruments (such as marimbas, rain sticks, and sound blocks) can also be used outside. For example, preschool teachers at Evergreen College created plastic circles by cutting away the inside circle of a margarine lid. They tied long colorful strips of plastic to the rings making a durable dance prop for outdoors. It is ideal if locked storage is available so that you can leave a collection of instruments and dance props in the play yard.

Julie Bullard

This outdoor music center provides children many musical opportunities.

The play yard can also contain permanently installed instruments such as a giant "thunder drum" made from steel or plastic barrels. You can create mallets by attaching softballs to each end of a dowel. To keep the mallets from being lost, attach them permanently to the drum. Jumbo chimes from metal pipes, a giant wooden xylophone, triangles, and sound pipes hung in trees are also good playground choices. At Curious Minds, a college student created a hanging xylophone from different sizes of wrenches. In Long Island, a program created a sound garden containing a music marimba, xylophone, metallophone, thunder wall, musical turtle, and arches with bamboo chimes and temple bells. When children climb a hill they can even find temple blocks (Schwartz,

2007). At Early Head Start, teachers created a music environment by hanging pots, pans, lids, and muffin tins along with strikers on the fence.

When establishing your outdoor environment, seriously consider a music and dance center. As demonstrated by the examples, there are many creative outdoor possibilities. Outdoor music and dance provides the same rich advantages as indoor music and dance in an environment with fewer constraints.

As you design the indoor or outdoor music and dance center, it is also important to consider music and dance standards and what materials and activities can be added to the center to address these standards. We will discuss this next.

Check Your Understanding 14.3
Click here to gauge your understanding of section concepts.

Appropriate Materials and Activities to Meet Music and Dance Standards

The National Coalition for Core Art Standards includes four overarching artistic processes— (see the anchor standards table in Chapter 13) for all the art disciplines and for all students, regardless of age. These are:

- Creating
- Performing
- Responding
- Connecting

While the music standards address creating, performing, and responding separately, connecting is embedded in the first three. The dance standards address each of the artistic processes separately, but stress that in practice all are often integrated into a lesson.

A well-rounded early childhood music and dance program emphasizes each of these processes and the content standards. Effective teachers ensure that the center includes developmentally appropriate materials to help children develop competencies related to these standards.

Antonio, a teacher of four- and five-year-old children, begins his circle each day by drumming a rhythm on the large gathering drum. As children join the circle, they also begin to play the rhythm.

Antonio noticed that several of the children were beginning to pound rhythms on other materials (tabletops, blocks, and snack dishes). Expanding upon their interest, he introduced several different types of drums, and added the drums and an iPod with drumming music to the music center. He also invited an American Indian drummer to spend the afternoon in the music center drumming with the children. Antonio initially sparked the children's interest in drumming by beginning circle time each day with a musical rhythm. However, when he observed the children's interest, he expanded upon it by adding new materials and resources.

Materials and Activities to Enhance Children's Ability to Create

The anchor standards for creating are:

- Generate and conceptualize artistic ideas and work.
- Organize and develop artistic ideas and work.
- Refine and complete artistic work (National Coalition for Core Arts Standards, 2014).

Ohman-Rodriguez (2005) states that composing music allows children to be "music insiders." Like other written symbols, it is important for children to have opportunities to

play with and use music symbols even if they are not connected to the sound the symbol represents (Ohman-Rodriguez, 2005). Children first learn to improvise music and then to write music. In dance, children also improvise before engaging in more formalized dance.

Amanda P. Smith (2011) enhanced four- and four-year-old children's ability to create music by first giving the children an experience and then a poem that represented that experience. Then she asked the children to provide ideas on how to sing the poem. She next created notes using the children's musical phrases. For example, she provided a shadow screen and flashlights. The children began to play that they were lightning bugs. She later provided the poem "Fireflies" and the children created a melody that she transcribed into musical notes. She also encouraged the children to create a melody to go with the poem on a barred instrument.

Following are materials that teachers can add to the music center to assist children in creating music and dance:

- Cards with a picture of a different body part on each card (hands, elbows, knees, and feet). Children then draw a card and create body music using the body part shown on the card.
- Examples of printed music such as songbooks. Charts of printed music hung on the wall can also provide examples. It is especially effective if the teacher introduces and uses the chart during a group activity, following the song and the notes with her finger as the children sing it.
- CD players and paper and pencils so that children can record their own songs. Campbell (1991) studied children ages five to seven and found that their own songs were rhythmically more complex than children's songs in the Caucasian, Native American, Hispanic, or most world cultures.
- Digital cameras, tablets, or video players that children can use to record each other as they dance.
- Different types of music that children can dance to.
- A variety of instruments that children can use for improvising and a CD player. This allows children to record themselves and listen to the music they have created.
- Paper and markers for children to make a visual image of their dance movements.
- Staff paper and note stickers or stamps so children can create their own music. After improvising music, children begin to write musical notation. To maximize learning, children need to hear the music they have composed soon after it is created. The teacher can play the music for the child. Another alternative is for the children to use a computer program to create music. For example, the creating music website by Morton Subotnik features a free program that allows children to choose an instrument that will play the music that they have created.

Materials and Activities to Enhance Children's Ability to Perform Music and Dance

The anchor standards for performing are:

- Select, analyze, and interpret artistic work for presentation.
- Develop and refine artistic techniques and work for presentation.
- Convey meaning through the presentation of artistic work (National Coalition for Core Arts Standards, 2014).

Singing. By the end of the preschool years, children should be able to play simple melodies on a variety of different instruments and sing many different types of songs. As children move through the preschool years they should sing in a more accurate pitch and rhythm (MENC, 1994). Songs using both actual words and nonsensical words (boo, bow, bah) can be included in the music center. When you choose songs, keep children's interests and voice ranges in mind (D4–A4). Short repetitive verses, descending intervals, and skipping patterns are popular with young children (Flohr, 2004, p. 94). If you are singing with children, keep your voice "high and light" to avoid damage to children's vocal cords (Shore & Strasser, 2006, p. 65). To promote singing in the music center, the early childhood teacher can do the following:

Julie Bullard

This stage and karaoke machine encourage children to sing. Dress-up clothes, chairs for an audience, and curtains all add to the allure.

- Provide earphones so that children can hear themselves singing. Teachers can create these by connecting two PVC joints to create a semicircular shape. The child holds one end at his mouth and the other at his ear.
- Develop props that children can manipulate as they sing a song. For example, you might provide a plastic spider to use as children sing "Eensey, Weensy Spider."
- Provide echo toys that children can sing to and easily play back.
- Construct a stage with a microphone (the microphone does not need to work).
- Supply picture books containing songs and music.
- Provide purchased sing-along recordings.
- Create your own tape for the music center by recording the class singing familiar songs.

Playing Instruments. Music centers are ideal for letting children independently experiment with a variety of instruments. Through playing musical instruments, children learn about **pitch** (how high or low), **timbre** (quality of the sound such as the difference between a clarinet and saxophone), and **texture** (how instruments interact with each other) (Carlton, 2006). To assist children to move beyond experimentation, provide recordings they can use as accompaniment and simple written music to play. Listed here are materials and ideas that can be added to the music center to help children learn about instruments.

- Provide a variety of high-quality instruments. The National Association for Music Education (1994) recommends that "drums, rhythm sticks, finger cymbals, triangles, cymbals, gongs, jingle bells, resonator bells, step bells, xylophone-type instruments with removable bars, chorded zithers, fretted instruments, electronic keyboard instruments, and assorted instruments representing a variety of cultures" be available for young children (National Association for Music Education, 1994, p. 3).
- Provide two sets of instruments with a screen between them. One child plays an instrument. The child on the other side of the screen tries to find the same instrument to play.
- Provide two sets of some instruments. One child can play a melody and another child can try to duplicate it.

- Provide music that children can play. Children can learn to play simple melodies on many different types of instruments if keys are color or number coded and the written musical notes are also color or number coded.
- Provide a recording of different beats for children to use when playing instruments.
- Make a recording of short rhythms. Include a pause after each rhythm so that children can create the same rhythm with their instrument.
- Encourage children to create their own instruments. It is important that the instruments are durable and easy to play if you want children to be able to successfully use them after they are created (see the "Create Your Own Rainstick" box and also Figure 14.1 for examples).
- Develop musical instruments out of household items. For example, you can add different levels of water to glasses or jars creating a homemade xylophone. Washboards, pots, pans, and wooden spoons can also be used as musical instruments.
- Provide instruments from different cultures. Authentic instruments can help children to learn about the cultures of others. Some cultural instruments that are appropriate for young children include marimbas, shaker eggs, tom-tom drums,

Create Your Own Rainstick

The rainstick is an example of a durable instrument that can enhance the music area. Authentic rainsticks are typically made from a dried cactus, which has the spines removed and nailed into the cactus. The rainstick makes a gentle sound and is played by shaking or tipping the stick.

Julie Bullard

Directions

1. Create the rainstick from a cardboard mailing tube.
2. Buy nails with large heads that are shorter than the inside diameter of the tube.
3. Pound nails into the tube, following a spiral pattern. On many tubes, this pattern is obvious on the outside of the tube.
4. Place a lid on one end of the tube and place sound making items into the tube, such as small pebbles, popcorn kernels, or recycled beads.
5. Place the lid on the top of the rainstick.
6. Decorate your rainstick. You can cover it with child- or adult-decorated paper, with contact paper, or you can add glue and roll the rainstick in sand.

Variations

Depending upon the age of the child, they can create all or part of the rainstick. They can also experiment with a variety of items to create different tones.

FIGURE 14.1
Durable, Easy-to-Play Instruments That Children Can Create

- ❑ Shakers—provide film canisters and a variety of found items (sand, pebbles, small sticks, seedpods) that could be used to create shakers. Larger shakers can be created using lengths of PVC pipes and PVC pipe caps.
- ❑ Drums can be created by removing the top and bottom of a metal coffee can. The plastic lid can be used for a drumhead. Or for better sound, cut a circle one inch larger than the circumference of the can out of an inner tube, a heavy plastic bag, rawhide, or a heavy balloon (only for older children). Attach the circle to the drum by securing the top to the coffee can side with heavy tape. You can also make a top and a bottom, punch holes around each, and lace them onto the can.
- ❑ Rain sticks can be created by pounding nails into postage mailing tubes. The nails should be nailed in a spiraling pattern around the tube. When this is completed, experiment with adding different small items that will trickle through the nails. For example, different sizes of pebbles will create different sounds.
- ❑ Gourd rattles can be created by cutting off the end of a gourd, scooping out the inside, and letting the gourd dry in the sun. After it has dried, the children can return the seeds to the gourd or add other small items and glue the lid back on. The gourd can be decorated with string and small beads, which will add more sound.
- ❑ Children can string bells on elastic and tie them to make bracelets for their wrists and ankles.
- ❑ Children can also use found materials to create their own unique instruments.

African tongue slit drums, afuche casaba (Lang, 1999), gourd shakers, tambourines, maracas, and rainsticks. Pictures of musicians playing the instruments along with short instrumentals can often be found on the Internet.

Watch a group of young children engaged in a rhythm activity. Which techniques make this an effective activity?

https://www.youtube.com/watch?v=58p6QtMYN1M

Maria, a teacher of first-grade children, labels each instrument with a picture of a musician playing the instrument on one side of a card and an outline of the country where the instrument is played on the other side. She adds a globe and a map so that children can locate the countries where the instruments come from. She also includes recordings of the different instruments being played and a computer game where children match the instrument to the recorded music.

- Hang a variety of bells from a frame (cowbells, jingle bells, or a hand bell) so that children can experiment with the different sounds.

Dancing. The music and dance center allows children to experiment with a variety of types of dance movements. To encourage dancing provide:

- Music with different types of beats.
- Videos of dancers.
- A bright light (overhead projector or a halogen flood light) so that children can shadow dance to the music (Stamp, 1992).
- Props such as streamers, costumes, and a large doll to use as a dance partner.
- A place to perform such as a small stage, or a few chairs for an audience.

Julie Bullard

The tape player with tapes and CD player with a CD allow children to play the rhythm instruments to the beat of the music. Notice the center has instruments from many different cultures.

Materials and Activities to Enhance Children's Ability to Respond to Music

The anchor standards for responding are:

- Perceive and analyze artistic work.
- Interpret intent and meaning in artistic work.
- Apply criteria to evaluate artistic work (National Coalition for Core Arts Standards, 2014).

As we've discussed, children naturally respond to movement and music from birth. However, for optimal development of skills, children need the opportunity to actively engage with the music, attending to the sounds and the changes in the sounds (Fox, 2000). Given next are several materials for encouraging this engagement in the music and dance center:

- Tape recordings of different classroom and outdoor sounds such as a car starting, vacuum cleaner running, and bird singing. Add picture cards of each of the sounds so that children can display the correct card when they hear the sound.
- A podium, a conductor's baton, and a music stand so that children can be conductors.
- Cards with pictures of a ball bouncing, hands clapping, feet tapping, and so forth. Children draw a card and demonstrate the beat of the music using the method shown on the card.
- A dancing scarf doll. Create the doll by putting batting and a square of fabric on a wooden spoon to form the doll's head. Tie the head with ribbon. The children can move the doll to the beat of the music (Kenney, 2004).
- Flannel-board pieces and songs that tell a story, such as *The Old Woman Who Swallowed a Fly*. Older children may be able to use story props for less obvious music (*Peter and the Wolf*).
- Providing props (masks, scarves, hats) so that children can choose the prop that fits the music and dance the way the music makes them feel.
- Providing music that tells a story and encouraging children to act it out.
- Paper and markers for drawing the beat of the music. Although many early childhood teachers have children draw to music, Flohr (2004) stresses that this typically does not constitute a music listening experience, since the music is often part of the background. To make it a musical listening experience, the music must be the primary activity.
- Instrumental music. Have pictures of each of the instruments being played. As children hear the instrument, they show the card (Flohr, 2004). One study in a preschool classroom found that children spent as much time in a listening center containing classical music as they did in any other center in the classroom, prompting the authors of the study to remind us that children as well as adults like to listen to music (Sims, Cecconi-Roberts, & Keast, 2011).
- Sound-matching games using film canister shakers containing different items.
- A CD with different pitches. Have a pause after each pitch so that children can try to imitate it.
- A variety of instruments with a few notes marked on each instrument so that children can listen to the same note on each of the different instruments.
- CD or iPad with different recorded rhythms. Children can have a card that they turn over to indicate if the two rhythms are the same or different. After a pause, the tape can give the answer.
- Videos of dancers for children to watch and critique.

Materials and Activities to Enhance Children's Ability to Connect

The anchor standards for connecting are:

- Synthesize and relate knowledge and personal experiences to make art.
- Relate artistic ideas and works with societal, cultural, and historical contexts to deepen understanding (National Coalition for Core Arts Standards, 2014).

This includes connecting dance and music and other arts and disciplines. Displaying personal preferences and meaning is another way that children connect with music and dance. One way we can assist this is to provide a rich variety of dance and music, allowing children to experience the social, cultural, and historical contexts.

TIP

Be cautious about playing music as children are engaged in center time activities. Carefully chosen, quiet music may at times assist in creating a calm environment. However, often music is just background noise, increasing the overall noise level in the classroom as children talk above it. The music might also act as a distracter, not allowing children to focus on the music or the activity they are engaged in. Or, the child might become trained to tune all music out and not learn the compositional aspects of music.

Music and Dance Materials and Activities for Infants and Toddlers

Infants and toddlers are natural movers and music makers and appear to understand the difference in music from their own culture and other cultures at a very young age. For example, research has found that infants prefer music that has a musical meter similar to their own (Soley & Hannon, 2010). As with preschool-aged and early-elementary-aged children, we can enhance this natural love of music and dance. Teachers at Children's Place do this by providing a variety of instruments, such as a lap harp, bongo drum, guitar, auto harp, basket of shaker eggs, and tambourines. They model how instruments are cared for and demonstrate ways the instruments might be played. The shaker eggs, lap harp, tambourines, and drums are left on a low shelf for children to explore. The guitar and autoharp are hung on the wall to be used with more adult supervision. Children point to them when they want to play. The center also has several musical toys that play songs when buttons are pushed. The children will play a song and dance to the music.

Julie Bullard

This music center provides toddlers a variety of choices.

Natasha, a teacher of infants, provides a basket of exploration items that make noise when banged. For example, she includes a basket of

Check Your Understanding 14.4
Click here to gauge your understanding of section concepts.

household items such as pots, pans, and metal and wooden spoons. She plays a variety of music for the children to listen to and dance to.

Tania has created a musical center for children who are just beginning to crawl. She found a play mat that makes sound when you crawl on the pad. She also has hung a bell at the top of the ramp to the climbing structure, so that when children crawl to the top they can ring the bell.

Each of these teachers has found ways to introduce active musical exploration in their settings. What are other ways that teachers help children to be successful in the music center?

Teachers' Facilitation of Learning in the Music Center

Provide Musical and Dance Experiences

The early childhood years are perfect for introducing children to a wide range of musicians, dancers, and musical and movement experiences. If possible, have the musician or dancer interact in the center with children coming and going as they wish. This allows children to interact with the musician or dancer individually and in small groups, according to their interests. To provide children with opportunities to see musicians or dancers that are not available in your community, you might provide short videos.

Thomas, a teacher of second graders, had visited Australia and returned with a didgeridoo. He brought the instrument into his classroom and introduced it by playing a short video of an Aborigine man playing the **didgeridoo**. *He also showed a video of people dancing to didgeridoo music. Thomas left the didgeridoo in the music center for several days, allowing children to experiment with creating sound using the instrument. The children also looked up information about the didgeridoo on the Internet and learned the instrument's history.*

There are many other options for exposing children to music and dance. Amanda brings her preschool children to a music store where they get to examine instruments and hear different selections of music. Samantha, a teacher of kindergarten children, takes her children to visit the high school band room where students describe and play instruments for the children. Curious Minds, a program for preschool children, brings children to short musicals where they see performers sing and dance.

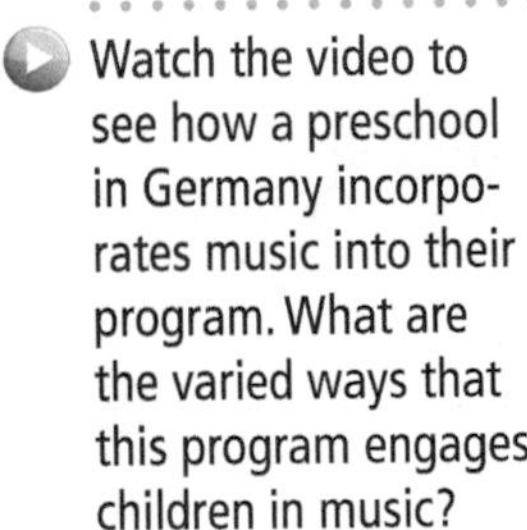

Watch the video to see how a preschool in Germany incorporates music into their program. What are the varied ways that this program engages children in music?

https://www.youtube.com/watch?v=0gdNMeFuzKQ

Include Music and Movement Throughout the Day

There are many opportunities throughout the day to incorporate music and movement. Natalie, a teacher of preschool children, sings a special song for many classroom transitions. For example, she has a special song for cleaning up, beginning lunch, and going outside. She has special calming music that she plays at the beginning of rest time. Each day, Natalie also emphasizes music and dance at the morning group time. During this time, children might play instruments, sing songs, or dance to music. If you struggle with planning music and dance activities, you might consider purchasing a curriculum such as *Music Together* or a book such as *Dance, Turn, Hop, and Learn* by Connie Bergstein Dow for dance activities.

Use Music and Dance to Help Children to Develop Skills in Other Curricular Areas

As we learned at the beginning of the chapter, music and dance can enhance skills in many other curricular areas. For example, teachers might:

- Choose songs or movements that reinforce concepts that children are working on (learning colors, body parts, the alphabet, numbers, and each other's names).
- Set items children are trying to memorize to music (addresses).

- Write songs you are learning on a flip chart so that children can increase their knowledge of the written word.
- Tell children about the history of a song or a dance, increasing their historical and cultural knowledge.
- Reinforce math concepts and terminology as children are reading music or clapping to a beat.

Introduce New Materials and Activities

For children to take full advantage of materials available in the music and dance center, you will need to introduce the materials and activities to them. For example, you will want to demonstrate how to use and care for instruments. You can introduce children to instruments and activities individually, in small groups, or at a group time. For example, during group time you can introduce a musical activity where children stand high for high notes and crouch low for low notes while singing the "Grand Old Duke of York." Then you can place the music in the music center with a picture of children standing high and crouching low to remind children of how to complete the activity. During a group time activity, you might introduce children to the idea of drawing a symbol or picture to portray a dance movement (this is one of the early childhood dance standards). You might then post dance symbols that the children can follow as they dance in the center.

Model Enjoyment of Music and Dance Yourself

Adults are powerful models. In one study, children using a music center during free play copied two-thirds of the teacher's modeled movements (Metz, 1989). Since children pick up their cues from adults, it is important to model enjoyment of a variety of types of music and dance.

Interact with Children to Deepen Their Knowledge

Your involvement can assist children in developing more advanced skills in music and dance. For example, you might demonstrate how to play an instrument or show children a new type of movement. You might also encourage children to take the next developmental step. For example, a child who has been improvising songs on a musical instrument may be ready to try to follow a pattern card or musical notes. Or, the child might be ready to write the notes down for others.

You might also present musical and dance challenges. For example, you might ask, "What would happen if you played the drum with just your hands? Does it sound different than when played with a drumstick?" or "What are all the different ways you can move to the music?"

Discuss Music and Model Musical Vocabulary

Children learn musical terms that are used by the adults in their environment. Following is a list of ways of increasing children's musical knowledge and vocabulary:

- Discuss the tempo, pitch, tonal quality, and rhythm of the music.
- Name musical terms (whole note, half note, quarter note, sharp, and treble clef) (Ohman-Rodriguez, 2005).
- Miche (2002) recommends that we teach preschool children the following words for dynamic levels: **piano** (soft), **mezzo** (medium), and **forte** (loud). Elementary students can learn **pianissimo** (very softly), piano, mezzo piano, mezzo forte, forte, and **fortissimo** (extremely loud) (Miche, 2002, p. 64).

- Discuss the size of the group that is playing (duet, orchestra, or band).
- Name the type of music being played (such as call and response, jazz, blues, western, or classical).
- Identify the instruments.

Discuss Dance and Model Dance Vocabulary

Dance also has its own unique vocabulary. For example you can expose children to terminology for ways of moving (swing, shake, tip, jump, hop, slide, do-si-do), pathways through space (curved, straight, zig-zag, random), dance elements (body, action, space, time, energy), dance phase (beginning, middle, end), names of body parts, or opposite qualities (smooth/jerky). You can also teach children about personal and community space.

Acknowledge Learners

Recognize children's musical and movement abilities by describing what they are doing, asking for information, discussing the aesthetic elements of their music or movements, or pointing out their progress and effort (Imiolo-Schriver, 1995). Another way to acknowledge learners is to make a video or audio recording of them playing an instrument, singing, or dancing. This allows children to revisit their work and share it with friends and family. However, be cautious about musical or dance performances. The standards emphasize the art-making process versus performances (NCAS, 2014).

Manage Special Challenges in the Music and Dance Center

There are two challenges that sometimes prevent teachers from developing a music center. These are a lack of instruments and the noise created by the center.

Lack of Instruments. You will need durable, quality-sounding instruments for your music center. If you cannot afford to buy instruments, there are many quality instruments that you or volunteers can make. Following are a few examples:

- Drums can be created with five-gallon buckets or metal barrels. There are many directions on the Internet for creating drums. For example, search for "Tips for Early Childhood Music: Building Music Centers" from the Texas School Music Project for directions and a video for making drums.
- Rhythm sticks can easily be created with dowels that are cut and rounded off at the ends.
- A xylophone can be created by cutting PVC pipe or 1/2" aluminium conduit pipe into different lengths and tying them onto a wooden frame or placing them on two strips of foam rubber. It is best if a little less than a third of the pipe extends off the frame. Xylophone pipes should be cut to the following lengths: 11", 10¼", 9¾", 9½", 8⅞", 8½", 7⅞", and 7⅝".

Julie Bullard

Sometimes common household items can become musical instruments. These pots and pans provide an inexpensive outdoor music area.

- Many instruments around the world are created from gourds, including water drums, temple gongs, stamping tubes, shakers, rattles, rain sticks, xylophones, drums, and lutes. For detailed directions on making all of the above instruments, see *Making Gourd Musical Instruments: Over 60 String, Wind, and Percussion Instruments and How to Play Them* (Summit & Widess, 1999).
- Tambourines may be made by tying flattened bottle caps with a hole in the center to the inside ring of an embroidery hoop and then fitting the rings together.

Watch the video to learn more about making an instrument from a gourd. How could the children be involved in creating the shekere?

https://www.youtube.com/watch?v=c70YJ02PBr4

Excessive Noise. As we discussed in Chapter 6, excessive noise can increase stress in children and adults and can negatively affect learning. However, following are several ways to decrease noise in the music area.

- Encourage children to explore the texture of sounds with purpose, not just make noise.
- Choose appropriate indoor instruments. For example, you might select small drums for indoors.
- Provide earphones for listening to music.
- Keyboards often come with a jack for headphones. It is important to use them as a way of reducing any unnecessary noise.
- Be consciously aware of the level of noise when children are dancing or moving to music. You might want to place a symbol on the CD player indicating where the volume dial should be set.
- Place sound-dampening materials on the floor, ceilings, and walls. For example, foam padding that is used under carpeting makes an excellent sound dampening material. You can staple the padding to the desired surface and paint it to add to the aesthetic quality.

Observe and Document Children's Musical and Dance Skills

Children in the music and dance center can be assessed on their ability to:

- Dance to music moving to different rhythms and tempos.
- Imitate movements.
- Use a variety of types of movements.
- Use dance movements to express an emotion or tell a story.
- Represent a dance movement through drawing.
- Use voices expressively.
- Sing a variety of simple songs.
- Sing in pitch.
- Play a variety of instruments.
- Keep rhythm when playing with a group or a recording.
- Play simple melodies.
- Improvise songs with their voice and instruments.
- Represent music through original or standard systems.
- Identify a variety of sounds.
- Indicate preferences in dance, music, and instruments.

Julie Bullard

This outdoor drum allows children at the Salish Kootenai College Childcare Center to practice a cultural tradition.

Meet the Needs of All Learners

Supporting Children from All Cultures. It is important to include examples of dance, music, and instruments in the classroom that represent children's cultural backgrounds.

The director at Birge Nest Early Head Start invited teachers to bring in their favorite child-friendly music to share with children. Since each of the three teachers had a different musical taste, this practice exposed children to a rich variety of music. However, one day Lisa, one of the teachers, heard Andre rapping and recognized that none of their music represented his cultural music. She realized that we must be intentional in the music we choose or we risk not including all children.

Music and dance provide the opportunity to learn about one's own culture and the culture of others. For example, children can study different instruments and songs, and the use of voice from different cultures to get a glimpse into the values and customs of the culture. Culture strongly influences how the voice is used (Flohr, 2004, p. 85). Some examples of this include Tuvan throat singing, Tibetan yodeling, and women singing in high pitches in Hindi music. Dance is also strongly influenced by culture.

Children can also learn about the people in the community in which they live. Inviting families with musical or dance skills and area dancers and musicians to visit the classroom can help children to learn about rich opportunities within their geographic area. Even elementary, middle school, and high school musicians or dancers can provide opportunities for children to experience a range of dances, songs, and instruments.

Supporting Children with Special Needs. All children need the opportunity to interact successfully in the music and dance center.

Check Your Understanding 14.5
Click here to gauge your understanding of section concepts.

Tori, a child who is blind, enjoys music and playing musical instruments. Janelle, her teacher, has found many ways to assist Tori in independently using the center. Tori is beginning to learn Braille. Therefore, Janelle labeled the CDs and location of each instrument in Braille. Janelle also created an outline of each instrument with sandpaper and placed it on the shelf. She labeled the CD player with tactile symbols. Through examining Tori's individual needs, Janelle was able to make environmental modifications so that she could be successful.

The music and dance center, based on our knowledge of standards and the children's own unique talents and interests, can provide a world of musical and movement opportunities for children. These opportunities are enhanced when a teacher shares the experience with children.

? Chapter Quiz 14
Click here to gauge your understanding of chapter concepts.

Throughout history, in all cultures, dance and music have been a natural part of children's experiences. Music and dance can enhance the quality of life, sometimes calming and other times exciting the participant. Music and dance also help to form our identity, teaching us about our culture. Through music and dance, children also learn about other cultures and enhance all areas of development.

Sample Application Activities

1. Make a homemade instrument to have for your classroom.
2. The school board in your community has just decided to cut the arts at the school. Write a short letter describing why the arts, particularly dance and music, are important.
3. Review songs that have won awards for children's music.
4. Create a three-ring binder with lyrics and music for children's songs. Make a list of the songs that would be appropriate to use during transition times and for music breaks.
5. Create a list of YouTube videos that you could use to introduce children to different types of dance.
6. Create a QR code that you could post in an early childhood music and dance center.
7. Assess a music and dance center using the environmental assessment in Figure 14.2.
8. Make a list of instruments from different cultures that you would like to have in your classroom. Develop cards for each instrument with information about the instrument on one side and a picture of a musician playing the instrument on the other side.
9. To learn more about incorporating music into the curriculum, visit these websites: Best Children's Music, the Children's Music Web, the National Association for Music Education (NAfME), or the Music Teachers National Association (MTNA) Websites for Kids.
10. To learn more about dance activities and standards, visit the National Dance Education Organization or the Kennedy Center Arts Edge.

FIGURE 14.2 Environmental Assessment: Music and Dance Center

- ❑ Is the center in an uncluttered area with enough space for dancing?
- ❑ Is the center located away from quiet areas?
- ❑ Is noise reduced through earphones and absorbent materials on floors, ceilings, and walls?
- ❑ Are there mirrors so that children can see themselves dance?
- ❑ Does the center include a variety of accessible, durable instruments that have a high-quality sound?
- ❑ Does the center contain a variety of dance props such as scarves, pieces of fabric, and clothing?
- ❑ Is there accessible, labeled storage for instruments and dance props?
- ❑ Is there sound equipment (toddlers, preschool, elementary) and video equipment (preschool and elementary) that children can operate themselves?
- ❑ Is there award-winning music from different genres, cultures, and historical time periods of music to listen to, play instruments with, and for dancing and moving?
- ❑ Are there videos of dancers from different genres, cultures, and historical time periods?
- ❑ Is there written music that children can see and play, including music for each pitched instrument?
- ❑ Does the center contain materials so that children can write their own music and dance movements (preschool and early elementary)?
- ❑ Are there computers and software for seeing dances, listening to music, creating and performing music and dance, playing musical games, and recording music?
- ❑ Are there books and other written and visual materials relating to music and dance including multicultural books?
- ❑ Does each musical activity have all the needed materials (e.g., audiotape to play rhythm instrument with, written music for keyboard)?
- ❑ Are there materials for music and dance to support all the standards?

Chapter 15

Integrating Technology

Learning Outcomes

After you have read this chapter, you will be prepared to:

- Describe how technology enhances children's development
- Discuss criteria for effectively using technology in the classroom
- Discuss multiple ways that technology can be used in the classroom to enhance the curriculum
- Explain how technology activities vary based upon children's age and development
- Describe multiple ways that teachers facilitate learning through technology

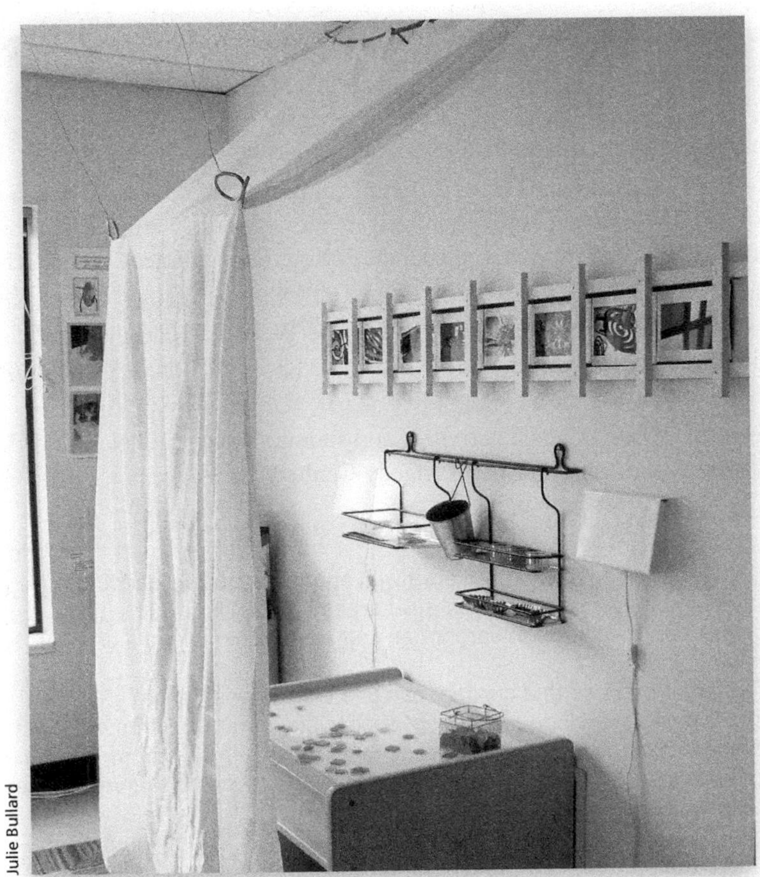
Julie Bullard

Terri, a teacher of preschoolers at Sunshine Academy, had a computer center that contained three computers. The computers were popular with the children and were always in use. However, Terri struggled with using the computers to support the curriculum. For example, although the computers were loaded with software programs for children to use in creating books, the children usually played games instead. Terri had loaded some streamed videos to support her farm animal unit. However, few children had watched them.

Terri decided to experiment with moving the computers to different areas of the classroom. She loaded programs onto the computer that would support the curriculum area where the computer was located and removed any unrelated programs. In the music area she loaded short videos of people playing instruments, a game where children matched sounds to the correct musical instrument, music that children could sing along with, and a program where children could write their own music and hear it played back. In the literacy center, she added Kid Pix (allowing children to write or dictate their story) and a drawing program (so they could add illustrations). They could also listen and follow along with computerized children's books. The computer in the science and math center included short videos on farm animals and webcams of different farm animals found at Farm Animals Webcams on Live Animals TV. The Building Blocks math program was also available.

After making these changes, the children used the computers for a variety of purposes rather than just to play games. Terri felt the computers supported her curriculum and increased children's learning. She stated, "I now think of the computer as a tool that when used appropriately can enhance learning." She plans to change the computers to different areas as needed. For example, she is thinking about adding a variety of hats from different cultures to the dramatic play area. She thinks that the children's play and learning may be supported by streamed videos of the different cultures that are represented by the hats.

Today the majority of children in the early years use some type of technology. For example, one-quarter of three-year-old children, almost half of five-year-old children, and two-thirds of eight-year-old children go online daily (Gutnick, Robb, Takeuchi, & Kotler, 2011). Mobile device usage is increasing, with 75% of children birth to age eight having a mobile device (smart phone, tablet) in their homes. Over one-third of children under two use a mobile device. On average, children birth to age eight have nearly two hours a day of screen time, with 60% of this time spent watching television (Common Sense Media, 2013).

Despite the widespread use, technology in the early childhood years continues to be debated, particularly in regard to computer use. For example, the Alliance for Childhood published two reports, *Fool's Gold: A Critical Look at Computers in Childhood* (Cordes & Miller, 2000) and *Tech Tonic: Towards a New Literacy of Technology* (Alliance for Childhood, 2004), warning of the danger of technology to children's physical health, creativity, and social well-being. *Strip Mining for Gold: Research and Policy in Educational Technology—A Response to Fool's Gold* responded with the many educational and social benefits of computers for young children (Clements & Sarama, 2003). Organizations such as NAEYC and the Fred Rogers Center for Early Learning and Children's Media have responded to this debate with position statements clarifying the appropriate use of technology (NAEYC, 2012).

Many consider computers or other forms of technology to have no inherent value or ability to harm; instead, they view it as a tool that can be appropriately or inappropriately used. "Just as pencils do not replace crayons but rather provide additional means of expression, computers, or cameras or any other form of technology do not replace other tools but add to the array of tools available to children to explore, create, and communicate" (Scoter, Ellis, & Railsback, 2001, p. 25). In thinking about using any type of technology, it is important to consider the following:

- Is it the best tool for the job?
- Will it produce added value to the activity?
- Is the activity of benefit to the child?
- What is the cost benefit? In thinking about the cost benefit, it is important to balance the cost of technology with the need and cost of other classroom learning materials (NAEYC, 1996).

Watch the video to learn more about the value of technology for young children. What reasons and warnings are given in this video clip for using technology with children?

Although there are many types of classroom technologies, this chapter will examine some of the most common, including the digital camera, video recorder, digital microscope, overhead projector, light table, whiteboards, and desktop and tablet computers. You will also find information about the application of technology integrated into the previous chapters.

How the Use of Technology Can Enhance Children's Development

Through the use of interactive technology, children learn technology skills while enhancing social and cognitive development.

Technology Skills

As children use the computer and other forms of technology, they have the opportunity to meet National Education Technology Standards (NETS). Established by the International Society for Technology in Education (ISTE), there are standards for children ages prekindergarten through second grade (ISTE, 2012). These include using technology to create stories, illustrate ideas, and produce presentations; conduct research; and engage with others through electronic means such as e-mail. In addition, the standards stress that children need to learn technology terminology and use technology independently, cooperatively, and safely. Young children also need to enhance their media literacy such as using more than one strategy to find answers, linking answers to specific evidence, and understanding that someone created the media and made choices about what to include, and that media technologies are tools (Rogoe 2015, p. 94).

Social Skills

Though initially some educators expressed concern that computers and related technologies might reduce socialization, researchers suggest that instead computers may increase the amount of communication and positive interaction between children (Clements, 1994; Haugland & Wright, 1997). For example, Muller and Perlmutter (1985) found that children participated in interactions with others during 63% of computer play versus 7% of puzzle play. Computers offer a unique environment that acts as a catalyst to share information, make decisions, and develop language (Tsantis, Bewick, & Thouvenelle, 2003). It often motivates children who typically do not interact with others to do so. Children engage in diverse social interactions when using the computer including asking for help; directing others' actions; providing information, assistance, and instruction; managing turn taking; acknowledging each other; commenting on each other's actions; and disagreeing (Heft & Swaminathan, 2002; Shahrimin & Butterworth, 2002). Although children seem to naturally assist each other when using the computer, one classroom developed rules to assure interaction. These included finding a friend (children were only allowed to play at the computer with a friend), helping a friend (pointing, discussing, providing information, and sharing the mouse), and taking turns (a timer helped to determine when it was the friend's turn) (Medvin, Reed, Behr, & Spargo, 2003).

Often computer "experts" arise in classrooms and become teachers of the other children. The experts are not assigned to this role by the teacher, but instead the other children bestow this title on them. Surprisingly, the computer expert often does not have a computer at home. Experts are usually not the most proficient children at academics or social skills, but they do gain communication and social skills as they help other children (Hutinger, 1999). For example, in one kindergarten program, the families were invited to send e-mails to their children. Since the children were not yet proficient readers, they had trouble reading the messages. That was when they discovered that Michael, a child with autistic behaviors, could read. Each day he went from classmate to classmate reading each of their messages. While in the past he'd been ignored by other children, he was now sought after.

Cognitive Skills

As a tool, the computer and other digital devices have several advantages that can aid in children's cognitive development.

- Computers are motivating for young children, increasing their on-task behavior. For example, one study found kindergarten children were on-task 90% of the time when they were on the computer (Bergin, Ford, & Hess, 1993).
- Computers provide consistent and frequent reinforcement (Parette, Hourcade, & Heiple, 2000).
- Computers allow children to work independently at their own pace (Parette et al., 2000).
- Software can provide extensive scaffolding of learning, which is very important in developing cognitive skills. Research has demonstrated increased achievement when using specifically designed apps. However, it is important to carefully match the app to the child's developmental level (Robb & Lauricella, 2015).
- Digital devices provide unique opportunities that may enhance learning. For example, computers can allow children to access the "largest information bank the world has ever known" (Parette et al., 2000, p. 245). With the computer, children can participate in simulations and manipulate variables that might not be possible in the real world (Scoter et al., 2001). With tablet computers and smartphones we can access this information from almost anywhere (identifying a bug on the playground).

The best academic results are found when the use of technology is clearly related to other classroom activities and curriculum. For example, research indicates that using a computer with supporting manipulatives increases children's skills more than using only the manipulatives or the computer alone (Clements, 1994; Haugland & Shade, 1994).

While there are many cognitive advantages to using computers, there is danger in using too much drill and skill software (Scoter et al., 2001). In one study, children's creativity was reduced by 50% after using this type of software (Haugland, 1992). Additionally, it is important to distinguish between using **interactive** and **noninteractive media**. The NAEYC position statement on technology and many other health organizations and child advocacy groups recommend that passive, noninteractive media be eliminated from early childhood settings (NAEYC, 2012). We must also be concerned about the total amount of screen time per day, even if the screen time is interactive. We will learn more about this later in the chapter.

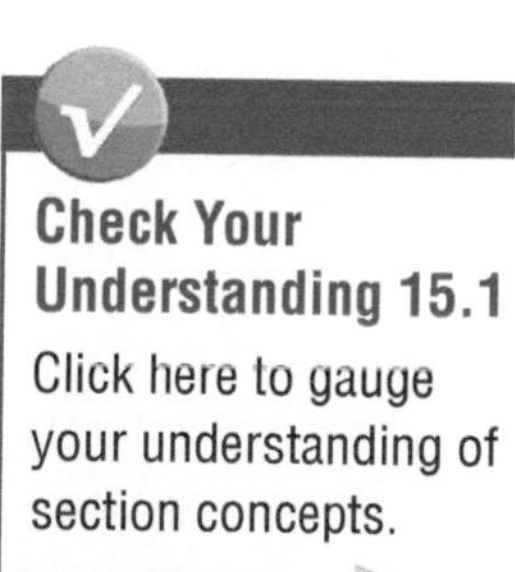

Criteria for Using Technology in the Classroom

While technology can be a separate classroom center, ideally teachers integrate it into other existing centers. As illustrated in the opening scenario, when teachers place computers or other technology devices in existing learning centers, there is often a more direct relationship between the curriculum and the technology. The computer or other technological device is used as a tool that expands and extends the curriculum, thereby increasing educational opportunities. Many programs are now choosing tablets and laptops over desktop computers because of the portability. However, regardless of where the technology is placed, there are important criteria to consider in designing a setting to support technology use. We will examine these next.

Take a Balanced Approach

In a balanced approach, technology does not replace actual experience but instead is a supplement to experiences. For example, if you live in an area where children can visit a farm, you would want to provide children with this experience. You might supplement this by watching carefully chosen videos of farm animals in preparation for your visit. During the visit, you might take videos and photos and use these to revisit the experience.

Design the Setting for Children's Independent Use

Design the technology devices and center so that children can use them independently.

- Mark audio players, CD players, overhead projectors, and other electronic devices with easy to recognize symbols so that children can turn them off and on. In some toddler classrooms, teachers mark the stop with a red sticker and the play with a green sticker.
- Make sure that everything that is needed to effectively use the technology device is easily accessible. For example, extra paper is stored near the printer.
- Place materials that children need within easy reach.
- Label shelves so that children can return the materials to the proper place.
- Pre-load programs onto the desktop or tablet computer, labeling the programs with easy to understand icons. To avoid "app jumping," it is helpful to have fewer programs or have children make a plan before using the device (Bailey & Blagojevic, 2015).
- Provide a mouse for each computer. Also, provide keyboards for older children. Although they are more difficult to use than a mouse, they offer more options and are preferred by children (Robinson, 1999).
- Establish a separate computer folder for each child where she can save her digital pictures, drawings, and stories.
- Provide instruction on how to use the technology.

> **TIP**
>
> When CDs are removed from covers, they may be difficult to tell apart. Some teachers draw pictures on the CDs to help children to locate their favorites. They also use color coding to help keep CDs with their appropriate cover.

Choose Appropriate Media

Media such as computer applications and programs and audio and visual recordings need to be developmentally appropriate, high quality, and free from bias. In choosing media you will want to consider the three Cs: content, context, and the individual child (Fred Rogers Center, 2012). See Figure 15.1 for information on choosing appropriate software.

TIP Ways to Find Appropriate Software

- Buy award-winning programs and apps—Some awards given for children's software include the Oppenheim Toy Portfolio Software Awards, Parents' Choice Awards, EDDIE Award, and REVERE Awards.
- Subscribe to a site that reviews **software**. (Children's Technology Review is an advertisement-free site that evaluates software for ease of use, educational value, design features, value for cost, and entertainment.)
- Review the **digital media** yourself using the checklist found in Figure 15.1.

Provide for Health and Safety

It is critical that electronic devices are set up in a safe and healthy manner.

- Reduce hazards by carefully placing cords to avoid tripping, avoiding extension cords, and never placing electrical devises near water.
- Reduce overall classroom noise through the use of earphones. Earphones need to be closely monitored so that loudness does not cause hearing damage.
- Reduce eye strain by providing proper light and placing screens to prevent glare.
- Prevent injuries and establish healthy computer habits by providing an ergonomic work station.
  - Workstations should be adjustable (18 to 26 inches). In one study of children's settings, it was found that the monitor and keyboard or mouse were often too high. This can cause pain in the neck, shoulder, back, arm, and hand (Kemp, 1999).
  - If the workstation is not adjustable, it is important to provide adjustable chairs to raise or lower the child to the proper position. Footstools can be provided so that children's feet are resting flat.
  - The monitor needs to be directly in front of the child and the top of the screen should be below the child's eye level so that the child is using a downward gaze.
- Avoid multiple-level desks with the keyboard and mouse below the computer. Instead, the keyboard should be placed directly in front of the user with room for the forearms to rest on the desk surface.
- Teach children to keep their wrists straight, to change positions frequently, and to take physically active breaks every 30 minutes (Straker, Maslen, Burgess-Limerick, Johnson, & Dennerlein, 2010).

Design the Setting to Encourage Co-Engagement

It is important to intentionally design the setting to encourage the children to interact while they are using the technology. For example, place two or three chairs at each computer station and place computers in areas where other children can watch. Research indicates that there are better outcomes when children use the computer together (Clements, 1999). Avoid placing computers in an isolated corner, since this tends

FIGURE 15.1 Choosing Appropriate Software

When screening software, consider the following criteria:

- ❑ Does the software have high educational or informational value? Is value added by using the software? Or would this information be better presented in a different format?
- ❑ Is the software developmentally appropriate for the children using it? According to Haugland (2005), only 20% of software is appropriate for children. Beware of software that is just an electronic work sheet page. The age limit, educational objectives, and educational philosophy should be clearly stated (Peterson, Verenikina, & Herrington, 2008).
- ❑ Is the software designed so that the child can use it independently (simple and clear directions, uses speech when appropriate, uses picture menus, and organized for intuitive use) (Prairie, 2005)?
- ❑ If providing simulations, they are realistic and real-world (Peterson, Verenikina, & Herrington, 2008).
- ❑ Is the child able to exercise control when using the software (sets the pace, can repeat a process, can stop and resume, chooses from multiple paths, and frequently saves)?
- ❑ Does the software encourage active learning (requires active participation and encourages exploration and further investigation, allows for trial and error)?
- ❑ Is the software exciting and interesting (utilizes many senses including sound, music, and voice; includes graphics and sounds that are motivating for young children; and is relevant to the group of children using the software)?
- ❑ Does the software scaffold children's learning (provides increasing challenges and a variety of levels, provides nonthreatening feedback allowing children to know their progress, provides hints and instruction, and does not penalize for mistakes)?
- ❑ Is the software anti-bias, containing respectful images of diverse cultures, multiple languages, people of different ages, abilities, colors, and diverse family structures (NAEYC, 1996)?
- ❑ Does the software promote prosocial values (no violence or implicit violence is present such as "blowing it up" to get rid of mistakes) (Tsantis, Bewick, & Thouvenelle, 2003)?
- ❑ Is the software preselected to match curricular goals, and is the software tied closely to other curricular activities? Software should support or be supported by the curriculum.
- ❑ Does the software have high-quality graphics and sounds? Graphics and sound need to add to the quality rather than being distracting.
- ❑ Is the software accessible for children with special needs?
- ❑ Does the software provide delight, enchantment, and adventure such as opportunities for free exploration, finding hidden secrets, and elements of surprise (Plowman, McPake, & Stephen, 2012)?

to separate children into users and nonusers. When there is room around the computer, children can watch what other children are doing and provide support and encouragement. They can also learn by watching (Haugland, 1997).

To encourage social interaction and a shared story experience, add multiple earphones to the audio or CD player. However, there may be times when individual use is more appropriate, and you will want to set up an environment to support this. For example, if children are recording individual stories you might want to set up a private booth to assist in concentration and to improve sound quality.

Provide Equal Access to Technology

Establish a management system to provide equal access to technology. Because computers and other technology devices are popular, it is often necessary to have a sign-up sheet so that everyone has an opportunity to use the equipment. Lists can prevent children from having to watch and wait their turn. Some early childhood classrooms use a timer to designate the amount of time that each child receives on the equipment. When the timer goes off, the child using the computer or other popular equipment crosses his name off the list and goes to get the next child on the list. If the child is engaged in another activity and does not want to leave it, she can leave her name on the list but let the next person have a turn first. In most classrooms, there are times during the day when technology devices are not available. For example, Becky, a teacher of preschool children, places a "computer sleeping" sign on the computer when it is not available.

Provide Ideas for Using Technology

Post ideas for use near the electronic device. You can use pictures to remind children of the different activities that they might accomplish with the device. For example, the audio player might be used to listen to music, listen to a story, record a story or song, or play a game of identifying sounds. Visual aids can help children to remember these varied choices.

Supply an Adequate Number of Computers and Other Technology Devices

There should be a computer for every four or five children. If this is not possible, you might consider combining your computers with those of other teachers and then rotating the computers on a predetermined schedule. Computer labs are not recommended for young children, because when computers are not in the classroom there is often a disconnect between the computer and the rest of the curriculum.

You will want to analyze the use of other media to determine the number of items needed. For example, one toddler classroom found that the light table was very popular, so they added another one.

Limit the Amount of Time Children Are Exposed to Media

The American Academy of Pediatrics recommends that children younger than two have no screen time (American Academy of Pediatrics, 2011). The joint position statement on technology by NAEYC and the Fred Rogers Center for Early Learning and Children's Media (2012) states that noninteractive media (DVDs, videos, television) should not be used in early childhood programs unless it promotes active engagement or interactions. However, in spite of these recommendations, research shows that children are engaged in many hours of screen time activity, much of it noninteractive. Screen time increases obesity rates, replaces interaction time, and decreases creative activities. There is also concern that excessive computer use by young children might lead to repetitive stress injuries and eyestrain (Cordes & Miller, 2000; Shields & Behrman, 2000).

Watch the video to see an example of a second- and third-grade class using Skype. How did this activity assist children in learning geography?

https://www.youtube.com/watch?v=5dN2rSGwtjk

Use the Internet Effectively

The Internet can be used to communicate with others (e-mail, **Skype**), locate information (websites, **WebQuests**), and share and publish projects. Research reveals that 30% of preschool children, 47% of kindergarten children, and 67% of third-grade children use the Internet daily (Straker et al., 2010). It is important that parents and teachers review and preselect Internet sites for children in the early childhood years. In addition, you might want to add protective software such as Net Nanny or CyberPatrol that will prevent children from inadvertently visiting inappropriate sites. Internet sites should meet

the same criteria as listed for appropriate software. In addition, sites should be commercial free and should not request any personal information from the child.

TIP Internet Sites to Consider for Young Children

- KidsClick provides a variety of websites divided into categories compiled by librarians.
- Fred Rogers Early Learning Environment includes children's e-books, apps, music, and games.
- WebQuest provides computer activities for kindergarten through adulthood.
- Ask Jeeves for Kids provides links that match children's questions with answers.
- National Geographic for Kids provides video clips, photos, and activities.

Check Your Understanding 15.2
Click here to gauge your understanding of section concepts.

Technology Activities to Support the Curriculum

Technology can be used to support all areas of the curriculum. Technology such as audio recorders, CD players, video recorders, light tables, overhead projectors, digital cameras, document cameras, and computers are tools that can provide children unique learning experiences, allow them to document their learning, and aid them in reflection.

Using Audio Recorders, CD Players, MP3 Players, and Smart Pens to Support the Curriculum

There are many types of audio recorders, from tape players, CD players, and MP3 players to digital pens. These players allow children to listen to stories, finger plays, or music. They also provide children with opportunities to engage in activities such as "guess the sound." With audio recorders, children are able to document their discussions, dramatic play episodes, storytelling, oral reading, singing, and instrument playing. These recordings can be used in a variety of ways. They can be transcribed so children can see their ideas in print, used as documentation of children's learning, analyzed to determine children's current competencies, and used for planning and facilitating deeper learning. Children and families can listen to children's stories and musical creations. Additionally, when recordings are made over a period of time, children and families can hear the improvement in children's skills. Recordings can also be used to provide directions. For example, digital pens easily capture the teacher's directions. When children touch the special coded dot they can listen to what is recorded. The pens also can record children's written stories and drawings and their verbal discussions about them.

Using Video Recorders to Support the Curriculum

George Forman has labeled video recording "a tool of the mind" (Forman, 1999), an aid for reflection for both teachers and children. For example, video recorders allow children to instantly revisit their experiences and to describe their thinking. It is easier for children to consider their thinking when they are not also engaged in the action. As children watch themselves participating in different interactions and then reflect upon them, they might also see the incident from another child's point of view. For example, they may see the look on the other child's face and hear the other child's statements better during reviewing.

Video recordings can also help children revisit group experiences. For example, Anya and her class of rural preschoolers were completing a project on tractors. As part of the project, they visited an implement dealer where they examined several different tractors and interviewed the manager. The children made a video of their visit. Upon returning to their program, they decided to make their own tractor. Over the next several weeks as dilemmas arose in building their tractor, they revisited the tractors they had videotaped.

As with audio recordings, video recordings can also be used to document children's learning. For example, Anya used video to document the children's questions and process as they created their tractor.

Julie Bullard

The light table highlights details in these natural items such as the different layers within the rocks or the veins of the leaves.

Using Light Tables to Support the Curriculum

Light tables allow children to experiment with light and shadows, color, transparency, layering, and textures. "The light takes everyday items and recreates them into objects of beauty and wonder for children" (Whited, 2003, p. 39). A variety of materials can be placed in clear containers on a shelf by the light table for exploration, including:

- Translucent items in different colors and shapes.
- X-rays.
- Sand.
- Colored gems and flat marbles.
- Colored cellophane and tissue paper.
- Natural items such as agates, crystals, feathers, leaves, bugs, shed snake skins, pressed flowers, dried rose petals, and shells.
- Found items such as bubble wrap and spiral pencil shavings.
- Interesting colored dishes.
- Bottles of colored water.

In addition to exploration, children can create interesting transitory designs with translucent objects, create masterpieces on the light table using art media (colored glue, shaving cream, and watercolors), mix colors in clear trays, trace items, or examine pictures, photos, and artwork that have been reproduced on transparencies.

Julie Bullard

Using the light table adds a new element to color mixing, with the light allowing the child to see the difference in even minor gradients of color.

Using Overhead Projectors to Support the Curriculum

Overhead projectors allow children the opportunity to explore color, transparency, and shadows. Because the

Create a Light Table

Julie Bullard

You can use a light table with all ages of children. This light table is inexpensive to create and is just the right size for one or two children.

Directions

1. Locate a suitable container such as this heavy-duty, cardboard shipping container.
2. Replace the lid of the container with a piece of frosted Plexiglas (glass stores can cut the size to order).
3. Drill a hole in the bottom side of your container.
4. Screw a one-pound coffee can with the top lid removed inside the bottom of the container.
5. Set a drop light facing up in the coffee can.
6. Thread the cord of the drop light through the hole you drilled earlier.
7. Insert a 120 vac 60 hv compact low-temperature fluorescent bulb into the clamp light (these can be replaced with colored bulbs if you wish).
8. Plug in and enjoy.

Variations:

You can use other types of light sources such as LED Christmas lights.

overhead projector shines onto a wall, it can also be used as a light source for creating shadows with objects and bodies and for creating shadow puppet plays.

When I was teaching Head Start, a group of children became enthralled with the overhead projector, often bringing items from home to see them projected on the wall. For example, one day Amber brought her doll to the classroom. Initially she was surprised that she did not see the shadow of the entire doll when she stood the doll on the projector. She spent the next half hour exploring shadows by positioning the doll in various poses to see the shadow that was created.

Adding a picture or photo transparency to the overhead projector can provide inspiration for art or a new backdrop for drama. Transparencies can also be used so that children can see their artwork and photos enlarged, creating a sense of wonder and pride. Enlarging pictures can also allow children the opportunity to study a subject in more detail. For example, the parts of a flower become more obvious when they are enlarged.

Overheads can also be used as a tool to help children think more deeply. A long-term project resulted in establishing a playground for birds. As part of the study, preschool children were trying to figure out a way to make a fountain for the birds (Forman & Gandini, 1994). They visited the city water fountain and took pictures. When they returned, the teachers put the photos on transparencies and shone them on the wall. They asked children to trace the fountain and show how they thought the water got into the fountain.

This helped to make the children's thinking visible and also caused children to think more deeply about their theories.

Using Document Cameras to Support the Curriculum

Document cameras, sometimes referred to as digital overheads or image presenters, allow one to magnify and to project a two-dimensional or a three-dimensional object or a transparency onto a wall. In many schools, they are replacing the overhead projector. You can use them for many purposes, such as projecting children's work so that it can easily be shared with the group. Picture books can be placed beneath the document camera and the enlarged image allows everyone to easily see the print and illustrations. Poems, finger plays, and songs can be shown on the wall enriching these activities by adding the written word. The document camera also provides the opportunity to make detailed observations of objects. For example, when children in Elisha's class were studying money, she placed different coins under the camera, which allowed the children to easily compare the coins. Additionally, you can use many document cameras with a microscope.

Messages for children or family can also be projected. For example, at Teeny Tots, teachers begin each morning with a daily message about special happenings for the day. They end each day with a list of what children did, with some child quotes. In the past, they wrote these on a poster. Since they have begun using the document camera, they can either type or write this on a piece of paper and project it, saving staff time.

Julie Bullard

The overhead projector provides many opportunities, such as allowing children to project their homemade slide shows. In addition, the projector provides the light source for shadow play.

Using Cameras to Support the Curriculum

Digital pictures and videos can support the curriculum in a variety of ways. Photos and video can be used to do the following:

- Record and document children's learning. Digital pictures can be shared on documentation boards or in documentation notebooks, placed on bulletin boards, or entered into individual children's portfolios. Videos and photos can also be shared on digital picture frames.
- Capture children's transitory work such as block buildings and sand creations.
- Display results of science experiments over time such as plants at different stages of growth.
- Record visitors for future discussion and study (children's pets, insects that have been caught and released, or birds that have visited the bird feeder).
- Allow children to see things from a different perspective.
- Revisit and reflect upon an experience such as a field trip.
- Create games and activities such as sorting, classifying, matching, graphing, puzzles, and expressing feelings.
- Create books. For example, you can create books of feelings, using actual photos. Books can also be created that show ways you can manage different types of emotions such as how you can calm down when feeling overly excited.

- Help children to feel valued through displaying pictures of them participating in various activities and successfully accomplishing tasks. Photos can also be ran off on transparency film and hung in windows.
- Introduce the staff, children, and families to each other.
- Soothe a child by providing individual family albums for children to look at and carry around.
- Make the transition from home to school easier. For example, Portland Oregon Public School Head Starts introduce the school to new children through sending photos to the child (Scoter et al., 2001, p. 28).
- Share information with parents and the community.
- To represent children in their play. For example, at the Portland Waldorf School, a photo of each child's full length portrait is cut out and mounted on cardboard. The children can then use their picture and the picture of friends as they play with their fairy house.
- Provide the schedule for the day in picture form. See the photo at the beginning of Chapter 3 for an example.
- Show the steps needed to complete a process (washing hands or cooking a snack).
- Provide nonverbal directions in a learning center.
- Show where items are to be placed on shelves and cupboards or to label a basket.
- Help establish management systems such as sign-up boards, attendance boards, and job charts. Some teachers place children's pictures on juice can lids and then use a magnetic board for their management systems.

Some classrooms have a child assigned as the photographer for the day or the week. This child is available for taking requested pictures. If the child is able, he is also responsible for downloading the pictures onto the computer.

School-aged children and preschoolers can successfully use digital cameras to document learning and to capture their perspectives. For example, here are some ways that children have used cameras in different programs:

- Children at the Discovery Preschool went on a neighborhood walk and took pictures of different kinds of homes. These were placed in the block area to inspire their building.
- A series of different types of books were created by the preschool and kindergarten class in an urban private school. One of the books was a "Guess Where I Am?" book. Each child took a picture using unusual angles or close-up shots to include in the book.
- Children at Burlington Little School took digital pictures of their pattern block designs. These were printed and placed in a three-ring binder for the children to revisit and use for future inspiration.
- In a kindergarten class where many children were homeless, the teacher gave each child a camera that she used to show her experiences. The photos were displayed in the school and in the community, highlighting the homeless experience through a child's eyes.
- Curious Minds has a stuffed bear named Tegar that travels to each child's house. A digital camera and journal accompany the bear so that children can record the bear's adventures. The pictures are discussed at a circle time and then posted on a bulletin board in the program.

Watch the video to see how one classroom used digital cameras. How did the teachers assist children to effectively use the camera as a learning tool?

Using Digital Microscopes to Support the Curriculum

Digital microscopes allow children to experience hidden worlds such as examining the scales of a butterfly's wings. With a wireless digital microscope and a tablet computer, children are able to go where their interesting object presides (Bailey & Blagojevic, 2015). For example, children might closely examine worms and bugs, leaves and flowers, or animal and human hair. Many microscopes also can take pictures, allowing children to save images. In one program, the images were created into a "Guess What I Am" book.

Using Computers and Whiteboards to Support the Curriculum

Like the previously discussed technology, computers are tools that can support all areas of the curriculum. There are many options including desktops, laptops, tablets, and smart phones. Tablets are becoming an increasingly popular choice in classrooms due to their portability and extra features such as a camera and video recorder. Many free applications are available for the devises. For example, when Trina was taking a walk with a group of children they saw a tree they wanted to identify. Trina took a picture of a leaf on her tablet and used an application called Leafsnap. Within seconds, she had the name of the tree, photos of the tree, and information about it. New applications are being constantly developed and are available for all areas of the curriculum. With Windows 8.1, you can also use the applications on a desktop or laptop computer. What are some ways that computers can enhance curriculum? We'll look at this next.

To Support the Arts. Computers can support the arts by providing tools for creating art, informative games, and research for supporting the topic of study. Programs such as Kid Pix Studio or HyperStudio can be used for drawing and creating products. Computers might actually enhance the drawing process for some children. One study examining preschool children's use of tablets for drawing discovered that the tablet attracted children who had not previously participated in drawing. Children stated they preferred drawing on the tablet to using other media because of the bright colors, ability to erase, and ease of use (Couse & Chen, 2010). An application such as Drawing Pad can change an iPad into an easel.

Children can also look up information about artists and see examples of the artists' work. For example, a preschool class was studying flowers and was able to examine more than 200 of Georgia O'Keefe's flower paintings. They compared the flowers painted by Georgia O'Keeffe, an American painter, with the flowers painted by Vladimir, a Russian artist.

Computer technology can also help children learn about music. With the computer, children can compose and record music and hear it played back using any instrument that they choose. They can play musical matching games, match instruments to their sounds, and hear and see musicians playing instruments, including instruments from other cultures. Apps such as Old McDonalds Piano can support music by letting children sing with accompaniment, play a piano, and record their voice. Or, if you want children to have access to a full recording studio, you might want to use the Garage Band app.

Dramatic play can also be enhanced with short, streamed videos of people using newly introduced props. For example, when Kirima introduced a fishing center she showed the children a short video of a fishing camp.

To Support Literacy. Computers can assist children with writing and reading by providing a motivating environment and tools that make the process easier. Research demonstrates that children write more when using computers than when using pencil and paper (Clements, Nastasi, & Swaminathan, 1993). This is most likely because writing is less laborious for children when they use the computer. The powerful editing tools can also help children to analyze and correct their work (Parette et al., 2000). Digital text can easily be arranged, rearranged, added to, and deleted, allowing children as young as three to create and organize stories (Ackermann, 2002). Many book creation apps are available such as Shadow Puppet, a free app that allows you to insert photo, video, text, maps, drawings, and music. Or you might want to try the Book Creator app, which allows children to insert photos, add narration and text, and draw pictures. The books can be viewed online or printed and placed in the classroom literacy center. This provides additional classroom reading material, an acknowledgment of the writer, and an authentic reason to write.

Computers also offer the unique opportunity to switch text to speech and speech to text. Voice synthesizers can read children's storybooks or their written text while highlighting the text that is being read. This assists children to link the written and spoken word. Some software even changes the story to a different language.

Visiting an author's or illustrator's website is another use of the computer to support literacy. This can add interest to an author's study. For example, Ezra Jack Keats, author of several children's books including *The Snowy Day*, provides story read-alouds, animated books, information, games, and activities on his website.

Many children's books are now available as an app, allowing the child to have additional interaction with the characters. The books are often designed so that you can read them yourself, have the story read as you turn the pages, or have auto read. For example, nearly all of Dr. Seuss's books are available as apps. One Globe Kids is an app that lets you hear stories from children around the world.

Children can use whiteboards as an interactive flannel board in retelling favorite stories. For example, a preschool teacher describes her children retelling the story of the three pigs. They could choose the background and manipulate the size of the pigs and the wolves. This led to discussions about how big the wolf needed to be to blow the house down (Lisenbee, 2009).

Although there was initial concern that computers might decrease children's oral language, research shows that children use similar amounts of language at the computer center as they do at other learning centers (Kelly & Schorger, 2001). Children often engage in self-talk as they first figure out how to use the computer. They then progress to using communication with others to solve problems and to discuss cause and effect (Bhargava & Escobedo, 1997).

To Support Social Studies. Computer programs and the Internet can expose children to a world beyond their normal experience. For example, they can learn about and communicate with children from other places. Clark (1998) describes how four teachers (prekindergarten, kindergarten, and first grade) electronically linked their classrooms. The children helped to develop websites, choosing items to place on the site and favorite links to share. The children also shared information through e-mail, asking each other questions such as "How many of you have pets?" In developing websites, children have the opportunity to think about what makes their community unique and how to capture that uniqueness to share with others. Programs can also assist children's emotional development by helping them feel powerful, develop persistence, and accept mistakes (Sharapan, 2015).

To Support Science. Computers can support science learning in a variety of ways. For example, a second-grade class in Atlanta was studying marine life. They enriched their learning through a variety of technological activities.

- They completed a WebQuest called Marine Life (McLaughlin, 2006). The WebQuest began by telling the child that one day she woke up to find that she had become a sea creature in her sleep. As she worked with her peers, she needed to figure out what marine animal she represented, how to survive, what she needed to eat, and who her enemies were.

- Before visiting the Georgia Aquarium, the children viewed webcams of the fish and learned about the fish through an online animal guide. Because of this exposure, they were prepared with a detailed list of questions to ask on their field trip.
- Using the StoryKit app the children wrote factual stories about a favorite sea animal using an online children's encyclopedia and preselected Internet sites (many featuring streaming videos) as references. They illustrated their storybooks and placed them in the class library for their classmates to read.

To Support Math. Computers can be successfully used with young children for a variety of math purposes, including self-guided instruction, exploration, problem solving, practice, and manipulation of math objects (Sarama & Clements, 2002). One advantage of using the computer for math is that children can manipulate math objects and easily save their work so they can continue it over a period of time. For example, when creating designs, they can continue to modify and add to them.

Several software programs have been developed to help young children learn math skills. One of these is *Building Blocks*, which combines manipulative and print activities, supported by computer learning. *Building Blocks* software provides activities and games including open-ended activities. Children's learning is scaffolded through a sequenced set of activities that provide needed encouragement and prompts as children progress through the program. This is a research-based, organized curriculum that helps to link children's formal and informal math knowledge. Research shows large gains for children who use the program versus those who do not (Sarama & Clements, 2004).

SMART Board. An electronic whiteboard, such as a SMART Board, can enhance the computer experience. When attached to a computer and projector, it becomes a large interactive screen that can be written on with a stylus or finger or used as a touch screen to manipulate images. It can also be used to project photos, powerpoints, or movies. A large display allows many children to see at once, making it an option for working with a small or large group. A computer projector can also be used to accomplish many of these tasks. For example, at Helen Gordan Child Development Center children were studying birds. As a short video of birds in flight played, children interacted with the scene by flapping their arms and flying with the birds.

Enhancing Family Support and Communication

A variety of digital media can allow teachers and families to communicate information, share student work and documentation, make digital classroom visits, and provide online learning communities. For example, family members can be a guest visitor through Skype, taking children through a virtual tour of their work site. Communication can also occur through text messages or e-mail. For example, Dakota cries frantically when her mother leaves. Imagine the mother's relief when she receives a text message a short time later with a photo of Dakota happily playing.

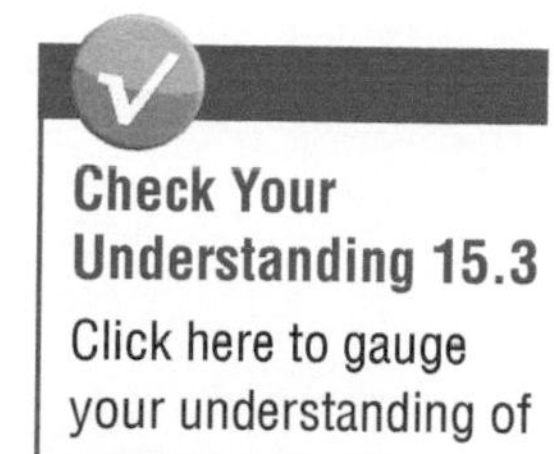

Student work, documentation, and e-portfolios can be shared electronically allowing families to easily share the information with other important people in the child's life. For example, one program develops a blog for each family and posts a work sample or anecdote about each child on a daily basis.

There are many other ways to use technology. Class news can be shared through electronic newsletters and photos of children can be shared through a photo sharing site. QR codes placed on bulletin boards can link photos or student work that is on the bulletin board to a video of the child creating or discussing the work (Puerling & Fowler, 2015). Online book clubs or discussion groups can allow families and staff to form learning communities. For example, participants might watch videos on current research or read articles or books about children and then have discussions about how to apply the information to the home and program settings (Guernsey & Levine, 2015).

Special Considerations for Infants and Toddlers

The American Academy of Pediatrics discourages media use in children under two, stating that there is no evidence that it is helpful and there is evidence of negative health and developmental consequences. They state that time could be used better in unstructured play and in interacting with others (American Academy of Pediatrics, 2011). However, two-thirds of children under two watch television or DVDs, averaging an hour of viewing a day (Common Sense Media, 2013). Higher levels of television watching are linked to sleep issues, obesity, and developmental lags (Lerner & Barr, 2014). Zero to Three, discuss research in *Screen Sense: Setting the Record Straight, Research-Based Guidelines for Children Under 3 Years Old* (2014). They state that there is no evidence that children learn from using devices independently. However, screen media can promote learning if the child is using developmentally appropriate, interactive media with adults who interact with the child around the media. Yet, explorations in the physical world result in greater learning. They also point out the dangers of background television. Research shows that background television interferes with language development, cognitive development, and executive function. This is especially worrisome, since research reveals that infants and toddlers average 5.5 hours of background television a day (Lerner & Barr, 2014; Rideout, 2014).

If you do choose to use digital media with infants and toddlers, carefully consider the content. Research findings indicate the importance of content that is relevant to the child and that features everyday themes. Avoid fast-paced programs and seek programs that are interactive (Lerner & Barr, 2014).

There are many less controversial forms of technology for infants and toddlers to use including audio players, overhead projectors, and light tables. Following is an example of how one group of young children explored technology.

Jennifer Whited from the Ohio University Child Development Center implemented a project on light with children aged six months to three years. Over a period of time, they experimented with different types of technology, such as a light table. They examined different objects such as transparent blocks, colored dishes, and bottles filled with tinted water. Transparent tissue paper was used to create designs. They painted, mixed colors, and experimented with clay, discovering how they looked on the table.

Jennifer and her colleagues eventually established a separate room for the exploration of light that included different types of technology such as a light table, an overhead projector, flashlights, rope lights, and battery-operated lanterns. They added a variety of props for experimentation (transparent materials, fabric, fishing line, art media, hair gel, ribbons, and mirrors). Dark curtains shaded the windows and sheer dark fabric was suspended from the ceiling to darken the room and help children to focus on the light source. They continued to experiment with a variety of media, such as drawing with markers, painting with watercolors, and making designs in shaving cream on the projector. Eventually the children understood that the design they were creating was the same as that transmitted onto the wall. Children also made designs with colored glue on Plexiglas and tissue paper on clear contact paper. The children placed their creations on the overhead projector enhancing the beauty of their designs. As stated by Whited, "Infants have a natural ability to reinvent the ordinary; boxes

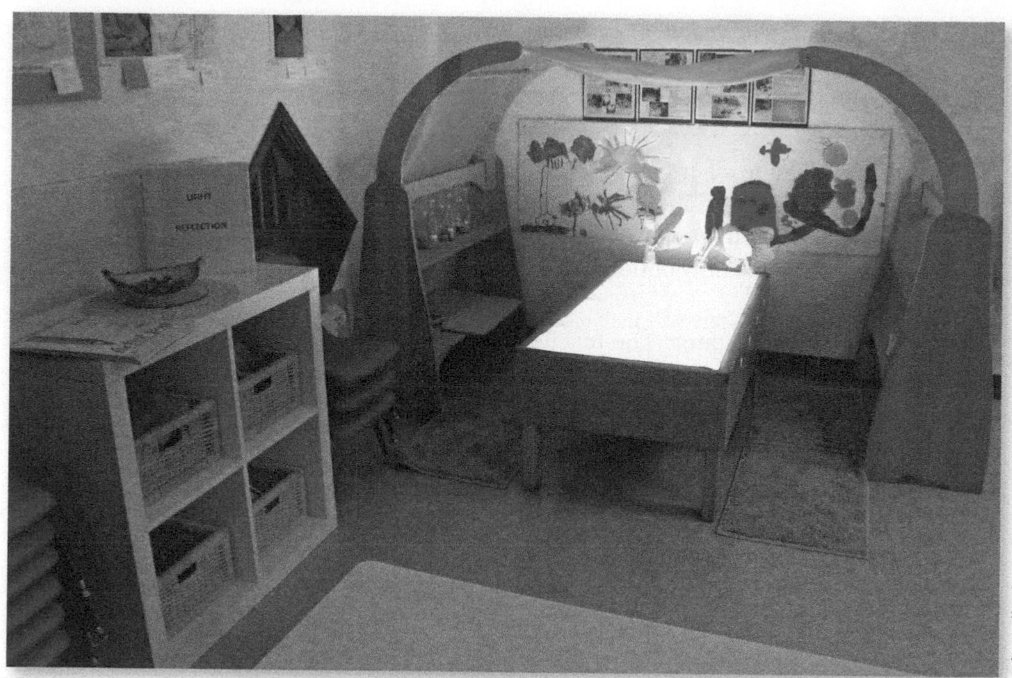

This light table in a toddler classroom at Mentor Graphics Child Development Center provides many learning opportunities. Note the documentation book that highlights some of the children's creations.

become houses, baskets become boats and plastic bottles become wonderful instruments. On the light table, plastic cups and plates become glowing blocks to build with" (Whited, 2003, p. 39).

Check Your Understanding 15.4
Click here to gauge your understanding of section concepts.

Apply Your Knowledge What are the ways that you might use audio recordings with infants and toddlers?

Teachers' Facilitation of Learning Through Technology

Teachers often take a hands-off approach to teaching technology. However, when teachers scaffold learning, children's knowledge increases. For example, children learn significantly more about computer technology and increase cognitive skills such as abstract thinking, vocabulary, planning, and visual motor coordination with teacher mediation (Shute & Miksad, 1997). Without teacher intervention, children often resort to trial and error "that is devoid of task conceptualization" (Samaras, 1996, p. 133).

Instruct, Model, Select Appropriate Technology, and Facilitate

According to Davis and Shade (1994), the teacher plays the following roles:

- Instructor. The teacher introduces new materials and software to children, providing initial instruction so that all children have an equal playing field. The instruction might be individual or small group. To be the most effective, children need to have the chance to actually use the technology while being instructed (Haugland, 1997).

- Role model. The teacher learns about technology, software, and websites and how and where to find appropriate ones. The teacher uses the computer and other technologies as classroom tools (creates portfolios, class books, classroom signs, and so on).
- Selector. The teacher carefully selects and evaluates appropriate technologies and media, thinking about whether this is the best tool to accomplish the goal. Is there value added by using technology? The teacher engages in ongoing evaluation to determine how children are using the media and whether they are learning from it.
- Mentor and facilitator. The teacher is a "sensitive observer, master questioner, and scaffolder of children's learning" (Samaras, 1996, p. 133). According to Nir-Gal and Klein (2004), the facilitator helps children to:
    - Focus on the task or the problem to be solved.
    - Expand their learning through discussion of what is happening, linking the learning to current curriculum and past experiences and knowledge, asking thought-provoking questions, providing challenges (What would happen if . . . ? Can you think of another way of . . . ?), discussing the thinking process, and helping children to predict outcomes.
    - Experience success.
    - Promote positive feelings through encouragement.
    - Regulate their behavior.

Watch the video to learn more about the role of the teacher in using technology. How is a child's learning impacted if the teacher is with the child as he uses the computer?

https://www.youtube.com/watch?v=29ylsrxof48

Observe and Document Individual Children's Learning

It is important to observe and document children's technological learning to provide appropriate experiences, determine ways to facilitate their learning, and document their current competency and growth in relation to technology. When observing children using technology, consider the following questions:

- Is the child able to effectively use the device (for example, turn the computer on and off, complete an activity independently, and problem solve if an issue arises)?
- Does the child follow the rules for technology use (taking turns and treating materials respectfully)?
- Does the child use ergonomically correct posture?
- Does the child interact with others while using technology (discusses work with others, provides assistance, asks questions, shares ideas, and works cooperatively)?
- What software can the child successfully use?
- Does the child use a systematic approach or a trial-and-error approach when using the device?

Meet the Needs of All Learners

It is important that all children have the opportunity to become proficient in using the computer and other forms of technology. However, this is not always the case. We will examine the digital divide where inequities exist due to race, parental educational levels, and income. We will also look at the ways that technology is being used to support learners with special needs.

The Digital Divide. Inequities in access to computers and other digital devices have created "the digital divide." While the digital divide is decreasing, computer and Internet use is still more common for Caucasians and Asians than for African Americans and Hispanics (Straker et al., 2010). About two-thirds of households in the United States now have computers and Internet access. Children in families with higher incomes have greater computer and Internet access. For example, while 86% of children in high income households have high speed Internet, only 46% of children in low income household do. While the number of families owning mobile devices have increased, there is a gap in the use of educational apps with 35% of children from low-income homes and 75% of children from higher-income homes using educational apps (Common Sense Media, 2013). Children who do not have computers at home typically have at least some access to computers at school. There is still concern, however, that school computer use and software may vary based upon the socioeconomic status of the children attending the program. For example, one study found a difference in the way that early childhood programs used computers. Those programs serving low-income children used computers to have fun while those serving children from higher-income families were more likely to use the computer for educational purposes (Judge, Puckett, & Cabuk, 2004). As teachers, it is important that we ensure that all children have equitable access to technology and high-quality technological experiences, especially those who might not have access in their home environments.

Provide Technology as a Support for Children with Special Needs. Technology may be especially important for children with special needs. "Technology can augment sensory input or reduce distractions. It can provide support for cognitive processing or enhance memory and recall. When used thoughtfully, these technologies can empower young children, increasing their independence and supporting their inclusion in classes" (NAEYC and the Fred Rogers Center for Early Learning and Children's Media, 2012, p. 9). For example, one study showed that a group of children with mild to moderate disabilities gained skills more rapidly in all developmental areas after the introduction of computers. Children's attention spans were also improved through using the computers. Children who had behavior problems and those having autism exhibited less negative behaviors and communicated more while using the computer (Hutinger, Rippey, & Johanson, 1999). Assistive technology can also help a child feel included. For example, a child with cerebral palsy might be able to build with blocks on a computer but not have the physical control to build with unit blocks. Today there are many different adaptive and assistive technologies that allow children to be more independent and that promote learning. In choosing the type of technology, it is important to consider each child's unique needs. In planning, you will also want to consider universal design for learning (UDL), which provides multiple ways of presenting and representing information, multiple ways for children to express their learning, and multiple ways of engaging with the activity, including choice and a range of participation options (Parette & Blum, 2015).

Technology can also be used to support English language learners. For example, teachers can find culturally relevant books and materials and create and modify existing materials using technology. When children have emigrated from another place, children and teachers can explore environments and interact with people from the child's earlier environments. Technology also provides the ability to translate and to hear accurate pronunciations of language (NAEYC and the Fred Rogers Center for Early Learning and Children's Media, 2012).

The teacher plays an important role in children's successful learning through technology. The teacher is an instructor, a role model, a critic who chooses appropriate

Check Your Understanding 15.5
Click here to gauge your understanding of section concepts.

technology, and a mentor and facilitator. She observes and documents children's individual learning and ensures that she meets the needs of all learners.

With thoughtful planning, children can use technology as a tool of inquiry to answer questions, to enhance creativity, to see things in a new way, or to bring items to life (Mitchell, 2007). Integrating technology into the curriculum can provide children with highly motivating activities that promote their development while preparing them for the future. By increasing our knowledge of appropriate technology resources and programs, we can be more effective in facilitating learning for all children, including those with special needs.

? Chapter Quiz 15

Click here to gauge your understanding of chapter concepts.

Sample Application Activities

1. Visit one of the Internet sites listed in this chapter. Make a list of ways that you could use the site.
2. Think of a topic of study. Look for technology and media that will support the topic.
3. Use the software evaluation in Figure 15.1 to critique three popular software programs for children.
4. Observe a classroom. What technology is being used? How is the adult supporting the children in using technology? Use the Environmental Assessment in Figure 15.2 to critique the environment.

FIGURE 15.2 Environmental Assessment: Technology

- ❑ Are there a variety of technology devices in the classroom that are available for children's use (computers, MP3 players, CD players, overhead projectors, light tables, digital cameras)?
- ❑ Can technology devices be used independently by the children?
- ❑ Do technology devices have the needed materials to make them effective, such as CDs for CD players, paper, and extra ink cartridges for printers?
- ❑ Are the materials organized and easily accessible (stored within reach)?
- ❑ Are ideas for usage posted near the electronic device?
- ❑ Are there enough devices to prevent long waits?
- ❑ Is there a management system to provide equal access to technology?
- ❑ Are electronic devices used in a safe and healthy manner (earphones, proper light, cords placed to reduce tripping, no extension cords)?
- ❑ Is the computer center ergonomic (adjustable 18–26-inch workstation or footstools, monitors directly in front of children with top of screen below child's eye level, keyboard and mouse directly in front of children, children encouraged to keep wrists straight)?
- ❑ Are computer programs loaded on the computer with easy to read icons?
- ❑ Is there at a minimum a drawing program and word processing program on the computer?
- ❑ Is there a mouse available for the computer?
- ❑ Is a keyboard available for older children?
- ❑ Is there a separate computer folder so that children can store their work?
- ❑ Are computers placed so that children can see them throughout the room?
- ❑ Is computer usage monitored?
- ❑ Is the technology area designed to encourage social use (two or three chairs at the computer, multiple earphones for CD player)?
- ❑ Are the media developmentally appropriate?
- ❑ Are the media free from bias?
- ❑ Do the media introduce children to other cultures?
- ❑ Are the media high quality?
- ❑ Are the media and technology devices accessible for children with special needs?

5. Learn more about technology and early childhood by reviewing articles and websites on the NAEYC Selected Resources on Technology in Early Childhood Education
6. Esteban, a four-year-old from Durango, Mexico, has just enrolled in your program. He only speaks Spanish and you only speak English. His older siblings as well as his extended family are still in Mexico. Develop a list of ways that technology might be used to assist Esteban and you as a teacher to facilitate Esteban's emotional, social, and intellectual development. Provide specific websites and programs that might be helpful.

Chapter 16

Special-Interest Centers

Learning Outcomes

After you have read this chapter, you will be prepared to:

- Discuss how to develop physical or fitness centers and defend the value of doing so
- Describe how to create puppetry centers and defend the value of doing so
- Explain how to create cooking and snack centers and defend the value of doing so
- Discuss how to create woodworking and carpentry centers and defend the value of doing so

Cathy Jackson

Miranda, a new preschool teacher, excitedly began the program year. However, after a few days she tearfully told the director that she was not sure that she could be a successful teacher. She said she had "several children who were out of control and nothing she did seemed to work." She described them as "very noisy, distractible, and destructive." The director agreed to observe the children and the environment. After the observation, the director and Miranda had a conference. The director suggested that Miranda add a classroom physical fitness area and a woodworking area that would provide for the high-energy needs of the children. Since the children were interested in taking things apart, the director also suggested that Miranda establish a special take-apart center. Miranda made these changes. She also began to observe each child more carefully, noting his or her interests and making sure all the classroom centers included materials of high interest to the children. After she implemented these changes, the children became more engaged and the behavioral issues were greatly diminished. Miranda, reflecting upon this, told her director, "I realize that when I initially set up the classroom, I put things out that I liked when I was young. I was a very quiet child who enjoyed passive activities. I had only prepared the environment to meet the needs of children who were just like me."

Apply Your Knowledge How does your temperament affect the materials and centers that you choose or would potentially choose for your classroom?

In this chapter, you will learn about several special-interest centers, including gyms and indoor physical centers, puppetry centers, cooking centers, and woodworking centers. These centers might occupy their own areas in the classroom or be included in other existing centers. For example, you might add puppetry to the literacy center or the dramatic play area. If the emphasis is on creating puppets and puppet stages, you might place puppetry in the art studio. The center may be a permanent addition or used on a rotating basis.

Indoor Physical or Fitness Center

Physical activity is essential so that young children can develop motor skills and maintain a healthy lifestyle, including a healthy weight (see Chapter 17 for more information). Childhood inactivity is contributing to the rising rate of obesity in children (Nelson, Carpenter, & Chiasson, 2006). The National Association for Sport and Physical Education (NASPE) recommends an accumulation of 30 minutes per day of structured physical activity for toddlers and 60 minutes per day of structured physical activity for preschoolers and elementary-aged children (Goodway, Getchell, Raynes, & NASPE, 2009). In addition, they recommend that children participate in one to several hours a day of unstructured physical activity. Gyms or fitness centers can be one way to meet this need.

Establishing the Indoor Physical Activity Space

How you set up and use your indoor physical area will depend upon your answers to the following questions:

- What is the developmental level of the children?
- How much space is available for the center?
- Is the space a dedicated gross motor area, or is the space for dual purpose?

- Can you permanently set up the space, or do you need to put away all the materials at the end of the session?
- What is the need for indoor gross motor? Are children able to play outside daily? Is the outside space established to promote physical activity?

Indoor physical centers can be placed in any large area such as a gym, lunchroom, or hallway. Generally, you will set up stations (similar to learning centers in the classroom) in this space. When using a large space, it is best to use the perimeter of the room for the stations, allowing several feet of space between each activity. Providing storage space with hooks or shelves at each station can make both set-up and clean-up more convenient.

Use the motor skill categories when developing your activity stations: locomotion skills such as running, hopping, and skipping; stability skills such as bending, jumping, stretching, and balancing; and manipulative skills such as catching, throwing, rolling, and kicking. Ideally, if all the children are using the space concurrently, six to eight activity stations (or at a minimum one station for every three children) will be available. Each station will typically focus on one or two skills such as throwing a ball at a target (Sanders, 2002). It is imperative that each station has enough equipment so that the children using the center will not have to wait for a turn (at least one ball per child at the target throwing center). You will want to consider the need for active adult supervision as you plan the stations. Most centers will need to be planned so that children can complete the center independently, freeing the teacher to actively supervise the group.

Watch this video about indoor physical fitness. How do the teachers in this video enhance physical fitness using indoor spaces?

https://www.youtube.com/watch?v=aHtD_63rjFQ&list=PLyizHCAockpoWzLf4kDaq3BirJXl5mEpR

Goodway and Robinson (2006) advocate that the teacher also establish a classroom physical fitness center. Ideally, this space is in a corner of the room. If a dedicated space in the classroom cannot be established, you might consider setting up a special gross motor activity each day in the circle area. Classroom fitness centers allow children to increase the overall time available to participate in physical activity and to practice motor skills. They also meet the needs of children with high levels of energy. In the next sections, we will examine skills and activities that will assist children to gain these skills. Many of the activities listed are appropriate for either a classroom fitness center or fitness stations in a gym.

Sample Fitness Materials and Activities: Locomotor

Following are suggestions for materials that you might include at fitness stations. Varying the materials helps to keep children interested while also creating new challenges.

Materials for Jumping and Hopping

- Bubble wrap to jump or hop on.
- Several hoops or circles to use for jumping or hopping from circle to circle. Lisa, a teacher of multiage children, made laminated colored circles and then glued a bath mat with suction cups underneath each circle to prevent slipping on the linoleum floor.
- A box platform or aerobic step stairs to jump or hop onto and off of.
- Foam noodles that are taped to the floor or made into a low hurdle by placing the noodle on a cone that has been cut for children to jump over.
- Hanging objects that children can bump into as they jump.
- Secured mats for broad jumping.
- A timer so children can hop as far as they can before the timer goes off.

- Hopscotch squares. Karl, a teacher of kindergarten children, cut pieces of rug into small squares and wrote numbers on the back of each square. Children place the rug squares into a hopscotch pattern or other patterns. They use these on a carpeted surface with the square carpet face down, preventing slipping.

Materials for Walking and Running

- A walking path with contact paper footsteps that show toes pointing in, toes pointing out, giant steps, short steps, and so on.
- Pictures on cards of different types of walking, such as uphill, downhill, lifting knees high, with floppy legs, with stiff legs, as if on ice, and on tiptoes. Children can draw a card and walk in the way shown from one side of the activity station to the other.
- An egg timer and mat so children can run in place until the timer goes off.
- A recorded drum beat, including fast and slow beats and beats that start and stop, for children to walk and run to.
- A course made from highway cones for children to run through.
- A course made of hanging empty plastic bottles with bells inside. The child tries to go through the course without ringing any bells or tries to ring every bell.

Materials for Galloping and Skipping

- A recorded drum beat or music with a skipping beat.
- Stick horses to ride.

Materials for Climbing

To keep children safe while climbing, it is critical that there are adequate fall surfaces under equipment and that toys are not left in fall zones.

- Climbing structures or a climbing wall mounted on the wall of the gym.
- A climbing rope attached at both the top and the bottom.

Materials That Combine Movements

- Streamers or scarves and music for dancing.
- Dance or exercise DVD.
- An obstacle course (such as a tunnel to crawl through, a jumping platform to jump from, a stick horse for galloping to a balance board, and footsteps indicating running to the end of the gym).

Sample Movement Materials and Activities: Stability Skills

Materials for Bending and Stretching

- Photos of children in yoga poses that children can copy.
- Scooter boards for moving across the room.

Materials for Balancing

- A timer that children can set to practice balancing on one foot. To help children remember the activity, Bellanca places a timer and a picture direction card in a basket. The picture direction card first shows a child setting the timer to one minute. The next picture shows the child balancing on one foot. The next picture shows the child jumping in the air in a celebratory pose.

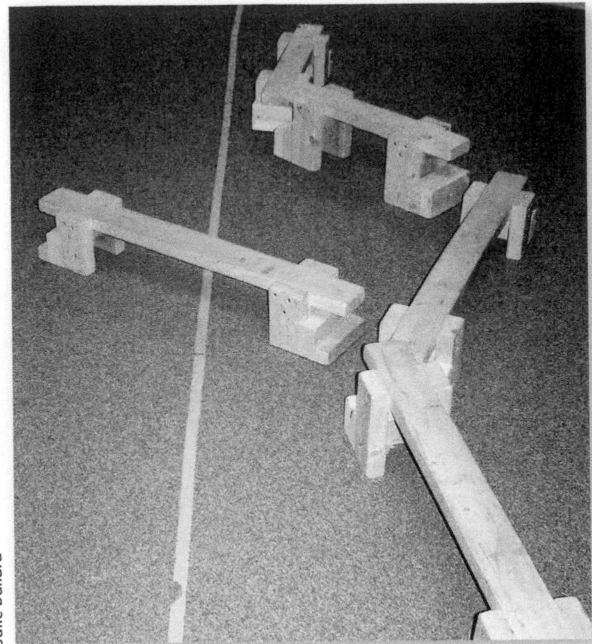
Julie Bullard

These teacher-made balance beams are used each day in the kindergarten hallway. When not in use they are stored under the hallway benches.

- Balance picture cards that children can follow. As children become familiar with following the photos, you can make the pictures more abstract by replacing the photos with stick people, and eventually symbols such as an × for arms and feet spread apart.
- A balance beam—can be a 2 × 4 on the floor or a piece of tape. As children become more proficient, you can create additional challenges such as providing a narrower board. Children can also walk backward or sideways on the board; step over an item like a bicycle tire or a traffic cone on the board; hold an item like a ball or beanbag while transversing the board; move to the center of the board, kneel down, and rise again; or hop on the beam. These various challenges can be provided in picture form.
- Animal cards in a basket that children can draw out and move like that animal.
- Tilt boards for learning to balance on an unstable surface.
- Stilts (these can be purchased or made with tin cans or buckets).
- Dumbbells for promoting stability skills and also strength and endurance. You can create dumbbells by filling two plastic bottles with sand and attaching one at each end of a dowel or old broomstick (Goodway & Robinson, 2006). Children can lift these from various positions—standing, sitting, lying on the floor, or squatting.

Sample Movement Materials and Activities: Manipulative Skills

Materials for Catching and Throwing. A large, soft ball is easiest to catch, while a small lightweight ball is easiest to throw. Until children are proficient at catching and throwing, it can be frustrating for them to throw and catch with each other.

- Scarves for throwing and catching (this is especially helpful for children who are afraid of balls).
- Different sizes, types, and weights of balls.
- Different weights of beanbags. Beanbags can easily be made by cutting a child's pair of pant legs into a beanbag size, filling it with sand, and sewing the ends.
- Scoops, such as one made from a plastic milk carton.
- Boxes or baskets for throwing into.
- An umbrella hung from the ceiling that children can throw Nerf balls into.
- Suspended hula hoops or a low basketball hoop for throwing beanbags and balls through.
- Targets taped to the wall for throwing at.
- A suspended, empty plastic bottle with a bell inside for hitting with a ball or beanbag.
- Rubber balls and plastic bottle bowling pins—sand can be placed inside the bottles to increase the challenge.
- Paper airplanes for throwing and catching.

climbing structure tunnels or tubes to crawl through balance beam balance boards exercise mats balls in a variety of kinds and sizes beanbags, Frisbees scoops, bats, paddles hoola hoops carpet squares	cones foam noodles ribbon sticks and scarves Bilibos jump ropes stilts in a variety of sizes scooter boards jumping platforms—wooden boxes or cardboard stuffed with newspapers music and music player portable boxes to keep equipment

FIGURE 16.1 Suggested Physical Equipment for Preschool and Early Elementary Age Children

Materials for Kicking. It is generally easier to kick a lighter-weight ball.

- A box of balls set near the corner of the room. The child kicks the ball into a corner so that the ball will come back to him.
- Targets to kick at.
- Obstacle course to dribble a ball through.
- Cards showing different parts of the foot—child practices dribbling the ball using that area of the foot.

Materials for Striking. The younger the child, the larger the striking object and instrument will need to be.

- Lightweight balls, a highway cone, and a plastic bat for hitting the ball off the cone.
- A foam noodle to bat a cloth-covered balloon or beach ball that is hung from the ceiling.
- A foam bladed hockey stick and balls for hitting.
- Nerf balls or cloth-covered balloons and racquets. You can create racquets by bending a wire coat hanger into a circular form and covering the racquet with a discarded calf-length nylon stocking. Make sure to bend the handle of the hanger into a loop to prevent eye injuries.

As the preceding sections have illustrated, it is important to have a variety of equipment available to enhance children's physical skills. For a list of suggested physical equipment, see Figure 16.1.

Special Considerations for Infants and Toddlers

Physical development rapidly occurs in the infant and toddler years. To develop important motor skills, and to develop a foundation for later physical development, children need abundant opportunities to engage in physical activity. They need adults to provide appropriate settings, ample materials, and scaffolding through encouragement, modeling, and instruction.

During this age span, children are developing locomotor skills such as crawling, walking, and jumping; non-manipulative skills such as balancing and turning; and manipulative skills such as throwing and kicking (Pica, 2013). To enhance physical development for young infants, you will want to provide short closely supervised periods of tummy time to strengthen the neck muscles. Placing toys slightly out of children's reach as they lie on their backs or sit up can enhance the young child's stretching and balance. As children begin to crawl and walk you will want multiple areas in the classroom dedicated to physical development. You can provide older infants and toddlers a variety of different objects

Julie Bullard

This climbing rail mirror takes little space and allows toddlers to see their image as they climb. The carpeted box provides a place for toddlers to climb into or support for infants to walk around.

so they can practice their developing skills. These include classroom climbing structures; tunnels and low rectangular boxes to crawl in and out of; risers, mattresses, low couches, or futons to crawl or step onto; and when ready for the challenge, steps such as a turned-over rocking boat to climb or a climbing rail mirror (Greenman, Stonehouse, & Schweikert, 2007). Securely anchored pull-up rails are another piece of equipment that is helpful for infants. When children become more proficient at walking, push-and-pull toys can provide enjoyment as children practice. If there is room in the classroom, indoor riding toys can also be provided.

Meeting the Needs of Children with Disabilities

Sensory processing (formally referred to as sensory integration) disorders are receiving attention in the early childhood field. There are different categories of sensory processing disorders and the disorders can involve different systems. One of these disorders involves the **vestibular system**, which includes the middle ears. This system helps us detect movement and change the position of our head accordingly. Another sensory disorder involves the **proprioceptive system**. This system provides a person with a subconscious awareness of body position, providing the ability to adjust one's body to new positions. While these disorders must be diagnosed by specialists such as occupational or physical therapists, there are some activities that can help all children develop these systems. This includes providing materials such as tactile stepping stones, moon shoes (little trampolines attached to the feet), spinning disks or sit and spins, rocker or wobble boards, scooter boards, balls for children to sit on and bounce (typically they have a handle), therapy balls or hot dog–shaped balls for children to roll on, stilts, and different types of sensory balls (nylon bath scrubbers or textured balls).

Teacher's Facilitation of Learning in the Fitness Center

For fitness learning stations to be successful, children will need to be able to independently complete most of the activities. To assist children to reach this goal, you will need to introduce each activity, helping children to understand how to complete the activity and safely use any equipment. Once you are confident that children can do this, they will be ready for station activities. For successful stations, you will need to have activities available as children enter the indoor physical fitness area. Some teachers handle this by having one teacher lead the children in a group activity as the other teacher sets up the stations. One or two children designated as helpers for the day can also assist in the station set-up.

Once children begin to use the stations you will circulate among stations offering assistance, providing encouragement, and assessing children's progress. You will also want to help all children to feel successful. You can do this by setting up the environment to encourage the right level of challenge. For example, in setting up a center for throwing, you might have different sizes of targets for children to throw at and encourage children to stand at any distance they wish from the target. Children will usually choose the right level of challenge for themselves, if allowed. It is also critical to avoid games or activities where children compete with each other. Also, avoid having a leader choose other children for teammates. This can be an agonizing experience for children who are chosen last.

One of your ultimate goals is to increase the physical activity for all children. Begin by eliminating waiting time through having enough stations and materials. Next, analyze games or activities to make sure they are encouraging activity. For example, in many circle games such as "Duck, Duck, Goose" only two children are running and the rest are sitting still. Finally, avoid elimination games. The children who go out first are often the ones who need the exercise the most. In addition, these children may feel unsuccessful, increasing their desire to avoid physical activities.

One of the special challenges that teachers deal with in physical centers is **rough and tumble play**. This type of play is very physically active. But, should you allow it? Many teachers are concerned about allowing rough and tumble play, particularly play fighting, because they believe it will lead to aggression or injury and that the play may escalate out of control or leave children agitated (Carlson, 2011). However, research shows that children distinguish between play aggression and real aggression where the intent is to harm and that the two rarely occur together. In fact, this occurs in only about 1% of cases (Smith, Smees, & Pellegrini, 2004). Moreover, children are often calmer after engaging in rowdy play (Carlson, 2011). Play fighting is typically seen more often in boys than girls. One study found that play fighting occurred daily for 40% of boys' dramatic play, even though it is the least tolerated form of play with 50% of teachers always banning it. Rough and tumble play is found in all animal species. While engaged in rough and tumble play, animals and children learn about social boundaries, practice and test their strength and agility, and develop self-regulation skills (Hart & Tannock, 2013; Logue & Harvey, 2010).

Check Your Understanding 16.1
Click here to gauge your understanding of section concepts.

Children need the opportunity to engage in daily physical activity. As they participate in the fitness center, they improve body composition, enhance physical skills, become more physically fit, and increase cardiovascular endurance, muscular strength, muscular endurance, and flexibility (Pica, 2013).

Puppetry Centers

With the help of a child, an inert puppet comes to life. Puppet centers can be as simple as a shoebox stage with a variety of finger puppets, or they can be as elaborate as a permanently established puppetry center housing a variety of types of stages and puppets. Puppets can be placed in a center of their own, or as mentioned earlier they might be included in the dramatic play, music, literacy, or manipulative centers. The art center can provide materials so that children can create a variety of different kinds of puppets.

How the Puppetry Center Enhances Children's Development

Puppets encourage imaginative, improvisational play and self-expression. They can enhance a story and encourage language development. Children can participate in informal dialogue, retell a favorite story, or make their puppet dance to the musical beat. Puppets allow children to act out a character, causing them to think about how that character might act, what the character might say, and how that character might look. They encourage the child to experiment with a variety of different voices.

Puppets also encourage social and emotional development through allowing children an acceptable way to express feelings, by letting them act out situations that they are currently experiencing, and by helping them brainstorm solutions to current or future problems. Because puppets draw attention away from the speaker, they can encourage the shy or scared child to talk. Many children feel safer when talking to or through a puppet, viewing the puppet as a "nonthreatening, sympathetic friend that can be trusted with thoughts and feelings without fear of ridicule or reprimand" (Hunt & Renfro, 1982, p. 17).

Designing an Effective Puppetry Center

A puppetry center is one way to encourage children to use puppets. An effective puppetry center contains these elements:

- A quiet space away from traffic with enough room for an audience.
- A simple puppet stage. Puppet stages help to define the puppet area and can add a playful touch. They can be store-bought or you can make your own by cutting a window out of an appliance box, turning a table onto its side, or creating a fabric curtain that hangs between two chairs. Small stages for finger puppets can be constructed using shoeboxes. Enquiring Minds Child Care created a puppet stage by removing a door from a storage closet and replacing it with a curtain. The teacher cut a hole in the curtain for the puppet play. A flap of cloth over the hole allowed the puppeteers to keep the audience in suspense.
- A variety of puppets for children to use. Puppets can be closely aligned with books, such as a Clifford puppet to go with the Clifford books, or they can be generic. Animal, people, and insect puppets are especially appropriate for young children. Choose puppets that can easily be controlled by the child, are durable, and, if possible, are washable.
- Storage that allows puppets to be visible, organized, and protected. You might put hand puppets into puppet tuckers such as milk cartons or soda bottles with the tops cut off, shoe bags, wine racks, or hanging baskets. Finger puppets might be stored in plastic divider boxes, muffin tins, or egg cartons (Hunt & Renfro, 1982).
- Materials for children to create their own puppets. Begin by making one type of puppet using simple materials (puppet made from a sock or paper bag). As children become more proficient, you can add materials to make new types of puppets, as well as additional materials for decorating puppets. Children should create puppets that they can use in their productions. For example, it is easy to create a puppet from a box. However, these puppets can be difficult to use. Some puppets that are appropriate for both creating and then using are listed in Figure 16.2.
- A list with pictures of puppet activities that children can act out (look sad, move arm, give a hug, hop, and clap).
- Books and recordings that children can use for puppet stories.

Julie Bullard

These child-created puppets are made from recycled materials. Children use them for shadow puppetry.

Role of the Teacher in Promoting Puppetry

If you have ever seen young children using puppets for the first time, you may have witnessed a scene similar to the following. Puppet number one, "Hi, how are you?" Puppet number two, "I'm fine." Then the puppets proceed to "wham-bam" each other. To prevent this, it is important to support the child's learning through introducing puppetry, providing information, and assisting children to learn techniques with puppets. To provide a successful puppetry experience you will want to introduce puppetry to children through modeling the use of puppets. You can use the puppets as a way of communicating with children. Many teachers have special puppets who have well-developed personalities. The puppet becomes a treasured classroom guest, interacting with individual children, small groups, and at

FIGURE 16.2
Child-Created Puppets

There are many different types of puppets that young children can make. A few of these are as follows:

- Sock puppets—Children can glue eyes, ears, mouth, etc., onto the sock. For a more sophisticated puppet, children can cut the toe of the sock, and sew in a circle of fabric to create a mouth.
- Mitten or glove puppets—Orphaned mittens and gloves can also become puppets. The thumb of the mitten can become the jaw allowing movement. Gloves might suggest unique types of puppets such as an octopus.Gloves can also be used for a family of finger puppets.
- Stick puppets—Puppets (often made from paper) attached to a Popsicle stick or rod can become a stick puppet. As children become more sophisticated puppet makers, they can use brads to create moving body parts.They can then attach each body part to a rod, allowing a range of movement.
- Finger puppets—Children can create finger puppets in a variety of ways.They can be made by creating a cone that fits on the finger, which becomes the body of the puppet. They also can be created by attaching a small puppet to a felt ring that fits on the finger. The individual finger of a glove can also become the base for a finger puppet. For children who are beginning to create finger puppets, you can make it easier by providing the base (completed cone, felt ring, individual glove finger).
- Paper bag puppets—These puppets, made from small paper lunch bags, use the flap of the bag for the mouth. While these are simple to make, they are more difficult to use than sock puppets.

You will want to supply a variety of materials for decorating the puppets. These might include sequins, beads, discarded jewelry, feathers, movable eyes, buttons, cotton balls, rickrack, ribbon, yarn, pompoms, pieces of fabric, felt, colored foam, construction paper, tag board, markers, needle and thread, brad fasteners, and glue.

After children have created the puppets, encourage them to use the puppets to talk. Puppets can enhance language skills by encouraging children to communicate with others, practice dialogue, and tell stories.

times the entire class. The puppet frequently has dilemmas that children help to solve. Children's dilemmas might also be solved by talking to the puppet. Anthony, a teacher in Head Start, often used his wise owl puppet to visit with an individual child who was having a difficult time. Engaging children in puppet exercises such as making the puppet talk is another way to introduce puppetry. This can be a group activity with each child holding a generic mitten puppet to use for practice. It is important to continue to support children in becoming puppeteers by participating in puppet activities with individual and small groups of children. Other excellent ways to introduce children to puppetry is through having puppeteers visit the classroom and taking children to puppet shows.

For puppetry to be effective you need dramas for the children to act out with their puppets, both recordings and books. This can include recordings of the teacher telling a puppet story. Some books that lend themselves to puppetry are *Caps for Sale*; *Five Little Monkeys Jumping on the Bed*; *Noisy Nora*; *My Crayons Talk*; *Silly Sally*; *Clarabella's Teeth*, *Where the Wild Things Are*; and classics such as *The Three Billy Goats Gruff*, *The Three Little Pigs*, and *Goldilocks and the Three Bears*. It is often easier for children to begin using puppets by only having to move the puppets without saying the words. As children become more proficient, they can do both.

Watch this video on shadow puppets. What are some of the different ways to use shadow puppetry in an early childhood curriculum?

https://www.youtube.com/watch?v=OsdMqNlcrls

Renew interest in puppetry by providing new puppets, backdrops, stories or by introducing children to a new form of puppetry, such as shadow puppetry. As children become more skilled at puppetry, they will often begin to develop and perform scripts that are more elaborate. Make sure that children understand the variety of roles in puppetry. Some children may be interested in making backdrops, turning the backdrops, or writing scripts. In this way, many children can be included in a child-initiated puppet production.

TIP

To create your own inexpensive puppets for children to use, remove the stuffing from a second-hand stuffed animal.

Check Your Understanding 16.2
Click here to gauge your understanding of section concepts.

Puppetry can bring joy to the child puppeteer and the audience, allow avenues for self-expression and creativity, and encourage language. Puppetry can also become an integrated unit of study. In Claudia's third-grade classroom, children became very interested in the puppetry corner. They composed and wrote special stories to perform. Claudia also found that the children were often working cooperatively in designing puppets and backdrops, and in performing. As children displayed interest in the puppets, Claudia decided to make this a topic of study for social studies. She introduced different types of puppets and puppetry that were used throughout the world, showing children short videos and inviting puppeteers to the classroom. As children learned about the puppets, they also learned about stories and traditions from different cultures.

Cooking and Snack Centers

A cooking and snack center may be permanently established or set up for a specific time of the day. For example, Curious Minds Child Care sets up a snack center each afternoon so that children can individually prepare their afternoon snack during choice time. Weeping Willow Kindergarten sets up a snack center for those children who have not eaten breakfast before they come to school. These centers are available during learning center time and children can choose when or if they want to eat. Therefore, it is not an interruption of their play.

What Children Learn Through Cooking

When children engage in the cooking and snack area, they learn the following skills (Foote, 2001):

- Food preparation skills such as washing their hands before beginning to cook, measuring and mixing skills, using small appliances, and safe cooking practices.
- Math skills such as one-to-one correspondence, measuring, fractions, and counting.
- Science skills such as observing, predicting, physical properties of matter, and changes in matter.
- Literacy skills such as sequencing, left to right progression, word and letter identification, reading for information, and new vocabulary.
- Fine motor skills. Cooking provides the opportunity to use hand strength and coordination (kneading or stirring), eye-hand coordination (pouring), and fine motor skills (cutting, peeling, or using a melon baller) (Colker, 2005).
- Appropriate nutrition and healthy eating habits. Food preferences begin when children are very young (Barbour, 2004). Children are more likely to experiment with and taste food they have helped to prepare. Through discussing healthy food choices and providing children opportunities to prepare healthy foods, we can help children to develop lifetime healthy habits.
- Cultural knowledge. Through cooking, children can learn about their own and other's cultures.
- Socioemotional development. As children cook, they develop initiative, responsibility, self-regulation, and a feeling of competence (Colker, 2005).

The cooking and snack center should include the following:

- An attractive place for a small group to sit and eat (you might add a tablecloth and a vase of flowers to the dining table).
- A counter or additional table for preparing the snack or setting out the tasting tray.
- A sink for ease of washing hands.
- A conveniently placed electrical outlet for the occasional use of a blender, toaster, or other small appliance.
- A system for designating the number of children that can use the center at one time. Some programs provide four aprons and require that all the children who are cooking wear an apron; others only set out four chairs at the table with the rule that you can only enter the area if there is an empty chair; and others post a sign with the number of children allowed.
- Aprons that are hung on hooks or a child-sized coat tree.
- Clean up supplies (covered garbage can, sponges, and child-sized sponge mop). Cooking and eating surfaces need to be cleaned and sanitized before and after use.
- Storage for small appliances, cooking equipment and utensils, and serving utensils.
- Recipe books, food magazines, and blank recipe cards for children to write their own recipes.
- Nutritional information (healthy-unhealthy snack poster or MyPlate poster).

Appropriate Cooking Center Activities

Many different types of activities can occur in the cooking center. The center can be used to prepare individual snacks (see Figure 16.3 for individual snack ideas), experiment with taste trays, or for small groups of children to prepare recipes.

One-Portion Recipes. Individual portion recipes allow many learning opportunities. Children are able to complete each step themselves, following sequenced directions, measuring and mixing ingredients, and finally eating the finished product. Because each child is completing the entire recipe, he is able to work independently as time is available, making it a perfect center activity. In addition, the child decides when he is hungry and prepares and eats the snack at that time rather than at a predetermined time established by someone else. This helps to establish a healthy approach to eating. Occasionally, you may have a child who is compelled to overeat if food is continually available. In this case, you will want to monitor the situation closely.

Choose recipes that children can complete themselves during the allocated time. The recipe needs to be nutritious, meeting childcare food program guidelines for a snack. Independent recipes are most successful if they can be completed in a few steps. Place each step of the recipe on a large index card that includes printed directions along with pictures or photos. You may want to laminate the cards to keep them for future cooking activities. Lay the cards out from left to right, beginning with a card that reminds children to wash their hands. Place the needed ingredients and measuring devices above each card. If the child is using measuring spoons or cups for more than one direction, it is helpful to have enough measuring devices that there can be one placed with each direction. See Figure 16.4 for a recipe that makes an individual portion of ice cream.

Taste Trays. Taste trays often provide three or more types of food for children to sample. At least some of these foods may be new to the children. The chosen foods often share some characteristic. For example, the taste tray might include a food item in different states (coconut in the shell, coconut milk, dried coconut). The highlighted foods

FIGURE 16.3 Examples of Individual Portion Recipes That Do Not Require Cooking

Following are nutritious cooking activities that a child can complete independently during center time. None of the recipes involve cooking, allowing the child to assemble and then immediately eat their creations. These recipes can be tailored to the developmental level of the children. For example, three-year-old children might assemble kebobs on toothpicks from precut meat and cheese. Older children will be able to cut the meat and cheese into cubes for their kebob before assembling them. Whenever you are planning cooking activities, it is very important to be aware of allergies in your classroom.

These are the easiest recipes. They require few ingredients and involve spreading and mixing, but not cutting or blending.

- ❑ Ants on a log—stuff celery with soft cheese and add raisins
- ❑ Round cracker with cream cheese and decorations to make faces
- ❑ Plain yogurt with a variety of stir ins (fruit, granola)
- ❑ Apple face (spread peanut butter on a half of an apple, use raisins to create face)
- ❑ Tortilla spread with refried beans and grated cheese
- ❑ Trail mix (mixture of raisins, nuts, dried fruits, cereal)

These recipes require children to follow more steps and to cut or blend ingredients.

- ❑ Fruit salad (older children can peel the fruit and make melon balls)
- ❑ Various types of kebobs (fruit, meat and cheese, cheese and cucumber)
- ❑ Peanut butter sandwiches (older children might make their own peanut butter by shelling ¼ cup peanuts and putting them in the blender with ½ tablespoon of vegetable oil). Make sure you check for peanut allergies before you do this activity.
- ❑ Smoothies (usually contains milk, fruit, and yogurt)
- ❑ Peanut butter balls (mixtures of peanut butter, honey, and dried milk, rolled in rice krispies)
- ❑ Banana pudding in a jar (shake 1 tablespoon plus 1 teaspoon of pudding mix in a baby food jar with ¼ cup milk, after shaking add ⅛ cup sliced banana)
- ❑ Boiled eggs to peel (after children have peeled the egg, they can follow the recipe to create egg salad sandwiches or deviled eggs)
- ❑ Raw vegetables with individually child prepared bean, spinach, or cottage cheese dip
- ❑ Carrot raisin salad

For additional recipe ideas, see *Cup Cooking, Individual Child-Portion Picture Recipes* by Barbara Foote *or The Cooking Book* by Laura Colker.

FIGURE 16.4 Recipe for an Individual Portion of Ice Cream

1 small plastic freezer bag
1 large plastic freezer bag
½ cup milk or half and half
1 tablespoon sugar
¼ teaspoon vanilla
Ice cubes
6 tablespoons rock salt

Combine the milk, sugar, and vanilla in a small plastic freezer bag. Securely seal the bag. Combine the ice and salt in the large bag until the bag is half full. Put the small bag inside the large bag and then seal the large bag. Shake the bag until the mixture thickens. When the mixture is the consistency of ice cream, take the smaller bag from the large bag and enjoy. If children have a long-handled spoon they can eat the ice cream out of the plastic bag.

might all come from one food group (different types of vegetables). Alternatively, the food might relate to a particular theme (from a certain area of the country, grows in trees, grow underground) (Colker, 2005).

Taura sets up a taste tray each week in the cooking center. She first discusses the foods that will be present with the children at circle time and allows them to see the food in an uncut form. For example, when they were tasting pineapples, she passed the pineapple around the circle where the children smelled it and felt the bumpy skin and prickly leaves. Next, she cut the pineapple open so they could see the core and flesh. She then placed the fresh pineapple chunks, along with canned pineapple chunks and fried pineapple, on the taste tray.

Watch the video on how one teacher uses taste trays. Why might the taste tray entice children to eat more fruits and vegetables?

Small-Group Cooking Activities. Many teachers plan a special small group, supervised activity in their cooking area each week. Small group cooking activities provide opportunities to engage in discussions about foods and for the teacher to model cooking techniques. However, the larger the group, the less opportunity the child has to be actively engaged in the process.

Dominique, a teacher of preschool children, valued the learning that occurred during cooking and had done this for several years. However, she was interested in helping children learn more about the diverse cultures in her community and wondered if cooking could be an avenue to explore culture. One day she and the children ate Irish soda bread for snack. Many of the children were unfamiliar with the bread and had questions about it. Dominique realized that breads might be a way to start to learn about different cultures. She invited families and community members to come in once a week and bake bread with the children in the cooking area. They then ate the bread for snack. Over the course of several months the children and their guests made scones (Scotland), tortillas (Mexico), chapattis (India), mandarin pancakes (China), okonomiyaki (Japan), pita bread (Middle East), crumpets (England), challah (Jewish braided bread), diphaphata (Botswana), and American Indian fry bread. Many of the guests also brought in cooking and eating utensils used in their culture, recipe books written in their native language, and other items such as photos of stoves and kitchens to show the children. As the children baked bread, they learned cooking techniques while also learning about other cultures.

Role of the Teacher in the Cooking Center

Children need to be supported in the cooking center by adults who effectively organize the center, supervise it, offer assistance as needed, and promote learning through conversations with children. The teacher needs to organize the center so that children can use it independently. For example, if using one-portion recipes, the individual cards with words and pictures detailing each step of the recipe, the ingredients, the cooking utensils and bowls would all be set out ahead of time. See Figure 16.5 for an example of how to set up a one-portion recipe activity.

You must also teach the children the skills they need to be successful (demonstrate how to measure ingredients, use small appliances, and use unfamiliar techniques). As with all skills we teach children, you will want to begin with simple cooking projects, and after children have mastered these, move to more complex recipes. For example, you

FIGURE 16.5 One-Portion recipe Setup

might begin with a two-step direction that does not require cooking and progress to multistep directions that require cooking. As you cook, discuss the food and processes with the children. For example, you can discuss background information about the food, name the food and processes, discuss the attributes of the food such as the texture, ask open-ended questions, and listen to children describe the steps they have taken.

Check Your Understanding 16.3
Click here to gauge your understanding of section concepts.

The center also needs to be safe and healthy. Food preparation and serving surfaces need to be washed and sanitized before and after using them. Food needs to be at the correct temperature to reduce bacteria. Additionally, you need to teach children healthy practices (washing hands before handling food, replacing a cooking spoon that has been licked) and safe practices (using appliances and utensils in a safe manner).

A cooking center allows children the gratifying experience of creating their own snacks while learning about healthy food choices. Children also gain literacy, science, and math skills as they cook.

Woodworking and Carpentry Centers

Although many teachers have concerns about the safety of woodworking, advocates stress that woodworking has many benefits and is a safe activity when children are taught the proper use of tools and there is adequate supervision. As children participate in woodworking, they enhance their creativity while practicing eye-hand coordination, large and fine motor skills, mathematical skills (measuring, one-to-one correspondence, and angles), science skills (properties of materials and the use of tools), and engineering skills (design process). Woodworking can also increase attention span and perseverance. For example, Thomas, a four-year-old, normally flitted from activity to activity. However, the combination of a specific goal, obvious visual progress, and the physical activity inherent in woodworking allowed him to stay focused. Like Thomas, many children find woodworking to be a preferred activity. Additionally, many programs find that woodworking centers encourage previously uninvolved families to participate in the program. For example, at Beautiful Beginnings Child Care, a father who is a carpenter now regularly brings in pieces of wood for the children to use. He carefully chooses wood that will be easy for the children to hammer and saw. He says, "I used to think that there was nothing I could contribute. But now that you've started the woodworking center, I can see a way I can help out." Two grandparents have been volunteering each week to assist in the woodworking center. One of the mothers, who makes wood signs, has invited the class to her workshop.

Young children's first woodworking activities can include pounding golf tees or large flat-headed nails into Styrofoam. As children's skills increase, they are able to pound nails into wood. For example, in one early childhood program in Hawaii, teachers placed a coconut tree cut lengthwise into the outdoor play yard. Children have pounded nails into the tree for many years.

By the end of the preschool years, most children can develop and follow a plan to create a self-chosen product. They are able to use a variety of tools in their creations and develop these creations over a period of time (Wellhousen & Crowther, 2004). See Figure 16.6 for more information on the developmental stages of woodworking.

Designing the Woodworking Center

Since woodworking is noisy, the center needs to be placed outside or in a noisy area of the classroom. If the center is inside, it might be placed next to the creative art area, so that children can use the art materials to decorate their creations. An effective woodworking center includes the following:

- Enough space for two to four children to work without interfering with each.
- A sturdy, stable woodworking bench (4×2.5 foot) with a vise at one end (Texas Child Care Quarterly, 2013).

Stage 1—Becoming acquainted with tools and wood. Children in this stage are exploring wood and tools. They might pound nails into a piece of wood simply for the joy of pounding.

Stage 2—Making simple skill attempts. In this stage, children begin to hammer, saw, and glue. They will attempt to make projects. For example, they might try to connect two pieces of wood by nailing them together. However, they often are not successful.

Stage 3—Developing simple constructions. As children become more proficient in woodworking, they are able to design and build simple constructions.

Stage 4—Refining skills. After children have built many constructions, they may begin to refine their skills. For example, they may glue before they nail wood together.

Stage 5—Functional construction. At this stage, children make realistic objects.

Stage 6—Decorative combinations. Children in this stage will preplan their woodworking to intentionally create a project that they can use. For example, they might make a doll bench to use in dramatic play.

Stage 7—Emergence of craft. In this stage, children try out new ideas, using carpentry for both functional and symbolic ideas (Huber, 1998, p.75).

FIGURE 16.6 Developmental Stages of Children's Woodworking

- Real tools (you might choose smaller-sized options). Appropriate tools for preschool and elementary children include hammers, pliers, vise grips, metal clamps, planes, levels, miter boxes, crowbars, files, handsaws (pull saw, crosscut, keyhole, or compass), screwdrivers (standard and Phillips), eggbeater drills and bits, rulers, small framing square, and retractable tape measures (Abraham, 2011; Huber, 1998).
- An abundance of pieces of soft wood (pine or poplar) that are a manageable size for the age group. Do not use hardwood (too difficult to nail into), plywood (can splinter), or treated wood (can contain harmful chemicals). You can often get free scrap lumber. However, you may need to buy wood so that you get the type of wood you want.
- Wood glue, nails (large headed), screws (Phillips), duct tape, and wire.
- Items for decorating creations (spools, bark, discarded knobs, latches, and paint).
- Items to use in building (wheels, latches, and knobs).
- Sandpaper.
- Carpentry pencils for marking wood and pencils and paper for drawing plans.
- Well-fitting safety goggles, work gloves (prevent blisters when sawing), and carpentry aprons (to hold nails) to provide for safety and convenience.
- A table covered with a plastic tablecloth for painting and gluing.
- Appropriate storage. All storage should be clearly labeled with an outline, photo, word, or in the case of small objects, with the actual item (screws and nails). You will want to have:
  - A place for hanging the tools. An outline of the tool allows children to know where to return each one. Avoid toolboxes since it is difficult to find a tool in the box and children can become injured as they dig through the box.
  - A chest with clear drawers for nails and screws.
  - A storage area for wood.
  - A shelf containing different baskets for goggles, work gloves, and items that can't easily be hung, such as miter boxes.
  - A place for children to display ongoing and completed work.
  - A magazine stand to provide storage for books of woodworking ideas, tool catalogs, and binders containing photos of children's woodworking process and products.

Julie Bullard

This preschool woodworking area at Helen Gordon Child Development Center has an abundance of tools and materials to create with.

Role of the Teacher in the Woodworking Area

Teachers play a crucial role in the success of the woodworking center through establishing an effective center, keeping the center stocked with materials, providing instruction and encouragement, and teaching and monitoring for safety. When introducing the tools, provide the name, discuss when you would use the tool, and demonstrate the proper usage of the tool. You may want to introduce one tool at a time, allowing children the opportunity to become competent with that tool before introducing another. Often the first tool introduced is a hammer. You will also want to introduce safety rules such as wearing goggles when using tools, using the tools in a responsible manner, keeping the work area clean, putting tools away when done, and following the work area participant limit signs. Until children are proficient, you may want to limit the number of children to one or two and provide close supervision.

Beginning woodworking activities need to be designed to acquaint children with tools and wood. It is important to provide activities that allow early success. These initial activities might include creating sculptures using wood glue, sanding a piece of wood, screwing a screw into a predrilled hole, nailing pre-set nails into wood and then pulling them out, or nailing flat-headed nails into Styrofoam. Providing colorful paper designs that children can nail around can increase motivation. Children can learn to saw by sawing pieces of Styrofoam and then move to sawing soft wood. As children become more competent with woodworking, you will want to provide the additional tools and materials they need to be successful. For example, children might be interested in creating a particular product such as a birdhouse. You might provide some pieces of wood containing cutout holes to assist with their process and simple plans and pictures of different types of simple birdhouses for inspiration and guidance. In addition, you might introduce children to the engineering process. As we discussed in Chapter 9, this process involves investigation, invention, implementation, and evaluation. Adding new materials and tools and presenting challenges can assist in keeping the area interesting.

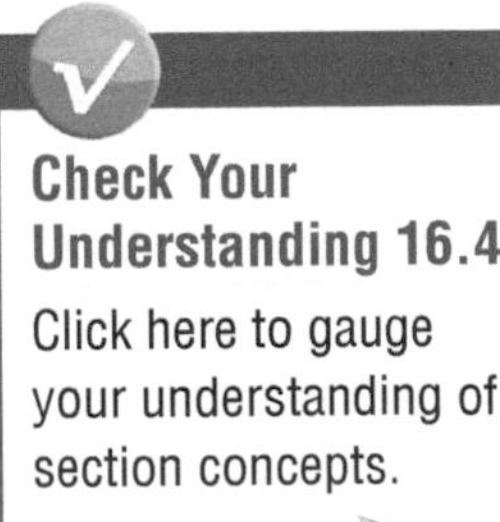

Check Your Understanding 16.4

Click here to gauge your understanding of section concepts.

Provide encouragement for children to make creative constructions and, as they become more skilled, to follow a plan. Typically, children will design and build their own constructions. However, at times it is appropriate to have a model for children to follow so that they can learn to follow a plan that includes structured steps. This can allow children to have a successful building experience. "Woodworking has not only a creative side but also a more structured side—following a design, pattern, set of instructions, or model" (Sosna, 2000, p. 38). You can also provide encouragement through documenting children's woodworking process and products with photos. Many teachers create a book of the constructions.

It is important to also offer assistance so that the child can be successful. This includes helping the child choose the appropriate tool for the job and assisting the child to use the tool in an effective manner, such as pointing the saw down at an angle.

Discuss constructions with children (ask children about the process used, the steps in the process, their next steps for continuing the project, and their challenges). Also, provide new vocabulary while talking with children (names of tools, types of wood, and processes).

Children's woodworking can be enhanced through experiences. Plan visits to lumberyards and woodworking shops so children can see tools being used in the real world. You can also invite carpenters and other woodworkers to visit the classroom.

TIP

To hold the nail steady, you might insert the nail through a large-tooth comb. The child can then hold the end of the comb. Alternatively, you might insert a piece of cardboard that will support the nail but will be torn away after the nail is securely embedded in the wood. Teachers might also use an awl to punch a hole for setting the nail.

Woodworking is an engaging center for both children and families. This center, where children get the chance to practice real-world skills, allows them to develop self-esteem and creativity and enhance social and fine motor skills (Foster & Hardison, 2000, p. 1).

Providing special-interest centers can meet children's unique needs while providing many additional learning opportunities. Special-interest centers can also help to prevent boredom. This is especially important for children who might be spending multiple years in the same classroom.

? Chapter Quiz 16

Click here to gauge your understanding of chapter concepts.

Sample Application Activities

1. Brainstorm a list of other special-interest centers. Choose one center and make a list of materials that would support the center.
2. Visit an early childhood classroom and observe the amount of physical activity that children receive during the day. Are they receiving the recommended amount? What options do you see for increasing indoor physical activity within the space?
3. Develop a cup-cooking recipe. Try the recipe with a group of children.
4. To learn more about puppetry throughout the world and how to create and use puppets, see the puppetry home page at Sagecraft.com.
5. Develop a puppet show that you can use to introduce children to puppetry.
6. Learn more about woodworking at the Child Care Lounge.

CHAPTER 17

Creating Outdoor Environments

Learning Outcomes

After you have read this chapter, you will be prepared to:

- Defend the value and rights of children to play outdoors
- Describe the advantages and disadvantages of different types of playgrounds
- Design effective outdoor environments
- Explain how to design outdoor environments for different age groups
- Describe multiple ways that teachers facilitate learning in the outdoor environment

Julie Bullard

The playground at Sunshine Academy, a preschool program, was too small and was cluttered with equipment that the children did not use. The equipment consisted of small plastic climbing sets that did not create developmental challenges for the children. As a result, children often used the equipment in unintended, unsafe ways. Additionally, none of the equipment developed upper-body strength. There were few natural materials in the playground, and the ground cover, once grass, had become very sparse. When it rained or the snow melted, the playground became a muddy bog.

Three years later the playground is blooming with flower and vegetable gardens, new trees have been planted, and a variety of ground surfaces (sand, wood chips, pavers, grass) are evident.

The playground, now much larger, is zoned into different areas and can be used in all types of weather. To develop gross motor skills, tires are embedded on their side to create a tunnel, and different heights of stumps are upended to form a place to climb on and jump from. An extensive white cedar play set offers climbing, sliding, and swinging opportunities. A climbing wall, overhead ladder, fire pole, and knotted climbing rope all increase upper-arm strength and development. Creative arts are enhanced through a music area that is attached to the fence and an art studio that is tucked under a tree. A small house and a golf cart with wheels removed create dramatic play opportunities.

The gardens and a bird feeder attract birds to the playground. The bird feeder is hung in the tree with a rope and pulley, making it easier to fill the feeder while also teaching about simple tools. Under the tree sits a small table that contains binoculars and a bird book for watching and identifying birds. A small cabinet that can be locked at night contains other equipment for watching and investigating (magnifying glasses, bug jars, and butterfly nets). A hammock and a basket of books are also under the tree, providing a quiet retreat area.

How did this transformation occur? First, the program developed a long-term plan. The plan began with what children needed and were interested in rather than what equipment to buy. A committee of parents, teachers, and administrators met for several months to develop the plan. Children were asked for their ideas, playgrounds were thoroughly researched, visits were made to high-quality playgrounds, and goals and timelines were developed. Critical to the success of the plan was an increase in the size of the playground. There was an area adjacent to the playground that was not being used. Although there had been many previous unsuccessful attempts to obtain this space, the playground research and planning made it easier to convince the manager that this area should be used for the playground. Work was phased in over a period of time. Costs were reduced through donated materials and labor (a youth group helped to bury the tires and stumps, a local college woodworking club built the playhouse). Finally, the administrator used the research the group had gathered to obtain a grant for the playground structure. Establishing long-term goals by involving all constituencies and seeking help from many sources allowed the program to transform their playground. Planning for children's needs and interests allowed the playground to become a fun, interesting, outdoor classroom filled with learning opportunities.

Value and Rights of Children to Play Outdoors

There are many benefits to a well-planned outdoor space. Outside, children can play vigorously, use loud voices, release excess energy, and engage in large, messy projects. In the outdoors, children can experience climate, openness, messiness, wildlife, and different landscapes such as hills, holes, streams, and mud puddles (Greenman, 1991). They can test and strengthen their physical skills and engage in social, cognitive, and creative pursuits. The outdoors provides invaluable learning opportunities, promotes health, encourages lifelong dispositions, and helps to instill an appreciation for nature (Cuppens, Rosenow, & Wike, 2007). Research indicates that children who play outdoors demonstrate better visual motor integration, imagination, and verbal and social skills than children who play inside (Yerkes, 1982). There are also health benefits to playing outdoors, including opportunities for exercise, exposure to sunlight necessary for the body to produce vitamin D, and an environment with less concentrated disease organisms than are found inside. Playing outdoors can also increase physical fitness and exercise, reduce obesity, and improve motor development.

Reducing Obesity and Increasing Physical Fitness

Prevalence of Obesity. In the United States, 8.4% of children two to five years old and 17.7% of six- to 11-year-olds are **obese** (weight for height is equal to or greater than the 95th percentile) (National Center for Health Statistics, 2014). There are both ethnic and income disparities in obesity. For example, one-third of low-income children ages two to four are **overweight** (weight for height is equal to or greater than the 85th percentile but less than the 95th percentile) or obese. American Indian, Alaska Native, and Hispanic children in this age group are more likely to be obese than other racial and ethnic groups (Sharma et al., 2009). Most other industrialized countries and many lower-income countries are also struggling with this epidemic (Han, Lawlor, & Kimm, 2010).

Dangers of Obesity. According to the World Health Organization (WHO), obesity is "one of the most serious public health challenges of the 21st century" (WHO, 2011). Children who are obese face both immediate and lifelong health problems. Obese children are more likely to have high blood pressure, high cholesterol, type 2 diabetes, asthma, sleep apnea, joint issues and discomfort, and liver and gallbladder disease. Children and adults who are overweight also face social discrimination, psychological problems, and poor self-esteem. Children who are obese face increased medical costs and have a greatly increased chance of being obese adults (Au, 2012; USDHHS, 2001).

Preventing Obesity. Excluding genetic factors, the strongest predictor for being overweight is lack of exercise (Nelson, Carpenter, & Chiasson, 2006). Let's Move! Active Schools, a comprehensive program based on the President's Council on Fitness, Sports and Nutrition recommends that children receive an hour of moderate to vigorous play each day to stay a healthy weight. Additionally, the National Association for Sports and Physical Education recommends children participate in one to several hours a day of unstructured physical activity (Goodway, Getchell, Raynes, & NASPE, 2009). Since many young children spend the majority of their day in early childhood programs, it is imperative that we promote higher activity levels and improved physical skills. In addition to the immediate advantages of exercise, physical skills and dispositions gained in early childhood can form a foundation for exercise throughout life.

Children engage in higher activity levels and burn more calories when they play outdoors rather than indoors (Sutterby & Frost, 2002). In fact, one study that tracked children's steps using pedometers found that children had 30% more steps during recess versus structured gym classes (Beresin, 2012). Children who spend more time outdoors are also more physically fit than their peers (Baranowski et al., 2000; Sallis et al., 1993). Ideally, the outdoor time is spent in child-chosen play, because this is the best way for children to accumulate physical activity (Pate, Baranowski, Dowda, & Trost, 1996). "For most children, outdoor play offers the only opportunity to engage in aerobic activities that enhance fitness, strength, flexibility, and endurance and helps compensate for faulty diets" (Sutterby & Frost, 2002, p. 38). To learn ways to enhance physical activity on playgrounds, see Figure 17.1.

FIGURE 17.1
Research Supported Interventions to Increase Playground Activity

Outdoor time can significantly contribute to needed exercise requirements if children participate in moderate-intensity play for 40% of the playtime (Ridgers, Stratton, & Fairclough, 2005). Try these research-supported interventions to increase playground activity:

- ❑ Develop obstacle courses (Scruggs, Beveridge, & Watson, 2003)
- ❑ Mark playgrounds with mazes, hop scotch, and snakes and ladders (Stratton, 2000)
- ❑ Plan high-activity games (Connolly & McKenzie, 1995)
- ❑ Improve the ratio of equipment (balls, bats, and jump ropes) to children
- ❑ Provide more play equipment (hurdles, tunnels, balance beams, targets, bean bags, balls, bats, jump ropes, hoops, and flying disks) (Broekhuizen, Scholten, & de Vries, 2014; Lopes, Lopes, & Pereira, 2009; Zask, van Beurden, Barnett, Brooks, Dietrich, 2001)
- ❑ Increase the number of permanent play facilities such as sand pits (Neilson, Taylor, Williams, & Mann, 2010)
- ❑ Assure activity is enjoyable for children (Weis & Ferrer-Caja, 2002)

Enhancing Motor Development

Children in the early childhood years are typically in the **fundamental movement** phase. Fundamental movements include running, walking, hopping, skipping, jumping, galloping, kicking, catching, striking, **dynamic balancing** (balancing while moving), **static balancing** (center of gravity remains stationary), and **axial movement** (such as bending, stretching, twisting, and turning) (Frost et al., 2004, p. 25; Gallahue, 1993).

Mastery of the fundamental movements is critical to participate successfully in many recreational games, sports, and activities. If these skills are not mastered, it leads to failure and frustration. While it is possible to learn these skills later in life, "the individual is … beyond the sensitive period during which it is easiest to master these skills; as a result, the skills frequently do remain unlearned" (Gallahue, 1993, p. 24). As people get older, they often are more self-conscious about poor skills, fear injury and peer rejection, and must unlearn bad habits, making skill development more difficult.

While maturation plays a role in the development of movement, it is not enough to assure competence. Children need opportunities to practice skills, encouragement to do so, and instruction (Gallahue, 1993). Free play that includes a range of physically challenging activities and equipment is the best way to provide movement activities (Frost et al., 2004, p. 25). Teachers who interact with children during outdoor free play can provide encouragement and individualized instruction, further enhancing skill development.

Enhancing Social Development

Play during outdoor time is linked to improved social skills and enhanced relationships between children (Gill, 2014, p. 12). Children develop social skills as they interact freely with peers, organize games, develop rules for play, and resolve conflicts (Jarrett, 2002, p. 1). As children create their own rules, they learn that rules are "not fixed and immutable but are man-made and refutable" (Elkind, 2006, p. 8).

In many schools, the playground may provide one of the limited opportunities for children to play freely with peers. In addition, playgrounds often combine children from different classrooms, allowing interaction with an expanded peer group.

Enhancing Cognitive Development

Research links outdoor time with improved cognitive skills and academic performance (Gill, 2014). Outdoors, children have unique intellectual learning opportunities. Through experience, they learn about the elements (earth, air, water, and fire) and cosmos (sun, moon, stars, and planets). They learn about **conservation** as they play. "Conservation, the understanding of continuity beneath apparent change, is a fundamental intellectual achievement aided and abetted by out-of-door experiences" (Elkind, 2006, p. 8). Additionally, as children interact in "rich" outdoor learning centers, they have opportunities to participate in math, science, music, art, and literacy, and to engage in communication. They also have ample opportunities to develop academic dispositions such as curiosity, initiative, engagement, persistence, imagination, invention, creativity, reasoning, problem solving, risk taking, responsibility, confidence, flexibility, and resilience (Banning & Sullivan, 2011).

Developing an Appreciation of Nature

A love of nature, and therefore the desire to preserve it, grows out of a child's frequent contact and play in the natural world (Schultz, Shriver, Tabanico, & Khazian, 2004; Sobel, 2004). If children do not have ample opportunities to play in the natural world in their early childhood years, they may never develop these attitudes (Sobel, 2002). Instead, children develop fears and phobias about nature and the natural world, referred to as **biophobia** (Mattenson, 2008; Sobel, 1996). Children not regularly exposed to nature refer to nature as "diseased," "disgusting," and "dirty." They also show fear of plants and insects (Bixler, Carlisle, Hammitt, & Floyd, 1994). Because children often spend 40 or more hours a week in early childhood programs, these places may be "mankind's last opportunity to reconnect children with the natural world and create a future generation that values and preserves nature" (White, 2004, p. 3).

Natural, ungroomed places are often favorites of children. For example, when asked to recall favorite environments in childhood, adults tend to remember more natural places than other settings (Jenson & Bullard, 2002). These are often places that they could manipulate (for example, build a fort) (Sobel, 1993).

Besides being preferred locations by children, research studies show that being in nature has many benefits for the child. This includes enhancement of creative play (Faber Taylor & Kuo, 2006) and increased attention spans (Wells, 2000). Being in natural areas also buffers the impact of stress on children (Wells & Evans, 2003). As children participate in natural settings, they acquire a sense of season and natural cycles, get a sense of themselves as nurturers, and develop a connection to something timeless and larger than themselves (Bohling-Philippi, 2006, pp. 49–51). Being in natural settings may also reduce the severity of symptoms in children with ADHD (Faber Taylor & Kuo, 2011).

Julie Bullard

Children learn to appreciate nature as they care for and observe the many different kinds of birds that visit the bird feeders.

Some programs have replaced blacktop, building natural environments that feature trees, ponds, and gardens. Studies in one school where this occurred showed that children had fewer playground injuries, and they experienced more joy, pride, and a sense of belonging after the transformation. In addition, there was a greater awareness of the environment (Moore, 1986).

You may be unable to transform the entire playground environment into a natural place. However, Frost et al. (2004) advocates designing a natural area in every playground, even if it is as simple as retaining an unmowed portion of grass to allow for wildflowers.

Because of the many benefits to outdoor play, the National Health and Safety Standards recommend that toddlers and preschoolers spend 60–90 minutes during a program day in outdoor play (American Academy of Pediatrics, American Public Health Association, & National Resource Center for Health and Safety in Child Care and Early Education, 2011). We have reviewed the importance of outdoor play. But, are children getting the recommended amounts of outdoor play? We will examine this question next.

Protecting Children's Right to Play Outdoors

Nearly 20 years ago, Rivken (1995), the author of *The Great Outdoors*, sounded the alarm that children's outdoor play was vanishing. "Children's access to outdoor play has evaporated like water in sunshine. It has happened so fast, along with everything else in this speed-ridden century that we have not coped with it well. If someone had said to our grandmothers, 'Bet your great-grandchildren won't know where to find worms,' they would not have believed it" (Rivken, 1995, p. 2). There is growing concern about the decrease in children's time outdoors. For example, between 1981 and 1997, the time outside for children between the ages of six and eight decreased by 27% (Hoffert & Sandberg, 2000). In one study, 70% of mothers played outside everyday when they were young, while only 31% of their children do (Clements, 2004). Children today have limited opportunities for free play or exposure to nature due in part to a "culture of fear" (White, 2004). Eighty-two percent of preschool and elementary children's parents stated the main reason they do not allow children to play outside is concern about crime and safety (Clements, 2004). Parents are concerned about injury, stranger danger, sun exposure, insect-carrying diseases, and pollution (Copeland et al., 2012; Pyle, 2002; Wilson, 2000). Additionally, children's time is often consumed with planned activities. As stated by Eric Nelson, author of *Outdoor Classrooms*, "The free-range childhood I enjoyed fifty years ago has yielded to one that is highly controlled, heavily scripted, and almost devoid of child-initiated, child-controlled activity" (Nelson, 2012, p. 17).

Since many children do not have the opportunity to play outdoors at home, it is especially important that they have opportunities for outdoor play in early childhood programs. However, children are typically not receiving the recommended physical activity in early childhood settings either. One study reveals that this is due to concerns with injury, lack of finances, and pressure to spend more time on academic skills. Even in preschools, research reveals that there is pressure to spend more time on academics at the expense of time outdoors (Copeland et al., 2012). This lack of free time to play outside has resulted in what some call a "childhood of imprisonment" (Stoecklin, 2000).

The trend to spend less time outside is also a concern in other countries. For example, the lack of time children spend outside, rising obesity, sedentary activities, and the amount of time children spend watching or using electronic media is a concern in Norway and several other Scandinavian countries. To counteract this, some kindergartens in Scandinavian countries are provided entirely outdoors. Results show that children in these programs are more creative in play, engage in increased play activities, have less illness, and are more physically fit than their peers (Fjørtoft, 2001, p. 112). These playgrounds are often natural spaces.

Are there differences in types of playgrounds and the results for children? Learn how research is beginning to answer this question by reading the next section.

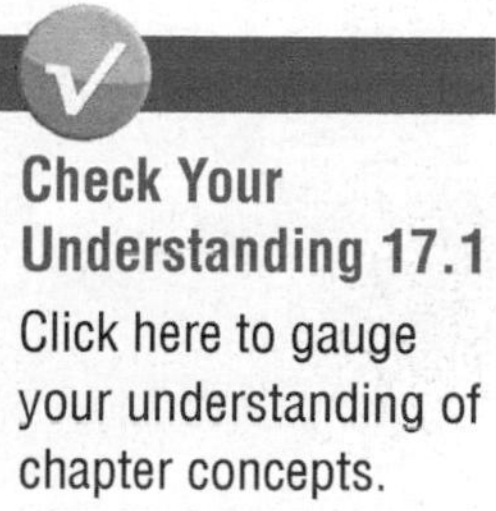
Check Your Understanding 17.1
Click here to gauge your understanding of chapter concepts.

Types of Playgrounds

Playgrounds in the United States began to appear in the 1800s (Moore, Bocarro, & Hickerson, 2007). Preschool playgrounds were influenced by Froebel, the father of kindergarten, and John Dewey, an American educator and philosopher who emphasized experiential learning. These playgrounds included gardens, sand play, woodworking, natural play materials, and equipment. The American parks movement, on the other hand, influenced elementary school playgrounds. These playgrounds emphasized equipment that contributed to physical development and were often placed on flat expanses of pavement or dirt (Dempsey & Frost, 1993, p. 316; Brown, Sutterby, & Thornton, 2001). The manufacturing era brought about the ability to create metal, steel, and wood playground structures, with many preschools following the trend found in elementary schools by replacing natural environments and gardens with equipment. Playgrounds have evolved from their early beginnings into several different types: traditional, contemporary, adventure, creative, and natural. Each type has advantages and disadvantages.

The traditional playground features fixed equipment such as jungle gyms, designed primarily for exercise. The contemporary playground often contains complex climbing equipment that is more aesthetically pleasing than the traditional. These playgrounds are sometimes referred to as Kit (purchased as a kit), Fence, and Carpet (landscaped with rubber surfaces) (KFC) playgrounds (Woolley & Lowe, 2012). Like the traditional playground, the contemporary playground mainly provides opportunities for exercise.

Watch the video to learn more about adventure playgrounds. Which skills do you see children using?

https://www.youtube.com/watch?v=kmrl8NZQ2e4

The adventure playground began in Europe after World War II when a designer noticed that children preferred playing with rubble and scraps rather than on traditional playground equipment. Using scraps of lumber, other building materials, nails, hammers, and saws, children build, design, and manipulate their own play environments. Adventure playgrounds are supervised by play workers or play leaders. While few exist in the United States, more than 1,000 adventure playgrounds exist in Europe (NPR, 2006).

Check Your Understanding 17.2

Click here to gauge your understanding of chapter concepts.

The creative playground is a combination of contemporary and adventure playgrounds. It contains both equipment and open-ended materials (Dempsey & Frost, 1993).

Natural playgrounds, sometimes called adventure gardens (Fjørtoft, 2001), use the natural habitat instead of equipment for learning, allowing children to play in unmanicured places. They may include elements such as water play in ponds and bogs, butterfly gardens, mud and sand play, secret hiding places, tree houses, and natural obstacles to climb on (White, 1997). One example is the Environmental Yard in Berkeley, California.

There are limited research studies comparing child outcomes on different kinds of playgrounds. Furthermore, because these studies have typically compared and contrasted only two types of playgrounds, it is difficult to make comparisons across all types of playgrounds. However, to see the current research that does exist on playground types and child outcomes, see Table 17.1.

To gain full advantage from outdoor play, children need an appropriate space. Joe Frost, a renowned author on children's play and play spaces, emphasizes that to achieve both development and fitness the ideal playground includes both natural playscapes and playground apparatus (Frost, 2010).

"Space is the backdrop to play, supplying content, context, and meaning. It is bound to communicate a variety of possible messages to children (Titman, 1994): welcome, dismay, excitement, intimidation, warmth, coldness" (Cosco & Moore, 1999). How do we design an effective space? In the next section, we will explore this question.

Christopher Bullard

This natural playground provides climbing and balancing surfaces.

Table 17.1 Comparison of Playground Types

Type of Playground	Research Findings
Traditional	Children spend most of their time in physical activity; favors children with high levels of physical skills (Barbour, 1999; Frost & Campbell, 1985; Frost & Strickland, 1985).
Natural environment	More effective in developing motor fitness, balance, and coordination than traditional playground (Fjørtoft, 2004). More effective in providing for fantasy play, creative play, sensory stimulation, and fine motor development than traditional or contemporary playgrounds (Woolley & Lowe, 2012).
Contemporary	Encourages children of all ability levels to interact. Children are more passive than in traditional playground. Children engage in more creative and pretend play than when playing on traditional playgrounds (Barbour, 1999; Hart & Sheehan, 1986; Susa & Benedict, 1994).
Adventure	Children engage in play for longer periods of time, engage in more cognitive play activities, participate in a wider range of activities, and participate in more adult interactions than in contemporary or traditional playgrounds (Hayward, Rothenberg, & Beasley, 1974; Moore, 1985).

Designing an Effective Outdoor Environment

An effective outdoor environment protects children's safety and health. It also contains an effective playground design, providing enhanced learning opportunities and social interactions. We will have an in-depth discussion of these criteria next.

Provide a Safe Playground

Safety must be a major consideration in designing, installing, and maintaining playgrounds. The goal is to reduce hazards while maintaining challenges. "A hazard is something a child does not see; a challenge is a risk the child can see and chooses to undertake or not. Children need to take risks to challenge their skills, gain confidence, and to promote resilience. A risk-free play area is neither possible nor desirable" (Kells, 2002, p. 22).

Each year in the United States, 200,000 children under the age of 12 are treated in emergency rooms for public playground–related accidents (U.S. Consumer Product Safety Commission, 2010). Most of these accidents occur in schools or in childcare centers (Phelan, Khoury, Kalkwarf, & Lanphear, 2001). In examining all playground injuries, girls are slightly more likely to be injured than boys, with children ages five to nine being at greatest risk (Phelan et al., 2001; Tinsworth & McDonald, 2001). Over 75% of injuries are related to falls (Vollman, Witsaman, Comstock, & Smith, 2009). While many children experience fear that inhibits them from climbing higher than they can safely handle, two groups are at special risk—infants, because they are often not aware of the risk, and children who have ADHD, which is characterized by impulsiveness and lack of fear (Frost et al., 2004).

So how can you prevent injuries on the playground? The National Program for Playground Safety (NPPS) stresses S.A.F.E. (supervision, age appropriateness, fall surfacing, and equipment maintenance) as a way of protecting children. After S.A.F.E. was implemented in one school district, there was a 27% decrease in severity and frequency of injuries (Tipping, 2007).

Supervision. Close supervision to assure that rules are followed and that children are not participating in unsafe behaviors is very important. To assist with supervision, the teacher child ratio needs to be the same outdoors as indoors. Teachers need to actively participate in supervision. This is sometimes done by teachers supervising different playground zones.

Teachers can also help children to feel emotionally and physically safe by helping to prevent and resolve conflict. Many conflicts can be prevented by having an effective environment and enough materials and equipment. When children do have conflicts that they are unable to successfully solve, it is important that the teacher assist the children in discussing and resolving the conflict.

Watch the video to learn more about supervision. What does ABC stand for?

https://www.youtube.com/watch?v=5YO8YbLcrYQ

Age Appropriateness. While it is crucial to limit serious playground accidents, it is important to allow children to experience physical challenges that are appropriate for their age and developmental level. "Being able to make informed decisions based on previous experience and through learning to manage challenges that are obvious or foreseeable is an important learning experience for a child. It assists in contributing to a child's holistic development, formulating positive self-image as well as competent living skills" (Mitchell, Cavanagh, & Eager, 2006, p. 122).

Children seek physical challenges. If there are no legitimate ways to challenge their skill levels, children will invent their own, sometimes with unintended risk. For example, they might climb on top of the small plastic playhouse. To meet the needs of children's rapidly developing skills, playgrounds need to contain graduated challenges. For example, teachers can provide balance beams that are different widths, climbers that can be accessed in different ways, partially buried stumps of different heights with different widths between them, different sizes of smooth rocks to climb, and overhead rings that are stationary at the beginning but become dynamic as you reach the far end.

Fall Surfacing. Since most public playground injuries relate to falls, it is critical that playgrounds have appropriate fall surfacing. However, in a survey of 1,000 playgrounds, only 25% met this criterion (Weintraub & Cassady, 2002). Appropriate surface materials such as sand, wood chips, or shredded rubber need to be installed and maintained under equipment from which children could fall and extending six feet in all directions (Bergen & Robertson, 2013). This includes providing appropriate surfaces under climbers, slides, swings, seesaws, and merry-go-rounds.

Equipment Maintenance. Playgrounds also need to be well maintained. A review of 24 Head Start Programs grantees in eight states that managed 175 facilities found that none complied fully with safety regulations. Violations included broken gates and fences, debris such as glass and nails, hazardous items within reach of children such as a machete and a gas-powered hedge trimmer, and playground equipment that was in poor repair (OIG, 2011). To keep children safe, playgrounds need to be inspected daily for debris or obvious safety hazards. In addition, there should be a regularly scheduled safety inspection to examine all the equipment and measure the ground cover to determine if compaction has occurred.

It is also important to be aware of your state licensing regulations. For example, childcare licensing standards often require that playgrounds be fenced to protect children from busy streets and other hazards.

Watch the video to learn more about safety. What are the dirty dozen for playground safety?

https://www.youtube.com/watch?v=NV-iLgSD7_g

Protect Children's Health

As discussed previously, being outdoors provides many benefits to children's health, including the opportunity to receive physical exercise. However, there are two potential concerns that we must be aware of so that we can provide protection against them. These are the use of arsenic on playground equipment and ultraviolet rays from the sun.

CCA. Arsenic from chromate copper arsenate (**CCA**), a pesticide used to treat wood in playground equipment, is a concern on children's playgrounds. The European Union banned CCA for residential use in 2003 (EC, 2003). Beginning in 2004, it became illegal for manufacturers to treat wood with CCA for most consumer uses in the United States. However, many playgrounds still contain CCA. Until the ban, CCA-treated wood was the most common wood used in playground construction (Hatlelid, Bittner, Midgett, Thomas, & Saltzman, 2004, p. 215). Arsenic can cause skin, lung, and bladder cancer after ingestion (ATSDR, 2000). This is a special concern for young children who may have hand-to-mouth contact. Studies find that children ages two to six typically ingest half of whatever is collected on their hands (Kwon et al., 2004).

So what can you do if you have a wood playground structure that might contain arsenic? The most effective solution, other than removing the equipment, is to have everyone who plays on the equipment wash their hands when they come in from the playground. Washing hands removes most of the arsenic (Kwon et al., 2004).

Ultraviolet Rays. Another outdoor danger is ultraviolet rays which can lead to skin cancer. To protect children, it is important to provide shade on the playground. This can include both natural shade from trees and bushes and human-made shade. Whenever possible, shades should be placed over areas where children will be spending extensive time, such as over platforms and sandboxes. In addition, it is important that all children wear sunscreen with UVB-ray and UVA-ray protection of SPF-15 or higher. Sunscreen should be applied to all exposed skin, except eyelids, 30 minutes before going outdoors and every 2 hours while in the sun. In addition, children should wear brimmed hats and sunglasses. The National Health and Safety Standards state that children's outdoor play should be limited between 10:00 AM and 2:00 PM (American Academy of Pediatrics et al., 2011). Infants under six months should be kept out of direct sunlight.

Use an Effective Playground Design

The design of the space is as important outdoors as indoors. Optimal playground design allows the playground to be functional and safe while providing increased learning opportunities and improved social interactions.

Provide Adequate Space That Is Divided into Zones. Most states require playgrounds to contain 75 square feet of space per child, but most experts recommend a minimum of 100 square feet (Pardee, Gillman, & Larson, 2005). Research demonstrates that when playgrounds do not have at least 75 square feet per child, moderate to vigorous activity is reduced (Dowda et al., 2009). When calculating the square feet needed, you must consider the maximum number of children that will be on the playground at any one time.

Most playground experts suggest that this space should be divided into zones that clearly delineate areas for different activities. Zones help to decrease conflicts, increase ability to focus, make areas more understandable, separate serene areas from more active areas, and keep areas from interfering with each other (Cuppens et al., 2007). In one study, nearly half of the play occurred in 10% of the playground, that which provided an enclosed area (Kirkby, 1989). Through zoning, we provide many enclosed areas.

The type of zones you plan will be based upon the developmental level of the children that you serve. Most design experts recommend semiprivate areas with specific places for gross motor activities, dramatic play, building and construction, art, sand and water, and literacy. The outdoors should also promote the exploration of the natural environment through providing plants, bushes, trees, and gardens.

In planning where to place the zones, Pardee et al. (2005) suggest you consider sun patterns, safety hazards such as overhead lines, the distance play materials will need to be transported before being used, and environmental features (shape of the space, the topography, and the placement of natural items like trees). For example, slopes may be used for sliding and trees for climbing or for building a bench around for reading and watching. It is also important to consider the points of access. Where will children enter the playground (Pardee, Gillman, & Larson, 2005, pp. 3–4)?

Zones can be divided using low, fragrant, nontoxic plants (mint, anise); low earth berms; brick walls; stumps; or fences from natural materials (Cuppens et al., 2007, p. 7). Zones can also be separated by providing unique surfaces in different areas.

Provide Circulation Paths. Clear routes around the playground prevent children from interfering with other children's play. They also help children to avoid safety zones around equipment. Plan a looping path with no dead ends. Looping paths are found to promote higher levels of activity in children than straight paths (Cosco, Moore, & Smith, 2014). By using a variety of materials (such as gravel, shredded wood bark, paving stones, sand, log cookies, or bricks) with different textures, you can create different moods and differentiate zones (Keeler, 2002). Paths can also be individualized by letting children create and decorate their own paving stone.

Design an Exciting Entry. It is ideal if classrooms can open directly onto playgrounds. As stated by Moore, "Progressive childcare programs are run outdoors as much as indoors . . . . Thus the need for wonderful visual and movement connections between in and out—low windows, wide doorways, etc." (Moore, 2002, p. 9).

However, if playgrounds do have separate entries, it is important to design the entryway. The entry provides "a visual clue that you are entering a special place." The entry welcomes children, helps to establish a mood, and controls the access into the area, encouraging children to create a thoughtful entry rather than a "mad dash" (Cuppens et al., 2007, p. 8). Entries might contain an arbor, interesting surface texture, or unique entry gate.

Provide Shade and Protection from the Elements. Natural and human-made shade protect children from ultraviolet rays and inclement weather. Natural shade can be provided under trees or vine enclosures. Canopies, umbrellas, awnings, parachutes, or netting covered with leafy branches can also provide shade. If you live in a hot climate, you might also want to help children cool down through providing water misters.

Include Sufficient Storage Areas. According to Nelson, an expert and author on outdoor environments, "lack of storage is the single most common playground design weakness discouraging teachers from being outside" (Nelson, 2006, p. 43). Needed materials must be readily available or they frequently are not used. Therefore, it is important to have storage throughout the playground. Appropriate storage is determined by what is being stored. For example, wood shelves with locking doors can store art or music supplies, storage benches can be used for loose parts, and a low parking garage can house tricycles or bikes. A built-in cabinet under the woodworking bench can store carpentry tools.

Provide Access to Toileting, Handwashing, and Drinking Water. Ideally, a bathroom or changing table (for children in diapers) is available on the playground. If possible, running water should also be available for washing hands and to provide drinking water. If running water is not available, you can bring pitchers of water and glasses outdoors. This is especially important on hot days when there is a risk of dehydration.

Create an Aesthetically Pleasing Environment. While playgrounds need to be functional, they should also be aesthetic or beautiful. Aesthetic playgrounds welcome children and adults and show the value we place on both them and the setting. In an aesthetic environment, participants are more likely to care about the setting and vandalism is reduced (Kelling & Coles, 1996). To create an aesthetic playground, consider the following:

Julie Bullard

This gazebo protects children from the sun as they draw and paint in this appealing outdoor center. The cloth adds sun protection and also interest to the center.

- Use materials and colors from nature. To learn about the environment and experience what it can offer us, "children need daily chances to interact with materials found in nature . . . like wood, stone, water, grass and nonpoisonous trees and shrubs" (Wilke, 2006). Bright, bold colors, often found on plastic playground equipment, can be overstimulating and can detract from nature (Pardee et al., 2005). Instead, a variety of colors and textures can be introduced through different ground covers, plants, trees, and flowers.
- Personalize the playground with children's ideas and art such as sculptures or murals created by children in the program. At the Helen Gordon Child Development Center in Portland, Oregon, children created gigantic murals on canvas. These hang in the playground enhancing the environment and providing documentation of children's learning.
- Design for rich sensory experiences—sound (wind chimes, water falling, and leaves rustling), sight (flowers and trees that change color), smell (different fragrant herbs in different areas such as lavender, lemon balm, mint, creeping thyme, and rosemary), and tactile (different types of fencing and diverse elements like wood, rock, dirt, and water) (Keeler, 2002).

- Provide a variety of ground covers.
- Pay attention to details (the water fountain can be beautiful as well as practical).
- Consider curved lines when creating walkways, flower beds, and divisions between zones.
- Create beauty (a basket of beautiful rocks, a miniature pond with floating plants, mosaic tables, or gazing balls to reflect light).
- Make sure the playground is clean and uncluttered and that materials and equipment are in good repair.

Create a Sense of Place. Today, many American playgrounds are cookie cutter designs, untouched by the influence of the children that use them or the community in which the children live. Instead, playgrounds should provide a "sense of place," giving children a feeling of belonging, identity, and ownership (Cosco & Moore, 1999). Landscape architects stress that each outdoor environment should be individualized, reflecting the location, culture, and values of the program. For example, at the East Stroudsburg University Childcare in Pennsylvania, a "sense of place" is created through playhouses representing the Adirondack shelters found on the Appalachian Trail. A mosaic-backed stage created by a community artist, students, and children also helps to create a "sense of place" and provides a beautiful backdrop for impromptu plays.

In creating a "sense of place," incorporate program and community values, along with local materials, plants, and cultures. Involve all participants in the planning and

Julie Bullard

This playground near the Columbia River incorporates a sense of place through the Lampson crane and fish.

ongoing development (children, families, and teachers). Even children as young as three are able to provide valuable insights that help to produce playgrounds that meet their needs and interests (Whiren, 1995). When planning, immerse children in the idea. Take them on field trips to see other parks, gardens, and natural habitats. Look at pictures of playgrounds and natural play settings. Let children express their ideas by discussing their experiences, drawing playground designs, and building dioramas and models (Keeler, 2002). When children have a "sense of place," they honor that place, cherishing it, remembering it, and taking care of it.

Create a Magical Space. As you design your outdoor environment, remember your own special spaces from childhood. Joe Frost, Sue Wortham, and Stuart Reifel (2012) describe several things that make a space magical. This includes providing opportunities for miniature worlds and opportunities to experience a colossal scale such as elevated platforms, time and space to act out the world of fairy tales, and real versus sham items such as real tools or a real rowboat over their plastic counterparts. Magical spaces are sensory rich, include loose parts, and unique and exotic items. There are places to do nothing and places that are special or sacred. Special or sacred spaces are naturally beautiful, enclosed areas with a serene atmosphere that children can transform to make their own.

Provide a Variety of Activity Areas

Playgrounds should contain a complete mix of activities: places to climb, crawl, swing, and slide; areas for riding wheeled toys; a large open area to run and play games; messy areas; places to play with water; places to grow things; places to observe nature; places to retreat; building areas; creative areas for music, movement, and art; and places for dramatic play (Greenman, 2005a). Areas need to be dynamic, allowing children and teachers to constantly reinvent the setting to meet the interests and the needs of the inhabitants.

Areas to Climb, Crawl, Develop Arm Strength, Jump, and Balance. As children climb, crawl, jump, and balance they master physical challenges, gain self-confidence, develop body awareness, and improve motor skills and fitness (agility, speed, balance, and coordination). They also develop spatial and directional awareness (Cuppens et al., 2007; Frost et al., 2004).

Places to Climb. Most playgrounds feature a structure to climb on. In addition to the physical benefits, high places allow children to see what is occurring around them and gives them a sense of power. You can purchase or build a stand-alone climbing structure. A variety of other climbing, jumping, and balancing options include:

- Platforms built around or in a tree.
- Large boulders—providing several different sizes allows children options that meet their developmental needs.
- Tree stumps of different heights embedded into the ground.

- Balance beams of different widths and heights.
- Planks laid on cable spools turned sideways.
- Suspension bridges made from tires placed side by side with a cable through the sides and attached to two poles at each end to hold the tires in place (Hogan, 1982).
- Suspension bridges from other materials.
- Tire trees.
- Tire walks made of tires set on the ground.
- Climbing walls.

Since children can climb up before they can climb down, make sure there is more than one way down, particularly on high structures (Pardee et al., 2005). For example, a child might climb up a climbing wall on a play structure and then climb down a set of steps. Also, allow ways for children to celebrate that they have mastered a challenge (Olds, 2001). This could include ringing a bell, flying a flag, blowing a bicycle horn, getting their picture taken, or getting a certificate. When buying climbing equipment, you might have the option to include features such as dinosaur panels, alphabet cutouts, or spinning tic-tac-toe games. However, these "items which only have one use or purpose, may have limited lasting appeal" (Pardee et al., 2005, p. 8). Instead, you might buy buckets with pulleys so that items can be brought up and down from the structure, colored fiberglass panels that allow the children to experience the world in a different way, or telescopes.

Places to Crawl. Options for children to crawl through include:

- Hollowed-out logs.
- A translucent crawl-through tunnel under a hill (Cuppens et al., 2007).
- Tires laid on their side and embedded into the ground.
- Concrete tunnels.
- Living willow tunnel—At St. Peter Chanel Primary School in England, parents, children, and staff collaborated to build a 5-foot-tall, 50-foot-long tunnel on their playground. Living willow has several advantages. It provides a natural environment that is inexpensive. It can take a variety of forms. Children can experience the changes in the willows during different seasons. While children feel hidden, they can still be seen by adults (Danks, 2003).

Places to Develop Arm Strength. Overhead equipment such as ladders, track rides, and overhead rings develop upper-body strength, coordination, lateral movement, and visual perception. Since children in the United States lack upper-body strength (Frost et al., 2004), this type of equipment is especially important. Overhead equipment must be challenging, yet usable by all children. Challenges are greater for children when dynamic elements such as free moving rings are added or when spacing is uneven (Frost, 1992). Some overhead equipment is developed on an incline, becoming higher and more difficult as it ascends and

Julie Bullard

This hollowed-out log at Spirit at Play provides opportunities for climbing and crawling.

allowing children with differing abilities to experience success. The equipment should be slightly above reaching height of 95% of the children using it (Frost, 1990, pp. 39–40). Balloon tires, standing upright, can be partially buried allowing a safe, accessible take-off and landing platform (Frost & Kim, 2000). Preschool children need assistance and encouragement when they are first introduced to overhead equipment. However, in one study, once assistance was given, most of the three- to six-year-old children were able to use the overhead ladder successfully. Within one month, they were able to travel the full distance of the ladder on their own (Frost et al., 2004). To assist the child, hold her by the waist as she moves from rung to rung.

Places to Swing. Young children prefer swings over many other activities on playgrounds (Holmes & Procaccino, 2009). Swings encourage rhythmic motion that can be relaxing and improve balance and coordination. In addition, "The pendulum action, gravitational force and speed physically experienced while swinging quickly translate into feelings of falling and flying—sensations that inspire imaginations" (Sutterby & Thornton, 2003, p. 1). Swings also provide children the opportunity to share and to work together, thereby assisting social development.

Providing a variety of swings can offer different advantages. For example, a horizontal tire swing lets several children swing at once. Traditional swings allow children to swing back and forth under their own power. Adaptive swings permit children with disabilities to enjoy swinging. However, avoid heavy metal swings such as those shaped like animals that have been banned due to the high incidence of injuries.

Teachers can help children to be more successful in swinging by encouraging them to lean their torso in sync with pumping. In addition, extending legs to the apex on top of the forward swinging arc provides additional momentum (Frost et al., 2004).

Places to Slide. Slides improve dynamic balance. In addition, unlike many other equipment options, slides present a low level of challenge to meet the needs of all children. Providing a variety of types of slides (spiral, tunnel, wide slides, and wave slides) in the playground adds interest and provides for children's differing ability levels. Slides can be provided as a stand-alone piece of equipment or attached to other equipment like a climber. For young children, embankment slides or slides placed upon a natural or human-made hill are often used, helping to prevent injury.

Area for Riding Tricycles, Scooters, Bikes, and Other Wheeling Toys. As children ride wheeled toys, they improve physical skills, coordination, muscle strength, and spatial perception. In designing this area, a hard-surfaced path is critical. Paths that are meandering, containing small hills, ramps, and drive-through tunnels, can add interest and challenge, and increase exercise. Requiring helmets will protect children from head injury and teach lifetime safety skills.

A Large Open Area for Gathering and Large Motor Play. The playground needs to include a large open area. Children can use this space as a gathering area. It also provides a place for playing games, running and dancing, flying kites, and throwing Frisbees and balls. Research indicates that large, open areas foster moderate to vigorous physical activity (MVPA) (Nicaise, Kahan, & Sallis, 2011). MVPA is associated with decreased obesity.

Messy Areas. Today many children live in sterile environments, not having the opportunity to dig in the dirt, make mud pies, or dash through mud puddles. However, when adults were asked about fond childhood memories, playing in the mud was frequently mentioned. "Even as adults we continue to enjoy the sensory experience of mud through mud baths, mud facials, gardening, and barefoot walks with mud oozing through our toes" (Jenson & Bullard, 2002, p. 16). To provide children with this opportunity, Curious Minds, a campus lab school created a mud center. The center included a non-working real stove with an oven; an assortment of pots, pans, and cooking utensils; a variety of found items for decorating (sawdust, pine cones, dried berries, pebbles, crushed leaves); an area with water for cleaning up; and of course large buckets of dirt and water. As the mud play developed, the children collected an increasing variety of items for decorating and stirring into their inventions and experimented with a variety of mud creations (stuffed pies, layered pies, soups, birthday cakes). The mud center was open-ended and allowed for a range of challenges. It included many curriculum areas, and was a favorite center for both adults and children.

While many other substances can be used for digging and creating, sand is probably the most popular medium. You will want to provide the sand area in a quiet space in the playground that has either natural or created shade. If you plant a buffer of plants or shrubs around the sand area, it may help to contain the sand. Cuppens et al. (2007) suggest creating an L-shaped sandbox, which allows more children to be involved in digging than does a rectangular box. However, if a sandbox is not available, you can create one by filling a child's wading pool or large tractor tire with sand.

To protect children's health, it is important to buy clean sand since collected sand may contain harmful toxins. Sandboxes need to be covered when not in use. One technique is to cover the sand area with fine mesh netting, allowing sand to air dry while keeping out cats.

TIP

If you install a grate or a series of grates where children enter the building from the playground, sand will come off their shoes, keeping the indoor space easier to care for.

Water Area. "Water comforts, fascinates, and instructs" (Rivken, 1995, p. 41). Although one must be cautious about water that is deep or stagnant, these restraints do not need to eliminate water play. Following are some suggestions on how to incorporate water play in the playground. Some of these suggestions may not be appropriate for areas that have limited water supplies. It is also important to check the licensing regulations in your state before developing a new water area.

- Allow children to run through a sprinkler.
- Provide water in tubs or water tables.
- Install an outdoor shower head.
- Provide a recirculating fountain. Depending on the size, children can observe and listen, or actually splash and wade into the fountain.
- Add a water source to your sand area; this can be as simple as a hose with a shut-off valve. By adding rain gutters or pipes, children can move water throughout the area. "The play value of sand is enhanced by the provision of a second fluid material, water" (Frost, 1992, p. 103).
- Install outdoor sinks and faucets. At the Pacific Oaks Infant/Toddler Program, a series of sinks (each with its own unique type of faucet) stair step down a slight incline. Water overflows into a shallow stream bed, allowing for more water adventures.

- Install a hand pump; this typically limits water consumption while providing exercise as the child pumps the water.
- Provide a very shallow creek. At a park in Salt Lake City, a very shallow creek meanders through the playground. Children learn hands-on physics as they experiment with large rocks they can move to divert the flow of water.
- Install a misting pipe from the side of a building or as a stand-alone structure.

Places to Observe and Interact with Insects, Animals, and Birds. Most playgrounds provide some exposure to living things. However, teachers can improve learning by attracting more birds, animals, and insects to the playground, and by providing tools to study what is found. Domesticated animals can also be part of the playground learning experiences.

To attract birds, animals, and insects, you must provide hospitable habitats. For example, teachers can provide bird feeders, birdhouses, and birdbaths; worm beds; squirrel feeders; and gardens and plants to attract butterflies and ladybugs. Long ungroomed grass and hedges for hiding might attract small native animals. Plants, shrubs, and trees are also important for wildlife habitats. In addition, they provide beauty, shade, and exposure to nature. Choosing plants that are indigenous to the region ensures a proven survival rate and helps children to learn about plants and trees that are native to the area (Schappet, Malkusak, & Bruya, 2003).

Binoculars, magnifying glasses, butterfly nets, and containers allow children a close-up view of animals and bugs. Learning can be extended by providing resources for animal, bug, and bird identification. For very young children, it might be helpful to provide laminated pictures of birds, bugs, and animals typically found in your playground. As children become more skilled, they can graduate to children's guidebooks and then to adult guidebooks. Teachers can place these along with magnifying glasses and binoculars into plastic containers with tight-fitting lids to protect them from unexpected rain showers.

Some programs have domestic animals such as rabbits or chickens in their play yards. At one preschool playground, a large ground-level rabbit hutch contains a small house to shelter the rabbit along with a fenced yard. Two children at a time can enter the yard to spend time with the rabbit. If the rabbit does not want contact, he enters his house. Children have learned that this means he does not want to be bothered. Many preschools and elementary schools also have chicken coops on their playgrounds. Children participate in feeding the chickens and gathering eggs.

A Place to Seek Refuge. Places to seek refuge, sometimes called stimulus shelters (Frost et al., 2004), are semi-private areas that allow a special place for dreaming and introspection, quiet exploration, solitary play, and a place to withdraw from the group when play becomes too intense. It also provides a place to watch others while deciding whether to participate with the group.

When planning a refuge, design it to be semi-enclosed. This allows adults to easily see inside the enclosure. Also, research shows that young children prefer semi-open rather than entirely closed structures by a five-to-one ratio (Dempsey & Frost, 1993).

Areas screened by vegetation (strategically planted vegetables or herbs can provide a safe and sensory area), a sunflower tepee, a living willow hut, a telephone booth, a playhouse, a tree house, or a tent can all provide places of refuge. A ceiling or canopy also helps to create a sense of refuge. For example, a hammock under a tree with overhanging branches could be a quiet place to retreat. A small house with various peepholes can allow the child to seek a retreat while also viewing the world in interesting ways. A small Zen garden can help establish a contemplative mood.

Places to Sit. Many different seating options add versatility and interest to the playground, while providing appropriate space for a variety of activities. These can include picnic tables and benches, seats built around trees, or mosaic tables and benches created by the children. Natural benches can be created from large, smooth boulders; logs placed on their side with a seat and back carved in; or log stools. Adult- and child-sized tables and seating, when placed throughout the play yard, allow for a variety of activities—games, resting, reading, art, eating, and cooking.

Julie Bullard

This outdoor fairy house and the loose parts encourage children to engage in imaginative play.

Loose Parts for Enhancing Possibilities. Loose parts add flexibility, increase creativity, and enhance and extend play (Daly & Beloglovsky, 2015). Loose parts such as balls also increase the amount of time that children spend engaged in exercise (Dowda et al., 2009). A variety of loose parts should be readily available. If outdoor storage is not available, it may be necessary to have crates, tubs, or baskets filled with items that can be brought out when you play outdoors. Although the list is limited only by one's imagination, following are some examples of loose parts:

- Natural materials to collect, sort, and use for decorating—pinecones, seashells, stones, leaves, seed pods, moss, rocks, and berries. One program collected a pile of left over pumpkins after Halloween that children explored and used in many different ways.
- Materials for water and sand exploration—hoses, spray bottles, sprinklers, turkey basters, paintbrushes, rain gutter, plastic tubing, buckets, cups, bowls, sifters, and containers in various sizes.
- Materials to explore nature—butterfly nets, magnifying glasses, magnifying boxes, binoculars, bird and insect identification books, and jars.
- Pulleys, ropes, and buckets for getting things in and out of tree houses and for getting bird feeders up and down.
- Things to throw, kick, jump, and bat—variety of types of balls, Frisbees, bats, jump ropes, and hoops.
- Things to fly—kites and airplanes.
- Things to ride and pull—trikes, bikes, wagons, and pull toys.
- Tools—hammers, saws, screwdrivers, nails, and rope.
- Materials to build with—spools, stumps, boards, tires, inner tubes, straw bales, long grass, crates, PVC pipe and elbows, plastic tubing, wooden pallets, cardboard, and sheets, tarps, or camouflage netting. Zip ties, strips of inner tubes, clamps, and duct tape can be used by children to hold structures together.

In one program, teachers collected trees after Christmas. Children used the trees in their play to create forts and forests. After the needles fell off the trees, the teachers assisted the children in cutting off the branches. The poles were then lashed together at the top to create tepee shaped structures. The children wrapped the structures with fabric to create continually changing play spaces.

Julie Bullard

This herb bed, created by parent volunteers, allows children to learn about gardening. Children care for the herb bed and pick the herbs to use in cooking projects. Also note in this photo how the bikes and helmets are stored in the bike corral.

Areas for Plants and Gardens. Caring for gardens allows children to gain a sense of responsibility, an enhanced appreciation and understanding of where food comes from, and increased knowledge of natural systems and seasons. Gardening can also help establish lifelong values. "If sustainable development values are to be created in society, we must recreate, as a matter of great urgency, viable educational habitat for children where they are able to learn on a daily basis the lessons of nature. Gardening is clearly an effective first step" (Moore, 1995, p. 68). Garden activities can also be a springboard for curriculum in math (charting, graphing), science (photosynthesis, plant needs, pests, composting, observation), social studies (food in different cultures, mapmaking), art (garden design), literacy (sign making, reading books), and health and nutrition (Stoecklin, 2001). Froebel believed that children should have both individual and group plots, promoting both responsibility and community (Brosterman, 1997). To enhance your garden you might consider adding a compost area, a worm bed, and a small greenhouse.

Check Your Understanding 17.3

Click here to gauge your understanding of chapter concepts.

The San Francisco Environmental yard provides examples of the many activities that gardening can promote. Children experimented with plants growing under different conditions. They kept garden logs where they recorded observations and documentation such as heights of plants and weight of produce. They learned about insects that assist and harm plants and developed ways to preserve food (Moore, 1995).

Depending upon space, gardens can be planted directly into the ground, in raised beds, in child-sized swimming pools, in tubs, or in flowerpots. By being creative, you can grow gardens even in very small spaces. For example, to grow potatoes you might consider growing them in a tire, and once the plants are two to three inches high you can add an additional tire and more dirt. As the season progresses, additional dirt and tires are added. This allows you to grow a crop of potatoes in a very small space. You might also plant in rain gutters that are attached to your chain link fence.

In many communities, there are garden clubs and greenhouses that will provide advice and assistance. In San Antonio, master gardeners volunteered to help elementary schools establish gardens. Ten thousand children, most in inner-city schools, participated in gardening each week. Children learned about nature by caring for and nurturing living things. They also learned about the need for cooperation and delayed gratification. Children indicated that school was more pleasurable after the gardening project began. The gardening project also increased parent involvement (Alexander, North, & Hendren, 1995).

TIP

For a quick, easy, gardening bed, buy a bag of potting soil, cut holes on top to insert plants, and cut holes in the bottom for drainage (Rivken, 1995, p. 43).

Create Your Own Palette Garden

Julie Bullard

Do you have a playground with little space for a garden? A pallet garden might be the answer. A pallet garden is inexpensive to create and takes little space since it can be secured to a fence. Because of the way that the pallet is divided, each child can have his or her own garden space.

Directions

1. Obtain a pallet. You can typically obtain them free at the many businesses that receive merchandise on pallets.
2. Paint your pallet any color you wish. If you paint the pallet with chalkboard paint, the children can label the pallet with the names of the plants that are growing.
3. Staple or nail a heavy-duty ground covering to the back of the pallet to keep dirt from escaping.
4. Pack potting soil into the space between each of the pallet boards.
5. Add moss to stabilize the potting soil and to hold moisture.
6. Plant your plants—strawberries and flowers grow well because of their relatively shallow root structure.

Outdoor Learning Centers (Block and Building, Art, Music and Movement, Science and Math, Literacy, and Dramatic Play). Outdoor learning centers are important additions to playgrounds. Playgrounds typically contain a block and building center (see Chapter 9), areas for dramatic play (see Chapter 7), an art area (see Chapter 13), and a music and movement center (see Chapter 14). Many programs also include science and math centers (see Chapters 11 and 12) and literacy centers (see Chapter 10). If outdoor centers are not yet permanent fixtures on your playground, you might develop play crates. For example, these could include a dress-up crate, music crate, bubble crate, sand and water play crate, and gardening crate (McGinnis, 2002).

Generally, when planning outdoor centers, it is important to take advantage of the extra freedom, space, and items available in the natural environment rather than duplicating what is available indoors.

Through appropriate playground design, we can provide rich experiences in a safe, healthy outdoor environment. However, in developing an appropriate design we must also consider the specific age group that will be using the playground.

Julie Bullard

The Mentor Graphics Child Development Center playground is adorned with art sculptures that were created by children and parents at the conclusion of a long-term project on bugs. Also, note the child-painted strips of roofing material woven into the fence.

Additional Considerations for Designing Outdoor Environments for Specific Age Groups

Although there are basic areas found on playgrounds for all age groups, to provide for safety and appropriate activities and experiences we must specifically design the playground for the ages using it. Following are recommendations for infant and toddler, preschool, and early elementary playgrounds.

Infants and Toddlers

Infants and toddlers experience rapid development of motor skills, including locomotor (running, jumping, climbing), small motor (throwing, hitting, kicking), and stability (bending, balancing). Children at this age are often practicing skills and engage in much repetition. For example, a toddler may repeatedly climb up and down a set of steps. Pretend play is also beginning to emerge. Sensory learning is especially critical at this age. Since children this age often mouth items, it is important that everything in the playground be safe to eat and either large enough or small enough that it does not create a choking hazard. Some unique features that are important to include in infant and toddler playgrounds are:

- 14- to 16-inch barriers that children can lean against and use to pull themselves to a standing position.
- Grassy places to roll, crawl, and move.
- Meandering pathways to crawl on or walk on—dirt, stone, planks, wood rounds, half logs, and brick (Greenman, 1991, p. 23).
- Different types of railing—poles, chains, iron, and rope (Greenman, 1991, p. 23).
- A house or lean-to that babies can crawl or toddle into. Flexibility can be provided by using skeletal structures. For example, a wide A-frame stepladder allows children to climb over and under. By adding fabric, the structure can also become a tent. Changing the type of fabric can provide additional variability (Greenman, 1991).
- Items to challenge newly developed gross motor skills—steps, inclines, things to crawl over, jump over, and climb on.
- Climbers with "varying levels and means of entry and exit, bells or pulleys to make sounds, dynamic components such as steering wheels to manipulate, and slides or climbers to promote action" (Dempsey & Frost, 1993, p. 23).
- Colored Plexiglas panels in climbers or on fences that allow babies to see the world in a different way.
- Cradle or bucket seat swings.
- Short tunnels to crawl into and play peek-a-boo.
- Slides built into a hill. A study of playground injuries resulting in visits to emergency rooms found that the most common source of injuries in children under age two were slides (McDonald & Greene, 2003). Building slides into a hill makes them safer.
- Elevated waterways with troughs to experiment with water.
- Things to hear—a variety of wind chimes and leaves rustling.
- Things to look at—mobiles, kites, banners, parachutes, wind socks, leaves, and patterns of sun and shade.
- Different textures to feel—"smooth round boulders, coarse bark and smooth sensual wood, soft and not so soft pine needles, and other vegetation to feel and rub up against" (Greenman, 1991, p. 23).

- Places to keep cool—human-made and natural shade.
- Places to sit alone and to sit with adults, such as small chairs, hammocks, or porch swings.
- Loose parts—fabric; baskets or buckets for collecting items; natural items to collect, carry, and dump; mats; inner tubes; dramatic play props; art materials; sand and water toys; riding toys; toys to push and pull; and balls.
- Diaper-changing tables.

Suzanne Clouzeau/Pearson Education

This playground provides a variety of activities for toddlers. Note the loose parts.

To protect infants from older toddlers who may injure infants due to running and throwing items, nonmobile infants need separate spaces. In addition, children need to be protected from equipment or areas that they are not yet developmentally ready to use. One way to accomplish this is by providing challenges that children must successfully navigate to reach the area. For example, at the Pacific Oaks Infant/Toddler Program, children must crawl over a boardwalk to reach the sand pit. In addition, they must transverse an obstacle of tires to reach the climber (Striniste & Moore, 1989).

Check Your Understanding 17.4
Click here to gauge your understanding of chapter concepts.

Preschool

Preschool children are in the fundamental movement phase of physical development, a phase of rapidly maturing physical skills. Sociodramatic play becomes more complex, with children participating in small-group cooperative play. Children at this age need additional challenges, more complex equipment, and a greater diversity of choices than infants and toddlers. All of the activity areas discussed earlier in the chapter should be included in the preschool playground.

Watch the video to see a toddler playground. What natural elements are included?

https://www.youtube.com/watch?v=kXtXkudaNrA

Early Elementary

Children ages six to eight are entering a more mature stage of fundamental movements (Gallahue, 1993) allowing them to learn new skills such as riding bikes and jumping rope. Games with rules become very important at this age. In addition to all the interest areas described earlier in the chapter, playgrounds need areas with firm surfaces for games such as basketball, hopscotch, and jump rope. Large surfaces are also needed for soccer, softball, and chase games. See Figure 17.2 to explore ideas if you have playground challenges.

Teachers working with this age group might have to be strong advocates for time outdoors. With the emphasis on academic achievement, many elementary programs are reducing outside time, instead using this time for more structured learning activities. This is especially true for programs that serve a higher percentage of children from low-income or minority families (Beighle, 2012; Jarrett, 2013).

However, research demonstrates that children who take time for physical activity have increased physical fitness, better attitudes, and score at least as well, if not better, on academic tests as children who spend all their time inside working on academics (Jarrett, 2013; Sallis et al., 1999). A meta-analysis of nearly 200 studies examining the effect of

FIGURE 17.2
Playground Challenges

Many programs continue to face extreme challenges in providing appropriate outdoor play spaces for children. For example, they may lack any playground space, the space they have might be unsafe, or it might be covered in blacktop. If you are faced with one of these or similar situations:

1. Begin by maintaining your commitment to provide outside time and experiences in green spaces.
2. Creatively brainstorm all existing possibilities to provide appropriate outdoor experiences for children. For example, the 5th Street Elementary School had an unused asphalt covered parking lot for an outdoor play space. The early childhood teachers began by creating outdoor crates to bring outside each day. Each crate contained a different type of activity (bubbles, art materials such as chalk to create murals, balls, and jump ropes). They also got permission to add some large tractor tires to the playground, they filled one with sand and the other became a garden. Next, they painted several games on the asphalt including hopscotch, foursquare, and scully. Classes also took turns setting up different types of obstacle courses and teachers took turns planning group games (kick the can, red light/green light).
3. Continue to advocate for appropriate spaces. The teachers as 5th Street Elementary School began by investigating and listing research that supported outdoor play in appropriate spaces. With the help of children, they drew up a plan for their desired playground. They first presented the research to the administration who agreed that if the teachers could get funding, they would support them in implementing their plan. They also provided the plan and an easy-to-read version of the research information to families, the school board, and the Parent Teacher Association (PTA). The PTA agreed to lead a fund-raising effort and sponsor workdays to change the playground.

physical activity on cognitive functioning supports this conclusion (Etnier et al., 1997). An interesting study in Canada examined children's achievement both before and after the school system implemented a new program where one-third of the day was devoted to the arts and physical activity. They found that children's achievement increased as did the children's physical fitness (Martens, 1982). Two reasons that achievement is increased may be because taking time for physical activity increases attention spans and reduces off-task behavior when children return to the classroom (Beighle, 2012; Jarrett et al., 1998).

Recess also allows children to engage in social interactions and practice communication skills, including negotiation. Further, physical activity outdoors reduces stress (Murray, Ramstetter, Council on School Health, & American Academy of Pediatrics, 2013).

Teachers' Facilitation of Learning in the Outdoor Environment

Teachers are critical, not only in the initial playground design but also in making the playground a dynamic environment that meets the needs and interests of the current group of children. For this to occur, the teacher must recognize the importance of outdoor play. As with indoor play, the teacher is responsible for planning additional daily activities and interacting with children to scaffold learning, promote positive social interactions, and encourage safe play while outdoors.

Recognize the Importance and Possibilities of Outdoor Play

Many teachers hold misconceptions about outdoor play, believing that it is a time for children to release excess energy, a time for a break for children and adults, or a place to develop gross motor skills (Frost et al., 2004). While each of these is true, the misconception is that these are the sole purpose for outdoor time. When teachers hold these misconceptions, they are often not fully supporting children's development through a "rich" environment or through their interactions. Additionally, teachers are the gatekeepers of outdoor time. One study found that teachers do not take children outdoors due to their own dislike of outdoors or inclement weather, the amount of work involved in taking children outdoors, their own health issues such as allergies, and the perceived chaos of outdoor time (Copeland, Kendeigh, Saelens, Kalkwarf, & Sherman, 2012).

Create a Rich, Challenging Environment

The outdoor environment needs to be continually assessed and adapted to meet children's needs and interests. In many programs, the outdoor environment is an afterthought with little funding or planning. Play materials are static, rather than dynamic, and there are few playground enhancements (Nelson, 2006; Wilke, 2006). In planning the outdoor play yard, it might help to think of it as an outdoor classroom containing all of the design features and areas described earlier in the chapter.

Provide a Schedule That Allows Time for Play Outdoors

When classrooms have adjacent playgrounds, children often are able to choose whether to play indoors or outdoors. When this is the case, outdoor play is available several hours a day. When it is not the case, it is important to have at least one period of extended outdoor play for a half-day program and two periods of extended outdoor play for a full-day program.

Children benefit from playing outdoors in most weather conditions. However, it is important that teachers and children are prepared with proper clothing. Many programs provide extra clothes for children who come unprepared. If the weather does occasionally prohibit outdoor play, teachers should use a gym, hallway, or lunchroom to provide similar activities. If there is no access to these environments, active play can be planned for the classroom. For ideas on indoor physical play, see Chapter 16.

Plan Special Activities for Outdoor Time

Special daily activities should be planned for outdoors. These activities provide additional choices for children, while enhancing learning opportunities. The ideas are limitless. Following are a few ideas to use as a springboard for planning.

- Provide mazes and hopscotch on the playground.
- Bury items in the sandbox, then give children brushes and screens to be archaeologists or paleontologists.
- Give children doll clothes to wash and hang out to dry.
- Fill spray bottles with water and food coloring—spray on snow in winter or on an old sheet in summer.
- Provide chalk for drawing around shadows.
- Supply bubble mixtures and a variety of bubble wands.
- Play games.
- Hang a hoop from a tree for children to throw balls through.
- Bring the musical instruments outside and have a band.
- Create streamers with plastic strips; children can use them for dancing and experimenting with wind.

- Provide kites to fly.
- Provide sheets of paper of different weights and sizes to create paper airplanes or pinwheels.
- Create challenges (e.g., a sand castle 2 feet high).

Obstacle courses are another way to provide variety. They can be created by teachers and children using the static features in the playground along with loose parts such as milk crates, tires, plastic hoops and bottles, planks, boxes, and cable spools. Tunnels can be created by cutting the bottom out of plastic trashcans. Plastic swimming pools can be filled with balls or Styrofoam to walk or crawl through (Griffen & Rinn, 1998). Obstacle courses can change and become more physically demanding when children master the current obstacle course or lose interest. Climbing, crawling, balancing, throwing, and kicking skills can all be incorporated into an obstacle course.

Provide Needed Props

Props can extend children's learning and can support children's developmental levels, interests, and program goals. For example, after a heavy rainstorm, water flooded into the basement at Curious Minds: Early Care and Education Center. The children were very interested in building a dam outside to "save their school." The teacher provided a variety of different materials for the children to experiment with, including sand bags and hay bales. The children then became interested in other ways to divert water. Children built waterways in the sand area including lakes and streams using the plastic and piping the teacher provided.

Interact with Children

It is crucial that teachers interact with children in the outdoors if children are to gain the full value from the outdoor experience. However, as with the indoor environment, you must be cautious about interfering with children's play unnecessarily. There are many important roles that the early childhood professional performs in the outdoor environment, including the following:

- Monitoring play and intervening if play is unsafe.
- Providing information (the name of a bug).
- Being a provocateur (asking what if questions) (Nelson, 2012).
- Being a play partner (throwing balls, playing games, and blowing bubbles).
- Providing additional materials to support the children's play.
- Demonstrating and teaching skills such as how to plant a garden or how to pump legs when swinging.
- Modeling enjoyment of nature and providing opportunities for children to experience nature. Rachel Carson, a well-known naturalist, stated, "If a child is to keep alive his inborn sense of wonder . . . he needs the companionship of at least one adult who can share it, rediscovering the joy, excitement, and mystery of the world we live in" (Carson, 1956, p. 46).
- Offering encouragement and providing recognition.
- Helping the excluded child to be included. For example, if you begin to play with the excluded child, often other children will join in the play. You can then continue to play, modeling appropriate interactions. Review Chapter 2 for a more in-depth discussion of this topic.

Meet the Needs of All Learners

Children at special risk need encouragement and opportunities to be active. This includes children who have fewer opportunities for exercise outside of the early childhood setting, children who are overweight, and children who are naturally less active.

Supporting Children from All Cultures. Research indicates that physical activity is lower in ethnic minority groups and also in recent immigrants (Dogra, Meisner, & Ardern, 2010). This may be due to fewer opportunities. Studies have found that "communities with low-SES populations and higher proportions of minority racial groups are also associated with the fewest community-level physical activity-related settings" (Powell, Slater, & Chaloupka, 2004, p. 143). For example, in Los Angeles, researchers conducted a study examining the acres of park per 1,000 people in different neighborhoods. Caucasian neighborhoods have 31 acres of parks, African-American neighborhoods have only 1.7 acres of parks, and Latino neighborhoods have only 0.6 acres of parks per 1,000 people (Wolch, Wilson, & Fehrenbach (2005)). These statistics are important, since the number and size of parks is linked to the amount of physical activity that people receive. Playgrounds in low-income areas also have more maintenance hazards than playgrounds in high-income areas (Suecoff, Avner, Chou, & Crain, 1999). As a result, children in the low-income areas might not be allowed to use the parks.

It is important that all children have access to outdoor play. If this is not possible in the home environment, it is even more crucial that there is ample opportunity for outdoor play in the childcare or school environment.

Supporting Children Who Are Overweight. Lack of activity is one of the primary predictors of being overweight as a child (Nelson et al., 2006). Observing the level of physical activity of each individual child will assist you in knowing when it might be helpful to intercede. Teachers can assist children to be more active by:

- Providing a range of challenges so all children can be successful (children who are overweight often have less developed physical skills than their peers).
- Setting up obstacle courses that everyone progresses through as they enter the playground.
- Providing encouragement and support when children are physically active.
- Engaging in physical activity with a child or small groups of children.
- Assisting children to master physical skills.
- Providing activities that appeal to a reluctant child's interests.

Several studies have found that boys spend more time in vigorous physical activity than do girls (Finn, Johannsen, & Specker, 2002; Pellegrini, Kato, Blatchford, & Baines, 2002; Ridgers et al., 2005). Therefore, it might be necessary to provide encouragement for girls to be more physically active.

Supporting Children with Disabilities. In addition to encouraging and providing opportunities for children who might engage in less physical activity, we must make sure that our playgrounds are accessible for all children, including those with disabilities. Boundless Playgrounds, a national organization dedicated to creating barrier-free playgrounds, lists their dream as, "For every child, A place to play: Every child, Every ability, Every where." In early childhood playgrounds, we need to make sure that all children in our program are able to realize this dream. We can be more successful if we use the following process to help a child with disabilities access the playground. First, we need to gather information about the child's interests, strengths, and challenges. Second,

Watch the video to learn more about boundless playgrounds. Which adaptations assist all children to be able to use the playgrounds?

https://www.youtube.com/watch?v=gfHR2B272D4

determine what opportunities and barriers exist on the playground. Third, brainstorm modifications to enhance playground opportunities for the child (Flynn & Kieff, 2002).

These modifications will vary from child to child. Following are a few examples of possible adaptations:

- Wind chimes, different textures to designate different platforms on a climbing structure, and different fragrant plants to mark different areas of the playground can help children with visual impairments to orient themselves (Moore, 1992).
- Circulation paths with firm surfaces that are 60 inches wide can accommodate a child in a wheelchair (Tipping, 2007).
- Multiple ways of getting on equipment, including ramps, allows access for children with reduced motor mobility.
- Structures with climbing and resting places at many levels help children who are physically challenged.
- Large swings with back supports allow children with physical disabilities to use swings.
- Various heights of water tables and sand tables allow children to stand or to sit in a wheelchair to access them.
- Side-mounted grips in tunnels allow children with limited use of their legs to still use the equipment.
- Wide slides allow children to slide down with someone else.
- Overhead ladders that are either low on one end or ramped allow use by children in wheelchairs.
- Adjustable-height basketball hoops allow all children to use them (Theemes, 1999).
- Low-demand activities encourage all children to participate and be successful. In one study, children with a range of disabilities were more likely to play cooperatively in low-demand activities (playing in the playhouse, swinging on a tire swing, climbing on equipment, or playing on slides) (Nabors et al., 1999).
- Peer buddies can help children with disabilities to be included in groups and can also provide needed physical assistance.
- Involvement in the play or activity by the teacher facilitates inclusion of children with special needs (Nabors et al., 1999).

For inspiration, you might consider the playground at Clemy Park in northern Virginia. The park features an accessible public playground that includes such unique features as a wheelchair drag race strip, a movable helicopter that allows a wheelchair to be attached, a flush-mounted carousel, spinning cups, and voice-activated components (Avrasin, 2007, p. 46).

Observe and Document Children's Learning

The outdoor environment provides an opportunity to observe many different skills. Two areas that are especially conducive to observing outdoors are gross motor skills and social/emotional development. While there are many ways to observe children outdoors, a checklist of physical skills may be helpful. As children demonstrate the skills in play, you can check them off the list. You might also set up an obstacle course and check the skills children use as they navigate the course. One way to document children's social skills is through anecdotal records. Following are a list of gross motor skills that can be observed on the playground.

- Walking
- Running

- Hopping
- Skipping
- Jumping
- Galloping
- Kicking
- Throwing
- Catching
- Striking (hitting with hand or object such as a bat)
- Dynamic balance (balancing while moving)
- Static balance (center of gravity remains stationary)
- Axial movement (bending, stretching, twisting, turning, etc.)
- Dominant hand and foot usage

Following are questions regarding social-emotional development that can be observed on the playground:

- Who does the child play with or does the child play alone?
- What are the child's favorite activities?
- How does the child gain play entry with his peers?
- What is the child's level of fear? Does the child seek new challenges?
- Is the child a leader or follower when participating in playground activities?
- Is the child able to take turns with others?
- Can the child negotiate and make compromises?
- Does the child express frustrations effectively?
- Does the child engage in appropriate interactions with new children and adults?

Check Your Understanding 17.5

Click here to gauge your understanding of chapter concepts.

In well-designed outdoor play environments, children experience rich learning, developing intellectual, social, creative, and physical skills. In addition, they have opportunities to engage in vigorous physical activity and to experience nature in ways that are typically not available indoors. They also have the opportunity to increase their physical activity. In this day of increased obesity, physical activity is critical. "To deny children the opportunity to reap the many benefits of regular, vigorous physical activity is to deny them the opportunity to experience the joy of efficient movement, the health effects of movement and a lifetime as confident, competent movers" (Gallahue, 1993). Furthermore, as outdoor play times decrease and natural environments shrink, the playground becomes one of the few places that children might still experience nature. Nurturing the joy of nature creates lifelong dispositions that are necessary to preserve the natural environment for future generations.

Chapter Quiz 17

Click here to gauge your understanding of chapter concepts.

Sample Application Activities

1. Learn more about obesity prevention by visiting the Lets Move Child Care website.
2. Learn more about the development of physical skills by visiting the PBS Child Development Tracker website.
3. See photos of adventure playgrounds by visiting adventure playgrounds: A Children's World in the City website or by visiting the website of the Anarchy Zone in Ithaca, New York.
4. Learn more about natural playgrounds by visiting the Natural Learning Initiative website.

5. Download the free book, *Nature Play and Learning Places,* from the National Wildlife Federation to learn more about designing natural spaces and to see a rich variety of play sites.
6. Locate additional websites that picture interesting playgrounds and share them with your class. Determine what type of playground you are reviewing (traditional, natural, contemporary, creative, adventure, or a combination).
7. Take an online visit to playgrounds to gain inspiration. You might begin by visiting Planet Earth Playscapes for a look at several project galleries of playgrounds.
8. Learn more about creating living willow structures by visiting the Living Willow Structures of the Hamptons website.
9. Assess a playground using the environmental assessment in Figure 17.3.
10. Develop a model of your ideal playground.
11. Gain current information on safety standards for playgrounds by visiting the National Program for Public Playground safety. The site provides information on several different sets of standards as well as training videos. Also, check on the licensing standards in your state.
12. Brainstorm a list of outdoor activities to enhance children's time on the playground.
13. Locate grants (for example, check with state block grant funds) and other funding resources (Boy Scouts seeking to become Eagle Scouts will sometimes develop a playground as a project) for developing a playground.

FIGURE 17.3 Environmental Assessment: Outdoor Environments

- ❑ Is the playground S.A.F.E. (appropriate supervision, developmentally appropriate equipment, appropriate fall zones and surfaces, well-maintained equipment)?
- ❑ Is there adequate space for the number of children using the playground?
- ❑ Are there safe, looping circular paths?
- ❑ Is the playground zoned? Are the zones visibly separated through different ground surfaces or dividers?
- ❑ Are nonmobile children protected from mobile children?
- ❑ Is there shade and protection from the elements?
- ❑ Are there different play surfaces?
- ❑ Is there sufficient storage space? Is the storage located near the location where the materials will be used?
- ❑ Is there access to toileting, handwashing and drinking water?
- ❑ Are there a variety of activity areas?
    - ❍ Areas to climb, crawl, jump, and balance
    - ❍ Areas to swing
    - ❍ Places to slide
    - ❍ Messy areas (mud, sand)
    - ❍ Water areas
    - ❍ Area for riding tricycles, scooters, and bicycles
    - ❍ Areas for plants and gardens
    - ❍ Places to observe and interact with insects, animals, and birds
    - ❍ Large area for gathering and large motor play
    - ❍ Place to seek refuge
    - ❍ Many different places to sit
    - ❍ Outdoor learning centers
        - ▪ Block and building
        - ▪ Art
        - ▪ Music
        - ▪ Dramatic play
        - ▪ Science and math
        - ▪ Literacy
- ❑ Are there loose parts available?
- ❑ Does the playground have the right amount of challenge?
- ❑ Are there a range of activities to meet the needs of different skill levels (balance beams at different widths, different types of swings, different ways to climb a structure)?
- ❑ Is the playground equipment accessible to all?
- ❑ Is the playground aesthetically pleasing (materials and colors from nature, personalized with children's ideas and art, designed for rich sensory experiences, created with beauty in mind, clean, uncluttered, attention to detail, curved lines)?
- ❑ Does the playground provide "a sense of place" (reflects location, climate, culture, values, local materials, and local plants)?

Adult/child interactions on the playground

- ❑ Are adults enforcing rules? If so, are the rules necessary for safety? Are children engaging in unsafe or harmful behavior that is being ignored?
- ❑ Are adults interacting with children? In what ways (playing, conversing)?
- ❑ Are adults scaffolding children's learning?
- ❑ Are adults nurturing dispositions (love of nature, respect for living things)?
- ❑ Are adults helping children who are in conflict?
- ❑ Are adults helping excluded children to be included?

Chapter 18

Creating Spaces for Families and Teachers

Learning Outcomes

After you have read this chapter, you will be prepared to:

- Discuss the value and methods of engaging families in their child's development and learning
- Describe how environmental design can assist in meeting the needs of families
- Discuss early childhood staff burnout
- Explain how environmental design can assist in meeting the needs of staff

Julie Bullard

Enquiring Minds Early Childhood Center strived to meet the needs of children and adults in their program. In addition to children's classrooms, they had a staff room and a family room. However, these rooms were rarely used.

Katie, a new director, wanted to rejuvenate the rooms. She began by meeting with the staff and families to ask what they needed to make their jobs (teaching or parenting) easier. The staff wanted a relaxing, rejuvenating environment for their breaks. They also needed a workroom. However, they stated that when both of these occurred in the same space, it was often ineffective. For example, staff found it difficult to relax when the copier machine was running. While the workroom needed to be functional with long tables, machines, and storage, the staff envisioned the relaxation room as a somewhat whimsical place with soft curtains and comfortable furnishings. The current room did not have space for both.

Katie then interviewed the families. She was surprised to find that they also wanted a quiet place to regroup after dropping children off or before picking them up. Like the staff, they also had a need to access resources and materials. Both staff and families concluded that designing the rooms to serve the needs of both groups would be the most effective way to use the space.

Katie and a committee of staff and families began the room design. The relaxation room had plants, a coffee table housing inspirational books, comfortable chairs, and windows covered with sheer curtains allowing light to flow into the room. Crystals hung in the window creating rainbows on the floor and surrounding walls. There was a refreshment bar with many kinds of tea, an espresso machine, a coffee pot, a mini fridge for snacks, and a microwave. A fountain, headphones with relaxation music, and natural oils for aromatherapy allowed additional relaxation opportunities. A bulletin board contained thank-you notes, an inspirational quote of the day, and a brainstormed list of 10-minute relaxation ideas generated by the staff and parents. One corner of the room was dedicated to yoga and stretching exercises. Because of a suggestion from some fathers who felt the rooms needed more materials to meet their needs, a computer with Internet hookup and headphones was added to play games, listen to music, or check e-mail. In addition, books focused on fathers were added.

The workroom contained a resource library, family learning backpacks to check out, a variety of office supplies, and machines such as computers, a laminator, and a copier. The room had large worktables as well as individual carrels. Although this room was designed for functionality, plants, framed pictures of children, families, and staff, and interesting baskets to hold supplies also helped it to be aesthetic. One family donated a beautiful rug that also created a more pleasant ambiance. Because of these changes, the rooms were in constant use. As families and staff began to use the rooms, a sense of community developed.

Apply Your Knowledge This center had two rooms available for staff and parents. Many programs do not have this amount of space. What are ways that you could still meet the parents' and staff's needs for relaxation and work space in a setting that had very little space?

Your environment provides a message about the respect and the value you place on the adults in children's lives. Effective environments meet the needs of both children and adults. They are aesthetic, comfortable, and emotionally and physically safe. Materials and displays represent and recognize the inhabitants. Environments for adults, like children, send the message, "This is a place where I belong, where I am valued, and where my basic needs are met. It is a place where I can effectively receive and give information."

Family Engagement: Value and Methods

To be effective educators, we must form partnerships with families and the community. Under the best scenario, the teacher "functions as a member of the extended family for both the parent and child" (Riley, San Juan, Klinkher, & Ramminger, 2008, p. 7).

Value of Family Engagement

Regardless of socioeconomic status, a parent's educational background, age, gender, ethnic, or racial background, numerous outcomes for children improve when families are engaged. Children whose families are involved experience greater school success and achievement in every academic area, better social skills, higher motivation, improved behavior and better attitudes about school, and increased attendance and retention (Harvard Family Research Project, 2014).

But, why is this so? Since children only spend 20% of their waking time in school, schools alone cannot meet children's educational needs (Harvard Family Research Project, 2014). Many experts now advocate an **anytime, anywhere learning** approach. But, there is a big gap between children's out-of-school experiences. For example, by the time that children complete elementary school, there is a 6,000-hour gap in out-of-school learning opportunities between the child who is from a low-income family versus a middle-income family (TASC, 2013). In one study, over half of the families wished that they knew how to use out-of-school time to create more effective learning opportunities for children (Patton & Caspe, 2014). Early childhood programs can help. Effective family engagement can create a bridge between what is taught at school and at home so that complementary learning can take place. With support, families can become better teachers of their children, become linked to community supports and resources, and find a place for social interaction. Families can also assist in creating stronger early childhood programs through their support, resources, and advocacy.

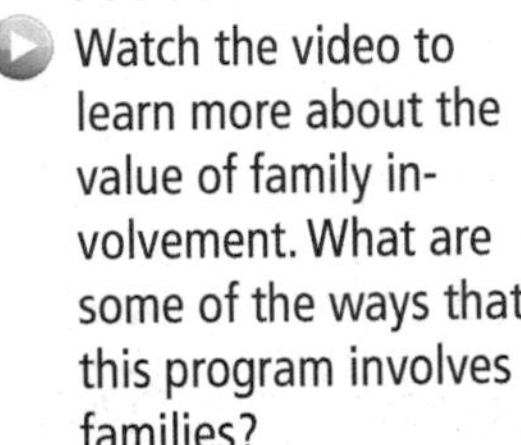

Watch the video to learn more about the value of family involvement. What are some of the ways that this program involves families?

https://www.youtube.com/watch?v=RTVLtln29I0&index=7&list=PLyizHCAockpoWzLf4kDaq3BirJXI5mEpR

Family engagement can assist teachers to know about families' **funds of knowledge**; improve their cultural competence; make them aware of home situations and the families' desires, values, and beliefs; and assist in the development of a positive trusting relationship with families. This can improve child–teacher relationships and learning.

Check Your Understanding 18.1

Click here to gauge your understanding of section concepts.

Ways to Engage Families in Children's Development and Learning

In planning for family engagement, we must examine the outcomes that we hope to achieve and plan activities to meet these outcomes. However, these outcomes can only be met if early childhood teachers have positive relationships with families, recognize the importance of families, and are willing to devote the time to support family engagement.

How can the environmental design assist in meeting these outcomes? We will examine this next.

Family Engagement Outcomes	Sample Activities to Achieve the Outcome
Family well-being	Help identify family interests and needs through building strong relationships. Link families with community supports, especially during times of family crises. Always show respect for the family.
Positive parent–child relationships	Provide parenting and child development classes. Assist families to find resources for challenging behaviors.
Families as life long educators	Share resources such as literacy backpacks with families.
Families as learners	Assist families to pursue their own educational goals by linking them to services.
Family engagement in transitions	Develop transition plans with families.
Family connection to peers and the community	Facilitate social connections through sponsoring parental support groups and facilitating social networks.
Families as advocates and leaders	Provide opportunities for families to learn about and engage in advocacy and leadership within the program.

Based on Office of Head Start & National Center on Parent, Family, and Community Engagement (2011). The Head Start Parent, Family, and Community Engagement Framework: Promoting Family Engagement and School Readiness from Prenatal to Age 8. Retrieved from http://eclkc.ohs.acf.hhs.gov/hslc/hs/sr/approach/pfcef

Meeting the Needs of Families Through an Effective Environment

Every program is unique in the amount of space available and the arrangement of this space. Some programs have long halls filled with child documentation, offices where parents are greeted, and well-stocked family resource rooms. In other programs, parents and children enter directly into the classroom. In still other programs, children arrive by bus. Each of these scenarios affects the placement of information for families, the type of family/child transition spaces, and the location of resources for families.

Julie Bullard

This entryway encourages parents to sit with their toddlers, rocking them and reading to them before they both begin their day.

The entry into the building creates the first impression of your program. It reflects your philosophy and gives a message to families and children. It also acts as a transition place, particularly when parents transport children to the program. With thoughtful design, halls

and entryways can be used to welcome and inform. Entries can provide different types of information, such as parent pamphlets, family displays, project webs, or children's documentation.

Even with limited space, creative teachers find ways to meet family and program needs. Regardless of space, we must develop a respectful environment where families feel they are valued and belong, that meets the families' basic needs as both individuals and parents, and where families can share and receive information about the child, parenting, and community services. Following are some suggestions for accomplishing this.

Establishing an Environment That Tells Families, "You Belong Here"

If we want families to feel that they belong in our programs we must be welcoming; make sure that our environments are inclusive of all cultures; assure that families recognize themselves in the images and information on our walls, in our materials, and in our different forms of communication; and reach out to under represented groups. We will examine each of these criteria in the following sections.

Develop a Welcoming Environment. "I belong here" begins with signage that greets families as they enter the program. At one school the sign said, "Everyone must report to the office immediately upon entering the building." At another school the sign read, "Please come to the office so that we can have the opportunity to personally greet you." Both asked families to comply with the same request. However, one made them feel like intruders while the other conveyed the image of welcoming treasured guests. To be effective and welcoming, signs need to have a positive tone and be written in the families' native language.

Be Inclusive of All Cultures. Environments that denote belonging are inclusive of all cultures. In thinking of culture, it is important to consider all dimensions of culture, including ethnic, racial, linguistic, geographic area or region, religion, economic status, and family composition. These dimensions of culture can affect family values and beliefs, historical and social influences, communication, and attitudes toward seeking help (Bradley & Kibera, 2006, p. 36). Norms of privacy and beliefs about child development are also highly dependent on a family's culture. It is important not to make assumptions about an individual family's culture based upon a particular characteristic. Instead, it is best to learn about the family by asking them to share information about their culture, values, beliefs, and desires for their children (Pipher, 2002, p. 353).

Assure That Images, Materials, and Communication Are Inclusive of All Families. To denote a sense of belonging we must make sure family resource materials, pamphlets, posters, flyers, newsletters, and children's books contain images that reflect cultural and family diversity, including fathers in caregiving roles and grandparents in the parenting role. We must also be conscious of the labels we apply to newsletters and bulletin boards. For example, family is more inclusive than mother, father, or parent. Paperwork can also give a sense of belonging or inclusion. Are the forms that families complete inclusive of all families (foster families, grandparents, or gay or lesbian families)?

Apply Your Knowledge Some schools have developed programs such as Muffins for Moms, where mothers are invited to school to have breakfast with their child, and Donuts for Dads, where fathers are invited to breakfast. What are the advantages and disadvantages of these programs? Are they inclusive of all families?

Using family photos is another way to include and highlight the diversity of families within your program. In one classroom, Becky, the teacher, made a family quilt. Each family created a quilt piece from construction paper that held a family picture and any other information or pictures the family wished to include. The teacher then laminated the papers and tied all the families' papers together with yarn to create the quilt. Becky displayed the quilt in the entry to the program.

This display created by a parent highlights a special family activity.

In another program, each family is highlighted for one week. During this week, a showcase is provided for the family to share artifacts, pictures, and stories. Best Beginnings child care encourages families to set up special interactive displays for the children in the program. One family had just taken a vacation to the ocean. They brought back seashells and set up a display for the children.

Providing materials (newsletters, flyers, informational packets, or parenting books) in the family's native language is also a way of letting families know that they belong, especially for parents who are just learning English. It is also an essential communication tool.

Reach Out to Under-Represented Groups. In the past few years, there have been several national initiatives to reach out to fathers. National leaders have recognized that fathers play a unique role in children's development, parenting in a different but complementary way with mothers (Fagan & Palm, 2004). Research shows that father's involvement is linked to better academic outcomes, higher IQs and cognitive abilities, enhanced social skills, greater self-regulation, and improved self-esteem in children (Jeynes, 2014; Rosenberg & Wilcox, 2006).

What are research-supported ways that early childhood programs can enhance fathers' involvement? These include ensuring the father's name and address are on forms, making a special effort to talk to fathers, providing specific invitations to fathers to participate in classroom events, inviting fathers to be on activity boards, and organizing special father events (Green, 2003). It's also important to design early childhood environments to include fathers. For example, display images of fathers with their children, establish resource libraries that include information specifically designed for fathers, spotlight examples of involved fathers, ensure that posters and brochures include fathers, and include a special column in your newsletter specifically devoted to dads.

Non-resident fathers also need to be included. A research meta-analysis shows a positive impact on children's social, behavioral, cognitive, academic, and social outcomes when non-resident fathers are involved with their children. More important than the quantity of time that fathers spend with children are the quality of time, the quality of the father–child relationships, and the father's involvement in children's activities (Adamsons & Johnson, 2013). How can early childhood programs assist non-resident fathers to meet these criteria? Ensure that non-resident fathers receive information from the early childhood program such as newsletters, notes home, and children's work; invite them to be involved in the program and their children's activities; provide equal access to parenting information and programs; and include them in family–teacher conferences. It is best to give separated or divorced parents the option of coming to the conference together or having separate conferences.

Establishing an Environment That Tells Families, "You Are Valued"

When we value a person, we acknowledge that person, seek his or her ideas, involve the person in decision making, and appreciate and utilize his or her expertise.

Acknowledge Family Members. One way to acknowledge someone is to provide a greeting to the person. Every person entering a program needs to be greeted. A brief personal message as family members pick up and drop off children can help to build relationships and let them know that you value them as persons and as parents. For example, as family members drop off children, Tanya notices a mother's new coat, discusses a child's upcoming birthday with another mother, asks a grandmother who has been receiving treatment for cancer how she is feeling, and asks a father who was in a race over the weekend how it went.

Seek Input from Families. When we value someone, we seek his or her ideas and opinions. You can obtain families' ideas in a variety of ways. An infant–toddler program added a box with a pad of paper and a pencil to their entry area so that families could express their joys and concerns. Families posted the joys on a bulletin board. They placed concerns in a box. The staff addressed the concerns at the next staff meeting. The director then posted the concern and the solution on the bulletin board. At another center, idea lists are posted on the bulletin board. For example, staff asked families about ideas for a playground renovation. As the project proceeded, the parent committee asked families for fund raising ideas.

Involve Families in Decision Making. When we value families, we also involve them in decision making about their child and about the program. Many programs have parent committees that are actively involved in program operations and decision making. For example, the composition of Head Start Policy Councils is more than 50% parents. Families are involved in decisions about hiring new staff, budgets, and curriculum.

In one program, families were actively involved in facility design. At Birge Nest Early Head Start, in Brattleboro, Vermont, a parent committee developed the entry space. The program was housed in an old industrial building. Although the classrooms and offices had been remodeled, the entry had been left with cement floors and drab undecorated walls. The families added several small café tables, a coffee bar, and a comfortable seating area where they could sit and read a book to their child or meet with other parents. Children's art work, a fountain, and a beautiful screen added to the ambiance.

To include more families in decision making, the Meadowlark School added poll boxes to the parent/child transition area. The current poll is whether to provide weekly potlucks at the center.

Recognize and Use Family Members' Expertise. We recognize and use others' expertise when we value them. In Ella's kindergarten room, family members are provided a choice of activities when they volunteer in the classroom. She has established a volunteer station that contains a list of the activities and all the materials and directions to complete the tasks. Ella respects that families have different interests and skills and so

Julie Bullard

At Mentor Graphics Child Development Center, each family creates a banner with their well wishes for their child. The banners stay up throughout the year, reminding staff of the families' hopes and dreams.

provides materials for a variety of options. Families help develop learning center materials, work with individual or small groups of children, and create homemade books and CDs. For example, two parents have been creating CDs in Spanish to use with some of the classroom books.

Brian, a teacher in a K–1 classroom, posts signs in each center with a list of what children are learning. Also posted are ways that adults can facilitate the learning. For example, he posts sheets with open-ended questions and background information in the science area. Brian states that since he has begun this, volunteers say that they feel more competent working with the children.

Amelia, a home childcare provider, posts a note on her door describing the theme she and the children are working on and invites parents to share materials, ideas, or expertise. The first time she did this, the theme was firefighters. One parent brought in a toy fire truck, another shared an authentic fire hat, and another arranged a visit by an uncle who was a firefighter.

At Curious Minds, a project web is hanging in the area where parents enter. Like Amelia's note, the project web informs families about the progress of the current project. Family members are encouraged to suggest ideas and to provide materials or assistance.

Establishing an Environment That Meets Families' Basic Needs

New families have the immediate need to successfully navigate the early childhood building and locate parking. Families also have the need to have their physical needs met as they use the early childhood facility, to feel comfortable leaving their children in your care, to have a peaceful transition when leaving or picking up their children, to have their resources protected, and to be considered as individuals as well as parents.

Assist Families to Easily Navigate the Setting. Entering a large program or school and trying to find the office can sometimes be intimidating, especially when there are multiple entrances. Recently I visited four programs. Each had a sign posted stating the need to check in with the office. However, the office was not easily located in any of the programs. When families first begin a program, we are setting the stage for future interactions. This first impression helps to answer the question, "Will my needs be met in this program?" Families need to be able to easily navigate the setting—to locate the office, their child's classroom, the gym, the parent resource room, and so forth. Classrooms and offices should be labeled in the language or languages used by the families. Floor plans posted by the door or arrows can direct families and others to the office. Diagrams, verbal directions, or a personal guide can assist families and guests to locate other program spaces.

Provide Convenient Parking. Easy-to-locate, convenient parking spaces are also important. Imagine a mother with a three-year-old and an infant. Even walking across a parking lot carrying the infant, a large bag of diapers, and a diaper bag with extra clothes, bottles, and formula, while trying to keep her three-year-old safe from traffic, can be very difficult.

Provide for Adults' Physical Needs. Adult-size chairs in classrooms, offices, meeting rooms, gyms, and other play spaces are critical to meet adults' physical needs. Many adults have difficulty sitting in small chairs or in sitting or rising from the floor. Maria Montessori stressed the need for child-sized furnishings as a way to demonstrate respect and provide comfort for the child. The same philosophy is true for adults.

Providing a comfortable place for nursing mothers is also important. While some mothers are comfortable nursing in the classroom, others desire a quiet, private space. You will want to accommodate both.

Assist Families to Feel Comfortable Leaving Children in Your Care. Families need to feel comfortable and safe leaving their children in your care. It is important for families to have information about the staff that works with their children. Many programs develop a showcase of staff, including cooks and janitors. The showcase includes pictures and professional information such as degrees, length working in the field, and awards. It also includes personal information to help families learn about staff members as individuals. For example, Tina described her interest in fly-fishing. This personal piece of information was a starting point for many conversations with families.

Watch the video to learn more on how to assist with peaceful transitions. How does the teacher help the children and families in this program to have a peaceful transition?

Assist with a Peaceful Transition. Families and children have a need for a peaceful transition between the program and home. Providing a quiet place where parents can engage in a transition activity such as reading a book can help to ease the transition for young children. Depending upon the climate and the child's age, you might need a place where parents can sit with children to help them remove boots and put on shoes or slippers. A waving window allows children and families to say their final goodbyes. For infants and toddlers, small, low windows can be placed slightly above the floor.

Help Protect Families' Resources. Families have the need to protect their resources. Having a lost and found box can help families find missing clothing, toys, and other items.

Meet the Needs of Parents as Individuals. Many programs also strive to meet the needs of parents as individuals. For example, each morning the Nurturing Center provides coffee and tea for families. They also provide a whiteboard for parents who wish to leave messages for other parents. Recently one parent wrote about a sale on children's clothing at a local store. Another parent let other families know about a free children's production at the local theatre.

Establishing an Environment That Allows the Family to Effectively Share and Receive Information About Their Child

There are many ways that we can encourage the sharing of information between families and staff. This includes providing multiple, frequent opportunities for two-way dialogue, taking advantage of daily communication opportunities, using your environment to provide information about what children are learning, and providing private places for conferences. We will examine each of these criteria in more depth in the following sections.

Provide Multiple, Frequent Opportunities for Two-Way Dialogue. The most effective family–teacher communication involves respectful two-way dialogue and frequent contact using varied forms of interaction (Crosser, 2005). When there is regular, effective communication, families rate teachers higher, feel more comfortable with the school, and are more involved in the school (Caplan, Hall, Lubin, & Fleming, 1997). Family–teacher communication is encouraged through family–teacher conferences, home visits, open houses, phone calls, e-mail exchanges, newsletters, and family-program activities such as child art shows, culminating events to projects, and parent luncheons. Many of the communication techniques that were discussed in Chapter 2 can assist in the development of respectful relationships with families such as reflective listening and using conflict resolution skills.

Take Advantage of Daily Communication Opportunities. Communication is also enhanced by having an environment that promotes daily interaction. It is important to design staff schedules so that someone is available to greet children and families as they arrive.

Family communication books or two-way journals are another way for families and teachers to exchange information. At the infant–toddler programs in Reggio Emilia, teachers and families create a "Notebook for Two Voices." These notebooks, which circulate between home and school, record children's developmental progression through notes, anecdotes, and personal reflections (Giovannini, 2001, p. 147). They also provide valuable documentation of the child's earliest years.

Individual family and teacher mailboxes can also be a place to share information. One program uses a hanging shoe holder for mailboxes. Another program uses plastic shoeboxes that are stacked on top of the children's cubbies. Both methods help to ensure that families and teachers receive notes and other correspondence.

When children are transported to school on buses, regular communication is more difficult. Terri, a teacher of kindergartners, sews 9″ × 12″ fabric pockets (a different design for each child) to hold information that goes between the family and teacher. The pockets are durable and obvious, and so are not easily destroyed or lost in backpacks.

Watch the video to learn more about parent–teacher conferences. How did the teacher help to ensure a successful conference?

Use Your Environment to Provide Information About What Children Are Learning. Your environment can also inform families about what children are learning. Many programs post the classroom schedule and lesson or project plans for families and volunteers to see. Like Brian, you can also post signs on the walls of each learning center telling what children are learning in that area. Project notebooks, documentation panels, and albums also inform families of children's learning. At the Burlington Little School, Deb Curtis creates documentation (photos, descriptions, and interpretations) of class and individual activities that she posts in the entry area for families to read. After all of the families have had a chance to read them, she places them in a three-ring binder that is also kept in the entry area. The Mentor Graphic Child Development Center has a file for each child that houses possible portfolio entries. The files and portfolios are placed next to the sign-in area, so that families can easily look at them.

Many programs also provide parents with information about what their child does each day. For example, when families drop children off at Curious Minds, there is a statement posted, "Today we are going to…." The families are encouraged to read the statement to their child or allow the child to read the statement to them. There is also a daily flash at the end of the day. On the "Daily Flash," the teacher lists at least one thing that the children did that day. A "Daily News Reporter," one of the children's rotating jobs, provides information from a child's point of view. In addition, teachers often place individual Happygrams, listing an accomplishment such as "Today I completed the ABC puzzle all by myself," in family mailboxes.

Teresa takes digital pictures on a daily basis. Using a digital picture frame, she

This continually changing bulletin board at Mentor Graphics Child Development Center is a favorite of families.

provides a slide show of images of the children engaged in activities for families to view as they pick up their children.

Provide Private Places for Impromptu and Scheduled Conferences. Within the environment, it is also important to have a private place for impromptu and scheduled family conferences. Adult-sized chairs and a round table can help to create a comfortable and egalitarian atmosphere. Sitting across from each other over a desk creates a barrier that some families might associate with the teacher having more power than they do.

Establishing an Environment Where the Family Can Gain Information and Materials That Will Assist Them in Providing for Their Child's Needs

Early childhood programs can be instrumental in providing information about parenting, home learning activities, and community resources. Each type of information can assist families in meeting children's needs.

Provide Parenting Information. You can share parenting information through parent lending libraries of books, DVDs, and videos. You can also offer tip sheets, placed near the sign-in area, that provide easy to read information about common issues for the age group. For example, an infant–toddler program might have tip sheets about subjects like toilet learning, starting solid foods, encouraging language, and sleeping through the night. Information can also be placed on bulletin boards. See Figure 18.1 for information on designing family bulletin boards.

Provide Information on Home Learning Activities. Many programs provide families with information and materials to assist with home learning activities. For example, Curious Minds creates math and literacy bags that include a children's book,

FIGURE 18.1
Family Bulletin Boards

Determine the purpose of the board (supply information about events, share documentation of what children are doing, provide parenting information)

Use design principles and placement so that the board is useful to families

- ❑ Ensure that the board is non-cluttered, with short, easy-to-read phrases and large type.
- ❑ Include interactive elements such as lifting a flap to find an answer to a question on the board.
- ❑ Provide a visual cue that changes have been made such as a different color background.
- ❑ Place the bulletin board at eye level in an area where families will notice it and have time to linger to read it.

Be creative

- ❑ Share children's artwork, answers to a question, photos of children engaged in an activity, or a photograph of a learning center or activity and a description of what children learned.
- ❑ Create a Give and Take Bulletin Board by dividing the board into featured spaces—Give Us A Hand (accomplishments), Learning Opportunities (training events), Things You Always Wanted to Know (program information), How About a Hand (volunteer opportunities), Picture This (photos of children), and I've Got an Idea (suggestions) (Child Care Plus, 1995).

a list of activities to use with the book, and all the materials to complete the activities. See the opening photo for an example of the bags. Backpacks or bags can also contain art kits, game kits, and science kits. Other programs provide writing briefcases containing paper, journals, a variety of writing implements, and story starters that families can check out.

While many programs stress that families should read to children, this may not be possible for all families. For example, some families may have difficulty accessing books in their native language. Encouraging storytelling is a way of respecting families while also meeting children's literacy needs. One program encouraged families to engage in storytelling by providing a digital voice recorder. Blank books and art supplies were also included for writing and illustrating a book, if the family wanted. Some families then lent the books and recording to the program so that other children could also listen to them.

Storytelling is also an important option for families with low reading skills. Through storytelling, children gain many of the same skills that they gain from being read to, including concept of story, the many strands of plot, internalization of character, prediction skills, the natural rhythms and patterns of language, listening and attending skills, vocabulary development, and learning figures of speech and metaphors. In addition, stories are often an important way of learning about and internalizing one's culture (Malo & Bullard, 2000).

Provide Information on Community Services. It is also helpful for programs to provide information about community services. Some programs sponsor one-stop services featuring a variety of social agencies in the family resource center (learn more about family resource centers by reading Figure 18.2). In other programs, teachers distribute booklets of available community services to each family. You might also display brochures from different community agencies in a prominent place.

Programs can assist families in many other ways as well. Some programs sponsor a clothing or toy exchange. For example, Santa Rosa Infant/Toddler Program has a clothing bin where families can drop off clean clothing. Any family can take clothing from the bin if they wish. Some programs provide families with the phone numbers of staff who are willing to provide after-hours or weekend childcare (with staff permission) as another way to assist families.

Check Your Understanding 18.2

Click here to gauge your understanding of section concepts.

FIGURE 18.2
Family Resource Centers

Some programs provide family resource centers. In the centers, families can obtain information, take classes, meet other parents, access community services, and assist in projects to make the program higher quality (Grant & Ray, 2010). Resource rooms might contain computers, libraries, clothing or toy exchanges, and private meeting spaces. In establishing a parent resource center, consider the following:

- ❑ Hold a meeting or survey families to see what they value in a resource center.
- ❑ Make the center visible and easy to find.
- ❑ Staff the center with volunteers.
- ❑ Clearly label all materials in the center.
- ❑ Make the center child friendly (even if families are using the center when their child is in the classroom, they might be bringing younger children with them).
- ❑ Provide multilingual information.
- ❑ Provide a welcoming environment (noncluttered, adult-sized soft furniture, coffee and tea pot).
- ❑ Provide informative posters, books, and pamphlets.
- ❑ Provide a suggestion box.
- ❑ Provide name tags where families can write their name and the name of their child as a way to build community.

Meeting the Needs of Staff

Through your environment, you can help to motivate, empower, and appreciate staff. Your environment can assist in developing or discouraging a sense of community and can reduce or contribute to job stress. It also serves as a model. If we create an aesthetic, effective environment for teachers it is likely that they will also see the value of this for children. Teachers, like children often spend eight or more hours in the early childhood setting. All aspects of the environment should allow staff to feel that this is a place where they belong, where their basic needs are met, where they are valued, where they can effectively share information with others, and where they can efficiently obtain the information and materials they need to be successful in meeting children's needs.

Reducing Stress and Burnout

Early childhood providers are particularly vulnerable to **burnout** (Evans, Bryant, & Owens, 2004). Leading researchers in the field describe burnout as including emotional exhaustion, depersonalization (distances self from others), and reduced accomplishment (Maslach, Jackson, & Leiter, 1996). Burnout leads to increased negativity about the job and children, a cynical attitude, feelings of inadequacy, and a reduced ability to cope. This has a negative impact on the care children receive in these environments (Evans et al., 2004).

There are many factors that contribute to early childhood caregiver stress and burnout, including undervalued work, poor communication, challenging relationships, low autonomy, isolation, insufficient time for all job demands, lack of involvement in decision making, and one of the greatest contributors, low wages (Corr, Davis, LaMontagne, Waters, & Steele, 2014; Evans et al., 2004; Wagner et al., 2013). The job itself is also very demanding. Children in the early childhood years require teachers who have abundant energy, continual positive interactions, and a high level of alertness.

Check Your Understanding 18.3
Click here to gauge your understanding of section concepts.

While occupational burnout can be reduced through equitable wages, it can also be reduced through stress management, networking and communicating with others, informal coping networks, and resources and materials to meet the high demands of early childhood (Evans et al., 2004). An effective environment can assist in providing these.

Meeting the Needs of Staff Through an Effective Environment

Establishing an Environment That Tells Staff, "You Belong Here"

Staff, like children and families, experience a sense of belonging when they see reflections of themselves in the environment (Carter & Curtis, 1998). This includes images and favorite items.

A sense of belonging is also reinforced by having a place for storing personal belongings. This needs to be secure so that children do not have access to medicines or other harmful items that might be found in purses or pockets. Teachers also need a space for storing personal teaching materials and private files and records.

Establishing an Environment That Tells Staff, "You Are Valued"

Some ways we show staff they are valued is by providing a comfortable, aesthetic environment, showing consideration for their time, involving them in decision making, and showing appreciation for them. In the next sections, we will examine each of these criteria more thoroughly.

Provide a Comfortable, Aesthetic Environment. Establishing comfortable, aesthetic, and clean adult environments (bathrooms, lounges, and staff rooms) is one very basic way that we let staff know that they are valued. For example, Susan, a principal of a kindergarten school, realized that she had been stressing the need for aesthetic places for children, while ignoring the aesthetics and comfort of adult spaces in her school. She began by redecorating the institutional adult bathroom, adding mirrors, plants, and a hand-woven rug. She placed lavender liquid soap and lavender lotion by the sink. A parent, who worked in a floral shop, brought in discarded but still beautiful fresh flowers that Susan placed in the bathroom. Like children, adults spend many of their waking hours in the early childhood environment. They need to be surrounded by "softness, art, beauty, natural materials, and living things" (Carter & Curtis, 1998, p. 125). It is important to create an environment where adults and children want to spend their time, rather than just enduring the experience.

Show Consideration of Staff's Time. Being considerate of someone's time is another way that we value him or her. For example, in early childhood facilities, having organized and convenient storage for program materials and supplies saves time and makes working conditions easier.

Seek Staff Input When Making Decisions. Encouraging staff input in decision making lets staff know that we appreciate their expertise, results in better decisions, and helps to reduce burnout. Some programs provide joys and concerns boxes for staff to express views. Others have a running dialogue on a staff bulletin board or discussion board. For example, one center was considering extending their hours. On the staff bulletin board was the question "What are the pros and cons of extending our hours?" Sticky notes and pens encouraged staff to add their views. One of the teachers then typed the notes, and they were used as a basis for discussion at a staff meeting.

Watch the video to listen to a song about teachers. How could this music video be used to show appreciation for teachers?

https://www.youtube.com/watch?v=40lVr6MQKtw

Show Appreciation for Staff Members. Many early childhood teachers feel undervalued. A director at Tiny Tots, understanding that feeling undervalued can lead to burnout, uses a variety of ways to show appreciation. For example, she places treats in the staff room with an appreciation note. She began an appreciation bulletin board and encourages families and staff to place notes on it. She collects free and inexpensive items and places them in a basket in the teachers' lounge for the teachers to take (sample lotions, pens, posters, magnets). She remembers birthdays with special treats. She also places individualized thank-you notes in teacher's mailboxes.

In a field with high turnover and high stress levels, it is important to remember to value staff. Establishing an environment of respect and appreciation, where all individuals are valued, can make the workplace more rewarding.

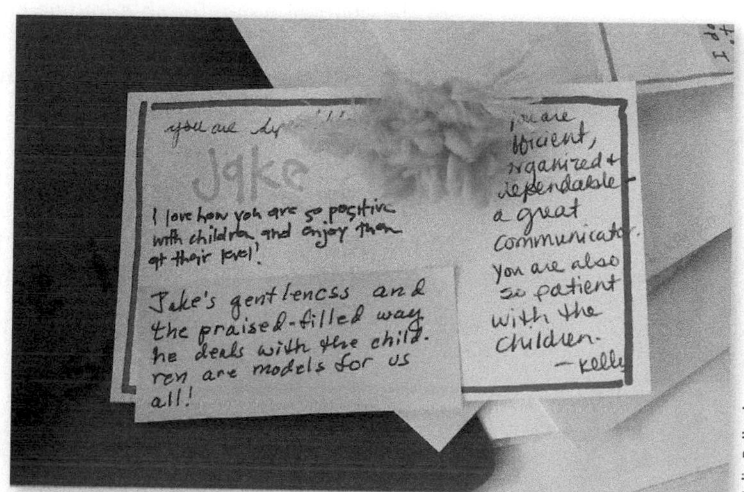

At Spirit at Play, staff write "warm fuzzies" to let other staff members know that they appreciate them.

Establishing an Environment That Meets Staff's Basic Needs

Teachers, like children, have a basic need for a safe and healthy environment with a place to keep personal belongings and materials. They also need a comfortable place to take a break where they can relax and rejuvenate. Providing for these basic needs helps to relieve staff stress and create a more pleasant working environment. This can lead to higher quality care for children.

Provide a Safe Environment. The most common adult injuries in early childhood settings are back injuries. They most frequently occur over a period of time rather than as an isolated incident (Wortman, 2001). To provide a comfortable environment and to protect teachers' backs, provide adult furniture. If adults are sitting on the floor, backrests should be provided. Steps that children can climb for diaper changing can also protect adults' backs. Another option that some centers use to protect an adult's back when changing a toddler is to have the toddler stand for diaper changes while the teacher sits on a low stool.

Provide a Healthy Environment. It is also critical to protect adults' health. "Improving the health of adults who work in child care pays double dividends. It not only helps the individual, but also everyone who depends on them" (Aronson, 2001, p. 1). Adequate airflow and noise, temperature, and humidity control protect the health of adults and children (see Chapter 6).

To protect from blood-borne diseases, it is imperative to have gloves easily available. Many centers have a supply of gloves in every room (classroom, bathrooms, gym, and lunchroom) and a fanny pack with gloves for taking outside. Teachers are more likely to use gloves when they are readily accessible.

To prevent illness, adults need to wash hands many times a day (for example, when they enter the program, before food preparation, and whenever assisting children with toileting or blowing noses). Providing lotion at every sink, can help to prevent the dry and cracked hands that can result from all the washing.

Assist Teachers to Reduce Stress. To be effective with children and to prevent burnout, staff need breaks from children. As discussed in the scenario at the beginning of the chapter, a comfortable lounge can decrease stress and assist staff to return to the children refreshed.

Some directors have found innovative ways to reduce stress for teachers. For example, the director at the First Steps Infant/Toddler Program brainstormed ways that she could support teachers and reduce their stress. Many of the teachers were single parents with multiple demands on their time. She realized that every day the program threw away quantities of food, since any food placed in serving bowls could not be served again. She encouraged staff to take home the remaining food at the end of the day. This saved the staff time and money while providing a nutritious meal for their family. The director also provided free yoga classes once a week that staff could attend with their children.

Establishing an Environment That Allows the Staff to Share Information with Others

Establishing a lounge and furniture groupings that encourage interaction can facilitate staff networking, sharing ideas, and problem solving of issues (Bentham, 2008). As people have the opportunity to know each other, they often form informal mentoring and support networks. While this is usually positive, at times it can become negative. When the Fifth Avenue School staff discussed creating a staff lounge, one of the teachers mentioned that in a previous school the lounge was dominated by negative talk about children and parents. She said that she ended up staying in her classroom during breaks rather than be influenced by the lounge atmosphere. The Fifth Avenue staff decided that they would prevent the possibility of this occurring by creating and posting a list of ground rules in the lounge. Two of their rules were "Freely share positive information about children, parents, and coworkers" and "Any problems or issues that are discussed are for the purpose of brainstorming solutions, no names will be used." The staff also made a commitment to remind each other of the rules. These guidelines have helped the Fifth Avenue School to have a positive staff lounge.

Individual staff mailboxes are also helpful in organizing and systematically getting mail and messages to staff members. Some programs also provide a list of staff phone numbers (with their permission) so that people can easily contact each other outside of work hours.

Curious Minds, a college lab school, has many students who work in the center each day. At the staff sign-in area, there is a communication book where the director, teachers, and lab and work-study students write pertinent information. This might include reminders about upcoming events, information a parent has provided that needs to be passed on to other staff members, a thank-you, and so forth.

Establishing an Environment Where the Staff Can Gain Information and Materials They Need to Provide for Children's Needs

To meet children's needs, teachers must have access to children's records, materials and supplies, references, and a work area for creating their own materials and supplies.

Provide Ready Access to Children's Files. Parents often fill out enrollment information that includes information about their child's interests, their goals for the child, and special talents they may have. If directors keep this information in a central office, teachers may never have the time to look at the material. Instead, locked files in each classroom can allow teachers to keep information readily available.

Provide Organized, Abundant Materials and Supplies. Teachers need enough materials and supplies to meet children's needs. While teachers will keep some of these in the classroom, there should also be storage for materials bought in bulk (paints, paper) and for recyclables. Supplies and materials should be visible, organized, and distributed fairly. Keeping a running list of additional materials, with the person's name requesting it, can help the person purchasing supplies get what teachers need. A workroom with a large table, copying machine, computer, and laminating machine can assist teachers in preparing additional materials.

Provide Teaching Resources. As demonstrated in the opening scenario, a resource area with a reference library, current educational journals, and access to a computer can

Julie Bullard

This light activity allows teachers to experiment with recycled materials and light sources.

Check Your Understanding 18.4
Click here to gauge your understanding of section concepts.

Click here to gauge your understanding of chapter concepts.

help teachers in planning classroom activities and researching a topic for their own background knowledge. These resources are also helpful in learning about new techniques or accessing information to meet the needs of a child or family with special needs. Some programs highlight new materials or books by placing them on an attractive display table (Bentham, 2008).

At the Kids World Learning Center, staff took turns writing a "Did you know … ?" on the resource room whiteboard. These tidbits of information provided teachers with educational ideas. For example, "Did you know that we should use one ounce of sunscreen per child at least 20 minutes before going outside?" The resource area can also contain announcements. For example, announcements about upcoming staff training, community workshops, and college courses can keep staff informed about educational opportunities.

To reduce adult stress and burnout and to provide high-quality care for children, families and staff must have their needs met. An effective environment meets adults' needs, encourages communication, provides access to resources, and lets adults know they belong and are valued.

Sample Application Activities

1. Develop a fact sheet about the value of family engagement. You can find additional information at the Harvard Family Research Project or the National Coalition for Parent Involvement in Education websites.
2. Discuss ways that you would develop a welcoming environment for a family who does not speak English.
3. Visit a program. Make a list of all environmental cues that tell families they belong in the program and that they are valued.
4. Brainstorm ways that stress could be reduced for staff in the program where you are working or completing labs.
5. Brainstorm a list of relaxing activities that can be completed in 10 minutes.
6. Use the environmental assessment in Figure 18.3 to critique an early childhood environment.

FIGURE 18.3 Environmental Assessment: Meeting the Needs of Families and Teachers

While there are many ways that we involve and appreciate adults, this checklist will focus on those that would be noticeable if you were observing the environment

Does the program meet the needs of families through

- ❑ Representing families in the program through photos, displays, and artifacts?
- ❑ Assuring that all materials used in the program represent cultural and family diversity (forms, posters, brochures, children's books, family resource books)?
- ❑ Providing materials in the families' native language?
- ❑ Seeking family input (for example, a suggestion box)?
- ❑ Involving families in decision making?
- ❑ Valuing families' expertise (such as a volunteer center, signs letting families know what the children are learning and how they can support the learning posted in learning centers, project webs with an invitation to add to it)?
- ❑ Easy-to-locate offices and classrooms?
- ❑ Signage that welcomes families in their native language?
- ❑ Convenient parking spaces?
- ❑ Adult-sized furniture and bathrooms?
- ❑ Staff displays that provide information to families about the people who are working with their children?
- ❑ Providing a space for peaceful transitions?
- ❑ Meeting the needs of parents as individuals (warm personal greetings, coffee and tea, parent lounge for relaxing)?
- ❑ A welcoming, informative entryway?
- ❑ Providing mechanisms for two-way communication (such as family mailboxes, communication books, individual greetings)?
- ❑ Providing information about what children are learning (for example, documentation panels, portfolios, daily flashes, happygrams)?
- ❑ Private places for conferences?
- ❑ Providing information that will assist families in providing for their child's needs (lending libraries, literacy backpacks, family resource centers, community pamphlet displays)?

Does the program meet the needs of staff through

- ❑ Providing reflections of staff (such as images and favorite items)?
- ❑ Supplying a place to store personal belongings and personal teaching materials?
- ❑ Providing a lounge for teachers to relax and rejuvenate?
- ❑ Providing adult-sized bathrooms?
- ❑ Valuing staff time by providing organized and convenient storage?
- ❑ Allowing staff input into decision making (such as joys and concerns boxes)?
- ❑ Appreciating staff's work (for example, posted thank-you notes, highlighting accomplishments on bulletin boards)?
- ❑ Protecting adults from back injuries by providing adult furniture, backrests for floor sitting, and diaper-changing steps?
- ❑ Improving the health of staff and children with adequate airflow, temperature, humidity, and noise control?
- ❑ Protecting staff from blood-borne diseases by having readily available gloves in every room?
- ❑ Encouraging hand washing through easily available sinks and providing lotion for protection from cracked hands?
- ❑ Providing a pleasant, aesthetic classroom environment?
- ❑ Supporting staff interactions (for example, a staff lounge, staff mailboxes, staff communication book)?
- ❑ Easily accessible children's files so that teachers have needed information?
- ❑ Providing enough materials and supplies so adults can meet children's needs?
- ❑ Providing teacher resources (such as a reference library, educational journals, computer with Internet access)?

Chapter 19

Meeting Environmental Challenges

Learning Outcomes

After you have read this chapter, you will be prepared to:

- Explain ways to create centers in small spaces
- Discuss ways to obtain materials on a limited budget
- Discuss how to develop a childcare in your home that meets the needs of both the family and the children in the childcare
- Describe techniques for sharing space between programs

Julie Bullard

An Early Head Start program invited a consultant to their classroom to help design their small space. The teachers were concerned because the mobile infants, who were beginning to crawl and walk, had limited space to move and play. In addition, there were no centers in the classroom, so it was difficult for children to find quiet places to look at a book or complete a simple puzzle. The room contained four highchairs, a large ramped loft, a small table and chairs, two adult-sized rocking chairs, and several teacher cabinets. A partial wall enclosed a sleeping area containing five cribs.

Although initially the teachers thought there was a need for each piece of equipment since at times they had five babies who were in cribs, after further analysis it was determined that equipment that was not in current use could be disassembled and stored elsewhere. This eliminated two cribs and two highchairs. Placing plastic storage bins under two of the remaining cribs eliminated the need for one of the teacher cabinets. High storage built on the wall eliminated the need for another storage cabinet. The removal of the equipment and storage cabinets created significantly more space for children to play.

The large loft could not be removed from the classroom, having been assembled within the space. However, the teachers felt that currently the loft wasn't being used to its full space potential. They decided to divide the loft platform with a gauzy curtain. They furnished the back half of the loft with soft cushions and books, creating a cuddly reading area. The bottom of the loft had been fully enclosed. A carpenter cut two child-sized holes into this area, making it usable for children to crawl in and out of.

The teachers also provided an illusion of more space by adding more mirrors to the walls and the ceiling. The napping area had a heavy wooden half door. This was replaced with a Plexiglas door, allowing children to see in and out of the napping area and also providing more light for this space.

By removing equipment that was not currently being used, rethinking storage options, reexamining their current space, and creating an illusion of space, the teachers were able to transform the room. Children and staff felt less confined in the newly designed room and children had more room for movement and play.

This chapter will examine a variety of challenges that programs face, including challenges with space, limited budgets, having an early childhood business in your home, and the need to share space.

Creating Centers in Small Spaces

Although most programs must meet minimum state standards for space of 35 square feet per child, most experts recommend a per child minimum of 50 square feet (White and Stoecklin, 2003). If you have only the minimum amount of space that is required by law, arranging your room can be challenging. However, there are several strategies to use if you are in this situation. They include removing any equipment or materials that you are not currently using, using all available space throughout the day, increasing space in a variety of innovative ways, using vertical surfaces, and creating an illusion of more space. For inspiration on creatively using space, visit loft apartments and tiny houses.

Effectively Use All Available Space

As in the opening scenario, as teachers we sometimes become so familiar with the equipment, materials, and space arrangement in our classrooms that we need to take a fresh look to determine if our space is being used to its full advantage. Some hints to take advantage of space include the following:

Julie Bullard

At Community Building Child Care, nestled in the heart of Spokane, Washington, the program took advantage of all available space to create a terraced playground that includes plants, a water feature, music, art, gross motor, and dramatic play.

- Collect data on the space used. For example, every 10 minutes during center play, tally where each child is playing. Are the children using every area within the classroom? If not, what changes could be made to better utilize the space?
- Remove all equipment and materials that are not currently being used.
- Reduce clutter (clutter takes space and makes small spaces seem smaller).
- Provide portable centers (a tote containing math manipulatives can be placed on the snack table and a beanbag throw can be put in the circle area during center time). The Oak Street Afterschool Learning Program provided additional space by having a play table that mounted to the ceiling with a pulley. The table was used for a train set. Children were taught to carefully lower the table for play and then raise it to provide space for circle time activities.
- Use tops of shelving for centers. For example, a science center might be placed on the top of the manipulative shelf.
- Think creatively and examine every space for possible use (bathrooms, closets, nap rooms, and coatroom). Can you replace a closet door with a curtain and use it for a puppet area? If there is a teacher's desk in the room, could an alone area be placed under the desk? Could the hall be used for cubbies, storage, or a separate center? For example, Karl Wolf, a teacher of kindergarten children, has a woodworking center and a gross motor area in the hallway outside his classroom.

Increase Usable Space

Programs might increase usable space in a variety of ways. This can include creating lofts, developing centers outdoors, carefully considering furniture options, and designing storage spaces that do not take floor space.

Create Lofts. Lofts allow centers to be placed in the upper platform and underneath. One Head Start program created an inexpensive option by converting bunk beds into lofts. When creating lofts, make sure that you contact your licensing agent or health department for requirements. You will also want to make sure that you have appropriate fall zones and surfaces.

Create Outdoor Centers. You might also be able to effectively use the outdoors for some of your centers. Many programs allow children to freely move back and forth between indoor and outdoor centers. If the weather allows you to spend significant time outside and space is an issue, you would not need to have the same centers inside and outside.

Use Dual-Purpose Furniture. Programs can also economize space by using movable or dual-purpose equipment. Blissful Beginnings Child Care has a lunch table that folds and latches against the wall when it is not needed for eating. The back of the table is a whiteboard that is used for drawing and writing when it is folded up. They also have a parent sign-in table that folds down for use and then folds and latches along the wall for the remaining part of the day. Another program uses folding chairs that they fold up when not in use to create more play space. Central Preschool has a specially designed sensory table with a lid that extends beyond the table. When the lid is placed on the sensory table, it can be used as a lunch table.

Use Smaller Furniture. Smaller furniture can also economize space. For example, a rectangular table takes less space than a kidney-shaped table. Typical shelves are wider than needed. Purchasing or building narrower shelving can save space.

Reconsider Storage Options. Effectively organizing and using storage can often eliminate floor storage. For example, like Andrea, consider using spaces under tables, cribs, window seats, or furniture for storage or placing storage high on the walls. Storage can also be increased by using the inside of cabinet doors, adding additional shelves between shelves that are spaced far apart, adding rotating trays, hanging shoe bags on the back of doors, and using square rather than round storage containers. At Loving Care, a parent who was a carpenter removed some sheetrock and built shelves between the studs for storage of small items. For inspiration on storage options, you might want to visit an RV dealership. RVs are typically built to take advantage of all possible storage spaces.

Julie Bullard

This teacher-created light table is just the right size for one or two children. Powered with a clamp light as a light source, it saves space and money.

Use Vertical Space Whenever Possible

Vertical surfaces are often an overlooked way to save space. For example, books hung in pockets on a divider can eliminate the need for a bookshelf. Wall pockets, felt surfaces, and whiteboards mounted to the wall, on the front of cabinets, or on the ends and backs of bookshelves can be used for activity centers. Pegboards mounted on the wall can provide access to materials such as dramatic play props, carpentry tools, or art supplies. Wall-mounted short lengths of rain gutter can be used to hold books or displays. Mounting easels on walls is another way to preserve floor space. You can change the materials on these vertical surfaces to provide new learning experiences. For example, an inexpensive magnetic oil pan mounted to the wall can be used to create artistic designs with magnetic craft sticks, learn science with magnetic gears and ball rolls, or as a word wall to enhance literacy.

Create the Illusion of More Space

Mirrors can make a room feel larger. Placing the mirrors so that they reflect an outdoor scene can be especially effective. You can also create the illusion of more space by keeping windows unobscured allowing the outside in. Painting everything in the room the same light color (including walls and furniture) also provides an illusion of greater space.

To create centers in small spaces, effectively use your available space and think creatively. One program had separate classrooms for three- and four-year-olds and for four- and five-year-olds. The classrooms were small and placed side by side. The

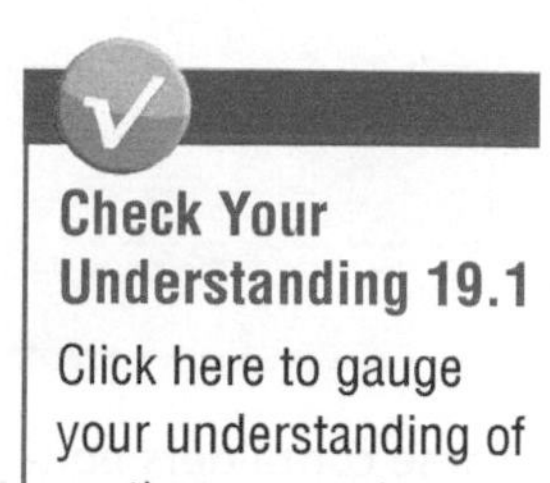

Check Your Understanding 19.1

Click here to gauge your understanding of section concepts.

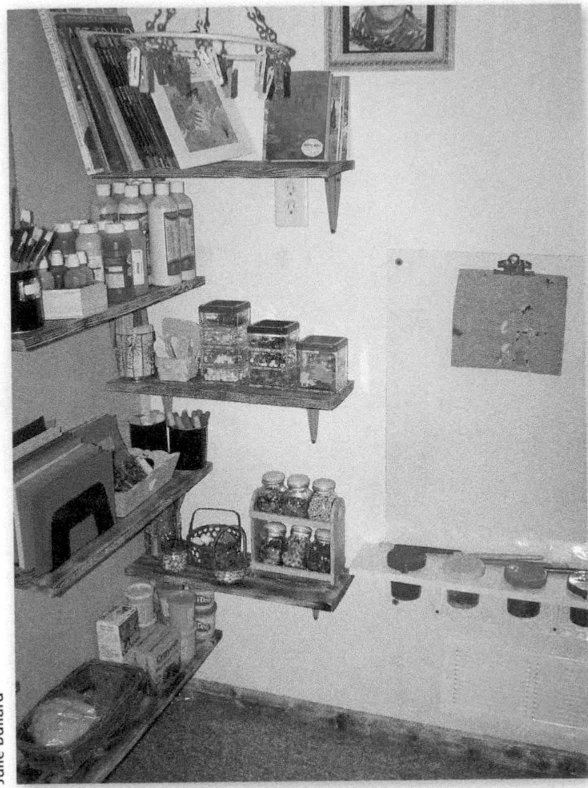

Floating shelves and an easel attached directly to the wall allow a home childcare provider to develop a functional, aesthetic art center in a very small space.

These containers bolted to the wall take advantage of vertical space. Because they are transparent, they give the illusion of taking less space.

teachers decided to share the classrooms, placing quiet areas (reading, art, manipulative, literacy, science) in one classroom and active areas (blocks, dramatic play, music, art) in the other. This allowed the teachers to provide every center and to make each center larger.

Free and Inexpensive Materials to Assist a Limited Budget

Teachers in early childhood classrooms are frequently looking for ways to expand their supply budget. You can obtain free and inexpensive materials by borrowing or creating materials, seeking donations of materials, buying materials secondhand, or obtaining materials through special fundraisers, contributions, or grants. Repairing what you have also reduces the need for a replacement.

Borrow Materials

- Literacy—check out books and tapes from the local library. Some children's librarians will have the books ready if you call ahead with a list or a topic.
- Resource trunks and packs—check with your local resource and referral agency and museums. Many have materials that can be checked out by teachers. The Department of Natural Resources and Fish, Wildlife, and Parks agencies also have teaching trunks available.
- Exchange with other childcare providers—in one community, family childcare providers meet monthly to exchange toys, manipulatives, and books. They also pooled their money to buy an indoor climber that they each take turns using.

Create Materials

Many materials can be handmade. One center had a committee of family and community volunteers who created and renovated materials. There were retired carpenters as well as people who enjoyed sewing and creating crafts. Throughout this book in the "Create your own" features, in figures, and in the text there are ideas for materials to create, including musical instruments, blocks, manipulatives, gross motor equipment, and puppets. You can also visit Pinterest for a wealth of ideas.

Furniture and shelving can be expensive for early childhood programs. If you are on a limited budget you can create child-sized tables using old doors and screw-on legs. Another option is to shorten the legs on an adult table. Shelving can be created by using bricks and boards, stackable crates, or heavy boxes duct taped together and spray-painted. You can make your own pillows or beanbag chairs using packing filling for the stuffing.

Seek Donations

Stores are often willing to donate unsold merchandise, samples, or promotional material. For example, after Halloween you might be able to obtain quality costumes and face paint either free or very inexpensively. Lumberyards, home improvement stores, and furniture outlets often have product samples (paint chip, counter, wallpaper, wallboard, rug, or fabric). As these become outdated, the store is often willing to donate them to you. Many businesses are also willing to donate promotional items to programs. For example, a bank had their name printed on Frisbees. They donated 25 to the local childcare. Another time, they donated sticky notes that the teachers and children used in a variety of ways.

Watch the video to learn more about how to make a play kitchen set. What other items could you make out of an entertainment center?

https://www.youtube.com/watch?v=1wu_yEhscEo

Merchants might also be willing to donate ends of rolls (fabric, paper, plastic, carpet, or contact paper). As you shop, look for items that are sold in rolls. If there are materials that you could use, ask the store if they would be willing to donate the roll ends to you. Also, ask for donations of other items that are typically thrown away, such as film canisters or reject keys.

In their book, *Beautiful Stuff: Learning with Found Materials*, Cathy Topal and Lella Gandini (1999) describe their invitation to children and parents to collect materials. Children helped to brainstorm a list of found and recyclable materials that they would like and the teachers sent home bags to hold the items. The returned bags were clipped shut until the grand opening, creating a sense of eager anticipation. When the bags were opened, the children determined ways to sort and classify the materials. Ultimately, the materials were displayed in clear or white containers. This allowed the children to see the contents, placed the emphasis on the materials rather than the container, and created a beautiful, enticing display. The materials became part of the classroom art studio.

Some communities have Reuse or **Remida Centers**. These centers contain donated discarded materials that are organized and typically given free to teachers. Visit the website of Reusable Resources Association or search for Remida Centers to find centers in your area and to learn more about using these discarded materials as classroom resources.

Buy Secondhand Materials and Equipment

Make a list of needed items that could be purchased secondhand. The Mother Goose Center had the following materials on their list: lamp, small loveseat, family sign-in table, beautiful trays, crystal dishes, interesting containers, and children's books, toys, and manipulatives. They had several parents who volunteered to look for these items when they went to garage sales and secondhand stores. By the end of the summer, they had found everything on their list. Craigslist or other similar online exchanges are another source for secondhand materials.

Julie Bullard

These donated mailboxes make an aesthetically pleasing place for family information at Curious Minds: Early Care and Education Center.

You might also be able to make special arrangements with a secondhand store for reduced rates or donations. Nearly New, a consignment store, allowed the funds from donations of used items to be credited to a local childcare.

Engage in Special Fundraisers and Seek Contributions and Grants

Some programs have parents who engage in fundraisers and seek contributions. It is often easier to receive contributions or to engage in fundraising if you have a specific project in mind. For example, you might be able to seek contributions for a specific piece of equipment, to paint the center, or to create a new learning center. This allows those donating to know how you will use their money. It also gives those participating in the fundraising a sense of accomplishment when the goal is met. When fundraising, you will want to make sure that the fundraiser fits with your organization's philosophy and mission. For example, many early childhood programs do not sell candy, since they have a goal of promoting healthy eating.

You might also receive needed program materials as gifts. For example, during the winter holiday season, many families give gifts to teachers. At one program, the teachers asked that families donate a puzzle, toy, or book to the center instead.

Many programs belong to book clubs. They sell children's books to families and earn points toward free books for their program. Programs serving a high percentage of children from low-income families can join First Book, which provides free and low-cost books to programs.

Grants can also assist in meeting program goals. As the need for quality early childhood programs becomes more visible, many states, corporations, and foundations are placing emphasis on this area. You might begin to look for grants by contacting your local resource and referral agency and inquiring about childcare block grants, state initiatives, and local businesses and foundations that award grants. To learn more about corporate and federal grants and to receive grant-writing tips visit the Grants Alert website.

Repair What You Have

Repairing what we have helps with limited budgets and demonstrates to children that we can be good stewards of resources. A program in Oregon contacted a local woodworking group, who agreed to repair any broken wooden items.

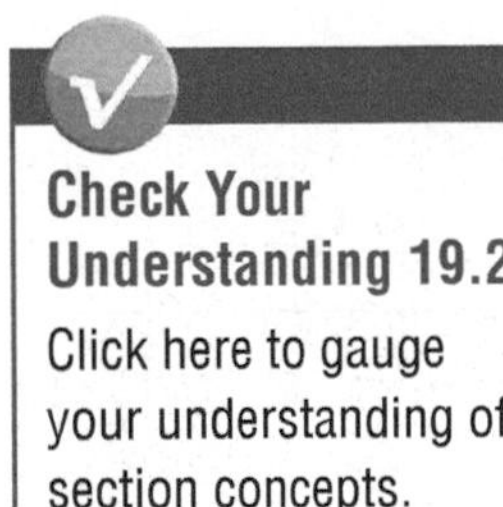

Another program had an "I Need Fixing Table" that families walked by as they dropped off and picked up their children. Families would often take an item home, repair it, and return it to the "I'm Fixed Box" that sat under the table.

Using found items, sharing materials, seeking donations of materials that would otherwise be thrown away, and repairing and fixing items we already own are earth-friendly options that help our budget, while supplying children with innovative, open-ended materials. Special fundraisers, contributions, and grants can help us to purchase materials that we cannot create or scrounge.

Establishing an Early Childhood Program in Your Home

Over 900,000 children under the age of five are cared for in **family childcare** homes (Laughlin, 2013). Family childcare home providers have the advantage of owning their own business, creating a naturally intimate environment for children, and establishing long-term relationships with children and families. While long-term relationships are important for all families, they may be especially important for families who have children with special needs or are culturally diverse. For example, as a parent of a child with special needs, it was important to me that I have a caregiver who intimately knew my child and the strategies that we had found successful in working with him. Our long-term relationship also helped to establish a level of trust that was needed when facing difficult dilemmas.

However, creating a business within your home is sometimes challenging. Family childcare providers list inadequate income, lack of colleagues, not being viewed as a professional, and separating work from home as stressors. While many family childcare providers begin care when their children are young, balancing the needs of your own child and the children in childcare can be demanding. Children who are used to having their own space must now share space as well as their parents' time. In family childcare, providers also play a multitude of roles (cook, janitor, administrator, or teacher) and may work extended hours. This also increases stress levels (Gerstenblatt, Faulkner, Lee, Doan, & Travis, 2014).

Whether children are in family childcare homes or centers, they have the same need for appropriate activities, experiences, and environments. According to the National Association for Family Child Care (2013), children in family childcare need materials for large- and small-motor development, language and literacy, art, math, science, and dramatic play. They also need child-sized furnishings. As with center care, children in family care have a need for retreat or alone spaces where they can seek solitude, escape noise and social interaction, release emotions, and calm themselves. Retreats in homes can be created by placing a lacy curtain over a table, adding space behind a couch or chair, replacing a closet door with a gauze curtain, or adding a play tent or loft (Weinberger, 2000). Unlike childcare centers that have a challenge in creating a comfortable, home-like environment, this typically already exists in family childcare. As with center care, it is important to eliminate clutter, use effective organization, and choose carefully what you place on your walls (Armstrong, 2012).

Watch this video to learn how one family childcare provider has arranged her environment. What makes this environment suitable for different ages?

https://www.youtube.com/watch?v=AVf091gMjXY

Previous chapters devoted to individual learning centers apply to family childcare as well as centers and schools. However, this may look different in a family childcare setting. Therefore, this section will address two unique issues for family childcares—how to meet the needs of the provider's family and how to meet the needs of a mixed-age group of children. We will also discuss how to create a professional identity as a family childcare provider.

Meeting the Needs of Children in Care and the Provider's Family

In addition to providing a special place with developmentally appropriate materials, activities, and environments for the children in care, the family childcare provider must also meet the needs of her family. Research indicates that this is accomplished best through clearly designating family and childcare space, ensuring private space and possessions for the provider's children, and making sure that the provider spends daily one-on-one time with her children (Goelman, Shapiro, & Pence, 1990).

Clearly Designate Childcare and Family Space. The environmental design of family childcares varies greatly. Some

Julie Bullard

A beautiful individual sand tray allows children in this family childcare an enticing retreat activity.

providers have a separate designated space for the childcare. Many have some separate designated space and some shared space. In other programs, all space used by the childcare is shared with the family. Family childcare providers must ensure that the space that is used by the childcare meets the square footage requirements of state licensing, while also meeting the needs of the family. To provide for everyone's needs, it is important to clearly define what space will be used for the childcare and what space will be used by the family. Keisha has solved this problem by placing a smiley face on the doors of rooms designated as childcare space and a stop sign on doors not used for childcare. This makes it clear to all, including Keisha's teenage children, that their private spaces will be protected. With shared space, it is also important to decide who is responsible for cleaning up the area.

Protect the Private Space and Possessions of the Home Provider's Child. Many providers have young children who must learn to share their space and their parent. It is important to make sure the child's possessions are respected, that they have their own private space, and that they have special time with their parent each day (Goelman et al., 1990). Some providers have a special closet or room for their child's toys. The same rule applies to these toys as to toys that children bring from home. For example, Amy has the rule that if a toy is brought from home the child must be willing to share that toy with others. This same rule applied to Christina, her daughter. If she takes a toy out of the special closet, she must share it with the other children.

Provide Parent–Child One-on-One Time. All children need the opportunity to have one-on-one time with their parent. Amy found that if she set aside 15 minutes to spend with Christina before the other children arrived each morning, then Christina was willing to share her mother the rest of the day.

Meeting the Needs of a Mixed-Age Group

The family childcare home typically includes a smaller group size and a wider range of ages (from babies to after school age children) than a center-based classroom. This allows families to keep all their children together, increasing sibling interaction and providing extended continuity of care with one provider. Children learn to interact with other children who are a variety of ages. Younger children have more competent models available who can scaffold their learning. Older children get the opportunity to be leaders and to increase their learning by teaching another. Additionally, because of the different age ranges, there may be less competition for the same toy or materials.

However, the wide range of age groups also creates challenges. Because you are caring for a mixed age group of children, your daily schedule is likely to be more flexible and it may be more difficult to complete structured activities. For example, you might plan to have a story time after lunch but it gets delayed due to the needs of a fussy baby. There is a need for a wider developmental range of materials. If you serve infants and toddlers with older children, you must provide materials for the older children, while protecting the younger children from choking hazards. You must also determine how to provide adequate materials for older children when you also have toddlers who are dumping items. Protecting babies from the rough and tumble play of older children is also critical. Given next are some ideas that can help to meet the needs of all children in a mixed-age setting.

- Provide more structured activities for older children as younger children nap.
- Use a wading pool as a protected area for an infant.
- Provide many open-ended materials that can be used by a range of ages, such as large blocks, balls, trucks, dolls, pieces of fabric, dress-up clothing, and hats.
- Develop shelving so that the materials at the bottom are appropriate for any age and the higher shelves contain older children's materials. For example,

a bookcase might have a basket of board books on the bottom with books that might get ripped by an infant on a higher shelf.

- Create a secure space where older children can use materials such as Legos that might be a choking hazard or a dumping issue. This could be a loft or a corner or hall that is blocked off by a gate. One provider uses a baby fence not for the babies but to create a protected place for the preschoolers to play with small manipulatives.

Establish a Professional Identity

When family childcare providers perceive themselves as professionals, they experience less work-related stress (Gerstenblatt et al., 2014). Providers who have established a professional identity are more likely to have parent–teacher handbooks, clearly defined policies, consistent hours for their own families and for childcare, clearly differentiated home and childcare space, more positive relationships, boundaries between work and home, and paid days off. They are also more likely to refer to themselves as teachers. While caregivers are sometimes worried about setting professional limits, research shown that those who do are more likely to have full enrollment and engage in higher professional practice (Gerstenblatt et al., 2014; Weaver, 2002).

Many family childcare providers face the challenges of balancing childcare and family interests and creating appropriate spaces for a wide age range of children. In addition, each family environment is unique and therefore has unique challenges. We'll examine the unique challenges of one family childcare provider, Maria, next.

The Story of Maria's Family Childcare Home

Each family childcare faces unique environmental challenges. Maria faces particularly difficult issues due to having a very small home, where most spaces need to be shared by the childcare business and by the family. This is made more challenging by the family's desire to have a home that does not look like a childcare during the evenings and weekends. Let's examine how Maria handles these challenges.

Maria worked in a childcare center for several years. However, now she has her own young child, Juliana, and she has decided to begin a family childcare business. Maria knew that she needed child-sized furnishings and learning centers to meet the needs of the children in the family childcare. However, she lives in a small house and she and her husband, Rafael, entertain their friends frequently. They want their house to look like a home rather than a family childcare business during the evenings and weekends. Although they have turned the guest bedroom into a dedicated space for childcare, they also need to use the living room, kitchen, and bathroom as shared space. They decide that their bedroom and Juliana's bedroom will be dedicated family spaces.

Because the kitchen has a linoleum floor, Maria uses this area for art, sensory play, and snacks and meals. A rolling cart (stored in the pantry when not in use) contains art supplies. The kitchen contains two child-sized tables. When children are not using them for eating, one is used for art materials and the other holds tubs for sensory play. Maria and Rafael fold the tables and place them on the porch if they need extra room for entertaining friends.

The living room is used for reading, writing, a quiet space, and a computer area. Beanbag chairs provide comfortable seating for both children and adults. Maria sewed several plastic pockets onto pieces of canvas to hold books and writing materials. Grommets at the top of the canvas slip over nails on the wall. Maria can easily remove the pockets from the wall, fold them, and place them in the living room closet. She places extra books in a basket by the beanbag chairs. Children use the living room coffee table for their writing activities.

Julie Bullard

This inexpensive round footstool is a safe place for Ember to practice her walking skills. At the end of the childcare day, the lid is placed on top and it becomes a footstool in the family living room.

The children's playroom contains dramatic play, block, and music areas. Knowing the importance of displaying children's images and work, Maria also added several bulletin boards to this room. One of Maria's concerns with this space was how to allow the older children to use the small manipulatives while protecting the infants and toddlers from choking hazards. She considered placing a partial door or gate on this room and only allowing the older children to use it. However, the toddlers loved to play with blocks and to dress up and Maria felt that developmentally they needed these opportunities. Maria solved the dilemma by building a loft in the room. The upper deck of the loft houses the manipulatives. A gate prevents the toddlers from using this area. Under the loft is an area enclosed on three sides, creating an intimate space for dramatic play. Framed children's artwork decorates the dramatic play area.

Children and families enter the childcare through the front door. At this door, a small porch contains a hook for children's coats and a wicker basket for each child's extra belongings. The porch enters into the living room. A secondhand roll top desk is a parent sign-in area. The desk has cubicles that serve as parent mailboxes. A bulletin board above the desk contains menus, weekly plans, and other parent information. At the end of the day, Maria closes the desk and flips the bulletin board over. On the other side of the bulletin board is a collage of family pictures.

Maria found that sometimes neighbors and relatives would drop in to visit during the day, not understanding that she was working. She created a sign to help solve this problem. On one side, the sign said "Welcome to our home." On the other side of the sign she wrote, "Maria's Childcare." Maria let friends and relatives know that they are welcome to visit when the welcome sign is displayed, but she is working when "Maria's Childcare" is displayed.

Through creative development and planning, Maria was able to develop a space that met the needs of her family and the childcare business. This allowed her to be an entrepreneur in a business that she found rewarding and that served a critical need. See Figure 19.1 for a list of ideas of how to share family and childcare space.

Check Your Understanding 19.3

Click here to gauge your understanding of section concepts.

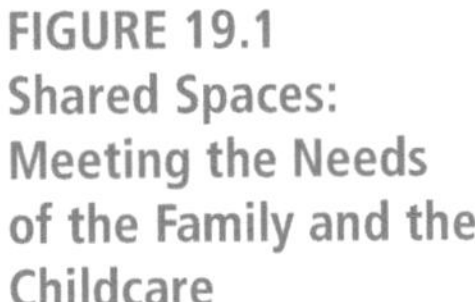

FIGURE 19.1 Shared Spaces: Meeting the Needs of the Family and the Childcare

In many family childcare homes, space is shared by the family and the children attending the childcare. To provide for the needs of the children in childcare, while also maintaining a family environment you might consider:

- ❑ Dual-purpose furniture (coffee table becomes a writing area for childcare)
- ❑ Beautiful baskets and containers such as hatboxes and trunks that store materials for the childcare but look natural in a home environment
- ❑ Rolling carts that hold material for the childcare but can easily be stored
- ❑ Closets that contain shelving units for children's materials—doors are open when the childcare is open, closed for family time
- ❑ Bulletin boards that contain business information on one side and family pictures on the other
- ❑ Incorporating childcare materials into the existing features of the house (children's books on the bottom of the family's book shelves)

Sharing Learning Spaces: Afterschool Programs

Many programs are challenged by needing to offer services in a shared space. For example, a morning and afternoon teacher may share a classroom, or a program may meet in a church space requiring teachers to put everything away each weekend. However, one of the most challenging space-sharing situations is one faced by many afterschool programs who meet in gyms or cafeterias. They have to set up and put away all materials on a daily basis. The Central Avenue Afterschool Program faced these challenges. They served approximately 30 children ages five to eight each day in the school cafeteria, setting up several tables with different activities on them (art, reading, and games). There was no clear division of space. The cafeteria also lacked soft spaces or places for children who wanted privacy. Because no active activities were available, some children invented their own. Children played tag, raced around the room, and slid under tables, bumping into other children and jarring tables. This led to arguments.

Tanya, a new teacher in the program, faced the challenge of how to change this pattern of behavior, while offering the children a quality program. She began by holding a circle time and asking children what they would like to do when they came to the afterschool program. She also had a meeting that included the afterschool and the cafeteria staff. A final meeting was held with families. Tanya had developed a relationship with families through personal contact as they picked up the children each day. She also communicated with families through maintaining a daily communication book, sending happy grams and newsletters, establishing a website with a discussion board for two-way communication, and creating a family board that assisted with decisions, promotion of the program, and family activities. Because of this relationship and the importance of the topic, most of the families came to the meeting. After Tanya received input from the different constituencies, she made a list of criteria. The space needed to:

- Be easy to set up and take down.
- Contain many varied activities (both quiet and active). There had been a request for a gross motor area and a woodworking area.
- Be divided into centers to allow for uninterrupted work.
- Provide a place for solitude.
- Contain storage for materials and works in progress.

Designing the Afterschool Space

In planning for the space, the teachers and children first determined what specific centers to include. They then created the following areas (see the diagram in Figure 19.2):

- Woodworking—The woodworking area is stationary. It includes a woodworking bench, a variety of tools, and scraps of wood. A broom and dustpan allows each woodworker to clean up when he or she is finished.
- Large motor—A rolling cart holds a variety of activities including balls, plastic hoops, beanbags, a lawn dart game, and a bowling game.
- Theatre—A trunk holds a variety of costumes and pieces of fabric that children can use to create their own costumes. The theatre is located on the stage and the trunk is stored there.
- Art and writing—The art materials are stored on a multi-shelf rolling cart. A tablecloth to protect the lunch tables is also stored on the cart.
- Hobby and game—These are placed on open shelves. The shelves have casters and they can be closed and latched when not in use.

FIGURE 19.2
Shared Space: Afterschool Room Arrangement

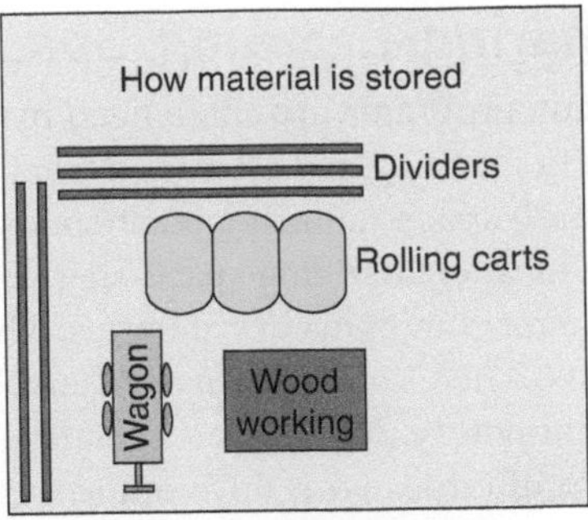

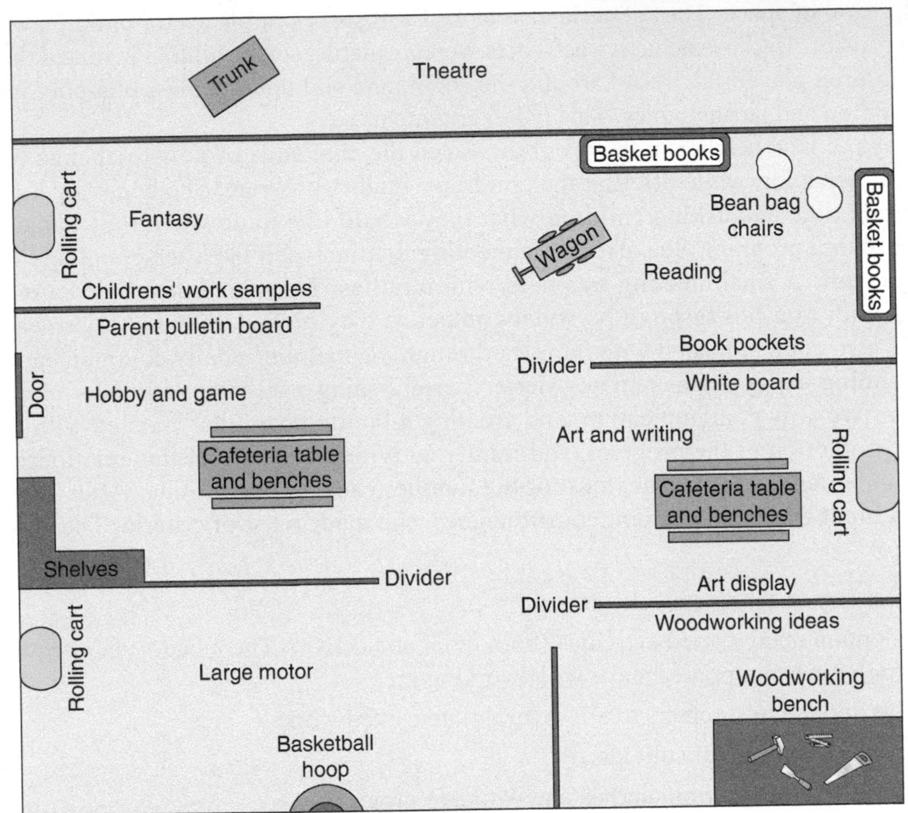

- Reading area—A wagon carries baskets of books, two beanbag chairs, and a rug to the reading area. This area also serves as a space where children can be alone.
- Fantasy play—A rolling cart holds a wooden barn with realistic-looking animals, people, and accessories (such as fencing, wagons, and milk cans), matchbox cars with a variety of play sets, and a Victorian dollhouse with furniture and dolls. Several lightweight, nonslip rugs are placed on the floor to define the area and to make floor play more comfortable.

In developing the space, the teachers used two open shelves that they currently owned and several lunchroom tables. They ordered a woodworking table and had a local carpenter create several rolling dividers. These dividers not only separate the space, but each is designed to serve at least one other function. For example, one divider has a white board on the side that faces the art area and book pockets on the side that faces the reading area. Another divider contains a parent bulletin board on one side and children's work on the other. To learn more about creating classroom dividers, see Figure 19.3.

FIGURE 19.3
Classroom Dividers

Classrooms can be divided by bookcases and furniture. However, if you are using shared space, you may need portable classroom dividers.

- ❑ Buy portable walls with locking wheels.
- ❑ Create portable walls from a trellis, pegboard, or old doors.
- ❑ Paint a sheet of plywood with chalkboard, whiteboard, or magnetic paint to create a portable wall and an activity center.
- ❑ Hang curtains from guide wires or create a frame from PVC pipe.

The program also purchased several rolling carts. At the end of the day, the children and teachers place all the rolling carts around the woodworking table. Then they roll the dividers over to the area, forming a barrier around the carts. This keeps the materials from being disturbed when the space is used for other purposes.

The teachers were stymied by how to store children's ongoing work (models, clay sculpture, beading). One of the cafeteria staff mentioned that they had an extra 6-foot-high rolling cart that held lunch trays. The teachers and children found this to be the perfect solution. Children placed their work on lunch trays and stored them on the cart.

After the redesign of the space, children were more engaged in activities, there were less discipline problems, and children and teachers enjoyed their time together more. Many techniques that the Central Avenue Afterschool Program used can be helpful to other programs seeking transformation. These include:

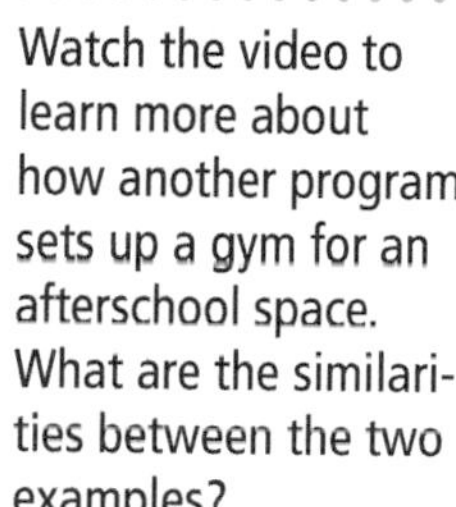

Watch the video to learn more about how another program sets up a gym for an afterschool space. What are the similarities between the two examples?

https://www.youtube.com/watch?v=F4o3cUmJs24&index=8&list=PLC4A141BF150B2397

- Involving all constituents in the planning.
- Providing a variety of engaging activities, both quiet and active.
- Separating the space according to use.
- Using portable screens for dividers that, whenever possible, are used for a dual purpose.
- Having adequate, convenient storage for putting materials away at the end of the day.
- Providing rolling carts, wagons, and shelving with wheels to make it easier and faster to move materials.
- Involving the children in setting up and taking down the space so that more of the teachers' time can be devoted to planning and preparing activities.

Check Your Understanding 19.4

Click here to gauge your understanding of section concepts.

Many programs face environmental challenges. When facing a challenge, it is wise to involve all constituencies. Receiving input can result in better designs and more support for the project. With the creative thinking generated by the group, even challenging spaces can be transformed to meet the needs of children and adults.

Throughout this book, we have learned that children can meet standards through a rich, play-based, intentionally designed environment where learning is facilitated by a skilled teacher. However, in many programs, this time-honored, research-based method of learning is being replaced with children spending the majority of their time in teacher-directed, small and large group instruction with little attention to children's individual needs or interests. Additionally, outdoor time is being reduced to provide more instructional time, even though research indicates that this is counterproductive. As early childhood educators, it is our responsibility to advocate for young children. Children deserve interesting, challenging play-based learning environments filled with wonder, discovery, and joy.

Chapter Quiz 19

Click here to gauge your understanding of chapter concepts.

Sample Application Activities

1. Visit a classroom or, if you are currently working with children, analyze the classroom that you are in. Make a list of innovative ways that the classroom could provide more play space for children.
2. Visit a thrift store to see what might be available to furnish a classroom. Make a list of materials that would be beneficial for an early childhood program.
3. Make a list of 10 materials that you could create for an early childhood setting. Make one of the materials and bring it to class to share with your classmates. Bring directions on how to create the item. These can be collected and made into a class booklet.
4. Visit Pinterest and search for family childcare. How do these programs meet the challenges of designing spaces for childcare and also for families?
5. Visit the National Association for Family Childcare website and review the accreditation standards, paying special attention to the environmental standards.
6. Interview a teacher or visit an afterschool program that is located in a gym or cafeteria. How have they managed this space challenge?

References

Chapter 1

Bodrova, E. & Leong, D. J. (2007). *Tools of the mind: The Vygotskian approach to early childhood education* (2nd ed.). Upper Saddle River, NJ: Merrill/Pearson.

Bullard, J. & Hitz, R. (1997). Early childhood education and adult education: Bridging the cultures. *Journal of Early Childhood Teacher Education, 18*(1), 15–22.

Ceppi, G. & Zini, M. (Eds.). (1998). *Children, spaces, relations: Metaproject for an environment for young children*. Washington, DC: Reggio Children.

Cooper, P. M., Capo, K., Mathes, B., & Gray, L. (2007). One authentic early literacy practice and three standardized tests: Can a storytelling curriculum measure up? *Journal of Early Childhood Teacher Education, 28*(3), 251–275. Retrieved from http://www.informaworld.com/10.1080/10901020701555564

Copple, C. & Bredekamp, S. (2009). *Developmentally appropriate practice in early childhood programs serving children from birth through age 8*. Washington, DC: National Association for the Education of Young Children.

Cosco, N. & Moore, R. (1999). *Playing in place: Why the physical environment is important in playwork*. 14th Play Education Annual Play and Human Development Meeting: Theoretical Playwork. Ely, Cambridgeshire, UK. Retrieved from www.naturalearning.org/PlayingPaper.html

Darling-Hammond, L. & Snyder, J. (1992). Curriculum studies and the traditions of inquiry: The scientific tradition. In P. W. Jackson (Ed.), *Handbook of research on curriculum* (pp. 41–78). New York: Macmillan.

DeVries, R. (2004). What is constructivist about constructivist education? *The Constructivist, 75*(1), 1–26.

Dickinson, D. K. & Tabors, P. O. (2002). Fostering language and literacy in classrooms and homes. *Young Children, 57*(2), 10–18.

Dolder, D. (2007). Handwork in the kindergarten (pp. 18–22). In J. Almon (Ed.), *What is Waldorf kindergarten?* Great Barrington, MS: Steiner Books.

Duckworth, E. (1964). Piaget rediscovered. *Journal of Research in Science Teaching, 2*(3), 172–175.

Early, D. M., Iruka, I. U., Ritchie, S., Winn, D.-M. C., Crawford, G. M., Frome, P. M., Clifford, R. M., Burchinal, M., Howes, C., Bryant, D. M., & Pianta, R. C. (2010). How do pre-kindergarteners spend their time? Gender, ethnicity, and income as predictors of experiences in pre-kindergarten classrooms. *Early Childhood Research Quarterly, 25*(2), 177–193.

Fraser, S. & Gestwicki, C. (2002). *Authentic childhood: Exploring Reggio Emilia in the classroom*. Albany, NY: Delmar.

Froebel, F. (1912). *Froebel's chief writings on education*. Retrieved from http://core.roehampton.ac.uk/digital/froarc/frochi/

Gandini, L. (2004). Foundations of the Reggio Emilia approach. In J. Hendrick (Ed.), *Next steps toward teaching the Reggio way* (pp. 13–26). Upper Saddle River, NJ: Merrill/Pearson.

Gandini, L. (2012). Connecting through caring and learning spaces. In C. Edwards, L. Gandini, & G. Forman (Eds.), *The hundred languages of children: The Reggio Emilia experience in transformation* (pp. 317–342). Santa Barbara, CA: Praeger.

Gill, T. (2014). The play return: A review of the wider impact of play initiatives. Retrieved from http://www.playscotland.org/who-we-are/playday/the-play-return-a-review-of-the-wider-impact-of-play-initiatives/

Ginsburg, K. R. (2007). The importance of play in promoting healthy child development and maintaining strong parent-child bonds. *Pediatrics, 119*(1), 182–191.

Greenman, J. (2005a). *Caring spaces, learning places: Children's environments that work*. Redmond, WA: Exchange Press, Inc.

Haight, W., Black, J., Ostler, T., & Sheridan, K. (2006). Pretend play and emotion: Learning in traumatized mothers and children. In D. G. Singer, R. B. Golinkoff, & K. Hirsh-Pasek (Eds.), *Play = learning: How play motivates and enhances children's cognitive and social-emotional growth* (pp. 209–230). New York: Oxford University Press.

Heckman, J. J., Pinto, R., & Savelyev, P. A. (2013). Understanding the mechanisms through which an influential early childhood program boosted adult outcomes. *American Economic Review, 103*(6), 2052–2086.

Hirsh-Pasek, K., Golinkoff, R. M., Berk, L. E., & Singer, D. G. (2009). *A mandate for playful learning*. New York: Oxford University Press.

Howes, C., Fuligni, A. S., Hong, S. S., Huang, Y. D., & Lara-Cinisomo, S. (2013). The preschool instructional context and child–teacher relationships. *Early Education & Development, 24*(3), 273–291.

International Play Association (IPA). Promoting the child's right to play. (1989). *IPA declaration of the child's right to play*. Retrieved from http://ipaworld.org/category/about-us/declaration/

Johnson, J. E., Christie, J. F., & Wardle, F. (2005). *Play, development, and early education*. Upper Saddle River, NJ: Merrill/Pearson.

Johnson, J. E., Sevimli-Celik, S., & A-Mansour, M. (2013). Play in early childhood education. In O. Saracho & B. Spodek (Eds.), *Handbook of research on the education of young children* (3rd ed., pp. 265–274). New York: Routledge.

Kostelnik, M. J., Gregory, K. M., Soderman, A. K., & Whiren, A. P. (2012). *Guiding children's social development & learning* (7th ed.). Belmont, CA: Wadsworth Cengage Learning.

Leong, D. J. & Bodrova, E. (2012). Assessing and scaffolding: Make-believe play. *Young Children, 67*(1), 28–34.

Miller, E. & Almon, J. (2009). *Crisis in the kindergarten: Why children need to play in school*. College Park, MD: Alliance for Childhood.

Milteer, R. M., Ginsburg, K. R., Mulligan, D. A., Ameenuddin, N., Brown, A., Christakis, D. A., Cross, C., et al. (2012). The importance of play in promoting healthy child development and maintaining strong parent-child bonds: Focus on children in poverty. *Pediatrics, 129*(1), 204–213.

Montessori, M. (1995). *The absorbent mind*. New York: Henry Holt Company. (First published in 1967.)

Montie, J. E., Xiang, Z., & Schweinhart, L. J. (2006). Preschool experience in 10 countries: Cognitive and language performance at age 7. *Early Childhood Research Quarterly, 21*(3), 313–331.

Mooney, C. G. (2000). *Theories of childhood: An introduction to Dewey, Montessori, Erickson, Piaget & Vygotsky*. St. Paul, MN: Redleaf Press.

National Scientific Council on the Developing Child. (2007). *The timing and quality of early experiences combine to shape brain architecture.* Working paper no. 5. Retrieved from http://www.developingchild.net

National Scientific Council on the Developing Child. (2010). *Early experiences can alter gene expression and affect long-term development.* Working paper no. 10. Retrieved from www.developingchild.harvard.edu

Olds, A. R. (2001). *Child care design guide*. New York: McGraw-Hill.

Oppenheimer, S. (2007). Human development through art. In J. Almon (Ed.), *What is Waldorf kindergarten?* (pp. 23–24). Great Barrington, MS: Steiner Books.

Piaget, J. (1964). Piaget rediscovered. In R. E. Ripple & U. N. Rockcastle (Eds.), *Piaget rediscovered: A report on the Conference on Cognitive Study and Curriculum Development*. Ithaca, NY: Cornell University Press.

Post, J. & Hohmann, M. (2000). *Tender care and early learning: Supporting infants and toddlers in child care settings*. Ypsilanti, MI: High/Scope Educational Research Foundation.

Rankin, B. (2004). Dewey, Piaget, Vygotsky: Connections with Malaguzzi and the Reggio approach. In J. Hendrick (Ed.), *Next steps toward teaching the Reggio way* (pp. 27–36). Upper Saddle River, NJ: Merrill/Pearson.

Rinaldi, C. (2001). Reggio Emilia: The image of the child and the child's environment as a fundamental principle. In L. Gandini & C. P. Edwards (Eds.), *Bambini: The Italian approach to infant/toddler care* (pp. 49–54). New York: College Press.

Sajaniemi, N., Suhonen, E., Hotulainen, R., Tormanen, M., Alijoki, A., Nislin, M., & Kontu, E. (2014). Demographic factors, temperament and the quality of the preschool environment as predictors of daily cortisol changes among Finnish six-year-old children. *European Early Childhood Education Research Journal, 22*(2), 286–306.

Schweinhart, L. J. & Wallgren, C. R. (1993). Effects of a follow-through program on school achievement. *Journal of Research in Childhood Education, 8*(1), 43–56.

Schweinhart, L. J. & Weikart, D. P. (1997). *Lasting differences: The High/Scope Preschool Curriculum Comparison Study through age 23.* Ypsilanti, MI: High/Scope Press.

Sluss, D. J. (2005). *Supporting play: Birth to age eight*. Canada: Thomson Delmar Learning.

Standing, E. M. (1957). *Maria Montessori: Her life and work.* New York: Plume.

Steiner, R. & Trostli, R. (1998). *Rhythms of learning: What Waldorf education offers children, parents & teachers*. Hudson, NY: Anthroposophic Press.

Strong-Wilson, T. & Ellis, J. (2007). Children and place: Reggio Emilia's environment as third teacher. *Theory into Practice, 46*(1), 40–47.

United Nations Convention on the Rights of the Child. (1989). UN General Assembly Document A/RES/44/25 *USA IPA*. Retrieved from http://www.ipausa.org/ipadeclaration.html

Wadsworth, B. J. (1989). *Piaget's theory of cognitive and affective development* (4th ed.). White Plains, NY: Longman.

Wohlwend, K. E. (2005). Chasing friendship: Acceptance, rejection, and recess play. *Childhood Education, 81*(2), 77–82.

Chapter 2

Addy, S., Engelhardt, W., & Skinner, C. (2013). *Basic facts about low-income children: Children under 6 years, 2011.* National Center for Children in Poverty. Retrieved from http://nccp.org/publications/pub_1076.html

Aud, S., Hussar, W., Kena, G., Bianco, K., Frohlich, L., Kemp, J., & Tahan, K. (2011). *The condition of education 2011* (NCES 2011-033). U.S. Department of Education, National Center for Education Statistics. Washington, DC: U.S. Government Printing Office.

Badanes, L. S., Dmitrieva, J., & Watamura S. E. (2012). Understanding cortisol reactivity across the day at child care: The potential buffering role of secure attachments to caregivers. *Early Childhood Research Quarterly, 27*(1), 156–165.

Bailey, C. S., Zinsser, K. M., Curby, T. W., Denham, S. A., & Bassett, H. H. (2013). Consistently emotionally supportive preschool teachers and children's social-emotional learning in the classroom: Implications for center directors and teachers. *NHSA Dialog, 16*(2), 131–137.

Bandura, A. (1993). Perceived self-efficacy in cognitive development and functioning. *Educational Psychologist, 28*(2), 117–148. Retrieved from http://www.informaworld.com/10.1207/s15326985ep2802_3

Bandura, A. & Locke, E. A. (2003). Negative self-efficacy and goal effects revisited. *Journal of Applied Psychology, 88*(1), 87–99.

Bernard, B. (2004). *Resiliency: What we have learned.* San Francisco, CA: WestEd.

Bowman, B. (2006). Resilience: Preparing children for school. In B. Bowman & E. K. Moore (Eds.), *School readiness and social-emotional development: Perspectives on cultural diversity* (pp. 49–57). Washington, DC: National Black Child Development Institute.

Brendtro, L. K., Brokenleg, M., & Van Bockern, S. (2002). *Reclaiming youth at risk: Our hope for the future* (Rev. ed.). Bloomington, IN: Solution Tree.

Brendtro, L. & Larson, S. (2006). *The resilience revolution.* Bloomington, IN: National Educational Service.

Coopersmith, S. (1981). *The antecedents of self-esteem.* Palo Alto, CA: Consulting Psychologists Press. (Original work published 1967.)

Center on the Developing Child at Harvard University. (2015). *Supportive relationships and active skill-building strengthen the foundations of resilience.* Working paper no. 13. www.developingchild.harvard.edu

Chapman, C., Laird, J., Ifill, N., Kewal Ramani, A., National Center for Education Statistics, Education Statistics Services Institute, & MPR Associates. (2011). *Trends in high school dropout and completion rates in the United States, 1972–2009: Compendium report.* Washington, DC: U.S. Department of Education, Institute of Education Sciences, National Center for Education Statistics.

Choi, J. Y. & Dobbs-Oates, J. (2014). Childcare quality and preschoolers' math development. *Early Child Development and Care, 184*(6), 915–932.

Cohen, J. (1988). *Statistical power for the behavioral sciences* (2nd ed.). Hillsdale, NJ: Lawrence Erlbaum Associates Inc.

Day, C. B. (2006). Leveraging diversity to benefit children's social-emotional development and school readiness. In B. Bowman & E. K. Moore (Eds.), *School readiness and social-emotional development: Perspectives on cultural diversity* (pp. 23–32). Washington, DC: National Black Child Development Institute.

Dunn, J. (2004). *Children's friendships: The beginning of intimacy*. Malden, MA: Blackwell Publishing.

Erikson, E. H. (1964). *Childhood and society*. New York: Norton.

Espinosa, L. M. (2006). Social, cultural, and linguistic features of school readiness in young Latino children. In B. Bowman & E. K. Moore (Eds.), *School readiness and social-emotional development: Perspectives on cultural diversity* (pp. 33–47). Washington, DC: National Black Child Development Institute.

Espinosa, L. (2010). *Getting it right for young children from diverse backgrounds: Applying research to improve practice*. Washington, DC: National Association for the Education of Young Children.

Federal Interagency Forum on Child and Family Statistics. (2011). *America's children: Key national indicators of well being 2011*. Washington, DC: U.S. Government Printing Office.

Fox, L., Dunlap, G., Hemmeter, M. L., Joseph, G. E., & Strain, P. S. (2003). The teaching pyramid: A model for supporting social competence and preventing challenging behavior in young children. *Young Children, 58*(4), 48–52.

Garcia, E. E. (1993). The education of linguistically and culturally diverse children. In B. Spodek (Ed.), *Handbook of research on the education of young children* (pp. 372–384). New York: Macmillan.

Gartrell, D. (2011). *A guidance approach for the encouraging classroom* (5th ed.). Belmont, CA: Wadsworth Cengage Learning.

Gorski, P. C. (2008). Peddling poverty for profit: Elements of oppression in Ruby Payne's framework. *Equity & Excellence in Education, 41*(1), 130–148.

Hazen, N. L. & Black, B. (1989). Preschool peer communication skills: The role of social status and interaction context. *Child Development, 60*, 867–876.

Honig, A. S. (2002). *Secure relationships: Nurturing infant/toddler attachment in early care settings*. Washington, DC: National Association for the Education of Young Children.

Honig, A. S. & Thompson, A. (1994). Helping toddlers with peer group entry skills. *Zero to Three, 14*(5), 15–19.

Howes, C. (1989). Friendships in very young children: Definition and functions. In B. H. Schneider, G. Attili, J. Nadel, & R. P. Weissberg (Eds.), *Social competence in developmental perspective* (pp. 107–121). Dordrecht, the Netherlands: Kluwer Academic Publishers.

Howes, C. & Hamilton, C. E. (1993). The changing experience of child care: Changes in teachers and in teacher-child relationships and children's social competence with peers. *Early Childhood Research Quarterly, 8*(1), 15–32.

Hulsey, L. K., Aikens, N., Kopack, A., West, J., Moiduddin, E., & Tarullo, L. (2011). *Head start children, families, and programs: Present and past data from FACES*. OPRE Report 2011–33a. Washington, DC: Office of Planning, Research and Evaluation, Administration for Children and Families, U.S. Department of Health and Human Services.

Kostelnik, M. J., Gregory, K. M., Soderman, A. K., & Whiren, A. P. (2012). *Guiding children's social development & learning* (7th ed.). Belmont, CA: Wadsworth Cengage Learning.

Kriete, R. & Davis, C. (2014). *The Morning Meeting Book* (3rd ed.). Turner Falls, MA: Northeast Foundtion for Children.

Marion, M. (2007). *Guidance of young children* (7th ed.). Upper Saddle River, NJ: Merrill/Pearson.

Maschinot, B. (2008). *The changing face of the United States: The influence of culture on early child development*. Washington, DC: Zero to Three.

Maslow, A. H. (1970). *Motivation and personality*. New York: Harper & Row.

McLeod, S. A. (2007). Maslow's hierarchy of needs. Retrieved from http://www.simplypsychology.org/maslow.html

McNelly, M. E. & Smith, J. (2013). Effects of social stories on the behaviors of typically developing preschoolers. *NHSA Dialog, 16*(4), 104–106.

Moffitt, T. E., Arseneault, L., Belsky, D., Dickson, N., Hancox, R. J., Harrington, H., Houts, R., Poulton, R., Roberts, B., Ross, S., Sear, M., Thomson, W. M., & Caspi, A. (2011). A gradient of childhood self-control predicts health, wealth, and public safety. *Proceedings of the National Academy of Sciences, 108*(7), 2693–2698.

Narvaez, D. & Gleason, T. (2013). Developmental optimization. In D. Narvaez, J. Pankesepp, A. Schore, & T. R. Gleason (Eds.), *Evolution, early experience and human development: From research to practice and policy* (pp. 307–325). Oxford Scholarship Online.

National Scientific Council on the Developing Child. (2004a). *Young children develop in an environment of relationships*. Working paper no. 1. Retrieved from http://www.developingchild.net/pubs/wp/Young_Children_Environment_Relationships.pdf

National Scientific Council on the Developing Child. (2004b). *Children's emotional development is built into the architecture of their brains*. Working paper no. 2. Retrieved from http://www.developingchild.net/pubs/wp/Childrens_Emotional_Development_Architecture_Brains.pdf

National Scientific Council on the Developing Child. (2007). *The timing and quality of early experiences combine to shape brain architecture*. Working paper no. 5. Retrieved from http://www.developingchild.net

Nieto, S. & Bode, P. (2012). *Affirming diversity: The sociopolitical context of multicultural education*. Boston: Pearson Education.

Nix, R. L., Bierman, K. L., Domitrovich, C. E., & Gill, S. (2014). Promoting children's social-emotional skills in preschool can enhance academic and behavioral functioning in kindergarten: Findings from Head Start REDI. *Early Education and Development, 24*(7), 1000–1019.

Odom, S. L., Zercher, C., Li, S., Marquart, J. M., Sandall, S., & Brown, W. H. (2006). Social acceptance and rejection of preschool children with disabilities: A mixed-method analysis. *Journal of Educational Psychology, 98*(4), 807–823.

Pianta, R., Howes, C., Burchinal, M., Bryant, D., Clifford, R., Early, D., & Barbarin, O. (2005). Features of pre-kindergarten programs, classrooms, and teachers: Do they predict observed classroom quality and child-teacher interactions? *Applied Developmental Science, 9*(3), 144–159. Retrieved from http://www.informaworld.com/10.1207/s1532480xads0903_2

Ramsey, P. G. (2003). The stress of poverty. In C. Copple (Ed.), *A world of difference: Readings on teaching young children in a diverse society* (pp. 86–87). Washington, DC: National Association for the Education of Young Children.

Ray, A., Bowman, B., & Brownell, J. O. N. (2006). Teacher-child relationships, social-emotional development, and school achievement. In B. Bowman & E. K. Moore (Eds.), *School readiness and social-emotional development: Perspectives on cultural diversity* (pp. 7–22). Washington, DC: National Black Child Development Institute.

Reardon, S. F. (2011). The widening academic achievement gap between the rich and the poor: New evidence and possible explanations. In R. Murname & G. Duncan (Eds.), *Whither opportunity? Rising inequality and the uncertain life chances of low-income children* (pp. 91–116). New York: Russell Sage Foundation.

Riley, D., San Juan, R. R., Klinkner, J., & Ramminger, A. (2008). *Social & emotional development: Connecting science and practice in early childhood settings*. Washington, DC: National Association for the Education of Young Children.

Rinaldi, C. (2001). Reggio Emilia: The image of the child and the child's environment as a fundamental principle. In L. Gandini & C. P. Edwards (Eds.), *Bambini: The Italian approach to infant/toddler care* (pp. 49–54). New York: College Press.

Rosas, J. & McCall, R. B. (2009). *Characteristics of institutions, interventions, and children's development*. Pittsburgh, PA: University of Pittsburgh, Office of Child Development.

Roser, S. L. (2012). *80 morning meeting ideas for grades K-2*. Greenfield, MA: Northeast Foundation for Children.

Sandall, S. R. & Schwartz, I. S. (2002). *Building blocks for teaching preschoolers with special needs*. East Peoria, IL: Paul H. Brookes Publishing Company.

Schunk, D. H. (1989). Self-efficacy and cognitive achievement: Implications for students with learning problems. *Journal of Learning Disabilities*, *22*, 14–22.

Sugai, G., Horner, R. H., Dunlap, G., Hieneman, M., Lewis, T. J., Nelson, C. M., Scott, T., Liaupsin, C., Sailor, W., Turnbull, A. P., Turnbull, H. R. III, Wickham, D., Wilcox, B., & Ruef, M. (2000). Applying positive behavioral support and functional behavioral assessment in schools. *Journal of Positive Behavior Interventions*, *2*(3), 131–143.

Sveinsson, A. & Morris, R. (2006). School bullying and victimization of children with disabilities. In R. J. Morris (Ed.), *Disability research and policies: Current perspectives* (pp. 187–204). Mahwah, NJ: Lawrence Erlbaum Associates.

Wien, C. A. (2004). From policing to participation: Overturning the rules and creating amiable classrooms. *Young Children Online*, 1–7. Retrieved from http://www.journal.naeyc.org/btj/200401/wien.asp

Wolpert, E. (2005). *Start seeing diversity: The basic guide to an anti-bias classroom*. St. Paul, MN: Redleaf Press.

Chapter 3

American Academy of Pediatrics, American Public Health Association, & National Resource Center for Health and Safety in Child Care and Early Education. (2011). *Caring for our children: National health and safety performance standards: Guidelines for out-of-home child care programs* (3rd ed.). Elk Grove Village, IL: American Academy of Pediatrics and Washington, DC: American Public Health Association. Retrieved from http://nrc.uchsc.edu

Bohn, C. M., Roehrig, A. D., & Pressley, M. (2004). The first days of school in the classrooms of two more effective and four less effective primary-grade teachers. *Elementary School Journal*, *104*(4), 269–287.

Booren, L. M., Downer, J. T., & Vitiello, V. E. (2012). Observations of children's interactions with teachers, peers, and tasks across preschool classroom activity settings. *Early Education & Development*, *23*(4), 517–538. doi:10.1080/10409289.2010.548767

Bowman, B., Donovan, M., & Burns, M. (2001). *Eager to learn: Educating our preschoolers*. Washington, DC: National Academy Press.

Buck, G. (1999). Smoothing the rough edges of classroom transitions. *Intervention in School and Clinic*, *34*(4), 224–227.

Butterfield, P. M. (2002). Child care is rich in routines. *Zero to Three*, *22*(4), 29–32.

Christie, J. F. & Wardle, F. (1992). How much time is needed for play? *Young Children*, *47*(3), 28–32.

Colvin, G., Sugai, G., Good, R. H., & Lee, Y. (1997). Effect of active supervisions and precorrection on transition behaviors of elementary students. *School Psychology Quarterly*, *12*, 344–363.

Copple, C. & Bredekamp, S. (2009). *Developmentally appropriate practice in early childhood programs serving children from birth through age 8*. Washington, DC: National Association for the Education of Young Children.

Davidson, J. (1982). Wasted time: The ignored dilemma. In J. F. Brown (Ed.), *Curriculum planning for young children* (pp. 196–204). Washington, DC: National Association for the Education of Young Children.

Dicarlo, C. F., Pierce, S. H., Baumgartner, J., Harris, M. E., & Ota, C. (2012). Whole-group instruction practices and children's attention: A preliminary report. *Journal of Research in Childhood Education*, *26*(2), 154–168. doi:10.1080/02568543.2012.657744

Early, D., Barbarin, O., Bryant, D., Burchinal, M., Chang, F., Clifford, R., Crawford, G., Weaver, W., Howes, C., Ritchie, S., Kraft-Sayre, M., Pianta, R., & Barnett, W. S. (2005). Pre-kindergarten in eleven states: NCEDL's multi-state study of pre-kindergarten & study of state-wide early education programs (SWEEP). Retrieved from http://fpg.unc.edu/node/4654

Early, D., Burchinal, M., Barbarin, O., Bryant, D., Chang, F., Clifford, R., Crawford, G., Weaver, W., Howes, C., Ritchie, S., Kraft-Sayre, M., Pianta, R., & Barnett, W. S. (2013). Pre-kindergarten in eleven states: NCEDL's multi-state study of pre-kindergarten and study of state-wide early education programs (SWEEP). Ann Arbor, MI: Inter-University Consortium for Political and Social Research. doi:10.3886/ICPSR34877.v1

Fromberg, D. P. (2002). *Play and meaning in early childhood education*. Boston: Allyn & Bacon.

Fukuda, K. & Asaoka, S. (2004). Delayed bedtime of nursery school children, caused by the obligatory nap, lasts during the elementary school period. *Sleep and Biological Rhythms*, *2*(2), 129–134.

Fuligni, A. S., Howes, C., Huang, Y., Hong, S. S., & Lara-Cinisomo, S. (2012). Activity settings and daily routines in preschool classrooms: Diverse experiences in early learning settings for low-income children. *Early Childhood Research Quarterly*, *27*(2), 198–209. doi:10.1016/j.ecresq.2011.10.001

Gareau, M. & Kennedy, C. (1991). Structure time and space to promote pursuit of learning in the primary grades. *Young Children*, *46*(4), 46–51.

Gill, T. (2014). The play return: A review of the wider impact of play initiatives. Retrieved from http://www.playscotland.org/who-we-are/playday/the-play-return-a-review-of-the-wider-impact-of-play-initiatives/

Greenman, J. (2006). The importance of order. *Exchange, 170*, 53–55.

Greenman, J. & Stonehouse, A. (1996). *Primetimes: A handbook for excellence in infant and toddler programs*. St. Paul, MN: Redleaf Press.

Hohmann, M. & Weikart, D. P. (2002). *Educating young children: Active learning practices for preschool and childcare programs*. Ypsilanti, MI: High/Scope Educational Research Association.

Kostelnik, M. J., Gregory, K. M., Soderman, A. K., & Whiren, A. P. (2012). *Guiding children's social development & learning* (7th ed.). Belmont, CA: Wadsworth Cengage Learning.

Kurdziel, L., Duclos, K., & Spencer, R. M. (2013). Sleep spindles in midday naps enhance learning in preschool children. *Proceedings of the National Academy of Sciences, 110*(43), 17267–17272. doi:10.1073/pnas.1306418110

Leinhardt, G., Weidman, C., & Hammond, K. M. (1987). Introduction and integration of classroom routines by expert teachers. *Curriculum Inquiry, 17*(2), 135–176.

Markova-Lama, I. (2013). Effects of academic and non-academic instructional approaches on preschool ELLs' English language development. *Doctoral Dissertations*. Paper 58. http://repository.usfca.edu/diss/58

McIntosh, K., Herman, K., Sanford, A., McGraw, K., & Florence, K. (2004). Teaching transitions: Techniques for promoting success between lessons. *Teaching Exceptional Children, 37*(1), 32–38.

McWilliam, R. A., Scarborough, A. A., & Kim, H. (2003). Adult interactions and child engagement. *Early Education and Development, 14*(1), 7–28.

Pattinson, C. L., Staton, S. L., Smith, S. S., Sinclair, D. M., & Thorpe, K. J. (2014). Emotional climate and behavioral management during sleep time in early childhood education settings. *Early Childhood Research Quarterly, 29*(4), 660–668. doi:10.1016/j.ecresq.2014.07.009

Pica, R. (2004). *Experiences in movement: Birth to age 8*. Clifton Park, NY: Thomson/Delmar Learning.

Reszka, S. S., Odom, S. L., & Hume, K. A. (2012). Ecological features of preschools and the social engagement of children with autism. *Journal of Early Intervention, 34*(1), 40–56. doi:10.1177/1053815112452596

Rimm-Kaufman, S. E., La Paro, K. M., Downer, J. T., & Pianta, R. C. (2005). The contribution of classroom setting and quality of instruction to children's behavior in kindergarten classrooms. *Elementary School Journal, 105*(4), 377–394.

Ritchhart, R., Palmer, P., Church, M., & Tishman, S. (2006). *Thinking routines: Establishing patterns of thinking in the classroom*. Paper presented at the annual meeting of the American Educational Research Association, San Francisco.

Rogers, L. (1988, October). Classroom management: Transitions and preschoolers. *Dimensions, 26*, 7–8.

Sainato, D. (1990). Classroom transitions: Organizing environments to promote independent performance in preschool. *Education and Treatment of Children, 13*(4), 288–297.

Sajaniemi, N., Suhonen, E., Hotulainen, R., Tormanen, M., Alijoki, A., Nislin, M., & Kontu, E. (2014). Demographic factors, temperament and the quality of the preschool environment as predictors of daily cortisol changes among Finnish six-year-old children. *European Early Childhood Education Research Journal, 22*(2), 286–306.

Salmon, A. (2008). Promoting a culture of thinking in the young child. *Early Childhood Education Journal, 35*(5), 457–461.

Shonkoff, J. P., Phillips, D., & National Research Council (U.S.). (2000). *From neurons to neighborhoods: The science of early child development*. Washington, DC: National Academy Press.

Tegano, D. W. & Burdette, M. P. (1991). Length of activity periods and play behaviors of preschool children. *Journal of Research in Childhood Education, 5*(2), 93–99.

Topal, C. W. (1983). *Children, clay and sculpture*. Worcester, MA: Davis Publications.

Vitiello, V. E., Booren, L. M., Downer, J. T., & Williford, A. P. (2012). Variation in children's classroom engagement throughout a day in preschool: Relations to classroom and child factors. *Early Childhood Research Quarterly, 27*(2), 210–220. doi:10.1016/j.ecresq.2011.08.005

Ward, T. M., Gay, C., Alkon, A., Anders, T. F., & Lee, K. A. (2008). Nocturnal sleep and daytime nap behaviors in relation to salivary cortisol levels and temperamentin preschool-age children attending child care. *Biological Research for Nursing, 9*(3), 244–253.

Wien, C. A. (1996). Time, work, and developmentally appropriate practice. *Early Childhood Research Quarterly, 11*(3), 377–403.

Wien, C. A. (2004). From policing to participation: Overturning the rules and creating amiable classrooms. *Young Children Online*, 1–7. Retrieved from http://www.journal.naeyc.org/btj/200401/wien.asp

Chapter 4

Morrow, L. M. & Smith, J. K. (1990). The effects of group size on interactive storybook reading. *Reading Research Quarterly, 25*(3), 213–231.

NAEYC (National Association for the Education of Young Children). (2009). *NAEYC standards for early childhood professional preparation programs* [Position statement]. Washington, DC: Author.

National Association for the Education of Young Children (NAEYC) & National Association of Early Childhood Specialists in State Departments of Education (NAECS/SDE) (2003). *Early childhood curriculum, assessment, and program evaluation: Building an effective, accountable system in programs for children birth through age 8. Position statement*. Washington, DC: NAEYC.

Solomon, P. G. (2003). *The curriculum bridge: From standards to actual classroom practice*. Thousand Oaks, CA: Corwin Press.

Chapter 5

Abbas, M. Y. & Othman, M. (2010). Social behavior of preschool children in relation to physical spatial definition. *Procedia – Social and Behavioral Sciences*, 5, 935–941.

American Academy of Pediatrics, American Public Health Association, & National Resource Center for Health and Safety in Child Care and Early Education. (2011). *Caring for our children: National health and safety performance standards: Guidelines for out-of-home child care programs* (3rd ed.). Elk Grove Village, IL: American Academy of Pediatrics and Washington, DC: American Public Health Association. Retrieved from http://nrc.uchsc.edu

Aronson, S. S. (1999). The ideal diaper changing station. *Child Care Information Exchange, 130*, 92.

Bartlett, S. (1993). Amiable space in the schools of Reggio Emilia: An interview with Lella Gandini. *Children's Environments, 10*(2), 23–38.

Bondavalli, M., Mori, M., & Vecchi, V. (Eds.). (1993). Children in Reggio Emilia look at their school. *Children, Youth, and Environments, 10*(2), 39–45.

Burke, K. & Burke-Samide, B. (2004). Required changes in the classroom environment: It's a matter of design. *Clearing House, 77*(6), 236.

Center for Disease Control and Prevention. (2012). *Sudden unexpected infant death and sudden infant death syndrome*. Retrieved from http://www.cdc.gov/SIDS/

Copple, C. & Bredekamp, S. (2009). *Developmentally appropriate practice in early childhood programs serving children from birth through age 8*. Washington, DC: National Association for the Education of Young Children.

Derman-Sparks, L. & Edwards, J. O. (2010). *Anti-bias education for young children and ourselves*. Washington, DC: National Association for the Education of Young Children.

Dunlap, G., DePerczel, M., Clarke, S., Wilson, D., Wright, S., White, R., & Gomez, A. (1994). Choice making to promote adaptive behavior for students with emotional and behavioral challenges. *Journal of Applied Behavior Analysis, 27*(3), 505–518.

Gramza, A. F. (1970). Preferences of preschool children for enterable play boxes. *Perceptual and Motor Skills, 31*, 177–178.

Greenman, J. (2005a). *Caring spaces, learning places: Children's environments that work*. Redmond, WA: Exchange Press, Inc.

Helm, J. H., Turckes, S., & Hinton, K. (2010, April). A habitat for 21st century learning. *Educational Leadership*, 66–69.

Johnson, J. E., Christie, J. F., & Wardle, F. (2005). *Play, development, and early education*. Upper Saddle River, NJ: Merrill/Pearson.

Legendre, A. (1999). Interindividual relationships in groups of young children and susceptibility to an environmental constraint. *Environment and Behavior, 31*(4), 463–468.

Lowry, P. (1993). Privacy in the preschool environment: Gender differences in reaction to crowding. *Children's Environments, 10*(2), 46–61.

Maxwell, L. E. (2007). Competency in child care settings: The role of the physical environment. *Environment and Behavior, 39*(2), 229–245.

McDougall, S. (2006). Furniture for the future. *21st Century Schools, 2*(1), 48–51.

Moore, G. T. (1986). Effects of the spatial definition of behavior settings on children's behavior: A quasi-experimental field study. *Journal of Environmental Psychology, 6*(3), 205–231.

Moore, G. T. (2002). Designed environments for young children: Empirical findings and implications for planning and design. Retrieved from http://www.arch.usyd.edu.au/documents/staff/garymoore/111.pdf

Moore, G., Lane, C. G., Hill, A. B., Cohen, U., & McGinty, T. (1994). *Recommendations for child care centers*. Milwaukee: University of Wisconsin–Milwaukee, Center for Architecture and Urban Planning Research.

Olds, A. R. (1989). Psychological and physiological harmony in child care center design. *Children's Environments Quarterly, 6*(4), 8–16.

Olds, A. R. (2001). *Child care design guide*. New York: McGraw-Hill.

Osborn, E. (2014). Eastern reveals 2014 TIMPANI toy study results. Retrieved from http://www1.easternct.edu/pressreleases/2014/12/01/eastern-reveals-2014-timpani-toy-study-results/

Pardee, M. (2005). *Equipping and furnishing early childhood facilities: Community investment collaborative for kids resource guide*. Local Initiatives Support Corporation. Retrieved from http://www.lisc.org/content/publications/detail/813

Patton, J. E., Snell, J., Knight, W. J., & Gerken, K. (2001). *A survey study of elementary classroom seating designs*. Paper presented at the annual meeting of the National Association of School Psychologists. Retrieved from http://eric.ed.gov/ERICDocs/data/ericdocs2/content_storage_01/0000000b/80/26/1e/37.pdf

Phelps, P. C. (2012). *Let's build: Strong foundations in language, math, and social skills*. Lewisville, NC: Gryphon House.

Readdick, C. A. (1993). Solitary pursuits: Supporting children's privacy needs in early childhood settings. *Young Children, 49*(1), 60–64.

Reinisch, S. & Parnell, W. (2006). *The 100 is there! Helen Gordon child development center*. DesignShare. Retrieved from http://www.designshare.com

Rushton, S. P. (2001). Applying brain research to create developmentally appropriate learning environments. *Young Children, 56*(5), 76–81.

Sajaniemi, N., Suhonen, E., Hotulainen, R., Tormanen, M., Alijoki, A., Nislin, M., & Kontu, E. (2014). Demographic factors, temperament and the quality of the preschool environment as predictors of daily cortisol changes among Finnish six-year-old children. *European Early Childhood Education Research Journal, 22*(2), 286–306.

Sajaniemi, N., Suhonen, E., Kontu, E., Rantanen, P., Lindholm, H., Hyttinen, S., & Hirvonen, A. (2011). Children's cortisol patterns and the quality of the early learning environment. *European Early Childhood Education Research Journal, 19*(1), 45–62.

Sheehan, R. & Day, D. (1975). Is open space just empty space? *Early Childhood Education Journal, 3*(2), 10–13.

The Partnership for 21st Century Skills. (2009). *P21 framework definitions*. Retrieved from http://www.p21.org/about-us/p21-framework

Tobin, J. J., Hsueh, Y., & Karasawa, M. (2009). *Preschool in three cultures revisited: Japan, China and the United States*. Chicago, IL: University of Chicago Press.

Vitiello, V. E., Booren, L. M., Downer, J. T., & Williford, A. P. (2012). Variation in children's classroom engagement throughout a day in preschool: Relations to classroom and child factors. *Early Childhood Research Quarterly, 27*(2), 210–220. doi:10.1016/j.ecresq.2011.08.005

Vygotsky, L. (1986). *Thought and language*. Cambridge, MA: MIT Press.

Waldecker, M. (2005). High class: Furniture and equipment selection. *American School and University, 78*(2), 30–34.

Wardle, F. & Cruz-Janzen, M. (2004). *Multiethnic and multiracial children in schools*. Boston: Allyn & Bacon.

White, R. (2004). *Adults are from earth; Children are from the moon; designing for children: A complex challenge*. Retrieved from http://www.whitehutchinson.com/children/articles/earthmoon.shtml

Zimmons, J. K. (1997). *The effect of spatial definition on preschool prosocial interaction.* (Doctoral dissertation, Texas Tech University, USA).

Chapter 6

21st Century School Fund. (2009). Research on the impact of school facilities on students and teachers – a summary of studies published since 2000. Retrieved from http://www.21csf.org/csf-home/Documents/ResearchImpactSchoolFacilitiesFeb2010.pdf

ALA (American Lung Association). (2014). *Asthma in children fact sheet.* New York: American Lung Association. Retrieved from http://www.lung.org/lung-disease/asthma/resources/facts-and-figures/asthma-children-fact-sheet.html

American Academy of Pediatrics, American Public Health Association, & National Resource Center for Health and Safety in Child Care and Early Education. (2011). *Caring for our children: National health and safety performance standards: Guidelines for out-of-home child care programs* (3rd ed.). Elk Grove Village, IL: American Academy of Pediatrics and Washington, DC: American Public Health Association. Retrieved from http://nrc.uchsc.edu

Barrett, P., Zhang, Y., Moffat, J., & Kobbacy, K. (2013). A holistic, multi-level analysis identifying the impact of classroom design on pupils' learning, *Building and Environment, 59*, 678–689.

Bartlett, S. (1993). Amiable space in the schools of Reggio Emilia: An interview with Lella Gandini. *Children's Environments, 10*(2), 23–38.

Buckley, J., Schneider, M., & Shang, Y. (2004). *The effects of school facility quality on teacher retention in urban school districts.* Washington, DC: National Clearinghouse for Education Facilities.

Butin, D. (2000). *Early childhood centers.* Washington, DC: National Clearinghouse for Education Facilities.

Ceppi, G. & Zini, M. (Eds.). (1998). *Children, spaces, relations: Metaproject for an environment for young children.* Washington, DC: Reggio Children.

Cheryan, S., Ziegler, S. A., Plaut, V. C., & Meltzoff, A. N. (2014). Designing classrooms to maximize student achievement. *Policy Insights from the Behavioral and Brain Sciences, 1*(1), 4–12.

Children's Environmental Health Network. (2010). *Eco-healthy childcare.* Retrieved from http://www.cehn.org/files/Checklist_English%201406.pdf

Curtis, D. & Carter, M. (2005). Rethinking early childhood environments to enhance learning. *Young Children, 6*(3), 34–38.

DeViney, J., Duncan, S., Harris, S., Rody, M. A., & Rosenberry, L. (2010). *Inspiring spaces for young children.* Silver Spring, MD: Gryphon House, Inc.

Doctoroff, S. (2001). Adapting the physical environment to meet the needs of all young children for play. *Early Childhood Education Journal, 29*(2), 105–109.

Earthman, G. I. (2004). Prioritization of 31 criteria for school building adequacy. Retrieved from www.schoolfunding.info/policy/facilities/ACLUfacilities_report1-04.pdf

Environmental Protection Agency (EPA). (2009). *Indoor air quality tools for schools reference guide.* EPA report no. EPA 402/K-07/008. Washington, DC: Author. Retrieved from http://epa.gov/iaq/schools/pdfs/kit/reference_guide.pdf

Evans, G. W. (2001). Environmental stress and health. In A. Baum, T. Revenson, & J. E. Singer (Eds.), *Handbook of health psychology* (pp. 365–386). Mahwah, NJ: Erlbaum.

Evans, G. W., Hygge, S., & Bullinger, M. (1995). Chronic noise and psychological stress. *Psychological Science, 6*(6), 333–338.

Evans, G. W. & Maxwell, L. (1997). Chronic noise exposure and reading deficits: The mediating effects of language acquisition. *Environment and Behavior, 29*(5), 638–656.

Fielding, R. (2006). *Learning, lighting and color: Lighting design for schools and universities in the 21st century.* Retrieved from http://www.designshare.com/articles/17133/fielding_light-learn-color.pdf

Fisher, A. V., Godwin, K. E., & Seltman, H. (2014). Visual environment, attention allocation, and learning in young children: When too much of a good thing may be bad. *Psychological Science, 25*(7), 1362–1370.

Fisher, J. (2006). *Creating place identity: It's part of human nature.* Retrieved from http://environmentpsychology.com/place_identity.htm

Gandini, L. (1984). Not just anywhere: Making child care centers into "particular" places. *Beginnings: The Magazine for Teachers of Young Children, 1*, 17–20.

General Services Administration (GSA). (2003). *Child care center design guide.* Retrieved from http://www.gsa.gov/gsa/cm_attachments/GSA DOCUMENT/designguidesmall_R2FD38_0Z5RDZ- i34K-pR.pdf

George, J. (1995). A loft-y idea for learning. *Educational Leadership, 53*(3), 56–57.

Graves, G. (1985). Shedding light on learning. *American School and University, 57*(7), 88–90.

Grebennikov, L. & Wiggins, M. (2006). Psychological effects of classroom noise on early childhood teachers. *The Australian Educational Researcher, 33*(3), 35–54.

Hathaway, W., Hargreaves, J., Thompson, G., & Novitsky, D. (1992). *A study into the effects of light on children of elementary school age—a case of daylight robbery.* Edmonton, Canada: Alberta Department of Education.

Haverinen-Shaughnessy, U., Moschandreas, D. J., & Shaughnessy, R. J. (2011). Association between substandard classroom ventilation rates and students' academic achievement. *Indoor Air, 21*(2), 121–131. doi:10.1111/j.1600-0668.2010.00686.x

Heschong Mahone Group. (2003). *Windows and classrooms: A study of student performance and the indoor environment.* Fair Oaks, CA: California Energy Commission.

Higgens, S., Hall, E., Wall, K., Woolner, P., & McCaughey, C. (2005). *The impact of school environments: A literature review.* CfBT: Research and Development. Retrieved from http://www.ncl.ac.uk/cflat/news/DCReport.pdf

Kantrowitz, E. J. & Evans, G. W. (2004). The relations between the ratio of children per activity area and off-task behavior and type of play in day care centers. *Environment and Behavior, 36*(4), 541–557.

Karre, A. (2003). *Lighting design and installation.* Cranhassen, MN: Creative Publishing International, Inc.

Kennedy, M. (2001). Into thin air. *American School & University, 73*(6), 32.

Kilgore, C. (2005). Toys' noise exceeds OSHA thresholds (Occupational Safety and Health Administration). *Pediatric News, 39*(7), 44.

Klatte, M., Lachmann, T., & Meis, M. (2010). Effects of noise and reverberation on speech perception and listening comprehension of children and adults in a classroom-like setting. *Noise and Health, 12*(49), 270–282.

Kryter, K. D. (1985). *The effects of noise on man* (2nd ed.). New York: Academies Press.

Legendre, A. (2003). Environmental features influencing toddlers' bioemotional reactions in day care centers. *Environment and Behavior, 35*(4), 523–549.

Loo, C. M. & Kennely, D. (1979). Social density: Its effects on behaviors and perceptions of preschoolers. *Environmental Psychology and Nonverbal Behavior, 3*(3), 131–146.

Manav, B. (2007). Color-emotion associations and color preferences: A case study for residences. *Color Research and Application, 32*(2), 144–150.

Maxwell, L. E. (1996). Multiple effects of home and day care crowding. *Environment and Behavior, 28*(4), 494–511.

Maxwell, L. E. (2003). Home and school density effects on elementary school children. *Environmental Behavior, 35*(4), 566–578.

Maxwell, L. & Evans, G. W. (1999). Design of child care centers and effects of noise on young children. DesignShare.com Retrieved from http://www.designshare.com/index.php/articles/chronic-noise-and-children/

Maxwell, L. E. & Evans, G. W. (2000). The effects of noise on pre-school children's pre-reading. *Journal of Environmental Psychology, 20*, 91–97.

Mendell, M. J. & Heath, G. A. (2005). Do indoor pollutants and thermal conditions in schools influence student performance? A critical review of the literature. *Indoor Air, 15*(1), 27–52.

Moore, G., Lane, C. G., Hill, A. B., Cohen, U., & McGinty, T. (1994). *Recommendations for child care centers.* Milwaukee: University of Wisconsin-Milwaukee, Center for Architecture and Urban Planning Research.

Mott, L. (1997). *Our children at risk: The 5 worst environmental threats to their health.* National Research Defense Council. Retrieved from http://www.nrdc.org/health/kids/ocar/ocarack.asp.

National Institute for Occupational Safety and Health (NIOSH). (2007). *Reducing pesticide exposure at school.* Washington, DC: Author.

National Lighting Product Information Program. (2005). Full-spectrum light sources. Retrieved from http://www.lrc.rpi.edu/programs/nlpip/lightingAnswers/fullSpectrum/claims.asp

National Research Council. (1993). *Pesticides in the diets of infants and children.* Washington, DC: National Academy Press. Retrieved from http://www.nap.edu/catalog.php?record_id=2126#toc

National Scientific Council on the Developing Child. (2006). *Early exposure to toxic substances damages brain architecture.* Working paper no. 4. Retrieved from http://www.developingchild.net/pubs/wp/Toxins.pdf

Olds, A. R. (1989). Psychological and physiological harmony in child care center design. *Children's Environments Quarterly, 6*(4), 8–16.

Olds, A. R. (2001). *Child care design guide.* New York: McGraw-Hill.

Read, M. A. (2003). Use of color in child care environments: Application of color for wayfinding and space definition in Alabama child care environments. *Early Childhood Education Journal, 30*(4), 233–239.

Read, M. A., Sugawara, A. I., & Brandt, J. A. (1999). Impact of space and color in the physical environment on preschool children's cooperative behavior. *Environment and Behavior, 31*(3), 413–428.

Readdick, C. A. & Bartlett, P. M. (1995). Vertical learning environments. *Childhood Education, 71*, 86–90.

Reinisch, S. & Parnell, W. (2006). *The 100 is there! Helen Gordon child development center.* DesignShare. Retrieved from: http://www.designshare.com

Sala, E., Laine, A., Simberg, S., Pentti, J., & Suonpaa, J. (2001). The prevalence of voice disorders among day care center teachers compared with nurses: A questionnaire and clinical study. *Journal of Voice, 15*(3), 413–423.

Schneider, M. (2002). *Do school facilities affect academic outcomes?* Washington, DC: National Clearinghouse for Educational Facilities.

Schneider, M. (2003). *Public school facilities and teaching.* Washington, DC, and Chicago. *National Clearinghouse for Educational Facilities.* Retrieved from http://www.21csf.org/csf-home/Documents/Teacher_Survey/SCHOOL_FACS_AND_TEACHING.pdf

Shield, B. M. & Dockrell, J. E. (2003). The effects of noise on children at school: A review. *Journal of Building Acoustics, 102*, 97–116.

Shonkoff, J. P., Phillips, D., & National Research Council (U.S.). (2000). *From neurons to neighborhoods: The science of early child development.* Washington, DC: National Academy Press.

Smith, P. K. & Connolly, K. J. (1986). Experimental studies on the preschool environment: The Sheffield Project. *Advances in Early Education and Day Care, 4*, 27–66.

Tarr, P. (2001). Aesthetic codes in early childhood classrooms: What art educators can learn from Reggio Emilia. *Art Education, 54*, 33–39.

Tarr, P. (2004). Consider the walls. *Beyond the Journal*, 1–6. Retrieved from http://www.journal. naeyc.org/btj/200405/ConsidertheWalls.pdf

Tiesler, G., & Oberdörster, M. (2008). Noise-A stressor? Acoustic ergonomics of schools. *Building Acoustics, 15*(3), 249–261.

Torelli, L. & Durrett, C. (2000). *Landscapes for learning: Designing group care environments for infants, toddlers and two-year-olds.* Retrieved from http://www.spacesforchildren.com/impact.html

Torelli, L. (2002). Enhancing development through classroom design in early head start. *Children and Families.* Retrieved from http://www.spacesforchildren.com/enhanc.html

Trancik, A. M. & Evans, G. W. (1995). Spaces fit for children: Competency in the design of daycare center environments. *Children's Environments, 12*(3), 43–58. Retrieved from http://www.colorado. edu/journals/cye/.

Weinstein, C. S. (1987). Designing preschool classrooms to support development. In C. S. Weinstein & T. G. David (Eds.), *Spaces for children: The built environment and child development* (pp. 159–185). New York: Plenum.

White, R. & Stoecklin, V. (2003). *The great 35 square foot myth.* Kansas City, MO: White Hutchinson Leisure & Learning Group.

Wien, C. A., Coates, A., Keating, B., & Bigelow, B. C. (2005). Designing the environment to build connection to place. *Young Children, 60*(3), 16–24.

Wilson, N. K., Chuang, J. C., Lyu, C., Menton, R., & Morgan, M. K. (2003). Aggregate exposures of nine preschool children to persistent organic pollutants at day care and at home. *Journal of Exposure Analysis and Environmental Epidemiology, 13*, 187–202.

Young, E., Green, H. A., Roehrich-Patrick, L., Joseph, L., & Gibson, T. (2003). *Do K-12 school facilities affect education outcomes?* Nashville, TN: Tennessee Advisory Commission on Intergovernmental Relations.

Chapter 7

Bafile, C. (2004). The prop box: Setting the stage for meaningful play. *Education World*. Retrieved from http://www.educationworld.com/a_curr/profdev101.shtml

Barbour, A., Desjean-Perrotta, B., & Rojas, M. (2002). *Prop box play: 50 themes to inspire dramatic play*. Ranier, MD: Gryphon House.

Beilinson, J. S. & Olswang, L. B. (2003). Facilitating peer-group entry in kindergartners with impairments in social communication. *Language, Speech, and Hearing Services in Schools, 34*, 154–166.

Bodrova, E. & Leong, D. J. (1998). Development of dramatic play in young children and its effects on selfregulation: The Vygotskian approach. *Journal of Early Childhood Teacher Education, 19*(2), 115–124.

Bodrova, E. & Leong, D. J. (2007). *Tools of the mind: The Vygotskian approach to early childhood education* (2nd ed.). Upper Saddle River, NJ: Merrill/Pearson.

Bodrova, E., Leong, D. J., Hensen, R., & Henninger, M. (1999). *Scaffolding early literacy through play: How to strengthen play, increase oral language, encourage symbolic thinking, and support the development of print and writing concepts*. New Orleans, LA: NAEYC Conference.

Boutte, G., Scoy, I. V., & Hendley, S. (1996). Multicultural and nonsexist prop boxes. *Young Children, 52*(1), 34–39.

Brown, P., Sutterby, J., & Thornton, C. D. (2001). Dramatic play in outdoor play environments. *Today's Playground*, 1(0), 10–11.

Calabrese, N. M. (2003). Developing quality sociodramatic play for young children. *Education, 123*(3), 606–608.

CDC (Centers for Disease Control and Prevention). (2013). *Head lice*. Retrieved from http://www.cdc.gov/parasites/lice/head/index.html

Christie, J. F. & Roskos, K. A. (2009). Play's potential in early literacy development. In R. E. Tremblay, R. G. Barr, R DeV. Peters, & M. Boivin (Eds.). *Encyclopedia on early childhood development* [online]. Montreal, Quebec: Centre of Excellence for Early Childhood Development (pp. 1–6). Retrieved from http://www.child-encyclopedia.com/documents/Christie-RoskosANGxp.pdf

Copple, C. & Bredekamp, S. (2009). *Developmentally appropriate practice in early childhood programs serving children from birth through age 8*. Washington, DC: National Association for the Education of Young Children.

Eggum-Wilkens, N. D., Fabes, R. A., Castle, S., Zhang, L., Hanish, L. D., & Martin, C. L. (2014). Playing with others: Head Start children's peer play and relations with kindergarten school competence. *Early Childhood Research Quarterly, 29*(3), 345–356.

Elias, C. L. & Berk, L. E. (2002). Self-regulation in young children: Is there a role for sociodramatic play? *Early Childhood Research Quarterly, 17*, 216–238.

Ferguson, C. J. & McNulty, C. P. (2006). Learning through sociodramatic play. *Kappa Delta Pi Record, 58*(3), 60–64.

Frost, J. L., Wortham, S. C., & Reifel, R. S. (2012). *Play and child development*. Boston: Pearson.

Gandini, L. (1984). Not just anywhere: Making child care centers into "particular" places. *Beginnings: The Magazine for Teachers of Young Children, 1*, 17–20.

Guralnik, M. J. & Hammond, M. A. (1999). Sequential analysis of the social play of young children with mild developmental delays. *Journal of Early Intervention, 22*(3), 243–256.

Hestenes, L. L. & Carroll, D. E. (2000). The play interactions of young children with and without disabilities: Individual and environmental influences. *Early Childhood Research Quarterly, 15*(2), 229–246.

Huffman, C. (2006). Supportive care for infants and toddlers with special health needs *Beyond the Journal: Young Children on the Web*, 1–8.

Jung, J. (2013). Teachers' roles in infants' play and its changing nature in a dynamic group care context. *Early Childhood Research Quarterly, 28*(1), 187–198.

Kim, S. (1999). The effects of storytelling and pretend play on cognitive processes, short-term and long-term narrative recall. *Child Study Journal, 29*(3), 175–191.

Kostelnik, M. J., Gregory, K. M., Soderman, A. K., & Whiren, A. P. (2012). *Guiding children's social development & learning* (7th ed.). Belmont, CA: Wadsworth Cengage Learning.

Krafft, K. C. & Berk, L. E. (1998). Private speech in two preschools: Significance of open-ended activities and make-believe play for verbal self-regulation. *Early Childhood Research Quarterly, 13*(4), 637–658.

Lee, S. (2007). Trimangles and kittens: Mathematics within socio-dramatic play in a New Zealand early childhood setting. In J. E. Watson, K. E. Beswick, & Mathematics Education Research Group of Australasia. *Mathematics: Essential Research, Essential Practice. Volumes 1 and 2. Proceedings of the 30th Annual Conference of the Mathematics Education Research Group of Australasia*. Mathematics Education Research Group of Australasia.

Leong, D. J. & Bodrova, E. (2012). Assessing and scaffolding: Make-believe play. *Young Children, 67*(1), 28–34.

Levin, D. (2003). Beyond banning war and superhero play: Meeting children's needs in violent times. *Young Children, 58*(3), 60–64.

Levy, A. D., Wolfgang, C. H., & Koorland, M. A. (1992). Sociodramatic play as a method for enhancing the language performance of kindergarten age students. *Early Childhood Research Quarterly, 7*, 245–262.

Lillard, A. S., Lerner, M. D., Hopkins, E. J., Dore, R. A., Smith, E. D., & Palmquist, C. M. (2013). The impact of pretend play on children's development: A review of the evidence. *Psychological Bulletin, 139* (1), 1–34.

Morrow, L. M. (1990). Preparing the classroom environment to promote literacy during play. *Early Childhood Research Quarterly, 5*, 537–554.

NAEYC (National Association for the Education of Young Children). (2006). *Imitating superheroes: Early years are learning years*. Washington, DC: Author.

Neeley, P. M., Neeley, R. A., Justen, J. E., & Tipton-Sumner, C. (2001). Scripted play as a language intervention strategy for preschoolers with developmental disabilities. *Early Childhood Education Journal, 28*(4), 243–246.

Paley, V. G. (2004). *A child's work: The importance of fantasy play.* Chicago, IL: University of Chicago Press.

Paley, V. G. (2010). *The boy on the beach.* Chicago, IL: University of Chicago Press.

Pardee, M. (2005). *Equipping and furnishing early childhood facilities: Community investment collaborative for kids resource guide.* Local Initiatives Support Corporation. Retrieved from http://www.lisc.org/content/publications/detail/813

Pellegrini, A. D. (1985). Social-cognitive aspects of children's play: The effects of age, gender, and activity centers. *Journal of Applied Developmental Psychology, 6*(2–3), 129–140.

Petrakos, H. & Howe, N. (1996). The influence of the physical design of the dramatic play on children's play. *Early Childhood Research Quarterly, 11*, 63–77.

Read, M. A., Sugawara, A. I., & Brandt, J. A. (1999). Impact of space and color in the physical environment on preschool children's cooperative behavior. *Environment and Behavior*, 31(3), 413–428.

Riley, D., San Juan, R. R., Klinkner, J., & Ramminger, A. (2008). *Social & emotional development: Connecting science and practice in early childhood settings.* Washington, DC: National Association for the Education of Young Children.

Russ, S. W., Robins, A. L., & Christiano, B. A. (1999). Pretend play: Longitudinal prediction of creativity and affect in fantasy in children. *Creativity Research Journal, 12*(2), 129–140.

Rybczynski, M. & Troy, A. (1995). Literacy-enriched play centers: Trying them out in "the real world." *Childhood Education, 72*(1), 7–12.

Shonkoff, J. P., Phillips, D., & National Research Council (U.S.). (2000). *From neurons to neighborhoods: The science of early child development.* Washington, DC: National Academy Press.

Smilansky, S. (1968). *The effects of sociodramatic play on disadvantaged preschool children.* New York: Wiley.

Smilansky, S. & Shefatya, L. (1990). *Facilitating play: A medium for promoting cognitive, socioemotional, and academic development in young children.* Gaithersburg, MD: Psychosocial and Educational Publications.

Trawick-Smith, J. (2014). *Early childhood development: A multicultural perspective* (6th ed.). Upper Saddle River, NJ: Pearson Education, Inc.

Vygotsky, L. S. (1978). *Mind in society: The development of higher psychological processes.* Cambridge, MA: Harvard University Press.

Chapter 8

American Academy of Pediatrics, American Public Health Association, & National Resource Center for Health and Safety in Child Care and Early Education. (2011). *Caring for our children: National health and safety performance standards: Guidelines for out-of-home child care programs* (3rd ed.). Elk Grove Village, IL: American Academy of Pediatrics and Washington, DC: American Public Health Association. Retrieved from http://nrc.uchsc.edu

Benbow, M. (1990). *Loops and other groups, a kinesthetic writing system.* Tucson, AZ: Therapy Skill Builders.

Bruni, M. (1998). *Fine-motor skills in children with Down syndrome: A guide for parents and professionals.* Bethesda, MD: Woodbine House.

Chalufour, I. & Worth, K. (2005). *Exploring water with young children.* St. Paul, MN: Redleaf Press.

Coleman-Jensen, A., Nord, M., & Singh, A. (2013). *Household food security in the United States in 2012.* Washington, DC: USDA ERS.

Crosser, S. (1994). Making the most of water play. *Young Children, 49*(5), 28–32.

Davis, E. E., Pitchford, N. J., & Limback, E. (2011). The interrelation between cognitive and motor development in typically developing children aged 4–11 years is underpinned by visual processing and fine manual control. *British Journal of Psychology, 102*(3), 569–584.

Dinwiddie, S. A. (1993). Playing in the gutters: Enhancing children's cognitive and social play. Retrieved from http://communityplaythings.com/resources/articles/sandandwater/PlayGutters.html

Exner, C. E. (1992). In-hand manipulation skills. In J. Case-Smith & C. Pehoski (Eds.), *Development of hand skills in children* (pp. 35–45). Bethesda, MD: American Occupational Therapy Association, Inc.

Feldman, R. S. (2012). *Child development* (6th ed.). Upper Saddle River, NJ: Pearson.

Giagazoglou, P., Fotiadou, E., Angelopoulou, N., Tsikoulas, J., & Tsimaras, V. (2001). Gross and fine motor skills of left-handed preschool children. *Perceptual and Motor Skills, 92*, 1122–1128.

Grissmer, D., Grimm, K. J., Aiyer, S. M., Marrah, W. M., & Steele, J. S. (2010). Fine motor skills and early comprehension of the world: Two new school readiness indicators. *Developmental Psychology, 46*(5), 1008–1017.

Herrington, S. & Lesmeister, C. (2006). The design of landscapes at child-care centres: Seven Cs. *Landscape Research, 31*(1), 63–82.

Hill, D. M. & Berlfein, J. (1977). *Mud, sand, and water.* Washington, DC: National Association for the Education of Young Children.

Hill, D. M. & Berlfein, J. (2000). *Mud, sand, and water* (3rd ed.). Washington, DC: National Association for the Education of Young Children.

James, K. H. (2010). Sensori-motor experience leads to changes in visual processing in the developing brain. *Developmental Science, 13*(2), 279–288.

James, K. H. & Atwood, T. P. (2009). The role of sensorimotor learning in the perception of letter-like forms: Tracking the causes of neural specialization for letters. *Cognitive Neuropsychology, 26*(1), 91–110.

Jarrett, O., French-Lee, S., Bulunuz, N., & Bulunuz, M. (2010). Play in the sandpit: A university and a child-care center collaborate in facilitated-action research. *American Journal of Play, 3*(2), 221–237.

Jarrett, O., Maxwell, D., Dickerson, C., Hoge, P., Daview, G., & Yetley, A. (1998). Impact of recess on classroom behavior: Group effects and individual differences. *The Journal of Educational Research, 92*(2), 121–126.

Johansson, R. S., Westling, G., Bäckström, A., & Flanagan, J. R. (2001). Eye–hand coordination in object manipulation. *The Journal of Neuroscience, 21*(17), 6917–6932.

Koch, C. J. (n.d.). *Not just for sand & water anymore: Your ultimate guide to sensory tables.* Retrieved from http://www.preschooleducation.com/ebook.shtml

Losse, A., Henderson, S. E., Elliman, D., Hall, D., & Knight, E. (1991). Clumsiness in children—do they grow out of it? A 10-year follow-up study. *Developmental Medicine and Child Neurology, 33*(1), 55–68.

Maldonado, N. (2006). Puzzles: Set the table for learning. *Texas Child Care*, Summer, 24–31.

Marr, D., Cermak, S., Cohm, E. S., & Henderson, A. (2003). Fine motor activities in Head Start and kindergarten classrooms. *The American Journal of Occupational Therapy, 57*(5), 550–557.

McDevitt, T. M. & Ormrod, J. E. (2013). *Child development and education* (5th ed.). Upper Saddle River, NJ: Pearson.

McHale, K. & Cermak, S. (1992). Fine motor activities in elementary school: Preliminary findings and provisional implications for children with fine motor problems. *American Journal of Occupational Therapy, 46*, 898–903.

Myers, C. A. (1992). Therapeutic fine-motor activities for preschoolers. In J. Case-Smith & C. Pehoski (Eds.), *Development of hand skills in children* (pp. 47–61). Bethesda, MD: American Occupational Therapy Association, Inc.

Olds, A. R. (2001). *Child care design guide*. New York: McGraw-Hill.

Piaget, J. (1954). *The construction of reality in the child*. New York: Basic.

Rosenblum, S., Weiss, P. L., & Parush, S. (2003). Product and process evaluation of handwriting difficulties. *Educational Psychology Review, 15*(1), 41–81.

Rule, A. C. & Stewart, R. (2002). Effects of practical life materials on kindergartners' fine motor skills. *Early Childhood Education Journal, 30*(1), 9–13.

Schwartz, B. (2007). Planting the seeds for a sound garden. *Early Childhood Newsletter, 13*, 12.

Seldin, T. & Wolff, J. (2007). *The exercises of practical life*. The Montesorri Foundation. Retrieved from http://www.montessori.org/story.php?id=58

Stevens, C. (2004). Playing in the sand. *The British Gestalt Journal, 13*(1), 18–23.

Stevenson, N. C. & Just, C. (2014). In early education, why teach handwriting before keyboarding? *Early Childhood Education Journal, 42*, 49–56.

Sweedler-Brown, C. O. (1992). The effect of training on the appearance bias of holistic essay graders. *Journal of Research and Development in Education, 26*(1), 24–29.

Texas Child Care. (2005). Manipulatives: Big learning from little objects. *Texas Child Care*, Fall, 30–37.

Thorne, G. (2006). Graphomotor skills: Why some kids hate to write. Center for development and learning. Retrieved from http://www.cdl.org/resource-library/articles/graphomotor.php?type=recent&id=Yes

Tomes, R. E. (1995). Teacher presence and child gender influences on children's activity preferences in preschool settings. *Child Study Journal, 25*(2), 123–140.

Trawick-Smith, J. (2014). *Early childhood development: A multicultural perspective* (6th ed.). Upper Saddle River, NJ: Pearson Education, Inc.

Walsh, M. (2007). Making the cut: Better understanding fine motor skill development in kindergarten students. Retrieved from http://origen.ed.psu.edu/pds_download/2007InquiryProjects/WalshMinquiry0607.pdf

Wehrmann, S., Chiu, T., Reid, D., & Sinclair, G. (2006). Evaluation of occupational therapy school-based consultation service for students with fine motor difficulties. *The Canadian Journal of Occupational Therapy, 11*, 225–236.

West, S. & Cox, A. (2001). *Sand and water play: Simple, creative activities for young children*. Beltsville, MD: Gryphon House.

Woolfolk, A. & Perry, N. E. (2015). *Child and adolescent development* (2nd ed.). Upper Saddle River, NJ: Pearson.

Yochman, A., Ornoy, A., & Parush, S. (2006). Perceptuomotor functioning in preschool children with symptoms of attention deficit hyperactivity disorder. *Perceptual and Motor Skills, 102*, 175–186.

Chapter 9

Andrews, A. O. (1999). Solving geometric problems by using unit blocks. *Teaching Children Mathematics, 5*(6), 318–325.

Bakawa-Evenson, L., Oesterreich, L., & Ouverson, C. (1995). *Making blocks*. Ames: Cooperative Extension Service, Iowa State University.

Bodrova, E. & Leong, D. J. (2007). *Tools of the mind: The Vygotskian approach to early childhood education* (2nd ed.). Upper Saddle River, NJ: Merrill/Pearson.

Bruce, T. (1992). Children, adults, and blockplay. In P. Gura (Ed.), *Exploring learning: Young children and block play* (pp. 14–26). Thousand Oaks, CA: Sage Publications, Ltd.

Cartwright, S. (1988). Play can be the building blocks of learning. *Young Children, 43*(5), 44–47.

Cartwright, S. (1990). Learning with large blocks. *Young Children, 45*(3), 38–41.

Casey, B. & Bobb, B. (2003). The power of block building. *Teaching children mathematics*. Reston, VA: National Council of Teachers of Mathematics.

Chalufour, I., Hoisington, C., Moriarty, R., Winokur, J., & Worth, K. (2004). The science and mathematics of building structures. *Science and Children, 41*(4), 30–34.

Chalufour, I. & Worth, K. (2004). *Building structures with young children*. St. Paul, MN: Redleaf Press.

Church, E. B. & Miller, K. (1990). *Blocks: A practical guide for teaching young children: Learning through play*. New York: Early Childhood Division, Scholastic.

Clements, D. H. & Sarama, J. (2000a). The earliest geometry. *Teaching Children Mathematics, 7*(2), 82–86.

Clements, D. H. & Sarama, J. (2000b). Standards for preschoolers. *Teaching Children Mathematics, 7*(1), 38–41.

Clements, D. H. & Sarama, J. (2000c). Young children's ideas about geometric shapes. *Teaching Children Mathematics, 6*(8), 482–488.

Clements, D. H. & Sarama, J. (2014). *Learning and teaching early math: The learning trajectories approach* (2nd ed.). New York: Routledge.

Cody, D. (1989). The building blocks of childhood. *Sky Magazine, 18*(11), 109–112.

Cohen, L. & Uhry, J. (2011). Naming block structures: A multimodal approach. *Early Childhood Education Journal, 39*(1), 79–87.

Dreier, E. (1996). Blocks in the elementary school. In E. S. Hirsch (Ed.), *The block book* (Rev. ed., pp. 103–116). Washington, DC: National Association for the Education of Young Children.

Elkind, D. (2006). The values of outdoor play. *Exchange Press, 171*, 6–11.

Ferrara, K., Hirsh-Pasek, K., Newcombe, N. S., Golinkoff, R. M., & Lam, W. S. (2011). Block talk: Spatial language during block play. *Mind, Brain, and Education, 5*(3), 143–151.

Gura, P. (1993). Becoming connoisseurs and critics: Making sense of blockplay. *Early Child Development and Care, 92*, 69–81.

Hanline, M. F., Milton, S., & Phelps, P. (2001). Young children's block construction activities: Findings from 3 years of observation. *Journal of Early Intervention, 24*, 224–237.

Hanline, M. F., Milton, S., & Phelps, P. C. (2010). The relationship between preschool block play and reading and maths abilities in early elementary school: A longitudinal study of children with and without disabilities. *Early Child Development and Care, 180*(8), 1005–1017.

Heisner, J. (2005). Telling stories with blocks: Encouraging language in the block center. *Early Childhood Research & Practice, 7*(2). Retrieved from http://ecrp.uiuc.edu/v7n2/heisner.html

Isbell, R. T. & Raines, S. (1991). Young children's oral language productions in three types of play centers. *Journal of Research in Childhood Education, 5*(2), 140–146.

Johnson, H. M. (1996). The art of block building. In E. S. Hirsch (Ed.), *The block book* (Rev. ed., pp. 9–26). Washington, DC: National Association for the Education of Young Children.

Johnson-Pynn, J. & Nisbet, V. (2002). Preschoolers effectively tutor novice classmates in a block construction task. *Child Study Journal, 32*(4), 241–255.

Kuschner, D. (1989). Put your name on your painting, but the blocks go back on the shelves. *Young Children, 45*(1), 49–56.

MacDonald, S. & Davis, K. (2001). *Block play: The complete guide to learning and playing with blocks*. Beltsville, MD: Gryphon House.

Miller, D. L. (2004). More than play: Children learn important skills through visual-spatial work! *Dimensions Educational Research Foundation*. Retrieved from http://www.dimensionsfoundation. org/media/findings/MoreThanPlayArticle.pdf

Miller, D. F. (2004). Science for babies. *Montessori Life, 16*(2), 25–27.

Moffitt, M. (1996). Children learn about science through block building. In E. S. Hirsch (Ed.), *The block book* (Rev. ed., pp. 27–34), Washington, DC: National Association for the Education of Young Children.

Nath, S. & Szücs, D. (2014). Construction play and cognitive skills associated with the development of mathematical abilities in 7-year-old children. *Learning and Instruction, 32*(6), 73–80.

National Council of Teachers of Mathematics. (2000). *Principles and standards for school mathematics*. Reston, VA: Author. Retrieved from www.nctm.org

Neuman, S. & Roskos, K. (1990). Play, print and purpose: Enriching play environments for literacy development. *The Reading Teacher, 44*(3), 214–221.

Newburger, A. & Vaughan, E. (2006). *Teaching numeracy, language, and literacy with blocks*. St. Paul, MN: Redleaf Press.

O'Hara, P., Demarest, D., & Shaklee, H. (2008). Early math skills: Building blocks for the future: Research brief. Retrieved from http://www.blockfest.org/2008_formatted%20research%20brief.pdf

Pasnak, R., Madden, S. E., Martin, J. M., Malabonga, V. A., & Holt, R. (1996). Persistence of gains for instruction in classification, seriation, and conservation. *Journal of Educational Research, 90*, 87–92.

Pasnak, R., McCutchen, L., Holt, R., & Campbell, J. W. (1991). Cognitive and achievement gains for kindergartners instructed in Piagetian operations. *Journal of Educational Research, 85*, 5–13.

Phelps, P. C. (2012). *Let's build: Strong foundations in language, math, and social skills*. Lewisville, NC: Gryphon House.

Piaget, J. (1947/62). *Play, dreams, and imitation in early childhood*. London: Routledge.

Piaget, J. (1967). *Play, dreams, and imitation in childhood*. New York: Norton.

Pickett, L. (1998). Literacy learning during block play. *Journal of Research in Childhood Education, 12*(2), 225–230.

Provenzo, E. F. & Brett, A. (1983). *The complete block book*. Syracuse, NY: Syracuse University Press.

Ramani, G. B., Zippert, E., Schweitzer, S., & Pan, S. (2014). Preschool children's joint block building during a guided play activity. *Journal of Applied Developmental Psychology, 35*(4), 326–336.

Reifel, S. (1984). Block construction: Children's developmental landmarks in representation of space. *Young Children, 40*(1), 61–67.

Reifel, S. & Yeatman, J. (1991). Action, talk and thought in block play. In B. Scales, M. Almy, A. Nicolopoulu, & S. Ervin-Tripp (Eds.), *Play and the social context of development in early care and education* (pp. 156–172). New York: Teachers College Press.

Sobel, D. (1993). *Children's special places: Exploring the roles of forts, dens, and bush houses in middle childhood*. Tucson, AZ: Zephyr Press.

Spencer, K. (2011, November 28). With blocks, educators go back to basics. *The New York Times*, p. A18.

Sprung, B. (2006). Yes you can: Meeting the challenge of math and science. *Scholastic Early Childhood Today, 20*(4), 44–51.

Stroud, J. E. (1995). Block play: Building a foundation for literacy. *Early Childhood Education Journal, 23*(1), 9–14.

Verdine, B. N., Golinkoff, R. M., Hirsh-Pasek, K., & Newcombe, N. S. (2014). Finding the missing piece: Blocks, puzzles, and shapes fuel school readiness. *Trends in Neuroscience and Education, 3*(1), 7–13.

Vygotsky, L. S. (1976). Play and its role in the mental development of the child. In J. S. Bruner, A. Jolly, & K. Sylvia (Eds.), *Play: Its role in development and evolution* (pp. 536–552). New York: Basic Books.

Vygotsky, L. S. (1978). *Mind in society: The development of higher psychological processes*. Cambridge, MA: Harvard University Press.

Walker, L. (1995). *Block building for children*. Woodstock, NY: Overlook Press.

Wellhousen, K. & Crowther, I. (2004). *Creating effective learning environments*. New York: Delmar Learning.

Wellhousen, K. & Kieff, J. E. (2001). *A constructivist approach to block play in early childhood*. Albany, NY: Delmar.

Wolfgang, C. H., Stannard, L. L., & Jones, I. (2001). Block play performance among preschoolers as a predictor of later school achievement in mathematics. *Journal of Research in Childhood Education, 15*, 173–180.

Chapter 10

Adams, M. J. (1990). *Beginning to read: Thinking and learning about print*. Cambridge, MA: MIT Press.

Adesope, O. O., Lavin, T., Thompson, T., & Ungerleider, C. (2010). A systematic review and meta-analysis of the cognitive correlates of bilingualism. *Review of Educational Research, 80*(2), 207–245.

Allington, R. L. (2011). What at-risk readers need. *Educational Leadership, 68*(6), 40–45.

Anderson, E. & Fenty, N. (2013). Integrating early literacy and other content curriculum in an era of increased accountability: A review of the literature. *Learning Across the Early Childhood Curriculum, 17*, 153–177.

Anti-Defamation League. (2003). Assessing children's literature. *New York State Association for the Education of Young Children (NYSAEYC) Reporter*. Retrieved from http://www.adl.org/education/assessing.asp

Beaty, J. J. (2013). *50 early childhood literacy strategies*. Upper Saddle River, NJ: Merrill/Pearson.

Berger, K. S. (2009). *The developing person through childhood and adolescence* (8th ed.). New York: Worth Publishers.

Bishop, R. S. (1992). Multicultural literature for children: Making informed choices. In V. J. Harris (Ed.), *Teaching multicultural literature in grades K–8* (pp. 37–53). Norwood, MA: Christopher-Gordon.

Bogart, D. & Blixrud, J. C. (2011). *Library and book trade Almanac*. Medford, NJ: Information Today, Inc.

Brabham, E., Buskist, C., Henderson, S. C., Paleologos, T., & Baugh, N. (2012). Flooding vocabulary gaps to accelerate word learning. *The Reading Teacher, 65*(8), 523–533.

Burchinal, M. & Forestieri, N. (2011). Development of early literacy? Evidence from major U.S. longitudinal studies. In D. K. Dickinson & S. B. Neuman (Eds.), *Handbook of early literacy research: Vol. 3* (pp. 85–96). New York: Guilford.

CDC Developmental Milestones. (2007). *Learn the signs*. Retrieved from www.cdc.gov/actearly

Chard, D. J. & Dickson, S. V. (1999). Phonological awareness: Instructional and assessment guidelines. *Intervention in School and Clinic, 34*(5), 261–270.

Child Trends Databank. (2014). *Dual language learners*. Retrieved from http://www.childtrends.org/?indicators=dual-language-learners

Diller, D. (2003). *Literacy work stations: Making centers work*. Portland, ME: Stenhouse.

Dollins, C. (2014). Expanding the power of read-alouds. *Young Children, 69*(3), 8–13.

Epstein, A. S. (2014). *The intentional teacher: Choosing the best strategies for young children's learning* (2nd ed.). Washington, DC: National Association for the Education of Young Children.

Espinosa, L. M. (2006). Social, cultural, and linguistic features of school readiness in young Latino children. In B. Bowman & E. K. Moore (Eds.), *School readiness and social-emotional development: Perspectives on cultural diversity* (pp. 33–47). Washington, DC: National Black Child Development Institute.

Farran, D. C., Aydogan, C., Kang, S. J., & Lipsey, M. W. (2006). Preschool classroom environments and the quantity and quality of children's literacy and language behaviors. In D. K. Dickinson & S. B. Neuman (Eds.), *Handbook of early literacy research* (pp. 257–268). New York: The Guilford Press.

Fernald, A., Marchman, V. A., & Weisleder, A. (2013). SES differences in language processing skill and vocabulary are evident at 18 months. *Developmental Science, 16*(2), 234–248.

Genesee, F., Paradis, J., & Crago, M. (2004). *Dual language development & disorders: A handbook on bilingualism and second language learning*. Baltimore, MD: Paul H. Brookes Publishing.

Gilbert, M. B. (2004). *Communicating effectively: Tools for educational leaders*. Lanham, MD: Scarecrow Education.

Girolametto, L., Hoaken, L., Weitzman, E., & van Leishout, R. (2000). Patterns of adult-child linguistic interaction in integrated day care groups. *Language, Speech, and Hearing Services in Schools, 31*, 155–168.

Hall, A. H. (2014). Interactive writing: Developmentally appropriate practice in blended classrooms. *Young Children, 69*(3), 34–38.

Halle, T., Calkins, J., Berry, D., & Johnson, R. (2003, September). Promoting language and literacy in early childhood settings. *Child Care and Early Education Research Connections*, 1–17.

Harris, J., Golinkoff, R. M., & Hirsh-Pasek, K. (2011). Lessons for the crib for the classroom: How children really learn vocabulary. In D. K. Dickinson & S. B. Neuman (Eds.), *Handbook of early literacy research: Vol. 3* (pp. 49–65). New York: Guilford.

Hart, B. & Risley, T. R. (1995). *Meaningful differences in the everyday experience of young American children*. Baltimore, MD: Brookes Publishing Company.

Hoffman, J. (2013). Sharing digital texts. In J. A. Schickedanz & M. F. Collins (Eds.), *So much more than the ABCs: The early phases of reading and writing* (pp. 71–72). Washington, DC: NAEYC.

IRA/NAEYC. (1998). Learning to read and write: Developmentally appropriate practices for young children joint position statement. In S. B. Neuman, C. Copple, & S. Bredekamp (Eds.), *Learning to read and write: Developmentally appropriate practices for young children* (pp. 3–28). Washington, DC: National Association for the Education of Young Children.

Jalongo, M. R. (2003). *Early childhood language arts* (3rd ed.). Boston: Allyn & Bacon.

Jalongo, M. R. (2008). *Learning to listen, listening to learn: Building essential skills in young children*. Washington, DC: National Association for the Education of Young Children.

Juel, C. (1988). Learning to read and write: A longitudinal study of 54 children from first through fourth grades. *Journal of Educational Psychology, 80*(4), 437–447.

Justice, L. M. (2004). Creating language—rich preschool classroom environments. *Teaching Exceptional Children, 37*(2), 36–44.

Lindsay, J. (2010). *Children's access to print material and education-related outcomes: Findings from a meta-analytic review*. Chicago, IL: Learning Point Associates.

Lucas, T. & Katz, A. (1994). Reframing the debate: The roles of native languages in English-only programs for language minority students. *TESOL Quarterly, 28*(3), 537–561.

MacDonald, S. (2006). *The portfolio and its use: A road map for assessment* (2nd ed.). Little Rock, AR: Southern Early Child Association.

Mayer, K. (2009). Emerging knowledge about emergent writing. In E. Essa & M. Burnham (Eds.), *Informing our practice: Useful research on young children's development* (pp. 111–118). Washington, DC: National Association for the Education of Young Children.

Miller, K. (2005). *Simple steps: Developmental activities for infants, toddlers, and two-year-olds*. Beltsville, MD: Pearson Education, Inc.

Mol, S. E. & Bus, A. G. (2011). To read or not to read: A meta-analysis of print exposure from infancy to early adulthood. *Psychological Bulletin, 137*(2), 267–296. doi:10.1037/a0021890

Morrow, L. M. (2012). *Literacy development in the early years: Helping children read and write*. Boston: Pearson.

Morrow, L. M., Freitag, E., & Gambrell, L. B. (2009). *Using children's literature in preschool to develop comprehension: Understanding and enjoying books*. Newark, DE: International Reading Association.

Morrow, L. & Gambrell, L. (2001). Literature-based instruction in the early years. In S. Neuman & D. Dickinson (Eds.), *Handbook of early literacy research* (pp. 348–360). New York: Guilford.

National Early Literacy Panel (U.S.), National Institute for Literacy (U.S.), & National Center for Family Literacy (U.S.). (2008). *Developing early literacy: Report of the national early literacy panel: A scientific synthesis of early literacy development and implications of intervention*. Washington, DC: National Institute for Literacy.

National Governors Association Center for Best Practices, & Council of Chief State School Officers. (2010). *Common core state standards*. Washington, DC: National Governors Association Center for Best Practices, Council of Chief State School Officers.

Neuman, S. B. (2006). Building vocabulary to build literacy: Creating a world of words in the classroom. *Early Childhood Today, 21*(2), 9.

Neuman, S. B. (2010). Sparks fade, knowledge stays: The national early literacy panel's report lacks staying power. *American Educator, 34*(3), 14.

Neuman, L. B., Celano, D., Greco, A., & Shue, P. (2001). *Access for all: Closing the book gap for children in early education*. Newark, DE: International Reading Association.

Neuman, S. B., Copple, C., & Bredekamp, S. (2000). *Learning to read and write: Developmentally appropriate practices for young children*. Washington, DC: National Association for the Education of Young Children.

Neumann, M. M. & Neumann, D. L. (2014). Touch screen tablets and emergent literacy. *Early Childhood Education Journal, 42*(4), 231–239.

Okagaki, L. & Diamond, K. E. (2009). Cultural and linguistic differences in families with young children: Implications for early childhood teachers. In E. Essa & M. Burnham (Eds.). *Informing our practice: Useful research on young children's development* (pp. 216–226). Washington, DC: National Association for the Education of Young Children.

Owocki, G. (2005). *Time for literacy centers: How to organize and differentiate instruction*. Portsmouth, NH: Heinemann.

Paley, V. G. (2004). *A child's work: The importance of fantasy play*. Chicago, IL: University of Chicago Press.

Pelatti, C. Y., Piasta, S. B., Justice, L. M., & O'Connell, A. (2014). Language-and literacy-learning opportunities in early childhood classrooms: Children's typical experiences and within-classroom variability. *Early Childhood Research Quarterly, 29*(4), 445–456.

Pilonieta, P., Shue, P. L., & Kissel, B. T. (2014). Reading books, writing books: Reading and writing come together in a dual language classroom. *Young Children, 69*(3), 14–21.

Reed, B. & Railsback, J. (2003). *Strategies and resources for mainstream teachers of English language learners*. Portland, OR: Northwest Regional Educational Laboratory.

Reutzel, D. R. & Morrow, L. M. (2007). Promoting and assessing effective literacy learning classroom environments. In J. R. Raratore & R. L. McCormack (Eds.), *Classroom literacy assessment* (pp. 33–49). New York: The Guilford Press.

Richgels, D. J. (2001). Invented spelling, phonemic awareness, and reading and writing instruction. In S. B. Neuman & D. Dickinson (Eds.), *Handbook of early literacy research* (pp. 142–55). New York: Guilford Press.

Roskos, K. & Christie, J. (2011). The play-literacy nexus and the importance of evidence-based techniques in the classroom. *American Journal of Play, 4*(2), 204–224.

Roskos, K. A., Christie, J. F., & Richgels, D. J. (2003). The essentials of early literacy instruction. *Young Children Beyond the Journal*. Retrieved from http://www.journal.naeyc.org/btj/200303/Essentials.pdf

Sandhofer, C. & Uchikoshi, Y. (2013). *Cognitive consequences of dual language learning: Cognitive function, language and literacy, science and mathematics, and social-emotional development*. Retrieved from www.cde.ca.gov/sp/cd/ce/documents/dllresearchpapers.pdf

Scarborough, H. S. (2009). Connecting early language and literacy to later reading (dis)abilities: Evidence, theory, and practice. In F. Fletcher-Campbell, J. Soler, & G. Reid (Eds.), *Approaching difficulties in literacy development: Assessments, pedagogy and programmes* (pp. 23–38). Thousand Oaks, CA: Sage Publications.

Searfoss, L. W., Readence, J. E., & Mallette, M. H. (2001). *Helping children learn to read: Creating a classroom literacy environment* (4th ed.). Needham Heights, MA: Allyn & Bacon.

Smith, C. B. (2003). *Skills students use when speaking and listening*. Bloomingdale, IN: ERIC Clearinghouse on Reading, English, and Language.

Snow, C. E., Burns, M. S., & Griffin, P. (Eds.). (1998). *Preventing reading difficulties in young children*. Washington, DC: National Academy Press.

Sonnenschein, S., Thompson, J. A., Metzger, S. R., & Baker, L. (2013). The importance of teachers' language and children's vocabulary to early academic skills. *NHSA Dialog, 16*(4), 107–112.

Strickland, D. S. & Riley-Ayers, S. (2006). Early literacy: Policy and practice in the preschool years: Preschool Policy Brief. *National Institute for Early Education Research, 10*, 1–11.

Timm, S. & Schroeder, B. L. (2000). Listening/nonverbal communication training. *International Journal of Listening, 12*, 109–128.

Tompkins, G. E. (2005). *Literacy for the 21st century: A balanced approach*. Upper Saddle River, NJ: Merrill/Pearson. 2014

Wessels, S. & Trainin, G. (2014). Bringing literacy home: Latino families supporting children's literacy learning. *Young Children, 69*(3), 40–46.

What Works Clearinghouse. (2007). *Direct instruction, DISTAR, and language for learning. What works clearinghouse intervention report*. What Works Clearinghouse, 2277 Research Boulevard, MS 5M, Rockville, MD 20850. Tel: 866-992-9799;

Fax: 301-519-6760; e-mail: info@whatworks.ed.gov; Web site: http://www.whatworks.ed.gov.

Wittmer, D. S. & Honig, A. S. (1991). Convergent or divergent? Teacher questions to three-year-old children in day care. *Early Child Development and Care, 68*(1), 141–147.

Chapter 11

Alpert, B. (2012). *A look at magnets*. Mankato, MN: Capstone Press.

American Association for the Advancement of Science (AAAS). (1993). *Benchmarks for science literacy: Project 2061*. New York: Oxford University Press.

Baylor, B. (1999). *Everybody needs a rock*. New York: Econo-Clad Books.

Blevins, W. (2003). *You can use a magnifying glass*. New York: Children's Press.

Boothroyd, J. (2011). *What floats? What sinks? A look at density*. Minneapolis, MN: Lerner Publications Company.

Bradley, K. B. (2001). *Pop! A book about bubbles*. New York: Scholastic.

Brenneman, K., Stevenson-Boyd, J., & Frede, E. (2009). *Early mathematics and science: Preschool policy and practice* (Preschool Policy Brief No. 19). New Brunswick, NJ: National Institute for Early Education Research.

Brimner, L. D. (1999). *Raindrops*. New York: Children's Press.

Broom, J. & Scott, K. (2014). *Animalium*. Somerville, MA: Big Picture Press.

Bulla, C. R. (2008). *What makes a shadow?* Columbus, OH: McGraw Hill/SRA.

Carle, E. (2015). *The tiny seed*. New York: Simon Spotlight.

Carnegie Task Force on Learning in the Primary Grades. (1996). *Years of promise: A comprehensive learning strategy for America's children: The report of the Carnegie Task Force on Learning in the Primary Grades*. New York: Carnegie Corp. of New York.

Chalufour, I. & Worth, K. (2012). Science in kindergarten. In C. Copple (Ed.), *Growing minds: Building strong cognitive foundations in early childhood* (pp. 137–148). Washington, DC: National Association for the Education of Young Children.

Charlesworth, R. & Lind, K. (2010). *Math & science for young children* (6th ed.). Belmont, CA: Wadsworth/Cengage Learning.

Charlesworth, R. & Lind, K. (2012). *Math & science for young children* (7th ed.). Belmont, CA: Wadsworth/Cengage Learning.

Cusick, D. (2014). *Animals that make me say wow!* Watertown, MA: Imagine! Publishing.

Dahl, M. (2006). *Roll, slope, and slide: A book about ramps*. Minneapolis, MN: Picture Window Books.

Danoff-Burg, J. (2003). Be a bee and other approaches to introducing young children to entomology. In D. Koralek & L. J. Colker (Eds.), *Spotlight on young children and science* (pp. 33–37). Washington, DC: National Association for the Education of Young Children.

DeVries, R. & Sales, C. (2011). *Ramps & pathways: A constructivist approach to physics with young children*. Washington, DC: National Association for the Education of Young Children.

Dunn, S. & Larson, R. (1990). *Design technology—children's engineering*. New York: Falmer Press.

Esbaum, J. (2009). *Apples for everyone*. Washington, DC: National Geographic.

Esbaum, J. (2009). *Seed, sprout, pumpkin, pie*. Washington, DC: National Geographic.

French, L. (2004). Science as the center of a coherent, integrated early childhood curriculum. *Early Childhood Research Quarterly, 19*(1), 138–149.

Frost, H. (2000). *Water as a liquid*. Mankato, MN: Pebble Books.

Gallenstein, N. (2005). Never too young for a concept map. *Science and Children, 43*(1), 44–47.

Gelman, S. A. (1999). Concept development in preschool children. In Forum on Early Childhood Science, Mathematics, and Technology Education, & Project 2061 (American Association for the Advancement of Science). *Dialogue on early childhood science, mathematics, and technology education* (pp. 50–61). Washington, DC: American Association for the Advancement of Science (AAAS).

Gelman, R. (2005). Learning from children—research in preschool settings. In A. Beatty (Rapporteur), *Mathematical and scientific development in early childhood* (pp. 5–7). Washington, DC: The National Academies Press.

Gelman, R. & Brenneman, K. (2004). Science learning pathways for young children. *Early Childhood Research Quarterly, 19*(1), 150–158.

Gelman, S. A. & Frazier, B. N. (2012). Development of thinking in children. In K. J. Holyoak & R. G. Morrison (Eds.). *The Oxford handbook of thinking and reasoning* (pp. 513–528). New York: Oxford University Press.

Glaser, L. (2001). *Wonderful worms*. New York: Scholastic.

Glenn, J. (2000). *Before it's too late: A report to the nation from the National Commission on Mathematics and Science Teaching*. Washington, DC: US Government.

Gold-Dworkin, H. (2000). *Fun with water and bubbles*. New York: McGraw-Hill.

Greathouse, L. E. (2011). *Melting and freezing*. Huntington Beach, CA: Teacher Created Materials.

Greenfield, D., Jirout, J., Dominguez, X., Greenberg, A., Maier, M., & Fuccillo, J. (2009). Science in the preschool classroom: A programmatic research agenda to improve science readiness. *Early Education & Development, 20*, 238–264.

Greenman, J. (2005). *Caring spaces, learning places: Children's environments that work*. Redmond, WA: Exchange Press, Inc.

Greenman, J., Stonehouse, A., & Schweikert, G. (2007). *Prime times, 2nd ed: A handbook for excellence in infant and toddler programs*. St. Paul, MN: Redleaf Press.

Heath, P. & Heath, P. (1982). The effect of teacher intervention on object manipulation in young children. *Journal of Research in Science Teaching, 19*(7), 577–585.

Hicks, K. (2011). *I use science tools*. Vero Beach, FL: Rourke Pub.

Himmelman, J. (2001). *An earthworm's life*. Chicago, IL: Children's Press.

Hughes, S. (2014). *Does it absorb or repel liquid?* New York: Crabtree Publishing.

Hughes, S. (2014). *Does it sink or float?* New York: Crabtree Publishing Company.

Hunter, R. (2007). *The facts about habitats*. London: Watts.

Iatridis, M. (1984). Teaching science to preschoolers. In M. McIntyre (Ed.), *Early childhood and science*. Washington, DC: National Science Teachers Association.

Kay, S. (2011). *Rocks and soil*. Monterey, CA: National Geographic School Publishing.

Klein, E. R., Hammrich, P. L., Bloom, S., & Ragins, A. (2000). Language development and science inquiry: The head start of science and communication program. *Early Childhood Research and Practice*. Retrieved from http://ecrp.unic.edu/v2n2/klein.html

Leckies, K. S. & Beerey, T. H. (2013). Everyone needs a rock: Collecting items from nature in childhood. *Children, Youth and Environments, 23*(3), 66–88.

Lind, K. (1999). Science in early childhood: Developing and acquiring fundamental concepts and skills. In Forum on Early Childhood Science, Mathematics, and Technology Education, & Project 2061 (American Association for the Advancement of Science). *Dialogue on early childhood science, mathematics, and technology education* (pp. 73–83). Washington, DC: American Association for the Advancement of Science.

Lind, K. K. (2005). *Exploring science in early childhood education: A developmental approach*. Albany, NY: Thomson Delmar Learning.

Linderman, K. W., Jabot, M., & Berkley, M. T. (2013). The role of STEM (or STEAM) in the early childhood setting. In L. E. Cohen & S. Waite-Stupiansky (Eds.), *Learning across the early childhood curriculum (Advances in early education and day care, volume 17)* (pp. 95–114). Emerald Group Publishing Limited.

Mason, A. (2005). *Move it! Motion, forces and you*. Toronto, ON: Kids Can Press.

Miller, D. F. (2004). Science for babies. *Montessori Life, 16*(2), 25–27.

Miller, R. & Sikkens, C. (2014). *Engineers solve problems*. New York: Crabtree Publishing.

Morgan, E. R. (2014). *Next time you see a maple seed*. Arlington, VA: NSTA Kids, National Science Teachers Association.

Murphy, P. J. (2002). *Push and pull*. New York: Children's Press.

National Research Council. (2005). *Mathematical and scientific development in early childhood: A workshop summary*. Alix Beatty (Rapporteur), Mathematical Sciences Education Board, Board on Science Education, Center for Education, Division of Behavioral and Social Sciences and Education. Washington, DC: The National Academies Press.

National Research Council (U.S.). (2012). *A framework for K-12 science education: Practices, crosscutting concepts, and core ideas*. Washington, DC: The National Academies Press.

National Science Foundation, Division of Science Resources Statistics. (2011). *Women, minorities, and persons with disabilities in science and engineering: 2011*. Special Report NSF 11–309. Arlington, VA. Available at http://www.nsf.gov/statistics/wmpd/

National Science Teachers Association. (2014). *NSTA position statement: Early childhood science education*. Retrieved from http//www.nsta.org/about/positions/earlychildhood.aspx

Nayfeld, I., Brenneman, K., & Gelman, R. (2011). Science in the classroom: Finding a balance between autonomous exploration and teacher-led instruction in preschool settings. *Early Education and Development, 22*(6), 970–988.

Nelson, R. (2003). *Freezing and melting*. Minneapolis, MN: Lerner Publications.

NGSS Lead States. (2013). *Next generation science standards: For states, by states*. Washington, DC: The National Academies Press.

Novak, P. O. B. (2010). *Engineering the ABC's: How engineers shape our world*. Northville, MI: Ferne Press.

Operation Physics. (1998). *Children's misconceptions about science*. Retrieved from http://www.amasci.com/miscon/opphys.html

Pascoe, E. (2005). *Soil*. Detroit, MI: Blackbirch Press.

Pfeffer, W. (2004). *Wiggling worms at work*. New York: HarperCollins Publishers.

Sherwood, I. (2005). The early years. *Science and Children, 43*(3), 20–23.

Shores, E. L. (2011). *How to make bubbles*. Mankato, MN: Capstone Press.

Sprung, B. & Froschl, M. (2006). Building diversity through science and science through diversity. *Connect, 19*(4), 7–10.

Squire, A. (2002). *Fossils*. New York: Children's Press.

Squire, A. (2002). *Rocks and minerals*. New York: Children's Press.

Stewart, M. (2014). *Beneath the sun*. Atlanta, GA: Peachtree Publishers.

Swinburne, S. R. (1999). *Guess whose shadow?* Honesdale, PA: Boyds Mill Press

Trundle, K., Miller, H., & Krissek, L. (2013). Digging into rocks with young children. *Science and Children, 50*(8), 46–51.

Tu, T. (2006). Preschool science environment: What is available in a preschool classroom? *Early Childhood Education Journal, 33*(4), 245–251.

Vogel, J. (2015). *Discover magnets*. Mankato, MN: The Child's World.

Weakland, M. (2011). *Bubbles float, bubbles pop*. Mankato, MN: Capstone Press.

Williams, R. A., Rockwell, R. E., & Sherwood, E. A. (1987). *Mudpies to magnets*. Mt. Rainier, MD: Gryphon House.

Worth, K. (2010). Science in early childhood classrooms: Content and process. Beyond this journal. *Early Childhood Research and Practice*. Retrieved from http://ecrp.uiuc.edu/beyond/seed/worth.html

Worth, K. & Grollman, S. (2003). *Worms, shadows, and whirlpools: Science in the early childhood classroom*. Portsmouth, NH: Heinemann.

Chapter 12

Achieve. (2010). *Achieving the common core: Comparing the Common Core State Standards in mathematics and NCTM's Curriculum Focal Points*. Retrieved from http://www.achieve.org/CCSSandFocalPoints

Baratta-Lorton, B. (1972). *Workjobs*. Menlo Park, CA: Addison-Wesley.

Beneke, S. J., Ostrosky, M. M., & Katz, L. G. (2008). Calendar time for young children: Good intentions gone awry. *Young Children, 63*(3), 12–16.

Berger, A., Tzur, G., & Posner, M. I. (2006). Infant brains detect arithmetic errors. *Proceedings of the National Academy of Sciences of the United States of America (PNAS), 103*(33), 12649–12653.

Bowman, B., Donovan, M., & Burns, M. (2001). *Eager to learn: Educating our preschoolers*. Washington, DC: National Academy Press.

Braswell, J. S., Lutkus, A. D., Grigg, W. S., Santapau, S. L., Tay-Lim, B., & Johnson, M. (2001). *The nation's report card: Mathematics 2000* (NCES 2001–517). Washington, DC: National Center for Education Statistics.

Caulfield, R. (2000). Number matters: Born to count. *Early Childhood Education Journal, 28*(1), 63–65.

Charlesworth, R. (2005). Prekindergarten mathematics: Connecting with national standards. *Early Childhood Education Journal, 32*(4), 229–236.

Clements, D. H. (2004). Part one: Major themes and recommendations. In D. H. Clements, J. Sarama (Eds.), & A. M. DiBiase (Assoc. Ed.), *Engaging young children in mathematics: Standards for early childhood mathematics* (pp. 1–72). Mahwah, NJ: Lawrence Erlbaum Associates.

Clements, D. H. & Sarama, J. (2014). *Learning and teaching early math: The learning trajectories approach* (2nd ed.). New York: Routledge.

Clements, D. H. & Stephan, M. (2004). Measurement in pre-K-2 mathematics. In D. H. Clements, J. Sarama (Eds.), & A. M. DiBiase (Assoc. Ed.), *Engaging young children in mathematics: Standards for early childhood mathematics* (pp. 299–317). Mahwah, NJ: Lawrence Erlbaum Associates.

Cooper, R. G., Jr. (1984). Early number development: Discovering number space with addition and subtraction. In C. Sophian (Ed.), *Origins of cognitive skills* (pp. 157–192). Mahwah, NJ: Lawrence Erlbaum Associates.

Copley, J. V. (2010). *The young child and mathematics* (2nd ed.). Washington, DC: National Association for the Education of Young Children.

Denton, K. & West, J. (2002). Children's reading and mathematics achievement in kindergarten and first grade. *Education Statistics Quarterly, 4*, 19–26.

DeVries, P. & Kohlberg, L. (1987). *Constructivist early education: Overview and comparison with other programs*. Washington, DC: National Association for the Education of Young Children.

Duncan, G. J., Dowsett, C. J., Claessens, A., Magnuson, K., Huston, A. C., Klebanov, P., Pagani, L. S., Feinstein, L., Engel, M., Brooks-Gunn, J., Sexton, H., Duckworth, K., & Japel, C. (2007). School readiness and later achievement. *Developmental Psychology, 43*(6), 1428–1446.

Edens, K. M. & Potter, E. F. (2013). An exploratory look at the relationships among math skills, motivational factors and activity choice. *Early Childhood Education Journal, 41*(3), 235–243.

Engel, M., Claessens, A., & Finch, M. A. (2013). Teaching students what they already know? The (mis)alignment between mathematics instructional content and student knowledge in kindergarten. *Educational Evaluation and Policy Analysis, 35*(2), 157–178.

Ethridge, E. A. & King, J. R. (2005). Calendar math in preschool and primary classrooms: Questioning the curriculum. *Early Childhood Education Journal, 32*(5), 291–296.

Freeman, R. & Swim, T. J. (2009). Intellectual integrity: Examining common rituals in early childhood curriculum. *Contemporary Issues in Early Childhood, 10*(4), 366–377.

Fuson, K. C., Clements, D. H., & Beckmann, S. (2010). *Focus in prekindergarten: Pre-K*. Reston, VA: National Council of Teachers of Mathematics.

Ginsburg, H. P. (2006). Mathematical play and playful mathematics: A guide for early education. In D. G. Singer, R. B. Golinkoff, & K. Hirsh-Pasek (Eds.), *Play = learning: How play motivates and enhances children's cognitive and social-emotional growth* (pp. 145–167). New York: Oxford University Press.

Grissmer, D., Grimm, K. J., Aiyer, S. M., Marrah, W. M., & Steele, J. S. (2010). Fine motor skills and early comprehension of the world: Two new school readiness indicators. *Developmental Psychology, 46*(5), 1008–1017.

Hachey, A. C. (2013). Research to practice: In early childhood mathematics education (ECME), teachers' beliefs count. *NHSA Dialog: The Research to Practice Journal for the Early Childhood Field, 16*(3), 165–171.

Hannibal, M. A. (1999). Young children's developing understanding or geometric shapes. *Teaching Children Mathematics, 5*(6), 353–358.

Hofer, K. G., Farran, D. C., & Cummings, T. P. (2013). Preschool children's math-related behaviors mediate curriculum effects on math achievement gains. *Early Childhood Research Quarterly, 28*(3), 487–495.

Houle, G. B. (1984). *Learning centers for young children*. West Greenwich, RI: Consortium Publishing.

Isbell, R. & Isbell, C. (2003). *The complete learning spaces book for infants and toddlers*. Beltsville, MD: Gryphon House, Inc.

Jordan, N. C., Levine, S. C., & Huttenlocher, J. (1994). Development of calculation abilities in middle- and low-income children after formal instruction in school. *Journal of Applied Developmental Psychology, 15*, 223–240.

Kamii, C. (2003). Modifying a board game to foster kindergartners' logico-mathematical thinking. *Young Children, 58*(5), 20–26.

Klibanoff, R., Levine, S., Huttenlocher, J., Vasilyeva, M., & Hedges, L. (2006). Preschool children's mathematical knowledge: The effect of teacher "math talk." *Developmental Psychology, 42*(1), 59–69.

Lantz, D. (1979). A cross-cultural comparison of communication abilities: Some effects of age, schooling, and culture. *International Journal of Psychology, 14*(3), 171–183.

Miller, K. (2005). *Simple steps: Developmental activities for infants, toddlers, and two-year-olds*. Beltsville, MD: Pearson Education, Inc.

Mix, K. S., Huttenlocher, J., & Levine, S. C. (2002). *Quantitative development in infancy and early childhood*. New York: Oxford University Press.

NAEYC (National Association for the Education of Young Children) & NCTM (National Council of Teachers of Mathematics). (2010 updated). *Early childhood mathematics: Promoting good beginnings: A joint position statement of the National Association for the Education of Young Children (NAEYC) and the National Council of Teachers of Mathematics (NCTM)*. Retrieved from http://www.naeyc.org/positionstatements/mathematics

National Assessment for Education Progress. (2011). Retrieved from http://nationsreportcard.gov/researchers.asp

National Council of Teachers of Mathematics. (2000). *Principles and standards for school mathematics*. Reston, VA: Author. Retrieved from www.nctm.org

National Council of Teachers of Mathematics. (2013). Mathematics in early childhood learning: A position of the National Council of Teachers of Mathematics. Retrieved from http://www.nctm.org/earlychildhoodmath/

National Governors Association Center for Best Practices, & Council of Chief State School Officers. (2010). *Common core state standards*. Washington, DC: National Governors Association Center for Best Practices, Council of Chief State School Officers.

National Research Council. (2009). *Mathematics learning in early childhood: Paths toward excellence and equity*. Washington, DC: The National Academies Press.

National Research Council (U.S.)., Bowman, B. T., Donovan, S., & Burns, M. S. (2001). *Eager to learn: Educating our preschoolers*. Washington, DC: National Academy Press.

Oberdorf, C. D. & Taylor-Cox, J. (1999). Shape up! Geometry and geometric thinking: Children's misconceptions about geometry. *Teaching Children Mathematics, 5*(6), 340–346.

Pruden, S. M., Levine, S. C., & Hutenlocker, J. (2011). Children's spatial thinking: Does talk about the spatial world matter? *Developmental Science, 14*(6), 1417–1430.

Sarama, J., Lange, A., Clements, D. H., & Wolfe, C. B. (2012). The impacts of an early mathematics curriculum on emerging literacy and language. *Early Childhood Research Quarterly, 27*, 489–502.

Seo, K. H. & Ginsburg, H. P. (2004). What is developmentally appropriate in early childhood mathematics education? Lessons from new research. In D. H. Clements & J. Sarama (Eds.), *Engaging young children in mathematics: Standards for early childhood mathematics education* (pp. 91–104). Mahwah, NJ: Lawrence Erlbaum Associates.

Sgarlotti, R. (Ed.). (2004). *Creating a sacred place for students in mathematics K-12*. Polson, MT: National Indian School Board Association.

Stipek, D. (2014). Mathematics in early childhood education: Revolution or evolution? *Early Education and Development, 24*(4), 431–435.

Taylor-Cox, J. (2003). Algebra in the early years? Yes. *Young Children, 58*(1), 14–21.

Verdine, B. N., Golinkoff, R. M., Hirsh-Pasek, K., & Newcombe, N. S. (2014). Finding the missing piece: Blocks, puzzles, and shapes fuel school readiness. *Trends in Neuroscience and Education, 3*(1), 7–13.

Vygotsky, L. S. (1978). *Mind in society: The development of higher psychological processes*. Cambridge, MA: Harvard University Press.

Wang, A. H., Shen, F., & Byrnes, J. P. (2013). Does the opportunity-propensity framework predict the early mathematics skills of low-income pre-kindergarten children? *Contemporary Educational Psychology, 38*(3), 259–270.

Young-Loveridge, J. M. (2004). Effects on early numeracy of a program using number books and games. *Early Childhood Research Quarterly, 19*(1), 82–98.

Zur, O. & Gelman, R. (2004). Young children can add and subtract by predicting and checking. *Early Childhood Research Quarterly, 19*(1), 121–137.

Chapter 13

Armario, C. (2012). Report: Arts classes at elementary schools reduced. *Star Tribune*. Retrieved from http://www.startribune.com/printarticle/?id=145804075

Bartel, M. (2006). *Teaching creativity*. Retrieved from http://www.goshen.edu/~marvinpb/arted/tc.html#skills

Bisgaier, C. S., Samaras, T., & Russo, M. J. (2005). Young children try, try again: Using wood, glue, and words to enhance learning. In D. Koralek (Ed.), *Spotlight on young children and the creative arts* (pp. 12–18). Washington, DC: National Association for the Education of Young Children.

Bresler, L. (1995). The case of the Easter bunny: Art instruction by primary grade teachers. In C. Thompson (Ed.), *The visual arts and early childhood learning* (pp. 63–66). Reston, VA: The National Art Education Association.

Burton, J. (2000). The configuration of meaning: Learner-centered art education revisited. *Studies in Art Education, 41*(4), 330–342.

Catterall, J. S., Dumais, S. A., & Hampden-Thompson, G. (2012). *The arts and achievement in at-risk youth: Findings from four longitudinal studies*. Washington, DC: National Endowment for the Arts.

Clayton, M. K. (2002). Displaying student work: An opportunity for student-teacher collaboration. *Responsive Classroom Newsletter, 14*(4), 1–4.

Colbert, C. B. & Taunton, M. (1988). Problems of representation: Preschool and third grade children's observational drawings of a three dimensional model. *Studies in Art Education, 29*(2), 103–114.

Cole, E. & Schaefer, C. (1990). Can young children be art critics? *Young Children, 45*(2), 33–38.

Copple, C. & Bredekamp, S. (2009). *Developmentally appropriate practice in early childhood programs serving children from birth through age 8*. Washington, DC: National Association for the Education of Young Children.

Danko-McGhee, K. & Shaffer, S. (2003). *Looking at art with toddlers*. Smithsonian Early Enrichment Center. Retrieved from http://www.seec.si.edu/resources.htm

Dunst, C. J. & Gorman, E. (2009). Development of infant and toddler mark making and scribbling. *CELL Reviews, 2*(2), 1–16.

Edwards, C. P. & Springate, K. W. (1995). *Encouraging creativity in early childhood classrooms* (ERIC Digest). Urbana, IL: ERIC Clearinghouse on Elementary and Early Childhood Education, ED389474.

Epstein, A. S. (2005). Thinking about art: Encouraging art appreciation in early childhood settings. In D. G. Koralek (Ed.), *Spotlight on young children and the creative arts* (pp. 52–57). Washington, DC: National Association for the Education of Young Children.

Epstein, A. & Trimis, E. (2002). *Supporting young artists: The development of the visual arts in young children*. Ypsilanti, MI: High/Scope Press.

Erickson, M. (1995). Art historical understanding in early childhood. In C. Thompson (Ed.), *The visual arts and early childhood learning* (pp. 63–66). Reston, VA: The National Art Education Association.

Forman, G. (1994). Different media, different languages. In L. G. Katz & G. Cesarone (Eds.), *Reflections on the Reggio Emilia approach* (pp. 37–46). Urbana, IL: ERIC Clearing House on Elementary and Early Childhood Education.

Forman, G. (2006). Negotiating with art media to deepen learning. In B. Neugebauer (Ed.), *Curriculum: Art, music, movement, drama* (pp. 34–36). Redmond, WA: Exchange Press.

Gandini, L. (2006). Teachers and children together: Constructing new learning. In B. Neugebauer (Ed.), *Curriculum: Art, music, movement, drama* (pp. 26–29). Redmond, WA: Exchange Press.

Gardner, H. (1991). *The unschooled mind.* New York: Basic Books.

Gross, T. & Clemens, S. G. (2002). Painting a tragedy: Young children process the events of September 11. *Young Children, 57*(3), 44–51.

Grossman, E. (1980). Effects of instructional experience in clay modeling skills on modeled human figure representation in preschool children. *Studies in Art Education, 22*(1), 51–59.

Hetland, L. & Winner, E. (2001). The arts and academic achievement: What the evidence shows. *Arts Education Policy Review, 102*(5), 3–6.

HMIE (Her Majesty's Inspectorate of Education). (2006). *Emerging good practice in promoting creativity: A report by HMIE.* Retrieved from http://www.hmie.gov.uk/documents/publication/hmieegpipc.html

Kerlavage, M. (1995). A bunch of naked ladies and a tiger: Children's responses to adult works of art. In C. Thompson (Ed.), *The visual arts and early childhood learning* (pp. 56–62). Reston, VA: The National Art Education Association.

Kim, K. H. (2011). The creativity crisis: The decrease in creative thinking scores on the Torrance tests of creative thinking. *Creativity Research Journal, 23*(4), 285–295.

Kindler, A. M. (1995). Significance of adult input in early childhood artistic development. In C. Thompson (Ed.), *The visual arts and early childhood learning* (pp. 10–14). Reston, VA: National Art Education Association.

Koster, J. B. (2005). *Growing artists: Teaching art to young children.* Clifton Park, NY: Thomson Delmar Learning.

Koster, J. B. (2012). *Growing artists: Teaching art to young children* (5th ed.). Belmont, CA: Wadsworth Cengage Learning.

Koster, J. B. (2015). *Growing artists: Teaching art to young children* (6th ed.). Stamford, CT: Cengage Learning.

Lasky, L. & Muderji, R. (1980). *Art: Basic for young children.* Washington, DC: National Association for the Education of Young Children.

Lowenfeld, V. & Brittain, W. L. (1987). *Creative and mental growth* (8th ed.). New York: Macmillan.

Mulcahey, C. (2009). *The story in the picture: Inquiry and artmaking with young children.* New York: Teachers College Press.

National Advisory Committee on Creative and Cultural Education. (1999). *All our futures: Creativity, culture and education.* London: DFEE.

National Coalition for Core Arts Standards (NCCAS) National Core Arts Standards: A Conceptual Framework for Arts Learning. (2014). Retrieved from http://nccas.wikispaces.com/file/view/Framework%2005%2022-14.pdf/513758852/Framework%2005%2022-14.pdf

National Governors Association Center for Best Practices, & Council of Chief State School Officers. (2010). *Common core state standards.* Washington, DC: National Governors Association Center for Best Practices, Council of Chief State School Officers.

Newton, C. (1995). Language and learning about art. In C. M. Thompson (Ed.), *The visual arts and early childhood learning* (pp. 80–83). Reston, VA: National Art Education Association.

Pelo, A. (2007). *The language of art: Inquiry-based studio practices in early childhood settings.* St. Paul, MN: Redleaf Press.

Robinson, K. (2005). *Education Commission of the States 2005 National Forum of Education Policy Chairman's Breakfast.* Denver, CO: Education Commission of the States.

Romberg, J. (2002). *Hooked on art! 265 ready-to-use activities in seven exciting media.* Paramus, NJ: Prentice Hall.

Schiller, M. (1995). Reggio Emilia: A focus on emergent curriculum and art. *Art Education, 48*(3), 45–50.

Seefeldt, C. & Waites, J. (2002). *Creating rooms of wonder: Valuing and displaying children's work to enhance the learning process.* Beltsville, MD: Gryphon House.

Smith, D. & Goldhaber, J. (2004). *Poking, pinching & pretending: Documenting toddlers' exploration with clay.* St. Paul, MN: Redleaf Press.

Spodek, B. (2006). Educationally appropriate art activities for young children. In B. Neugebauer (Ed.), *Curriculum: Art, music, movement, drama* (pp. 23–25). Redmond, WA: Exchange Press.

Tarr, P. (1997). Creating connections: Adding "art" to your art program. *Canadian Child Care Federation.* Retrieved from http://www.cccf-fcsge.ca/docs/cccf/00000980.htm

The College Board. (2012). *The arts and the common core: A Review of connections between the Common Core State Standards and the National Core Arts Standards Conceptual Framework.* New York, NY: The College Board.

Thompson, S. C. (2005). *Children as illustrators: Making meaning through art and language.* Washington, DC: National Association for the Education of Young Children.

Topal, C. W. (2006). Fostering experiences between young children and clay. In B. Neugebauer (Ed.), *Curriculum: Art, music, movement, drama* (pp. 30–33). Redmond, WA. Exchange Press.

Vecchi, V. & Giudici, C. (2004). *Children, art, artists: The expressive languages of children, the artistic language of Alberto Burri.* Italy: Reggio Children Modena.

West, N. T. (2006). Art for all children: A conversation about inclusion. In B. Neugebauer (Ed.), *Curriculum: Art, music, movement, drama* (pp. 15–19). Redmond, WA: Exchange Press.

Wien, C. A., Keating, B.-L., Comeau, A., & Bigelow, B. (2012). Moving into uncertainty: Sculpture with three- to five-year-olds. In C. Copple (Ed.), *Growing minds: Building strong cognitive foundations in early childhood* (pp. 75–82). Washington, DC: National Association for the Education of Young Children.

Winner, E. & Vincent-Lancrin, S. (2013). The impacts of art education. In E. Liebau, E. Wagner, & M. Wyman (Eds.), *International yearbook for research in arts education* (pp. 71–78). Münster: Waxman.

Chapter 14

Aquino, F. (1991). *Songs for playing.* Mexico, DF: Trillas.

Caine, J. (1991). The effects of music on the selected stress behaviors, weight, caloric and formula intake, and length of hospital stay of premature and low birth weight neonates in a newborn intensive care unit. *Journal of Music Therapy, 28*(4), 180–182.

Campbell, P. S. (1991). The child-song genre: A comparison of songs by and for children. *International Journal of Music Education, 17, 14–23.*

Carlton, E. B. (2006). Learning through music: The support of brain research. In B. Neugebauer (Ed.), *Curriculum: Art, music, movement, drama: A beginnings workshop book* (pp. 45–48). Redmond, WA: Exchange Press.

Carlton, E. B. & Weikart, P. S. (1994). *Foundations in elementary education music.* Ypsilanti, MI: High/Scope Press.

DeCasper, A. & Spence, M. (1986). Prenatal maternal speech influences newborns' perception of speech sounds. *Infant Behavior and Development, 9*, 133–150.

Federico, G. F. (2002). Fetal responses to a musical stimulation: Music therapy and pregnancy. In J. Fachner & D. Aldridge (Eds.), *Dialogue and Debate Conference Proceedings of the 10th World Congress on Music* (pp. 530–546). Witten, Germany: Music Therapy World.

Ferguson, L. (2005). The role of movement in elementary music education: A literature review. *Applications of Research in Music Education, 23(2), 23–33.*

Flohr, J. W. (2004). *The musical lives of young children.* Upper Saddle River, NJ: Pearson.

Fox, S. B. (2000). Music and the baby's brain: Early experiences. *Music Educators Journal, 87*(2), 23–27.

Frega, A. L. (1979). Rhythmic tasks with 3-, 4-, and 5-year-old children: A study made in Argentine Republic. *Bulletin of the Council for Research in Music Education, 59*, 32–34.

Greata, J. D. (2006). *An introduction to music in early childhood education.* Clifton Park, NY: Thomson Delmar Learning.

Hetland, L. & Winner, E. (2001). The arts and academic achievement: What the evidence shows. *Arts Education Policy Review, 102*(5), 3–6.

Imiolo-Schriver, D. A. (1995). *Developmentally appropriate practice: The creation, implementation, and assessment of learning centers in the kindergarten music curriculum.* St. Paul, MN: University of St. Thomas.

Jordan-DeCarbo, J. & Galliford, J. (2011). The effect of an age-appropriate music curriculum on motor and linguistic and nonlinguistic skills of children three to five years of age. In S. L. Burton & C. C. Taggart (Eds.), *Learning from young children: Research in early childhood music* (pp. 215–230). Lanham, MD: Rowman & Littlefield Education.

Keeler, R. (2002). *20 ways to create play environments for the soul.* Retrieved from http://www.planetearthplayscapes.com/20souls.html

Kelley, L. & Sutton-Smith, B. (1987). A study of infant musical productivity. In J. C. Peery, I. W. Peery, & T. W. Draper (Eds.), *Music in child development* (pp. 35–53). New York: Springer-Verlag.

Kenney, S. (2004). The importance of music centers in the early childhood class. *General Music Today, 18*, 28–37.

Koster, J. B. (2015). *Growing artists: Teaching art to young children* (6th ed.). Stamford, CT: Cengage Learning.

Lang, S. (1999). *Cornell University child-care center rings with music to develop young brains.* Retrieved from http://www.planetearthplayscapes.com/soundart.html

Lobo, Y. & Winsler, A. (2006). The effects of creative dance and movement program on the social competence of Head Start preschoolers. *Social Development, 15*, 501–519.

McCarney, S. B. (1992). *The preschool evaluation scale.* Columbia, MO: Hawthorne Educational Services.

MENC. (1994). *National standards for arts education.* Reston, VA: Music Educators National Conference. Retrieved from http://www.menc.org

Metz, E. (1989). Movement as a musical response among preschool children. *Journal of Research in Music Education, 37*(1), 48–60.

Miche, M. (2002). *Weaving music into young minds.* Australia: Delmar Thomson Learning.

Moyeda, I., Gomez, I., & Flores, M. (2006). Implementing a musical program to promote preschool children's vocabulary development. *Early Childhood Research and Practice, 8*(1). Retrieved from http://ecrp.uiuc.edu/v8n1/galicia.html

Music Educators National Conference, & MENC, the National Association for Music Education. (1994). *Opportunity-to-learn standards for music instruction: Grades preK-12 curriculum and scheduling, staffing, materials and equipment, facilities.* Reston, VA: Music Educators National Conference.

National Coalition for Core Arts Standards (NCCAS). (2014). National Core Arts Standards: A Conceptual Framework for Arts Learning. Retrieved from http://nccas.wikispaces.com/file/view/Framework%2005%2022-14.pdf/513758852/Framework%2005%2022-14.pdf

National Dance Education Organization. (2015). *Standards for dance in early childhood: Philosophy underlying early childhood standards.* Retrieved from http://www.ndeo.org/content.aspx?page_id=22&club_id=893257&module_id=55419

Ohman-Rodriguez, J. (2005). Music from the inside out: Promoting emergent composition with young children. In D. G. Koralek (Ed.), *Spotlight on young children and the creative arts* (pp. 44–49). Washington, DC: National Association for the Education of Young Children.

Peery, J. C. & Peery, I. W. (1986). Effects of exposure to classical music on the musical preferences of preschool children. *Journal of Research in Music Education, 34*(1), 24–33.

Putkinen, V., Tervaniemi, M., & Huotilainen, M. (2013). Informal musical activities are linked to auditory discrimination and attention in 2–3-year old children: An event-related potential study. *European Journal of Neuroscience, 37*, 654–661.

Ries, N. L. L. (1982). *An analysis of the characteristics of infant-child singing expressions.* Thesis (Ed.D.), Arizona State University, Abstract from ProQuest File: Dissertation Abstracts Item: 8223568.

Sawyers, K. & Hutson-Brandhagen, J. (2004). Music and math: How do we make the connection for preschoolers? *Exchange, 158*, 46–49.

Schellenberg, E. G. (2004). Music lessons enhance IQ. *Psychological Science, 15*(8), 511–514.

Schwartz, B. (2007). Planting the seeds for a sound garden. *Early Childhood Newsletter, 13*, 12.

Shaw, G. (2003). *Keeping Mozart in mind* (2nd ed.). San Diego: Academic.

Shonkoff, J. P., Phillips, D., & National Research Council (U.S.). (2000). *From neurons to neighborhoods: The science of early child development.* Washington, DC: National Academy Press.

Shore, R. & Strasser, J. (2006). Music for their minds. *Young Children, 61*(2), 62–67.

Sims, W. L., Cecconi-Roberts, L., & Keast, D. (2011). Preschool children's uses of a music listening center during free-choice time. In S. L. Burton & C. C. Taggart (Eds.), *Learning from young children: Research in early childhood music* (pp. 131–140). Lanham, MD: Rowman & Littlefield Education.

Smith, A. P. (2011). The incorporation of principles of the Reggio Emilia Approach in a North American Preschool music curriculum. In S. L. Burton & C. C. Taggart (Eds.), *Learning from young children: Research in early childhood music* (pp. 79–94). Lanham, MD: Rowman & Littlefield Education.

Soley, G. & Hannon, E. E. (2010). Infants prefer the musical meter of their own culture: A cross-cultural comparison. *Developmental Psychology*, *46*, 286–292.

Stamp, L. N. (1992). Music time? All the time! *Early Childhood Education Journal*, *19*(4), 4–6.

Summit, G. & Widess, J. (1999). *Making gourd musical instruments: Over 60 string, wind & percussion instruments and how to play them.* New York: Sterling Publishing Co., Inc.

The College Board. (2012). *The arts and the common core: A Review of connections between the Common Core State Standards and the National Core Arts Standards Conceptual Framework.* New York, NY: The College Board.

Trehub, S. (2001). Musical predispositions in infancy. *Annals of the New York Academy*, *930*, 1–16.

Van de Carr, R. & Lehrer, M. (1986). Enhancing early speech, parental bonding, and infant physical development using prenatal intervention in standard obstetric practice. *Pre- and Perinatal Psychology Journal*, *1*(1), 20–30.

Whitcomb, R. (2010). Rhythmic characteristics of improvisational drumming among preschool children. *Research and Issues in Music Education*. Retrieved from http://go.galegroup.com/ps/Ldo? id=GALE%7CA269028863&v=2.1&u=mtlib_1_1134&it=r&p=AONE&sw=w

Winner, E. & Vincent-Lancrin, S. (2013). The impacts of art education. In E. Liebau, E. Wagner, & M. Wyman (Eds.), *International yearbook for research in arts education* (pp. 71–78). Münster: Waxman.

Winsler, A., Ducenne, L., & Koury, A. (2011). Singing one's way to self-regulation: The role of early music and movement curricula and private speech. *Early Education and Development*, *22*(2), 274–304.

Zentner, M. & Eerola, T. (2010). Rhythmic engagement with music in infancy. *Proceedings of the National Academy of Sciences of the United States of America*, *107*(13), 5768–5773.

Chapter 15

Ackermann, E. (2002). Language games, digital writing, emerging literacies: Enhancing kids' natural gifts as narrators and notators. In A. Dimitracopoulou (Ed.), *Information and communication technologies in education*. Proceedings of 3rd Hellenic Conference, with international participation, September 26–29, 2002, University of Aegean, Rhodes, Greece, Kastaniotis.

Alliance for Childhood. (2004). *Tech tonic: Towards a new literacy of technology*. College Park, MD: Alliance for Childhood.

American Academy of Pediatrics. (2011). Policy statement: Media use by children younger than 2 years. *Pediatrics*, *128*(5), 1040–1045.

Bailey, M. & Blagojevic, B. (2015). Innovate, educate, and empower: New opportunities with new technologies. In C. Donohue (Ed.), *Technology and digital media in the early years: Tools for teaching and learning* (pp. 162–182). New York, NY: Routledge.

Bergin, D. A., Ford, M. E., & Hess, R. D. (1993). Patterns of motivation and social behavior associated with microcomputer use of young children. *Journal of Educational Psychology*, *85*(3), 437–445.

Bhargava, A. & Escobedo, T. H. (1997). *What the children said: An analysis of the children's language during computer lessons.* Paper presented at the Annual Meeting of the American Educational Research Association, Chicago, IL (ERIC Reproduction Service No. ED409561).

Clark, L. (1998). *When young children use the Internet: A report of benefits for families, children and teachers.* Retrieved from http://www.wiu.edu/users/mimacp/wiu/articles/

Clements, D. H. (1994). The uniqueness of the computer as a learning tool: Insights from research and practice. In J. L. Wright & D. D. Shade (Eds.), *Young children: Active learners in a technological age* (pp. 31–49). Washington, DC: National Association for the Education of Young Children.

Clements, D. H. (1999). Young children and technology. *Dialogue on early childhood science, mathematics, and technology education.* Washington, DC: American Association for the Advancement of Science, Project 2061. Retrieved from http://www.project2061.org/newsinfo/earlychild/experience/clements.htm

Clements, D. & Sarama, J. (2003). Strip mining for gold: Research and policy in educational technology: A response to "Fool's Gold." *AACE Journal*, *11*(1), 7–69.

Clements, D. H., Nastasi, B. K., & Swaminathan, S. (1993). Young children and computers: Crossroads and directions from research. *Young Children*, 48(2), 56–64.

Common Sense Media. (2013). *Zero to eight: Children's media use in America 2013.* San Francisco, CA: Common Sense Media. Retrieved from https://www.commonsensemedia.org/research/zero-to-eight-childrens-media-use-in-america-2013

Cordes, C. & Miller, E. (2000). *Fools gold: A critical look at computers in childhood.* College Park, MD: Alliance for Childhood.

Couse, L. J. & Chen, D. W. (2010). A tablet computer for young children? Exploring its viability for early childhood education. *Journal of Research on Technology in Education*, *43*(1), 75–98.

Davis, B. C. & Shade, D. D. (1994). *Integrate don't isolate: Computers in the early childhood curriculum.* ERIC Digest. EDO–PS–94–17. Urbana, IL: ERIC Clearinghouse on Elementary and Early Childhood Education, University of Illinois.

Forman, G. (1999). Instant video revisiting: The video camera as a "Tool of the Mind" for young children. *Early Childhood Research and Practice*, *1*(2), 1–6. Retrieved from http://ecrp.uiuc.edu/v1n2/forman.html

Forman, G. & Gandini, L. (1994). *The amusement park for birds* (video). Amherst, MA: Performanetics.

Guernsey, L. & Levine, M. H. (2015). Pioneering literacy in the digital age. In C. Donohue (Ed.), *Technology and digital media in the early years: Tools for teaching and learning* (pp. 104–114). New York, NY: Routledge.

Gutnick, A. L., Robb, M., Takeuchi, L., & Kotler, J. (2011). *Always connected: The new digital media habits of young children.* New York: The Joan Ganz Cooney Center at Sesame Workshop. Cooney Center at Sesame Workshop.

Haugland, S. (2005). Selecting or upgrading software and web sites in the classroom. *Early Childhood Education Journal*, *32*(5), 329–340.

Haugland, S. W. (1992). Effects of computer software on preschool children's developmental gains. *Journal of Computing in Childhood Education*, *3*(1), 15–30.

Haugland, S. W. (1997). Computers in the early childhood classroom. *Early Childhood News*, *9*(4), 6–17.

Haugland, S. W. & Shade, D. D. (1994). Software evaluation for young children. In J. L. Wright & D. D. Shade (Eds.), *Young children: Active learners in a technological age* (pp. 63–76). Washington, DC: National Association for the Education of Young Children.

Haugland, S. W. & Wright, J. L. (1997). *Young children and technology: A world of discovery*. Boston: Allyn & Bacon.

Heft, T. M. & Swaminathan, S. (2002). The effects of computers on the social behavior of preschoolers. *Journal of Research in Childhood Education, 16*(2), 162–174.

Hutinger, P. (1999). *Preschool classroom computer experts*. Retrieved from http://www.wiu.edu/users/mimacp/wiu/articles/

Hutinger, P., Rippey, R., & Johanson, J. (1999). Findings of research study on effectiveness of a comprehensive technology system demonstrate benefits for children and teachers. Retrieved from http://www.wiu.edu/users/mimacp/wiu/articles/

International Society for Technology in Education. (2012). NETS for students 2007 profile. Retrieved from http://www.iste.org/standards/nets-for-students/nets-for-students-2007-profiles#PK-2#PK-2#PK-2#PK-2#PK-2#PK-2#PK-2#PK-2

Judge, S., Puckett, K., & Cabuk, B. (2004). Digital equity: New findings from the early childhood longitudinal study. *Journal of Research on Technology in Education, 36*(4), 383–396.

Kelly, K. L. & Schorger, J. R. (2001). "Let's play 'puters": Expressive language use at the computer center. *Information Technology in Childhood Education Annual, 13*, 125–138.

Kemp, C. (1999). Computer stations get failing grade. *American Academy of Pediatrics News, 15*(5), 2.

Lerner, C. & Barr, R. (2014). Screen sense: Setting the record straight research-based guidelines for screen use for children under 3 years old. Retrieved from http://www.zerotothree.org/parenting-resources/screen-sense/

Lisenbee, P. (2009). Whiteboards and web sites: Digital tools for the early childhood curriculum. *Young Children, 64*(6), 92–96.

McLaughlin, K. (2006). *Marine life Webquest*. Retrieved from http://webquest.org/questgarden/lessons/14095-060117134552/

Medvin, M. B., Reed, D., Behr, D., & Spargo, E. (2003). Using technology to encourage social problem solving in preschoolers. In G. Marshall & Y. J. Katz (Eds.), *Learning in school, home and community: ICT for early and elementary education*. International Working Conference on Learning with Technologies in School, Home and Community, Manchester, United Kingdom.

Mitchell, L. M. (2007). Using technology in Reggio Emilia inspired programs. *Theory into Practice, 46*(1), 32–39.

Muller, A. A. & Perlmutter, M. (1985). Preschool children's problem-solving interactions at computers and jigsaw puzzles. *Journal of Applied Developmental Psychology, 6*, 173–186.

NAEYC (National Association for the Education of Young Children) & Fred Rogers Center for Early Learning and Children's Media at Saint Vincent College. (2012). *Interactive media as tools in early childhood programs serving children from birth through age 8* [Position statement]. Washington, DC: Author.

NAEYC (National Association for the Education of Young Children). (1996). *Technology and young children—ages 3–8* [Position statement]. Washington, DC: Author. Retrieved from http://www.naeyc.org/resources/position_statements/pstech98.htm

Nir-Gal, O. & Klein, P. S. (2004). Computers for cognitive development in early childhood: The teacher's role in the computer learning environment. *Information Technology in Childhood Education Annual, 16*, 97–119.

Parette, H. P. & Blum, C. (2015). Including all young children in the technology-supported curriculum: A UDL technology integrated framework. In C. Donohue (Ed.), *Technology and digital media in the early years: Tools for teaching and learning* (pp. 129–149). New York, NY: Routledge.

Parette, H. P., Hourcade, J. J., & Heiple, G. S. (2000). The importance of structured computer experiences for young children with and without disabilities. *Early Childhood Education Journal, 27*(4), 243–250.

Peterson, R., Verenikina, I., & Herrington, J. (2008). Standards for educational, edutainment, and developmentally beneficial computer. Retrieved from gameshttp://ro.uow.edu.au/edupapers/62/

Plowman, L., McPake, J., & Stephen, C. (2012). Extending opportunities for learning: The role of digital media in early education. In S. Suggate & E. Reese (Eds.), *Contemporary debates in childhood education and development* (pp. 95–104). New York: Routledge.

Prairie, A. (2005). *Inquiry into math, science, and technology for teaching young children*. Clifton Park, NY: Thomson Delmar Learning.

Puerling, B. & Fowler, A. (2015). Technology tools for teachers and teaching: Innovative practices and emerging technologies. In C. Donohue (Ed.), *Technology and digital media in the early years: Tools for teaching and learning* (pp. 183–198). New York, NY: Routledge.

Robb, M. B. & Lauricella, A. R. (2015). Connecting child development and technology: What we know and what it means. In C. Donohue (Ed.), *Technology and digital media in the early years: Tools for teaching and learning* (pp. 70–85). New York, NY: Routledge.

Robinson, L. (1999). *Engaging young children in computer activities*. Retrieved from http://www.wiu. edu/users/mimacp/wiu/articles/

Rogoe, F. (2015). Media literacy in early childhood education: Inquiry-based technology integration. In C. Donohue (Ed.), *Technology and digital media in the early years: Tools for teaching and learning* (pp. 91–103). New York, NY: Routledge.

Samaras, A. P. (1996). Children's computers. *Childhood Education, 72*, 133–136.

Sarama, J. & Clements, D. (2002). The role of technology in early childhood learning. *Teaching Children Mathematics, 8*(6), 340–343.

Scoter, J. V., Ellis, D., & Railsback, J. (2001). *Technology in early childhood education: Finding the balance*. Portland, OR: Northwest Regional Educational Laboratory.

Shahrimin, M. I. & Butterworth, D. M. (2002). Young children's collaborative interactions in a multimedia computer environment. *Internet and Higher Education, 4*, 203–215.

Sharapan, H. (2015). Technology as a tool for social-emotional development: What we can learn from Fred Roger's approach. In C. Donohue (Ed.), *Technology and digital media in the early years: Tools for teaching and learning* (pp. 12–20). New York, NY: Routledge.

Shields, M. K. & Behrman, R. E. (2000). Children and computer technology: Analysis and recommendations. *Children and Computer Technology*, 10(2), 4–30.

Shute, R. & Miksad, J. (1997). Computer assisted instruction and cognitive development in preschoolers. *Child Study Journal, 27*(3), 237–253.

Straker, L., Maslen, B., Burgess-Limerick, R., Johnson, P., & Dennerlein, J. (2010). Evidence-based guidelines for the wise use of computers by children: Physical development guidelines. *Ergonomics, 53*(4), 458–477.

Tsantis, L. A., Bewick, C. J., & Thouvenelle, S. (2003). Examining some common myths about computer use in the early years. *Beyond the Journal, Young Children*. Retrieved from www.journal.naeyc.org/btj/200311

Whited, J. (2003). *Experiences with light*. Retrieved from http://www.ohiou.edu/childdevcenter/DOCUMENTS/lightbook.pdf

Chapter 16

Abraham, C. (2011). Woodworking: A constructive learning center. *Texas Child Care Quarterly, 35*(3). Retrieved from childcarequarterly.com

Barbour, J. (2004). *Children's eating habits in the U.S.: Trends and implication for food marketers*. Rockville, MD: Packaged Facts. Retrieved from www.packagedfacts.com

Carlson, F. M. (2011). *Big body play: Why boisterous, vigorous, and very physical play is essential to children's development and learning*. Washington, DC: National Association for the Education of Young Children.

Colker, L. J. (2005). *The cooking book: Fostering young children's learning and delight*. Washington, DC: National Association for the Education of Young Children.

Foote, B. J. (2001). *Cup cooking: Individual child-portion picture recipes*. Mt. Ranier, MD: Gryphon House.

Foster, R. R. & Hardison, R. (2000). Can a woodworking center be safe? *Healthy Child Care: Health and Safety Ideas for the Young Child, 3*(4). Retrieved from http://www.healthychild.net/articles/sf16wood.html

Goodway, J. D. & Robinson, L. E. (2006). SKIPing toward an active start: Promoting physical activity in preschoolers. *Beyond the Journal*. Retrieved from http://www.journal.naeyc.org/btj/200605/GoodwayBTJ.asp

Goodway, J., Getchell, N., Raynes, D., & National Association for Sport and Physical Education. (2009). *Active start: A statement of physical activity guidelines for children from birth to age 5*. Reston, VA: National Association for Sport and Physical Education.

Greenman, J., Stonehouse, A., & Schweikert, G. (2007). *Prime times, 2nd ed.: A handbook for excellence in infant and toddler programs*. St. Paul, MN: Redleaf Press.

Hart, J. L. & Tannock, M. T. (2013). Young children's play fighting and use of war toys. In R. E. Tremblay, M. Boivin, & R. DeV. Peters (Eds.), *Encyclopedia on early childhood development*. Montreal, Quebec: Centre of Excellence for Early Childhood Development and Strategic Knowledge Cluster on Early Child Development. Retrieved from http://www.child-encyclopedia.com/documents/Hart-TannockANGxp1.pdf

Huber, L. K. (1998). Woodworking in my classroom? You bet! *Early Childhood News*, 10(2), 72–75.

Hunt, T. & Renfro, N. (1982). *Puppetry in early childhood education*. Puppetry in Education Series. Austin, TX: N. Renfro Studios.

Logue, M. E. & Harvey, H. (2010). Preschool teachers' views of active play. *Journal of Research in Childhood Education, 24*(1), 32–49.

Nelson, J. A., Carpenter, K., & Chiasson, M. A. (2006). Diet, activity, and overweight among preschool-age children enrolled in the Special Supplemental Nutrition Program for Women, Infants, and Children (WIC). *Preventing Chronic Disease*. Retrieved from http://www.cdc.gov/pcd/issues/2006/apr/05_0135.htm

Pica, R. (2013). *Experiences in movement and music: Birth to age 8* (5th ed.). Belmont, CA: Wadsworth.

Sanders, S. W. (2002). *Active for life: Developmentally appropriate movement programs for young children*. Washington, DC: National Association for the Education of Young Children.

Smith, P. K., Smees, R., & Pellegrini, A. D. (2004). Play fighting and real fighting: Using video playback methodology with young children. *Aggressive Behavior, 30*, 164–173.

Sosna, D. (2000). More about woodworking with young children. *Young Children, 55*(2), 38–39.

Texas Child Care Quarterly. (2013). Back to basics: Woodworking. Retrieved from childcarequarterly.com

Wellhousen, K. & Crowther, I. (2004). *Creating effective learning environments*. New York: Delmar Learning.

Chapter 17

Alexander, J., North, M., & Hendren, D. K. (1995). Master gardener classroom garden project: An evaluation of the benefits to children. *Children's Environments, 12*(2), 123–133.

American Academy of Pediatrics, American Public Health Association, & National Resource Center for Health and Safety in Child Care and Early Education. (2011). *Caring for our children: National health and safety performance standards: Guidelines for out-of-home child care programs* (3rd ed.). Elk Grove Village, IL: American Academy of Pediatrics and Washington, DC: American Public Health Association. Retrieved from http://nrc.uchsc.edu

ATSDR. (2000). *Toxicological profile for arsenic*. Atlanta, GA: U.S. Department of Health and Human Services—prepared by Syracuse Research Corporation for Agency for Toxic Substances and Disease Registry.

Au, N. (2012). The health care cost implications of overweight and obesity during childhood. *Health Services Research, 47*(2), 655+. Retrieved from http://go.galegroup.com.proxyserver.umwestern.edu/ps/i.do?id=GALE%7CA284552048&v=2.1&u=mtlib_1_1134&it=r&p=AONE&sw=w

Avrasin, M. (2007). Creating a powerhouse of play. *Parks and Recreation, 42*(4), 42–47.

Banning, W. & Sullivan, G. (2011). *Lens on outdoor learning*. St. Paul, MN: Redleaf Press.

Baranowski, T., Mendlein, J., Resnicow, K., Frank, E., Cullen, K. W., & Baranowski, J. (2000). Physical activity and nutrition in children and youth: An overview of obesity prevention. *Preventive Medicine, 31, S1–S10.*

Barbour, A. (1999). The impact of playground design on the play behaviors of children with differing levels of physical competence. *Early Childhood Research Quarterly, 14*(1), 75–98.

Beighle, A. (2012). *Research brief: Increasing physical activity through recess*. Active Living Research. Retrieved from http://www.activelivingresearch.org/node/12481#alldownloads

Beresin, A. R. (2012). Play counts: Pedometers and the case for recess. *International Journal of Play, 1*(2), 131–138.

Bergen, S. & Robertson, R. (2013). *Healthy children, healthy lives: The wellness guide for early childhood programs*. St. Paul, MN: Redleaf Press.

Bixler, R. D., Carlisle, C. L., Hammitt, W. E., & Floyd, M. F. (1994). Observed fears and discomforts among urban students on field trips to wildland areas. *Journal of Environmental Education, 26*(1), 24–33.

Bohling-Philippi, V. (2006). The power of nature to help children heal. *Child Care Exchange, 171*, 49–53.

Broekhuizen, K., Scholten, A. M., & de Vries, S. I. (2014). The value of (pre) school playgrounds for children's physical activity level: A systematic review. *International Journal of Behavioral Nutrition and Physical Activity, 11*(1), 59.

Brosterman, N. (1997). *Inventing kindergarten*. New York: Harry N. Adams.

Brown, P., Sutterby, J., & Thornton, C. D. (2001). Dramatic play in outdoor play environments. *Today's Playground, 1*(0), 10–11.

Carson, R. (July 1956). Help your child to wonder. *Woman's Home Companion*, 25–27, 46–48.

Clements, D. H. (2004). Part one: Major themes and recommendations. In D. H. Clements, J. Sarama (Eds.), & A. M. DiBiase (Assoc. Ed.), *Engaging young children in mathematics: Standards for early childhood mathematics* (pp. 1–72). Mahwah, NJ: Lawrence Erlbaum Associates.

Connolly, P. & McKenzie, T. L. (1995). Effects of a games intervention on the physical activity levels of children at recess. *Research Quarterly for Exercise and Sport, 66* (Suppl.), A60.

Copeland, K. A., Kendeigh, C. A., Kalkwarf, H. J., Sherman, S. N., & Saelens, B. E. (2012). Societal values and policies may curtail preschool children's physical activity in child care centers. *Pediatrics, 129*(2), 265–274.

Cosco, N. & Moore, R. (1999). *Playing in place: Why the physical environment is important in playwork*. 14th Play Education Annual Play and Human Development Meeting: Theoretical Playwork. Ely, Cambridgeshire, UK. Retrieved from www.naturalearning.org/PlayingPaper.html

Cosco, N. G., Moore, R. C., & Smith, W. R. (2014). Childcare outdoor renovation as a built environment health promotion strategy: Evaluating the preventing obesity by design intervention. *American Journal of Health Promotion, 28*, S27–S32.

Cuppens, V., Rosenow, N., & Wike, J. (2007). *Learning with nature idea book: Creating nurturing outdoor spaces for children*. Lincoln, NE: National Arbor Day Foundation.

Daly, L. & Beloglovsky, M. (2015). *Loose parts: Inspiring play in young children*. St. Paul, MN: Redleaf Press.

Danks, S. G. (2003). Green mansions: Living willow structures enhance children's play environments. *Children, Youth and Environments, 13*(1). Retrieved from http://cye.colorado.edu

Dempsey, J. D. & Frost, J. L. (1993). Play environments in early childhood education. In B. Spodek (Ed.), *Handbook of research on the education of young children* (pp. 306–321). New York: Macmillan Publishing.

Dogra, S., Meisner, B. A., & Ardern, C. I. (2010). Variation in mode of physical activity by ethnicity and time since immigration: A cross-sectional analysis. *International Journal of Behavioral Nutrition and Physical Activity, 7*, 75–86.

Dowda, M., Brown, W. H., McIver, K. L., Pfeiffer, K. A., O'Neill, J. R., Addy, C. L., & Pate, R. R. (2009). Policies and characteristics of the preschool environment and physical activity of young children. *Pediatrics, 123*(2), e261–e266.

EC (European Commission). (2003). Commission Directive 2003/2/EC of 6 January 2003 relating to restrictions on the marketing and use of arsenic (10th adaptation to technical progress to Council). Retrieved from http://eurlex.europa.eu/LexUriServ/LexUriServ.do?uri=0J:L:2003:004:0009:0011:EN:PDF

Elkind, D. (2006). The values of outdoor play. *Exchange Press, 171*, 6–11.

Etnier, J. L., Salazar, W., Landers, D. M., Petruzzello, S. J., Han, M., & Nowell, P. (1997). The influence of physical fitness and exercise upon cognitive functioning: A meta-analysis. *Journal of Sport and Exercise Psychology, 19*(3), 249–277.

Faber Taylor, A. & Kuo, F. E. (2006). Is contact with nature important for healthy child development? State of the evidence. In C. Spencer & M. Blades (Eds.), *Children and their environments: Learning, using, and designing spaces*. Cambridge: Cambridge University Press.

Faber Taylor, A. & Kuo, F. E. (2011). Could exposure to everyday green spaces help treat ADHD? Evidence from children's play settings. *Applied Psychology: Health and Well-Being, 3*, 281–303.

Finn, K., Johannsen, N., & Specker, B. (2002). Factors associated with physical activity in preschool children. *The Journal of Pediatrics, 140*(1), 81–85.

Fjørtoft, I. (2001). The natural environment as a playground for children: The impact of outdoor play activities in pre-primary school children. *Early Childhood Education Journal, 29*(2), 111–117.

Fjørtoft, I. (2004). Landscape as playscape: The effects of natural environments on children's play and motor development. *Children, Youth and Environments, 14*(2), 21–44. Retrieved from http://www.colorado.edu/journals/cye/

Flynn, L. L. & Kieff, J. (2002). Including everyone in outdoor play. *Young Children, 57*(3), 20–26.

Frost, J. L. (1990). Young children and playground safety. In J. Frost & S. Worthman (Eds.), *Playgrounds for young children: National survey and perspectives* (pp. 29–48). Reston, VA: American Alliance for Health, Physical Education, Recreation and Dance.

Frost, J. L. (1992). *Play and playscapes*. Albany, NY: Delmar.

Frost, J. L. (2010). *A history of children's play and play environments: Toward a contemporary child-saving movement*. Marceline, MO: Routledge.

Frost, J. L., Brown, P., Sutterby, J. A., & Thornton, C. D. (2004). *The developmental benefits of playgrounds*. Olney, MD: Association for Childhood Education International.

Frost, J. & Kim, S. (2000). *Developmental progress in preschool-age children's using an overhead bar*. Unpublished manuscript.

Frost, J. L. & Campbell, S. D. (1985). Equipment choices of primary-age children on conventional and creative playgrounds. In J. L. Frost & S. Sunderlin (Eds.), *When children play* (pp. 89–92). Wheaton, MD: Association for Childhood Education International.

Frost, J. L. & Strickland, E. (1985). Equipment choices of young children during free play. In J. L. Frost & S. Sunderlin (Eds.), *When children play. Proceedings of the international conference on play and play environments*. Wheaton, MD: Association for Childhood Education International.

Frost, J. L., Wortham, S. C., & Reifel, R. S. (2012). *Play and child development*. Boston: Pearson.

Gallahue, D. L. (1993). Motor development and movement skill acquisition in early childhood education. In B. Spodek (Ed.), *Handbook of research on the education of young children* (pp. 24–41). New York: Macmillan.

Gill, T. (2014). The play return: A review of the wider impact of play initiatives. Retrieved from http://www.playscotland.org/who-we-are/playday/the-play-return-a-review-of-the-wider-impact-of-play-initiatives/

Goodway, J., Getchell, N., Raynes, D., & National Association for Sport and Physical Education. (2009). *Active start: A statement of physical activity guidelines for children from birth to age 5*. Reston, VA: National Association for Sport and Physical Education.

Greenman, J. (1991). Babies get out: Outdoor settings for infant toddler play. *Child Care Information Exchange, 79*, 21–24.

Greenman, J. (2005a). *Caring spaces, learning places: Children's environments that work*. Redmond, WA: Exchange Press, Inc.

Griffen, C. & Rinn, B. (1998). Enhancing outdoor play with an obstacle course. *Young Children, 53*(3), 18–23.

Han, J. C., Lawlor, D. A., & Kimm, S. Y. (2010). Childhood obesity. *The Lancet, 375*(9727), 1737–1748.

Hart, C. R. & Sheehan, R. (1986). Preschoolers' play behavior in outdoor environments: Effect of traditional and contemporary playgrounds. *American Educational Research Journal, 23*(4), 668–678.

Hatlelid, K. M., Bittner, P. M., Midgett, J. D., Thomas, T. A., & Saltzman, L. E. (2004). Exposure and risk assessment for arsenic from chromated copper arsenate (CCA)-treated wood playground equipment. *Journal of Children's Health*, 2(3), 215–241. Retrieved from http://www.informaworld.com/10.1080/15417060490930056

Hayward, D. G., Rothenberg, M., & Beasley, R. R. (1974). Children's play and urban playground environments: A comparison of traditional, contemporary, and adventure playground types. *Environment and Behavior, 6*(2), 131–168.

Hoffert, S. & Sandberg, J. (2000). *Changes in American children's time 1981–1997*. Center for the Ethnography of Everyday Life. Retrieved from ceel.psc.isr.unich.edu/pubs

Hogan, P. (1982). *The nuts and bolts of playground construction*. West Point, NY: Leisure Press.

Holmes, R. M. & Procaccino, J. K. (2009). Preschool children's outdoor play area preferences. *Early Child Development and Care, 179*(8), 1103–1112.

Jarrett, O. S. (2002). *Recess in elementary school: What does the research say?* Champaign, IL: ERIC Clearinghouse on Elementary and Early Childhood Education. Retrieved from http://purl.access.gpo.gov/GPO/LPS43139

Jarrett, O. (2013). A research-based case for recess. US Play Coalition. Retrieved from www.usplaycoalition.clemson.edu

Jarrett, O., Maxwell, D., Dickerson, C., Hoge, P., Daview, G., & Yetley, A. (1998). Impact of recess on classroom behavior: Group effects and individual differences. *The Journal of Educational Research, 92*(2), 121–126.

Jenson, B. J. & Bullard, J. A. (2002). The mud center: Recapturing childhood. *Young Children, 57*(3), 16–19.

Keeler, R. (2002). *20 ways to create play environments for the soul*. Retrieved from http://www.planetearthplayscapes.com/20souls.html

Kelling, G. L. & Coles, C. M. (1996). *Fixing broken windows: Restoring order and reducing crime in our communities*. New York: The Free Press.

Kells, P. (2002). Safety vs. challenge—the playground dilemma. *Interaction, 16*(2), 21–22.

Kirkby, M. (1989). Nature as refuge in children's environments. *Children's Environments Quarterly, 6*(1), 7–12.

Kwon, E., Zhang, H., Wang, Z., Jhangri, G. S., Lu, X., Fok, N., Gabos, S., Li, X., & Le, X. C. (2004). Arsenic on the hands of children after playing in playgrounds. *Environmental Health Perspectives, 112*(14), 1375–1380.

Lopes, L., Lopes, V., & Pereira, B. (2009). Physical activity levels in normal weight and overweight Portuguese children: An intervention study during an elementary school recess. *International Electronic Journal of Health Education, 12*, 175–184.

Martens, F. L. (1982). Daily physical education—a boon to Canadian elementary schools. *Journal of Physical Education, Recreation, & Dance, 53*(3), 55–58.

Mattenson, K. A. (2008). Too young for rainforests? The impact of a rainforest curriculum on elementary students' affective responses to nature. *Dissertation Abstracts International*, 69–04, Section A, 1267–1430.

McDonald, J. & Greene, M. (2003). Special study: Injuries and death involving children under age two associated with playground equipment. Directorate for Epidemiology, U.S. Consumer Product Safety Commission.

McGinnis, J. L. (2002). Enriching outdoor environments. *Young Children, 57*(3), 28.

Mitchell, R., Cavanagh, M., & Eager, D. (2006). Not all risk is bad, playgrounds as a learning environment for children. *Injury Control and Safety Promotion, 13*, 122–124.

Moore, G. T. (1986). Effects of the spatial definition of behavior settings on children's behavior: A quasi-experimental field study. *Journal of Environmental Psychology, 6*(3), 205–231.

Moore, G. T. (2002). Designed environments for young children: Empirical findings and implications for planning and design. Retrieved from http://www.arch.usyd.edu.au/documents/staff/garymoore/111.pdf

Moore, R. (1985). Neighborhoods as childhood habitats. Special issue. *Children's Environments Quarterly, 1*(4), 1–14.

Moore, R. (1992). *Helping children to understand and love planet earth: International Federation of Landscape Architects Handbook*. Washington, DC: ASLA.

Moore, R. C. (1995). Children gardening: First steps towards a sustainable future. *Children's Environments, 12*(2), 66–83.

Moore, R. C., Bocarro, J., & Hickerson, B. (2007). Natural surroundings. *Parks and Recreation, 42*(4), 36–41.

Murray, R., Ramstetter, C., Council on School Health, & American Academy of Pediatrics. (2013). The crucial role of recess in school. *Pediatrics, 131*(1), 183–188.

Nabors, L., Willoughby, J., & Badawi, M. A. (1999). Relations between activities and cooperative playground interactions for preschool-age children with special needs. *Journal of Developmental and Physical Disabilities, 11*(4), 339–352.

National Center for Health Statistics. (2014). NCHS fact sheet: NCHS obesity data. Retrieved from http://www.cdc.gov/nchs/data/factsheets/factsheet_obesity.htm#about

Neilson, G., Taylor, R., Williams, S., & Mann, J. (2010). Permanent play facilities in school playgrounds as a determinant of children's activity. *Journal of Physical Activity & Health*, *7*(4), 254–261.

Nelson, E. (2006). The outdoor classroom: No child left behind. *Child Care Exchange*, *171*, 40–43.

Nelson, E. (2012). *Cultivating outdoor classrooms: Designing and implementing child-centered learning environments*. St. Paul, MN: Redleaf Press.

Nelson, J. A., Carpenter, K., & Chiasson, M. A. (2006). Diet, activity, and overweight among preschool-age children enrolled in the Special Supplemental Nutrition Program for Women, Infants, and Children (WIC). *Preventing Chronic Disease*. Retrieved from http://www.cdc.gov/pcd/issues/2006/apr/05_0135.htm

Nicaise, V., Kahan, D., & Sallis, J. F. (2011). Correlates of moderate-to-vigorous physical activity among preschoolers during unstructured outdoor play periods. *Preventive Medicine*, *53*, 309–315.

NPR (Producer). (2006). *Fun & games: Adventure playgrounds a dying breed in the U.S.* Retrieved from http://www.npr.org/templates/story/story.php?storyId=5254026

Office of Inspector General (OIG). (2011). *Review of 24 head start grantees' compliance with health and safety requirements*. Washington, DC. Retrieved from http://oig.hhs.gov/oas/reports/region10/11102503.pdf

Olds, A. R. (2001). *Child care design guide*. New York: McGraw-Hill.

Pardee, M., Gillman, A., & Larson, C. (2005). *CICK resource guide—volume 4: Creating playgrounds for early childhood facilities*. Local Initiatives Support Corporation. Retrieved from http://www.lisc.org/content/publications/detail/814/

Pate, R. R., Baranowski, R., Dowda, M., & Trost, S. G. (1996). Tracking of physical activity in young children. *Medicine and Science in Sports and Exercise*, *28*(1), 92–96.

Pellegrini, A. D., Kato, K., Blatchford, P., & Baines, E. (2002). A short-term longitudinal study of children's playground games across the first year of school: Implications for social competence and adjustment to school. *American Educational Research Journal*, *39*(4), 991–1015.

Phelan, K. J., Khoury, J., Kalkwarf, H. J., & Lanphear, B. P. (2001). Trends and patterns of playground injuries in United States children and adolescents. *Ambulatory Pediatrics*, *1*(4), 227–233.

Powell, L. M., Slater, S., & Chaloupka, F. J. (2004). The relationship between community physical activity settings and race, ethnicity and socioeconomic status. *Evidence-Based Preventive Medicine*, *1*(2), 135–144.

Pyle, R. (2002). Eden in a vacant lot: Special places, species and kids in community of life. In P. H. Kahn & S. R. Kellert (Eds.), *Children and nature: Psychological, sociological and evolutionary investigation* (pp. 305–328). Cambridge: The Massachusetts Institute of Technology Press.

Ridgers, N. D., Stratton, G., & Fairclough, S. J. (2005). Assessing physical activity levels during recess using accelerometry. *Preventative Medicine*, *41*(1), 102–107.

Rivken, M. S. (1995). *The great outdoors: Restoring children's right to play outside*. Washington, DC: National Association for the Education of Young Children.

Sallis, J., McKenzie, T., Kolody, M., Lewis, M., Marshall, S., & Rosengard, P. (1999). Effects of health-related physical education on academic achievement: Project Spark. *Research Quarterly for Exercise and Sport*, *70*(2), 127–134.

Sallis, J., Nader, P., Broyles, S., Berry, C., Elder, J., McKenzie, T., & Nelson, J. (1993). Correlates of physical activity at home in Mexican-American and Anglo-American preschool children. *Health Psychology*, *12*(5), 390–398.

Schappet, J., Malkusak, A., & Bruya, L. D. (2003). *High expectations: Playgrounds for children of all abilities*. Bloomfield, CT: National Center for Boundless Playgrounds.

Schultz, P. W., Shriver, C., Tabanico, J. J., & Khazian, A. M. (2004). Implicit connections with nature. *Journal of Environmental Psychology*, *24*(1), 31–42.

Scruggs, P. W., Beveridge, S. D., & Watson, D. L. (2003). Increasing children's school time physical activity using structured fitness breaks. *Pediatric Exercise Science*, *15*(2), 156–169.

Sharma, A. J., Grummer-Strawn, L. M., Dalenius, K., Galuska, D., Anandappa, M., Borland, E., Mackintosh, H. & Smith, R. (2009) Obesity prevalence among low-income, preschool-aged children-United States, 1998–2008. *Morbidity and Mortality Weekly Report*, *58*(28), 769–773.

Sobel, D. (1993). *Children's special places: Exploring the roles of forts, dens, and bush houses in middle childhood*. Tucson, AZ: Zephyr Press.

Sobel, D. (1996). *Beyond ecophobia: Reclaiming the heart in nature education*. Great Barrington, MA: The Orion Society.

Sobel, D. (2002). *Children's special places: Exploring the role of forts, dens, and bush houses in middle childhood*. Detroit, MI: Wayne State University Press.

Sobel, D. (2004). *Place-based education, connecting classrooms & communities*. Great Barrington, MA: The Orion Society.

Stoecklin, V. L. (2000). Creating playgrounds kids love. White Hutchinson Leisure & Learning Group. Retrieved from http://www.whitehutchinson.com/children/articles/playgrndkidslove.shtml

Stoecklin, V. (2001). *Developmentally appropriate gardening with children*. White Hutchinson Leisure and Learning Group. Retrieved from http://www.whitehutchinson.com/children/articles/gardening.shtml

Stratton, G. (2000). Promoting children's physical activity in primary school: An intervention study using playground markings. *Ergonomics*, *43*(10), 1538–1546.

Striniste, N. A. & Moore, R. C. (1989). Early childhood outdoors: A literature review on the design of childcare environments. *Children's Environments Quarterly*, *6*(4), 25–31.

Suecoff, S. A., Avner, J. R., Chou, K. J., & Crain, E. F. (1999). A comparison of New York City playground hazards in high and low-income areas. *Archives of Pediatrics and Adolescent Medicine*, *153*, 363–366.

Susa, A. M. & Benedict, J. O. (1994). The effects of playground design on pretend play and divergent thinking. *Environment and Behavior*, *26*(4), 560.

Sutterby, J. A. & Frost, J. L. (2002). Making playgrounds fit for children and children fit for playgrounds. *Young Children*, *57*(3), 36–40.

Sutterby, J. & Thornton, C. D. (2003, September). Swinging stimulates both bodies and brains. *Today's Playground*, *3*(5), 10–11.

Theemes, T. (1999). *Let's go outside! Designing the early childhood playground*. Ypsilanti, MI: High/Scope Press.

Tinsworth, D. & McDonald, J. (2001). *Special study: Injuries and deaths associated with children's playground equipment*. Washington, DC: U.S. Consumer Product Safety Commission.

Tipping, E. (2007). Safe ground: Building, maintaining and inspecting playgrounds to ensure all kids can play safely. *Recreation Management*. Retrieved from http://www.recmanagement.com/features. php?fid=200701fe01&ch=5

Titman, W. (1994). *Special places, special people. The hidden curriculum of school grounds*. WWF UK (World Wide Fund for Nature)/Learning Through Landscapes. doi: 10.1080/03004430214553

U.S. Consumer Product Safety Commission. (2010). *Public playground safety handbook*. Bethesda, MD: U.S. Consumer Product Safety Commission. Retrieved from http://www.cpsc.gov/cpscpub/pubs/325.pdf

U.S. Department of Health and Human Services, Public Health Service, Office of the Surgeon General [USDHHS] (2001). *The Surgeon General's call to action to prevent and decrease overweight and obesity 2001*. Rockville, MD: Author.

Vollman, D., Witsaman, R., Comstock, R. D., & Smith, G. A. (2009). Epidemiology of playground equipment-related injuries to children in the United States, 1996–2005. *Clinical Pediatrics, 48,* 66–71.

Weintraub, R. & Cassady, A. (2002). *Playing it safe: The sixth nationwide safety survey of public playgrounds*. Retrieved from http://www.consumerfed.org/backpage/PlayingItSafeJune2002.pdf

Weiss, M. R. & Ferrer-Caja, E. (2002). Motivational orientations and sport behavior. In T. S. Horn (Ed.), *Advances in sport psychology* (pp. 101–183). Champaign, IL: Human Kinetics Publishing.

Wells, N. M. (2000). At home with nature: Effects of "greenness" on children's cognitive functioning. *Environment and Behavior, 32*(6), 775–795.

Wells, N. M. & Evans, G. W. (2003). Nearby nature: A buffer of life stress among rural children. *Environment and Behavior, 35*(3), 311–330.

Whiren, A. P. (1995). Planning a garden from a child's perspective. *Children's Environments, 12*(2), 250–255.

White, R. (1997). Sometimes, you just gotta make mud pies: Children's adventure play gardens. *Tourist Attractions and Parks Magazine*. Retrieved from http://www.whitehutchinson.com/leisure/articles/84.shtml

White, R. (2004). *Adults are from earth; Children are from the moon; designing for children: A complex challenge*. Retrieved from http://www.whitehutchinson.com/children/articles/earthmoon.shtml

WHO. (2011). *Childhood Overweight and Obesity*. Retrieved January 5, 2012 from http://www.who.int/dietphysicalactivity/childhood/en/.

Wilke, J. (2006). Why outdoor spaces for children matter so much. *Child Care Exchange, 171*, 44–48.

Wilson, R. A. (2000). *Outdoor experiences for young children* (ERIC Digest). Charleston, WV: ERIC Clearinghouse on Rural Education and Small Schools (ERIC Identifier ED 448013).

Wolch, J., Wilson, J. P., & Fehrenbach, J. (2005). Parks and park funding in Los Angeles: An equity-mapping analysis. *Urban geography, 26*(1), 4–35.

Woolley, H. & Lowe, A. (2013). Exploring the relationship between design approach and play value for outdoor play spaces. *Landscape Research, 38*(1), 53–74.

Yerkes, R. (1982). *A playground that extends the classroom*. Report No. RC 014 562, ERIC Document 239802. Oxford, OH: Department of Health, Physical Education, and Recreation.

Zask, A., van Beurden, E., Barnett, L., Brooks, L. O., & Dietrich, U. C. (2001). Active school playgrounds: Myth or reality? Results of the 'Move It Groove It' project. *Preventive Medicine, 33*(5), 402–408.

Chapter 18

Adamsons, K. & Johnson, S. K. (2013). An updated and expanded meta-analysis of nonresident fathering and child well-being. *Journal of Family Psychology, 27*(4), 589–599.

Aronson, S. S. (2001). Taking care of caregivers: Wellness for every body. *Child Care Information Exchange*. Retrieved from https://secure.ccie.com/catalog/search.php?search=taking+care+of+care givers&category=50

Bentham, R. (2008). Rich environments for adult learners. *Young Children, 63*(3), 72–74.

Bradley, J. & Kibera, P. (2006). Closing the gap: Culture and the promotion of inclusion in child care. *Young Children, 61*(1), 34–40.

Caplan, J., Hall, G., Lubin, S., & Fleming, R. (1997). *Literature review of school-family partnerships*. Retrieved from http://www.ncrel.org

Carter, M. & Curtis, D. (1998). *The visionary director*. St. Paul, MN: Redleaf Press.

Child Care Plus. (1995). Keys to building partnerships with families. *Child Care Plus Newsletter, 5*(2), 1–4. Retrieved from http://www.ccplus.org/newsletters/5-2.pdf

Corr, L., Davis, E., LaMontagne, A. D., Waters, E., & Steele, E. (2014). Childcare providers' mental health: A systematic review of its prevalence, determinants and relationship to care quality. *International Journal of Mental Health Promotion, 16*(4). doi: 10.1080/14623730.2014.931067

Crosser, S. (2005). *What do we know about early childhood education? Research based practice*. Clifton Park, NY: Thomson Delmar Learning.

Evans, G. D., Bryant, N., & Owens, J. S. (2004). Ethnic differences in burnout, coping, and intervention acceptability among childcare professionals. *Child Youth Care Forum, 33*(5), 349–371.

Fagan, J. & Palm, G. (2004). *Fathers and early childhood programs*. Canada: Thomson Delmar.

Giovannini, D. (2001). Traces of childhood: A child's diary. In L. Gandidi & C. P. Edwards (Eds.), *Bambini* (pp. 146–151). New York: Teacher College Press.

Green, S. (2003). Reaching out to fathers: An examination of staff efforts that lead to greater father involvement in early childhood programs. *Early Childhood Research & Practice, 5*(2). Retrieved from http://ecrp.uiuc.edu/v5n2/green.html

Harvard Family Research Project. (2014). *Redefining family engagement for student success*. Retrieved from http://www.hfrp.org/family-involvement/publications-resources/redefining-family-engagement-for-student-success

Jeynes, W. H. (2014). A meta-analysis: The relationship between father involvement and student academic achievement. *Urban Education*. doi: 0042085914525789

Malo, E. & Bullard, J. (2000). *Storytelling and the Emergent Reader* (ED448464). Paper presented at the International

Reading Association World Congress on Reading, Auckland, New Zealand.

Maslach, C., Jackson, S. E., & Leiter, M. P. (1996). *Maslach burnout inventory manual* (3rd ed.). Palo Alto, CA: Consulting Psychologists Press.

Office of Head Start & National Center on P, Family, and Community Engagement. (2011). *The Head Start parent, family, and community engagement framework: Promoting family engagement and school readiness from prenatal to age 8*. Retrieved from http://eclkc.ohs.acf.hhs.gov/hslc/hs/sr/approach/pfcef

Patton, C. & Caspe, M. (2014). *Finding time together: Families, schools, and communities supporting anywhere, anytime learning*. Cambridge, MA: Harvard Family Research Project. www.hfrp.org/content/download/4607/121749/file/Finding_Time_Together_091714_Harvard-Family-Research-Project.pdf

Pipher, M. (2002). *The middle of everywhere: Helping refugees enter the American community*. Orlando, FL: Harcourt.

Riley, D., San Juan, R. R., Klinkner, J., & Ramminger, A. (2008). *Social & emotional development: Connecting science and practice in early childhood settings*. Washington, DC: National Association for the Education of Young Children.

Rosenberg, J. & Wilcox, W. B. (2006). *The importance of fathers in the healthy development of children*. Washington, DC: U.S. Department of Health and Human Services, Administration for Children and Families.

TASC. (2013). *Reinventing school: Summary and materials from 6,000-hour learning gap forum*. Retrieved from http://www.expandedschools.org/policy-documents/reinventing-school-summary-and-materials-6000-hour-learning-gap-forum#sthash.ZOHphq9a.dpbs

Wagner, S. L., Forer, B., Cepeda, I. L., Goelman, H., Maggi, S., D'Angiulli, A., Wessel, J., Hertzman, C., & Grunau, R. E. (February 1, 2013). Perceived stress and Canadian early childcare educators. *Child & Youth Care Forum*, *42*(1), 53–70.

Wortman, A. M. (2001). Preventing work-related musculoskeletal injuries. *Child Care Exchange*, *140*, 50–53.

Chapter 19

Armstrong, L. J. (2012). *Family child care homes: Creative spaces for children to learn*. St. Paul, MN: Redleaf Press.

Gerstenblatt, P., Faulkner, M., Lee, A., Doan, L. T., & Travis, D. (2014). Not babysitting: Work stress and well-being for family child care providers. *Early Childhood Education Journal*, *42*, 67–75.

Goelman, H., Shapiro, E., & Pence, A. R. (1990). Family environment and family day care. *Family Relations*, *39*(1), 14–19.

Laughlin, L. (2013). *Who's minding the kids? Child care arrangements: Spring 2011*. Current Population Reports, P70-135. Washington, DC: U.S. Census Bureau.

National Association for Family Child Care. (2013). *Quality standards for NAFCC accreditation* (4th ed.). Author. Retrieved from http://legacy.nafcc.org/index.php?option=com_content&view=article&id=289&Itemid=325

Topal, C. W. & Gandini, L. (1999). *Beautiful stuff: Learning with found materials*. Italy: Davis Publications.

Weaver, R. H. (2002). Predictors of quality and commitment in family child care: Provider education, personal resources, and support. *Early Education and Development*, *13*(3), 265–282.

Weinberger, N. (2000). Overcoming obstacles to create retreats in family child care. *Young Children*, *55*(5), 78–81.

White, R. & Stoecklin, V. (2003). *The great 35 square foot myth*. Kansas City, MO: White Hutchinson Leisure & Learning Group.

Index